JOB ANALYSIS

JOB ANALYSIS

A HANDBOOK FOR THE HUMAN RESOURCE DIRECTOR

Jai Ghorpade, Ph.D.
Professor of Management
San Diego State University

Prentice Hall, *Englewood Cliffs, New Jersey 07632*

Library of Congress Cataloging-in-Publication Data

Ghorpade, Jai, date.
Job analysis.

Bibliography:
Includes index.
1. Job analysis. I. Title.
HF5549.5.J6.G48 1987 658.3'06 87–14350
ISBN 0–13–510256–1

Editorial/production supervision and
interior design: Madelaine Cooke
Cover design: Edsal Enterprises
Manufacturing buyer: Ray Keating

To the memory of my father, mother, and brother

A Division of Simon & Schuster
Englewood Cliffs, New Jersey 07632

Printed in the United States of America

10 9 8 7 6 5 4 3 2 1

ISBN 0-13-510256-1 01

Prentice-Hall International (UK) Limited, *London*
Prentice-Hall of Australia Pty. Limited, *Sydney*
Prentice-Hall Canada Inc., *Toronto*
Prentice-Hall Hispanoamericana, S.A., *Mexico*
Prentice-Hall of India Private Limited, *New Delhi*
Prentice-Hall of Japan, Inc., *Tokyo*
Prentice-Hall of Southeast Asia Pte. Ltd., *Singapore*
Editora Prentice-Hall do Brasil, Ltda., *Rio de Janeiro*

Brief Contents

Contents

Exhibits

Preface

The survival and effectiveness of every organization is determined ultimately by how well it is able to combine and utilize its human, material, and other resources in the service of its mission and goals. Job analysis, the subject of this book, is one of the concepts that can aid management in ensuring effective combination and utilization of resources. The particular thrust of this concept is with providing management with information about jobs for use in redesign of jobs and for hiring, training, compensating, appraising, and directing the work force.

This book is designed to serve as a comprehensive guide to job analysis. It is addressed primarily to human resource professionals working in modern organizations. It should also be of value as a teaching device in courses on job analysis, as a sourcebook for attorneys and other legal users, and as a guide to the literature for researchers.

Noteworthy Features

The contents of this book were assembled after careful study of available publications on the subject. The following are the noteworthy features of the book:

- Crystallization of the role and applications of job analysis in the human resource management process.
- Systematic presentation of the proven techniques and methods of job analysis.
- Practical, ''how-to-do-it'' guides for constructing job descriptions, specifications, compensable factors, and other products of job analysis.
- Demonstration of applications of job analysis results to human resource planning, selection, performance appraisal, training, compensation, and equal employment opportunity.
- A collection of questionnaires, checklists, and other standardized instruments that can be used in designing job analysis programs and investigations.
- Reviews of laws, agency rules, and court decisions relating to job analysis issues and problems.

How This Book Is Organized

This book is organized into six chapters. The first chapter presents a capsule review of the concept of job analysis, its rationale, and its place in human resource management. The approach to the study of the subject that is used in the book is also presented through simple, graphic illustrations.

The remaining five chapters are logical extensions of the framework presented in Chapter 1. Chapter 2 deals with the nature and measurement of job information. Chapter 3 reviews the methods and systems or the *how* of job analysis. Chapters 4 and 5 deal with two of the principal *results* of job analysis: job descriptions and specifications, respectively. The final chapter is concerned with the *uses* of job analysis results in the performance of key human resource management functions. The appendices at the end of the book provide questionnaires, checklists, and other ready-made job analysis instruments. These are intended as resources to be used in the performance of job analysis activities. They should be of particular value to human resource professionals for use in in-house job analysis programs.

Acknowledgments

Many people influenced the content and structure of this book, and I am grateful to them. Ultimately, any errors that remain in the book are mine, and I bear responsibility for them. My special thanks to Thomas J. Atchison and Stephen P. Robbins, both on the faculty of the Department of Management, San Diego State University, for their comments on the initial drafts of this book. Two people at Prentice Hall were particularly helpful in providing guidance, encouragement, and support in getting the job done: Alison Reeves, editor, and Madelaine Cooke, production editor. Three reviewers provided valuable ideas that improved the final product: Donald P. Schwab, University of Wisconsin, Madison; Jerry T. Edge, Solar Turbines Inc., San Diego; and Catherine M. Jett, Teledyne Ryan Aeronautical, San Diego. Finally, I am grateful to my wife, Suzanne, for her patience and help in enabling me to complete the book.

Acronyms and Abbreviations

AFHRL	Air Force Human Resource Laboratory
ARS	Ability Requirements System
BCM	Behavioral Consistency Method
BFOQ	Bona Fide Occupational Qualities
CIT	Critical Incidents Technique
CODAP	Comprehensive Occupational Data Analysis Programs
DOL	U.S. Department of Labor
DOT	*Dictionary of Occupational Titles*
EEO	Equal Employment Opportunity
FES	Factor Evaluation System
FJA	Functional Job Analysis
GED	General Educational Development
HSMS	Health Services Mobility Study
ILO	International Labour Organisation
JCI	Job Characteristics Inventory
JDS	Job Diagnostic Survey
JEM	Job Elements Method
JIMS	Job Information Matrix Systems
JRF	Job Rating Form
KSAO	Knowledges, Skills, Abilities, and Other Human Characteristics
MBO	Management by Objectives
MTEWA	Machines, Tools, Equipment, and Work Aids
PAQ	Position Analysis Questionnaire
QWL	Quality of Work Life
SME	Subject Matter Expert
SVP	Specific Vocational Preparation
TM	Techniques and Methods
TTA	Threshold Trait Analysis
USES	U.S. Employment Service
VERJAS	Versatile Job Analysis System
WPSS	Work Performance Survey System
YJI	Yale Job Inventory

1 Introduction to Job Analysis

Human resource management staffs spend their time in two kinds of activities. First, they take care of the day-to-day administrative needs of the organization relating to the management of human resources. This typically entails assisting managers with staffing, compensation, performance appraisal, and training; assuring compliance with equal employment opportunity legislation and safety and health requirements; administering the labor contract if one exists; and handling complaints, gripes, and queries from employees.

Besides taking care of day-to-day affairs, human resource staffs also engage in system maintenance and development activities. These are aimed at making sure that the organization is able to meet its future human resource needs and to accommodate to changes. Examples of such activities are assisting top management in shaping human resource strategy and policy, forecasting future human resource needs and formulating action plans for meeting those needs, and assisting managers in redesigning jobs and work systems (Janger, 1977; Klatt, Murdick & Schuster, 1985).

Much has been developed over the years to assist the human resource director in fulfilling the varied obligations that accompany the role. Many theories have been advanced, and models of the human resource management function have been built. The literature is also rich with methods, tools, and techniques for the performance of human resource management functions (Tead & Metcalfe, 1933; Heckmann & Huneryager, 1962; Rowland & Ferris, 1982; Fombrun, Tichy & Devanna, 1984).

Job analysis, the subject of this book, is a part of the inventory of the ideas that is available to the human resource director. The focus of this concept is with providing the human resource director with information about jobs that can be used in the performance of other human resource functions. While not a cure-all for all the employment problems that beset modern industry, job analysis does have something to contribute to all the significant challenges encountered by the human resource director. It is a pivotal link in the chain of activities that constitutes modern human resource management.

1.1 Job Analysis: An Overview

The term *job analysis* currently accommodates a diverse range of undertakings that vary widely in regard to purposes, scope, and methods. At one extreme can be placed studies that are aimed at solving one or more job-related problems faced by a particular organization at a particular time. An example of such an undertaking would be a study aimed at clarifying the missions of a group of jobs within an organization. This could be accomplished simply by holding a set of meetings with the affected parties. At the other extreme can be placed institutionalized job analysis programs that function as ongoing parts of organizations or even entire industries. In such instances, job analysis would be considered an integral part of the managerial system of the enterprise. (Excellent reviews of varieties of job analysis programs are provided in Wilson, 1974, and McCormick, 1979.)

Within this variation, however, a couple of characteristics stand out as being the distinguishing features of job analysis. The first, and most obvious, of these is that the unit of analysis of job analysis is the job. This focus separates job analysis from organizational analysis, task analysis, management by objectives, time and motion study, person analysis, and other fields that operate at different levels and that have as their subject matter units that are larger or smaller in scope.

But job analysis is not the only field that deals with jobs. Other roles within organizations that also have interests in jobs are industrial engineers, compensation analysts, recruiters, and trainers. What distinguishes job analysis from these other job-related fields is its distinctive thrust: the mandate of the job analyst is to provide the others with information about jobs. Job analysis thus has no independent existence; it is always a part of other activities. It is an instrumental activity that is undertaken, either on an ad hoc or an ongoing basis, to fulfill the informational needs experienced by other specialists in the performance of their various functions.

A DEFINITION OF JOB ANALYSIS

Taking the foregoing features into account, we can now offer a definition of job analysis.

> Job analysis is a managerial activity, performed within organizations, and directed at gathering, analyzing, and synthesizing information about jobs, information that serves as the foundation for organizational planning and design, human resource management, and other managerial functions. (Based on Ghorpade and Atchison, 1980, p.136)

This definition of job analysis is in keeping with the emerging view of the concept. We use it hereafter as a basis for our study of the subject.

REASONS BEHIND JOB ANALYSIS

Why is job analysis necessary? Or, to put it in the language of our definition, why is it necessary to gather, analyze, and synthesize information about jobs? Four reasons can be offered as providing the rationale behind job analysis. They stem partly from the nature of managerial work and partly from the structure of modern industrial society.

- Jobs serve as the building blocks of organizations. They are the primary action units of the organization. What the organization achieves (or fails to achieve) can ultimately be traced to its ability to muster the energies of its human resources in making the products and services that it needs for its survival and effectiveness. An ongoing program of job analysis is thus an operating requirement. Without such a program, managers lack the information that they need for bringing about an efficient allocation of resources. (The properties of jobs from an organizational perspective are summarized in Exhibit 1.1.)
- In the modern enterprise, jobs are consciously created. This is in contrast to the workings of a nonindustrial society in which jobs tend to evolve as social roles, with tradition and custom playing a significant part in their evolution. Since jobs are consciously created, it makes sense to subject them to scrutiny from time to time to make sure that they are attaining the goals that were intended. If the goals have changed, then job analysis is essential for redesigning jobs (Davis & Taylor, 1979, p. x).
- Jobs are frequently created by people who will not be performing them. In large manufacturing companies, it is common for jobs to be designed by industrial engineers. The job design

EXHIBIT 1.1 What Is a Job?

The term ''job'' is one of those words that is commonly encountered in everyday speech but that turns out to be quite complex upon closer examination. One point on which there is agreement is that jobs are subunits of organizations. Using this fact as a point of departure, it is possible to isolate the general properties of jobs as well as the factors that distinguish jobs from each other. The following are some of the general properties of jobs viewed as subunits of organizations:

- Jobs are made up of material, ideational, and human resources.
- Jobs and organizations maintain a mutually beneficial relationship: organizations make available the resources, and the jobholders produce goods and services needed by the organization.
- Jobs serve as the building blocks of organizations; they provide the basis for the formation of work groups, departments, and other larger divisions.
- Jobs link people with organizations; there is no place within an organization without a formal or informal work assignment.

Although all jobs share these features, no two jobs are entirely alike. In fact, differentiation is simultaneously the basis and the result of job formation. The following are the key factors that distinguish jobs from each other:

- Missions—each job provides the organization with unique products or services.
- Material resources—machines, tools, equipment, and work aids; raw materials used in the job.
- Human characteristics—knowledges, skills, abilities, and other attributes (KSAOs) required of workers to perform the job.
- Methods—the processes, techniques, or the ''know-how'' that form the basis for transformation of resources into usable outputs.
- Tasks and behaviors—the nature of the human involvement in the work.
- Status—place of the job within the organization's hierarchy.

practices in the service sector vary widely. In both sectors, little opportunity is provided for active involvement of job incumbents and potential workers in the design of jobs. Even with the best of intentions, it is thus possible for the designer to fail to take note of the peculiarities of particular situations and to bring about allocations that are dysfunctional. Job analysis provides an opportunity to remedy defects in the design of jobs (Davis & Taylor, 1979; Hackman & Suttle, 1977; Klatt, Murdick & Schuster, 1985, pp. 128–167).

- Modern organizations are constantly faced with rapid, and frequently dislocating, changes in their products, clienteles, and supply markets. Some of these changes can be attributed to the tremendous strides made in recent years on the technological front, particularly the harnessing of the computer in manufacturing. Others have their roots in global developments and pressures on scarce resources from emerging nations and growing populations. Structural changes erode the currency of role prescriptions. Job analysis provides a means for realigning the goals of the organization with those of their jobs.

ANALYTIC CONCERNS OF JOB ANALYSIS

Job analysis is an analytical activity. To analyze something is to dissect it, to separate its components and see how they fit. When the unit being analyzed is a part of a larger system, the analyst is faced with a twofold task: to study the interrelations among its component parts, and to isolate how the unit fits into the larger whole. This automatically entails tracing of the exchanges that take place between the unit and the larger system.

Both these general analytical concerns are characteristic features of job analysis. Viewing jobs as components of organizations, job analysts study the internal compositions of jobs as well as their interrelations with the organization. The following are the analytical thrusts of job analysis.

- *Outputs*. What are the specialized products or services that result from the job? In what ways do they differ from the outputs of other jobs within the organization?
- *Inputs*. What knowledges, skills, and abilities are required of the workers performing the job? What material, capital, and other nonhuman resources are utilized in the job?
- *Throughput*. How are the resources transformed into the desired outputs or services? What are the processes, techniques, and methods used in the transformation process? How are functions allocated between machines and people? What human activities, behaviors, and contacts are involved in the work?
- *Context*. Where is the job found within the organization? What is the flow of authority and responsibility? What are the physical and psychological demands of the environment in which the work takes place? What are the terms and conditions under which the job is performed by the worker? What are the laws and other legal mandates that apply to the work situation?

USES OF JOB INFORMATION

Job analysis was introduced into managerial practice around the turn of the century. During the initial years, it was viewed largely as an aid in time and motion analysis. Over the years, however, the scope of applications of job information has widened considerably. A summary of the major uses of job analysis data in modern enterprises is provided in Exhibit 1.2. In considering this list, it needs to be emphasized that job analysis is currently not linked with any specific use. Instead, it is emerging as a highly versatile tool that is capable of serving a very wide range of managerial interests. (For historical accounts of the enlarging scope of job analysis, see Zerga, 1943; Shartle, 1959; Sparks, 1982.)

SOURCES OF JOB INFORMATION

A variety of sources are available to the job analyst for gathering job-related information. These can be sorted roughly into three categories:

- *Industry sources*—generic job descriptions, occupational data, and other information contained in government publications, union, and industry sources. The *Dictionary of Occupational Titles*, published by the U.S. Department of Labor and now in its third edition, is the best known and most comprehensive source of generic job data. (See also Oldham & Seglin, 1984; Grego & Rudnik, 1970.)
- *Company documents*—policies and procedures manuals, prior job descriptions, union contracts, and other written documents.
- *Human sources*—job incumbents, co-workers, supervisors, customers, and other human resources associated with the job.

AGENTS OF DATA GATHERING

In most situations, the agent of data gathering is the job analyst. It is also possible for job incumbents, supervisors, and other persons to serve in this capacity. In recent years, nonhuman agents such as cameras, recorders, and other devices are being used in job study (Niebel, 1982).

METHODS AND SYSTEMS OF DATA GATHERING

Three principal methods are used in data gathering in job analysis: observation, interview, and written instruments such as questionnaires, checklists, and diaries. In practice, the format of these methods can be varied; they can also be combined for greater efficiency. Thus, interviews with human agents can be conducted by one analyst or by a group. A checklist can be used to structure observations. Multiple versions of a questionnaire can be administered at the same time.

EXHIBIT 1.2 Uses of Job Information

	Salaried (n = 638)	Hourly (n = 430)
Job evaluation	98	95
Setting wage and salary levels	92	88
Appraising personnel	59	44
Establishing incentives	11	14
Determining profit sharing	6	2
Other	2	1
Recruiting and placing	95	93
Making job specifications	74	75
Promoting, transferring, and rotating	72	67
Constructing tests	14	18
Indicating sources of employees	18	16
Counseling (vocational)	25	26
Matching men with jobs	65	61
Placing the handicapped	17	25
Structuring jobs	58	54
Diluting jobs	19	19
Enriching jobs	26	25
Other	3	4
Conducting labor and personnel relations	83	79
Developing performance standards	48	42
Establishing responsibility	70	56
Establishing authority	64	44
Establishing accountability	66	46
Handling grievances	17	44
Conducting labor negotiations	8	34
Establishing channels of communication	32	24
Organizing personnel records	35	36
Other	1	1
Utilizing workers	72	67
Organizing and planning	56	47
Engineering jobs	17	16
Controlling costs	22	29
Controlling quality	14	16
Predicting changes	13	11
Avoiding excess task duplication	45	40
Other	1	1
Training	61	63
Developing courses	33	36
Selecting trainees	34	34
Orienting employees	36	36
Programming teaching machines	2	2
Other	1	1

Source: *Summary of National Job Analysis Methods Survey* (Long Beach: California State College, Bureau of Business Research, 1968), as presented in E. J. McCormick, Jr., *Job Analysis: Methods and Applications*, AMACOM, Division of American Management Association, New York, 1979, p. 18.

In addition to these primary methods, systems of job analysis have been developed over the years to facilitate the gathering and analysis of job information. These consist of structured, or ready-made, packages of job analysis concepts, techniques, and methods. There currently exist over 15 job analysis systems. (The major ones are described in Chapter 3 and in Appendix A at the back of the book.)

1.2 Job Analysis for Human Resource Management

The preceding review has made clear that job analysis is capable of serving a wide range of interests. Our purpose in this section is to chalk out the territory of the field as it relates to human resource management.

LINKS BETWEEN JOB ANALYSIS AND HUMAN RESOURCE MANAGEMENT

Job analysis has been a part of human resource management since its early beginnings. In recent years, however, it has come to occupy a pivotal role in human resource management. Its particular mission is to provide human resource specialists with the job-related information that is needed for the performance of their various functions.

The links between job analysis and human resource management are shown in Exhibit 1.3. On the right side of this illustration are the human resource functions served by job analysis. This list represents the traditional and emerging interests of human resource professionals in job analysis.

The informational outputs typically sought through job analysis for human resource management are shown on the left side of Exhibit 1.3. They are described more fully in Exhibit 1.4. It is a tradition within the job analysis literature to refer to these as the products or derivatives of job analysis (Tead & Metcalfe, 1933; BNA, 1966, p. 13; Byars & Rue, 1984, p. 33; Mathis & Jackson, 1985, pp. 182–184).

The products of job analysis differ from each other over the following dimensions: unit of analysis, order in which they are derived, types of information provided, level of specificity, and purposes to be served in the human resource management process.

The primary, first-level product of a job analysis is the job description. This document focuses on the job as a whole as the unit of analysis and provides, in varying levels of specificity,

EXHIBIT 1.3 Links Between Job Analysis and Human Resource Management

Job information → Products (Results) of Job Analysis:

- Job description
- Worker specification
- Performance criteria
- Compensable factors
- Job families

→ Uses of Job Analysis Products in Human Resource Management

Function	Uses
Job design	Job redesign Quality of work life Safety and health programs
Human resource planning	Forecasting demand and supply of labor Human resource (skills) inventories Action plans
Recruitment and selection	Application blanks Realistic job previews Matching jobs and people Test validation
Equal employment opportunity	Test validation Job-relatedness and bona fide occupational qualifications Comparable worth of jobs Mobility paths
Performance appraisal	Performance criteria and standards Clarifying roles Performance counseling and guidance
Compensation	Job evaluation Job classification Contract negotiations Comparable worth
Training and development	Training needs analysis Career counseling and guidance

EXHIBIT 1.4 Description of the Principal Products of Job Analysis

Job description	Description of the job as a whole, explaining in detail what the worker does, why, how, and where.
Worker specification	Specifications of the knowledges, skills, abilities, and other human characteristics required of the workers to be assigned to the job. (Also referred to as *job specifications.*)
Performance criteria	Yardsticks to be used in appraising worker success in job performance.
Compensable factors	Job and human characteristics to be used as basis for compensation decisions.
Job families	Grouping of jobs according to common job, worker, and environmental descriptors.

answers to the fundamental analytic questions of job analysis noted earlier. It serves as a basis for the derivation of all other products and as a source document for a variety of direct uses in human resource management.

All the other products are specific-purpose derivatives of the job description. Each has its own unit of analysis and a relatively specific set of uses. Some of these differences are evident in Exhibit 1.4. Others are brought out in the discussion that follows.

Individual products of job analysis are used in two principal ways in human resource management. The first is to derive other products. The need for doing this stems from there being a natural order in the gathering, analyzing, and synthesizing of job information. Thus, the analyst's ability to understand the knowledges, skills, and abilities required of the worker hinges on the existence of a job description. Compensable factors can only be assembled after the relevant job and worker factors are known. Job families can only be created after the job, the worker, and context variables are described.

The second use of the products of job analysis is in the performance of various human resource management functions. This is their natural and ultimate justification. As shown in Exhibit 1.3, job analysis contributes something of value to all the key human resource management roles. To the job designer, job analysis provides the information needed for job redesign, quality of work life (QWL), and safety and health programs. The job and worker variables uncovered through job analysis can be used by the human resource planner in forecasting human resource needs, constructing personnel inventories, and formulating action plans. Recruiters can use the job description and its derivatives to gain familiarity with the job, for constructing and validating application blanks, and for providing potential employees with realistic job previews. In promoting equal employment opportunity (EEO), job analysis provides the data base needed for establishing job-relatedness, bona fide occupational qualifications (BFOQs), comparable worth of jobs, and the tracing of mobility paths. The criteria needed for performance appraisal come from descriptions of job mission, technology, tasks, and the context. When these are combined with worker specifications, they can also serve as a basis for clarifying roles and for providing employees with guidance and counseling. Compensation analysts can use job and worker factors for conducting job evaluation, for classification, and for contract negotiations. Job descriptions and specifications can be used by trainers in conducting training needs analysis, an activity that is central to all training and development.

THE PROCESS OF JOB ANALYSIS IN HUMAN RESOURCE MANAGEMENT

The various activities and elements involved in job analysis have been discussed individually in the previous pages. It is time now to bring them all together and to provide a depiction of the total process from the beginning to the end. Our concern at this stage is with the process of job analysis as it relates to human resource management.

Viewed as a series of activities, job analysis for human resource management consists roughly of six phases as shown in Exhibit 1.5. (As all these activities are discussed in detail in

EXHIBIT 1.5 The Process of Job Analysis in Human Resource Management

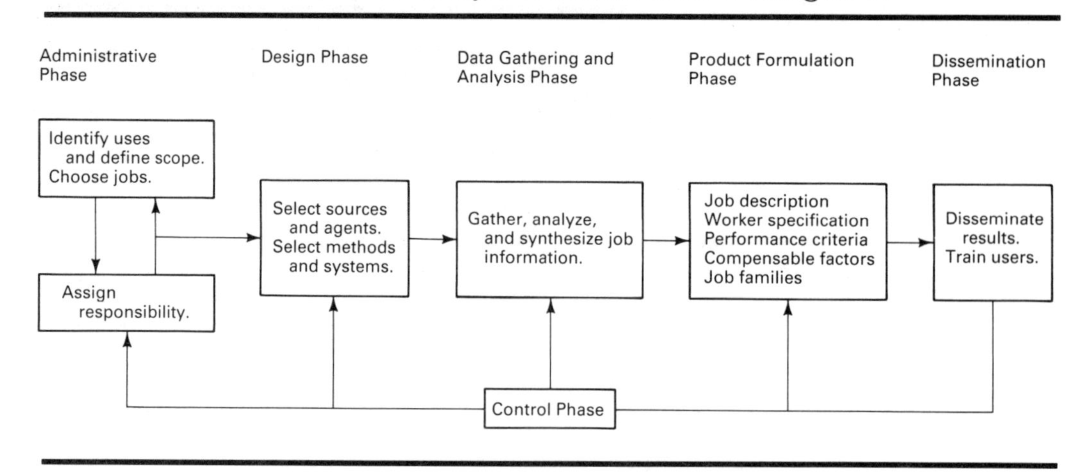

later chapters, the discussion relating to them here is limited to providing an overview of the "what," "why," and "how" of job analysis.)

Administrative Phase. These are the preliminaries; they determine the "what" and "why" of the undertaking. The following types of issues are resolved at this stage:

- Identification of the uses to be made of the job information.
- Selection of the job(s) to be analyzed.
- Demarcation of the types and scope of information to be gathered.
- Assignment of responsibility for the conduct of the activity.

Job analysis begins by identification of the uses to be made of the job information. Basically, this amounts to pinpointing the problems that are to be resolved through job analysis. This step defines the type of information that is to be gathered and the scope of the effort. The jobs to be analyzed are then selected, and responsibility for its conduct is assigned.

Many options are available to management in making these decisions. Thus, a job analysis could cover one or several jobs. It could be single-purposed (test validation) or multipurposed (all uses listed in Exhibit 1.3). The analyst could be a person or a subunit of the organization.

Design Phase. This relates to the "how" of the activity and calls for resolution of the following concerns:

- Selection of sources and agent of information.
- Selection of methods or systems of job analysis.
- Selection of data analysis techniques (if not provided for in the system used).

Here, the significant decision faced is the classic business choice: make or buy. If the problem addressed is fairly routine, it might be possible to utilize a ready-made system. (Available systems of job analysis are described in Chapter 3, and in Appendix A.)

Data Gathering and Analysis Phase. This is the heart of job analysis and consists roughly of three interrelated activities:

- Gathering the desired information according to methods and procedures chosen by the analyst.
- Analyzing, that is, describing, classifying, and evaluating the job factors studied.
- Synthesizing, that is, interpreting, translating, and organizing the information into useful categories.

The manner in which this phase is fulfilled will be determined largely by the choices made in the design phase. Structured systems contain analytic procedures that are integral parts of their methodologies. When data gathering is unstructured, post hoc content analysis will have to be conducted.

Product Formulation Phase. The thrust of this phase is on composing the desired products. The informational outputs typically sought through job analysis in human resource management were shown in Exhibit 1.4. When the preceding steps are conducted systematically, product formulation turns out to be largely a clerical task.

Dissemination Phase. This phase is concerned with the promotion of the use of the job analysis results. It consists of two activities:

- Making the results available to the recruiters, trainers, and other ultimate users.
- Training the users in the proper utilization of the results.

Training of users is particularly important in instances where legal issues are involved (Bemis et al., 1983).

Control Phase. The roots of this phase stem from the dynamic nature of organizations. Changes in technology and other work arrangements can erode the currency of job analysis products. Control is thus an ongoing concern; it consists of studying the feedback from the users and updating or revising the job description and other products of job analysis.

1.3 Job Analysis and the Law

Job analysis developed originally as a response to coordinative problems that resulted from growth in size and complexity of industrial organizations. In recent years, however, developments on the legal front have provided another motivation behind job analysis. More and more, the government is getting involved in the regulation of the employer-employee relationship. Since job analysis is a pivotal human resource function, its conduct has come under the scrutiny of governmental agencies.

LEGAL FRAMEWORK

To understand the legal status of job analysis, it is useful briefly to examine the legal framework governing the employer-employee relationship. Roughly four types of legal materials govern this relationship at the federal level:

Constitutional provisions	First, Fifth, Thirteenth, and Fourteenth Amendments and Civil Rights Acts of 1866, 1870, and 1871
Statutes	The National Labor Relations Act, civil rights/equal employment opportunity laws, and other employment relations laws
Executive orders	Notably Executive Orders 11141 (1964), 11246 (1965), 11478 (1969)
Agency rules and guidelines	Notably the *Uniform Guidelines* (1978)

Exhibit 1.6 provides details relating to the coverage of the constitutional provisions, statutes, and executive orders. The focus of the constitutional provisions is on protection of religious freedom, due process, and equality of opportunity. Even though these mandates have been around

EXHIBIT 1.6 Employment Relations Laws and Orders

Federal Law	Type of Employment Discrimination Prohibited	Employers Covered
U.S. Constitution, First and Fifth Amendments	Deprivation of employment rights without due process of law	Federal government
U.S. Constitution, Fourteenth Amendment	Deprivation of employment rights without due process of law	State and local governments
Civil Rights Acts of 1866 and 1870 (based on Thirteenth Amendment)	Race discrimination in hiring, placement, and continuation of employment	Private employers, unions, employment agencies
Civil Rights Act of 1871 (based on Fourteenth Amendment)	Deprivation of equal employment rights under cover of state law	State and local governments (private employers if conspiracy is involved)
National Labor Relations Act	Unfair representation by unions, or interference with employee rights, that discriminates on the basis of race, color, religion, sex, or national origin	Private employers and unions
Equal Pay Act of 1963	Sex differences in pay for substantially equal work	Private employers (state and local governments uncertain)
Executive Order 11141 (164)	Age discrimination	Federal contractors and subcontractors
Title VI, 1964 Civil Rights Act	Discrimination based on race, color, or national origin	Employers receiving federal financial assistance
Title VII, 1964 Civil Rights Act (as amended by the Equal Employment Act of 1972)	Discrimination or segregation based on race, color, religion, sex, or national origin	Private employers with 15 or more employees; federal, state, and local governments; unions and apprenticeship committees; employment agencies
Executive Orders 11246 and 11375 (1965)	Discrimination based on race, color, religion, sex, or national origin (affirmative action required)	Federal contractors and subcontractors
Age discrimination in Employment Act of 1967	Age discrimination against those between the ages of 40 and 65	Private employers with 20 or more employees, unions with 25 or more members, employment agencies, apprenticeship and training programs (state and local governments uncertain)
Title I, 1968 Civil Rights Act	Interference with a person's exercise of rights with respect to race, religion, color, or national origin	Persons generally
Executive Order 11478 (1969)	Discrimination based on race, color, religion, sex, national origin, political affiliation, marital status, or physical handicap	Federal government
Revenue Sharing Act of 1972	Discrimination based on race, color, national origin, or sex	State and local governments receiving revenue-sharing funds
Education Amendments of 1972	Sex discrimination	Educational institutions receiving federal financial assistance
Rehabilitation Act of 1973; Executive order no. 11914 (1974)	Discrimination based on physical or mental handicap (affirmative action required)	Federal contractors, federal government
Vietnam Era Veterans Readjustment Act of 1974	Discrimination against disabled veterans and Vietnam era veterans (affirmative action required)	Federal contractors, federal government
Age Discrimination Act of 1975	Age discrimination	Employers receiving federal financial assistance
State laws		
State fair employment practices laws	Similar to Title VII and Equal Employment Act of 1972	Varies by state; passed in about 85 percent of states

From W. F. Glueck, *Personnel: A Book of Readings* (Dallas, Tex.: Business Publications, 1979), pp. 346–347.

for some time, their applications to the employment relations arena are of recent origin. The statutory enactments seek to regulate employer-employee relations in the interests of national goals and priorities. The National Labor Relations Act addressed itself to the regulation of union-management relations. The civil rights/EEO laws are concerned with preventing discrimination and promoting equal employment opportunity at the workplace. The executive orders have

EXHIBIT 1.7 Excerpts from Title VII of the Civil Rights Act (as Amended by the Equal Employment Opportunity Act of 1972)

Sec. 703. (a) It shall be an unlawful employment practice for an employer—

(1) to fail or refuse to hire or to discharge any individual, or otherwise to discriminate against any individual with respect to his compensation, terms, conditions, or privileges of employment, because of such individual's race, color, religion, sex, or national origin.

(2) to limit, segregate, or classify his employees or applicants for employment in any way which would deprive or tend to deprive any individual of employment opportunities or otherwise adversely affect his status as an employee, because of such individual's race, color, religion, sex, or national origin.

(e) Notwithstanding any other provision of this title, (1) it shall not be an unlawful employment practice for an employer to hire and employ employees, for an employment agency to classify, or refer for employment any individual, for a labor organization to classify its membership or to classify or refer for employment any individual, or for an employer, labor organization, or joint labor-management committee controlling apprenticeship or other training or retraining programs to admit or employ any individual in any such program, on the basis of his religion, sex, or national origin in those certain instances where religion, sex, or national origin is a bona fide occupational qualification reasonably necessary to the normal operation of that particular business or enterprise, and (2) it shall not be an unlawful employment practice for a school, college, university, or other educational institution or institution of learning to hire and employ employees of a particular religion if such school, college, university, or other educational institution or institution of learning is, in whole or in substantial part, owned, supported, controlled, or managed by a particular religion or by a particular religious corporation, association, or society, or if the curriculum of such school, college, university, or other educational institution or institution of learning is directed toward the propagation of a particular religion.

(h) Notwithstanding any other provision of this title, it shall not be an unlawful employment practice for an employer to apply different standards of compensation, or different terms, conditions, or privileges of employment pursuant to a bona fide seniority or merit system, or a system which measures earnings by quantity or quality of production or to employees who work in different locations, provided that such differences are not the result of an intention to discriminate because of race, color, religion, sex, or national origin, nor shall it be an unlawful employment practice for an employer to give and to act upon the results of any professionally developed ability test provided that such test, its administration or action upon the results is not designed, intended or used to discriminate because of race, color, religion, sex or national origin. It shall not be an unlawful employment practice under this title for any employer to differentiate upon the basis of sex in determining the amount of the wages or compensation paid or to be paid to employees of such employer if such differentiation is authorized by the provisions of section 6(d) of the Fair Labor Standards Act of 1938, as amended (29 U. S. C. 206(d)).

(j) Nothing contained in this title shall be interpreted to require any employer, employment agency, labor organization, or joint labor-management committee subject to this title to grant preferential treatment to any individual or to any group because of the race, color, religion, sex, or national origin of such individual or group on account of an imbalance which may exist with respect to the total number or percentage of persons of any race, color, religion, sex, or national origin employed by any employer, referred or classified for employment by any employment agency or labor organization, admitted to membership or classified by any labor organization, or admitted to, or employed in, any apprenticeship or other training program, in comparison with the total number or percentage of persons of such race, color, religion, sex, or national origin in any community, State, section, or other area, or in the available work force in any community, State, section, or other area.

the same goals as do the civil rights/EEO laws. However, the former are directed at contractors doing business with the federal government. An additional provision contained in these orders is that they require the covered employers to undertake affirmative action. The law that has had the greatest impact on the regulation of employer-employee relations in recent years is the Civil Rights Act of 1964. Excerpts from Title VII of this law are given in Exhibit 1.7.

A patchwork of governmental agencies is involved in the application and policing of the laws and orders. Chief among these is a set of regulatory agencies created for the enforcement of specific statutes and the system of courts. The federal agencies that are active in the enforcement of employment laws are

Agency	**Enforcement Responsibility**
National Labor Relations Board (NLRB)	National Labor Relations Act
Equal Employment Opportunity Commission (EEOC)	Title VII of the Civil Rights Act, Age Discrimination in Employment Act, Equal Pay Act
Office of Federal Contract Compliance Programs (OFCCP)	Executive orders
Justice Department	Title VII in cases involving states, local governmental agencies, or political divisions

In enforcing the laws under their charge, the governmental agencies are entitled to make rules for their enforcement. The most notable of these in the civil rights/EEO fields are the *Uniform Guidelines on Employee Selection Procedures* published jointly by the U.S. Civil Service Commission, the Department of Justice, the Equal Employment Opportunity Commission, and the Department of Labor in 1978. Portions of these guidelines that relate directly to job analysis are given in Appendix L. (These guidelines are hereafter referred to as the *Uniform Guidelines*.)

The regulatory agencies have no direct enforcement or punishment powers. They are expected to bring about settlement of grievances through conciliation. When conciliation fails, they must petition the courts for enforcement of their findings and orders. The rules and guidelines formulated by them are also subject to review and approval by the courts. The courts may choose to approve their rules, modify them, or overturn them in their entirety. However, the courts typically honor the rules formulated by the agencies. In the famous *Griggs* v. *Duke Power Company* case, the Supreme Court stated that the *Uniform Guidelines* are entitled to "great deference." (For more extensive reviews of the state of the employment relations law, see Sovereign, 1984, and Twomey, 1986.)

LEGAL STATUS OF JOB ANALYSIS

With the foregoing as background, we can now put in perspective the legal status of job analysis. Let us begin by noting that job analysis is not mandated by law. By this we simply mean that there does not exist, either at the state or local level, any law that requires organizations to conduct job analysis. However, agency rules and court decisions now make it virtually impossible for companies, particularly large companies with heterogeneous labor forces, to be in compliance with the laws without conducting systematic job analysis. This applies particularly to the civil rights/EEO laws listed in Exhibit 1.6.

To understand the underlying linkages, it is useful to stand back and examine the central goals of the civil rights/EEO laws. Stripped of their legal technicalities, these laws are aimed at promoting the upward mobility of blacks, women, and other traditionally underprivileged groups. There are two parts to this effort: preventing unfair discrimination and facilitating their movement into the system through affirmative action and other proactive requirements and exhortations. The first calls for a ban on the use of race, religion, sex, and national origin as a basis for treating people unequally. The second calls for the removal of practices that result in unequal consequences for the underprivileged and the taking of proactive steps to bring them into the fold of opportunity (Ledvinka, 1982, p. 37).

Given these twin goals, job analysis has a prominent place in the arena of equal employment opportunity. Its most notable use in the EEO arena has been as an employer defense against charges of unfair discrimination in the presence of adverse impact. These linkages are brought out in the following excerpts from the *Uniform Guidelines*:

> The fundamental principle underlying the guidelines is that employer policies or practices which have an adverse impact on employment opportunities of any race, sex, or ethnic group are illegal under Title VII and the Executive Order unless justified by business necessity. (Supplementary Information, Section II)

> Once an employer has established that there is adverse impact, what steps are required by the guidelines? . . . the employer can modify or eliminate the procedure which produces the adverse impact, thus taking the selection procedure from the coverage of these guidelines. If the employer does not do that, then it must justify the use of the procedure on grounds of "business necessity." This normally means that it must show a clear relation between performance on the selection procedure and performance on the job. In the language of industrial psychology, the employer must validate the selection procedure. (Section IV)

In the presence of adverse impact, the employer thus must either mend its ways or undertake validation. The foundation of the validation strategies recognized in the *Uniform Guidelines* is job analysis. The procedural requirements are explained in Appendix L.

Employer defense against charges of unfair discrimination has not been the only impetus behind job analysis in the EEO arena. Fear of being in violation of the EEO laws has been another moving force. Large employers, particularly public utilities, have a lot to lose by the negative publicity that results from EEO cases. In addition, some employers pride themselves on being "good citizens." They actively subscribe to the spirit of the EEO laws.

As a result of these various interests, the scope of applications of job analysis in the EEO arena has widened considerably. The following are some of the uses to which it is being put in this area:

- Identification of the existence of differential validity.
- Validation of tests and other decision-making instruments.
- Verification of the job-relatedness of selection criteria.
- Demonstration of the bona fide occupational qualification status of selection criteria.
- Demonstration of business necessity.
- Identification of mobility paths and job ladders for the promotion of upward mobility of minorities.

The chapters that follow provide additional details relating to the application of job analysis in EEO activities. An entire section of Chapter 6 is dedicated to this issue.

1.4 Comparisons of Job Analysis with Other Fields

Modern society's interest in the systematic study of jobs dates back to the Industrial Revolution and the emergence of the factory system. Job analysis is but one of the fields that has emerged as a result of this interest. Over the years, other fields have developed that also deal in one way or the other with jobs. Before proceeding further, therefore, it is useful to examine these other fields and to point out the similarities and differences between them and job analysis in regard to fundamental concerns and methods. The following fields are discussed in the paragraphs that follow: work study, job design, job enlargement, job enrichment, and management by objectives. Our comparisons of these fields with job analysis focuses on the following points: unit of analysis, goals and concerns of the field, and characteristic methods.

WORK STUDY

The label *work study* is a catchall that historically accommodated a variety of specialized fields dealing with the organization of work. The most famous persons associated with these fields were Frederick W. Taylor and Frank and Lilian Gilbreth, the originators of the scientific management movement (Niebel, 1982).

Currently, work study consists of two major specializations: method study and work measurement (Exhibit 1.8). Method study, which is also referred to as motion study, is concerned with finding the ideal or best method of doing the work. Work measurement, which is also referred to as time study, is concerned with determining the standard time required to perform the work. The goal of both these specializations is enhancement of productivity.

EXHIBIT 1.8 Work Study and Its Components

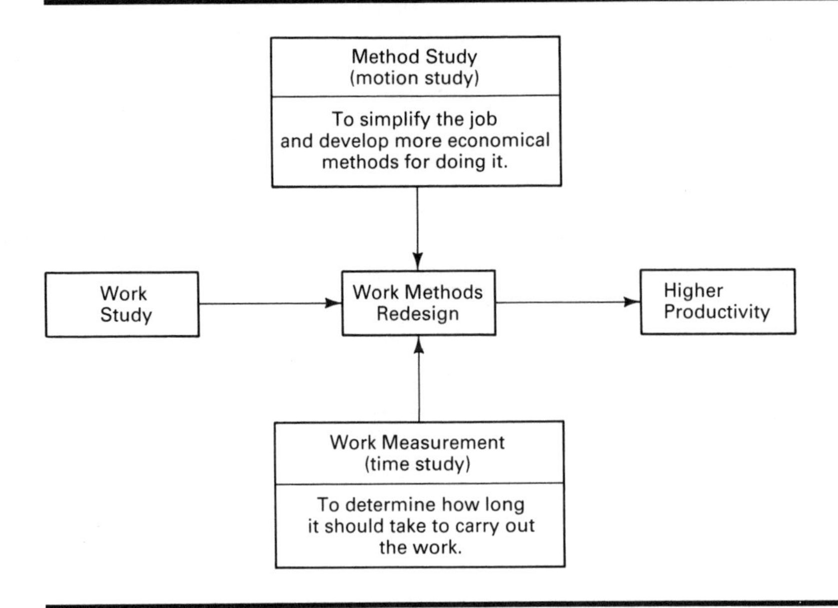

The basic procedure of work study consists of eight steps:

1. Select a job or process to be studied.
2. Record from direct observation everything that happens, using the most suitable of the recording techniques, so that the data will be in the most convenient form to be analyzed.
3. Examine the recorded facts critically and challenge everything that is done, considering in turn, the purpose of the activity, the place where it is performed, the sequence in which it is done, the person who is doing it, and the means by which it is done (Exhibit 1.11).
4. Develop the most economic method, taking into account all the circumstances.
5. Measure the quantity of work involved in the method selected and calculate a standard time for doing it.
6. Define the new method and the related time so that it can always be identified.
7. Install the new method as agreed standard practice with the time allowed.
8. Maintain the new standard practice by proper control procedures (International Labour Organisation, 1979, p. 35).

Steps 1, 2, and 3 occur in every work study. Step 4 is part of method study, while step 5 relies on work measurement (Exhibit 1.8).

The rationale behind work study is illustrated in Exhibit 1.9. In this schema, *work content* refers to the amount of work contained in a given product measured in worker-hours or machine-hours. *Basic work content* is the irreducible minimum time theoretically required to produce one unit of output. Excess work content is added to by defects in design or product specifications, inefficient methods of manufacturing, and shortcomings of management and workers.

The role that work study can play in improving the efficiency of existing processes is shown in Exhibit 1.10. A company faced with unacceptably low levels of productivity has two options: (1) invest capital in developing new processes and installing machinery that is more efficient or (2) reduce work content and ineffective time through better management. The first option is always available but is costly or requires time to attain results. Work study offers the alternative of keeping the existing processes and making them more efficient.

With this background as a basis, we can now compare work study with job analysis. There is evident an immediate difference in the unit of analysis of the two specializations. The focus of work study is on processes, methods, and techniques involved in manufacturing; that of job

EXHIBIT 1.9 How Manufacturing Time Is Made Up

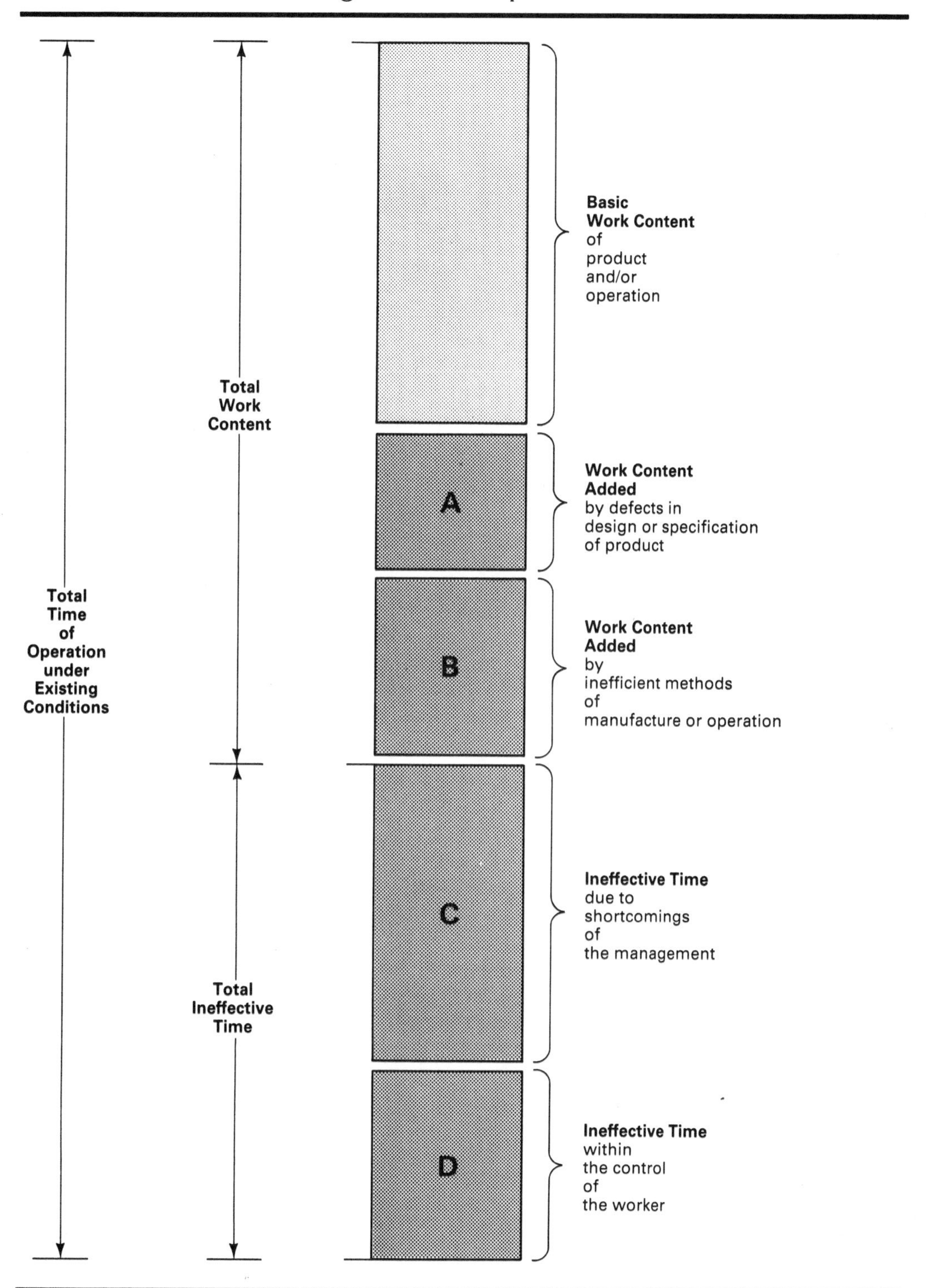

From International Labour Organisation, *Introduction to Work Study*, 3rd ed. (Geneva: ILO, 1979), p. 14. Copyright © 1979 by the International Labour Organisation, Geneva. Reprinted by permission.

analysis is on the job. Differences are also noticeable with regard to goals. Work study has a definite commitment to productivity, with enhancement of productivity being the primary justification behind the effort. Enhancement of productivity is compatible with job analysis; however, it would be one of many concerns.

EXHIBIT 1.10 Role of Work Study in Improving Productivity

Approach	Type of Improvement	Means	Cost	How Quickly Can Results be Achieved?	Extent of Improvement in Productivity	The Role of Work Study
Capital investment	1. Development of new basic process or fundamental improvement of existing ones	Basic research Applied research Pilot plant	High	Generally years	No obvious limit	Method study to improve ease of operation and maintenance at design state
	2. Install more modern or higher-capacity plant or equipment or modernize existing plant	Purchase Process research	High	Immediately after installation	No obvious limit	Method study in plant layout and to improve ease of operation when modernizing
Better management	3. Reduce the work content of the product	Product research Product development Quality management Method study Operator training Value analysis	Not high compared with 1 and 2	Generally months	Limited—of the same order as that to be expected from 4 and 5. Should *precede* action under those heads	Method study (and its extension, value analysis) to improve design for ease of production
	4. Reduce the work content of the process	Process research Pilot plant Process planning Method study Operator training Value analysis	Low	Immediate	Limited, but often of a high order	Method study to reduce wasted effort and time in operating the process by eliminating unnecessary movement
	5. Reduce ineffective time (whether due to management or to workers)	Work measurement Marketing policy Standardization Product development Production planning and control Material control Planned maintenance Personnel policy Improved working conditions Operator training Incentive schemes	Low	May start slowly but effect grows quickly	Limited, but often of a high order	Work measurement to investigate existing practice, locate ineffective time and set standards of performance as a basis for— A. Planning and control B. Utilization of plant C. Labor cost control D. Incentive schemes

EXHIBIT 1.11 The Primary Questions of Work Study

Purpose	What	is actually done?	*Eliminate* unnecessary parts of the job.
	Why	is the activity necessary at all?	
Place	Where	is it being done? Why is it done at that particular place?	*Combine* wherever possible
			or
Sequence	When	is it done? Why is it done at that particular time?	*Rearrange* the sequence of operations for more effective results.
Person	Who	is doing it? Why is it done by that particular person?	
Means	How	is it being done? Why is it being done in that particular way?	*Simplify* the operation.

From International Labour Organisation, *Introduction to Work Study*, 3rd ed. (Geneva: ILO, 1979), p. 101. Copyright © 1979 by the International Labour Organisation, Geneva. Reprinted by permission.

To appreciate the significance of this difference, consider the all too common situation where the enterprise is experiencing internal conflict but its productivity is at a level that management considers acceptable. In such cases, work study would serve little purpose. An analysis of the job structure of the company, along with surveys and other information gathering activities, might be more helpful in diagnosing the reasons behind the problems. The work study expert might be called in at a later stage if the arrangement of work were found to be a problem. A third difference between the two specializations pertains to scope of their respective involvement in bringing about change. The work study expert would be involved in all stages of the effort, from helping management diagnose the shortcomings of the processes to devising improved processes (Exhibit 1.11). The job analyst, on the other hand, is a provider of information; the actual implementation would be done by supervisors, recruiters, and other line roles (Exhibit 1.3).

JOB DESIGN

As currently construed in the human resource management literature, *job design* is a specialization that deals with the structuring of jobs in organizations. Once the need for a job is acknowledged, the job designer brings the job into existence by specifying the mission of the job, the machines, tools, equipment, and work aids to be used in its performance; the methods, processes, and techniques to be followed in doing the work; the tasks involved; and the depth and scope of the worker's involvement in the job. In short, the job designer grapples initially with the questions that the job analyst later investigates.

The relationship between job design and job analysis is nicely captured in a model presented in a new textbook on human resource management (Exhibit 1.12). Both fields have jobs as their common unit of analysis, but there are significant differences in the stage of involvement of the two with jobs and their underlying concerns. Job design is an aspect of work design or those activities aimed at creating the structure of the organization. It is the responsibility of the job designer to create the job, to spell out its mission and methods, and to place it within the broader network of interrelations that constitute the organization. The cycle of activities involved in job design ends with the creation of jobs. Job analysis, when performed, comes at a subsequent stage; it is performed on actual jobs, and it has as its central concern the study of the job as an organizational subunit. It may be undertaken routinely as a monitoring device or as a response to some managerial concern about effectiveness and efficiency. The information uncovered by the job analyst could be used by the job designer to redesign the job.

EXHIBIT 1.12 Relation Between Job Design and Job Analysis

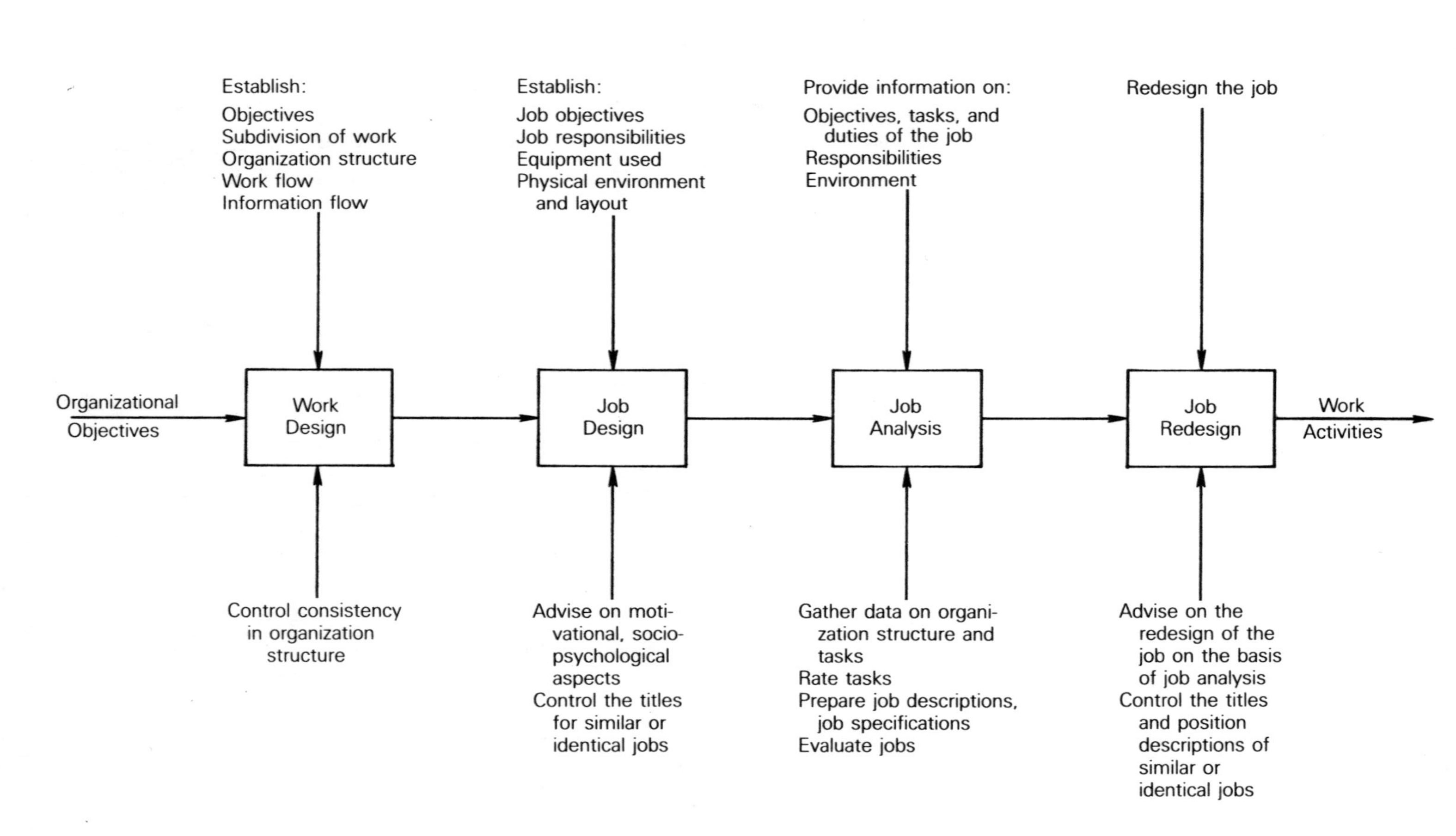

Source: L. A. Klatt, R. G. Murdick, and F. E. Schuster, *Human Resource Management* (Columbus, Ohio: Charles E. Merrill Company, 1985), p. 132. Copyright © 1985 by Bell & Howell Company. Reprinted by permission of the publisher.

JOB ENLARGEMENT AND ENRICHMENT

Job enlargement is a conscious redesign of a job to increase the scope of the job, that is, the number of tasks performed by the employee. *Job enrichment*, on the other hand, increases job depth or the degree of control that the worker has over the work. Under job enlargement, variety is added to the work, while under enrichment, the worker is given greater freedom, independence, and responsibility. Both these concepts are part of a movement to make work more interesting, challenging, and rewarding for the worker while at the same time enhancing productivity (see Davis & Taylor, 1979; Hackman & Suttle, 1977; Hackman & Oldham, 1980).

The three fields being compared here (job enlargement, job enrichment, and job analysis) have jobs as their common unit of analysis. However, they differ in regard to levels of analysis and underlying concerns. Enlargement and enrichment are concerned primarily with job-person relationships. More specifically, they seek to regulate the scope and depth of involvement of the worker in task performance. The object of this regulation is enhancement of worker satisfaction and productivity. They are both action-oriented fields with definite agendas and goals to attain. Job analysis, on the other hand, is concerned with a broader range of issues relevant to job performance (Exhibit 1.3). Also, job analysis is relatively neutral in regard to goals. It has the potential for providing management with a description of the current state of the job-person relationship. This information might be used to enlarge and enrich the job or to simplify and narrow its scope further. But the concept itself is not intrinsically linked with any agenda or action scheme.

MANAGEMENT BY OBJECTIVES

Management by objectives (MBO) is a participative approach to management that relies on tangible, verifiable, and measurable performance factors in assigning work to subordinates and in monitoring their performance. The process involved in this approach is shown in Exhibit 1.13. An important characteristic of MBO is that it relies heavily on participation by subordinates in the setting of performance goals (Morrissey, 1977; Drucker, 1954).

Comparison between MBO and job analysis yields the following similarities and differences. Both fields study jobs, but they differ widely in regard to aspects of jobs studied, goals, and methods. MBO is focused on an important, but specific, element: results of jobs and the monitoring of performance for the attainment of those results. Compare this with the multitude of interests pursued by job analysts shown in Exhibit 1.3. Also, MBO has a definite administrative concern: setting goals and monitoring performance. In contrast, job analysis has no commitment to any particular administrative goal beyond the provision of job-related information for decision making.

From a methodological perspective, MBO and job analysis have much to gain from each other. The analysis of an existing job can provide the supervisor with three categories of information that are an integral part of the MBO process: missions, objectives, and standards (Exhibit 1.13). The experiences gained from the operation of MBO programs, on the other hand, can provide valuable information for the job analyst regarding the role of the job and its place within the wider organizational context.

1.5 Job Analysis and the Human Resource Director: Questions and Answers

The preceding discussion has covered many and diverse issues relating to job analysis. The purpose of this section is to summarize the basics and to crystalize the role of job analysis in human resource management by using the question and answer format.

Q. What is job analysis and why should a company invest resources in conducting it?

A. Broadly viewed, job analysis refers to gathering, analyzing, and synthesizing information about jobs. There are two reasons for a company to invest resources in job analysis. First, job

EXHIBIT 1.13 The Management-by-Objectives and Results Process

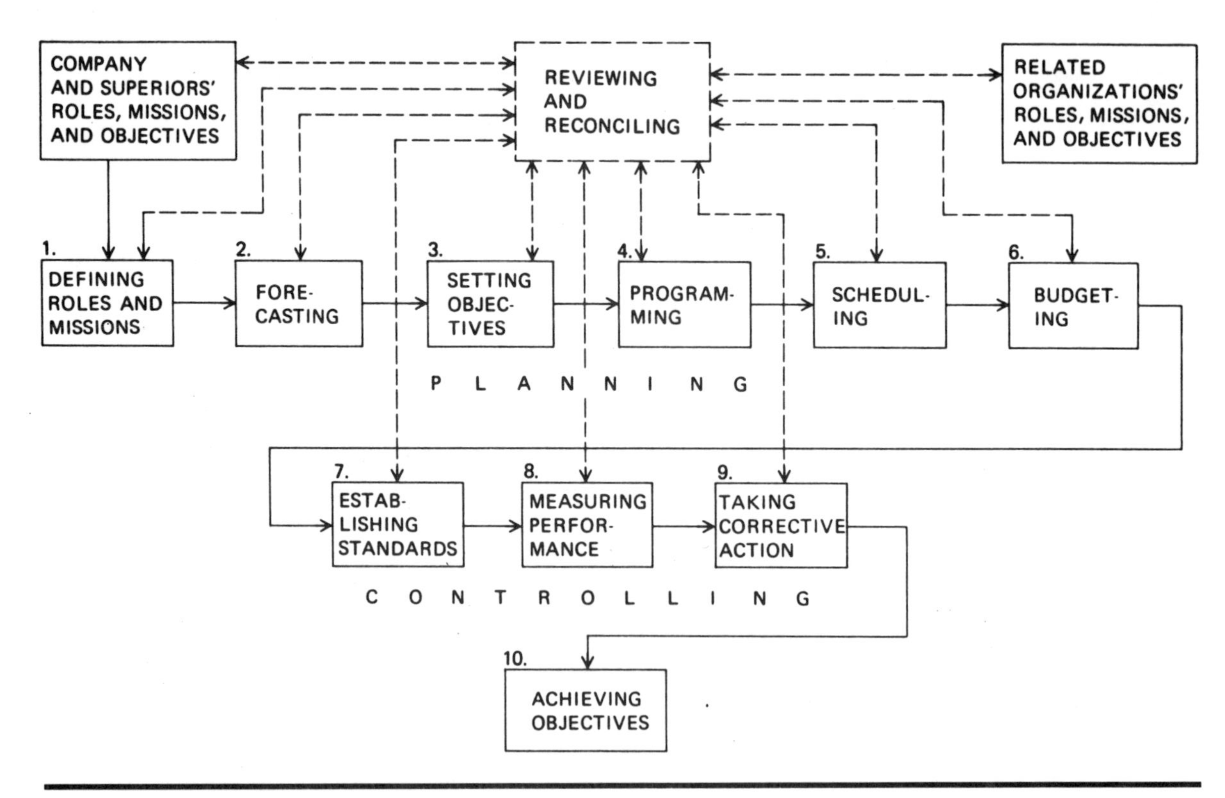

From G. L. Morrissey, *Management by Objectives and Results for Business and Industry*, © 1977, Addison-Wesley Publishing Company, Inc., Reading, Massachusetts. Page 19, Fig. 2.1. Reprinted with permission.

analysis, in some form, is an inherent part of management. There is no choice in this matter. Without access to job information, managers cannot design the workplace, assign work to individuals, appraise performance, and perform the many other duties that go with their role. Job analysis provides a systematic way of fulfilling this ongoing need for job information. Without systematic job study, managers would be performing these functions in a vacuum or with unreliable, biased, or incomplete information.

Second, although job analysis is not mandated by law, agency guidelines and court decisions look upon job analysis very favorably. Job analysis is strongly recommended in the *Uniform Guidelines*, particularly in cases where adverse impact has been found. In adjudicating EEO cases, the courts look for evidence of systematic job study in the human resource programs of defendant corporations. The mere presence of a job analysis is not enough from a legal point of view. But evidence showing a sincere effort on the part of the employer to base human resource decisions on objectively and systematically gathered data does add to the credibility of the defense.

Q. Why should the human resource director invest resource in this activity?

A. People, the main charge of the human resource director, must ultimately relate to their employing organizations through their jobs. There is no place within an organization for an individual without some formal or informal work assignment. This being the case, job analysis should have a natural appeal for the human resource director. Systematically gathered job information can provide the foundation for the performance of all other human resource management functions. Involvement of the human resource department in this activity can also broaden the outlook of its staff, establish links with the industrial engineers, and generally contribute toward the development of better human resource management programs.

Q. What is the mission of the job analyst, and what tasks and interfaces are involved in this role?

A. The mission of the job analyst is to provide management with valid, accurate and reliable information about jobs. A description of the tasks involved in the job analyst's job provided in the *Dictionary of Occupational Titles* is reproduced in Exhibit 1.14. Combining the generalities stated in this description with our preceding discussion of the job analysis process, four principal activity dimensions and interfaces of the job analyst's role can be identified.

1. Consulting with managers and human resource staffs to determine the purposes and scope of the analysis. The job analyst is a specialist with a distinctive mission. But the determination of the thrust of the activity is a prerogative of management.
2. Analyzing jobs and formulating job descriptions, worker specifications, and other products of job analysis. The number of products developed and their contents are determined by the purposes to be served.
3. Training of recruiters, compensation analysts, trainers, and other specialists in the proper use and applications of the job analysis products. This is necessary since the connections between the products of job analysis and their practical applications are not readily evident. Also, the development of these products might call for changes in operating procedures and practices.
4. Recommending changes in methods, procedures, and practices. Attempts to study jobs place the job analyst in a position to uncover inefficiencies and inequities in the operations of the organization. It is natural, therefore, to expect the analyst to pass these on to interested parties. But the job analyst would not have the primary responsibility for the implementation of changes.

Note the highly specialized conception of the job analyst's role. As we see it, the technical side of the activity begins with identification of the job-related informational needs of the functions to be ultimately served; it ends with the derivation of the products of job analysis. The training obligation of the job analyst is a facilitative function. Here, the job analyst serves as a counselor, trainer, and guide; the actual implementation is to be done by the users. The recommender role is also a facilitative function. Unlike the work study expert, the job analyst does not get involved in bringing about changes in methods and procedures.

Q. How is job analysis conducted, that is, how is job-related information gathered, analyzed, and synthesized?

EXHIBIT 1.14 A Partial Description of the Job Analyst's Job

166.267–018 JOB ANALYST (profess. & kin.) personnel analyst.

Collects, analyzes, and prepares occupational information to facilitate personnel, administration, and management functions of organization: Consults with management to determine type, scope, and purpose of study. Studies current organizational occupational data and compiles distribution reports, organization and flow charts, and other background information required for study. Observes jobs and interviews workers and supervisory personnel to determine job and worker requirements. Analyzes occupational data, such as physical, mental, and training requirements of jobs and workers and develops written summaries, such as job descriptions, job specifications, and lines of career movement. Utilizes developed occupational data to evaluate or improve methods and techniques for recruiting, selecting, promoting, evaluating, and training workers, and administration of related personnel programs. May specialize in classifying positions according to regulated guidelines to meet job classification requirements of civil service system and be known as POSITION CLASSIFIER (gov. ser.).

Source: U.S. Department of Labor, *Dictionary of Occupational Titles*, 4th ed. (Washington, D.C.: U.S. Government Printing Office, 1977).

A. There is no set way of conducting job analysis. Job data are gathered by using the methods that are common to all research involving human subjects: observation, interview, and questionnaires. Job analysts today have access to a number of ready-made systems that can be used as aids in gathering, analyzing, and synthesizing job data. (These are described in Chapter 3 and in Appendix A.)

Q. Who should be assigned the responsibility for the conduct of job analysis, and what are the knowledges, skills, abilities, and other human characteristics required of those performing this work?

A. The *who* in job analysis could be a subunit of the organization or a person. Assigning the responsibility to a subunit makes sense if the organization is large, has a highly differentiated job structure, employs a heterogeneous labor force, and is characterized by rapid changes in its methods and procedures. Small organizations, on the other hand, can get by with delegating this responsibility to one or more persons within the organization.

Precise specification of the KSAOs involved in job analysis work is not possible at this time. Ironically, the job has yet to be studied from this perspective. Even though the role has been in existence for some time, and even though the concept itself offers ways of remedying this deficiency, the KSAOs of this job have yet to be established systematically. (Qualitative descriptions of the job analyst KSAOs are found in the following: Tead & Metcalfe, 1933, pp. 241–242; International Labour Organisation, 1979, pp. 43–45.)

The absence of research on the KSAOs involved in job analysis work creates a dilemma. Given this void, to attempt a specification is to violate a principle that we strongly advocate: KSAOs for jobs need to be determined after systematic description of the job. An entire chapter is dedicated to showing how this can be attained (Chapter 5). But to pass over this area without some commentary is to leave the reader in the dark about a critical ingredient of job analysis.

Our compromise is as follows. The activities involved in job analysis are discussed at length in the chapters that follow. While these are not a substitute for a concise statement of the required KSAOs, they do provide some understanding of the demands made by the job on those assigned to perform it. At this stage, it suffices to offer a caution: the responsibility for job analysis should not be assigned to clerks. There is need for clerical skills in job analysis. But the demands of the activity call for an array of KSAOs that go beyond those required in clerical work. The basis for this statement will become clearer as the analysis unfolds.

1.6 Plan of This Book

This chapter has provided an overview of the role of job analysis in human resource management. This final section reveals the plan of the book and highlights the key features of the approach.

CHAPTER SEQUENCE AND CONTENTS

This book consists of six chapters. Our concern in this chapter has been with introducing the reader to job analysis. Chapter 2 follows up with a discussion of job information or the subject matter of job analysis. Chapter 3 presents the *how* of job analysis or the methods used in gathering, analyzing, and synthesizing job information. A major commitment of this chapter is the description of systems of job analysis that have been developed to aid the analyst in the conduct of the activity.

Chapter 4 deals with *job description*, which is the primary, first-level product of job analysis. Chapter 5 is concerned with *worker specification* or the derivation of the KSAOs needed for effective job performance.

Chapter 6 is dedicated to showing the *uses* of job analysis results in human resource management. The focus is on tracing the linkages between job analysis products and human resource management functions.

The rest of this section is concerned with highlighting the key features of the approach used in this book. Links are shown between the ideas that were expressed in this chapter in rudimentary form and the chapters to follow.

APPROACH TO JOB ANALYSIS

As this book is to serve as a practical guide, discussion of theories and models has been minimized. Nevertheless, all books need to have an approach to the subject or preconceptions of the interrelations among the factors studied. This book is no exception; it does rest on some preconceptions. They are contained in several of the illustrations given in this chapter. Stated in propositional terms, they are as follows.

- Jobs are subunits of organizations (Exhibit 1.1).
- Job analysis consists of sets of activities that are directed at uncovering information about jobs, information that can be used in the performance of various managerial functions (Exhibit 1.2).
- While job analysis has potential for uncovering a wide range of job-related information, the thrusts of particular analyses will be determined by their purposes (Exhibits 1.3 and 1.4).
- The methods used in job analysis are determined by the nature of the data gathered, which in turn are influenced by the purposes to be served. There are no standard or universal means of data gathering and analysis.
- The job analyst is a specialist. The primary responsibility of this role is the construction of job descriptions, worker specifications, compensable factors, and other job-related informational outputs (Exhibits 1.3, 1.4, 1.5, and 1.14).

The chapters that follow are elaborations of these preconceptions. The diagrams provided in the introductory sections of the chapters are of particular relevance to our approach (Exhibits 1.1 to 1.5).

COVERAGE OF LAWS

Legal developments have been a significant influence behind the current popularity of job analysis. But these developments are many in number and relate to a wide range of issues in job analysis. To attempt to cover them in one place would be both cumbersome and confusing. Coverage of laws is therefore handled as follows.

The overview of the laws provided earlier in this chapter is supplemented with discussions of specific applications and requirements as they relate to the topics covered in the chapters that follow. Chapters 3, 4, and 5 contain sections showing the legal requirements relating to the topics covered in those chapters. The discussion of laws in Chapter 6 is interspersed throughout the chapter.

COVERAGE OF TECHNIQUES

A variety of techniques have been developed in recent years to aid the analyst in gathering, analyzing, and synthesizing job information. An attempt is made in this book to bring these together around the central activities of job analysis. Chapter 3 is dedicated entirely to explaining the techniques, methods, and systems of job analysis. Every chapter that follows has some discussion of techniques. Additionally, a collection of selected instruments is provided in the appendices to the book. These instruments, along with the many illustrations provided, should make this handbook a fairly complete guide for the job analyst.

TERMINOLOGY OF JOB ANALYSIS

Even though job analysis as a concept has been around for a while, its terminology is still loose and suffers from inconsistent usage. An attempt is made in this book to remedy this situation. Sections containing definitions of terms are included in Chapters 2 to 5. Specialized terms encountered in Chapter 6 are defined as the need arises.

2 Job Information: Nature and Measurement

Job analysis is concerned with gathering, analyzing, and synthesizing information about jobs. The purpose of this chapter is to provide an overview of the types of information that constitute the subject matter of job analysis. The following are the specific goals of this chapter:

1. To define a set of basic terms encountered in job analysis.
2. To sort job information into useful conceptual categories.
3. To present the substantive properties of jobs that need to be taken into account in attempts to analyze them.
4. To take note of the difference in job factors according to their measurement properties.
5. To discuss issues that are relevant to the measurement of job properties.

2.1 Basic Terminology of Job Analysis

The following are definitions of the basic terms encountered in job analysis. Their interrelations are highlighted in the discussion that follows.

Job output	Results stemming from the performance of the job. In the job analysis literature, outputs are typically broken down into products and services.
Resources	The material, human, and ideational resources used in the work.
Input	Broadly viewed, any factor that influences the performance of the job.
Throughput	Activities undertaken to transform resources into desired outputs.
Operation	The intentional changing of a part to attain the desired size, shape, or form.
Process	A series of operations that advance a product toward its ultimate size, shape, or form.
Techniques and methods	Ways of combining resources through the use of tools for attaining the purposes of the job.
Task	A set of interrelated activities, performed by the worker, and directed at attaining job outputs.
Behaviors	The nature of the human involvement in task performance.

Job context	The physical, cultural, and psychological environment in which the work takes place.
Job information	Any data, qualitative or quantitative, that are descriptive of the job being studied. These could encompass factors that constitute the job itself, as well as characteristics of the worker, and the context in which the work takes place.
Job descriptor	Any job information that is consciously chosen to serve as a basis for describing, analyzing, classifying, or evaluating the job.

Jobs are rooted in the fabric of the organization. Attempts to study them bring the analyst in contact with a wide array of cultural, technological, and physical factors. For analytic purposes, however, it is possible to view job information in two ways: substantive properties of jobs and form of information. The substantive view looks upon jobs as parts of organizations. The concern here is with isolating the inherent attributes of jobs as organizational units. Alternatively, job information can also be considered for its form. The concern in this case is with noting the properties of job factors from a measurement perspective. Additional details on this fundamental distinction are given in the discussion that follows.

2.2 Job Information: Substantive Considerations

Jobs are the building blocks of organizations. They are created by organizations for the attainment of specific goals relevant to the attainment of their ultimate missions. Viewed as organizational units, jobs reveal a set of inherent properties. To highlight these properties, Exhibit 2.1 shows the interrelations among common elements of the job situation by using the terminology of system theory. This diagram is used as a basis for the discussion that follows.

OUTPUTS

Jobs are an expression of division of labor. They are formed and sustained by organizations for the production of outputs that are needed for the functioning of the organization. Broadly viewed, an *output* is any result that emanates from the job and is relevant to the functioning of the organization. In the job analysis literature, job outputs are classified roughly into two types: products and services (U.S. Department of Labor, 1972; Gael, 1983, p. 54).

EXHIBIT 2.1 Interrelations Among Common Elements of Job Situations

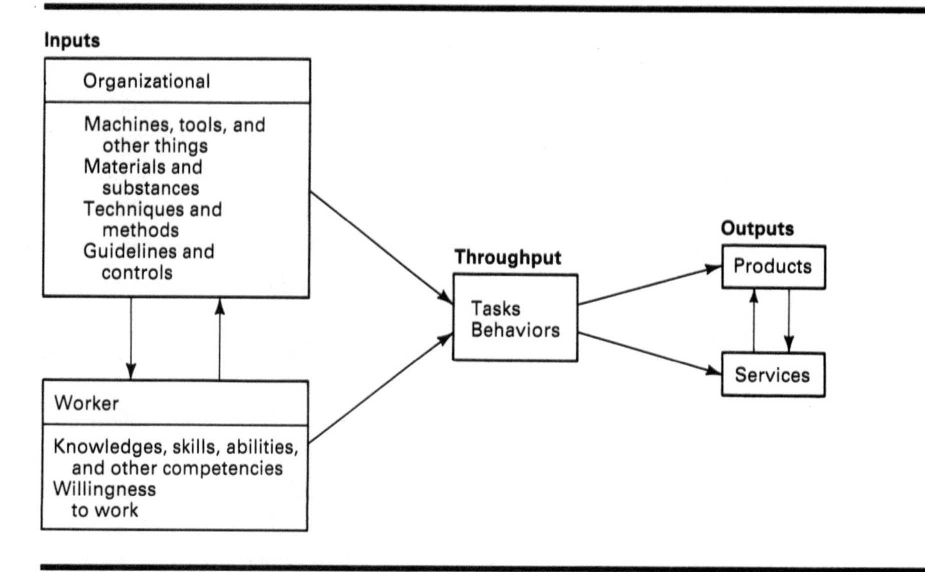

Products. The label *product* in job study is used to refer to outputs of a tangible nature. Products are visible, "hard," directly measurable things. They can include finished products or goods in process. Examples of products from various walks of life are

Radiologist	Administers barium mixture. Takes spot films. Approves radiographs.
Job Analyst	Develops job descriptions. Sets worker specifications. Establishes compensable factors. Establishes performance standards. Creates job families.
Professor	Grades term papers. Grades examinations Publishes scholarly papers.

Services. These can be viewed as a residual category of outputs. They include results or performance expectations that cannot be neatly identified as products. Their relevance stems from the reality that the results of many jobs cannot be expressed in tangible terms. This is so in some cases because the work consists of mental activities that may not result in immediate, tangible things. Examples of such services are the functions performed by managers and thinking processes engaged in by scientists. In other cases, outputs are classified as services because the performance expectations of the job holder are behavioral in nature. Examples of these are found in the activities of an assisting nature, for example, nurse assisting surgeon during an operation.

While the categorization of outputs into products and services is useful in a conceptual sense, a couple of difficulties are encountered in implementation. To begin with, service activities can sometimes be measured, and hence could be treated as products for decision-making purposes. Thus, the services provided by nurses can be counted, for example, physical motions, movements, trips. Also, the unit of measurement can be changed in reaching job outputs. Thus, the performance of managers can be evaluated on the basis of the outputs of their work units. The focus here shifts from what they do to what they attain in their roles as managers.

The responsibility for choosing the appropriate unit in studying outputs rests with the job analyst. The distinction between products and services can be used as a preliminary guide. Once the relevant outputs are identified, they serve thereafter as the rudder for the rest of the analysis. Outputs reflect the purposes of the job and provide a basis for tracing the linkings with other job factors.

INPUTS

Inputs are the things that are put into the job for the attainment of the desired outputs. Inputs can be classified roughly into two categories according to their source: organizational and worker (Exhibit 2.1).

Organizational Inputs. Roughly four types of inputs are provided by organizations to job holders for the performance of the work as shown in Exhibit 2.1. Each of these is discussed briefly in the paragraphs that follow.

In the modern enterprise, work is accomplished through the use of *things* of various kinds. The following are definitions and examples of the things that are commonly encountered, and need to be accounted for, in job analysis.

Machines	Devices that are a combination of mechanical parts with the framework and fastenings to support and connect them, designed to apply force to do work

	on or to move materials or to process data. Examples: computers, typewriters, drill presses, conveyors, and computers.
Tools	Implements that are manipulated to do work on or move materials. Examples: hand tools, electric cutters, paint-spray guns, and electric screwdrivers.
Equipment	Devices that generate power, communicate signals, or have an effect upon material through application of light, heat, electricity, steam, chemicals, or atmospheric pressure. Examples: ovens, stills, forges, cameras, and P.B.X. switchboards.
Work aids	Miscellaneous items that cannot be included in the preceding categories. Examples: jigs, fixtures, and clamps used to secure workpiece in place for future operations; special measuring devices such as micrometers, calipers, and gauges that are manipulated by hand; graphic instructions (blueprints, sketches, maps, charts) and other formalized job instructions and manuals; and musical instruments (adapted from U.S. Department of Labor, 1972, pp. 5–6).

The acronym MTEWA is commonly used in the job analysis literature to refer to machines, tools, equipment, and work aids. These elements are so referred to hereafter in this presentation.

A second type of input provided by organizations to job holders is *materials*. These can be sorted roughly into three categories:

Basic materials	Raw ingredients used in the manufacture of goods and services. Examples: wood, metal, and fabric.
Goods-in-process	Partially completed products on their way to being finished. Examples: unfinished furniture, auto chassis heading for assembly, and spokes for wheels of bicycles.
Data	Information to be used in the compilation of final or other documents. Examples: raw data for the construction of billings, financial statements, and insurance policies.

A third type of organizational input into jobs consists of *techniques and methods* (*TMs*) or the ways in which the MTEWAs are to be used in job performance. In most cases, the TMs are implied in the MTEWAs used. However, it is possible (and frequently desirable) to isolate the TMs that go with the job. In the job analysis literature, the common practice is to depict TMs through method verbs. The following are some examples of TMs expressed through method verbs for various occupations.

Hunting, fishing	Baiting, bleeding, camouflaging, clubbing, hooking, shooting, snaring, spearing.
Machining	Calibrating, forming, measuring, shaping.
Accounting	Auditing, disbursing, tabulating, verifying.

A fourth type of organizational input consists of *guidelines and controls* under which the work is to be performed. The roots of this input can be traced to division of labor, which is a central characteristic of all organizations. Every job within the organization is expected to contribute a specialized product or service. Not only that, but the job product or service must meet the specifications of the organization. Guidelines and controls aid in retaining job focus and assure that the work meets both the quantity and quality requirements of the organization.

Guidelines and controls come in the form of prescriptions. Their subject matter can encompass the entire range of factors associated with jobs. They can address

- *What* the worker is to produce or serve, including prescriptions relating to quantity and quality of output.

- *How* the work is to be performed or specifications relating to the MTEWAs, materials, and techniques and methods to be used in job performance.
- The *activities* and *behaviors* required of the worker.
- *Where* and *when* or the place at which the work is to be done and the sequence of the operations.

As a job analysis concern, study of guidelines and controls has traditionally been linked with compensation decisions. In recent years, however, this factor has aroused considerable interest among behavioral scientists; it forms a central concern of the quality-of-work-life (QWL) movement. A principal claim of this movement is that allowing workers greater discretion at work promotes both high productivity and job satisfaction (Hackman & Suttle, 1977).

Worker Inputs. Workers bring two principal inputs to the job: competencies and a willingness to work. Competencies refer to the knowledges, skills, abilities, and other human characteristics (KSAOs) essential for job performance. Collectively, they signify the capability of the worker for performing the tasks, operations, and other demands of the job. Willingness, on the other hand, is in the realm of motivation. It is basic to the amount of effort the worker is willing to expend in job-related activity. (The elements of both of these worker inputs are discussed in more detail in Chapter 5.)

THROUGHPUT

The concept that links outputs with inputs is the notion of throughput. This is the dynamic aspect of jobs, and it is concerned with the transformation of the inputs into the desired products and services (Katz & Kahn, 1978).

While the notion of *throughput* has gained wide acceptance in the literature, there is lacking a consensus on how to express this aspect of job performance. The concepts shown under throughput in Exhibit 2.1 are commonly found in discussions of how work is performed. They help in exemplifying the dynamics that underlie the transformation of resources into outputs. In all of them, the main actor is the worker. A *task* consists of a set of interrelated activities directed at attaining job outputs. Tasks are performed by workers and constitute a necessary step in the transformation of the resources into the desired outputs. *Behaviors* are the specific human actions that are necessary for task performance. Exhibit 2.2 shows the connection between a task and its accompanying behaviors. A task statement spells out what needs to be accomplished in the form of activities with reference to a particular goal. Behaviors, on the other hand, show the nature of the human involvement called for by the work.

JOB CONTEXT

The context of the job refers to the environment or setting in which the work takes place. An inventory of factors that comprise the environment of jobs is given in Exhibit 2.3.

The need for studying job context is widely recognized in the literature. The basis for the interest in study of context stems from an established fact about organizations: context prescribes the modus operandi and could influence the *who*, *how*, *when* and other specifics relating to job performance. This means that jobs with common outputs can vary widely in regard to the arrangment of the work system and expectations relating to performance requirements.

To illustrate this claim, consider the partial descriptions of the airline pilots' jobs given in Exhibit 2.4. All these jobs have a common purpose—to pilot airplanes. But what a world of difference exists among them in regard to the specifics relating to tools, tasks, and performance requirements. Note in particular the variations in the nature and number of tasks performed by the various pilots, with the executive pilot performing a distinctively nonpilot task—representing the company on the executive level when dealing with business associates, officials, and customers. Glaring differences are also evident in regard to the physical and psychological climates in which the various pilots work. The commercial passenger pilot goes from airport to airport,

EXHIBIT 2.2 Interrelations Between Tasks and Behaviors: An Example from the Housing Industry

JOB: HOUSING INSPECTOR

General Responsibilities

Under supervision to do work of more than ordinary difficulty and complexity in the inspection of existing dwellings in investigating complaints and in the enforcement of applicable laws or ordinances and to do related work as required.

Task

Investigates complaints and makes routine inspections of dwellings, premises, nondwelling structures, and vacant lands to determine compliance with the housing maintenance code, zoning ordinance, and other applicable laws and ordinances.

Behaviors

1. Drives car to inspection site.
2. Gains entrance.
3. Observes, or looks for, "problems" that don't meet code in these areas: structure, electrical, plumbing, heating, ventilation, fire hazards, health hazards, safety hazards.
4. Records these observations in written form.
5. Based on findings, in line with the nature and seriousness of the problems, fills out forms, writes tags, or refers elsewhere.
6. Follows up later to see if conditions were improved by visiting site, telephoning, or writing.

From S. J. Mussio and M. K. Smith, *Content Validity: A Procedural Manual* (Minneapolis: Minneapolis Civil Service Commission, 1973), pp. 58–59.

which are typically air-conditioned, and encounters passengers, flight attendants, and other co-workers. The agricultural pilot typically flies alone but may have a farmer as a companion from time to time; this pilot's world consists of fields, pesticides, and livestock.

Description of the context of jobs is thus not simply a matter of recording the presence of a set of factors within the environment. To understand how work actually gets done, it is essential to select those factors that have potential for explaining variations in performances of groups and individuals. Recognizing that the list of context variables that can affect performance is very large, we present now a set of factors that are fruitful to investigate from a human resource management perspective.

Work Flow and Plant Layout. This component refers to the arrangement of machines, equipment, and work aids to facilitate the flow of materials in the processing of the goods and services. There are four types of layouts: fixed position, process or function, product or mass production, and group. Exhibit 2.5 shows the differences among these in schematic terms.

The fixed position layout is used when the material to be processed is fixed in one place and the workers, machines, equipment, and tools are brought to it. Examples are shipbuilding, aircraft, and automobile manufacture.

Under the process layout, all the operations of the same nature are grouped together. This layout is used when a large number of products that share the same machinery are being made and where the individual products have a low volume of output. Examples are cutting of materials in the making of garments, auto workshops, and sewing and stitching garments.

The product layout is used in situations where the demand is for standardized products and where the operations are broken down in a sequence. Examples are soft drinks, car assembly, and canning.

The group production layout is of relatively recent origin and stems from the quality-of-work-life movement. Under this arrangement, groups of workers team up for the making of a product or part and distribute work among themselves; they may also rotate tasks. This arrangement

EXHIBIT 2.3 Major Factors Affecting Employees' Job Performance and Productivity

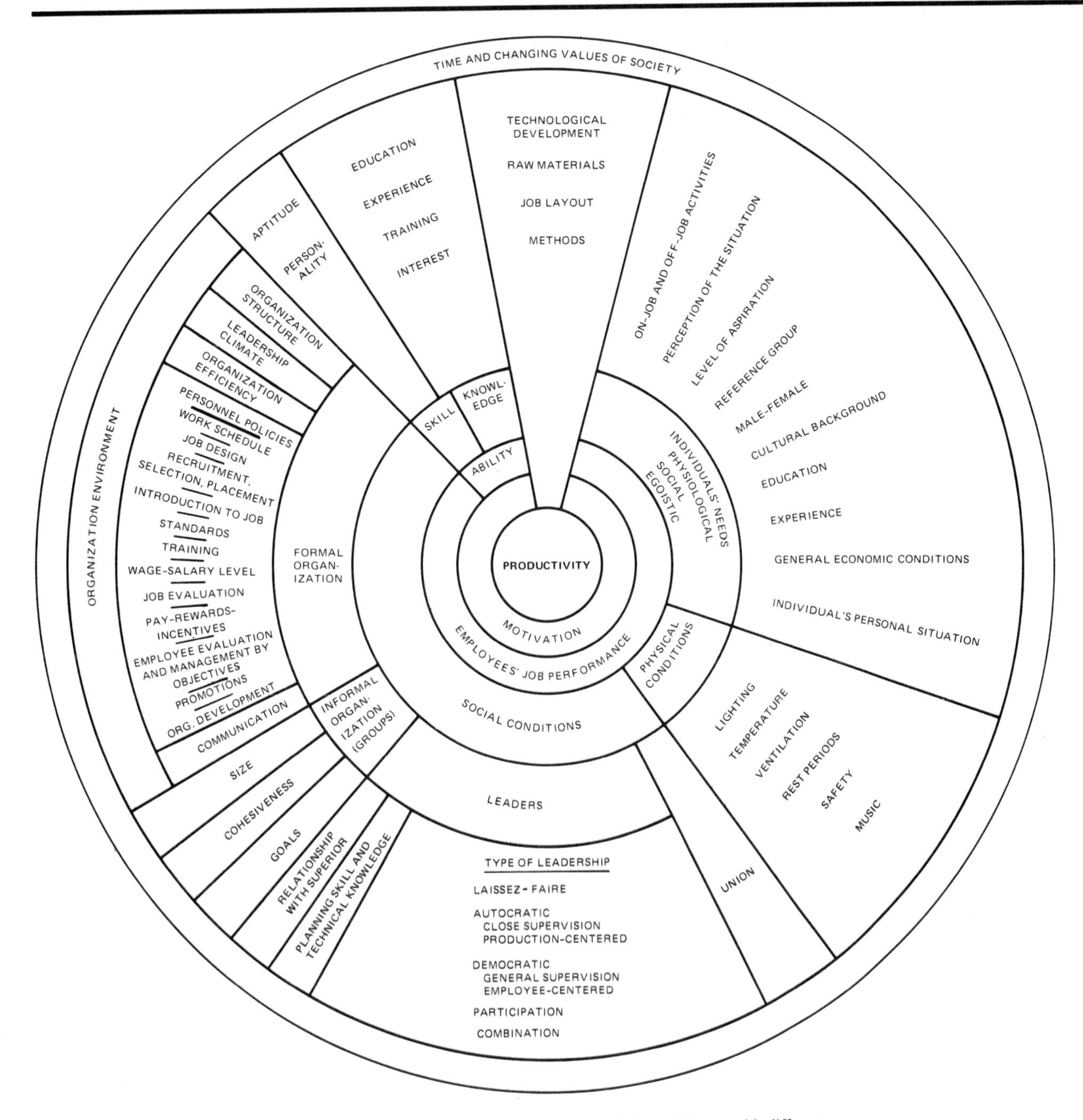

Note: The size of each segment has no relationship to its relative importance, which would vary with different organizations, different departments, and even different individuals with their own distinct needs. The factors in each segment affect factors in the corresponding segment of the next smaller circle; they may also affect and be affected by other segments in the same circle or other circles.

From: Robert A. Sutermeister, *People and Productivity*, 3rd ed. (New York: McGraw-Hill Book Company, 1976).

EXHIBIT 2.4 Partial Descriptions of Seven Airline Pilots Jobs

196.263–010 AIRPLANE PILOT (agric.) aerial-applicator pilot; agricultural-aircraft pilot; aircraft pilot; airplane pilot, crop dusting.

Pilots airplane or helicopter, at low altitudes, over agricultural fields to dust or spray fields with seeds, fertilizers, or pesticides: Flies over field together with FARMER (agric.) to become acquainted with obstacles or hazards, such as air turbulences, hedgerows, and hills peculiar to particular field. Arranges for warning signals to be posted. Notifies FARMERS (agric.) to move livestock from property over which harmful material may drift. Signals AIRPLANE-PILOT HELPER (agric.) to load aircraft. Observes field markers and flag waved by AIRPLANE-PILOT HELPER (agric.) on ground to prevent overlaps of application and insure complete coverage. May specialize in application of pesticides and be designated as PEST-CONTROL PILOT (agric.).

196.263–014 AIRPLANE PILOT, COMMERCIAL (air trans.) commercial pilot; pilot.

Pilots airplane to transport passengers, mail, or freight, or for other commerical purposes: Reviews ship's papers to ascertain factors, such as load weight, fuel supply, weather conditions, and flight route and schedule. Orders changes in fuel supply, load, route, or schedule to insure safety of flight. Reads gages to verify that oil, hydraulic fluid, fuel quantities, and cabin pressure are at prescribed levels prior to starting engines. Starts engines and taxies airplane to runway. Sets brakes, and accelerates engines to verify operational readiness of components, such as superchargers, carburetor-heaters, and controls. Contacts control tower by radio to obtain takeoff clearance and instructions. Releases brakes and moves throttles and hand and foot controls to take off and control airplane in flight. Pilots airplane to destination adhering to flight plan and regulations and procedures of Federal Government, company, and airport. Logs information, such as time in flight, altitude flown, and fuel consumed. Must hold Commerical Pilot's Certificate issued by Federal Aviation Administration. May instruct students or pilots in operation of aircraft. May be designated according to Federal license held as TRANSPORT PILOT (air trans.), or type of commerical activity engaged in as AIRLINE PILOT (air trans.) or CORPORATE PILOT (air trans.). When piloting airplane over pipelines, train tracks, and communications systems to detect and radio location and nature of damage is designated AIRPLANE-PATROL PILOT (bus. ser.). When in command of aircraft and crew is designated as AIRPLANE CAPTAIN (air trans.), or when second in command is designated AIRPLANE FIRST-OFFICER (air trans.) or COPILOT (air trans.).

196.263–018 AIRPLANE PILOT, PHOTOGRAMMETRY (bus. ser.)

Pilots airplane or helicopter at specified altitudes and airspeeds, following designated flight lines, to photograph areas of earth's surface for mapping and other photogrammetric purposes: Sights along pointers (window blocking) on aircraft to topographical landmarks. Adjusts controls to hold aircraft on course, to insure required overlap with photographs taken on previous flight line, and to select landmark points as guide for next flight line. Observes dials and moves controls to hold aircraft in level flight to eliminate contour errors in photographs caused by forward and lateral tilt of aircraft.

196.263–030 EXECUTIVE PILOT (any ind.) company pilot; corporation pilot; private pilot.

Pilots company-owned aircraft to transport company officials or customers, and makes preflight and inflight tests to insure safety of flight: Files flight plan with airport officials. Obtains weather data and interprets data based on flight plan. Operates radio equipment aboard airplane. May maintain and repair aircraft according to limitations set by A & E license. May represent company on executive level when dealing with business associates, officials, and customers.

196.263–034 FACILITIES-FLIGHT-CHECK PILOT (gov. ser.)

Operates airplane equipped with special radio, radar, and other electronic equipment to conduct in-flight testing of air navigational aids, air traffic controls, and communications equipment, and to evaluate sites of proposed equipment installation: Plans flight activities in accordance with test schedule. Pilots flight pattern and files flight plan. Informs crewmembers of flight and test procedures. Coordinates flight activities with ground-support crews and air-traffic-control. Operates aircraft over designated area at specified altitudes in all types of weather to determine receptivity and other characteristics of airport-control signal and navigation and communications equipment and systems, such as racon, tacan, scater, and atis. Prepares evaluation reports of each flight. Conducts periodic preflight checks of aircraft to insure proper maintenance and safe operation.

196.263–038 HELICOPTER PILOT (any ind.)

Pilots helicopter to transport people, cargo, mail, fight fires, or to spread seed for reforestration. May instruct students in operation of helicopter and equipment, such as water buckets, seed spreaders, and hoisting slings. Must hold Commercial Pilot's Certificate with Helicopter Rating issued by Federal Aviation Administration. May be designated as PILOT-REPORTER (radio & tv broad.) when piloting craft over assigned area to observe and report on traffic conditions.

196.263–042 TEST PILOT (aircraft-aerospace mfg.)

Pilots new, prototype, experimental, modified, and production aircraft to determine their airworthiness: Inspects aircraft prior to flight by examining items, such as quantity of fuel and operation of controls. Starts and warms engine, listens to engine sounds at various speeds, and monitors instruments to detect malfunctions. Taxies aircraft to test controls, brakes, and shock absorbers. Radios control tower for takeoff instructions, releases brakes, and moves throttles and hand and foot controls, to take off and control aircraft in flight. Puts aircraft through maneuvers, such as stalls, dives, glides, rolls, turns, and speed runs, to test and evaluate stability, control characteristics, and aerodynamic design. Observes recording and operating instruments during test to evaluate airplane performance. Files report of test results. May give instructions for adjustments or replacement of parts. May deliver aircraft from factory or airport to designated receiving point.

From U.S. Department of Labor, *Dictionary of Occupational Titles*, 3rd ed. (Washington, D.C.: U.S. Government Printing Office, 1977).

is currently being tried out in companies in Europe and the United States (the foregoing summary is based on International Labour Organisation, 1979, p. 109).

Knowledge of the work flow and plant layout is useful in understanding the physical place of the job in the production process. This information could be useful to job designers and safety experts.

Physical Context. This component refers to the natural factors encountered at the workplace. It could also encompass the consequences arising from the combinations of materials and substances used in the work. The following are the major categories of factors that can be listed under the physical context of the job:

- Whether the work is inside or outside.
- Natural conditions such as temperature, heat, wetness, and humidity.
- Consequences stemming from the operation of the machinery such as noise, vibration, and radiant energy.
- Consequences stemming from the combination of the materials used in the production process such as fumes, odors, dusts, mists, and gases.

Knowledge of the physical context of work provides the basis for understanding health and safety conditions at work. It might also have implications in the compensation area, as the factors just described determine the attractiveness of the work.

Interrelations with Other Jobs. This has two dimensions: hierarchical and horizontal. The hierarchical dimension refers to the place of the job within the organizational hierarchy and paths of progression and movements. This is established quite simply by finding out to whom the worker reports and the jobs to which transfers and promotions are possible.

The horizontal dimension of job interrelations refers to the process or functional connections between the job under study and other jobs. Viewed in this way, jobs fall into three categories: independent, successive, coordinate.

In independent jobs, the incumbent works alone in performing significant portions of the work activities. Examples are mail delivery, outside sales, and forest rangers.

In successive jobs, jobs are a link in a chain of operations. Jobs in process and product plant layouts are examples of successive jobs.

EXHIBIT 2.5 Four Types of Plant Layouts

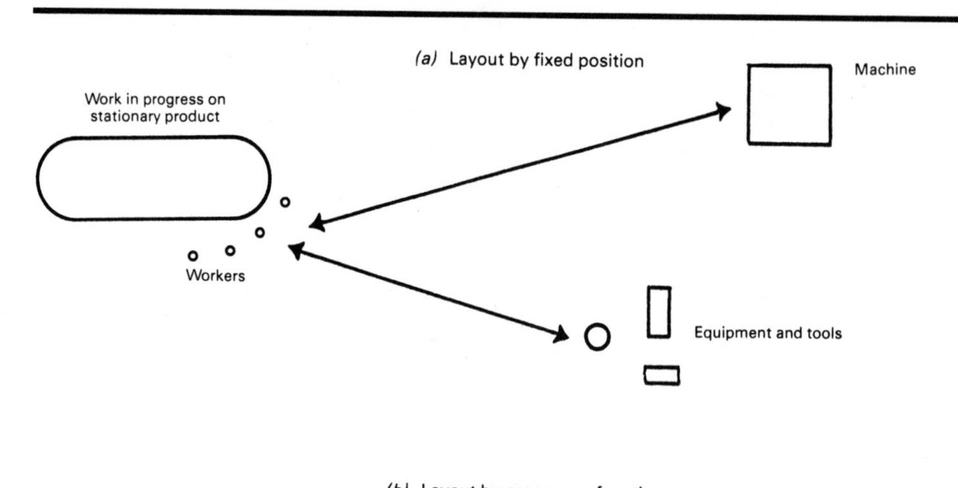

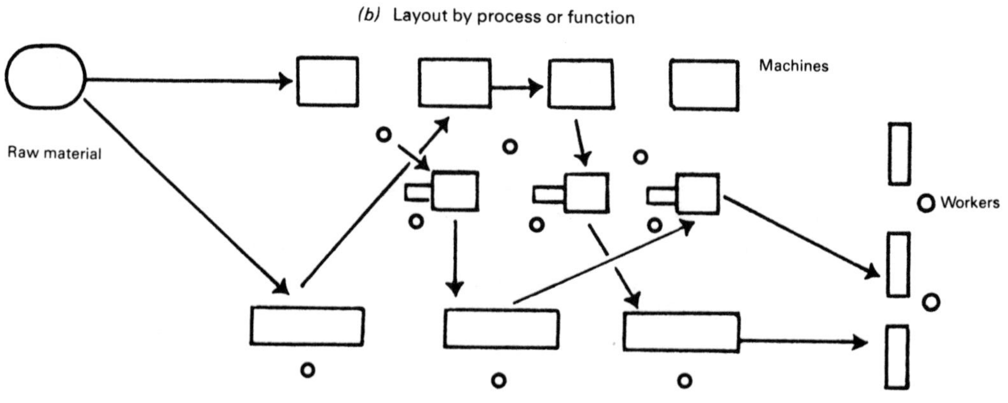

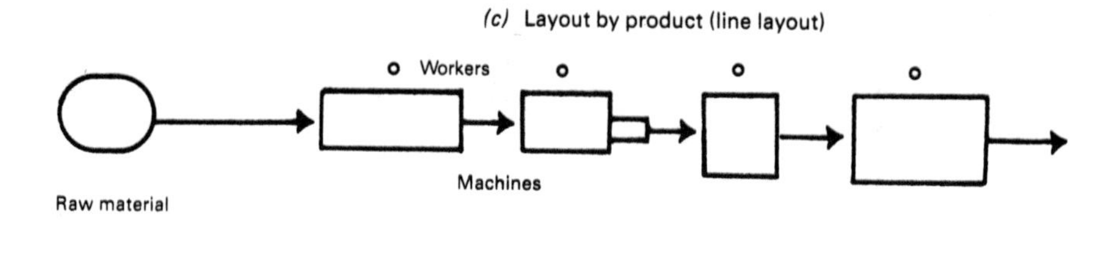

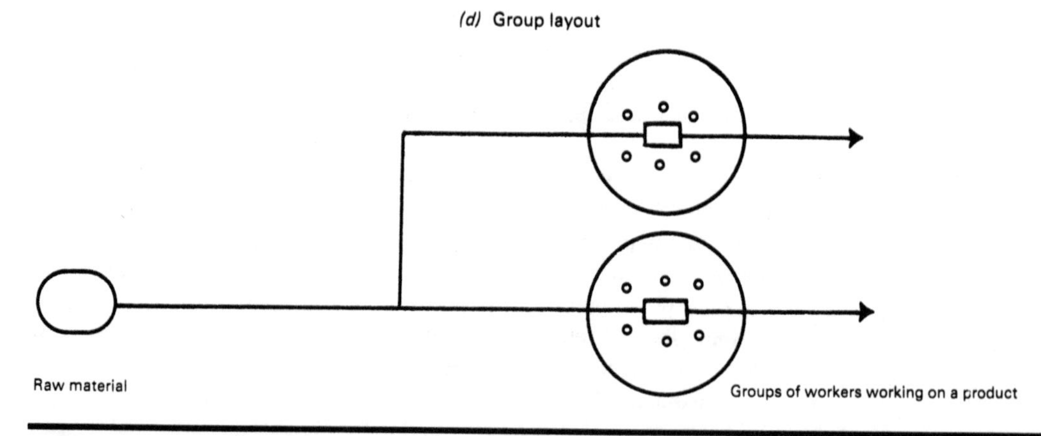

Source: International Labour Organisation, *Introduction to Work Study*, 3rd ed. (Geneva: ILO, 1979). Copyright © 1979 by International Labour Organization, Geneva. Reprinted by permission.

Coordinate jobs rely on a team work approach. Holders of coordinate jobs assist each other in the attainment of a common output, with each job providing a specialized service. Examples are operating room teams, athletic teams, and ship crews (Cascio, 1982, pp. 257–258).

Job interrelations are a fruitful area of investigation for human resource management purposes. To begin, this factor provides information relating to mobility paths, an item of vital interest to counselors and trainers. Each category of jobs brings with it certain attractions and problems. Thus, independent jobs provide autonomy and possibly variety for the worker. Maintaining control over quantity and quality is a problem for such jobs. Successive jobs tie the worker into a chain of linkings and are thus easier to control. Boredom is a major complaint relating to such jobs. Coordinate jobs foster interaction and closeness among the job holders. In such cases, however, it is difficult to single out individual contributions.

Terms and Conditions of Employment. This context factor which can cover a wide range of subjects, includes:

- Wage and salary rates and ranges.
- Incentives, if any.
- Benefits packages.

As a job analysis concern, the study of terms and conditions of employment needs to focus on the factors that form the basis of the employment contract for the particular job in question. The patterns of compensation for the company as a whole are relevant only in a comparative sense.

Legal Requirements. Many labor sectors are now affected by laws and agency rules. The concern in job analysis needs to be with identifying those constraints and requirements that relate to the job.

The table of laws and rules given in the first chapter of this book provides a starting point. Companies doing business with the government, governmental agencies, and unionzed companies may need to consult additional industry sources relating to laws and rules.

2.3 Job Information: Forms of Data

The job factors described in the preceding section are the ultimate substantive concerns of job analysis. To analyze them, however, it is essential to consider them from a measurement or mathematical perspective. Viewed accordingly, a different picture emerges of these job factors. The following are some of the ways in which job factors can be viewed from a measurement perspective. (Note that the term *factor* is used broadly to encompass objects, events, and all other units of interest.)

MEASUREMENT: FACTORS AND ATTRIBUTES

In its broadest sense, measurement has been defined as the orderly assignment of numbers to objects, events, and other factors. Actually, the focus of measurement is on the *attributes* of factors. The differences between some job factors and their attributes are illustrated as follows:

Job Factors	Attributes
Machines	Sizes, fuel consumption, brand names
Rules	Number, clarity, fairness
Tasks	Difficulty, criticality, importance

The distinction between factors and attributes is critical to all discussion of measurement. It emphasizes that factors encountered in job analysis are seldom of interest in themselves. They attain relevance because of the attributes or qualities that they bring with them to the workplace. An attribute is said to be measured when it is labeled and placed within an ordered numerical matrix (Schneider & Schmitt, 1986, p. 177).

QUALITATIVE VERSUS QUANTITATIVE

For measurement purposes, job information can be sorted roughly into two categories: qualitative and quantitative. *Qualitative* attributes are differences in kind. They are viewed in a plus or minus sense, without reference to amounts of differences. Examples of qualitative attributes of jobs are job titles, identification numbers, and classifications. Numbers can be used to signify qualitative differences, but only as marks of identification. Qualitative differences cannot be added, subtracted, multiplied, or divided. To do so would result in the attainment of useless (and misleading) results.

Quantitative attributes, on the other hand, take on numerical values. Here, numbers can be used to signify degrees or amounts of differences among job factors with reference to the attributes. Within the quantitative set, it is frequently useful to distinguish between attributes that yield *relative* (*or ordinal*) differences from those that yield *absolute* differences.

Relative differences are ones of degree or magnitude. Examples of job attributes that yield relative differences are job status, task difficulty, and hardness of materials used in the process. When such attributes are encountered, the job factors can only be ranked in terms of higher or lower, more or less, without reference to precise distance among the factors. There is no zero from which to begin the measurement. Absolute differences, on the other hand, refer to distance among factors. Examples of attributes that yield absolute differences are time spent on tasks, productivity, temperature, and dollar value of output attained. Here, a zero is encountered, and the differences among factors can be calculated by using the basic mathematical operations of addition, subtraction, division, and multiplication. (For a more detailed discussion of the differences in forms of data, see Ghiselli, Campbell & Zedeck, 1981.).

2.4 Selected Measurement Issues Relating to Job Information

Measurement is an intrinsic part of job analysis. All attempts to gather, analyze, and synthesize job information require the assignment of numbers to job attributes. This section is dedicated to bringing out a set of measurement issues that are of particular relevance to job analysis.

STATISTICAL CONCEPTS

It should be apparent to the reader by now that job analysis entails more than the construction of narrative descriptions of job factors and their attributes. To serve the many functions of human resource management that rely on job information for their activities, the analyst needs to summarize job information in systematic terms. This brings out the relevance of statistics in job analysis. The analyst needs to be able to describe as well as to draw inferences from bodies of data that are gathered in numerical form.

Since human resource professionals typically have some familiarity with common statistical concepts, it is not essential here to present an elaborate discussion of this subject. Appendix 2.1 at the end of this chapter presents a review of basic statistical concepts and their application to areas of importance to job analysis. The reader should note in particular the applications shown for the calculations of reliability and validity, which are two of the central measurement concepts encountered in job analysis. The ideas relating to these two concepts presented in the appendix to this chapter should be studied in conjunction with the validation requirements contained in the *Uniform Guidelines*, which are summarized in Appendix L at the end of the book.

SUBJECTIVE VERSUS OBJECTIVE

This distinction has its roots in the part played by human judgment in the gathering and analysis of data. Strictly viewed, data are viewed to be *subjective* when human judgment has played a part in their coming into being. *Objective* data, on the other hand, are found naturally or are derived through nonhuman agents. Taking the job factor of temperature as a basis, the differences between subjective and objective measurement of this factor would be as follows:

Subjective	Agreement among persons about the degree of the temperature
Objective	Agreement among instruments about the degree of the temperature

While this distinction is conceptually clear, and useful for classifying data, problems are encountered at the operational level. To begin, it is not always possible to place neatly all data that are encountered in these two categories. Consider the case of estimates and ratings provided by experts on the basis of rational study of the facts. Such data are frequently used in forecasting human resources, studying job characteristics such as complexity, importance, and criticality and in rating human performance. Although influenced by human judgment, decisions must be based on objective considerations. Also, it is difficult to avoid the exercise of human judgment even when dealing with overtly objective facts. Thus, accounts provided by witnesses to crimes frequently contain a measure of personal interpretation. Subjectivity can creep in even in the choice of objective criteria. Thus, ''words typed per minute'' is an objective criterion. But the decision to use it as a basis for measuring performance stems from human preferences.

For these reasons, caution needs to be exercised in passing evaluative judgments about the worth of data. Subjective does not automatically imply bad or polluted. Conversely, objective does not automatically mean good or free from bias. It is particularly important not to equate the qualitative-quantitative distinction with the subjective-objective distinction. It is tempting in this regard to view quantitative data as objective, while relegating qualitative data to the realm of subjectivity. This could be misleading and erroneous. Thus, the ratings given in beauty contests are quantitative but inherently subjective. On the other hand, narrative descriptions of jobs are nonquantitative, but could be highly accurate in depicting the reality that exists (Cook & Reichardt, 1979; Van Maanen, 1983).

USE OF DESCRIPTORS IN JOB ANALYSIS

Broadly viewed, any job-related information can qualify as a descriptor of a job. It is a convention within the job analysis literature, however, to limit the use of this term to those attributes that are consciously chosen as a basis for describing, classifying, and evaluating jobs. A job attribute thus becomes a descriptor when it is included as part of the analytic tool kit of the job analyst.

As with all job attributes, descriptors can be classified according to their substantive or measurement properties. A substantive descriptor is one that reflects a property of a job as an organizational unit. Substantive descriptors can be further broken down into two categories: inherent and cosociative. *Inherent* descriptors include those properties that are inherent attributes of jobs, such as those discussed in an earlier section. *Cosociative* descriptors, on the other hand, are variables of interest to the analyst that are not inherent attributes of jobs, but with which the job can be identified for analytic purposes. Examples of cosociative descriptors are union affiliations of job, legal classifications (exempt/nonexempt), and abilities of workers performing the job (McCormick, 1979, pp. 157–161).

Viewed from a measurement perspective, descriptors can be sorted into qualitative and quantitative categories, depending on their inherent form. The quantitative descriptors can be further refined according to the subcategories given earlier.

Job descriptors can also be classified according to the functions that they serve in job analysis. The most common use of job descriptors in job analysis is in describing the reality that exists. Descriptors can also serve an evaluative function. A simple example of an evaluative descriptor is cleanliness of the workplace. Such a descriptor goes beyond the substantive reality and arrives at a judgment about the job based on external criteria. Evaluative descriptors serve as basis for rating, ranking, and passing judgment on the worth of the job. They are central to human resource management; their uses in the performance of various human resource management functions are illustrated in later chapters of this book.

APPENDIX 2.1 STATISTICAL CONCEPTS AND VALIDATION PRINCIPLES: A SHORT REVIEW

Some Basic Statistics

THE MEAN

Possibly the most frequently encountered statistical index in psychological research is the mean or the average. The mean of a series of scores consists of simply adding up the scores to form a total, and dividing this sum by the number of scores. Operationally, the mean is calculated by the following formula:

$$\bar{x} = \frac{\Sigma x}{n},$$

where

$\bar{x}$ = the mean,
x = a particular score,
Σ = the sum of the scores,
n = the number of scores.

For example, suppose a manager had the following test scores for ten employees: 21, 26, 23, 15, 21, 17, 18, 19, 21, and 24. The mean or average of this distribution of scores is calculated to be:

$$\bar{x} = \frac{205}{10} = 20.5.$$

The mean is a statistic that summarizes a distribution of scores into the single most representative value.

STANDARD DEVIATION

Distribution of scores often tends to fall into a particular shape, sometimes referred to as a ''bell-shaped'' (because the distribution resembles a bell) or normal curve. Exhibit 2.A. illustrates two such curves. While each of these two distributions demonstrates ''properties'' of a normal curve (e.g., the distribution ''peaks'' at the mean; the shape of each curve is not disproportionate), the two distributions differ in that one has a greater ''spread'' than the other. Distribution (a) in Exhibit 2.A has scores which are more dispersed than the scores in distribution (b). A useful statistic that helps to summarize a distribution of scores is the standard deviation. The standard deviation is an index of the amount of spread or dispersion among a set of scores. When a standard deviation is used to summarize the amount of spread among scores in a *sample* it is represented by the letters S.D. (when the standard deviation is computed for a total *population* of scores it is typically represented by the Greek symbol σ). For two distributions with the

From R. D. Arvey, *Fairness in Selecting Employees*, © 1979, Addison-Wesley Publishing Company, Inc., Reading, Massachusetts. Pages 10–38 (Chapter 2). Reprinted by permission.

EXHIBIT 2.A Two Distributions With Same Means but Different Standard Deviations

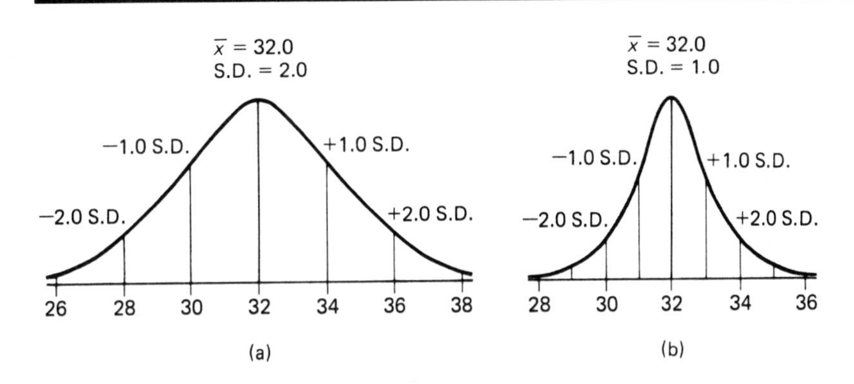

same mean, the distribution with the larger standard deviation (S.D.) will have relatively more spread, or variability, around the mean.

One may use the standard deviation to calculate the interval within which most of the scores will lie. Specifically, the interval $\bar{x} \pm 1$ S.D. will contain approximately 68 percent of the scores and the interval $\bar{x} \pm 2$ S.D. will contain approximately 95 percent of the scores. Thus, for distribution (a) in Exhibit 2.A, 95 percent of the scores will fall between $\bar{x} \pm 1$ S.D. $= 32.0 \pm 2.0$, or 30.0 to 34.0.

The formula for calculating the standard deviation is as follows:

$$\text{S.D.} = \sqrt{\frac{\Sigma(x - \bar{x})^2}{n}}.$$

Thus, the standard deviation of the test scores for the ten employees given above would be calculated in the following way:

$x - \bar{x}$	$(x - \bar{x})^2$
$21 - 20.5 = .5$	$(\ .5) = .25$
$26 - 20.5 = 5.5$	$(\ 5.5) = 30.25$
$23 - 20.5 = 2.5$	$(\ 2.5) - 6.25$
$15 - 20.5 = -5.5$	$(-5.5) = 30.25$
$21 - 20.5 = .5$	$(\ .5) - .25$
$17 - 20.5 = -3.5$	$(-3.5) = 12.25$
$18 - 20.5 = 2.5$	$(\ 2.5) = 6.25$
$19 - 20.5 = -1.5$	$(-1.5) - 2.25$
$21 - 20.5 = .5$	$(\ .5) = .25$
$24 - 20.5 = 3.5$	$(\ 3.5) = 12.25$
	$\Sigma(x - \bar{x})^2 = 100.5$

$$\text{S.D.} = \sqrt{\frac{\Sigma(x - \bar{x})^2}{n}} = 3.17.$$

THE *t*-TEST

Researchers using statistics often are interested in making inferences about the population from which samples have been drawn. For example, suppose a researcher had administered an employment test to ten male and ten female applicants. The researcher might have asked the question:

Are the means of the population from which these samples were drawn equal or unequal? The classical statistical procedure for a researcher to follow is to start by proposing *no* differences between the population means. This is commonly referred to as stating the *null hypothesis*. The *alternative hypothesis* states that there is, indeed, a difference between the means of the two populations. The next step is to review the data to determine if the empirical results support one or the other of these two hypotheses. Based on the sample data, if the two means are very different from each other, researchers typically reject the null hypothesis and indicate that the observed data are more consistent with the alternative hypothesis; that is, the observed difference between the means is so great as to be considered essentially true in general, rather than a chance occurrence, or "fluke." Researchers will typically reject the null hypothesis when the odds are less than 5 out of 100 that the results obtained were due to chance factors and accept that the difference between the two groups is real. This cut-off point is known as the .05 significance level. When a researcher reports that the difference between the means of two groups is significantly different, this is a way of expressing that the probability is less than 5 chances out of 100 that the sample means would be this different from each other purely by chance, *if* the null hypothesis were indeed true and the two population means are equal. Researchers will also adopt a significance level of .01 indicating that the odds of finding such data solely by chance (if the null hypothesis were true) are less than 1 out of 100.

A statistic commonly employed in detecting whether the means are different is the t-test (although the t-test is used frequently in other applications). To illustrate this test using the example above, suppose the researcher found that the ten males and ten females who took the employment test displayed the following means and standard deviations:[1]

Males	Females
$\bar{x}_1 = 26.7$	$\bar{x}_2 = 35.4$
S.D. = 1.7	S.D. = 1.4
$N_1 = 10$	$N_2 = 10$

where the subscripts 1 and 2 indicate from which group the statistical indices were derived (1 = males, 2 = females). If the two distributions have similar spread or variability around their means (technically, this is known as homogeneous or equal variances), a t-test may be computed according to the following formula:

$$t\text{-value} = \frac{\bar{x}_1 - \bar{x}_2}{\sqrt{\left[\frac{(N_1 - 1)\,\text{S.D.}^2\ (N_2 - 1)\,\text{S.D.}^2}{N_1 + N_2 - 2}\right] \cdot \left[\frac{1}{N_1} + \frac{1}{N_2}\right]}}.$$

Following this formula, the computation of the t-value based on the data given above for the male and female employees is as follows:

$$t\text{-value} = \frac{26.7 - 35.4}{\sqrt{\left[\frac{(10 - 1)(1.7)^2 + (10 - 1)(1.4)^2}{10 + 10 - 2}\right] \cdot \left[\frac{1}{10} + \frac{1}{10}\right]}}$$

$$= \frac{-8.7}{\sqrt{\left[\frac{26.01 + 17.64}{18}\right] \cdot [.2]}} = \frac{-8.7}{\sqrt{.415}} = \frac{-8.7}{.64}$$

$$= -13.59.$$

[1] When a standard deviation is computed in situations where its values will be used to estimate the standard deviations of the population from which the sample was drawn, the formula for its calculation is

$$\text{S.D.} = \sqrt{\frac{(x - \bar{x})^2}{N - 1}}.$$

After the t-value is calculated, it is compared to a theoretical distribution (technically known as the t-distribution) which allows the researcher to determine the probability of obtaining a mean difference of this observed magnitude if, in fact, there is no difference between the population means of the two groups. In the present example, the probability of finding a difference of this magnitude by chance is less than .001, or 1 time in 1,000. Thus, the researcher would reject the null hypothesis of no difference between the two population means and assert that there is a difference between them.

It should be noted, however, that one must *not* always adhere to this .05 convention. One could instead reject the null hypothesis if the probability (also called the p-value) is less than .10 or .15 (or any p-value, for that matter). The decision depends on the researcher's notion of what constitutes a relatively rare event. But, in almost all court cases that deal with research associated with discrimination issues, the .05 level of significance is adopted as the basic indicator of a statistical difference.

A further concept which should be explored in t-tests is the idea of one- versus two-tailed tests. Without going into great detail, when a researcher has no prior knowledge concerning which group might exhibit the larger mean value, a *two*-tailed t-test is conducted. However, if specific differences are expected (e.g., if one suspects that a particular group will score higher), then a *one*-tailed t-test is conducted. A two-tailed test is sensitive to significant differences in either direction, greater *and* less. The one-tailed test is sensitive to differences in only one direction, greater *or* less. A researcher should employ a one-tailed test only when the direction in which the difference will occur can be specified ahead of time. An advantage of using a one-tailed test is that it is relatively easier to find statistical significance compared to a two-tailed test.

TYPE I ERROR, TYPE II ERROR, AND POWER

Researchers use statistics in order to make "best guesses" about the true state of affairs when incomplete data or measurement error exists. These best guesses may either be true or false. A framework for examining the accuracy of the inferences drawn is provided in most statistics texts under the rubric of Type I and Type II errors.

As we have noted above, researchers employ a procedure in which a null hypothesis and an alternative hypothesis are stated. They then collect data, conduct a specific statistical test (e.g., t-test), and make a decision about which hypothesis is correct based on the results of the statistical test. For example, a researcher will make a decision concerning whether the null hypothesis is true or false. In actuality, the situation will be either one of these alternatives: The null hypothesis will be true or it will be false. In other words, the two groups actually may not differ, except by chance, or they may indeed differ. Thus, there are four possible outcomes when a researcher makes an inference or a decision based on a statistical study.

1. The researcher could reject the null hypothesis when it is in fact true. This error in the researcher's decision is called a Type I error and is represented by the Greek letter α. It is also referred to as alpha or the probability of rejecting the null hypothesis when it is actually true.
2. The researcher could fail to reject the null hypothesis when it is actually false. This is referred to as a Type II error and is represented by the Greek letter β. This value corresponds to the probability of accepting the null hypothesis when it is *not* true.
3. The researcher may decide that the null hypothesis is true when it does, in fact, represent the actual state of affairs. This, of course, would be a correct decision. It is often symbolized as $1 - \alpha$.
4. The researcher may decide that the null hypothesis is false when, in fact, the alternative hypothesis is true. This too would be a correct decision. It is often referred to as the *power* of a statistical test. It represents the probability that a researcher will detect a difference when it exists, and is often symbolized by $1 - \beta$.

We might represent these four outcomes as shown in Exhibit 2.B.

EXHIBIT 2.B Types of Errors Made as a Function of the True Status of the Null Hypothesis

		Null Hypothesis True	Null Hypothesis False
Researcher's decision (based on data from a sample of the population)	Accept null hypothesis	$1 - \alpha$	Type II error (β)
	Reject null hypothesis	Type I error (α)	Power ($1 - \beta$)

Researchers are most interested in the fourth outcome, *statistical power*. They want their tests to have as much power as possible, so that if the null hypothesis is false they are able to detect it. The power of a test is affected by essentially three variables:

1. Sample size—the larger the sample, the greater the statistical power.
2. Degree of actual differences—the larger the differences among the means of the groups, the greater the power to detect these differences.
3. Stated alpha level—researchers who use a .01 significance level will have less power than those who use a larger (e.g., .05) alpha level.

Thus researchers can increase the power of their statistical tests by increasing sample sizes in their studies and by less stringent significance levels. More will be said about power in a later chapter.

CORRELATION COEFFICIENT

Another statistic frequently encountered in psychological research is the correlation coefficient. This statistic summarizes the degree of *linear association* between two variables. Consider a situation in which a group of 15 employees were administered a psychological test. Suppose further that their supervisor also rated each employee's "overall" performance using a 10-point scale (1 = poor performance, 10 = superior performance). In order to examine the relationship between the test score and the job-performance rating, these data would be plotted on a graph such as that shown in Exhibit 2.C. Each point represents a single individual. Thus, employee

EXHIBIT 2.C Scatterplot for Test Scores and Performance Ratings Based on 15 Employees

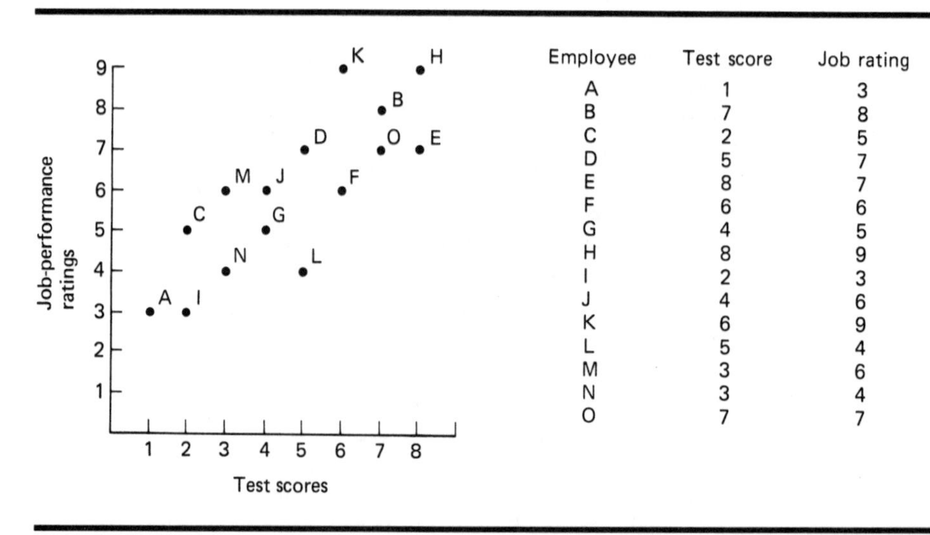

Employee	Test score	Job rating
A	1	3
B	7	8
C	2	5
D	5	7
E	8	7
F	6	6
G	4	5
H	8	9
I	2	3
J	4	6
K	6	9
L	5	4
M	3	6
N	3	4
O	7	7

A had a test score of 1 and had a job-performance rating of 3. The coordinates of point A on the graph represent these two scores for this individual. A graph of this sort is commonly referred to as a "scatterplot."

While this graph is a good *visual* representation of the degree of relationship, it would also be useful to have a number that would summarize those data. This number, called the *correlation coefficient*, is computed according to the following formula:

$$r_{XY} = \frac{N\Sigma XY - (\Sigma X)(\Sigma Y)}{\sqrt{[N\Sigma X^2 - (\Sigma X)^2]\,[N\Sigma Y^2 - (\Sigma Y)^2]}},$$

where

r_{XY} = correlation coefficient,
X = score on first variable,
Y = score on second variable,
ΣX = summation over first variable,
ΣY = summation over second variable,
ΣX^2 = summation over first variable squared,
ΣY^2 = summation over second variable squared,
ΣXY = first score multiplied by second score summed over people,
N = number of people with both scores.

The correlation coefficient for the data presented is calculated as follows:

Employee	X	X^2	Y	Y^2	XY
A	1	1	3	9	3
B	7	49	8	64	56
C	2	4	5	25	10
D	5	25	7	49	35
E	8	64	7	49	56
F	6	36	6	36	56
G	4	16	5	25	20
H	8	64	9	81	72
I	2	4	3	9	6
J	4	16	6	36	24
K	6	36	9	81	54
L	5	25	4	16	20
M	3	9	6	36	18
N	3	9	4	16	12
O	7	49	7	49	49
	$\Sigma X = 71$	$\Sigma X^2 = 407$	$\Sigma Y = 89$	$\Sigma Y^2 = 581$	$\Sigma XY = 471$

The resulting r_{XY} is .82. The values of a correlation coefficient range between +1.00 and −1.00. A correlation of +1.00 represents a perfect positive relationship and indicates that if you know the value of one variable, the exact value of the other variable can be determined. A correlation of zero indicates that no relationship exists, and a correlation of −1.00 represents a perfect negative correlation between two variables. Obviously, there are a great many relationships that are less than perfect, and the correlation calculated here using the employee data given in Exhibit 2.C is just one example. Our correlation here of .82 indicates that if one knows the particular test score of an employee, one may fairly accurately predict his or her job-performance rating. In other words, a person with a high test score is more than likely to receive a high job-performance rating.

Additional types of relationships are shown in Exhibit 2.D. Part (a) depicts a high positive relationship between the variables X and Y. Part (b) shows a high negative relationship. Part (c) depicts a situation where there is essentially no relationship. And part (d) shows the same thing as (a)—a high positive correlation—by means of an *ellipse diagram*. Frequently, instead of plotting each individual point, an ellipse is used to show the relationship.

The correlation coefficient may also be tested for statistical significance in order to determine

EXHIBIT 2.D Several Kinds of Correlational Relationships

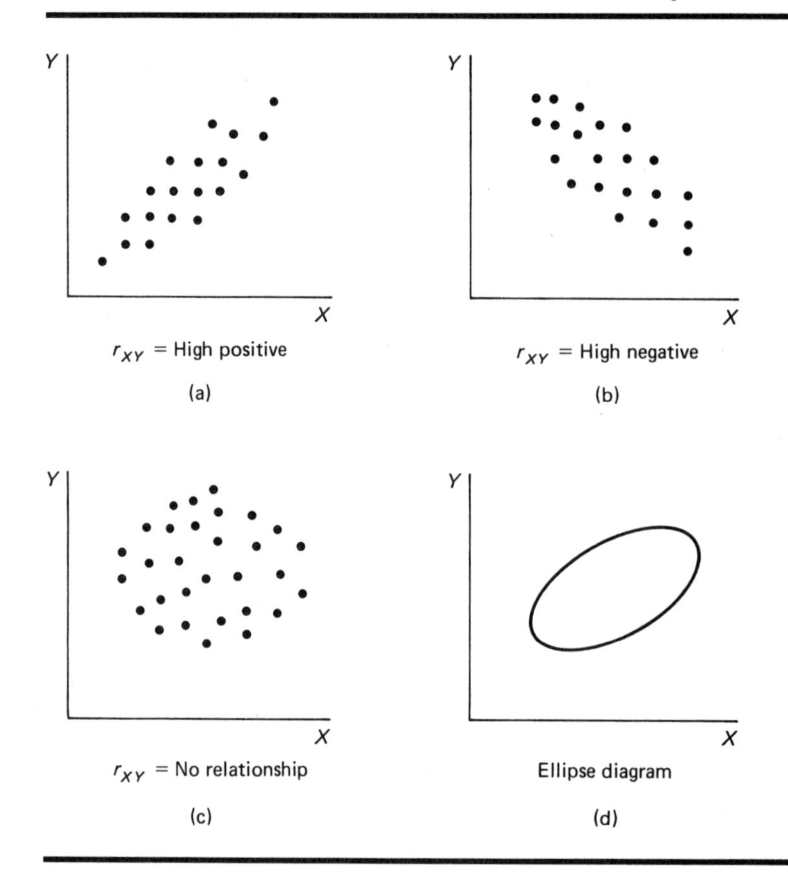

whether the correlation is "real" or whether it was simply a chance finding and the "true" correlation or relationship in the population is zero.

It is possible to determine the probability of achieving a particular correlation in a sample of people purely by chance if the population was actually zero. Most frequently, if the probability is equal to or less than .05, the correlation is considered to be statistically significant—that is, the "real" relationship is *not* likely to be zero.

In order to determine if the correlation is stastically significant, one must consult a table of the minimum correlation needed to achieve significance (sometimes called the critical value). There is a different critical value for each sample size used, as shown in Exhibit 2.E. The magnitude of the obtained correlation is compared with the correlation needed to be significant (as derived from Exhibit 2.E or any statistics text). If the observed correlation equals or exceeds the value in the table, it is said to have reached the level of statistical significance.

For example, given a sample size of 15, one would need a correlation of .51 to be significant at the .01 level. The correlation computed in the example was .82. Going to Exhibit 2.E, this computed or obtained value (.82) is higher than either .51 or .64. Thus, we may say that the correlation is significant beyond the .01 level. This is often communicated symbolically by $p < .01$.

It is worthwhile here to point out the special relationship between sample size and the magnitude of the correlation needed to achieve significance. In general, the smaller the sample size, the larger the size of the correlation needed to reach significance. For example, a correlation of .35 based on a sample of 20 people is not large enough to be considered significant. But, if the same correlation of .35 were found based on a sample of 50, the correlation *would* be considered significant. This is due simply to the fact that correlations computed on smaller samples tend to fluctuate more than correlations based on larger samples.

EXHIBIT 2.E Magnitude of Correlations Needed to Achieve Significance for Various Sample Sizes

Sample Size	.05 Level	.01 Level
3	.98	1.00
4	.95	.99
5	.88	.96
6	.81	.92
7	.75	.87
8	.71	.83
9	.66	.80
10	.63	.76
11	.60	.73
12	.57	.71
13	.55	.68
14	.53	.66
15	.51	.64
20	.44	.56
25	.40	.50
30	.36	.46
35	.33	.43
40	.31	.40
50	.27	.36
70	.23	.30
100	.19	.25

Another fact to keep in mind is that the correlation coefficient is based on variables assumed to have a linear (that is, a straight-line) relationship. When two variables are related in a nonlinear fashion, as in Exhibit 2.F, the correlation coefficient *under*estimates the true relationship.

REGRESSION EQUATIONS

On many occasions, researchers would like to be able to predict one variable from knowledge about another. For example, a personnel manager may wish to predict a prospective employee's job performance on the basis of his or her score on an employment test. A method of analysis that permits these predictions is called *regression analysis*. Exhibit 2.G illustrates the situation discussed earlier in which a manager had available both the test scores and the job-performance ratings for 15 employees. In this instance, a way of summarizing these data is through the use of a "straight" line, usually called a regression line. This line has been statistically derived so that its path represents the best possible "fit" to the data (that is, the distance from the regression line to the various data points is at a minimum).

EXHIBIT 2.F A Nonlinear Relationship between Test X and Job-Performance Rating

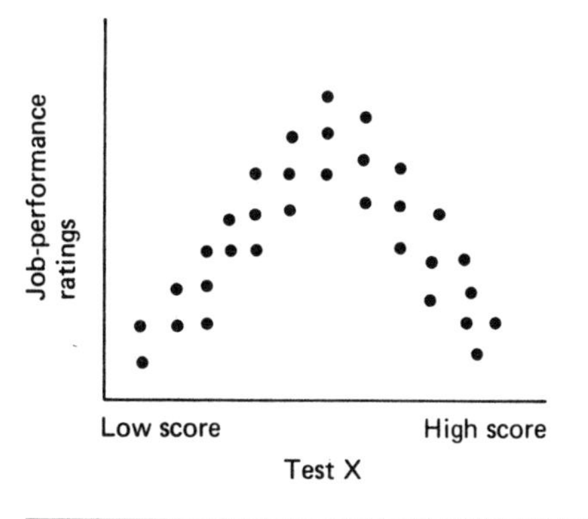

EXHIBIT 2.G Regression Line Based on Test Scores and Job-Performance Data

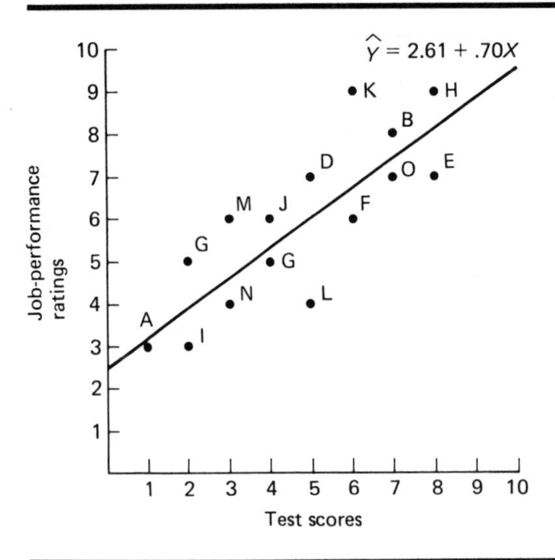

Some readers will recall from an early course in algebra that any straight line may be represented mathematically by the formula:

$$Y = a + bX,$$

where

Y = score on the Y-variable,
a = intercept value,
b = slope of regression line,
X = score on the X-variable.

For example, the regression line depicted in Exhibit 2.G is summarized by the regression equation: $\hat{Y} = 2.61 + .70(X)$, where $\hat{Y}$ = predicted job performance. The intercept value (2.61) is the distance from the zero point on the Y-axis to the point where the regression line crosses the Y-axis. The slope value (.70) indicates the amount of change in the Y-variable that occurs with every unit of change in the X-variable. That is, for every one-unit increase in test score, one should expect a .70 increase in the Y-value. It is also possible to derive a negative slope, which would be indicated by a negative sign (−) for the slope value. These slope values are referred to as "regression" weights.[2]

The regression equation may be used to predict scores of one variable from the value of the second variable. Suppose a job applicant scored 8 on a selection test. Using the regression equation we could incorporate this value into the equation and derive a *predicted* job-performance value:

$$\hat{Y} = 2.61 + .70(8) = 8.21,$$

where

$\hat{Y}$ = predicted job performance.

Suppose another job applicant scored a 3 on the same test. Using the equation, predicted job performance is 4.71. The manager would probably want to hire the first applicant, who had a higher predicted score on the job-performance variable.

Another method of using regression lines for estimating job performance is simply to look

---

[2] Occasionally, these weights are calculated in a different fashion (according to a procedure using "standardized scores") and are called "Beta weights."

at the diagram to obtain a predicted score. For example, Exhibit 2.H presents a regression line of the formula $\hat{Y} = 2.61 + .70(X)$. Suppose again we are interested in knowing the predicted Y-value for an individual with a test score of 8. Using the diagram, one would find 8 on the X-axis, look up from this score to the regression line, and then look over to the Y-axis following the dashed lines. The predicted Y-value is 8.21.

It should be obvious that the predictions based on regression-line equations are not perfect. In fact, while some of the data points in Exhibit 2.G fall close to the regression line, only a few points fall exactly on the line. A way of summarizing the degree of error in prediction is through the use of a statistic known at the *standard error of estimate*. This statistic is computed according to the formula:

$$\sigma_{Y \cdot X} = \sigma_Y \sqrt{1 - r_{XY}},$$

where

$$\sigma_{Y \cdot X} = \text{standard error of estimate,}$$
$$\sigma_Y = \text{standard deviation of } Y,$$
$$r_{XY} = \text{correlation between } X\text{- and } Y\text{-variables.}$$

The standard error of estimate may be treated as a standard deviation of the errors made in predicting Y from X. We expect about two-thirds (68 percent) of the observed Y-values to lie within the limits of plus and minus one standard error of estimate from the predicted value of Y. The standard error of estimate for the data shown in Exhibit 2.G is 1.31. Theoretically, about 68 percent of those who score 8 on the test will be expected to receive performance ratings within the limits of 8.21 ± 1.31, or between 6.90 and 9.52.

Finally, it should be noted that it is also possible to construct a regression equation predicting X from a knowledge of Y, e.g., $X = a + bY$. In most situations in this text, however, the variable predicted (Y) will be some form of *job performance* (which we call the *dependent* variable) and the variables used to make the predictions (X) will frequently be some form of *test score*, or other standard used in making selective decisions (which we generally call the *independent* variable).

A question which often arises is why should one want to make predictions about some T-variable (e.g., job performance) when one already has knowledge about these scores. The answer is simply that these data points are used to determine whether a relationship exists and to describe the relationship. Then the equation derived can be used to make predictions *in the future* for prospective employees for whom job-performance data are *not* available. A basic assumption is that the relationship found among one group of employees will hold up in the future.

EXHIBIT 2.H Finding Predicted Y-Value by Visually Using Regression-Line Diagram

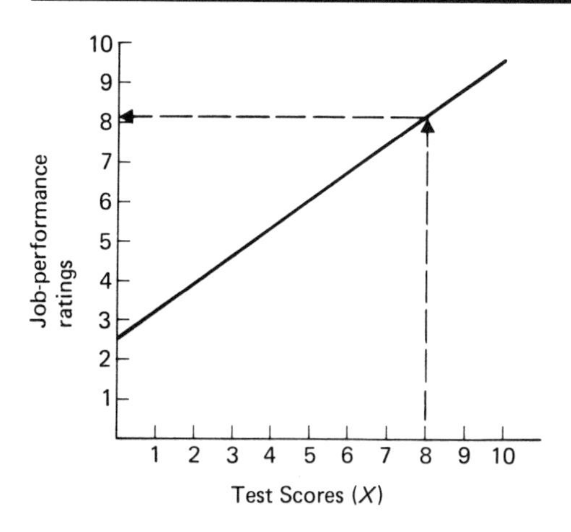

MULTIPLE REGRESSION

Occasionally researchers want to make predictions about one variable from knowledge based on *more* than one other variable. When there are more than one independent or predictor variables in the equation, researchers use a method of analysis known as *multiple regression.* In general form, the multiple-regression equation looks like the following:

$$\hat{Y} = a + b_1X_1 + b_2X_2 + \cdot \cdot \cdot + b_NX_N,$$

where

$$\begin{aligned} \hat{Y} &= \text{predicted value of the } Y\text{-variable}, \\ b_1, b_2, \ldots, b_N &= \text{regression weights associated with the various predictors}, \\ X_1, X_2, \ldots, X_N &= \text{scores on the various predictors}, \\ a &= \text{intercept value}. \end{aligned}$$

Similarly, a multiple-correlation coefficient may be calculated by correlating the *observed* values of Y with the *predicted* values of Y ($\hat{Y}$) across the number of individuals.

For example, suppose a personnel manager had two tests (Test X and Test Z) which were positively correlated with job performance. The manager might calculate[3] the regression equation to be as follows:

$$\hat{Y} = .75 + .41(\text{Test X}) + .24(\text{Test Z}).$$

For an applicant with a score of 5 on Test X and a score of 7 on Test Z, the predicted Y-score would be

$$Y = .75 + .41(5) + .24(7) = 3.36.$$

It should be noted that the same applicant might have achieved nearly this same predicted Y-score in a different fashion. That is, if his or her score on Test X were 3 and score on Test Z was 9, the predicted Y-score would have still been 3.41, which is quite close to the previous predicted value. The regression model has been called *compensatory* because high scores on one of the predictor variables will sometimes compensate for low scores on the other predictor(s).

Reliability of Measurement

As we will see, the *reliability* of specific measuring instruments is critical when evaluating them for evidence of potential bias. Thus, it is important to define reliability in some detail for use in later chapters.

Reliability concerns the consistency of measurement. When we measure the same thing twice, do we obtain the same scores? Of particular concern is whether selection tests and job-performance measures demonstrate consistency. Suppose we administered an employment test on one day and subsequently readministered the same test the following day. We would not be too surprised if the scores were highly correlated; however, we would have grave doubts about the potential usefulness of the test if the correlation was low! If a test does not correlate well with itself, how can we expect it to demonstrate a relationship with some other variable?

Many psychologists have dealt with reliability by representing the variation among people's scores on a selection test as being composed of two components: (1) variation due to the individuals' "true" scores (that is, the scores that accurately represent the characteristics of the individuals) and (2) variation due to "error." That is,

$$\sigma_t^2 = \sigma_\infty^2 + \sigma_e^2,$$

[3] Methods for calculating multiple-regression equations are given in Guilford and Fruchter (1965) and other standard statistics texts.

where

$$\sigma_t^2 = \text{observed score variation.}$$
$$\sigma_\infty^2 = \text{variation due to ``true'' scores,}$$
$$\sigma_e^2 = \text{variation due to ``error.''}$$

To the extent that there is relatively little error in the measuring system, reliability will be high. Thus, one definition of reliability is:

$$r_{tt} = 1 - \frac{\sigma_e^2}{\sigma_t^2},$$

where r_{tt} = reliability of the test (or correlation of the test with itself).

The error component may have a variety of sources. Dunnette (1966) has described four sources of error in psychological measurement:

1. *Errors due to inadequate sampling of content.* The correlation between two tests designed to measure the same thing may not be perfect (+1.00) due to the fact that the test items for the two exams may have been slightly different.
2. *Errors due to chance response tendencies.* Occasionally, individuals will simply guess on test items, or answer at random the test items that seem to be meaningless. Any tendencies toward guessing or random responding contribute to error.
3. *Errors due to changes in testing environment.* Physical conditions such as the lighting, music level, temperature, or time of day, may affect test scores. Similarly, the particular manner in which a test is administered may contribute to error in test scores.
4. *Errors due to changes in the person taking the test.* An individual could score differently on a test given on different occasions due to factors peculiar to the individual. For example, health factors, fatigue, and mood shifts may contribute to error. In addition, individuals may actually develop new competence in the same area being measured, but this is not considered measurement error.

There are various ways of estimating the reliability (r_{tt}) of measurement. A common method is to obtain a remeasure after a period of time. For example, employees might be asked to retake an employment test after a month or so, or supervisors might be asked to rerate their employees on job performance. The scores over these two administrations are then correlated. This procedure is commonly referred to as computing a *test-retest reliability coefficient*, or an estimate of *stability*. There is one major factor which inflates this estimate of reliability: People tend to recall the test questions and their answers to them, and they tend to repeat their answers. Similarly, supervisors remember how they rated employees from one rating to the next.

Another way to measure reliability is to correlate one *part* of the test with some other part of the test. If the test is measuring the same ability or aptitude reliably, it should do so throughout the entire test. For example, in a 40-item test of mechanical ability, the scores individuals receive on the first 20 items of the test can be correlated with their scores on the second 20 items. This practice is referred to as computing a *split-half reliability*. Alternatively, a score for each individual based on all the *even*-numbered items of the test can be correlated with a score based on all the *odd*-numbered items. This is called an *odd-even reliability coefficient*.

When a researcher computes an odd-even or split-half reliability coefficient, the coefficients are computed based on a test half the length of the original test. In a sense, half the items on the test have to be "folded back" to correlate with the other half of the test in order to establish the reliability of the test. It is possible, however, to estimate what the reliability of the test would be if it were at "full strength" with *all* the items. The Spearman-Brown formula provides this estimate:

$$r_{tt} = \frac{2r_{xx}}{1 + r_{xx}},$$

where

r_{tt} = reliability of a total test estimated from the reliability of one of its halves,
r_{xx} = correlation between halves of a test.

For example, suppose a personnel manager administered a 100-item test to 200 employees and calculated a split-half reliability coefficient of .45. He wished to determine what the reliability would be for the full-length test. Using the Spearman-Brown formula, the estimate would be

$$r_{tt} = \frac{2(.45)}{1 + .45} = .62.$$

An additional method of correlating the parts of a test with one another is to correlate each test item with every other item. These are usually referred to as *internal-consistency* measures of reliability, and several formulas for calculating estimates along these lines may be found in Guilford (1965).

A method of establishing reliability through the construction of different forms of a test is called *equivalent-forms* reliability. Employees are again asked to take two tests, except that the two tests differ in the specific items contained in the tests. An advantage of this method is that it eliminates the problem of memory effects found in the test-retest method. However, the construction of equivalent forms of the same test is quite difficult and expensive, and thus is not frequently used.

A method of establishing the reliability of *supervisory ratings* of job performance (versus *test* scores) is to obtain independent ratings or measurements from two or more supervisors on each employee. While it is likely that different supervisors appraise employee behavior differently, it is usually desirable that some degree of agreement be achieved among the raters.

STANDARD ERROR OF MEASUREMENT

A statistic that indicates the amount of error in a measurement system is called the *standard error of measurement*. One way to understand this concept is to consider a situation where a person is measured and tested repeatedly. If we were able to secure a large number of measurements on an individual, we would expect to find the scores distributed in a normal-curve fashion. The mean of this distribution is considered to be the individual's "true score"—or error-free score, as discussed earlier. The standard deviation of this distribution represents the degree of error in the measuring system. About 68 percent of the scores fall within plus or minus one standard deviation. This standard deviation is referred to as the standard error of measurement and may be estimated by the following:

$$\text{S.E.M.} = \sigma_x\sqrt{1 - r_{xx}},$$

where

S.E.M. = standard error of measurement,
σ_x = standard deviation of test,
r_{xx} = reliability of test.

This statistic is helpful in estimating a person's "true score" when we are able to test that person only once. For example, if a person is administered a test and obtains a score of 80 and the S.E.M. of the test is 3.0, we can conclude with fair confidence that the individual's true or error-free score is somewhere between 86 and 92 (89 + 3.0).

Validity: A Review of the Basic Concepts

While reliability has to do with the stability and consistency of measurement, validity involves whether a test or measuring instrument is measuring what it is supposed to measure. One could have an extremely reliable measuring instrument but be using it to measure the wrong attribute.

For example, a ruler, which is an extremely reliable instrument, would not be a valid measuring device for the assessment of I.Q. Dunnette (1966) defines validation as the process of learning more about the meaning of a measuring device.

Because the concept of validity is so important in the context of the present text, the basic strategies and principles of validity are reviewed. However, we will not be able to provide in-depth coverage of all the various strategies; readers might also consult other standard texts in selection. A particularly important guide to validation principles was issued in 1975 by the Division of Industrial-Organizational Psychology (American Psychological Association) entitled *Principles for the Validation and Use of Personnel Selection Procedures*. This 14-page booklet details the various validation methods and considerations. Below is a summary of several acceptable and frequently used validation strategies.

CRITERION-RELATED VALIDITY

This form of validity is perhaps the most commonly used. In fact, it was given almost a "preferred" status in the 1970 EEOC testing guidelines and in court decisions. Criterion-related validity means that a *predictor* (or "test") is associated (correlated) with a *criterion* (a measure of job performance). The most frequent example is the correlation of employee test scores with supervisory ratings of job performance. There are two basic variations of this strategy: predictive and concurrent validity.

Predictive validity refers to employees being tested prior to employment and hired on some basis other than the test scores. Then, at a later time, job-performance measures are collected and correlated with the test scores. This strategy is said to be one of the best for accurately assessing the validity of a test, but it does have problems. First, many organizations have neither the time nor the resources to conduct a longitudinal predictive study. Sometimes it is necessary, especially under court pressure, to obtain an estimate of a test's validity as soon as possible.

A second problem is that organizations (e.g., civil service) are sometimes required by law to make decisions on the basis of tests. Thus, it would be difficult, if not impossible, for an organization suddenly to forego testing and use other devices for selection. A recent court decision highlighted this problem. In *U.S.* v. *City of St. Louis* (1976) the court ruled that a predictive-validity design was inappropriate due to the length of time required to conduct such a study in view of the legal duty of the organization to establish a valid selection procedure immediately.

A variation of the predictive-validity design is to use the test in making the selection decisions (e.g., by establishing a cutoff score), and to collect job-performance data later. Then, measures of association between the test and job performance are computed. A problem with this design is that it *under*estimates the true test validity due to "restriction in range" on the test, as shown in Exhibit 2.I. Suppose the true relationship between a test and job performance is represented by the scatterplot in Exhibit 2.I(a). These data portray a reasonably high relationship, say, $r = .50$. Suppose, though, that the organization had been using a cutoff score at point A to select employees and that only individuals who had scored above that point on the test had been hired. Now, if the organization decided to conduct a validation study, the only individuals for whom data would be available are those represented in Exhibit 2.I(b). It is easy to see that a correlation computed on these subjects would be considerably reduced due to less variation on scores in this sample, e.g., $r = .10$. This phenomenon is known as a reduction in the correlation due to *restriction of range on the predictor*. There is also a reduced range of scores on the measure of job performance. Thus, restriction of range on the *criterion* may also occur at the same time.

The second (and most frequent) criterion-related validation strategy is to collect the test scores and the criterion measures at the same time. This is referred to as *concurrent validity*. For example, the test is given to a group of current employees, measures of job performance based on these same employees are collected, and the two sets of data are correlated. This design has been criticized on several counts:

1. Because test scores are obtained from individuals already employed in the job, the results may not apply to others. Individuals tend to move into jobs for which they are best qualified

EXHIBIT 2.1 Illustration of Restriction-of-Range Phenomena

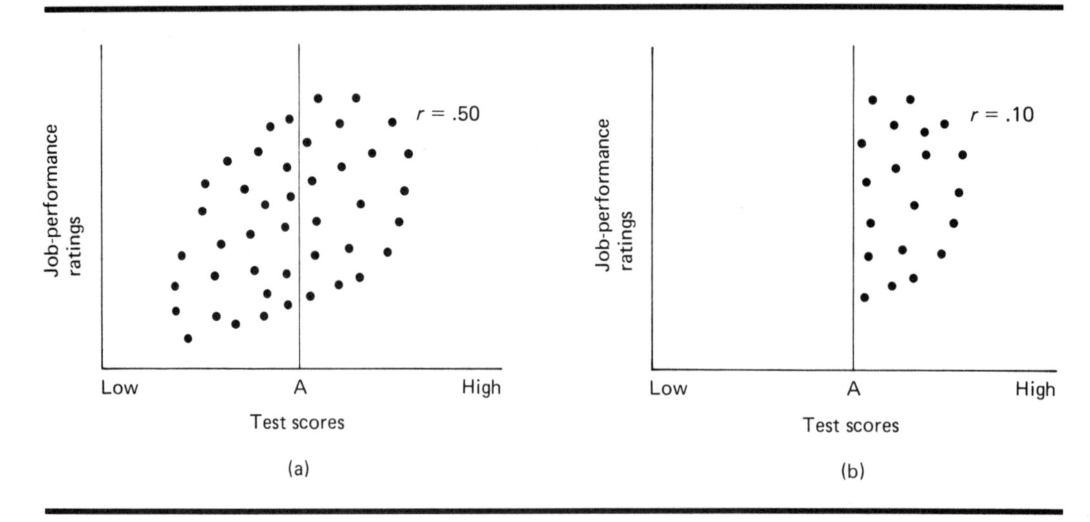

and in which they will be satisfied. Their particular skills and personality patterns may fit the job, while individuals who leave the job may not have found such a good "fit" between the job and their own needs. Thus, the test-score range for the employee pool may be more homogeneous (restricted) than the range for job applicants. For this reason, it is important to collect information on job applicants and compare their test scores with those of job incumbents to determine whether any differences exist between the two groups.

2. It is possible that current employees change by developing particular skills necessary for success on the job. For example, a job that requires a certain amount of arithmetic is bound to have an effect of "sharpening up" the arithmetic skills of employees who may have let those skills get rusty prior to employment.

3. Job incumbents may also respond differently while taking the tests than job applicants. That is, incumbents may be less likely to "fake" tests than individuals who are applying for jobs. Again, to determine whether this could be the case, test scores of job applicants should be compared to the test scores of current employees. When performing concurrent validation studies, subjects should be asked to adopt an applicant "mental set" and be encouraged to do as well as they can on the tests.

The concurrent design is more expedient and less costly than predictive validity, so it is the more commonly used procedure.

CONTENT VALIDITY

Content validity concerns the adequacy of the test in *sampling* job behaviors, knowledge, and skills necessary for job performance. That is, a test is content valid if the items on the test directly reflect observed behavior skills and knowledge considered essential for adequate job performance. The classic example of context validity is a typing test, which directly samples skills necessary for the job. Only recently has the content-validity strategy been given serious attention by industrial psychologists and the courts.

There are three steps usually considered necessary for content validity to be established. First, *job-analysis* procedures are used to describe the basic tasks, skills, and responsibilities involved in the job and to determine those behaviors that are the most relevant, important, or frequently performed. Second, test items are written, or "work samples" are developed, which reflect the essence of the job. Efforts are made to develop these so that they *directly* reflect what is performed in the job. Third, experts (e.g., supervisors, job incumbents) who are familiar with the job evaluate the items (or work samples) and agree that the test procedure is an accurate reflection of the job. These experts should be able to identify items which are also irrelevant to the job in question.

Content validity is an inappropriate strategy for validating ability, intelligence, interest, and other abstract tests. The basic logic behind content validity is to build tests that reflect *directly* the behaviors and skills involved in the job rather than the aptitudes or underlying abilities *presumed* to be involved in the job. "Simply stated, a content-valid selection procedure should sample the job for the applicant and give the applicant a fair chance to demonstrate his or her competence to perform the job" (Sharf, 1976, p. 6).

Content validity is often confused with "face validity." A test which appears to the *test taker* as if it is related to a job is said to be "face valid." A content-valid test will almost always demonstrate "face" validity; however, a test with face validity may *not* have content validity.

THE OUTCOMES OF PREDICTIONS

It is not enough to obtain a significant validity coefficient and pronounce a test useful. There are other factors that influence the relative value of a selection test.

Suppose a personnel manager was able to collect test-score data on 100 employees who were eventually hired and that at a later date, he or she was able to collect job-performance data on all of these individuals using a 1–5 rating scale. Assume that the correlation between the test scores and job-performance ratings was calculated to be .70. Exhibit 2.J depicts this relationship graphically using an ellipse diagram. Assume that the heavy horizontal line in the diagram represents a dividing line: Those individuals rated at or above this line were considered successful in the job as rated by their supervisor; those rated below the line were considered not successful.

The heavy vertical line represents the cutting point (C) on the test when individuals scoring above this point would be selected (in the future) and those scoring below the point would be rejected. These two lines allow the division of the diagram into four quadrants.

1. *Quadrant I* (true positive) represents those individuals for whom success was predicted, and who were indeed successful.
2. *Quadrant II* (false negative) represents those individuals for whom success was not predicted, but who actually would succeed if hired.

EXHIBIT 2. J Quadrant Analysis to Help Determine Utility of a Test

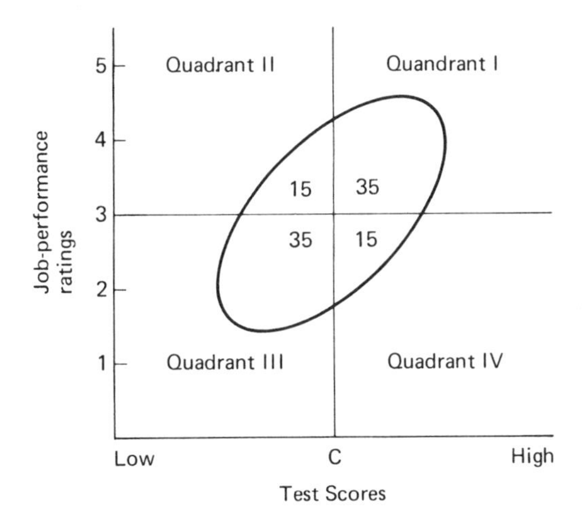

3. *Quadrant III* (true negative) represents those individuals for whom success was not predicted, and who actually did not succeed in the job.
4. *Quadrant IV* (false positive) represents those individuals for whom success was predicted, but who did not succeed in the job.

In Exhibit 2.J the number of individuals who fell into the different quadrants is given. For example, the number of individuals for whom job success was predicted and who actually were successful (Quadrant I) is 35.

The first question we might ask is "How accurate were the predictions made by the test?" This could be calculated by applying the following formula:

$$\frac{\text{I} + \text{II}}{\text{I} + \text{II} + \text{III} + \text{IV}} = \frac{70}{100} = .70.$$

That is, 70 percent of the predictions made using the test were correct. This seems to be fairly impressive evidence in favor of the test. However, a second question which must be asked in evaluating a predictor is "How accurate would I have been if no predictor was used?" This figure may be calculated using the following formula:

$$\frac{\text{I} + \text{II}}{\text{I} + \text{II} + \text{III} + \text{IV}} = \frac{35 + 15}{35 + 15 + 35 + 15} = .50.$$

This is referred to as the *base rate*—the proportion of applicants who would succeed on the job if tests were not used to select them. In the example given, the accuracy of the predictions made using the test was .70 compared to a base rate of .50. Thus, the use of the selection system represents a gain in the accuracy of predictions made compared with using no selection test.

It should be noted that, as the base rate increases, it becomes relatively more difficult for a selection system to show improvement. For example, if 95 percent of employees selected are successful, it becomes difficult to improve on the current system.[4]

A further concept which is important in evaluating a selection device is the notion of the *selection ratio*. The selection ratio is defined as the proportion of individuals actually hired to those who applied. For example, there may be 200 applicants and only 10 individuals are hired. This would represent a selection ratio of 10/200 or .05 percent. Generally speaking, a selection system has greater value when the selection ratio is small—that is, when there are many more applicants than jobs. Taylor and Russell (1939) provide methods for estimating the practical effectiveness of tests given different selection ratios.

To summarize, the value of a prediction system varies as a function of three basic variables:

1. *The magnitude of the validity coefficient*—As validity increases, so does the value of the system.
2. *The base rate*—As the base rate approachs 50 percent, the selection system demonstrates greater value.
3. *The selection ratio*—As selection ratios become smaller, the value of a selection system increases.

The Concept of Utility

Utility refers to the *overall* usefulness of a selection system. The concept includes the accuracy of the decisions made, but also concerns a consideration of the costs of using the selection system and the costs associated with the *errors* in the decisions made. Wiggins (1973), Cronbach

[4] Wiggins (1973) has pointed out that a test with greater than zero validity will be better than random selection, no matter what the base rate.

and Gleser (1965), and Dunnette (1966) have shown how these costs may be considered in evaluating a selection system. First, the kinds of costs must be made explicit and estimated. Dunnette (1966) groups the different kinds of costs into actual and potential costs:

1. *Actual costs* are those expenses incurred when an applicant is hired. These costs would include the costs of recruitment and testing, the cost of orientation programs, and the cost of training.
2. *Potential costs* involve the costs associated with incorrect selection decisions. These are of two types: (a) Costs associated with hiring an individual who subsequently fails (false positives). These costs may involve termination costs, costs of undesirable job behavior (e.g., damaged equipment, accidents, loss of customers) and may represent one of the major personnel costs to an organization. Traditionally, managers have focused on these kinds of costs. (b) Costs associated with rejecting a person who could have been successful on the job (false negatives). While these costs are typically indirect, they may eventually come back to affect the organization. For example, minority-group members rejected during the selection process, but who could actually do the job if hired, may eventually become passive, frustrated, and hostile. Such feelings may eventually erupt in actions against specific organizations or society in general.

The estimation of costs is, according to Cronbach and Gleser (1965), the "Achilles heel" of utility in personnel decision making. Dunnette (1966) and Wiggins (1973) provide excellent examples of how utility estimates, although clearly subjective in nature, may be made. Each specific outcome (e.g., false positive, valid negative, etc.) is assigned a "utility value" that indicates the relative worth or favorableness of an outcome for an institution.

Some courts have informally considered the utility of selection systems. For example, one court earmarked the use of age as a variable on which selection decisions may be made because its use resulted in a decrease in expensive false positive—in this case, a decrease in accident rates when driving buses (*Usery* v. *Tamiami Trail Tours, Inc.* [1976]).

In sum, the relative costs of selection errors are an important consideration in the evaluations of selection systems. We will return to this topic in a later chapter.

Summary

This chapter was meant to provide sufficient information for the reader to pursue the topics developed in later chapters. Some of the statistical terms and concepts are obviously more sophisticated than others. For a more comprehensive treatment, the reader is advised to consult a standard statistics text. However, if the reader has grasped most of the principles developed here, the statistical analyses presented in later chapters should present few problems.

3 Methods and Systems of Job Analysis

The preceding chapter has described the types of information that are encountered in job analysis. This chapter is concerned with the *how* of job analysis. It presents the steps involved in data gathering and analysis and reviews the methods and systems that are available for performing this phase of job analysis. The following are the specific goals of this chapter:

1. To define a set of method terms relevant to job analysis.
2. To outline the steps involved in data gathering and analysis.
3. To describe and evaluate the available methods and systems of job analysis.
4. To review the legal requirements relating to choice of methods and systems of job analysis.
5. To provide the human resource director with suggestions relating to choosing methods and systems of job analysis.

The organization of the chapter follows the sequence of the purposes just noted. To retain the flow of the discussion, background information relating to the job analysis systems introduced in this chapter is presented in Appendix A.

3.1 Definition of Method Terms

The term *method* tends to be used loosely to refer to a wide range of action concepts dealing with the gathering and analysis of data. It can be used both as a noun and as a verb. When used as a noun, it refers to ready-made or set ways of gathering and analyzing data. When used as a verb, it refers to sets of actions undertaken to gather and analyze data. To establish a common frame of reference, it is useful to define the key terms that are encountered in data gathering and analysis.

Data — Any information, qualitative or quantitative, that is descriptive of the object being studied. In job analysis, data are synonymous with job-related information. They could encompass information relating to the job itself as well as worker characteristics, environmental factors, and other elements of the job situation.

Tool — A primary instrument used in data gathering and analysis. Exam-

	ples of tools used in job analysis are human agents, computers, questionnaires, and diaries.
Techniques and methods (T&Ms)	Ways of combing and using tools; modes of data gathering and analysis. Examples of techniques and methods used in job analysis are structured questionnaires, regression analysis, and observations based on a checklist.
Theory (model)	Preconceptions about the interrelations among the objects studied; explanations of the "whys" behind the functioning (or malfunctioning) of persons and systems. Examples of theories used in job analysis are the data, people, and things schema of Functional Job Analysis, and information-input mediation processes work-output model of the Position Analysis Questionnaire.
System	Arrangement of techniques and methods on the basis of theory to solve problems, to advance knowledge, or to perform an administrative function. Established systems of job analysis are discussed in this chapter and in Appendix A. (The definitions provided draw heavily on Wallace, 1983, p. 6.)

While the foregoing method concepts can be conceptually differentiated from each other, there are frequently overlaps in application. The place of the concept within the hierarchy can be influenced by the stage of the investigation and the nature of the questions addressed. What is a tool in one context can emerge as a system in another. Take the computer as an example. It can be considered to be a tool when used as an instrument in data gathering. But in its own right, the computer is a highly complex system consisting of various mechanical parts arranged according to sets of rules and known interactive properties of the parts.

3.2 Steps in Data Gathering and Analysis

The total set of activities involved in the conduct of job analysis were outlined in Chapter 1 (Exhibit 1.5). The focus here is on providing additional details relating to the steps involved in the actual gathering and analysis of job information. We also implicitly cover issues relating to the design phase of analysis.

Assuming that the jobs to be analyzed have been selected, the design and data gathering phases consist roughly of the following five steps.

Step 1. Crystalize the purposes to be served by the analysis.

Job information is needed for the performance of a wide range of human resource management functions (Chapter 1, Exhibit 1.3). Before data can be gathered, therefore, it is essential that the analyst crystalize the exact uses to be made of the information. In fulfilling this requirement, it is not enough merely to indicate the broad human resource management function to be served. The analyst needs to go beyond that and to specify, in fairly clear terms, the particular use to be made of the information within the function. The items listed on the right side of Exhibit 1.3 (Chapter 1) provide examples of specific applications. If multiple purposes are to be served, then the analyst needs to arrive at priorities and to take note of the interrelations among the data needs of the users.

Step 2. Identify the attributes of the job factors that are of relevance to the purposes.

The job factors of interest in job analysis were presented in Chapter 2 (Exhibit 2.1). This step calls for the specification of the particular attributes of the factors that meet the informational needs of the functions to be served. An example of how this can be done is shown in Exhibit 3.1. The job factor that serves as the example in this illustration are tasks. The guide shows the links between common attributes of tasks and the ultimate purposes to be served.

EXHIBIT 3.1 A Guide for Selecting Task Attribute Questions

PURPOSE \ QUESTIONS	Do You Perform This Task?	How Significant/Important Is This Task To Your Job?	How Difficult Is This Task?	How Much Time Do You Spend Performing This Task?	How Frequently Do You Perform This Task?
Describe Jobs	√	√		√	√
Design/Redesign Jobs	√	√	√	√	√
Match Skill & Job Requirements	√		√		
Develop Staffing & Span Of Control Requirements	√			√	√
Establish Training Requirements	√	√	√	√	√
Conduct Operations Reviews Actual Vs. Desired Task Performance	√			√	
Compare Jobs Similarities & Differences	√	√		√	
Develop Task By Task Performance Evaluation	√	√			

From Sidney Gael, *Job Analysis* (San Francisco: Jossey-Bass, Inc., 1983), p. 95.

Step 3. Select the agent of data gathering and the sources of job information.

In most human resource management situations, the agent can be expected to be the analyst. The sources could be job incumbents, their co-workers, supervisors, and other persons associated with the job. The analyst might also wish to consult existing job descriptions and other written company sources.

Step 4. Select the methods of data gathering and analysis.

A wide variety of tools, techniques, and methods are currently available to the job analyst for gathering and analyzing job information. For analytic puposes, however, it is convenient to sort them roughly into two categories: primary methods and systems. There are basically three primary methods of data gathering: observation, interview, and written instruments. The systems consist of collections of techniques and methods organized around theories of jobs and people. They are ready-made ways of gathering and analyzing job data.

A major purpose of this chapter is to review and evaluate the methods and systems of job analysis that are currently in use. Suggestions relating to choosing methods and systems are given in the last section of the chapter.

Step 5. Gather, analyze, and synthesize job information.

The three elements of this step (gather, analyze, synthesize) cannot be neatly distinguished from each other operationally. Their collective thrust is on deriving the informational outputs that are needed for the purposes to be served.

3.3 Primary Methods of Data Gathering

As has just been noted, there are basically three methods of data gathering in job analysis: observation, interview, and written instruments. In practice, each of these methods can be combined with the others. Thus, an observer can use a checklist as an aid in observation. An interviewer can spend some time observing interviewee behavior during the interview. Variations in uses of methods can also be attained through alterations in structure, format, and mode of operations.

OBSERVATION

This is the oldest method of data gatering in job analysis. Most of the pioneering work on job analysis grew out of observational accounts of work (Uhrbrock, 1922).

The basic procedure in observation is quite straightforward. The analyst observes workers and other objects of interest and records what is seen; the account is then summarized in light of the uses to be made of the information. While simple in conception, there are several variations in the observational method. One variation stems from the degree of involvement of the observer in the culture studied. Thus, the observer could be a participant or a nonparticipant. Under participant observation, the observer would actually assume a role within the group studied and act out a part. Under nonparticipant observation, the observer would have no direct role in the functioning of the group. He or she would be a detached third party, mechanically observing, recording, and summarizing behaviors, activities, and interactions.

Variation in the observational method can also be gained by building structure into the effort. The following are some of the ways in which observation can be structured:

- Limiting what is observed, that is, worker-machine interactions, specific human behaviors, time and motion involved in work, the workings of the informal organization.
- Requiring the observer to be fixed in place.
- Placing limits on the duration of observation.
- Requiring the observer to use a structured questionnaire in gathering, recording, and reporting the data.

As a method of data gathering, observation has much to offer the job analyst. A major strength of this method is that it enables the gathering of a wide range of data. A trained observer can observe formal and informal behaviors, work activities, time and motion relationships, and interactions among people and things. He or she can permeate work groups and learn about their attitudes, values, and beliefs. Prolonged interaction between observer and subject can add to the depth of understanding of hidden variables. The outsider perspective of the observer can provide a valuable check against the biases exhibited in self-reports. When combined with a structured questionnaire, observation can be made to yield systematic measurements of multiple categories of data (see Jenkins et al., 1975; Mintzberg, 1973).

The problems faced in the use of observation in data gathering revolve around two issues: capabilities of the observers and the amount of structure built into the study. The full benefits of observation are attained when it is conducted by trained observers, in a fairly open-ended fashion, and over a long period of time. Seasoned professionals can provide a picture of the underlying reality that cannot be matched through any other method. The alternative is to rely on nonprofessionals, and to control their output through tight structuring of the observations. This increases the costs of the effort. More important, there is missing in the results of such undertakings the sparks of insights and depths of understandings that only professionals can provide. The results of structured observation are only as good as the system guiding the study.

Given these pluses and minuses, the place of observation in job analysis can now be crystallized. Observation is most appropriate (and even inevitable) in exploratory analysis or in situations where little is known in advance about the work group to be studied and the underlying issues are unclear. It is also a proper means of gathering data when self-reports by workers cannot be relied upon. Observation is inappropriate and wasteful as a means for verifying information that is already known and for testing specific theories. It is particularly unsuited for cases in which large numbers of workers have to be reached within a short period of time.

INTERVIEW

The interview can be defined as a conversation with a purpose. In job analysis, the purpose of interviewing is to gather useful information about jobs. Variations in interview formats revolve around the following factors: parties to the interview, role of the interviewer, and amount of structure. Most typically, job analysis interviews are encounters between two individuals: the analyst and a worker. It is also possible for there to be multiple parties on both sides. Thus, a worker could be interviewed by a panel, a group of workers could be interviewed by a single analyst, or a group of workers could be interviewed by a panel of analysts.

The role of the interviewer can range from that of a passive note taker to that of an active generator of information. As a note taker, the main responsibility of the interviewer is to gather the desired information according to an established schedule. Interviewer success in this case would be judged according to the completeness of the data gathered. On the other end of the continuum, the interviewer would go beyond the written agenda to generate additional information. This would be attained through probing, following leads and clues provided by the worker, and pursuing issues that may not be a part of the agenda. The scope and usefulness of the information gathered would be the considerations in judging interviewer effectiveness at this end.

The structure of the interview provides a third variation in format. The following are some of the ways in which interviews can be structured:

- Limiting the types of information to be gathered through the interview.
- Specifying the content of the questions to be asked.
- Specifying the contents of the answers to be received.
- Specifying both the contents and the answers to be received.
- Specifying the form in which the question is to be asked.
- Specifying the form in which the answer is to be received.
- Specifying the form in which the questions are to be asked and the answers are to be received.

With this as background, we can now offer some evaluative comments on interviewing as a method of data gathering in job analysis.

The following are the positive features of interviewing. First, being a personal confrontation between two parties, interviewing enables exploration of a wide range of issues: characteristics of jobs as perceived by the worker; the worker's attitudes, values, beliefs, and opinions; and their mastery of the language and technical matters. About the only phenomenon that cannot be readily reached through interviews is intrapersonal dynamics or what is really going on in the interviewee's mind. Second, the interviewer can provide respondents with assistance in the answering of questions. This is particularly relevant for workers who have difficulty understanding the written word. Third, the interviewer can remedy the deficiencies of interview schedules and guides. Even with the best of intentions, problems can creep into interview formats. Fourth, the interviewer can control the size of the respondent sample. Uncooperative respondents can be reasoned with, by showing them the benefits that they can gain from participating. In cases where respondents refuse to cooperate, others can be selected to take their place. Fifth, the interview offers an opportunity for on-the-spot assessments of the validity of the responses. The interviewer is in a position to note not only what the respondent says but also how he or she says it. Contradictory statements can be followed up through additional questions or by using variations of questions to check for consistency (Selltiz et al., 1959, pp. 236–243; Henerson et al., 1978).

Along with the foregoing benefits, the interview brings with it some problems. First, the interview is susceptible to all the biases that plague human encounters. In a job analysis interview, a major danger is that the interviewer might allow the characteristics of the worker to influence judgments about the job. Racial and sexual stereotypes might color the analyst's vision of the job and its requirements. Second, interviewing takes time and disrupts work schedules. To be fruitful, interviews need to be conducted in a relaxed atmosphere without disruptions. Both parties need to be given enough time to cover the issues. This requirement is difficult to meet in practice, particularly if large numbers of respondents are to be interviewed and the interview protocol covers a wide range of issues. Third, the interview sacrifices anonymity and thus raises the possibility of dishonest or self-serving responses. This danger is particularly great when work relations are strained and mutual respect and trust are lacking between labor and management.

WRITTEN INSTRUMENTS

Written instruments go under various labels. The ones commonly encountered in job analysis are questionnaire, inventory, diary, and checklist. Choice of a label for a written instrument hinges on the purposes of the analyst, amount of structure attained, and the circumstances surrounding its use. The label *questionnaire* is the most encompassing; it could be attached to all written instruments. In the job analysis literature, however, it is reserved for highly structured but multipurpose instruments. The *inventory* is also a highly structured instrument, but in job analysis, inventories are typically seen as specific-purpose documents. They are relied upon for studying tasks, behaviors, and other specialized concerns. A *diary* could be structured or unstructured. Its distinguishing feature is that it relies on the worker as the agent of data gathering. A *checklist* could be any list, long or short, single-purposed or multipurposed, that is of interest to the analyst. However, it is typically relatively unstructured in format. (Examples of the various types of written instruments identified are provided in the discussions that follow, and in the appendices to the book.)

Other sources of variation in the questionnaire method are provided by differences in the sources of data, agents of data gathering, and modes of administration. The prime sources of data in job analysis are humans: workers, supervisors, and customers. Written instruments can also be used to accumulate and structure information from company documents, industry, and other secondary sources. Humans are again the primary agents of data gathering. In recent years, devices such as cameras and videos are also being used in job study (see Niebel, 1982). Written instruments can be administered to individuals or groups. They can require the respondents to identify themselves or to remain anonymous. Written instruments can be delivered personally to the respondents, or they can be mailed to them.

As a method of data gathering in job analysis, written instruments offer some distinct advantages. First, they can reach large numbers of people in a short time. They can literally be mailed to thousands of potential respondents. Second, they facilitate uniformity of responses. This is particularly the case with instruments that contain specific questions anchored to scaled responses. Third, written instruments can be readily structured to enable quantification of the results. In fact, the rules for quantification can be built into the instrument itself. Fourth, the anonymity of respondents can be preserved. The mailed questionnaire is the best device for attaining this goal. When completely structured, all that the respondents have to do is to circle their choices, making it unnecessary for them even to divulge samples of their handwriting! The mailed, anonymous questionnaire comes about as close as it is possible to the secret ballot used in political elections. Fifth, respondents can reply at their convenience, without the pressure of an immediate reply. This raises the chances of receiving thoughtful answers (Henerson et al., 1978).

The disadvantages of written instruments are readily apparent. First, they are costly to develop. The best gains from this method are attained when the instrument is highly structured, requiring the respondent only to check or verify preferences. To reach this stage of development, however, takes considerable pilot work and time. All the major instruments used in job analysis (described later) were the result of years of research and experimentation on the part of the researchers. It is quite common for questionnaire development to be preceded by observation and interviewing. This feature makes it difficult, if not impossible, to rely on questionnaires when the need is urgent. Second, the quality of the responses received can be affected by a wide range of variables when the instrument is administered without any assistance. Thus, uniformity of responses can be lost if the items on the instrument are subject to varying interpretations. Technical terms may not be understood by some respondents. The items on the questionnaire may turn out to be incomprehensible to some respondents. This is a very significant problem and has been a source of considerable concern to researchers. A Harris poll found the following about the comprehension levels of the U.S. population: (1) 13 percent of the population 16 years of age or over have serious literacy problems that impair their daily lives, (2) 34 percent of the sample could not fill out a simplified Medicaid application, (3) 8 percent with some college training had serious literacy problems (as summarized in Dunnette, 1976, p. 382).

3.4 Systems of Job Analysis

A job analysis system is a collection of tools, techniques, and methods brought together around some theory about the interrelations among jobs, people, and organizations. There currently exist dozens of systems of job analysis. Some are comprehensive undertakings, built around elaborate and systematically articulated theoretical frameworks. Others are specific-purpose systems aimed at satisfying specialized needs. Still others are parts of families of systems that share certain features in common, but vary from each other in relation to operational details. (The reader should review the background information of the systems provided in Appendix A before proceeding further.)

OVERVIEW OF JOB ANALYSIS SYSTEMS

Job analysis systems can be distinguished from each other over the following dimensions: unit of analysis, theory behind the system, form of data, agents and sources of job information, techniques and methods of data gathering and analysis, and amount of structure.

Orientations to Job Analysis. The unit of analysis of job analysis is the job. For this reason, many systems of job analysis focus directly on studying the missions, tasks, and other substantive features of jobs. However, the study of a particular job does not have to begin directly with the job itself. It is possible to arrive at some understanding of the dynamics of the job by studying the abilities, skills, and other characteristics of the workers performing the job. Some systems of job analysis follow this orientation. It is a convention within the job analysis literature to refer to those systems that focus directly on the job as *job oriented*. Conversely, systems that focus on the worker as a point of departure are called *worker oriented*. The following is a breakdown of the systems according to their orientation:

Job Oriented

FJA: Department of Labor, Sidney Fine's FJA, and Job Information Matrix System (JIMS)

Task Inventories: CODAP and WPSS

HSMS—Health Services Mobility Study

Worker Oriented

PAQ—Position Analysis Questionnaire

CIT—Critical Incidents Technique

JEM—Job Elements Method
BCM—Behavioral Consistency Method
TTA—Threshold Traits Analysis
ARS—Ability Requirements Scales

Variations within these two sets of systems revolve around their scope of coverage. The job-oriented systems study jobs, but the scope of their reach varies. Thus, the FJA systems have whole jobs as their units of concern. The job component of concern of the task inventories and the HSMS are tasks. Finer breakdowns within the worker-oriented systems revolve around the aspect of human involvement studied. Some focus on generalized human behaviors required for task performance. Examples of this focus are found in the PAQ, OAI, and CIT. Others have aptitudes, abilities, and other human characteristics as their focus of concern. Systems that fall within this subset are JEM, TTA, and ARS. (For more detailed discussions of orientations to job analysis, see Heneman et al., 1986, pp. 73–76; Prien, 1977; Ash, 1982.)

Theory. All job analysis systems rest on some explicit or implicit preconceptions about the nature of the interrelations between their units of analysis and the wider organizational context. Unfortunately, the preconceptions underlying many of the systems reviewed here are not clearly articulated. In general, the job-oriented systems tend to draw on the system framework. Jobs are viewed as subunits of organizations. The most systematically articulated theory of jobs and people within organizations is contained in Sidney A. Fine's version of functional job analysis. This is reproduced in its entirety in Appendix A under his system.

The worker-oriented systems typically rest on some preconceptions about the nature of interrelations between human characteristics and job factors and dynamics. According to Prien (1977, p. 169), most of the worker-oriented approaches are based on the notion that there exists a finite set of dimensions—aptitudes, abilities, or characteristics—that can be used to describe a job and that account for the variability in job performance effectiveness. An articulation of this viewpoint is contained in the PAQ and is reproduced under that system in Appendix A (also see Ash, 1982).

Outputs. The informational outputs provided by systems in job analysis follows their orientations and theoretical preconceptions. The job-oriented systems yield information about job outputs, guidelines and controls, tasks, and other job factors. These can then be used for drawing inferences about worker characteristics and other derivatives.

The worker-oriented systems yield information about behaviors, aptitudes, abilities, and other human characteristics. These in turn can be used for gaining insight about jobs. However, it is important to emphasize that descriptions of worker characteristics cannot always be relied upon to draw accurate inferences about job properties. This is because many human abilities, skills, and other characteristics are common to different jobs. Thus, mathematicians are expected to be able to perform complex mathematical operations. But they are not the only ones who need this ability; it is also expected of engineers, scientists, and a variety of other trades that make use of mathematics in their work. For this reason, all worker-oriented systems make use of job information, either explicitly or implicitly, in performing their analysis (Heneman et al., 1986, pp. 75–76). (The processes and steps involved in deriving outputs from job analysis systems are discussed in more detail in Chapters 4 and 5.)

Forms of Data. Job analysis systems vary widely in regard to this dimension. The differences in regard to data can be viewed on a continuum. On one end of the continuum are data that consist of verbal, narrative descriptions of the units studied. On the other end are data that are strictly quantitative, describing the units involved in precise, numerical terms.

Viewed in this way, the PAQ and the task inventories can be placed on the quantitative side of the continuum. These were designed specifically to yield quantitative descriptions of their respective units of analysis. In fact, these systems are structured so that their respective outputs can be entered into computers and tabulated through packaged statistical programs.

None of the available systems can be placed in their entirety on the nonquantitative end of the continuum. All have provisions for some quantification of data at some stage of the analysis. Many systems seek a mix of data, with narrative descriptions being a part of some aspects of the analysis. Thus, the three FJA systems have provisions for narrative descriptions of tasks and context variables; they also contain provisions for numerical ratings of certain job factors and human traits. The JEM, and its recent derivative the BCM, requires the gathering of descriptive data relating to critical incidents during the initial phases of the analysis.

With this as background, we now examine in more detail the contents of the systems of job analysis that are the subject of this review. Since many details have already been presented in Appendix A, our analysis focuses on general approaches and methods of sets of systems that can be combined for discussion purposes. The bulk of the review focuses on the systems given in the appendix. In addition, we also review ideas contained in work study (introduced in Chapter 1) and some job inventories, known as job characteristics inventories, that are becoming a part of the tool kit of job analysis.

FUNCTIONAL JOB ANALYSIS

The label *functional job analysis* (*FJA*) is applied to an approach to job analysis developed by the Department of Labor in the 1930s to meet its mandate relating to the creation of a nationwide public employment service. FJA currently consists of three systems: the original system, referred to here as the Department of Labor (DOL) system, Sidney Fine's Functional Job Analysis, and the Job Information Matrix Systems (JIMS).

All three of the FJA systems are based on a common theory of jobs and people. A detailed statement of this theory is given in Sidney Fine's FJA in the Appendix A. Briefly, this theory states that all job situations call for some involvement on the part of the worker with *data, people, and things*. These are the central elements of the system; they are defined as follows:

Data: Information, knowledge, and conceptions, related to data, people and things, obtained by observation, investigation, interpretation, visualization, and mental creation. Data are intangible and include numbers, words, symbols, ideas, concepts, and oral verbalization.

People: Human beings; also animals dealt with on an individual basis as if they were human.

Things: Inanimate objects as distinguished from human beings, substances or materials; machines, tools, equipment and products. A thing is tangible and has shape, form, and other physical characteristics. (U.S. Department of Labor, *Dictionary of Occupational Titles*, 1977, pp. 1369–1371)

The worker's involvement with these factors is expressed through sets of common functions or activities that are characteristically carried out in relation to data, people, and things. Exhibit 3.2 presents the worker functions contained in the three systems. Note that the functions are arranged in a hierarchy, with the simplest function being at the bottom, and each higher function reflecting a progressively higher level of complexity. Thus, for data, comparing is considered to be a more elementary activity than copying. (Note that in Fine's system, progressively higher numbers are assigned to higher functions, while the reverse is the case with the other two.)

The worker functions hierarchy serves as the pivotal part of the FJA systems. The approach to analysis consists of placing jobs within the hierarchy by comparing their task contents with the breakdown in the hierarchy. Thus, under the DOL system, a job that requires "compiling" of data would receive a score of 3. In placing jobs within the hierarchy, it is assumed that the assigned level includes the requirements of lower functions but excludes the requirements of higher functions. Thus, when a job is placed at the "compiling" level, it is assumed that the worker may be required also to "compute, copy, and compare," but not to "analyze, coordinate, or synthesize."

Functional job analysis contains an extensive network of derivative concepts and instruments to serve as aids in just about all aspects of job analysis. Their applications are discussed in the chapters that follow. The following is a summary and guide to these concepts and instruments.

EXHIBIT 3.2 Worker Functions Hierarchies

Data	People	Things
Department of Labor		
0 Synthesizing	0 Mentoring	0 Setting up
1 Coordinating	1 Negotiating	1 Precision working
2 Analyzing	2 Instructing	2 Operating, controlling
3 Compiling	3 Supervising	3 Driving, operating
4 Computing	4 Diverting	4 Manipulating
5 Copying	5 Persuading	5 Tending
6 Comparing	6 Speaking, signaling	6 Feeding, offbearing
	7 Serving	7 Handling
	8 Taking instructions, helping	
Sidney Fine's Functional Job Analysis*		
6 Synthesizing	7 Mentoring	3A Precision working, setting up
5B Coordinating	6 Negotiating	2A Manipulating
5A Innovating		2B Operating, controlling
		2C Driving, controlling
4 Analyzing	5 Supervising	
3A Computing	4A Consulting	
3B Compiling	4B Instructing	
	4C Treating	
	3A Coaching	1A Handling
	3B Persuading	1B Feeding, offbearing
	3C Diverting	1C Tending
2 Copying	2 Exchanging information	
1 Comparing	1A Taking instructions, helping	
	1B Serving	
Job Information Matrix Systems		
10 Synthesizing	20 Mentoring	30 Setting up
11 Coordinating	21 Negotiating	31 Precision working
12 Analyzing	22 Educating	32 Operating, controlling
13 Discriminating	23 Superintending	33 Driving, operating
14 Figuring	24 Diverting	34 Manipulating
15 Compiling	25 Persuading	35 Tending
16 Copying	26 Speaking, signalling	36 Feeding, offbearing
	27 Serving	37 Handling

* As presented in Fine and Wiley (1971, pp. 31–70). Revised version of Fine's scales are given in Appendices B, E, and J. Examples of Fine's system given in the text are based on original scales as given in the sources cited.

(The references to the appendices contained in the following discussion are to the appendices to the book.)

Worker Functions. All three FJA systems contain elaborate definitions and examples of each of the items in the worker functions hierarchies (Exhibit 3.2). These are reproduced in Appendix B. Although similar in substance, there are important variations. The DOL's version is task oriented, while that of Fine is relatively more behavior oriented. This difference is evident in the choice of verbs that begin the descriptions. The verbs used in Fine's system are closer to the human actions involved in the work.

Another difference between the DOL's and Fine's systems pertains to scoring provisions. Both systems contain provisions for *level* of activity with the data, people, and things hierarchy. This is simply a placement for the work done within the hierarchy. In addition, Fine's system provides for measurement of *orientation* or the relative involvement of the worker in the functions. This is expressed as a percentage in increments of 5 units adding up to 100. An example is provided in Exhibit 3.3. The task in question is from welfare work. The level scores correspond to the breakdown in the worker functions hierarchy. The orientation scores or relative involvement of the worker is 35 percent with data, 60 percent with people, and 5 percent with things.

EXHIBIT 3.3 Some Job Analysis Results from Fine's FJA System

Data	People	Things	Data	People	Things		Reas.	Math.	Lang.	
W.F.—Level			W.F.—Orientation			Instr.	G.E.D.			Task No.
3B	3A	1A	35%	60%	5%	3	3	1	4	W.E.6
GOAL:						OBJECTIVE:				
TASK: Suggests/explains to client reasons for making favorable appearance, and specific areas in which he needs improvement to conform to local standards/expectations, in order that client makes job applications appropriately dressed and groomed.										

From Sidney A. Fine, *Functional Job Analysis Scales: A Desk Aid.* (Kalamazoo, Mich.: W. E. Upjohn Institute, 1973), p. 20.

The JIMS version of worker functions contains an interesting and valuable extension of the DOL hierarchy. Worker functions are broken down into finer activity components through definitions and synonyms found in dictionaries and through consultation with experts. An example of an extension within the Data category for the function ''figuring'' follows:

14—FIGURING	Performing arithmetic operations on and/or carrying out a prescribed action in relation to them. Does not include counting.
Estimate	To determine roughly the size, extent, or nature of. Not the same as forecast in *Synthesizing*.
Compute	To arrive at an answer by simple (arithmetic) means. Compute is not to be confused with calculate (under *synthesize*), which applies to highly abstruse and problematical questions.
Plot	To determine the physical position of, by mathematical means.

This extension of the worker functions hierarchy enables greater precision in finding the closest approximation to the activity. As of the last edition of the JIMS, the activity verbs lists for the data and peoples hierarchy were completed. They are reproduced in Appendix B in the JIMS section.

Work Fields. A work field is a standardized summary of the MTEWA, methods, materials, and tasks involved in a job or occupation. The DOL system contains 100 work fields organized for the purpose of classifying all the jobs within the economy. Examples of work fields are given in Appendix D.

Sentence Analysis Technique. A special technique has been devised for describing job-worker situations by using the terminology and procedures of functional job analysis. Examples of applications of this technique are given in Appendix D. Its usage in job description activity is illustrated in the next chapter.

Scale of Worker Instructions. This is contained in Fine's system and deals with what we have labeled as guidelines and controls (Chapter 2, Exhibit 2.1). It is reproduced in Appendix E. This scale is based on the assumption that all tasks have two components: prescribed and discretionary. The prescribed components represent those areas where the worker has no choice over what is done. The discretionary components consist of areas of tasks where the worker is expected, even required, to use judgment in planning and execution of the task. The higher the score on the scale, the higher the discretion in task performance. Thus, in Exhibit 3.3, the task described received a score of 3, indicating little discretion in task performance.

Worker Traits. The DOL system contains an elaborate schema for studying human traits relevant to job performance. The items included under worker traits are as follows: training time (general educational development and specific vocational preparation), aptitudes, temperaments, interests, physical demands, and environmental conditions. Each of these traits is scaled to enable classification. Definitions of these traits and their accompanying scales are given in Appendices J and K.

Fine's system also contains a general educational development (GED) scale. It is similar to the DOL in conception, but is somewhat more descriptive of the behavioral demands on the worker. It is also reproduced in Appendix J. Use of FJA concepts in worker specification activity is illustrated in Chapter 5.

JOB INVENTORIES

Strictly construed, to inventory is to take stock of goods, people, and other objects. When an inventory is conducted with this definition as a guide, the person conducting the inventory would have at hand a list of the objects of concern, and specifications relating to desired amounts, sizes, and other attributes. A count would be taken and the results would provide data on whether the objects are in stock, short, or over.

While the foregoing is a common view of inventories, the act of inventorying can be extended to appraising of the objects. Besides taking stock of objects, questions can be raised about their goodness. A further extension would involve raising questions about new items to add to the existing lines or as replacements of existing objects. When viewed in this broad way, inventorying is a particular approach to appraising and evaluating.

The inventory concept has enjoyed considerable popularity among job analysts. Dozens of job inventories currently exist. They go under various labels and address diverse analytical and theoretical interests. Exhibit 3.4 contains a partial list of the job inventories currently in existence. Before examining these individually, it is useful to present the general properties of job inventories.

Characteristics of Inventories. In their intrinsic form, job inventories are highly structured instruments. The items within job inventories are scaled to yield numerical data relating to the objects studied. A job inventory is thus in reality a questionnaire.

All the job factors of interest to job analysts can be studied in some way through inventories. Typically, however, inventories are constructed for tangible factors that can be observed and described in quantitative terms. The factor most commonly studied through inventories is job tasks.

The items contained within inventories are finite. This means that the inventory in its completed form contains a set number of items. Of course, items can be added to inventories, and existing items can be removed or substituted with others. But for any particular administration, the items on the inventory would be a closed set.

A wide range of analytical questions can be pursued through inventories about job factors.

EXHIBIT 3.4 A Partial List of Job Inventories and References to Sources

Inventories	Sources
Ability Requirements Scales	Fleishman & Quaintance, 1984
CODAP	Christal & Weissmuller, 1977
Generic Skills	Randhawa, 1978
Job Characteristics Inventory	Brief & Aldag, 1978
Job Components Inventory	Banks et al., 1983
Job Diagnostic Survey	Hackman & Oldham, 1980
Job Rating Form	Hackman & Oldham, 1980
Occupational Analysis Inventory	Cunningham et al., 1971
Position Analysis Questionnaire	McCormick et al., 1969
Threshold Trait Analysis	Lopez et al., 1981
Yale Job Inventory	Hackman & Lawler, 1971

EXHIBIT 3.5 A Scaled Task Inventory Item

Data Processing Task Inventory	Page ____ of ____ Pages	
Listed below are a duty and the tasks which it includes. Check all tasks which you perform. Add any tasks you do which are not listed, then rate the tasks you have checked.	CHECK	TIME SPENT
K. Programming Computers	If Done	1. Very much below average 2. Below average 3. Slightly below average 4. About average 5. Slightly above average 6. Above average 7. Very much above average
1. Adapt programs written in symbolic language to different computer configurations.	✓	4
2. Analyze applications to select appropriate utility programs and subroutines.	✓	2
3. Analyze computer inputs prior to test run and follow-up.	✓	1
4. Analyze programming documentation.		
5. Audit computer inputs after test run and follow-up.	✓	6
6. Code computer applications using a reports program generator.		
7. Code programs utilizing more than one language.	✓	7

From William H. Melching and Sidney D. Borcher, *Procedures for Constructing and Using Task Inventories* (Columbus: Center for Vocational and Technical Education, Ohio State University, 1973), p. 36.

A fixed concern of all inventories is finding out whether or not the factor is *present or absent* in the job. This is a basic requirement and is met through a simple yes/no type scale as illustrated under the "Check If Done" column in Exhibit 3.5. This concern can be readily expanded to include counts relating to sizes, amounts, and frequencies.

If the job factor is quantifiable, there is virtually no theoretical limit to the types of evaluative concerns that can be pursued through inventories. The following are some of the evaluative concerns that have been pursued by job analysts through job inventories:

- *Relationship of factor with other factors.* Example: allocation of functions between people and machines.
- *Relevance of factor to job mission.* Example: the extent to which current process contributes to attainment of job goals.
- *Impact of factor on health and safety*: Example: the extent to which materials and processes used in job pose a danger to health and safety.
- *Mutual dependence of factor with other factors.* Example: the knowledges, skills, and abilities required for performance of task.
- *Employee reactions to job factors.* Example: the extent to which job provides a challenge for the job incumbent. Does the employee like the job as currently structured?

With this as background, we now examine some of the ready-made job inventories that are available. A partial list is given in Exhibit 3.4. As several of these are reviewed in Appendix

A, the details presented there are not repeated here. For discussion purposes, the inventories can be grouped according to their unit of analysis.

Task Inventories. The unit of analysis of these inventories are tasks. The entire range of analytical questions, from finding out whether a task is part of the job to evaluation of the task from various perspectives, can be pursued through task inventories.

Inventorying of tasks is generally done on a job-by-job basis. In recent years, however, the accumulation of information on the job structure of the economy has resulted in the compilation of task inventories on an occupational basis. Thus, the *Dictionary of Occupational Titles* published by the Department of Labor, which is now in its fourth edition, provides descriptions of tasks in about 20,000 jobs found within the U.S. economy (U.S. Department of Labor, 1977). The descriptions of the airline pilots jobs given in Exhibit 2.4 (Chapter 2) provides an example of the types of materials contained in this source.

Another Department of Labor publication was assembled primarily to serve as a basic source of information on 22 broad occupational areas. This publication uses concepts from the JIMS system already described. For the occupational areas covered, it lists the tasks characteristically performed in the occupation, relevant educational requirements, the MTEWAs typically used, and the environmental setting in which the work takes place. Exhibit 3.6 shows a portion of the inventory dealing with administrative and management occupations. Note that the boxes on

EXHIBIT 3.6 A Portion of a Task Inventory Dealing with Administrative and Management Occupations

Inventory

What the Worker Does

Listed below are activities that might be involved in a job-worker situation. Record an "X" after each activity relating to the job being analyzed.

Analyzes and controls expenditures . . . . . ☐
Analyzes market and forecasts trend reports . . . . . ☐
Appoints department heads . . . . . ☐
Authorizes promotions and transfers of personnel . . . . . ☐
Contracts for sale, purchase, and delivery of goods or services . . . . . ☐
Coordinates maintenance and repair activities . . . . . ☐
Coordinates marketing and sales programs . . . . . ☐
Coordinates personnel and safety programs . . . . . ☐
Coordinates production, distribution, and sales activities . . . . . ☐
Coordinates and revises production schedules . . . . . ☐
Develops and executes plans for utilization of machines, manpower, and material . . . . . ☐
Develops personnel recruitment methods . . . . . ☐
Directs departmental operations . . . . . ☐
Directs personnel and industrial training programs . . . . . ☐
Directs studies, investigations, and surveys . . . . . ☐
Enforces administrative policies, operating procedures, and safety rules . . . . . ☐
Interprets policies, procedures, and company regulations . . . . . ☐
Formulates, initiates, and executes policy and programs . . . . . ☐
Negotiates contracts . . . . . ☐
Negotiates with government, commissions, or management officials . . . . . ☐
Plans and directs research and development programs . . . . . ☐
Plans and organizes department or office practices and procedures . . . . . ☐
Plans and implements safety programs . . . . . ☐
Plans and directs advertising, sales, and marketing activities . . . . . ☐
Plans and directs production activities . . . . . ☐
Prepares operating and work schedules . . . . . ☐
Prepares operations budget . . . . . ☐
Reviews and revises budget allocations . . . . . ☐
Recommends changes in production procedures . . . . . ☐
Resolves customer or client complaints . . . . . ☐
Recommends changes or revision of operating procedures . . . . . ☐

From U.S. Department of Labor, *Task Analysis Inventories: A Method for Collecting Job Information* (Washington, D.C.: U.S. Government Printing Office, 1973), p. 5.

the right are left blank. In using the inventory, the analyst would place an X in the boxes for items that are pertinent to the job being analyzed. These items could then serve as a starting point for a more in-depth study of the job (see U.S. Department of Labor, 1973).

Two of the task inventories that have figured prominently in the development of the task inventory method are CODAP and WPSS. Exhibit 3.7 provides an example of the type of output that results from CODAP. In this case, the tasks are from the jobs of journeymen medical services laboratory specialists. The informational results obtained through the inventory were percentage of members performing the tasks and three counts of time spent. (More is said about task inventories in the section in Chapter 4 that deals with task descriptions.)

Behavior Inventories. The unit of analysis of these inventories are behaviors. The *Position Analysis Questionnaire* (*PAQ*) is currently the most popular of the behavior-oriented inventories. This inventory consists of 187 job elements of a worker-oriented nature that tend to characterize,

EXHIBIT 3.7 Task Analysis Results from CODAP (*Task Job Description for Journeymen Medical Laboratory Specialists* [*N* = *394*])

Disk		Task Title	Percent of Members Performing	Average Percent Time Spent by Members Performing	Average Percent Time Spent by All Members	Cumulative Sum of Average Percent Time Spent by All Members
M	5	Prepare Reagents and Standards	75.38	1.01	0.76	39.32
J	27	Perform Hematology Procedures for Prothrombin Time	79.19	0.95	0.76	40.08
J	4	Perform Spinal Fluid Cell Counts	84.52	0.88	0.74	40.82
I	1	Examine Specimens Macroscopically	79.95	0.92	0.73	41.55
I	6	Identify Protozoans, Cestodes, Nematodes, or Trematodes	74.62	0.95	0.71	42.26
F	19	Collect Fecal or Urine Specimens Directly from Patients	52.79	1.33	0.70	42.96
J	28	Perform Hematology Procedures for Reticulocyte Count	84.26	0.82	0.69	44.65
N	8	Perform Urinalyses for Bile Tests	85.28	0.80	0.68	44.34
I	3	Perform Concentration and Flotation Techniques	72.84	0.93	0.68	45.02
J	13	Perform Hematology Procedures for Coagulation Times by Capillary Method	79.70	0.85	0.68	45.70
M	34	Perform Biochemical Procedures for Uric Acid Tests	70.81	0.96	0.68	46.37
N	3	Perform Kidney Function Tests	76.14	0.89	0.68	47.05
J	30	Perform Hematology Procedures for Thrombocyte Count	80.46	0.83	0.67	47.72
J	14	Perform Hematology Procedures for Coagulation Times by Lee-White Method	82.23	0.81	0.66	48.38
M	37	Utilize Methods for Colormetric Procedure	52.03	1.25	0.65	49.03
J	11	Perform Hematology Procedures for Cerebrospinal Fluid Count	80.96	0.80	0.65	49.68
M	32	Perform Biochemical Procedures for Total Cholesterol and Esters Tests	68.27	0.93	0.63	50.32
M	17	Perform Biochemical Procedures for Chlorides Tests	71.07	0.89	0.63	50.95
N	12	Perform Urinalyses for Occult Blood Tests	82.49	0.76	0.63	51.58
E	5	Maintain Files of Clinical Laboratory Requests	54.82	1.14	0.63	52.20
J	8	Perform Hematology Procedures for Bleeding Time, Duke Method	71.83	0.86	0.62	52.82
M	38	Utilize Methods for Electrolyte Determinations	61.68	1.00	0.61	53.43
J	20	Perform Hematology Procedures for Erythrocyte Indices	79.44	0.75	0.59	54.03
M	11	Perform Biochemical Procedures for Calcium and Phosphorus Tests	64.72	0.92	0.59	54.62
E	7	Maintain Files of Laboratory Records or Reports	51.27	1.14	0.59	55.20
J	25	Perform Hematology Procedures for L. E. Test	75.38	0.77	0.58	55.79
L	5	Draw Blood for Transfusions	64.47	0.90	0.58	56.36
K	13	Perform Serological Procedures for Heterophile Presumptive and Differential Antibody Test	63.45	0.90	0.57	56.94
J	18	Perform Hematology Procedures for Eosinophile Count	80.46	0.71	0.57	57.51
M	2	Operate Flame Photometer	64.97	0.88	0.57	58.08
G	8	Perform Sperm Counts	79.44	0.71	0.57	58.65
J	29	Perform Hematology Procedures for Sickle Cell Preparations	82.74	0.68	0.56	59.21
M	14	Perform Biochemical Procedures for Carbon Dioxide Determinations	67.26	0.83	0.56	59.77
E	11	Receive Incoming Supplies	55.58	0.96	0.53	60.31
L	15	Store Blood According to Grouping and Factor	59.90	0.89	0.53	60.84
F	20	Collect Pus Specimens Directly from Patients	65.99	0.80	0.53	61.37

From Raymond E. Christal, *The United States Air Force Occupational Research Project* (Lackland Air Force Base, Tex.: Occupational Research Division, Air Force Human Resource Laboratory, 1974), p. 62.

EXHIBIT 3.8 Organization of the Position Analysis Questionnaire: Major Divisions and Examples of Job Elements

1. *Information input.* (Where and how does the worker get the information he uses in performing his job?)
   Examples: Use of written materials
   Near-visual differentiation
2. *Mental processes.* (What reasoning, decision-making, planning, and information-processing activities are involved in performing the job?)
   Examples: Level of reasoning in problem solving
   Coding/decoding
3. *Work output.* (What physical activities does the worker perform and what tools or devices does he use?)
   Examples: Use of keyboard devices
   Assembling/disassembling
4. *Relationships with other persons.* (What relationships with other people are required in performing the job?)
   Examples: Instructing
   Contacts with public, customers
5. *Job context.* (In what physical or social contexts is the work performed?
   Examples: High temperature
   Interpersonal conflict situations
6. *Other job characteristics.* (What activities, conditions, or characteristics other than those described above are relevant to the job?)

or to imply, the human behaviors that are involved in jobs. These job elements are organized under six divisions. Exhibit 3.8 shows the divisions within the PAQ, their definitions, and examples of elements that fall within each division. The primary scales used in the PAQ for rating the elements are shown in Exhibit 3.9. Every item in the PAQ is linked to a scale. In using the PAQ, ratings are assigned item by item according to the scale that goes with each item. An illustration of the PAQ format and procedures for analyzing job elements is given in Exhibit 3.10. In this case, the job elements in question are visual sources of job information that fit within the first division of the questionnaire (Information input, in Exhibit 3.8). The analytic interest is in finding out the extent to which each of the listed sources is used by the worker as a source of information in performing the job. The raters' judgments are expressed through the Extent of Use (U) scale shown at the top right of the exhibit. If the rater feels that element 1 (Written Materials) are nominally/infrequently used, a score of 1 would be assigned.

Worker Traits Inventories. The units of analysis of these inventories are human aptitudes, abilities, and personal traits. As a basic source in job analysis, these inventories provide lists of basic human capabilities, their definitions, and scales for rating them. Their primary use in job analysis is in establishing the ability requirements of jobs. Inventories from our list (Exhibit 3.4) that fall into this category are

Job Components Inventory
Fleishman's Ability Requirement Scales
Generic Skills Project, Canadian Department of Manpower Administration
Threshold Trait Analysis (TTA)

As trait inventories are of primary use in establishing worker requirements, they are discussed in more detail in Chapter 5 of this book, which deals with that topic. Note that portions of some of these inventories are reproduced in Appendices J and K at the end of the book.

EXHIBIT 3.9 Scales Used in the PAQ for Rating Job Elements

Code	Extent of Use (U)	Code	Importance to the Job (I)
N	Does not apply	N	Does not apply
1	Nominal/very infrequent	1	Very minor
2	Occasional	2	Low
3	Moderate	3	Average
4	Considerable	4	High
5	Very substantial	5	Extreme
Code	**Amount of Time (T)**	**Code**	**Possibility of Occurrence (P)**
N	Does not apply (or is very incidental)	N	No possibility
1	Under one-tenth of the time	1	Very limited
2	Between one-tenth and one-third of the time	2	Limited
3	Between one-third and two-thirds of the time	3	Moderate
3	Over two-thirds of the time	4	Fairly high
5	Almost continually	5	High
Code	**Applicability (A)**		**Special Scales (S)**
N	Does not apply		Special scales developed for job elements that cannot be rated with the other five scales. Some special scales do not have an "N" (does not apply) provision because the statements in these scales apply in some degree to all jobs.
1	Does apply		

From E. J. McCormick, P. R. Jeanneret, and R. C. Mecham, *Position Analysis Questionnaire* (West Lafayette, Ind.: Occupational Research Center, Purdue University, 1969). Copyright © 1969 by Purdue Research Foundation, West Lafayette, Indiana 47907. Adapted with permission.

Job Characteristics Inventories. These are a relatively recent addition to the tool kit of the job analyst and have not yet been fully utilized in job analysis investigations. Their origins go back to theories of motivation at work proposed by various scholars. The approach to be discussed here, which provided the inspiration behind the job characteristics inventories, was developed by Hackman, Lawler, and Oldham (Hackman & Suttle, 1977; Hackman & Oldham, 1980).

The theoretical framework behind this approach is illustrated in the diagram in Exhibit 3.11. The underlying proposition is that jobs vary in terms of their potential to bring about desirable work outcomes such as internal work motivation, personal growth and job satisfaction, and work effectiveness. Differences among jobs in this respect can be traced back to their standing on the core job characteristics that are skill variety, task identity, task significance, autonomy, and feedback. The immediate impact of these core characteristics is on the critical psychological states. The higher the first three characteristics for a job, the higher the experienced meaningfulness of the work. Autonomy affects experienced responsibility for the work, and feedback influences the knowledge of the actual results of the work activities. The model recognizes, however, that the relations among its three components (job characteristics, critical psychological states, and outcomes) may not hold for all workers at all times. The three moderators are worker knowledge and skills, growth need strength, and context satisfactions.

Of the inventories listed in Exhibit 3.4, the following fall within this category:

Job Characteristics Inventory (JCI)
Job Diagnostic Survey (JDS)
Job Rating Form (JRF)
Yale Job Inventory (YJI)

EXHIBIT 3.10 Illustration of the PAQ Format and Rating Procedure

INFORMATION INPUT

1 INFORMATION INPUT

1.1 Sources of Job Information

Rate each of the following items in terms of the extent to which it is used by the worker as a source of information in performing his job.

Code	*Extent of Use (U)*
N	Does not apply
1	Nominal/very infrequent
2	Occasional
3	Moderate
4	Considerable
5	Very substantial

1 U____ Written materials (books, reports, office notes, articles, job instructions, signs, etc.).

2 U____ Quantitative materials (materials which deal with quantities or amounts, such as graphs, accounts, specifications, tables of numbers, etc.).

3 U____ Pictorial materials (pictures or picturelike materials used as *sources* of information, for example, drawings, blueprints, diagrams, maps, tracings, photographic films, x-ray films, TV pictures, etc.).

4 U____ Patterns/related devices (templates, stencils, patterns, etc., used as *sources* of information when *observed* during use; do *not* include here materials described in item 3 above).

5 U____ Visual displays (dials, gauges, signal lights, radarscopes, speedometers, clocks, etc.).

6 U____ Measuring devices (rulers, calipers, tire pressure gauges, scales, thickness gauges, pipettes, thermometers, protractors, etc., used to obtain visual information about physical measurements; do *not* include here devices described in item 5 above).

7 U____ Mechanical devices (tools, equipment, machinery, and other mechanical devices which are *sources* of information when *observed* during use or operation).

8 U____ Materials in process (parts, materials, objects, etc., which are *sources* of information when being modified, worked on, or otherwise processed, such as bread dough being mixed, workpiece being turned in a lathe, fabric being cut, shoe being resoled, etc.).

9 U____ Materials *not* in process (parts, materials, objects, etc., not in the process of being changed or modified, which are *sources* of information when being inspected, handled, packaged, distributed, or selected, etc., such as items or materials in inventory, storage, or distribution channels, items being inspected, etc.).

10 U____ Features of nature (landscapes, fields, geological samples, vegetation, cloud formations, and other features of nature which are observed or inspected to provide information).

11 U____ Man-made features of environment (structures, buildings, dams, highways, bridges, docks, railroads, and other "man-made" or altered aspects of the indoor or outdoor environment which are *observed* or *inspected* to provide job information; do not consider equipment, machines, etc., that an individual uses in his work, as covered by item 7).

From E. J. McCormick, P. R. Jeanneret and R. C. Mecham, *Position Analysis Questionnaire* (West Lafayette, Ind.: Occupational Research Center, Purdue University, 1969), p. 4.

Of these, the YJI is the original version developed by Hackman and Lawler (1971) based on earlier research by Turner and Lawrence (1965). The JDS is a modification of the YJI, and the JCI is an extension and refinement of the JDS. The JRF is a companion instrument to the JDS.

While all four instruments have something of value for the job analyst, the JRF is closest to the central interests of job analysis. It is designed to be used by observers and others outside the job for objective assessment of the core job characteristics within the model. The items contained with this instrument parallel the concerns in the guidelines and controls factor discussed in Chapter 2. The JRF is reproduced in Appendix E.

Job inventories are thus a structured, disciplined mode of job analysis. The advantages and disadvantages of such written instruments in general were discussed earlier. A particular feature of the existing inventories that needs to be highlighted is their specialization. An inventory that satisfies all the needs of the job analyst currently does not exist. It is possible, however, to

EXHIBIT 3.11 The Complete Job Characteristics Model

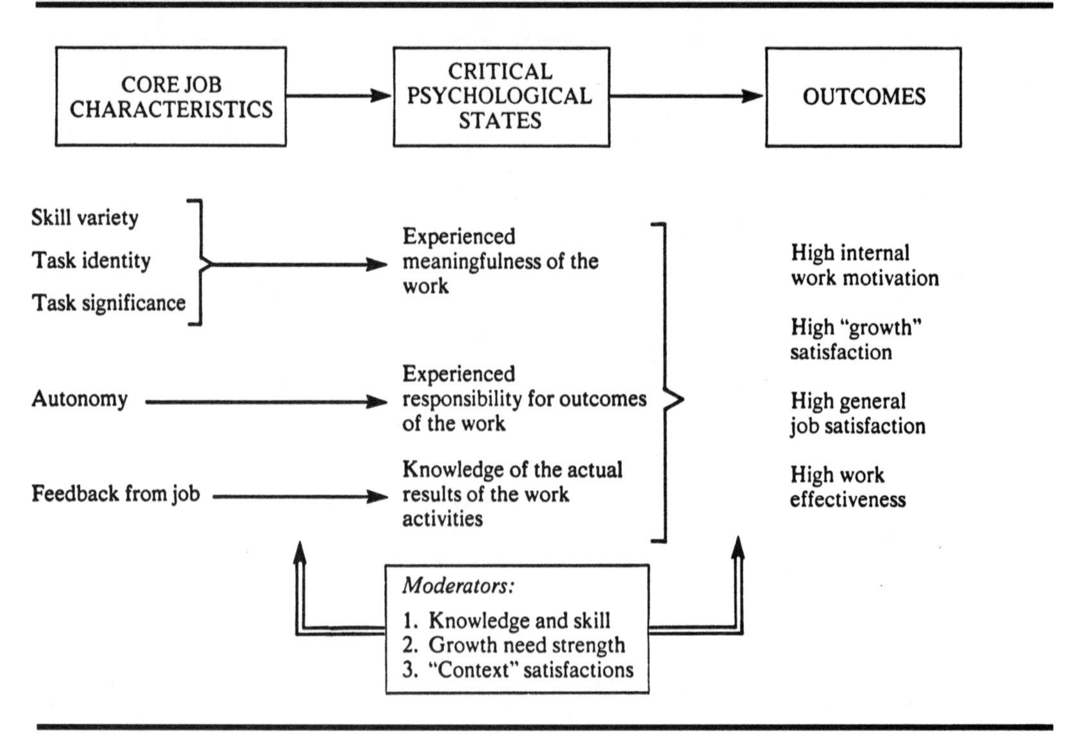

From J. R. Hackman and G. R. Oldham, *Work Redesign*, © 1980, Addison-Wesley Publishing Company, Inc., Reading, Massachusetts. Page 90, Fig. 4.6. Reprinted with permission.

borrow bits and pieces from different inventories to compile a tailor-made approach. More is said on this subject later in this chapter.

WORK STUDY METHODS

Work study is not a system of job analysis. Rather, it is a collection of methods that can be used in analyzing work systems for enhancing productivity and efficiency. Three of the work study methods that are useful for human resource management concerns are diagramming, charting, and work sampling.

Diagramming and Charting. These are two of the primary techniques of work study. The differences between the two revolve around guidelines used in constructing them. A diagram is a schematic depiction of processes, flows, and other interrelations among objects, ideas, and concepts. It is not done to scale, and the elements of a diagram have no mathematical properties. A chart, on the other hand, is relatively more structured and relies on common symbols. The elements of a chart could depict mathematical interrelations. To use an analogy from the building trades, a diagram corresponds roughly to the architect's rendering of a building, while a chart is closer to the working drawings.

Since diagrams are not done according to any rules, little can be said by way of providing guidelines. When diagramming job situations, the analyst needs to create pictures, by whatever means that are necessary, to depict the essential interrelations. Many examples of diagrams can be found in this book, beginning with the exhibits in Chapter 1. An example of how diagrams can be used in conjunction with charts is given later in this section.

Rules have been developed for charting. The major advance here is the creation of a set of symbols that have gained common recognition. Exhibit 3.12 shows five symbols that have been

EXHIBIT 3.12 Work Study Symbols and Examples

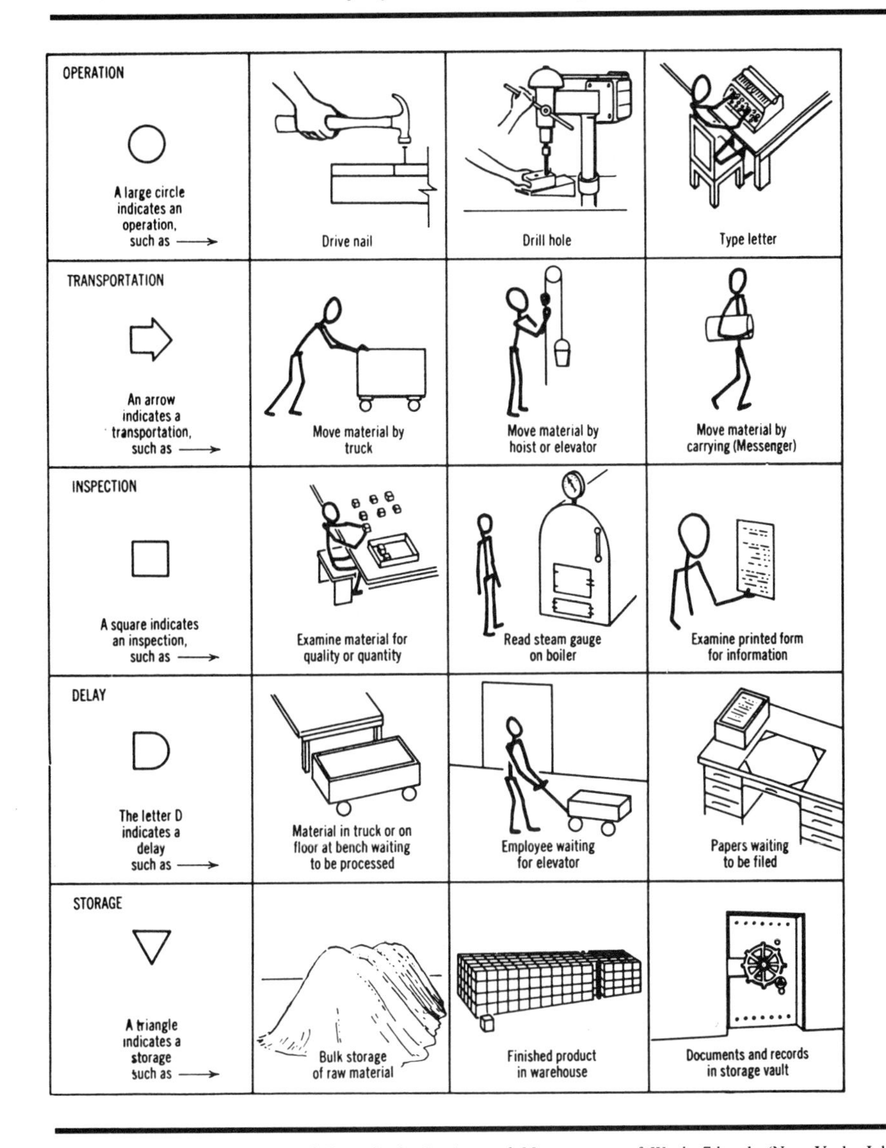

From R. M. Barnes, *Motion and Time Study: Design and Measurement of Work,* 7th ed. (New York: John Wiley, 1980), p. 62.

accepted as standard by the American Society of Mechanical Engineers. An *operation* is said to occur when an object (raw material, component, or service) is intentionally changed in one or more of its characteristics. It represents a major step in the process and usually occurs at a machine or a work station. A successful operation takes the object a step closer toward its ultimate form or completed product. *Transportation* refers to the movement of workers, materials, equipment, and other objects from place to place, but does not include movements that are an integral part of an operation or an inspection. *Inspection* occurs when an object is examined for identification or is compared with a standard as to quantity or quality. A *delay* is said to take place when the performance of the next planned operation in the sequence does not take place immediately. *Storage* occurs when an object is kept under control through some form of authorization that regulates its entry and removal. The difference between a delay and storage is that a requisition, chit, or some other formal authorization is required to get an article out of storage but not out of a situation involving a delay. Two symbols can be combined to show that their activities are being performed at the same work station or when they are being performed concurrently as one activity. Thus, a circle within a square would represent a combined operation and inspection (Barnes, 1980; International Labour Organisation, 1979).

A variety of standard charting formats have been developed to serve different descriptive purposes. The available charts fall roughly into two groups: process sequence charts, which portray a series of events or happenings in the order in which they occur, but which do not depict the events to scale, and time scale charts, which record events, also in sequence, but on a time scale, depicting more precisely the interaction among related events. The following are the descriptions of the charts within these two groups:

Sequence Charts

Outline process chart—provides an overall picture of the situation by recording in sequence only the main operations and inspections.

Process flowchart—shows the sequence of the flow of a product or a procedure by recording all events under review using the appropriate process chart symbols. There are three types of process flowcharts:

Person type—records what the worker does.

Material type—shows how material is handled or treated.

Equipment type—records how the equipment is used.

Two-handed process chart—records the activities of a worker's hands (or limbs) and their relations to each other.

Time Scale Charts

Multiple activity chart—records the activities of more than one subject (worker, machine, or equipment) on a common time scale and shows their interrelationship.

Simo chart—using film analysis, this chart records simultaneously on a common time scale the *therbligs* or groups of *therbligs* performed by different parts of the body of one or more workers (see International Labour Organisation, 1979).

In work study, charts are to the methods analyst as a hammer is to a carpenter. They are a highly versatile tool that can be used in a wide variety of situations. Exhibit 3.13 provides a summary of the variety of job situations that can be depicted and analyzed through the use of charts and related techniques.

The work study literature contains many concrete examples of utilization of diagrams and charts in the solution of job-related industrial problems. Exhibits 3.14 and 3.15 show one such application. In this case, the organization was a hospital ward containing 17 beds and the problem related to serving meals (Exhibit 3.14). Under the original method, the food was first brought from the kitchen on trays, placed on the serving table, dished and served (one plate at a time) to the patients individually. Under the revised method (dashed line in Exhibit 3.14), the serving table was removed, the nurse was provided with a trolley, being required to carry two dished plates at a time and serve meals directly to the patients from the trolley. The process flow chart shown in Exhibit 3.15 shows these movements graphically and accounts for the savings in time, operations, and distance. (An excellent discussion of charting techniques can be found in International Labour Organisation, 1979.)

A couple of limitations of charts may be noted in closing this discussion. One obvious drawback of charts is that they are limited in what they can describe. Charting is most feasible when the subject matter described is visible and tangible. Also, charts cannot accommodate too many variables without losing their appeal and effectiveness. The more variables that are introduced into the chart, the more clouded the interrelations become.

EXHIBIT 3.13 Job Situations That Can Be Analyzed Through Charts

Type of Job	Examples	Recording Technique
Complete sequence of manufacture	Manufacture of an electric motor from raw material to dispatch. Transformation of thread into cloth from preparation to inspection. Receipt, packing, and dispatch of fruit.	Outline process chart Flow process chart Flow diagram
Factory layout: movement of materials	Movements of a diesel engine cylinder head through all machining operations. Movements of grain between milling operations.	Outline process chart Flow process chart—material type Flow diagram Travel chart Models
Factory layout: movement of workers	Laborers servicing spinning machinery with bobbins. Cooks preparing meals in a restaurant kitchen.	Flow process chart—man type String diagram Travel chart
Handling of materials	Putting materials into and taking them out of stores. Loading lorries with finished products.	Flow process chart—material type Flow diagram String diagram
Workplace layout	Light assembly work on a bench. Typesetting by hand.	Flow process chart—man type Two-handed process chart Multiple activity chart Simo chart Cyclegraph Chronocyclegraph
Gang work or automatic machine operation	Assembly line. Operator looking after semiautomatic lathe.	Multiple activity chart Flow process chart—equipment type
Movements of operatives at work	Females operatives on short-cycle repetition work. Operations demanding great manual dexterity.	Films Film analysis Simo chart Memotion photography Micromotion analysis

From International Labour Organisation, *Introduction to Work Study*, 3rd ed. (Geneva: ILO, 1979), p. 84.

Work Sampling. This is a loose designation for a set of methods that rely on sampling for gathering and analyzing work-related factors. In theory, anything that exists and can be counted is reachable through sampling. In practice, work sampling is used to study work activities, behaviors, and time expenditures. The usual procedure for carrying out a work sampling program are as follows:

Establish the objectives of the study.

Identify the activity elements to be used in the study.

Carry out a preliminary study to get estimates of percentages of time of activity elements, or otherwise estimate percentage of time of least frequently occurring element.

Set level of desired accuracy.

Set level of desired statistical significance.

Determine number of observations necessary to fulfill specified conditions.

Determine the method of survey and individuals to be surveyed.

Prepare appropriate record forms.

Carry out survey.

Summarize and analyze results (McCormick, 1979, p. 91).

The following is a simple example demonstrating the logic behind work sampling. Suppose

EXHIBIT 3.14 Flow Diagram: Serving Dinner in a Hospital Ward

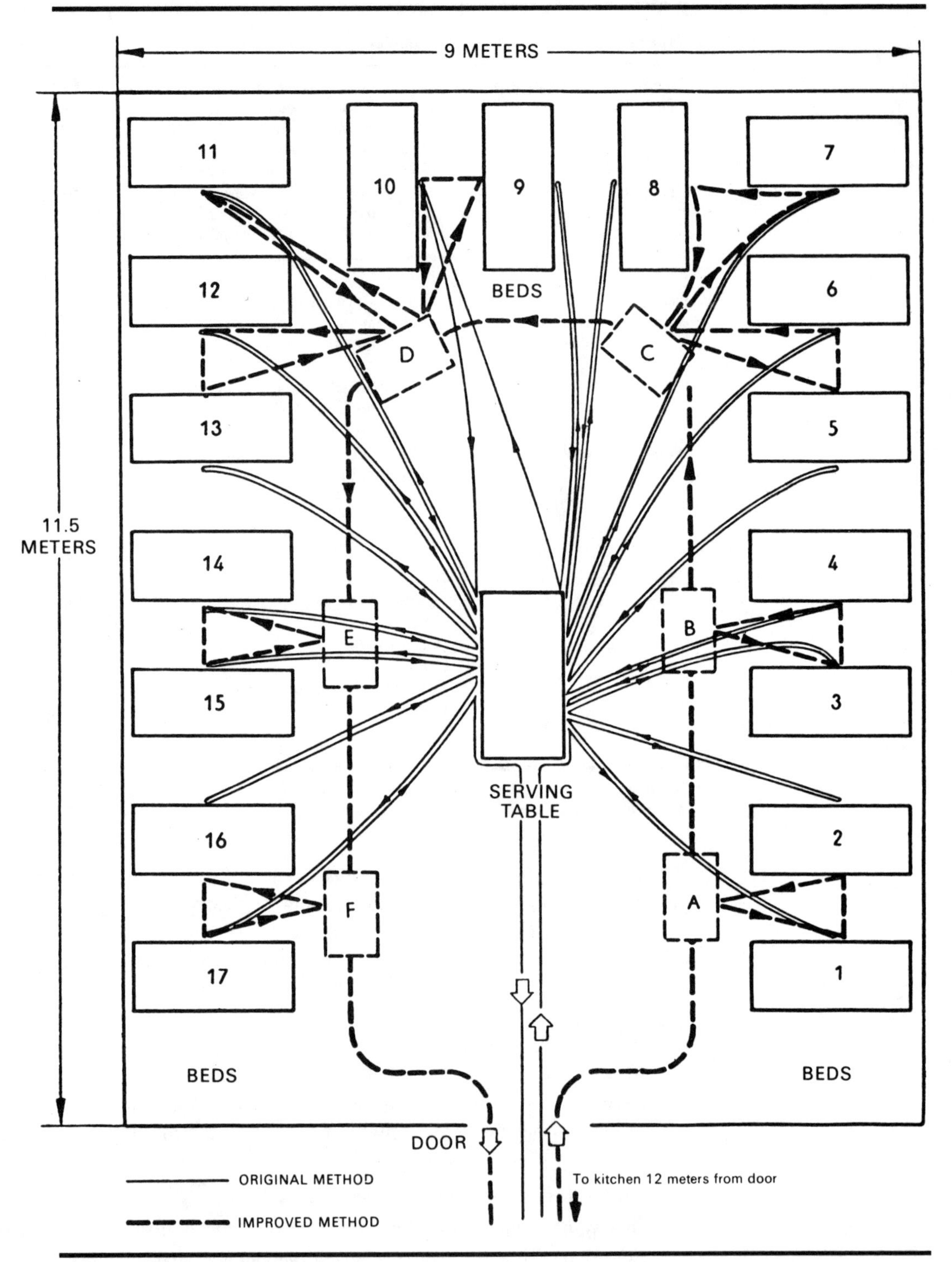

From International Labour Organisation, *Introduction to Work Study*, 3rd ed. (Geneva: ILO, 1979), p. 134. Copyright © 1979 by International Labour Organisation, Geneva. Reprinted by permission.

EXHIBIT 3.15 Person-Type Process Flow Chart: Serving Dinner in a Hospital Ward

FLOW PROCESS CHART		MAN/~~MATERIAL/EQUIPMENT~~ TYPE			
CHART No. *7* SHEET No. *1* OF *1*		SUMMARY			
Subject charted: *Hospital nurse*		ACTIVITY	PRESENT	PROPOSED	SAVING
		OPERATION ○	*34*	*18*	*16*
		TRANSPORT ⇨	*60*	*72*	*(—12)*
ACTIVITY: *Serve dinners to 17 patients*		DELAY D	—	—	—
		INSPECTION □	—	—	—
		STORAGE ▽	—	—	—
METHOD: PRESENT/PROPOSED		DISTANCE (m)	*436*	*197*	*239*
LOCATION: *Ward L*		TIME (man-h)	*39*	*28*	*11*
OPERATIVE(S):	CLOCK No.	COST:	—	—	—
		LABOUR	—	—	—
CHARTED BY:	DATE:	MATERIAL *(Trolley)*	—	*$24*	—
APPROVED BY:	DATE: –	TOTAL *(Capital)*		*$24*	

DESCRIPTION	QTY. *(plates)*	DISTANCE (m)	TIME (min)	○	⇨	D	□	▽	REMARKS
ORIGINAL METHOD									
Transports first course and plates – kitchen to serving table on tray	*17*	*16*	*.50*						*Awkward load*
Places dishes and plates on table	*17*	—	*.30*						
Serves from three dishes to plate	—	—	*.25*						
Carries plate to bed 1 and return	*1*	*7.3*	*.25*						
Serves	—	—	*.25*						
Carries plate to bed 2 and return	*1*	*6*	*.23*						
Serves	—	—	*.25*						
(Continues until all 17 beds are served. See figure 42 for distances)									
Service completed, places dishes on tray and returns to kitchen	—	*16*	*.50*						
Total distance and time, first cycle		*192*	*10.71*	*17*	*20*	—	—	—	
REPEATS CYCLE FOR SECOND COURSE		*192*	*10.71*	*17*	*20*	—	—	—	
Collects empty second course plates		*52*	*2.0*	—	*20*	—	—	—	
TOTAL		*436*	*23.42*	*34*	*60*				
IMPROVED METHOD									
Transports first course and plates – kitchen to position A – trolley	*17*	*16*	*.50*						*Serving trolley*
Serves two plates	—	—	*.40*						
Carries two plates to bed 1; leaves one; carries one plate from bed 1 to bed 2; returns to position A	*2*	*1.5 / 0.6 / 1.5*	*.25*						
Pushes trolley to position B	—	*3.0*	*.12*						
Serves two plates	—	—	*.40*						
Carries two plates to bed 3; leaves one; carries one plate from bed 3 to bed 4; returns to position B	*2*	*1.5 / 0.6 / 1.5*	*.25*						
(Continues until all 17 beds are served. See figure 32 and note variation at bed 11)									
Returns to kitchen with trolley	—	*16*	*.50*						
Total distance and time, first cycle	—	*72.5*	*7.49*	*9*	*26*				
REPEATS CYCLE FOR SECOND COURSE	—	*72.5*	*7.49*	*9*	*26*				
Collects empty second course plates	—	*52*	*2.00*	—	*20*				
TOTAL	—	*197*	*16.98*	*18*	*72*				

that the concern is with determining whether a given machine is idle or not. In such a case, the observations would be aimed at detecting one of two possibilities:

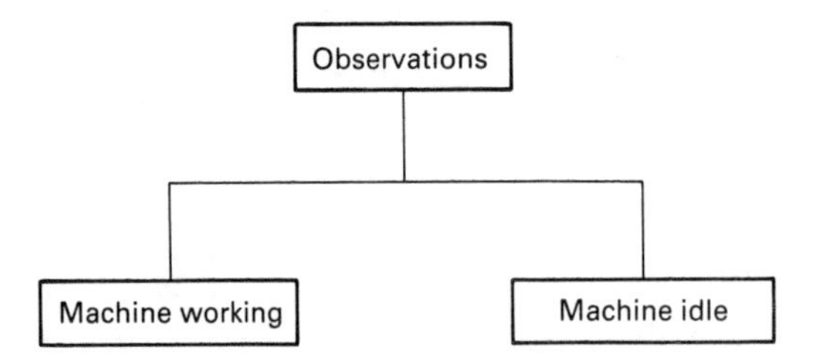

The objective could be expanded to find out the cause of the stoppage of the machine:

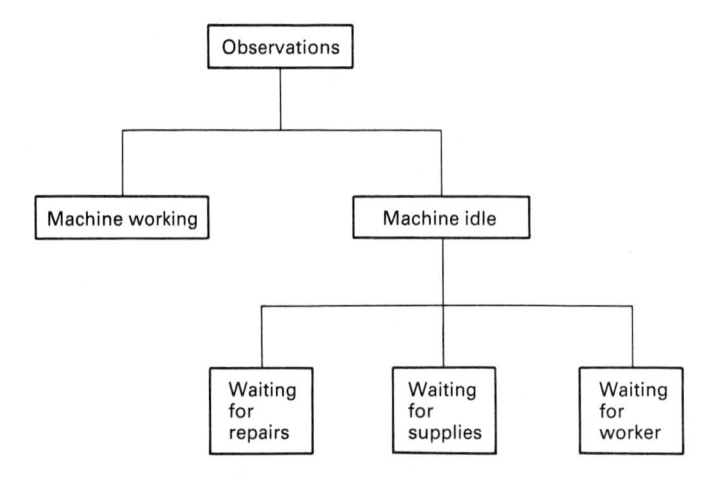

The results of this sampling study can be summarized as in Exhibit 3.16. Depending on the preferences of the analyst, details relating to desired levels of accuracy, confidence, and significance can be built into the analysis (see International Labour Organisation, 1979 for a more complete review of work sampling techniques).

Work sampling has traditionally been associated with industrial engineering. In recent years, however, attempts have been made to expand its applications to areas of human resource management concerns. Thus, Carroll and Taylor (1969) applied the technique to the study of time allocations of clerical workers. The concern was with comparing estimated time with actual time allocations in various work activities. Sixteen workers were asked to estimate the proportion of time each spent on various job activities during a routine workday. While this was happening,

EXHIBIT 3.16 Summaries of Observations Acquired Through Work Sampling

Date:	Observer:	Study No.:	
Number of observations: 75		Total	Percentage
Machine running	卌 卌 卌 卌 卌 卌 卌 卌 卌 卌 卌 卌 II	62	82.7
Machine idle	卌 卌 III	13	17.3

EXHIBIT 3.16 *(cont.)*

Date:		Observer:	Study No.:	
Number of observations: 75			Total	Percentage
Machine running		卌 卌 卌 卌 卌 卌 卌 卌 卌 卌 卌 卌 II	62	82.7
Machine idle	Repairs	II	2	2.7
	Supplies	卌 I	6	8.0
	Personal	I	1	1.3
	Idle	IIII	4	5.3

From International Labour Organisation, *Introduction to Work Study*, 3rd ed. (Geneva: ILO Press, 1979), p. 203. Copyright © 1979 by the International Labour Organisation, Geneva. Reprinted by permission.

an independent observer obtained random observations of their work activities 16 times a day for a period of two weeks. The results are given in Exhibit 3.17. Note that the absolute differences are not very large, being at the most 6 percent (for machine operations). An interesting finding was that differences in idle and personal time, which might have been expected to be the least accurately estimated by employees due to their sensitive nature, was off by only 4.7 percent.

Another example of work sampling applications is provided in a study by Haas et al. (1969). In this case, the subjects were 355 managers in a large metropolitan bank. The objective was to determine the differences, if any, between how managers actually spend their time versus

EXHIBIT 3.17 Proportions of Time Spent in Various Work Activities as Determined by Estimates and by Work Sampling

	Job Time Proportions as Determined by Work Sampling		**Job Time Proportions as Determined by Estimates**	**Differences in Average Time Allocation**
Work Activity	*n*	%	%	%
Conversation	246	10.3	7.5	2.8
Filing	202	8.5	10.8	2.3
Idle and personal	169	7.1	2.4	4.7
Machine operation	155	6.5	12.4	5.9
Mail handling	11	.5	.8	.3
Telephone	108	4.6	7.9	3.3
Typing	179	7.5	6.3	1.2
Walking	89	3.7	5.0	1.3
Writing, research and review*	1,074	45.1	46.8	1.7
Other	75	3.2	0.0	3.2
Unknown	72	3.0	0.0	3.0
Totals	2,380	100.0	100.0	

* These were originally separated in the study but were combined because the observer and *Ss* had difficulty in differentiating among them.

From S. J. Carroll and W. H. Taylor, Validity of estimates by clerical personnel of job time proportions, *Journal of Applied Psychology*, 53, 1969, p. 165. Copyright © 1969 by the American Psychological Association. Reprinted by permission of the author.

EXHIBIT 3.18 Means and Standard Deviations for Time Managers Believe They Actually Spend and Time They Think They Should Spend in Six Managerial Activities

Present Study $N = 355$							Mahoney et al. (1965)* $N = 492$	
Actual				Should				
Mean	S.D.	Rank	Activity	Mean	S.D.	Rank	Mean	Rank
24.19	20.30	1	Negotiating	25.39	21.52	1	7.8	6
20.72	16.17	2	Supervising	20.07	16.47	2	28.4	1
13.15	9.39	3	Evaluating	13.69	10.19	4	12.7	4
13.13	8.67	4	Coordinating	12.03	7.43	5	15.0	3
12.79	11.07	5	Investigating	9.23	8.04	6	12.6	5
12.15	9.60	6	Planning	14.61	10.13	3	19.5	2

* Staffing, which accounted for 4.1 percent of the time, was omitted. The sample was taken from 13 companies in various industries.

From J. A. Haas, A. M. Porat, and J. A. Vaughan, "Actual vs. Ideal Time Allocations Reported by Managers: A Study of Managerial Behavior," *Personnel Psychology*, vol. 22 (1969), p. 66. Copyright © 1969 by Personnel Psychology, Inc. Reprinted by permission.

how they think they should spend their time. The data were gathered by means of a written questionnaire that measured actual versus ideal behavior patterns as perceived by the respondents. The results are given in Exhibit 3.18. The highest expenditure of time, both actual and ideal, was in negotiating. This is understandable for bank officers since they have to deal with customers, especially in the consumer loans area. There were no major differences in the last four activity categories under "Actual." An interesting difference was found in the "Should" responses. Note that the amount of time that the respondents felt should be spent in planning increased, while the time attributed to investigating decreased. The authors suggest that such data could be useful in bringing about changes and in training new managers.

3.5 Job Analysis Methods and the Law

As noted in the first chapter, job analysis is looked upon very favorably by the Equal Employment Opportunity regulatory agencies and the courts. This section summarizes the requirements relating to choice of methods of job analysis.

· Neither the *Uniform Guidelines* nor the courts have expressed any preference for particular methods of job analysis. The analyst is thus free to choose the methods that suit the purposes of the analysis.

· The sources used in data gathering must be up to date and close to the job. The human sources that have received approval are job incumbents, their supervisors, administrators, and other persons with firsthand or specialized knowledges about the job. In addition, nonhuman resources such as company training manuals, prior job descriptions, and standardized questionnaires and checklists may also be used.

· The job analyst and other agents of data gathering should be experts. However, the expertise of the agents is not sufficient in itself to prove that the job analysis was valid.

· Objective data are generally preferred to subjective data. Objective data consist of "hard" data (productivity, sales, absenteeism rates) and descriptions of tasks and other job factors that can be independently verified. Subjective data, on the other hand, consist of information that is influenced by human judgment. Examples of such data are ratings of tasks and other job factors and opinions expressed by individuals that cannot be directly substantiated by hard facts (Kleiman & Durham, 1981).

· According to the *Uniform Guidelines*, the methods that are chosen must be open, clearly explained, and conform to the technical standards laid down in the *Guidelines*. The courts, however, do not consider these technical standards to be the final word. In judging the appropriateness of a particular job analysis method, the courts consider the totality of the undertaking. No one technique, source, agent, or procedure is considered appropriate or sufficient in itself. Consequently, the courts sometimes reach contradictory conclusions on the acceptability of particular methods. The following review of case law provides a glimpse into the varied and inconsistent responses of federal courts to job analysis issues. The first set of cases are instances where the job analysis methods were approved by the courts (summarized from Thompson & Thompson, 1982).

> The content validity claims made by a Board of Examiners for their test was rejected because it rested on a job analysis that was cursory and consisted of statements of duties and opinions of experts. The Court would have preferred an empirical analysis by experts and professionals that systematically studied: the job, the performance of those already occupying it, and the elements, aspects, and characteristics that made for successful job performance (*Chance* v. *Board of Examiners*, 1971).
>
> An examination used by a state Civil Service Commission was found to lack content validity. In this case, the witness for the defense, the Assistant Chief of the Division of the Department of Personnel, testified that he had never performed a job analysis and that the examination was prepared by gathering together the file on the previous examination, the former notice of the exam, the class specifications, and a magazine published by the Personnel Department. In rejecting the claim, the Court asserted that the knowledge, skills, abilities, and other human characteristics (KSAOs) tested in the examination must be those that are required for successful job performance. It also provided a definition of job analysis for test validation purposes:
>
> > a thorough survey of the relative importance of the various skills involved in the job in question and the degree of competency required in regard to each skill. It is conducted by interviewing workers, supervisors, and administrators; consulting training manuals; and closely observing the actual performance of the job. (*Vulcan Society* v. *Civil Service Commission*, 1973)

In a case where a Department of Correctional Services was the defendant, the Court went into greater depth regarding job analysis procedures (*Kirkland* v. *Department of Correctional Services*, 1974). It stated that job analysis is the cornerstone in the construction of a content valid examination and went on to point out that

> Without such an analysis to single out the critical knowledge, skills and abilities required by the job, their importance relative to each other, and the level proficiency demanded as to each trait, a test constructor is aiming in the dark and can only hope to achieve job relatedness by blind luck. (cited in Thompson & Thompson, 1982, p. 867)

The test was judged to be invalid for the following reasons. First, it did not meet three criteria of content validity that the judge had assembled from his reading of professional publications and case law: (1) the KSAOs must be critical and not peripherally related to successful job performance, (2) portions of the exams should be accurately weighted to reflect the relative importance to the job of the attributes for which they test, and (3) the level of difficulty of the exam material should match the level of difficulty of the job. Second, written evidence such as a job description was not provided to show that a job analysis had indeed been performed. Third, the actions taken in lieu of a job analysis were unacceptable to the Court; these consisted of job audits of a different job (correction officer and not correction sergeant), outdated materials, a one-paragraph class specification containing cursory information, KSAO statements that were actually descriptive of five examination subsets rather than the KSAOs demanded by the job, and the rule book for the job.

The Job Elements Method (JEM) was tested in a case where the defendents were prominent state and federal governmental agencies. In this case, an examination for selection of troopers was constructed and used by the State of New York with technical assistance from the U.S. Civil Service Commission. In rejecting this content validation effort, the Court gave the following reasons: the method used (JEM) did not focus on what troopers actually do on the job, but only on the underlying traits or characteristics that troopers believe characterize successful job performance; a task-oriented analysis was not done, and hence there was no documented linkage between the content domain of the exam and the actual tasks and duties of the New York State Trooper (*U.S.* v. *State of New York*, 1979).

· The review of cases by Thompson and Thompson also documented cases where job analysis procedures were accepted by the courts. These cases involved public employers around the country. In the interest of space, only the outcome and the general reasoning are given here.

> KSAOs for the job of police sergeant derived through the critical incidents technique were accepted by the Court. Reliance on informed and expert testimony was instrumental in swaying the Court (*Davis* v. *Washington*, 1972).
>
> A job analysis judged to be insufficient by a court was declared to be sufficient by the same court because the judge was impressed with the qualifications of an expert who rendered an opinion stating that the resultant Sergeant's Promotional Examination was content valid (*Shield Club* v. *City of Cleveland*, 1974).
>
> An exam was declared to be content valid even though it was acknowledged that its preparation departed from the APA standards (*Bridgeport Guardians* v. *Police Department*, 1977).
>
> A job analysis was deemed adequate but the test was disallowed because it did not reflect the findings in the job analysis (*Firefighters Institute for Racial Equality* v. *City of St. Louis*, 1977).
>
> A job analysis conducted by the Civil Service Commission of the City of New York failed to meet the tests laid out in the *Guidelines*. However, it was judged to be acceptable by the court. The judge appeared to have been impressed by the amount of detail provided by the city in defending its approach (*Guardians Association of NYC Police Department* v. *Civil Service Commission of New York*, 1980).

Given the dynamic state of modern human resource management, it is not possible to attain closure in any discussion of the state of the law that governs its functioning. Perhaps the best guide for the analyst when choosing a method is to respect the traditional principles of science—openness of procedures, sufficiency of detail, objectivity of data gathering and analysis, and a willingness to experiment with different methods until the most suitable one is found.

3.6 Suggestions Relating to Data Gathering and Analysis

Data gathering and analysis is a disciplined activity. The steps involved in this activity, and the techniques and methods of data gathering and analysis that are currently available, were reviewed in the preceding sections. We close this discussion by offering some suggestions for aiding the human resource director in fulfilling this phase of job analysis.

MODE OF OPERATION

Given the complexity of the subject and the variety of ways in which job information can be gathered and analyzed, an important decision facing the analyst is that of choosing an appropriate mode of operation. This can be placed on a continuum. On one end of the continuum would be a mode where the analyst makes himself or herself the star of the activity. Under this mode, the analyst assumes direct and personal responsibility for gathering, analyzing, and interpreting job information. The analyst serves as the agent of data gathering and relies solely on his or her judgment in fulfilling all significant aspects of the task. On the other end of the continuum would be a mode where the analyst relies entirely on a ready-made system, with built-in provisions for gathering, analyzing, and synthesizing job information. Under this mode, exercise of the analyst's judgment is limited to defining the purposes of the effort and in choosing the system to be used.

Neither mode is practicable in its extreme in most situations. But the options are clear, and their feasibility and relative benefits can be pointed out in general terms. The first mode, where the analyst serves as the star performer, assumes a highly trained and experienced analyst. It would be appropriate in instances where the scope of the investigation is limited and the focus is on objective attributes of jobs. This mode, however, would be inappropriate in instances where large numbers of jobs have to be analyzed, multiple purposes are to be served, and the opinions of the affected parties are of importance. Its major limitation is that it relies entirely on the judgment (and possible fallibility) of the analyst.

The second mode, where the analyst relies on a ready-made system, has the advantage of capitalizing on institutional experience. The analyst does not need to "reinvent the wheel" every time a job analysis has to be conducted. The major problem with this approach, relied upon in the extreme, is that it assumes the existence of a ready-made system that can provide the analyst with the needed information.

Given these options, an appropriate way of closing this discussion is by providing a framework for making the decisions encountered and by pointing out some competencies that are needed on the part of the analyst.

CRITICAL DECISION: MAKE OR BUY?

The basic choice that is faced in selecting methods and systems is the classic business decision: make or buy. The *make* option, exercised in the extreme, would entail devising all the forms and procedures from scratch. The *buy* option, on the other hand, would involve adoption of some other company's program or the purchase of a packaged system of the type discussed earlier.

Each option has its own set of attractions. These are stated in the following comparative terms:

Advantages of Making	Advantages of Buying
Involvement of outsiders is avoided.	Outsiders can provide different and impartial perspective.
Consultation and other fees are saved.	Savings are realized in developmental costs.
Internal staff derives benefits that come with doing the whole thing by themselves.	Experts can provide guidance and professional training.
System can be tailored to suit the particular needs of the company.	A ready-made, standardized system can provide industry norms and practices against which the results can be compared.

The pivotal administrative consideration in making the make or buy decision is the availability of internal talent and capability. If the company has qualified persons on its staff, it would make sense to keep the effort local. The absence of internal talent would force reliance on ready-made systems, in varying degrees. Time is another significant consideration. If the need is urgent, a ready-made system would have to be adopted. The results can then be used to develop a program that suits the company's long-term needs.

CRITERIA FOR CHOOSING SYSTEMS

A variety of criteria can be used in choosing systems of job analysis. Exhibit 3.19 shows three sets of criteria and their interrelations. Each set reflects a different vantage point in making decisions relating to choice of systems (based on Sistrunk & Smith, 1982; Astin, 1964; Landy & Farr, 1983).

EXHIBIT 3.19 A Classification of Criteria for Selecting Methods and Systems of Job Analysis

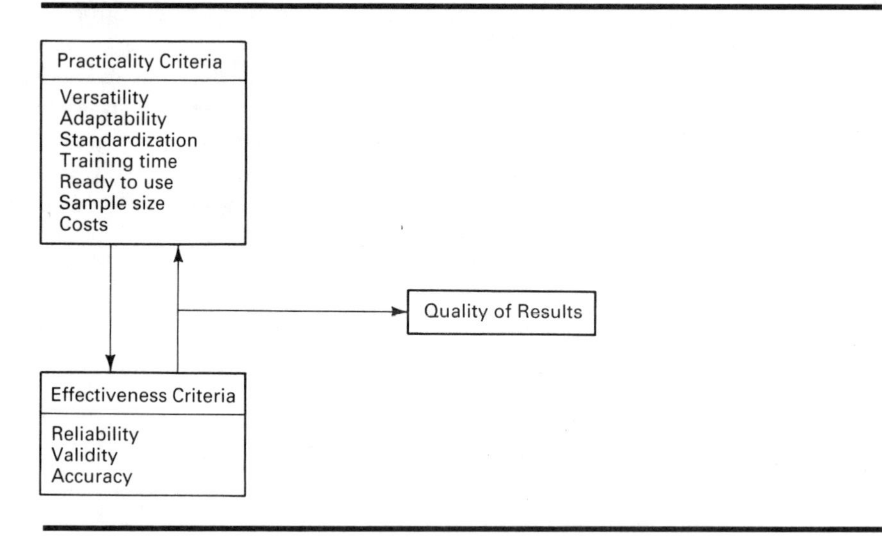

The ultimate criterion in choosing or retaining a system of job analysis is the quality of the results attained. This is judged, over a period of time, by finding out the extent to which the information provided is relevant, translatable, and useful for fulfilling the informational needs of the organization. The chances of acquiring quality of results are enhanced if the system meets the tests of effectiveness and practicality criteria shown in Exhibit 3.19.

System Effectiveness. The focus of these criteria is on the system itself, and the underlying evaluative concern is with assessing its effectivness or ability to provide the information needed.

Reliability	The consistency of the results attained through the system. A method is judged to be reliable if it yields the same (or very similar) results under similar conditions of usage and application. Thus, a task inventory is judged to be reliable if it yields the same task information over repeated applications.
Validity	The conformance between what was expected and what was attained. A system is judged to be valid if it provides the type of information that it was designed to provide. Thus, a task inventory is valid if it yields the desired task information.
Accuracy	The ability of the system to provide an assessment of the true value of factor being measured. Accuracy implies both reliability and validity, but the reverse is not always true. Thus, to qualify as accurate, a rating received by a job factor on some attribute (such as prestige, importance, or criticality) must reflect the true standing of the factor on that attribute.

Practicality Concerns. A system might meet all the effectiveness criteria noted, but yet not be very useful to the analyst. It might fall short on practicality considerations. The following are some criteria that can be used to judge practicality. (These are based on Sistrunk & Smith, 1982.)

Versatility	Ability of the system to analyze different jobs and to serve multiple purposes.
Adaptability	Extent to which it is possible to adapt the method to different job situations without losing its effectiveness.

Standardization	There are two dimensions to standardization: internal and external. The internal dimension refers to uniformity of terminology and modes of data gathering and analysis. A method that is standardized in this sense should yield data that are comparable across jobs and over different applications. External standardization refers to conformance with practices within the industry. This type of standardization enables comparison of results across organizations.
Training time	The amount of time required to train job analysts to use the method. The emerging notion of "user friendly" in the computer field is relevant to the assessment of training time.
Ready to use	Extent to which the method is tested, refined, and operational.
Sample size	Number of respondents or agents needed to ensure adequate or dependable results.
Costs	Both developmental and administrative costs.

RESEARCH ON JOB ANALYSIS SYSTEMS

Job analysis systems have accumulated over a period of time. They have been devised by different sponsors and are built on very divergent theoretical foundations. For this reason, study of their effectiveness in relative terms is rendered difficult. There is currently a dirth of research that evaluates their workings in terms of hard data. The bulk of what is available consists of data acquired through surveys of opinions about various systems. One such study was published by the Center for Evaluation Research of the University of South Florida. The raters of job analysis systems in this study were 93 participants with experience in human resource management fields. Two issues were investigated: (1) effectiveness of a set of systems in serving various organizational purposes and (2) ratings of the systems according to a set of criteria. These data are provided in Exhibit 3.20. The results are based on a five-point scale.

To begin with purposes (Exhibit 3.20a), wide ranges of scores were received by the systems in relation to the purpose dimensions. A couple of generalities, however, are evident. Note that the two job-oriented systems (CODAP and FJA) tended to do quite well over all the purpose dimensions. Neither earned the lowest score on any of the dimensions. In fact, CODAP earned the highest score over 7 of the 11 dimensions.

A difference in performance of the systems might be expected when the purpose factors are broken down according to worker versus job concerns. Thus, the job-oriented systems might be expected to do better over the job dimensions, while the reverse could be expected for the worker-oriented systems. This was not generally the case. On only one worker-related dimension did a worker-oriented system receive the highest score (TTA for Personnel Requirements/Specifications).

The results relating to practicality concerns are given in Exhibit 3.20b. The PAQ attained the highest score in 6 out of the 11 concerns. This is as expected since the PAQ was specifically designed with these criteria in mind—it is a standardized, operational, off-the-shelf instrument. But note the results relating to occupational versatility/suitability and quality of outcomes. The highest scores were attained here by the two job-oriented systems—CODAP and FJA.

The results presented in Exhibit 3.20 cannot be taken as the final word on the relative worth of job analysis systems. They do, however, offer a couple of valuable lessons for choosing systems. One point that stands out is the possible trade-offs in regard to effectiveness versus practicality. A system that is valid, reliable, and accurate may rate low when judged in terms of costs, training time, and other practical considerations. Compare, for example, the ratings of the two job-oriented systems in regard to quality of outcome and costs in Exhibit 3.20(b).

Another critical question is relevancy. A system might score high on both sets of criteria (effectiveness and practicality), but not have the potential for producing the type of information desired by the analyst. Consider the performance of the ARS system in this regard. This is a highly developed system and does quite well in relation to the two sets of criteria shown in

EXHIBIT 3.20 Comparative Research on Job Analysis Systems: Purposes and Practicality

Purposes	Job Analysis Methods: Threshold Traits Analysis	Ability Requirements Scales	Position Analysis Questonnaire	Critical Incident Technique	Task Inventory/ CODAP	Functional Job Analysis	Job Elements Methods	F[b]	p<	η^2
(a) Effectiveness Ratings of 7 Job Analysis Methods for 11 Organizational Purposes[a]										
Job description	2.95[c] (1.01)	2.15 (.97)	2.86[c] (1.09)	2.59[c] (1.15)	4.20[d] (.94)	4.07[d] (.97)	2.66[c] (1.03)	54.58	.0001	.32
Job classification	3.11[c] (1.00)	2.61[d] (1.07)	3.67[e] (.97)	2.19 (.95)	4.18[f] (1.00)	3.81[ef] (.97)	2.73[cd] (1.11)	50.82	.0001	.30
Job evaluation	2.80[c] (.93)	2.44[cd] (1.04)	3.70[e] (1.03)	2.37[d] (1.13)	3.46[e] (1.08)	3.52[e] (.90)	2.72[cd] (1.06)	26.91	.0001	.18
Job design	2.73[cd] (1.03)	2.28[e] (1.09)	2.99[c] (1.13)	2.52[de] (1.10)	3.72[f] (1.13)	3.64[f] (.99)	2.59[de] (1.08)	28.25	.0001	.18
Personnel requirements/specifications	3.68[c] (.87)	3.51[cd] (1.09)	3.36[cd] (1.03)	2.86[e] (.98)	3.19[de] 1.13)	3.58[c] (.94)	3.64[c] (1.19)	9.24	.0001	.07
Performance appraisal	2.80[cd] (1.11)	2.75[c] (1.14)	2.72[c] (1.06)	3.91[e] (1.12)	3.24[df] (1.15)	3.58[ef] (1.13)	3.07[cd] (1.12)	18.07	.0001	.13
Worker training	2.74[c] (1.13)	2.78[c] (1.13)	2.76[c] (1.03)	3.42[d] (.96)	3.65[d] (1.03)	3.63[d] (1.07)	3.33[d] (1.06)	16.03	.0001	.12
Worker mobility	2.67[c] (1.01)	2.47[cd] (1.05)	2.78[ce] (1.05)	2.20[d] (.96)	3.34[f] (1.09)	3.07[ef] (.94)	2.62[c] (.98)	18.60	.0001	.11
Efficiency/safety	2.34[cd] (1.02)	1.90[c] (.95)	2.46[de] (1.09)	3.08[f] (1.30)	2.79[ef] (1.05)	2.81[ef] (1.08)	2.30[cd] (1.07)	14.28	.0001	.10
Manpower/work force planning	2.61[cd] (.98)	2.32[ce] (.93)	2.83[df] (1.06)	2.24[e] (.88)	3.41[g] (1.14)	3.11[fg] (1.06)	2.60[cde] (1.11)	20.65	.0001	.12
Legal/quasi-legal requirements	2.65[cd] (1.06)	2.44[c] (1.13)	3.03[de] (1.06)	2.66[cd] (1.14)	3.67[f] (1.17)	3.38[ef] (1.09)	2.79[cd] (1.14)	17.45	.0001	.11

[a] Means are the top numbers. Standard deviations are the numbers in parentheses. The same size ranges from 91 to 93.

[b] *F*-ratios, probability, and η^2 values are for the effect of the job analysis method, as derived from a two-way repeated measures ANOVA (job analysis method × organizational affiliation).

[cdefg] Means in each row with the same superscripts are not significantly different from each other.

Practicality Concerns	Job Analysis Methods: Threshold Traits Analysis	Ability Requirements Scales	Position Analysis Questionnaire	Critical Incident Technique	Task Inventory/ CODAP	Functional Job Analysis	Job Elements Method	F[b]	p<	η^2
(b) Ratings of 7 Job Analysis Methods for 11 Practicality Concerns[a]										
Occupational versatility/suitability	3.74^{gh} (1.04)	3.61^{g} (1.14)	3.82^{gh} (1.09)	3.86^{gh} (1.22)	4.13^{h} (1.04)	4.06^{h} (.94)	3.58^{g} (1.12)	3.29	.01	.02
Standardization	3.37^{g} (1.01)	3.40^{g} (1.18)	4.28^{h} (.89)	1.99^{j} (.78)	3.97^{hi} (1.11)	3.54^{gi} (1.02)	2.88 (1.05)	52.03	.0001	.31
Respondent/user acceptability	2.96^{g} (.98)	3.00^{g} (.98)	3.12^{gh} (1.00)	3.19^{gh} (1.10)	3.43^{h} (1.09)	3.44^{h} (.98)	3.16^{gh} (1.03)	3.09	.01	.03
Amount of job analyst training required[c]	2.73^{gh} (1.07)	3.00^{g} (1.01)	2.78^{gh} (1.04)	3.04^{g} (1.08)	2.39^{h} (1.21)	2.57^{gh} (1.04)	2.68^{gh} (1.06)	2.60	.05	.02
Operational	2.96^{g} (1.09)	3.09^{gh} (1.01)	4.20^{i} (1.01)	3.42^{hj} (1.26)	4.04^{i} (1.12)	3.85^{ik} (.95)	3.52^{jk} (1.08)	20.59	.0001	.14
Sample size[d]	2.78^{gh} (.84)	2.51^{gi} (.98)	3.53^{j} (1.15)	3.04^{hk} (1.26)	2.08^{i} (1.21)	3.26^{jk} (.86)	3.16^{hjk} (.92)	18.02	.0001	.13
Off-the-shelf	3.20^{g} (1.17)	3.27^{g} (1.23)	4.51^{h} (.93)	2.43 (1.33)	2.98^{g} (1.36)	3.28^{g} (1.29)	3.03^{g} (1.28)	28.58	.0001	.19
Reliability	3.04^{g} (.93)	3.10^{g} (.85)	3.84^{h} (.86)	2.67^{i} (.95)	4.05^{h} (.80)	3.49 (.88)	2.93^{gi} (.88)	27.68	.0001	.18
Cost[e]	2.87^{g} (.87)	3.23^{h} (.90)	3.29^{h} (1.15)	2.57^{gi} (1.00)	2.29^{i} (.96)	2.80^{g} (.84)	2.96^{gh} (1.07)	14.54	.0001	.11
Quality of outcome	2.67^{g} (.86)	2.61^{g} (.82)	3.17^{h} (.99)	2.74^{g} (1.00)	3.63^{i} (1.07)	3.53^{hi} (1.02)	2.76^{g} (1.04)	17.54	.0001	.13
Time to completion[f]	3.31^{gh} (.95)	3.36^{g} (1.03)	3.43^{g} (1.07)	2.17^{ij} (.97)	1.93^{i} (1.11)	2.57^{jk} (.90)	2.93^{hk} (1.05)	42.70	.0001	.25

[a] Means are the top numbers. Standard deviations are the numbers in parentheses. The sample size ranges from 88 to 92.

[b] *F*-ratios, probability, and η^2 values are for the effect of job analysis method, as derived from a two-way repeated measures ANOVA (job analysis method × organizational affiliation).

[c] The higher the rating the less training required.

[d] The higher the rating the fewer respondents required.

[e] The higher the rating the lower the cost.

[f] The higher the rating the less time required for completion.

[ghijk] Means in each row with the same superscripts are not significantly different from each other.

Exhibit 3.19 when it is used for the purposes for which it was designed. However, it simply does not have the content to service the different needs of the human resource director (Exhibit 3.20(a)).

Given these complications, the most relevant guide to system selection is clarity of purposes to be served. Before even considering the adoption of a system, the analyst should very clearly delineate the scope of the analysis, the uses to be made of the data, and the exact types and forms of data needed for the uses. In short, the analyst should take care of the preliminaries discussed in the introductory chapter.

TWO IMPORTANT COMPETENCIES: QUESTION FORMULATION AND INTERVIEWING

Regardless of the scope of the job analysis and other specifics, there are two competencies that the job analyst needs to develop: question formulation and interviewing.

Question Formulation. Much of the data gathering in job analysis is done through asking questions of job incumbents and other human sources and agents. All three primary methods of data gathering (observation, interview, and questionnaires) rely, explicitly or implicitly, on questions relating to the issues being investigated. The analyst's ability to devise questionnaires and even to formulate a plan of action hinge ultimately on his or her ability to ask the right questions. Formulating questions is thus one of the important competencies needed of a job analyst. The following are some suggestions relating to question formulation assembled from various sources (based on Bouchard, 1976; U.S. Department of Labor, 1972; Sudman & Bradburn, 1982).

- Restrain the impulse to write a question until you have thought through the issue to be resolved. Ask yourself the following questions: What do I want to know and why? Where does it fit into the broader issues to be investigated and resolved?
- Examine questions in other sources that deal with the issues to be investigated and build on prior experiences. Chief among these would be ready-made questionnaires and inventories (if available), prior job analysis schedules, and textbooks and industry publications. If written sources are not available, critical incidents should be gathered according to the procedures outlined in the CIT system (see Appendix A).
- Include only questions that are necessary for resolving the issues to be investigated.
- Put the questions in a logical sequence. Start with easy, salient, nonthreatening, but necessary questions.
- Construct a preliminary instrument and conduct a pilot study involving a small number of respondents.
- Examine the results and modify or remove problem questions as noted:

    Modify unclear questions.

    Remove repetitious questions unless they are needed for respondent reliability checks.

    Split double-barreled questions into two; if they cannot be split, remove them from the list.

    Remove questions that lie outside the competence of the respondent.

    Place distance between questions that are likely to bias responses when placed close together.

- Construct a revised list of questions after making the foregoing changes.
- Scale questions by noting the form of the data sought through them. For qualitative data, simple yes/no formats are sufficient. For ordinal and higher levels of data, it may be possible to obtain comparative or absolute measures.
- Conduct a second pilot study. This time the focus is on checking for the adequacy of the questions and the scales.
- Construct the final instrument after examining the results of the second pilot study.

Guidelines for Interviewing. The interview is one of the primary methods of data gathering in job analysis. It has a place in all the stages of data gathering and analysis. At the developmental stage, interviews are necessary to formulate the goals and scope of the study and to construct questionnaires, checklists, and other instruments and tools of analysis. Interviews can also be used in the final stage for actually gathering the data needed for the analysis. Knowing how to interview is thus one of the requirements for success in job analysis.

A variety of general guides and rules have been constructed over the years to assist those who need to conduct interviews. The following is a set of issues encountered in job analysis interviewing and some suggestions relating to them.

· Clarify interview objectives and methods before the confrontation. Remember that the interview is a conversation with a purpose. In job analysis, the purpose is to gather useful information about jobs. Before confronting the respondent, the analyst should therefore have a very clear idea about the what, why, and how of the interview.

· Make sure that the interview is the appropriate vehicle for securing the desired information before proceeding further. To accomplish this, the analyst should examine the question schedule and ask the following questions: Might any of the questions embarrass the respondents? Might the respondent be threatened by any of the questions? Are there any items in the schedule that would cause the respondent to freeze or to give evasive or untruthful answers? Can the required information be acquired more cheaply through observation, company records, and other means? If any of these questions is answered in the affirmative, the analyst should reconsider the decision to interview. Observations, anonymous questionnaires, and other impersonal methods might be more appropriate. If alternative methods are closed, the analyst then needs to recognize that specialized knowledges and competencies are needed for pursuing sensitive questions. Training should be acquired before proceeding further (see Sudman & Bradburn, 1982).

· Choose respondents to suit the nature of the information sought, the modes of data gathering, and other specifics of the study. Large numbers of respondents are needed for sampling opinions, values, attitudes, and other emotional variables. A small number of knowledgeable persons is sufficient for understanding job methods, processes, and other objective features of the work environment. In matters that have legal implications, it may be essential to document the qualifications of the respondents. In all cases, there must be a match between the comprehension levels of the respondents and the levels of questions asked.

· Gain the support of the respondent for accomplishing your purpose. This is particularly important in a job analysis interview since the respondent's job might be affected by the interview outcome. One way of gaining support is by explaining the purposes of the interview and the potential payoff, if any, for the respondent and the work group.

· Control the interview and keep it focused on the objectives. The following are some guidelines for steering the interview:

> Help the respondent to think and talk according to the logical sequence of the questions.
>
> Allow the respondent sufficient time to respond.
>
> Secure specific and complete information before moving from one question to the next; if the discussion wanders, be sure to come back to the points that were not fully covered.
>
> Provide periodic summaries of what has been accomplished; such summaries are useful in retaining focus and bringing the respondent back to the schedule if straying has taken place.

· Control personal mannerisms, behaviors, and involvements in the interview that might adversely affect the outcomes. The following are some guidelines relating to this issue:

> Conduct the interview in plain, easily understood language.
>
> Do not take issue with the respondent's statements and viewpoints.

Do not show any partiality in the issues discussed.

Show politeness and courtesy throughout the interview.

Do not "talk down" to the respondent.

Be impersonal without appearing disinterested.

Do not allow yourself to be influenced by your personal likes, dislikes, and viewpoints.

· Take extensive notes, particularly on information that is new or unplanned or deviates from the formal schedule (based on U.S. Department of Labor, 1972).

4 Job Description

The methods that can be used in gathering job information were reviewed in Chapter 3. This chapter deals with the job description, which is a primary product of job analysis. A unique feature of the job description is that it focuses on the job as a whole as the unit of analysis. Job analysis is the activity; job description is a result of that activity. Guided by this preconception, the goals of this chapter are as follows:

1. To define a set of terms that are relevant to job description.
2. To crystalize the uses of job descriptions in human resource management.
3. To present the contents of job descriptions.
4. To review the techniques of job description.
5. To review legal developments affecting job descriptions.
6. To offer some suggestions relating to selected issues in job description.

4.1 The Terminology of Job Description

Most of the terms that are encountered in job description activity were defined in earlier chapters. A useful starting point for bringing things together is the interrelations among common elements of job situations shown in Exhibit 2.1 in Chapter 2. The definitional task is essentially one of translating the abstract terms contained in that illustration into the language of job description.

Mission, results, objectives

In contemporary business practice, these terms are used in reference to the outputs of jobs. Although they are frequently used interchangeably in the literature, it is possible to use them with some precision. They are used as follows in this book:

Mission: A qualitative statement of the specialized contribution expected of the job holder. The mission statement identifies the role or purpose of the job within the organization's action scheme. The mission of the job is implied in its title.

Results: Description of the outputs expected in the form of products or services. Statements of results could also specify expectations relating to quality.

Objectives: Specification of the amounts of products or services and time frames for their achievement.

Duty, responsibility: Two of the most widely and indiscriminately used terms in the job analysis field. They have been used in the trade literature, singly or in combination, to describe expectations relating to products, services, tasks, behaviors, contacts, and even to personal characteristics of workers (see Oldham & Seglin, 1984; Bemis et al., 1983, pp. 66–67; Stoner, 1982, pp. 314–315; Ulery, 1981; Grego & Rudnik, 1970).

Our recommendation is that these terms not be made a formal part of job descriptions. However, if the need should arise for using them, we suggest the following distinctions:

Duty: Portion of the work assignment consisting of tasks. A duty can consist of one task or several related tasks. To qualify as a duty, however, the task or tasks must actually be a part of the assignment of the worker and not consist of generalized expectations of roles.

Responsibility: A grammatical variation of terms dealing with job outputs. Can be used to depict the results or objectives for which the worker can be held accountable through the act of delegation. Most appropriately used in describing results expected of managerial personnel.

Job function: Refers to a collection of tasks grouped together for administrative convenience.

Position description: A limited and specialized description of job factors addressed to subgroups within the job family. Work assignment of an individual.

4.2 Job Description: An Overview

A job description is a principal product of job analysis. This section provides an overview of the contents, uses, and formats of job descriptions. Before proceeding, it is important to emphasize that the form of the job information entered on the description is determined by the method used to gather it. Thus, unstructured observation and interviews typically result in qualitative, narrative types of descriptions. Inventories, on the other hand, yield quantitative data that can be presented in statistical terms. It is the responsibility of the analyst to figure out in advance the form in which the information is desired and to choose the appropriate methods for acquiring it.

CONTENTS OF JOB DESCRIPTIONS

Much has been written in recent years about job descriptions. An examination of this literature suggests a couple of areas of agreement relating to the contents of job descriptions. A major point on which most authorities agree is that a job description, to qualify as such, must contain information on the common properties that help to distinguish jobs from each other. The items that tend to be linked with job descriptions most often are job titles, purposes, work activities, tasks, things and materials used, methods, and context. The distinguishing characteristics of a job description is that it provides a picture of the *what*, *why*, *how*, *where* of the job in capsule form.

A second area of agreement pertains to the items that should not be included in job descriptions. One category of information that has no place on a job description are the qualifications of the workers assigned to the job. These are to be inferred from the job description and are hence entered in a separate document called the Worker or Job Specification. Another category of information that is to be omitted from job descriptions is the work assignments of particular

EXHIBIT 4.1 Contents of Job Descriptions

Job Identification	Title, subtitles, codes, grades, wage classifications, location, and reporting relationships
Job Summary: Mission	Concise but complete statement of the mission or purpose of the job and the products or services expected of the worker.
MTEWA	Machines, tools, equipment, and work aids.
Materials	Raw materials, goods in process, substances, data, and other materials used in the work.
Techniques and Methods	Characteristic ways of transforming resources into outputs.
Guidelines and Controls	Modes of supervision and prescriptions relating to quantity and quality of output, techniques and methods, behaviors, and work sequence.
Tasks/Behaviors	Description of the work performed, inclusive of interactions of the worker with data, people, things, and the guidelines under which the work is done.
Context	Physical, psychological, and emotional context of the job, terms and conditions of employment; and interrelations with other jobs.
Supplementary Information	Details not accommodated in the above sections, but that are essential or useful for operational purposes; definition of terms.

individuals. These are placed in another specialized document known as the Position Description. The construction of Position Descriptions is the repsonsibility of the managerial personnel in charge of individuals and work units.

A pure job description is thus a summary of the job itself as an organizational unit. Although the job is eventually to be performed by one or more workers, the description itself contains no reference to worker characteristics or the names of workers associated with the job or the work assignments of particular individuals (Cascio, 1982, p. 51; Gael, 1983, p. 59–60; *Uniform Guidelines*, 1978; Chruden & Sherman, 1984; McCormick, 1979; Oldham & Seglin, 1984; Ulery, 1981; Grego & Rudnik, 1970).

Building on this, we present in Exhibit 4.1 a summary of the items that qualify for inclusion in job descriptions. Most of these are from the theoretical diagram presented in Exhibit 2.1 in Chapter 2. There are, however, a couple of variations. The first two items, Job Identification and Summary, accommodate the outputs of jobs but in a particular way. The Job Title (contained in the Job Identification section) signifies the role of the job within the organization, while the Summary crystalizes the mission of the job or the specialized products or services expected of the job holder. A second variation pertains to the order or sequence of the items. Our interest in Chapter 2 was with explaining the interrelations among common elements of job situations. The focus here is on job factors that provide a basis for describing concrete jobs.

PURPOSES SERVED BY JOB DESCRIPTIONS IN HUMAN RESOURCE MANAGEMENT

The job description has roughly three categories of uses in human resource management: as a basis for deriving other informational outputs, as a source document for some direct uses, and as a tool in basic research relating to jobs. These interrelations are shown schematically in Exhibit 4.2.

Basis for Deriving Other Informational Outputs. In the chain of activities that constitutes job analysis, the job description is the first and primary product of job analysis. It serves as the foundation for the derivation of worker specifications, performance criteria, compensable factors, job families, and other informational outputs needed for human resource management. In this sense, the job description can be viewed as a basic source document, a starting point for the

EXHIBIT 4.2 Uses of Job Descriptions

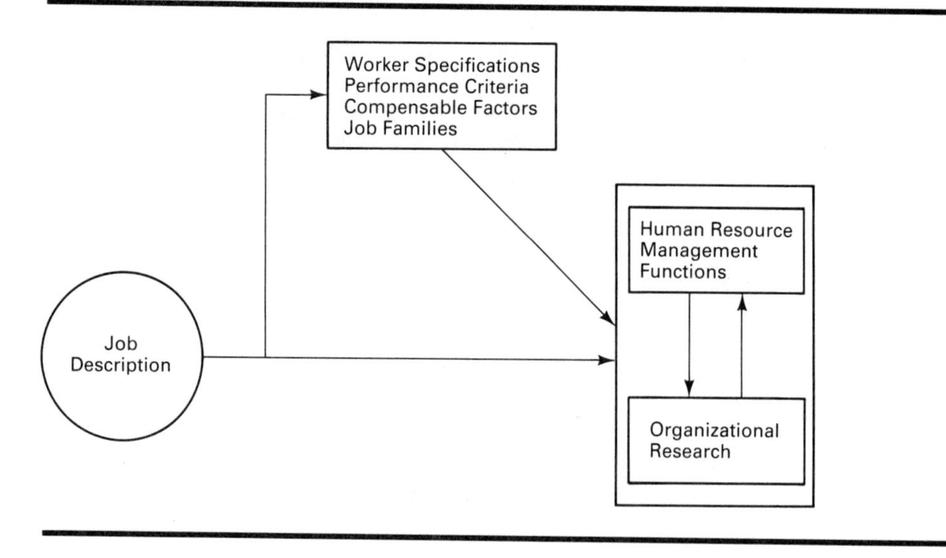

derivation and refinement of application blanks, performance appraisal forms, job classifications, and other personnel instruments needed for administrative purposes (see Exhibit 1.3, in Chapter 1).

Direct Uses. Job descriptions can be used directly as a source of information in the performance of various supervisory and human resource management activities. Supervisors can use job descriptions as a basis for assigning work, for clarifying missions and performance expectations, and for guiding and monitoring individual performance.

Industrial engineers and job designers can use job descriptions for verifying the currency of job design, for making sure that the various roles comprising the total work system are in alignment, and for correcting health and safety hazards. In the absence of job descriptions, such information has to be gathered on an ad hoc basis every time a job design issue arises.

Job descriptions have many uses in human resource planning, recruitment, selection, and placement. In conjunction with worker specifications, job descriptions provide the information needed for the development and operation of human resource inventories. Recruiters can use job descriptions for familiarizing themselves with the contents and demands of jobs. Advertisements and internal postings for vacancies are based on summaries of jobs. Job descriptions provide information needed for validation of selection tests, application blanks, and other predictor instruments. A new and growing use of job descriptions is in providing realistic job previews to potential employees (Wanous, 1980; Wanous & Dean, 1984).

Job descriptions are a primary tool in performance appraisal. Their major institutional use here is in the formulation of performance criteria and standards. Descriptions are also the basis for understanding the critical human behaviors involved in job performance.

The major use of job descriptions in the compensation area is in job evaluation. In conjunction with the information contained in job specifications and context descriptions, job descriptions aid in the formulation of compensable factors. Objective descriptions can also be of use in explaining the basis of wages rates and ranges to employees. In this sense, they can help human resource specialists in handling employee complaints, gripes, and queries relating to their pay and benefits (Milkovich & Newman, 1984).

Job descriptions can serve as a valuable tool in training, development, and career guidance. It is an ideal vehicle for understanding and depicting the mobility paths and interlinkings among jobs. This information can be used by career counselors, supervisors, and trainers in advising employees of promotion and advancement opportunities (Schein, 1978).

Tool in Basic Research. A third category of use of job descriptions is in basic research relating to jobs. This is typically not of much concern to small, private companies. However, large companies, governmental agencies, the armed forces, and other organizations that employ large numbers of workers need to pay attention to the composition of their labor forces. Knowledge of job contents and structures is also sought by the Department of Labor and other governmental agencies that are involved in the regulation of the labor markets in the economy as a whole. Objective and standardized descriptions of jobs can aid in tracking changes relating to demands on workers, employment levels by occupation, and other basic types of concerns.

FORMAT OF JOB DESCRIPTIONS

The job factors listed in Exhibit 4.1 serve as the substance of job descriptions. However, there has not yet emerged a standard format or terminology for composing job descriptions. Companies typically allow the uses to be made of the information to guide the coverage, sequence, and details presented. The scope of descriptions thus ranges from one or two items to elaborate descriptions of a wide number of items.

There is also little consistency in the terminology used in organizing materials in job descriptions. All the terms defined in the initial section of this chapter as well as those contained in Exhibit 4.1 are encountered in contemporary job description practice. However, considerable variation is found from industry to industry, and sometimes within organizations in the same industry, regarding labeling of items on job descriptions (see Oldham & Seglin, 1984, pp. 3–10; Grego & Rudnik, 1970, pp. 12–14; Ulery, 1981, pp. 5–8).

We therefore use the factors listed in Exhibit 4.1. as a rough guide for this discussion. The intent in each case is to describe them in more detail and to show how and where to present them in job descriptions. In each case, alternative terms used for these factors are discussed.

In undertaking this exposition, it is assumed that the sequence of activities leading to the job description, specified in Exhibit 1.5 in Chapter 1, have been completed. Specifically, it is assumed that the analyst has access to the information needed for compiling job descriptions. Also, our concern is not with the compilation of specific job descriptions. Rather, the focus is on lining up the categories of information that could be included in job descriptions, their sequence, and the options in presenting them.

4.3 Job Identification and Summary

These are two of the universal concerns of job descriptions. Without any exception, all job description formats contain some provisions for identifying the job and for providing a capsule statement of the essence of the job.

JOB IDENTIFICATION

The thrust of this section is on capturing the identity of the job within the enterprise. Roughly four types of materials can be included under this section: job title, other identifying labels, location of the job, and reporting relationships.

Job Title. The title signifies the role that is to be played by the worker within the organization. It is the mark of identification that distinguishes the job from all other jobs.

Assigning a title appears on the face of it to be a simple matter. In practice, several complications and choices are encountered. Consider the following options:

Clerk-typist versus typist-clerk
Programmer-analyst versus analyst-programmer
Liaison-engineer versus engineer-liaison
Doctor–medical consultant versus medical consultant–doctor

In each case, the word that is used first conveys the primary commitment of the assignment. But there is no settled way of arriving at this decision. It is up to the analyst to decide which of the labels most accurately captures the essence of the job. The completed title should convey the purpose of the job, its level within the organization, and the domain of its reach in relating to outputs and activities.

Other Identifying Labels. The title signifies the official role of the job holder. In addition, jobs typically acquire a variety of other labels. Here are some examples of additional labels identified according to their sources:

Codes in the *Dictionary of Occupational Titles*
Codes in industry publications
Subtitles and alternative titles resulting from tradition and custom
Grades within jobs resulting from wage classifications (i.e., clerk I, clerk II, clerk III)
White-collar, blue-collar
Exempt/nonexempt distinction made by the Fair Labor Standards Act

Inclusion of these additional details rounds out the identification of the job. The extent to which they are actually entered for particular jobs in a description would vary widely from company to company and from industry to industry. The analyst must make this decision after taking note of the needs of the company.

Location of the Job. This refers to the place where the job is physically located. For large private corporations, location is stated by naming the division, department, or branch that harbors the job. However, the terminology used in designating organizational units varies considerably. Thus, police officers are assigned to police stations, but work on different beats. Sentries are assigned to posts. Sales representatives work in different territories. Postal jobs are found in post offices. The burden is on the analyst to find the label that is characteristic of the trade, industry, or organizational sector.

Reporting Relationship. This item places the job within the organizational hierarchy. It states the title of the higher job to which the job incumbent reports. In constructing a job description, the name of the person to whom the job incumbent reports is not identified. The relationship is between titles and signifies the chain of authority within the organization.

JOB SUMMARY: MISSION

The job summary is an established tradition in job analysis. It follows the identification section and is intended to provide an overview of the job as an organizational unit. While considered to be a mandatory part of a job description, there is little agreement on the scope of its coverage or the style for expressing its contents. A minimal expectation is that the summary state, as clearly as possible, the mission or basic purpose of the job. Beyond that, job summaries found in the literature vary widely in regard to coverage and mode of expressions used. The alternative labels found in the literature for job summaries are job functions, accountability, and basic responsibility or purpose.

To aid in understanding of the options, Exhibit 4.3 provides examples of job summaries found in different sources. The summaries from the Department of Labor's publication are linked with its system of functional job analysis. They convey the *what and why* of jobs within the data, people, and things framework. The words used in the summary facilitate capturing of the involvement of the worker with the three sets of worker functions. These involvements, and their corresponding levels, are given in brackets at the end of the each summary.

The summaries from the manufacturing industries source also follow the *what and why* format. However, the wording also contains suggestions relating to quality of results expected.

EXHIBIT 4.3 Variations in Job Summaries

U.S. Department of Labor System (1972)

Operates loading machine to load coal into mine cars (things relationship, nonmachine-handling level)
Totals customer accounts and posts results in recapitulation ledger (data relationship, computing level)
Portrays role in dramatic production to interpret character to audience (data and people relationships, synthesizing and diverting levels)

Job Descriptions in Manufacturing Industries (Ulery, 1981)

Programmer	To interpret systems, programs, and job flow specifications developed by project leader, systems, to produce meaningful and efficient logic programs and operating techniques that will satisfy user requests (p. 92)
Tooling engineer	To recommend tooling requirements for the injection molds used at all plant locations and to provide follow-up to ensure that appropriate tooling is purchased and used in accordance with different objectives (p. 100)

Council on Library Technology (Grego & Rudnik, 1970)

Library clerk III	Under general supervision from a designated supervisor, to be responsible for the performance of clerical library duties involving exercise of independent judgment and, in some positions, supervision of clerical personnel (p. 27)
Library technical assistant I	Under general supervision from a designated supervisor, to perform technical work in the processing, recording, filing, and circulation of library materials, the performance of which requires the application of standards of judgment based upon a knowledge of the purposes and work processes of library science (p. 29)

The summaries from the library source attempt to combine a description of purposes with type of supervision and level of discretion available to the job incumbent in the performance of job tasks. This type of summary is typical of governmental agencies whose job descriptions are modeled on the Factor Evaluation System of the U.S. Office of Personnel Management (see U.S. Office of Personnel Management, 1979).

The analyst thus has considerable discretion in the compilation of job summaries. All the models shown in Exhibit 4.3 can be defended. The critical consideration in making the decision is serving the interests of the users. However, to avoid repetition, and to retain the uniqueness of the summary as a part of the job description, we recommend the following:

- Keep the summary brief, preferably to a one-sentence statement.
- Use the summary to crystalize the basic purpose of the job and its rationale for existence or the *what and why* of the job.
- If the job description is constructed according to some theoretical framework or is a part of a system of analysis, use the language that is appropriate to the system (exemplified in the DOL and Library Council summaries in Exhibit 4.3).
- Avoid inclusion of results expected, tasks, time frames, and other details that go beyond the job purpose and rationale. Such details belong in other parts of the job description. They erode the uniqueness of the job summary as an independent item.

4.4 Resources and Methods

Job outputs are attained through the transformation of resources. For job description purposes, resources can be sorted roughly into two categories: machines, tools, equipment, and work aids (MTEWA) and materials such as raw ingredients, goods-in-process, and data.

The need for including a description of resources in job descriptions is widely recognized in the literature. However, this item is usually not an independent item on job descriptions. Discussions of resources is typically fused with descriptions of techniques, methods, and task performance.

There are basically two ways in which resources and methods can be accommodated into job descriptions. One is by providing an inventory of resources and the accompanying techniques and methods that are characteristic of the trade. This is the approach followed by the DOL system under the notion of work fields. A second is by extending the scope of task descriptions to include descriptions of resources, techniques, and methods. Both approaches are complementary. The work field approach is discussed first. Techniques for incorporating descriptions of resources and methods into task descriptions are discussed in the next section.

WORK FIELDS

Work fields are an integral part of the DOL system of job analysis. A work field is defined as follows in the DOL handbook:

> Work Fields are organizations of specific methods either (1) characteristic of machines, tools, equipment, or work aids, and directed at common technological objectives, or (2) characteristic of the techniques designed to fulfill socio-economic purposes. (1972, p. 5)

The DOL system contains 100 work fields that are organized for the purpose of classifying all the jobs in the economy. Each work field has a title, a definition, and a three-digit identification number. An alphabetical list of the work fields contained in the DOL system and some completed examples of work fields are given in Appendix D at the end of the book.

A work field thus consists roughly of four components. One is a description of the broad socioeconomic purposes served by the work field. This is given at the beginning of each work field. Description of purposes is followed by an inventory of methods associated with the work field. The inventory is given in the form of method verbs that tell how the outputs of the work field are attained. Next is an inventory of the MTEWA characteristically used in performing the work. The final section, at the bottom, contains the outputs that result from the work field.

PLACE IN JOB DESCRIPTION

The amount of space that is allotted to descriptions of resources and methods on a job description would hinge entirely on the purposes to be served by the description. An inventory, such as that exemplified in work fields, can be a valuable aid in several human resource management functions. Knowledge of resources and methods used in the work can serve as basis for beginning the process of deriving worker specifications. Trainers can use this information for organizing the contents of training programs. Safety experts would have an interest knowing the interactions among MTEWA, materials, and methods.

Our general suggestion is that the analyst compile an inventory of the MTEWA, resources, and characteristic methods used in the work. Inclusion of such an inventory in the body of the description itself, however, would probably detract from the flow of the description; it would also be at variance with contemporary business practice. A good compromise would be to place it in the supplementary section of the job description. Significant elements of this inventory can then be incorporated in task and context descriptions.

4.5 Guidelines and Controls

As an organizational variable, the purpose of guidelines and controls is to aid the worker to retain focus on the mission of the job. They consist of prescriptions relating to quantity and quality of outputs expected, techniques and methods, task performance, behaviors, and sequence of activities. These prescriptions can come in many forms: operating procedures and policies, manuals of methods and style, traditional practices within the industry, engineering handbooks, personnel manuals, and styles of supervision.

In the job analysis literature, the study of guidelines and controls has taken a particular thrust. The focus is on understanding the impact of the prescriptions on the amount of discretion left to the worker in job performance. Viewed in this way, jobs can be differentiated from each other according to the amount of input that the worker is allowed over outputs, resource combinations, methods, pace, and sequence.

INSTRUMENTS FOR MEASURING GUIDELINES AND CONTROLS

Most job analysis systems have portions that deal with guidelines and controls. Instruments that have gained wide recognition are reproduced in Appendix E. All are designed to yield measures of worker discretion. There are, however, significant differences among them with reference to theoretical vantage points and techniques. These are brought out in the discussion that follows.

Fine's Scale of Worker Instructions. This is a part of Sidney Fine's Functional Job Analysis. An example illustrating the application of this scale was given in Chapter 3, Exhibit 3.3. Note that Fine's scale of worker instruction is to be used task by task.

Factor Evaluation System (FES). This system is part of the human resource management program of the U.S. Office of Personnel Management. It is used for classifying jobs in the General Schedule (GS) (see U.S. Office of Personnel Management, 1979).

The FES has two scales that deal with guidelines and controls. Both are reproduced in Appendix E. The Supervisory Controls scale has three parts: (1) how work is assigned—the direct or indirect controls exercised by the supervisor in relation to priorities, deadlines, objectives, and boundaries; (2) employee's responsibility for carrying out the work—extent to which the employee is expected to develop the sequence and timing of various aspects of work, to modify or recommend modifications of instructions, and to participate in establishing priorities and defining objectives; and (3) how work is reviewed—nature and extent of review, ranging from close and detailed review of each phase of the assignment to spot check of finished work for accuracy to review for adherence to policy.

The Guidelines scale focuses more directly on the discretion issue. It measures two dimensions: (1) presence of written guidelines—desk manuals, dictionaries, handbooks, and the federal *Personnel Manual* and (2) judgment needed in using guidelines—extent to which the written guidelines limit the opportunity to interpret or adapt the guidelines.

Health Services Mobility Study (HSMS). This system contains two scales relating to guidelines and controls. Both are given in Appendix E. A couple of variations offered by these scales can be noted. Both scales address issues that are fairly specific: choice of method and quality of output. Note also that the descriptions are spelled out as skills.

Job Rating Form (JRF). This instrument is not a part of the mainstream of job analysis practice. It is a part of the Job Diagnostic Survey, an instrument that was designed by industrial psychologists to diagnose the need for job redesign. It is based on a theory that postulates interrelations among job characteristics, critical psychological states, growth needs strengths, and affective outcomes. The theoretical framework underlying this model was reviewed in Chapter 3 (see particularly Exhibit 3.11).

The JRF is reproduced in Appendix E. It is included here for consideration by job analysts for studying guidelines and controls because it contains a couple of interesting additions to the conventional views on this subject. To begin, the JRF uses a rating scale format. This is in contrast to all the other instruments described earlier that are essentially ways of classifying jobs or factors. Also, the JRF measures a set of job characteristics that are important in understanding potential employee responses to jobs, but that have not received much attention in the job analysis literature. The job characteristics that are included in the instrument are skill variety, task identity, task significance, autonomy, feedback from the job itself, feedback from the agents, and dealing with others. Each of these factors is of significant concern from an employee perspective. Collectively, they yield an index of the overall potential of a job for fostering internal work motivation on the part of the job incumbents. The formula for calculating this score is given after the JRF in Appendix E. (For a summary of research on the JDS, see Hackman & Oldham, 1980, pp. 313–315.)

PLACE IN JOB DESCRIPTION

The study of guidelines and controls has been an important preoccupation of job analysts for some time. Finding a place for this item on a job description, however, has proven to be a problem. The most common practice is to fuse discussions of guidelines and controls into task descriptions and even job summaries. An example of how they can be included in job summaries is provided in Exhibit 4.3 within the summaries of the two library jobs. Ways of including them in task descriptions are reviewed in the next section.

Another approach to handling this issue is by making descriptions of guidelines and controls an independent item on the job description. This course of action would be appropriate, and even necessary, when the description is being prepared for a specific purpose where knowledge of guidelines and controls is essential for deriving the required output. Thus, fairly detailed understanding of guidelines and controls is essential for job evaluation purposes. When the description is prepared for this purpose, considerable space would be given to this item in the body of the description itself (see Milkovich & Newman, 1984, pp. 91–156).

Yet another approach is to treat guidelines and controls as a context issue. This approach has gained some support in recent years. It is based on the premise that the structure of guidelines and controls varies from situation to situation and hence is appropriately treated as a contingency. This approach is followed by the VERJAS system. It is discussed more fully in the section on context of this chapter.

4.6 Task Descriptions

All job descriptions contain some description of the tasks involved. The alternative labels that are given to this aspect of the job description are work performed, duties and responsibilities, job functions, and accountabilities. We prefer the label task descriptions as it is the most neutral. Also, the notion of task as theoretically developed today has potential for accommodating most of the other items on our list of job factors shown in Exhibit 4.1.

The discussion of tasks presented here consists of seven subsections. The first subsection is concerned with defining the notion of task and showing its components. The next four subsections deal with the mechanics of task description. They are somewhat theoretical and abstract. Readers who do not have an immediate need for mastering the mechanics of task description might wish to postpone the study of these materials until their operational needs are clear. The next to the last subsection reviews approaches to task description found in the literature and gives examples of contemporary practices. The final subsection shows how to handle task descriptions in job descriptions.

DEFINITION AND COMPONENTS OF TASKS

The notion of task has emerged as an important vehicle for the description of work. It is useful, therefore, to begin this discussion with a definition. The HSMS contains the following definition of task:

> A task is a series of work activities (elements) which are needed to produce an identifiable output that can be independently consumed or used, or that can be used as an input in a further stage of the production by an individual who may not be the performer of the task. (Gilpatrick, 1977b, p. 2–1)

A task is thus a grouping of activities that are targeted at producing outputs. But task performance does not take place in isolation. It is a part of larger sets of activities and processes that characterize organizations and that are subject to the rules and modes of operation of the organization. When viewed as parts of larger collectivities, the components of tasks encompass, on a small scale, most of the components of jobs. Expressed in the language of job analysis, the *who*, *what*, *why*, and *how* of tasks take the following forms:

Who — The performer of tasks is assumed to be the worker.

What — This refers to the activities involved in the task, which may be physical, mental, or interpersonal.

Why — This refers to the outputs that take the form of products or services. Outputs of tasks, however, are not synonymous with the outputs of jobs. Rather, task outputs are a stage of production of job outputs; they serve as inputs in the making of products or services with which the job is identified.

How — This encompasses MTEWA, materials, techniques, and methods and guidelines and controls.

For analytic and administrative purposes, tasks can be further broken down into *elements*. The elements of tasks are the operations or steps required to initiate the task, to carry it out, and to terminate it. Elements have all these properties, but on a smaller scale. The outputs of elements serve as inputs to the task (Gilpatrick, 1977b, p. 2–2).

RULES AND GUIDES FOR IDENTIFYING TASKS

Given the wide reach of tasks, identification of tasks is no easy matter. The HSMS provides eight rules and some accompanying guides for identifying tasks and their components. They are summarized in the discussion that follows. (The page references here are to Gilpatrick, 1977b.)

1. In principle, someone other than the performer of the task must be able to use or consume the output of the task.

This rule emphasizes that the outputs of tasks are to be consumed or used as inputs in a further stage of production. A very broad view is taken of task outputs by the HSMS:

> An output is an altered physical state of a thing or person, a changed mental state of a person, or a new item. It can be storable, or can be consumed as it is produced. It can be physical (tangible) or non-physical (intangible). (p. 2–10)

The *persons* connected with task performance are the performer, recipient, respondent, and co-worker. The performer is the worker. The person to whom the performer gives things to, or does things for, is the recipient. A respondent is a person from whom the performer gets information from or talks with on matters relating to task performance. A person who helps, or works in conjunction with the performer, is the co-worker (pp. 2–20 and 2–21).

Consumption of an output means that is it used at the point of production or in a further stage of production. Examples of outputs that are used at the point of production are served food, administered injection, and counseled patient. Examples of those that are used in further stages of production are (1) prepared procedure tray to be used in a special medical procedure and (2) subassembly to be used in the manufacture of a television set.

2. Theoretically, time should elapse between tasks.

If there can be no lapse of time in a sequence of activities, it is likely that the same person must do the next sequence. The task should then include the sequence as elements. For example, the injection of a contrast medicine is typically followed by a series of X-ray exposures. Since all the exposures ordered are outputs of the same task, and since it is not appropriate to wait between exposures, the same person must carry out all the steps in sequence.

3. A task includes all the possible conditions or circumstances with which a single performer is expected to deal in connection with the production stage or the output involved.

The task should include all the instances leading to a given type of output. The elements should reflect any likely situations or emergencies that can be anticipated or covered, including fine details of a nonrepetitive nature that are carried out from one instance to another. For example, when patients enter an emergency ward, it becomes essential to determine how urgently they need attention. But the conditions in which patients arrive are varied and impossible to predict in advance. The task elements, therefore, cover all the possible patients and conditions in which they arrive to be evaluated.

4. A task includes all the elements that require continuous judgments or assessment by the same performer to assure the quality of the output.

Quality of output is the key consideration in assembling tasks. This is a particular concern in health care since overfragmentation of work assignments can endanger the patient. For example, some neuroradiology examinations include tomography (a technique for making X-ray pictures of a predetermined section of the body by blurring out the images of other parts) as an element in the task rather than as a separate task. This is because the radiologist carrying out the original examination is cumulatively assessing the patient's condition and hence should be the one to direct the tomography.

5. A task includes all the elements needed to produce an output that can be independently used or acted upon without special explanations to the next performer in the next stage of production.

6. A task includes all the elements needed to complete an output to a point at which another performer (who would continue with the production sequence) would not have to redo major elements or perform extra steps in order to continue.

A task is not completed if the next steps in a sequence cannot be done by a different person without a major repetition of prior steps. For example, setting the technical factors for an X-ray examination is not a separate task because a radiologic technologist should never expose a patient to radiation without having personally selected and set the technical factors. Similarly, ''making repairs'' would be an incomplete description of a task if the person making the repairs is also the one who assesses the problem and chooses the appropriate means for making the repair. The assessment and the decision relating to what to do are also elements, since repetition would be necessary were someone else to make the repair.

7. A task must include minor alternative elements to cover a wide variety of institutional arrangements so that another performer can continue with the next stage in a production sequence within current institutional arrangements.

The roots of this rule can be traced to the reality that organizational practices vary over minor procedural matters. Thus, in some organizations, forms are used for reporting work results; in others, results may be communicated orally to other performers. In one department, documents may be placed in trays for filing; in another, they may be handed down to a clerical worker. Such minor procedural variations that do not significantly affect the structure of the task can be considered as contingencies.

8. A task must be sufficiently broad in statement that it can be rated on its frequency of occurence.

If a task cannot be rated for frequency, it has not been properly identified. The basic HSMS definition of a task excludes one-time assignments given to specific individuals with specific training and that are not to be repeated. Examples of these are assignments that deal with the design of a special piece of equipment or a program.

The eight rules just given are abstract in conception, but they cover just about all the issues encountered in task identification. Their applications are brought into later discussions that present examples of task descriptions.

WRITING TASK DESCRIPTIONS

Task descriptions are intended to communicate the dynamic aspects of the job. By their very nature, they accommodate multiple and diverse types of information. It is important, therefore, that they be written in unambiguous terms. The following is a compilation of rules that have accumulated in regard to writing style.

- The present tense should be used throughout.
- The actor in the action is assumed to be the worker.
- A terse, direct style should be used in describing the action. Every task statement should begin with an active verb.
- Avoid passive sentences where the agent-action-goal order is reversed. Example:

Passive	**Active**
The tools are to be cleaned at the end of the shift by the worker.	Cleans tools at the end of the shift.

- Specific verbs are preferred over those that describe broad processes, job functions, or accountabilities. Examples of verbs that should be avoided are assure, determine, indicate, ensure, and supervise (Gael, 1983, p. 57).
- The verbs that are used should reflect the behaviors involved or be readily amenable to translation into behaviors. Examples:

Drives tractors to plow . . .

Turns valves to regulate coolant flow . . .

Feeds materials into machine that stamps out parts . . .

- Only one action and one object should be included in a task statement. Examples:

Multiple Actions or Objects	**Single Actions and Objects**
Review and prepare cost estimates.	Review cost estimates. Prepare cost estimates.
Review files, reports, and correspondence.	Review files. Review reports. Review correspondence.

The rule can be violated when the actions or objects are closely related and form a unit of work. Examples:

Locate and repair short in wiring.

Place labels on envelopes and packages.

Address letters, packages, and boxes.

- Use quantitative words were possible. Rather than saying "pushes loaded trucks," write "pushes hand truck loaded with 100 to 500 pounds of steel plate" (Grego & Rudnik, 1970, p. 10).
- Tasks should be described in language that is familiar to the job incumbents. Technical terms, acronyms, and other specialized or uncommon terms should be singled out and underlined; they should then be defined or explained with liberal use of examples and applications in the supplementary section of the description. (The foregoing was based on Melching & Borcher, 1973, and Gael, 1983, pp. 51–73.)

COMBINING TASKS INTO JOB FUNCTIONS

Tasks could be presented individually, or they could be combined into groups. The need for combining arises when the number of tasks is large or when the job entails multiple and dissimilar performance obligations. When tasks are combined, the resulting groups are called *job functions.*

Grouping of tasks into functions entails two interrelated activities: choosing of descriptors for classifying tasks and developing a procedure for allocating tasks according to the chosen descriptors.

Descriptors for Combining Tasks. Numerous descriptors are available for classifying tasks for deriving job functions. The following six are commonly used in industry under varying labels.

1. *Managerial versus nonmanagerial tasks.* Many jobs that are not classified as managerial entail some managerial activities: Examples:

Senior waiters can assist in the training and overseeing of the work of new hires.

Professors direct the work of teaching and research assistants.

Cashiers at banks supervise tellers.

This distinction is very commonly adhered to in industry and provides a fairly solid foundation for grouping tasks. The managerial function would contain tasks that entail supervisory, training, or directing activities. The nonmanagerial functions would be comprised of tasks associated directly with the production of outputs.

2. *Nature of the activity itself.* Many tasks, although performed in different locations or aimed at different objects, entail the same type of activity. Examples:

Labeling—boxes, letters, and cans.

Negotiating—with customers, suppliers, and fellow workers.

Filing—folders, letters, documents.

When activity is used as the basis for grouping, the objects of the activity take second place in the classification. If the objects modify the activity in any significant way, subclassifications can be developed.

3. *Demands on workers.* The demands made by tasks on workers can range from mental to physical or a combination of the two. Examples:

Physical—stooping, kneeling, and lifting.

Mental—reasoning, thinking, problem solving.

Combination—composing, drawing, drafting.

While these distinctions are simple in concept, caution needs to be exercised in using them in classifying tasks. These distinctions are useful only in extreme cases. Their usefulness diminishes with job complexity.

4. *Worker contacts.* Contacts can be classified in several ways for grouping tasks:

Objects of contacts—data, people, things. These can be further refined. Examples:

People—superiors, respondents, recipients, co-workers, and customers.

Things—MTEWA, materials, and substances.

Data—qualitative versus quantitative, financial, biodata.

Frequency of contacts—number of times worker comes into contact with different objects.

Purpose of contacts—to acquire and give information, to direct, to serve.

All the foregoing, singly or in combination, can be used as a basis for grouping tasks. Contacts figure prominently in the FJA systems schema of data, people, and things. Some specifics are provided later in this section.

5. *Nature of outputs*. Classification of tasks (and even jobs) on the basis of outputs has gained wide acceptance in industry. It is the basis generally for the blue-collar/white-collar distinction. Jobs that are classified as blue collar are typically the ones that yield tangible products. White-collar work, on the other hand, is characterized by services.

6. *Job goals versus system maintenance activities*. This distinction has a great deal of theoretical support and is also adhered to in industry. Job goal activities are the tasks undertaken by the worker for fulfilling the mission of the job. They are directed at attaining the products or services with which the job is identified and that form the rationale for its existence. System maintenance activities, on the other hand, are directed at enhancing the survival, stability, and effectiveness of the organization. They are not a regular part of the job. Rather, they are supportive of the system in which the work takes place. The following example brings out the differences for the job of teller:

Job Goal Activities	**System Maintenance Activities**
Accepts cash deposits.	Recommends future budgetary needs of department.
Balances cash.	Participates in bank's community projects.
Cashes checks, etc.	Relays customer complaints to management.

While the need for this distinction is widely recognized, the terminology used varies considerably. What we have referred to as system maintenance activities can also be referred to as accountabilities, subsidiary or supportive activities, and organizational relationships (Oldham & Seglin, 1984; Ulery, 1981; Grego & Rudnik, 1970).

Function Identification. The choice of descriptors is one of the requirements for combining tasks into functions. The second is the development of a procedure or method for sorting tasks according to the chosen descriptors. Fortunately, much is available to the analyst in fulfilling this requirement. The choice ranges from methods that are highly statistical to those that are intuitive. Exhibit 4.4 contains a summary of a method that relies on the logic of content analysis.

EXHIBIT 4.4 The "Eyeball" Method of Function Identification

1. Write each task statement on a separate slip of paper or card.
2. Sort task statements into piles or clusters according to a rule aimed at grouping tasks that have something in common. All tasks involving the same broad work activity, such as negotiating with customers, maintaining equipment, distributing supplies, and so on, should be placed in the same cluster. You may find it necessary to further subdivide some of the task clusters; for instance, maintaining equipment may be subdivided into preventive maintenance and corrective maintenance. At least two analysts working independently, but under the same guiding rule, should sort the task statements.
3. Compare the clusters of task statements developed by each analyst to determine where they agree and disagree.
4. Bring analysts together to discuss their task clusters, the rationale they used to assign tasks to clusters, and the reasons for disagreements in the number of types of clusters formed and assignments of tasks to clusters.
5. Refine task clusters by moving task statements between clusters or developing new clusters in accordance with the discussion. Consensus is the goal; if the analysts cannot agree, however, another sort by a third analyst is warranted. The third sort does not necessarily have to start from scratch. The results from all three sorts should be compared as above and a consensus reached.
6. Name each cluster in accordance with the type of work represented. The cluster name is the name of the function.

From Sidney Gael, *Job Analysis: A Guide to Assessing Work Activities* (San Francisco: Jossey-Bass, Inc., Publishers, 1983), pp. 64–65.

This method is a part of the Work Performance Survey System (WPSS) of the American Telephone & Telegraph Company. It should be sufficient for most companies for preparing in-house job descriptions. (For a review of factor analysis and other statistical techniques, see McCormick, 1979, pp. 167–173.)

QUANTIFYING TASK INFORMATION

Tasks are typically described in narrative terms. However, aspects of tasks can be expressed in quantitative terms. Quantitative expressions of task data are of two types: descriptive or evaluative. The descriptive type is simply a numerical expression of the primary managerial interests in tasks:

- Part of job (whether or not task is a part of the job).
- Performance (whether or not the incumbent performs the task).
- Frequency of performance (how often the task is performed).
- Time spent on the task (in hours or minutes).
- Relative time spent on task compared to other tasks.
- Relative involvement with data, people, and things.

Information of this type, when expressed in quantitative terms, provides more precise information about the worker's involvement in the task. It can serve as the foundation for basic decisions relating to work assignments, division of labor, and time allocations. Some scales for the measurement of worker involvement in tasks are given in Appendix F of the book.

The evaluative measurements of task data are aimed at arriving at judgments about the tasks. The following are the types of task attributes that form the basis of such measurements:

- Complexity of the task.
- Criticality of the task.
- Importance of the task.
- Difficulty of learning the task.
- Costs of error.

Evaluative judgments of this type provide the basis for decisions relating to compensation, training, and performance appraisal. They go beyond depiction of the worker involvement in the task, to placing a value on the task as a component of the job. Some scales for the evaluation of task attributes are given in Appendix G. Additional examples and illustrations of quantification of task information is provided in the discussion that follows.

VARIATIONS IN TASK DESCRIPTIONS: SOME EXAMPLES

The preceding section have provided an overview of the *what*, *why*, and *how* of tasks in abstract, theoretical terms. It is time now to apply this theory and to illustrate the options available to the analyst in describing tasks.

The critical decision facing the analyst in describing tasks revolves around scope of the description. The choice in this regard ranges from simply identifying the *what* of the task to compiling descriptions that also accommodate *why*, *how*, *where*, *when*, and *how much*. All these variations are illustrated in the examples that follow.

Special Agent Task Inventory. This is an actual inventory of tasks within the job of special agent in the Florida Department of Law Enforcement. This inventory is useful in understanding the mechanics, benefits, and limits of the task inventory approach to task description. As this inventory is somewhat lengthy, it is reproduced in its entirety, along with the rules followed in constructing it in Appendix 4.1 at the end of this chapter.

The Special Agent Task Inventory consists of 105 tasks. These tasks were assembled initially by analysts from inventories and other written materials on closely related jobs. The preliminary draft of the inventory consisted of 158 tasks. This draft was reviewed by subject matter experts (SMEs), first individually and then in a group. The review resulted in a revised inventory of 112 tasks. This revised inventory was subjected to a pilot test with the same SMEs serving as subjects. A final version of the task inventory was constructed and scaled to measure four task attributes: relative time spent, relative time spent under ideal conditions, level of difficulty, and criticality of error. These scales are described in the text of Appendix 4.1.

The final inventory was mailed to job incumbents. One hundred and fifteen responses were received, which represented a return rate of 85 percent. The data were then keypunched and entered into the computer. At this point, the analysts had a choice relating to sorting of tasks into functions. Functions could have been derived by quantitative techniques such as factor analysis and cluster analysis. The analysts chose instead to go with preset function categories found within the trade. The data were then tabulated to yield the results shown in Appendix 4.1.

With this as background, it is useful to examine the contents of the Special Agent Task Inventory as an approach to task description. Note that the statement of tasks is quite limited; it signifies the *what* behind the tasks. This feature is an essential requirement (and a limitation) of quantification. To acquire ratings on attributes through scales, the description of tasks by necessity has to be limited to one performance dimension; it cannot accommodate multiple dimensions and interactions in the body of the task statement.

Taking the limitation as given, the task inventory approach yields a wealth of information about task characteristics. Note the ratings of individual tasks according to their task importance value (TIV) in Appendix 4.1. This was arrived at according to the following formula:

$$\text{Task importance} = (\text{difficulty} \times \text{criticality}) + \text{actual time spent}$$

A summary of the job functions within the special agent's job according to their mean importance value in given in Exhibit 4.5. The three most important functions in the special agent's job are legal proceedings (e.g., testifying and preparing evidence), practice and procedures (e.g., determining the justification for use of deadly force, assuming cover identities in undercover operations, and participating in raids), and intelligence (e.g., utilizing, maintaining contact with, or otherwise handling informants).

As stated in our introductory discussion of job analysis systems in Chapter 3, the task inventory approach is a highly disciplined, quantitative way of describing and organizing task information. The foregoing example illustrates the advantages and disadvantages that go with this approach. It provides a useful background for reviewing other approaches that yield different types of results along with attendant benefits and limitations.

EXHIBIT 4.5 Special Agent Task Inventory: Function Categories Ranked in Order of Importance Based on Mean Function Values

Function	Area No.	Number of Tasks	Mean Importance Value
Legal proceedings	(8)	3	24.1
Practice and procedures	(1)	29	21.2
Intelligence	(5)	8	19.7
Evidence collection and preservation	(4)	17	16.9
Self-development	(7)	4	16.3
Public contacts	(6)	8	15.5
Equipment use and maintenance	(2)	16	14.4
Reports and forms	(3)	20	14.2
Grant mean of all functions = 17.4			

From Frank Sistrunk and Philip L. Smith, *Multimethodological Job Analysis for Criminal Justice Organizations* (Tampa: Center for Evaluation Research, University of South Florida, 1982), p. 87.

Sentence Analysis Technique (SAT). This technique is found in the DOL system. It is linked with the worker functions hierarchy and provides an approach to describing work activities in the standardized terminology of functional job analysis. Examples illustrating the results that flow from this technique are given in Appendix D. The following are the rules that are used in describing work activities:

1. The subject of the action is always the worker (implied but not expressed).
2. The verb, which always begins the sentence, is synonymous with the worker function.
3. The immediate object is data, people, or things. For a data function, the object is information in some form. For a people function, the object is the people to whom the service is being rendered; and for a thing function, the object is the machine, tool, equipment, or work aid (MTEWA) through which the action of the verb is performed.
4. The infinitive phrase reflects the purpose or the why of the activity. The objective here is the result to be attained by the worker.

The top half of the SAT examples in Appendix D shows the application of the technique according to the rules just given. The bottom half contains the classification of the work according to its place within the worker function hierarchy and the coding schemes contained with the DOL system (U.S. Department of Labor, 1972, p. 7).

Fine's FJA. The approach to task description used by Fine is an extension of the basic FJA concepts. It provides for accommodating *what*, *why* and *how* plus information relating to guidelines and controls, levels, and orientation. An example illustrating all these features, along with a dissection of the *who*, *what*, *why* and *how*, is given in Exhibit 4.6.

Under Fine's FJA, study of level and orientation is an integral part of task description. The *level* measure indicates the relative complexity or simplicity of a task when it is compared to other tasks. This is assigned by selecting the function within the worker functions hierarchy (described in Chapter 3, Exhibit 3.2) that best describes the pattern of behavior in which the worker engages to perform a given task effectively. The task described in Exhibit 4.6 fell at the copying level for data, exchanging information level for people, and handling for things.

The *orientation* measure in Fine's system indicates the relative involvement of the worker

EXHIBIT 4.6 Task Description from Sidney Fine's Functional Job Analysis

TASK: *Asks client questions, listens to responses, and writes answers on standard intake form, exercising leeway as to sequence of questions, in order to record basic identifying information (items 1–8).*

Area	Functional Level	Orientation (Percent)
Data	Copying (2)	50
People	Exchanging information (2)	40
Things	Handling (1A)	10

The components of the above task statement are as follows:

Who — Is assumed to be the worker.

What — Asks clients questions.
Listens to responses.
Writes answers on standard intake form.

Why — . . . to record basic identifying information (on items 1–8 on the intake form).

How — Tools: intake form and pen.
Instructions received:
Prescribed content: standard intake form (items 1–8).
Discretionary content: exercising leeway as to sequence of questions.

From Sidney A. Fine and Wretha W. Wiley, *An Introduction to Functional Job Analysis* (Kalamazoo, Mich.: W. E. Upjohn Institute for Employment Research, 1971), p. 17. Copyright © by Sidney A. Fine. Adapted by permission.

EXHIBIT 4.7 Level of Complexity of Worker Functions

Level of Complexity	Data	People	Things
High	Synthesizing Coordinating	Mentoring Negotiating	Precision working, setting up
Medium	Analyzing Computing, compiling	Supervising Consulting, instructing, treating Coaching, persuading, diverting	Manipulating; operating, controlling; driving, controlling
Low	Copying Comparing	Exchanging information Taking instructions; helping, serving	Handling, feeding, offbearing; tending

From Wretha W. Wiley and Sidney A. Fine, *A Systems Approach to New Careers* (Kalamazoo, Mich.: W. E. Upjohn Institute for Employment Research, 1969), p. 15.

with data, people, and things as the task is performed. It is expressed by assigning a percentage in units of 5 or 10 to each of the three functions so that the total adds up to 100 percent. The task described in Exhibit 4.6 received orientation scores of 50 percent for data, 40 percent for people, and 10 percent for things.

The Scale of Worker Instructions, given in Appendix E, is to be used for rating the discretion available to the worker in task performance. The task described in Exhibit 4.6 would receive a score of 2 (this summary was taken from Fine & Wiley, 1971, pp. 5–30).

The scores received by tasks can be used to gain an index of level of complexity of the work. An arrangement of the worker functions according to high, medium, and low level of complexity is given in Exhibit 4.7.

HSMS Approach. The HSMS system contains an elaborate network of rules, guidelines, and procedures for constructing and writing task descriptions. The definition of task followed in the system and the rules for identifying tasks were presented earlier. Exhibit 4.8 presents a task description compiled according to these rules. This example is from the "patient care grouping" of tasks.

The HSMS task description has five components:

Task outputs (1): These include the main output, by-products, any decisions and/or records made, any intangibles, and the results of contingencies. The form used for outputs are noun or nounforms that require the past form of a verb to describe the result of the work activity. Outputs are stated in a single sentence, with different outputs being separated by semicolons. Exhibit 4.9 shows the guide to be used in identifying task outputs.

What is used in task performance (2): The focus is on "things," with the narrative providing details relating to level of discretion. In describing things, generic terms are used rather than brand names. Exhibit 4.10 gives the guide to be followed in identifying things used in the job.

Recipient, respondent, or co-worker involved in task (3 and 4): (generic terms such as "co-worker" or "clerical worker" are used when it is clear that the person is involved due to particular institutional procedures and is not an essential part of the task's identification): The correct, specific occupational term for the co-worker or the condition of the recipient is used when this has been used to determine the task's identification. The guide for identifying recipients, respondents, and co-workers is given in Exhibit 4.11.

Name of the task (5): The name of the task is constructed so that it reflects the first four items. This is accomplished by naming the chief output and the recipient of the task and adding the word "by," which is then followed by the task elements and things used. There are two names: abbreviated and extended. The abbreviated task name presents the activity verb, output, things used, and person(s) involved. The extended task name includes the abbreviated name,

EXHIBIT 4.8 Task Description from the Health Services Mobility Study, Patient Care Grouping

1. *What is the output of this task*? (Be sure this is broad enough to be repeatable.)

   Patient and suction machine readied for suctioning; tracheal passageway cleared or machine turned on and off as ordered; patient cleansed and/or machine cleansed; matter removed shown to MD.

2. *What is used in performing this task*? (Note if *only* certain items must be used. If there is choice, include everything or the kinds of things chosen among.)

   MD's orders; patient's chart or checklist; suction machine; antiseptic soap, water; tubing and sterile catheter(s) for suction machine; trap and drainage bottles; cup; gauze, saline solution; sheet; clock or watch.

3. *Is there a recipient, respondent, or co-worker involved in the task*? Yes ( ) No ( )

4. *If Yes to q. 3*: Name the *kind* of recipient, respondent, or co-worker involved, with descriptions to indicate the relevant condition; include the kind with whom the performer is not allowed to deal if relevant to knowledge requirements or legal restrictions.

   Any patient to be treated with use of suction machine; physician; co-worker?

5. *Name the task* so that the answers to questions 1–4 are reflected. Underline essential words.

   Setting up and using suction machine to clean airway or to assist with gastric lavage, by obtaining materials and machine, preparing patient, checking machine, turning machine on and off as ordered for gastric lavage, or inserting catheter into tracheal opening and clearing airway; clean up afterwards.

List elements fully:
Performer uses suction machine for purposes such as gastric lavage (when MD inserts catheter) or with patient who has had a tracheostomy performed for the insertion of a tube for breathing. Performer uses suction machine as a result of:

a. Verbal or written request of physician.
b. Own decision based on observation of patient's need.

1. Performer reads physician's orders on chart or checklist, listens to verbal orders, or considers own decision.
2. Performer obtains necessary materials from storage area or checks that these are with machine. If obtained separately, performer places on table near patient or machine.
3. Performer wheels suction machine near patient or wheels patient to machine if stationary wall unit. (May check that the machine is clean; may decide to clean or have cleaned.) If not already done, plugs machine's cord into wall outlet.
4. Performer may explain to patient what will be done. May drape patient with sheet.
5. Performer checks machine by turning on suction and checking suction outlet with finger to feel suction. If machine is not functioning, decides to report; obtains another (portable) machine or wheels patient to another machine.
6. Attaches prepackaged tubing and catheter set to machine by connecting tubing to machine and catheter to tubing.
7. If gastric lavage, performer turns machine on and off at physician's orders after he or she has inserted catheter. Stands by during process.
8. If patient has had a tracheostomy and needs passage cleared, performer inserts the suctioning catheter with appropriate force to enter the tracheal opening. When inserted to appropriate level, performer turns on suction and attempts to clear mucus from passageway. Turns off machine when done.

   Performer may reassure or comfort patient during process; determines whether passage has been cleansed.

   If not, performer uses fresh catheter(s) and repeats suctioning until the airway is clear.
9. Performer may clean the area surrounding the tracheal opening with gauze and saline solution.
10. After use, performer discards the tubing and catheter(s). May place some of the matter removed from the patient in a cup, pouring it from the drainage bottle or glass, and may show to physician (if requested to do so).
11. Discards cup or matter in bottle; may decide to wash machine and bottles or have subordinate wash (using antiseptic soap and water). Returns machine or has it returned (if portable).
12. Records what was done and time on patient's chart or checklist, or informs physician that task is completed.

From Eleanor Gilpatrick, *The Health Services Mobility Study Method of Task Analysis and Curriculum Design*, Research Report No. 11, Vol. 2 (New York: Hunter College, City University of New York. The Research Foundation, 1977), pp. 4-25–26.

EXHIBIT 4.9 Health Service Mobility Study Guide for Identifying Task Outputs

1. Decisions, judgments, and evaluations can be outputs of separate tasks or outputs of elements within a task. If they are left in the head of the decider, the judge, or the evaluator, they are outputs of elements. If they are *regularly expressed in transmittable form*, such as spoken to someone or written down, they are outputs of separate tasks. Only then are the outputs usable by someone other than the performer.
2. When performers carry out activities that cover a variety of instances of a similar type of activity, such as administering a range of tests, exercises, or treatments, repairing objects or equipment, or doing other work activities which are neither sets of unexpected occurrences nor minute, regularly recurring functions, task grouping is required.
3. If the performer *must choose* among varieties of tests, exercises, etc., and does not make the choice as part of a separate task (by recording it or transmitting it), and must be prepared for all instances, one broad task exists which includes the decision and all the alternatives in the same task. Both the decision and the execution are outputs of the same task.
4. If the performer has a variety of similar activities to do, each of which is *prescribed*, the activities should be grouped; there are as many tasks as groupings according to the following rules:
   a. If the varieties of the tests, exercises, treatments, repairs, etc., can all be covered by the same set of skills and knowledge, then each is an instance of the same task and the task is defined in terms of what the varieties of outputs have in common.
   b. If the varieties of the tests, exercises, treatments, repairs, etc., are covered by different skills and knowledges, then the varieties of outputs should be grouped according to their skill and knowledge requirements, and each task is defined in terms of the distinguishing characteristics of the output grouping.

From Eleanor Gilpatrick, *The Health Services Mobility Study Method of Task Analysis and Curriculum Design*, Research Report No. 11, Vol. 2 (New York: Hunter College, City University of New York, The Research Foundation, 1977), p. 2–16.

EXHIBIT 4.10 Health Services Mobility Study Guide for Identifying What Is Used in Task Performance

1. The range of things used in the task must correspond to the range of contingencies and options covered by the task's output.
2. Tasks are not differentiated by minor differences in what is used if these have no effect on skill or knowledge requirements. Differences in brands, sizes, colors, and similar details are minor unless they require different skills and knowledges.
3. If the performer *must choose* among the things used to produce a given output and does not make the choice as part of a separate task (by recording or transmitting it), and must be prepared to use any of the materials or equipment chosen among, one broad task exists which includes the decision and all the alternative methods.
4. If the performer has a variety of materials and/or equipment to work with to obtain a given output, and each is *prescribed*, the things used should be grouped; there are as many tasks as groupings according to the following rules:
   a. If the varieties of things can all be covered by the same set of skills and knowledge, then each is an instance of the same task, and the task is defined in terms of the output and what the things have in common.
   b. If the varieties of things used require different skills and knowledges, the things used should be grouped according to their skill and knowledge requirements, and each task is defined in terms of the output and the distinguishing characteristics of the groupings of things used.

From Eleanor Gilpatrick, *The Health Services Mobility Study Method of Task Analysis and Curriculum Design*, Research Report No. 11, Vol. 2 (New York: Hunter College, City University of New York, The Research Foundation, 1977), p. 2–20.

EXHIBIT 4.11 Health Services Mobility Study Guide for Identifying Recipients, Respondents, and Co-workers

1. If a task activity requires the performer to deal with a range of recipients, respondents, or co-workers as an intrinsic aspect of the task activity, a single task is identified that covers the range.
2. If a task procedure relating to a given output and things used is carried out differently depending on the age, sex, condition, or status of the recipient, respondent, or co-workers involved, and the differences reflect differences in the skills and/or knowledges required, there is more than one task involved. There are as many tasks as there are significant variations in the way the procedure is done as determined by the kind of individuals involved, provided that the differences in the individuals can be *anticipated* before the tasks begin.
3. Minor variations in the total number and kinds of recipients, respondents, and co-workers that do not result in different skill or knowledge requirements should not be used to differentiate tasks. Such minor variations should be treated as instances of the same task.

From Eleanor Gilpatrick, *The Health Services Mobility Study Method of Task Analysis and Curriculum Design*, Research Report No. 11, Vol. 2 (New York: Hunter College, City University of New York, The Research Foundation, 1977), p. 2–23.

followed by the chief elements of the task in order, reflecting the range of outputs, things used, and persons involved that identify the task and make it unique.

PLACE, SCOPE, AND FORMAT OF TASK DESCRIPTIONS

The preceding discussions have presented an overview of the options available to the analyst in compiling task descriptions. We now discuss how to handle task descriptions in job descriptions.

Place in Job Descriptions. Task descriptions are an integral part of job descriptions. The common practice is to place them after the job summary. The order of the tasks is determined by the nature of the work. The *DOL Handbook* (1972) gives four possibilities and some ways of handling them.

1. The worker performs a specific cycle or sequence of operations. In such cases, tasks are listed according to the sequence in which they are performed.
2. The worker has no regular cycle of operations. In such situations multiple work and operationally unrelated assignments are encountered. It might be useful to organize tasks according to functions.
3. The worker frequently changes from one set of tasks to another. In such cases, the analyst must first make sure that all the tasks are performed by all the workers. They are then recorded on one schedule according to whatever institutional criteria are relevant to the situation.
4. The worker performs a given set of tasks, although in emergencies, he or she performs other sets of tasks involved in other jobs. Such situations really reflect different jobs, and their tasks should not be combined (U.S. Department of Labor, 1972, pp. 3–4).

Scope of Task Descriptions. We have presented the range of possibilities in this regard. The most basic coverage is exemplified in the Special Agent Task Inventory (Appendix 4.1). More inclusive descriptions were contained in all the others, with the HSMS providing the most comprehensive approach to task description.

The simple description is most appropriate as a part of structured inventories. It expresses one dimension at a time and, hence, lends itself to quantitative assessments of worker involvement and task attributes. This approach, however, enlarges the length of the task description as happened in the special agent job (Appendix 4.1). Also, it fails to capture the interrelations among the *what*, *why*, and *how* of the task. To convey these interrelations, it may be essential to construct supplements containing the relevant details.

The narrative, comprehensive-type description exemplified in the other approaches reviewed is intended to convey a picture of the totality of the task components. However, such descriptions do not lend themselves to quantitative assessments of task characteristics. In fact, the more inclusive the description, the less can it be quantified. Also, inclusive descriptions present operational problems in applications. Thus, trainers would have to break down the descriptions into finer elements to put together training materials.

Format. The choice here ranges from pure task descriptions to a fusion of tasks with functional responsibilities, authority, behaviors, and "good citizenship" obligations. These variations are brought out in the descriptions contained in Exhibits 4.12, 4.13, and 4.14. The dough mixer's description (Exhibit 4.12) falls on the purer side of the task description. The focus is on the work itself, and the analysis covers in neutral, clinical terms the *what*, *why*, and *how* of the dough mixer's job. The description of the nurse's role conveyed in Exhibit 4.13 is an extreme example of fusion of tasks, personnel practices, and good citizenship expectations. The description of the relief teller work (Exhibit 4.14) reflects a compromise between the two. Note the functional statement of the duties and also the use of phrases such as "has authority to cash checks" (duties), "has an inherent duty and responsibility to make recommendations" (organization), and "is to conduct relationships in a manner that will enhance the overall marketing effort" (relationships).

Both approaches have their advantages and limitations. A pure description of tasks focuses attention on the specifics of outputs, methods, and activities. This can serve as a basis for

EXHIBIT 4.12 Partial Description of Job of Dough Mixer from the Department of Labor *Handbook*

Establishment Job Title: DOUGH MIXER
Industry Assignment: Baker Products
SIC Code and Title: 2051 Bread and Other Bakery Products
DOT Code: 520–782

Job Summary

Operates mixing machine to mix ingredients for straight and sponge (yeast) doughs according to established formulas, directs other workers in fermentation of dough, and cuts dough into pieces with hand cutter.

Description of Tasks

1. *Dumps ingredients into mixing machine*: Examines production schedule to determine type of bread to be produced, such as rye, whole wheat, or white. Refers to formula card for quantities and types of ingredients required, such as flour, water, milk, vitamin solutions, and shortening. Weighs out, measures, and dumps ingredients into mixing machine. (20%)
2. *Operates mixing machine*: Turns valves and other hand controls to set mixing time according to type of dough being mixed. Presses button to start agitator blades in machine. Observes gauges and dials on equipment continuously to verify temperature of dough and mixing time. Feels dough for desired consistency. Adds water or flour to mix measuring vessels and adjusts mixing time and controls to obtain desired elasticity in mix. (55%)
3. *Directs other workers in fermentation of dough*: Prepares fermentation schedule according to type of dough being raised. Sprays portable dough *trough* with lubricant to prevent adherence of mixed dough to trough. Directs DOUGH-MIXER HELPER in positioning trough beneath door of mixer to catch dough when mixing cycle is complete. Pushes or directs other workers to push troughs of dough into fermentation room. (10%)
4. *Cuts dough*: Dumps fermentated dough onto work table. Manually kneads dough to eliminate gases formed by yeast. Cuts dough into pieces with hand cutter. Places cut dough on proofing rack and covers with cloth. (10%)
5. Performs miscellaneous duties: Records on work sheet number of batches mixed during work shift. Informs BAKE SHOP FOREMAN when repairs or major adjustments are required for machines and equipment. (5%)

Adapted from U.S. Department of Labor, *Handbook for Analyzing Jobs* (Washington, D.C.: U.S. Government Printing Office, 1972), pp. 42–45.

EXHIBIT 4.13 Partial Description of Job of Nurse, Cleveland Lutheran Hospital, 1887

In addition to caring for your 50 patients each nurse will follow these regulations:

1. Daily sweep and mop the floors of your ward, dust the patient's furniture and window sills.
2. Maintain an even temperature in your ward by bringing in a scuttle of coal for the day's business.
3. Light is important to observe the patient's condition. Therefore, each day, fill kerosene lamps, clean chimneys, and trim wicks. Wash the windows once a week.
4. The nurse's notes are important in aiding the physician's work. Make your pens carefully, you may whittle nibs to your individual taste.
5. Each nurse on day duty will report every day at 7 A.M. and leave at 8 P.M. except on the Sabbath on which day you will be off from 12:00 noon to 2:00 P.M.
6. Graduate nurses in good standing with the director of nurses will be given an evening off each week for courting purposes, or two evenings a week if you go regularly to church.
7. Each nurse should lay aside from each pay day a goodly sum of her earnings for her benefits during her declining years, so that she will not become a burden. For example, if you earn $30 a month you should set aside $15.
8. Any nurse who smokes, uses liquor in any form, gets her hair done at a beauty shop, or frequents dance halls will give the director good reason to suspect her worth, intentions, and integrity.
9. The nurse who performs her labors and serves her patients and doctors faithfully and without fault for a period of five years will be given an increase by the hospital administration of five cents a day, provided there are no hospital debts that are outstanding.

EXHIBIT 4.14 Relief Teller Duties and Responsibilities

JOB DESCRIPTION: Relief Teller
DEPARTMENT/DIVISION: Branch
REPORTS TO: Vice President and Branch Administrator
SUPERVISES: Has no supervisory responsibility.

JOB SUMMARY

Performs usual paying and receiving teller functions plus may handle savings deposits and withdrawals, loan payments, savings bond redemption, collections, night deposit, etc. Relieves tellers who are absent in whatever capacity and location needed. Required extensive knowledge of all teller operations and flexibility in the performance of teller duties. Considerable customer contact required. Exercises independent judgment in some instances under limited supervision.

DUTIES

1. Accepts demand deposits.
2. Accepts savings deposits.
3. Has authority to cash checks up to a certain limit.
4. Accepts loan payments, commercial and installment.
5. Accepts payments on collection items.
6. Prepares collection letters and tracers.
7. Writes expense checks.
8. Orders money for branch.
9. Countersigns charge tickets.
10. Balances cash drawer.
11. Helps get out customer statements.
12. Verifies cash.
13. Redeems savings bonds.

ORGANIZATION

Has an inherent duty and responsibility to make recommendations to supervisor concerning possible methods to improve department.

EXHIBIT 4.14 *(cont.)*

FINANCES

Has the responsibility to make recommendations to supervisor concerning the budgetary needs of the department.

RELATIONSHIPS

1. Responsible to the Vice President and Branch Administrator for the fulfillment of functions, responsibilities, and authority and for their proper interpretation.
2. Will have extensive contact with customers and the public, and is to conduct relationships in a manner that will enhance the overall marketing effort of the bank.
3. Will be called upon from time to time to participate with community organizations and in community projects.

From Frank Oldham, Jr., and Jeffrey L. Seglin, *Job Descriptions in Banking* (Boston: Bankers Publishing Company, 1984), pp. 146–147.

additional refinements and extensions for use in training, selection, performance appraisal, and other functional areas. The alternative approach conveys a picture of the totality of expectations of the role, including the possible moral obligations that go with the job. But the specifics of task performance are lost in such descriptions. These would have to be addressed in manuals and other supplementary materials.

4.7 Context Information

The context of the job refers to the environment in which the work is performed. The set of context factors that qualify for consideration in job analysis were discussed in Chapter 2 (see particularly Exhibit 2.3).

The need for paying attention to context variables stems from the fact that the environment in which the work is done can shape the design of the job, work assignment practices, and performance expectations and outcomes. These interdependencies are shown in schematic terms in Exhibit 4.15. Considerable support is found in the literature for the inclusion of context information in job descriptions. However, there has yet to emerge any standard set of practices relating to what to include, where to place it in the job description, and how to depict the interrelations. We now review some approaches and methods for depicting context factors in job description.

APPROACHES TO DESCRIBING CONTEXT FACTORS

Approaches and specific procedures for describing context factors are found in three systems: VERJAS, FES, and the DOL. Each is reviewed briefly in the paragraphs that follow.

VERJAS. Documentation of context variables in job description is an integral part of VERJAS. The following definition of job context is used in the system:

> The term job context refers to the degree of accountability and responsibility the employee has in the job, the amount of supervision he or she exercises, as well as the kinds of physical, personal, and emotional demands he or she will sustain. (Bemis et al., 1983, pp. 70–71)

This definition resulted in the identification of nine context factors. These are reproduced, along with the accompanying questions, in Exhibit 4.16. Note that VERJAS considers supervision (received and given) and guidelines to be context variables.

The VERJAS manual contains a form for studying the context factors shown in Exhibit 4.16. An example of how this form is used in context description is shown in Exhibits 4.17 and 4.18 for the job of clerk typist/receptionist. Under VERJAS, context variables are identified

EXHIBIT 4.15 Interrelations Among Components of Tasks

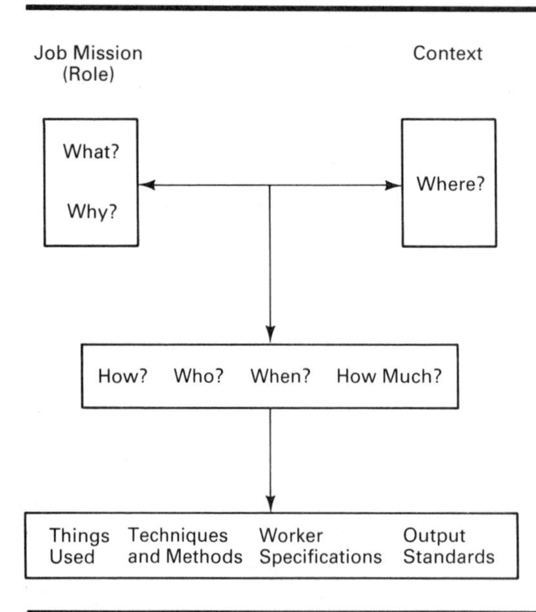

EXHIBIT 4.16 Job Context Factors and Questions from VERJAS

1. How much and what kind of *supervision is received*? How are assignments given? What kind of assistance is available? When is work reviewed—in progress, at completion, or in the course of another's work? Is the employee physically separated from supervision? What is the frequency of contact? How much decision making is left to the incumbent? What freedom does the employee have to act? Mark the appropriate boxes on proximity and frequency, and note relevant facts in row I of the worksheet.

2. What *guidelines*—manuals, policies, procedures, forms— are available? What judgment is needed to apply them? What is prescribed and what is left to the workers' discretion? What responsibility does the worker have for decision making? Does equipment require the operator to make independent judgments based on fine discriminations? The fourth part of the task statements should provide the information needed for this factor. Indicate whether the factor is applicable and, if so, note relevant facts in row II of the worksheet.

3. To what extent are *research and analysis*—fact finding, interpretation, investigation—required by the position? What *reports* are prepared? Who receives the reports? Is information compiled, studied, reported, and used as a basis for deciding on a plan of action? To what extent is complex interpretation required? Task statements should provide data for this factor. Indicate whether the factor is applicable and, if so, note relevant facts in row III of the worksheet.

4. What is the degree of *accountability* and potential *consequence of error*, or both? Is the employee responsible for the security of, or maintaining records on, money or other valuables? Is the employee responsible for the operation or maintenance of expensive equipment? To what extent is the employee responsible for the accomplishment of a goal or profit? Could others be threatened by injury or loss of life? Could others be inconvenienced, and face loss of time, money? Indicate whether the factor is applicable, and if so, indicate the nature of consequences of error and note relevant facts in row IV of the worksheet.

5. What *personal contacts* are required by the job? What internal contacts are involved—co-workers, other departments, upper levels of management? What external contacts are required—customers, representatives of regulatory agencies, job applicants? What is the purpose of these contacts—to provide information, to obtain information, to persuade? Task statements should provide data for this factor. Indicate whether the factor is applicable in row V of the worksheet. If it is applicable, make a note of the kinds of internal and external contacts in the space provided.

6. What *supervision is exercised*? What is the complexity of supervision—train, hire/fire, assign work, review work, evaluate performance? How many employees of what kind are supervised—skilled or semi-skilled, clerical, professional or technical? Task statements should be reviewed for references to this factor. Indicate in row VI of the worksheet whether supervision is exercised, and if it is, indicate the number of people supervised and the nature of this supervision. Also make a note in row VI about information relevant to supervision exercised.

EXHIBIT 4.16 (*cont.*)

7. What are the *physical demands* of the job? What are the mobility requirements of the job—standing, walking, sitting, stooping, kneeling, crouching, crawling, climbing? What are the lifting requirements—is the work sedentary, light, medium, heavy, or very heavy? Is vertical or horizontal reaching required? Indicate in row VII of the worksheet whether the job has any physical demands. If it does, indicate the nature of any lifting or mobility requirements in the spaces provided and note any other physical demands.

8. What are the *work hazards*? These might be mechanical, electrical, fire, chemical, explosive, or radiation. The source of hazards might be equipment operated or the physical environment in the work place. Is the work done at heights or underground? Are there bad atmospheric conditions (i.e., fumes, odors, dusts, mists, gases, stagnant air)? Indicate in row VIII of the worksheet whether the job has any work hazards, and if so, the nature and severity of those hazards.

9. Does the job make *personal demands* in addition to work hazards? Does the job involve work in heat, cold, dampness, confined space, or around noise or vibration? Does the job involve shift work, availability for call out during nonworking periods, or mandatory overtime during emergency situations? Are there *stress* factors built into the job, such as interruptions for a typist in a reception area, demanding customers in a sales clerk situation, or competing demands, such as in a dispatcher or control operator position? Indicate in row IX of the worksheet whether the job imposes any personal demands, and if so, the nature of those demands.

EXHIBIT 4.17 Individual Position Summary Form for Clerk Typist/Receptionist from VERJAS

Job Title: Clerk Typist/Receptionist   Position No.: 327   Page No: 1

1. Duties	2. Tasks	3. Performance Criteria	4. Performance Standards	5. Indicators of Performance
I. Typing*	1. Types letters, memos, and reports*			
	2. Types/transcribes letters, memos, and reports*			
	3. Types forms and form letters*			
	4. Proofreads and corrects			
II Answering telephone/ greeting visitors*	5. Answers telephone*			
	6. Greets visitors*			
III Filing	7. Files			
	8. Searches files/ pulls documents			

Signature—Supervisor: Joanna Margais   Signature—Employee: Roberta Wood   Date: 6-11-83

* Duties and tasks that are critical to performance in positions.

EXHIBIT 4.18 Job Context Worksheet for Clerk Typist/Receptionist from VERJAS

PART A—SCOPE AND EFFECT	Clerk Typist/Receptionist	Page 1 of 2	Position No.: 327
I.	SUPERVISION RECEIVED Proximity: ☒ Visual ☐ Physical Sep. ☐ Geog. Sep. Frequency: ☐ Constant ☒ Hourly ☐ Daily ☐ Weekly ☐ Less Than Weekly	NOTES Sits in reception room but can be seen from manager's office. Sometimes may go for several days without supervision during heavy travel periods for manager.	TASKS WHICH REQUIRE THIS FACTOR
II.	GUIDELINES ☐ Not Applicable ☒ Applicable	NOTES Style manual. Much of guidance is oral. Some areas of work not covered by guidelines—must exercise judgment.	1, 2, 5, 6, 7
III.	RESEARCH ANALYSIS REPORTS ☒ Not applicable ☐ Applicable	NOTES	
IV.	ACCOUNTABILITY CONSEQUENCES OF ERROR ☐ Not Applicable ☒ Applicable ☐ Life ☐ Property ☐ Injury ☐ Inconvenience ☒ Monetary	NOTES Contracts can be lost.	
V.	PERSONAL CONTACTS ☐ Not Applicable ☒ Applicable	NOTES (INTERNAL) Does typing for 5 people.	1, 2, 3
		NOTES (EXTERNAL) Key source of contact with clients and other outsiders.	5, 6

From Stephen E. Bemis, Ann Holt Belenky, and Dee Ann Soder, *Job Analysis* (Washington, D.C.: The Bureau of National Affairs, Inc., 1983), pp. 72–73.

task by task. Exhibit 4.17 gives the task involved in the clerk typist/receptionist job, and Exhibit 4.18 identifies the relevance of the context factors to those tasks.

Context description in the VERJAS system is viewed as a step in job evaluation. Thus, the factors contained in the worksheet (Exhibit 4.16) also happen to be the factors that are commonly found in popular job evaluation systems. They are to be combined with information relating to worker knowledge and skill requirements for assembling compensable factors. (A clean copy of the VERJAS context worksheet is given in Appendix I.)

Factor Evaluation System. The work environment is one of the nine factors that comprise this system. It is defined as

> The risks and discomforts imposed by physical surroundings and the safety precautions necessary to avoid accidents or discomfort. (U.S. Office of Personnel Management, 1979, p. 30)

EXHIBIT 4.18 *(cont.)*

		NOTES	
VI.	SUPERVISION EXERCISED ☒ Not Applicable ☐ Applicable Number Supervised: _____ Skilled/Semiskilled _____ Clerical _____ Prof./Technical _____ Other Nature: ☐ Hire/Fire ☐ Train ☐ Assignments ☐ Review Work ☐ Eval. Perf.		
	PART B—ENVIRONMENT		
VII.	PHYSICAL DEMANDS ☐ Not Applicable ☒ Applicable Lifting: ☒ 10 lb max. ☐ 20 lb max. ☐ 50 lb max. ☐ 100 lb max. ☐ Over 100 lb Mobility: ☐ Standing ☒ Walking ☒ Sitting ☐ Stooping ☐ Reaching ☐ Kneeling ☐ Crouching ☐ Crawling ☐ Climbing	NOTES Mostly sitting—some walking. Stooping and reaching required when filing or retrieving materials.	1, 2, 3, 4, 6 7, 8
VIII.	WORK HAZARDS ☒ Not Applicable ☐ Applicable ☐ Mechanical ☐ Explosives ☐ Electrical ☐ Radiation ☐ Fire ☐ Atmospheric ☐ Chemical ☐ Weight	NOTES	
IX.	PERSONAL DEMANDS/STRESS ☐ Not Applicable ☒ Applicable ☒ Overtime ☐ Climate ☐ Shift Work ☒ Stress ☐ Split Shift ☒ Repetitious Operations	NOTES Some overtime. Can be stressful when proposal must get out by deadline and there are phone calls. Repetitious during periods of heavy typing.	1, 2, 5

Under the FES, the work environment is a compensable factor. The description of the factor, along with the levels and point assignments, are given in Appendix I. The greater the risks, discomfort, and stress involved in the job, the higher the points that the job receives in the job evaluation system.

DOL System. The environment portion of the job analysis schedule of the DOL system is linked closely with the demands made by the job on the physical capacities required of the worker to perform the job effectively. Environmental conditions are defined as

> Environmental conditions are defined as those physical surroundings of job-worker situations which make specific demands upon a worker's physical capacities. (U.S. Department of Labor, 1972, p. 325)

The system recognizes seven environmental conditions. These are as follows:

1. Inside versus outside work
2. Extreme cold with or without temperature change
3. Extreme heat with or without temperature change
4. Wetness and/or humidity
5. Noise and/or vibration
6. Hazards—conditions that pose danger to life and health or could result in bodily injury, for example, moving mechanical parts, electrical shock, working on scaffolding and high places, exposure to burns, radiant energy, explosives, toxic chemicals and biological agents
7. Atmospheric conditions: fumes, odors, dusts, mists, gases, and ventilation

The DOL manual contains a form for presenting environmental conditions. This is reproduced in Appendix I, along with a modified version found in the JIMS system.

PLACE IN JOB DESCRIPTION

Context information can be accommodated in two ways in a job description. The first is as integral parts of the preceding items. This happens naturally as information is gathered on the job title, MTEWA, materials, techniques and methods, guidelines, and tasks. Thus, attempts to track down the title of the job will inevitably lead to inquiries relating to its location within the organization and the reporting relationships. Similarly, study of MTEWA, materials, and techniques and methods naturally yields information not only on the practices common to the trade but also the mode of operation of the organization. Displaying sensitivity to organizational particulars adds to the richness and authenticity of the description.

Context variables can also be reported separately on the job description, either in an independent section or in the supplementary section. This course of action would be justified when the reporting of particular environmental factors is deemed to be essential for the derivation of informational inputs needed for human resource functions. Thus, job evaluation schedules typically include environmental conditions as compensable factors. This was illustrated in the VERJAS and FES systems. Separate treatment of environmental factors can also be beneficial in deriving worker specifications. Thus, the presence of particularly hazardous or stressful factors can moderate the requirements relating to human characteristics needed for job performance.

4.8 Supplementary Information

This is a residual item and its contents and scope will hinge entirely on the decisions made for all the preceding factors on the description (Exhibit 4.1). In general, the shorter the job description, the greater the need for buttressing it with supplementary information. Supplementary information can be presented for the job as a whole or factor by factor. It can include descriptive or evaluative data. It can also be extended to account for historical, current, and emerging issues relating to the job.

JOB DESCRIPTION SUPPLEMENTS

These would relate to the job as whole and could encompass the following:

Job Identification. All items discussed here except the job title could be included as supplements. In addition, the analyst might consider compiling a staffing schedule and reviewing the place of the job in the company's affirmative action plan. Exhibit 4.19 is a staffing schedule from the DOL manual.

EXHIBIT 4.19 Portion of a Staffing Schedule from U.S. Department of Labor, Job Analysis Handbook

U.S. Department of Labor
Manpower Administration

OMB44-R0722

CONFIDENTIAL STAFFING SCHEDULE
(Title Sheet)

UNIT NAME ADMINISTRATIVE

Title Sheet No. 1/3

No. Employees in Unit 4

Establishment No. 360-150-392

Job No.	Job Title	In-ex	Number Employed			Dictionary of Occupational Titles				Tr.	Comments (Enter additional comments on reserve side)
			M	F	T	Title	Code	Suf Code	WTA Gr.		
1	Plant Superintendent		1		1	PRODUCTION SUPERINTENDENT (any ind.)	183.118	014	237	0	
2	Billing Clerk	X		1	1	BILLING CLERK (clerical) II	219.388	026	280	0	
3	Shift Supervisor		2		2	GENERAL FOREMAN (any ind.)	183.168	022	245	0	
UNIT NAME: CARD ROOM							No. of Employees in Unit 32				
1	Card Room Supervisor		1		1		680.180			A	360-150-392-84
2	Card Machine Operator	X	4		4		680.885		447	A	360-150-392-85
3	Carding Machine Technician	X	3		3		680.380			A	360-150-392-86
4	Section Supervisor (Drawing & Roving)	X	3		3		680.280			A	360-150-392-87
5	Draw Frame Operator	X	6		6	DRAWING-FRAME TENDER (textile)	680.885	034	447	C	360-150-392-88

MA 7-37

From U.S. Department of Labor, *Handbook for Analyzing Jobs* (Washington, D.C.: U.S. Government Printing Office, 1972), p. 21.

Context Variables. Environmental factors that cannot be conveniently accommodated in the body of the description itself can be discussed in a supplement. The following are some of the context factors that are of immediate relevance to the job description but that cannot readily be accommodated into the text of the description:

- Work flow and plant layout
- Physical environment
- Psychological and emotional climate
- Horizontal and vertical job relations
- Terms and conditions of employment
- Legal requirements

In addition, this section can contain information relating to job history and anticipated changes in technology, labor markets, and other institutional conditions that are relevant to future decisions about the job.

Ratings. It is a common practice in industry to assign ratings to jobs for classification and other purposes. Thus, the job analysis schedule of the DOL assigns ratings according to the place of the job in the worker functions hierarchy. Shartle's classic publication on occupational information has provisions for prestige ratings of occupations and even entire industries (Shartle, 1959, pp. 54–77).

FACTOR SUPPLEMENTS

Supplements can also be constructed factor by factor. The following are some supplementary data that can be constructed factor by factor:

MTEWA, Materials, and Techniques and Methods. Supplementary information for these factors would be essential when their treatment is fused with task descriptions. One approach is to construct work fields such as those contained in the DOL system and reproduced in this book in Appendix D.

The supplement relating to these factors can also be extended to include commentary on their currency or obsolescence. This is particularly relevant in "hi-tech" jobs that are organized around rapidly changing technology. Appendix H provides a checklist of questions that can be raised about MTEWA, materials, and techniques.

Guidelines and Controls. As indicated earlier, the current thrust among job analysts in describing this factor is on understanding the discretion available to the worker in task performance. Those data could be fruitfully supplemented with documentation of the manuals, dictionaries, handbooks, and other written materials that exist and that define the worker's role in job performance. In fact, study of such materials is a requirement for using the supervision and guidelines factors in the FES system (U.S. Office of Personnel Management, 1979, pp. 14–18).

Tasks. Assuming that the task component factors are adequately described, the supplementary information on tasks can address the following concerns:

- Assuring standardization in task description. This would entail specifying the terminology followed in task description and encouraging its use in task description activity.
- Diagrams, charts, and other depictions that show the mechanics of the interrelations among things, and task elements. (See examples from work study in Chapter 3.)

DEFINITION OF TERMS

Occupational groups and trades tend to develop their own jargon. Use of this jargon in job description adds to its authenticity for the job incumbents. However, it can create problems for persons who do not have firsthand knowledge of the job. It is useful, therefore, to add a section to the job description supplement that clarifies usage of terms or meanings that are not commonly encountered.

Definition of terms might also be essential for occupations where specialized and uncommon terms are a deliberate part of the trade. Medicine, law, and computer science are examples of such fields.

In closing this section, it is important to emphasize the difference between a supplement to and a derivative of a job description. A job description supplement is a body of information that adds to or expands the base of information about the job or its factors. A derivative, on the other hand, is an informational product that is inferred from the job description. The derivatives of job descriptions are worker specifications, performance criteria, compensable factors, and job families.

4.9 Job Descriptions and the Law

As emphasized in prior chapters, job analysis is highly favored by the EEOC guidelines and the courts as a basis for the making of personnel decisions. Much of what was said earlier in regard to the legal requirements and preferences relating to job analysis also applies to job descriptions. The following are some principles and developments that apply more specifically to job descriptions.

· Written job descriptions are preferred over unwritten ones. In fact, an unwritten job description has no legal standing.

· Descriptions must deal with jobs as they are actually found within the company. Generic descriptions are of questionable value.

· There is currently no consensus from a legal perspective on the scope of job descriptions viewed in terms of factors to be covered. A minimal expectation is that the job description contain statements of the tasks involved in the work. The following other job factors have also been viewed favorably: behaviors, duties, activities, and elements (Thompson & Thompson, 1982; Lilienthal & Rosen, 1980).

· Job descriptions are viewed as the proper basis for the making of a wide range of personnel decisions. Their presence (or absence) has been a significant issue in court deliberations involving employee complaints relating to unfair employer practices. The following is a sampling of the cases addressing this issue:

> One of the reasons offered by a female employee in support of her claim of wrongful discharge was that she was not given a job description (*Donaldson* v. *Pillsbury Company*, 1977).
>
> The absence of a written job analysis was held to be one of the limitations of a test validation study offered by an employer as defense in a charge of racial discrimination (*Watkins* v. *Scott Paper Company*, 1976).
>
> The company was required to post more definite job descriptions when vacancies occurred to remedy charges of discrimination in working conditions by black employees (*Patterson* v. *American Tobacco Company*, 1978).
>
> A charge of unfair discharge by new minority employee was sustained by a district court as employer had failed to explain duties and priorities fully and accurately to employee (*Weahkee* v. *Perry*, 1978).

· The inferences drawn from job descriptions relating to worker qualifications, performance requirements, and other derivatives need to be justified on the basis of relevancy. The mere presence of a job description thus is not enough. The description must address the tasks and behaviors that are critical to the job. It must also show, rationally or through a systematic validation procedure, the connections between job factors and worker specifications, performance criteria, and other informational products derived from the description (Bemis et al., 1983, p. 135).

4.10 Selected Issues and Suggestions Relating to Job Descriptions

The potential contents of job descriptions were presented in the preceding sections. This final section addresses a set of issues and dilemmas that are encountered in job description and offers some suggestions for resolving them.

LENGTH OF JOB DESCRIPTIONS

It is commonly agreed that the job description should not be very long. While this rule needs to be respected, it is important to point out that setting an arbitrary limit on its length might be self-defeating. A better rule, and one that we strongly advocate, is that the length of the description be guided by the purposes that it is designed to serve. It should present all the information that is needed by the recruiters, trainers, and other users for the performance of their respective functions.

LEVEL OF SPECIFICITY

Job factors can be described at varying levels of specificity. Thus, noise at the workplace can be described simply by noting its source—trumpets, grading, or blasting; it can also be described more precisely by measuring loudness in decibels. Heat can be described by the use of everyday expressions such as hot or cold; it can also be measured and recorded more precisely through the use of thermometers. To crystalize the options relating to detail more clearly, consider the following pairs of task descriptions:

Slides fingertips over machine edges to detect ragged edges and burrs.	Raises right hand 1 foot to table height, superimposes hand over mechanical part, and, by depressing the first and second fingers to the machined part and moving the arm slowly sidewise about 6 inches, feels with fingertips for snags or pricks that are indicative of surface irregularities (U.S. Department of Labor, 1972, p. 31).
Completes daily route work log to close out day's assigned route.	Completes daily route work log by computing mileage driven on route (subtract mileage out from mileage in shown on tachograph at end of day), posting mileage information and work accomplished per stop, and presenting completed route work log with key to supervisor in order to close out day's assigned route (Gael, 1983, p. 61).

The dilemma that is created by the existence of this choice is clear. The more the detail that is provided, the greater the readiness of the description as a source of information and as an instrument of action. The more the detail, however, the larger the investment of resources in terms of money and time.

The solution for this dilemma lies in deciding in advance the place of the job description in the total human resource management program. Two options are available. First, make the job description the only source of information on the job. If this option is followed, then it would make sense to be generous in terms of the details provided. The other option is to make the job description a general statement, with the additional details being covered in supplementary manuals and guidelines.

The qualifications of the users of job information are a critical consideration in making decisions relating to scope and detail. In general, experienced employees would require less detail than inexperienced employees. In fact, in the case of highly experienced employees, it may not be essential to go beyond identification of the job functions involved. Thus, an experienced machinist would search for ragged edges and burrs as part of the general function of machining a part. Employees who have been at the job for a while would know how to close out the daily work route log without having to follow a detailed, written procedure.

THE POSITION DESCRIPTION

The term *position description* is encountered in the job analysis literature frequently. Unfortunately, there is little consistency in its usage. It can be used in four ways. One is as a synonym for job description. This use is characteristic of the U.S. Office of Personnel Management and other public agencies. Another is to refer to the work assignments of subgroups within a job family. The jobs falling into the family would be similar, but not identical, with respect to the work performed and place in the organization. The differences might hinge on experience (advanced versus entry level), proficiency required of employees (craftsman versus apprentice), time of work (day versus night shifts), or some other organizationally specific factor. In such cases, the term *job description* would be reserved for description of the generalities of the job as an organizational role. The position descriptions would then contain the information describing the work assignments of the subgroups. A third way is as a description of the work assignments of individuals within a group or subgroup. This is an extension of the second usage taken to the level of individuals. The existence of extreme variations in the work performed would be the justification for such an extension. A fourth is to refer solely to the outputs and other results expected of workers in the job. The description in this instance would not contain any information about tasks and other job factors. It would be the basis of communication between manager and subordinate relating to what the subordinate is expected to attain within a time frame. When used in this way, the position description is the same as the agreements found between superiors and subordinates in management by objectives programs (Oldham & Seglin, 1984, p. 14; U.S. Office of Personnel Management, 1979; Morrissey, 1977).

Because of the existence of these varied views on the meaning of the position description, it is pointless to subscribe rigidly to a particular view. To facilitate grammatical consistency, however, we find it useful to keep it separate from job description. The position description is therefore viewed in this book as a limited, specialized, and particular purpose description of job factors addressed to subgroups within the job family. This definition accommodates the last three views reviewed.

DESCRIPTION VERSUS PRESCRIPTION

As emphasized in Chapter 1, job analysis has a dual mandate. One portion of this mandate is concerned with understanding the state of affairs as it exists. This is a descriptive concern and is fulfilled when the analyst creates an accurate picture of what is being done, why it is being done, and how. But a pure description may not be sufficient or useful. This is because organizations are dynamic entities; their missions and structures are constantly subject to forces of change. Continuation of existing arrangements may not be in the interest of the organization. The second part of the job analyst's mandate is thus to arrive at prescriptions for change.

Reconciliation of the actual with the desired is a persistent and endemic problem in job description. There are no easy solutions to this problem. Our general suggestion is that the task of describing jobs be viewed as a series of progressively prescriptive steps. At the initial steps of the data gathering, the analyst needs to take stock of the realities of the situation. No judgments would be passed at this stage. After a picture of the realities is created, an evaluation of what is found would be undertaken in light of the current and emerging needs of the organization. At this stage, the analyst would work closely with managers, industrial engineers, union representatives, and other interested parties in arriving at the desired courses of action. The final job description would be by nature prescriptive. It would reflect a plan of action that addresses the current and emerging needs of the organization.

VERIFICATION OF THE JOB DESCRIPTION

The job description is a primary product of job analysis. The completed job description is to be used as a basis for deriving other informational outputs, for the performance of various human resource management functions, and as a tool in research (Exhibit 4.2). Given these connections, a job description can be viewed as an instrument for administrative action. As an instrument, a job description must meet all the tests of effectiveness that are applied to instruments: it must be reliable, valid, and accurate. In the job analysis literature, the term *verification* is used to refer to the activities undertaken to assure that the job description meets these tests.

Before proceeding further, it is essential to point out that it is frequently difficult (if not impossible) to arrive at evaluative judgments of the job description as a whole. This is so for two reasons. First, the description is made up of multiple factors (Exhibit 4.1). It is thus possible for some portions of it to be acceptable, while others are not. Second, the factors that make up a description vary considerably in regard to form—some are qualitative, others are quantitative. Differences in form require different methods of verification and result in judgments with varying levels of confidence.

For these reasons, it makes sense to view the verification process factor by factor, with the actual amount of time and energies expended in verification being determined by the relevance of the factor to the ultimate uses. Once the decision to verify is made, the methods that are used would be determined by the form of the factor.

Reliability. As a concept, reliability refers to consistency of outcomes. There are two facets to reliability: *stability*, or the extent to which the instrument yields the same results over repeated applications, and *equivalence*, or the extent to which the instrument yields similar results over multiple applications at the same time.

A description of a job factor could be judged to be stable if the reader's understanding of its contents remained the same over repeated readings, spread over a period of time. The reader could be the job incumbent, a new hire, or a trainee. Procedurally, one or more of the subjects could be asked to read the description and to convey their understanding of its contents at two sessions spread over a two-week span of time. If the description is in the form of a task inventory, the ratings given to tasks over involvement (e.g., frequency of performance) or attributes (e.g., importance) at two time periods could be compared. The higher the correlation between the two sets of ratings, the greater the reliability.

Alternatively, the factor description could be judged to be equivalent if multiple readers gained the same understanding at one reading. Thus, an index of equivalence in regard to task attributes would be the level of agreement among the raters.

It is important to emphasize that reliability, strictly viewed, would not inquire into the goodness or appropriateness of the prescriptions. Thus, two people can agree completely on what is conveyed, but the message may be faulty, inaccurate, or even misleading. These are important concerns, but they are not within the concerns of reliability.

Reliability is thus largely a communication issue. As an effectiveness concern, it is targeted at making sure that the description conveys what it is intended to convey. The chances of meeting this requirement are enhanced when attention is paid to choice of words and writing style in composing descriptions. The rules relating to these were given in an earlier section. In our judgment, the description of the dough mixer's job in Exhibit 4.12 is more in conformity with these rules than those contained in Exhibits 4.13 and 4.14. (For a review of accumulated research on the reliability of task inventories, see Gael, 1983, pp. 24–25.)

Validity. When applied to job descriptions, validity refers to the goodness or worthwhileness of the description as an instrument for action. As an instrument, a job description is judged to be valid if it fulfills the purposes that it was intended to serve. The ultimate test of validity is the extent to which it fulfills the three categories of uses that it is intended to serve: derive other products, aid the human resource specialists in their work, and serve as a tool in research (Exhibit 4.2).

The operational procedures used to test the validity of job descriptions hinge on how the description versus prescription issue stacks up. Establishing the validity of a "descriptive" job description is fairly straightforward. Basically, the concern is with documenting the correspondence between the contents of the description with the realities of the job situation; the closer the description is to the actual job situation, the greater its validity. The following are some of the ways in which the validity of such descriptions can be established and enhanced:

- Ask different groups to read the description, to comment on its accuracy, and then to compare the results. The most common practice is to compare the responses of job incumbents with those of their supervisors.
- Have trained observers compare the description with the actual job performance through observation. (A standardized and quantitative procedure for doing this is reported in Jenkins et al., 1975).
- Correlate the results of factor descriptions arrived at through different methods. For example, actual time spent on tasks arrived at through the inventories can be compared with clocked time for the same tasks.
- Use data on reliability as a substitute for validity. The basis for doing this rests on the assumption that high levels of agreement among respondents signifies a form of validity, known as consensual validity (Gael, 1983, p. 27; McCormick, 1979, pp. 133–134).

The ''descriptive'' job description is most appropriate when the design of the job and its mode of performance are in harmony with current and emerging organizational needs. It would not be sufficient or even desirable in instances where the job analysis is part of a program of change or when the organization is experiencing change. In such instances, the description itself becomes an instrument of change.

Verifying the validity of a ''prescriptive'' job description presents a different challenge. There are both immediate and long-term considerations. An immediate judgment of validity must rest on the opinions of management, industrial engineers, and other experts. The job analyst would do well to involve as many viewpoints and interests as can be accommodated in arriving at this evaluation. The phrasing of the questions, and the incisiveness of the inquiries are critical in arriving at the final product. This is an area in which the job analyst has much to learn from work study. Appendix H provides a checklist of questions that can aid the analyst in this endeavor.

The long-term validity of a ''prescriptive'' job description is judged by its ability to fulfill the informational needs of the users. This is the bottom line and the ultimate test of effectiveness. It is for this reason that our basic model provides a feedback loop in the entire process of job analysis (Chapter 1, Exhibit 1.5). The following are a couple of ways in which judgments can be arrived at about ultimate validity:

- Secure assessments of the description from recruiters, trainers, supervisors, and other final users. An endorsement from this source would provide a fairly authoritative statement on validity.
- Draw inferences relating to validity from study of human resource management outcomes. This is the ''firing line'' test and is directed at finding out the extent to which the description has actually contributed to better human resource management practice. Incidents (both positive and negative) relating to role clarity, fairness and equity in compensation, promotions, and other significant personnel issues can provide some indication of whether the description has made a positive contribution.

Accuracy. When applied to job descriptions, accuracy refers to the extent to which the descriptions provided on the instrument reflect the true values of the job factors described. Establishing the accuracy of hard, quantitative, and objective factors is typically not a problem. Consider descriptions relating to amount of time spent on particular tasks by the worker. What is stated in the job description can be readily compared against the reality—the greater the conformance, the more accurate the description.

Verification of the accuracy of the subjective factors, however, presents a different challenge. Consider ratings on evaluative descriptors of tasks such as complexity, difficulty, and importance. Such ratings cannot be correlated in any way with objective indices. For this reason, internal correlations have to be relied upon as proof of accuracy. Thus, high correlations among ratings given by multiple raters can be taken as an index of accuracy. Confidence in such results is increased if the raters reflect different organizational levels, skills, and demographic characteristics (see Landy & Farr, 1983, pp. 22–23).

APPENDIX 4.1 FLORIDA DEPARTMENT OF LAW ENFORCEMENT SPECIAL AGENT TASK INVENTORY

Part I. Familiarization

After gaining approval and support of the agency, the job analyst should review existing class specifications, training materials, and position description questionnaires. Written rules and procedures should also be reviewed. If time permits, observation of at least one full tour of duty should be undertaken. This process should take no more than two to three days including observation, less if the job analyst has already gained sufficient familiarity with the job class in question.

Part II. Task Inventory

A. PRODUCTION OF FIRST DRAFT OF TASK STATEMENTS

1. Collect task inventories prepared for similar jobs.
2. Review for content against written materials available to the analyst.
3. Revise and edit the task statements, arrange them into approximately ten function categories, and produce a first draft.

This process should take two days including typing.

B. REVIEW OF TASK STATEMENTS BY SUBJECT MATTER EXPERTS (SMES)

1. Identify at least three (but no more than six) experts (two incumbents and one supervisor). These experts should have at least two years experience and exposure to a variety of assignments performed by incumbents at several locations. If female and minority SMEs are available, their inclusion is very desirable for legal reasons.
2. After securing their cooperation, the analyst should provide SMEs with the draft and request that they delete irrelevant tasks, add overlooked tasks, review the function clusters, and combine statements so that the inventory reflects a complete but concise survey of the work performed. The inventory should contain no more than 100 task statements when the SMEs have completed their work.
3. The revised inventories are collected by the job analyst.

This process should take one day of analyst time, one to two days of SME time, and the entire process one to two weeks including mailing.

C. INTEGRATION OF SMEs INPUTS AND PREPARATION OF THE PILOT FORM OF THE INVENTORY

1. The job analyst should review the SMEs' inputs and prepare an inventory with no more than 100 task statements.
2. These task statements should be put into a questionnaire format with suitable instructions and the following scales:
   a. *Relative time spent*—Amount of time spent on this task relative to time spent on other tasks.
      0 = Not performed
      1 = Extremely small amount of time

2 = Small amount of time
3 = Below-average amount of time
4 = Average amount of time
5 = Above-average amount of time
6 = Large amount of time
7 = Extremely large amount of time

b. *Relative Time Spent Under Ideal Circumstances*—Amount of time that *should be* spent on this task relative to time spent on all other tasks.

c. *Task Difficulty*—Difficulty in doing a task correctly relative to all other tasks in the job.

1 = One of the easiest of all tasks
2 = Considerably easier than most tasks
3 = Easier than most tasks performed
4 = Approximately one-half tasks are more difficult, one-half less
5 = Harder than most tasks performed
6 = Considerably harder than most tasks performed
7 = One of the few most difficult tasks

d. *Criticality of Error*—The seriousness of consequences that arise from inadequate or incorrect performance of a task relative to the other tasks.

1 = Negligible or trivial
2 = Not too serious
3 = Somewhat serious
4 = Average seriousness
5 = Slightly above average in seriousness
6 = Extremely serious
7 = Disastrous (e.g., life threatening)

This process should take two days of analyst time and up to a week for production of the questionnaire (typing, proofing, etc.).

D. PILOT TESTING AND PRODUCTION OF FINAL VERSION

1. Give questionnaire to six SMEs in local area; have them fill it out as expert informants and comment in conversation with the analyst. If necessary, the same SMEs who edited the task list could serve as the informants. In their role as informants, they would respond to the questionnaire, not based on their own job, but based on how they think a representative worker in the target job would respond.
2. Prepare final questionnaire, including any revisions indicated in pilot testing. Include a demographic data section.

This process should take one day of analyst time, one day of SME time, and one additional day for production of final form.

E. PRODUCTION OF INVENTORIES, ADMINISTRATION, AND ANALYSIS

1. Make a sufficient number of copies to cover all incumbents and their direct supervisors. The concluding table contains a prototype inventory form.
2. Distribute the questionnaire with a cover memo from the department head that specifies a completion date. Respondents should complete the questionnaire on the basis of their current assignment.
3. Collect and keypunch data.
4. Analyze data to produce most important tasks and functions according to the formula, task

importance = difficulty × criticality + actual time spent. Function importance is the sum of task importance for all tasks within the function. This combination yields an index of task importance for the personnel administration purposes of recruitment, selection, training, and performance appraisal.

This process should take only one day of analyst time and up to three to four weeks including mailout, receipt of returns, and data processing.

F. PREPARE LISTING OF FUNCTIONS IN ORDER OF IMPORTANCE AND THE COMPONENT TASKS LISTED UNDER EACH FUNCTION IN THEIR ORDER OF IMPORTANCE

This process should take a few hours of analyst time and one day of typing.

This concludes the task inventory phase.

Florida Department of Law Enforcement Special Agent Task Inventory

Function	Task Importance Value (TIV)	Standard Deviation (SD)
Legal Proceedings		
8–3 Assist in preparation of evidence for use by prosecution	25.5	8.9
8–1 Testify at legal proceedings	25.4	8.9
8–2 Participate in pretrial conference	21.2	8.4
Practice and Procedures		
1–22 Determine the justification for use of deadly force	36.0	12.5
1–19 Assume cover identities in undercover operations	34.1	11.3
1–6 Overtake and stop/approach/control occupants of stopped felony suspect vehicles	30.6	9.7
1–4 Participate in raids	30.4	9.4
1–9 Execute search warrants	28.5	10.6
1–7 Make warrantless arrests and/or searches	27.9	10.2
1–25 Coordinate regional investigations involving multiregional or interstate violators	20.5	9.9
1–8 Execute arrest warrants	27.4	10.0
1–15 Conduct interviews and/or interrogations	23.7	8.5
1–1 Conduct surveillances (i.e., physical, electronic) using surveillance equipment	22.6	8.6
1–5 Search arrested persons	22.4	10.0
1–2 Observe and describe people, places, objects, and events	21.0	8.2
1–29 Utilize and justify T&E funds and flashrolls	20.9	9.8
1–23 Assist local low enforcement agencies during civil disturbances	20.8	11.4
1–16 Make searches of individuals	20.7	9.5
1–13 Prepare investigative notes, rough sketches, and diagrams	20.5	8.1
1–24 Coordinate the apprehension and extradition activities for the return of alleged or known violators	20.5	9.9
1–21 Examine records and files to detect fraud-related crimes	20.4	7.9
1–18 Evaluate injury patterns of homicide/suicide victims	20.3	9.3
1–11 Perform VIP security duties	18.4	11.7
1–12 Determine legal authority and jurisdiction	17.9	9.7
1–17 Prepare and transport persons who are in custody	17.2	9.5
1–10 Conduct line-ups (i.e., physical, photographic)	14.2	6.6
1–26 Transport valuables, money, checks, or other legal tender as an official duty	13.1	7.7
1–20 Arrange and witness autopsies	12.9	7.7
1–3 Administer rights warnings to suspects and obtain waivers	11.9	6.7
1–27 Secure technical assistance from other departments and/or state offices	11.3	6.9
1–14 Conduct field testing of suspected drugs	10.3	6.4
1–28 Serve subpoenas	9.0	5.3
Intelligence		
5–5 Utilize, maintain contact with, or otherwise handle informants	27.7	11.0
5–4 Recruit informants	22.9	9.4

Florida Department of Law Enforcement Special Agent Task Inventory *(cont.)*

Function	Task Importance Value (TIV)	Standard Deviation (SD)
Intelligence *(cont.)*		
5–3 Identify potential informants	20.8	10.0
5–1 Gather information for criminal intelligence purposes	19.4	8.9
5–2 Read, review, and analyze criminal intelligence information	17.6	9.3
5–8 Maintain informant records and files	17.4	11.3
5–7 Process and disseminate intelligence information	17.1	8.0
5–6 Assign rating codes to information obtained for intelligence purposes	14.6	8.5
Evidence Collection and Preservation		
4–2 Collect physical evidence (i.e., hair and fiber, documentary, toolmark, firearms, bloodstain, glass)	22.2	8.4
4–1 Conduct searches for physical evidence	22.0	8.0
4–3 Seize evidence or contraband	21.7	9.0
4–5 Take special precautions to preserve fragile or perishable evidence	20.7	8.6
4–4 Protect and/or preserve evidence at crime scene	20.1	8.0
4–15 Collect homicide evidence during autopsies	19.9	8.3
4–16 Obtain fingerprints from deceased persons	18.7	8.9
4–9 Detect and lift latent fingerprints	18.5	8.8
4–6 Maintain evidence in safe storage	17.6	7.8
4–14 Maintain gunpowder residue evidence	17.4	9.4
4–11 Make plaster casts	16.0	10.0
4–12 Obtain handwriting exemplars and standards	13.2	6.2
4–7 Transport or transmit evidence to the crime lab	12.2	7.0
4–10 Roll fingerprint impressions	12.0	7.9
4–13 Apply identification markings to evidence	11.9	6.2
4–8 Relinquish evidence to designated evidence custodian	11.6	6.7
4–17 Estimate monetary value of drug evidence	10.1	6.9
Self-development		
7–1 Learn and comply with FDLE policies and procedures	18.9	10.1
7–3 Maintain personal physical fitness	18.8	9.2
7–4 Conduct personal study/research of job-related subjects	14.6	6.6
7–2 Attend training/educational programs for career development	12.8	6.1
Public Contacts		
6–1 Provide assistance during natural disasters or in civil defense emergencies	17.8	10.5
6–4 Provide technical assistance to other law enforcement agencies	16.8	6.7
6–2 Make liaison contacts with other law enforcement or criminal justice agencies	16.6	7.6
6–6 Interact with government, business and private persons, or groups	15.9	6.8
6–7 Represent the department at meetings or conferences	14.7	7.9
6–3 Provide teaching and/or training support	14.5	7.1
6–5 Make public presentations upon request at approved meetings	14.5	6.3
6–8 Attend special training seminars, workshops or conferences for the purpose of obtaining additional knowledge or exchanging information	12.8	5.8
Equipment Use and Maintenance		
2–13 Fire handgun or shotgun in the line of duty	29.1	14.1
2–3 Utilize electronic monitoring/surveillance equipment	19.5	8.1
2–15 Apply handcuffs to arrested persons	17.2	8.7
2–16 Use gas mask, bullet proof vest, or other special protective devices	17.2	9.7
2–4 Perform field maintenance on electronic monitoring/surveillance equipment	15.8	8.5
2–12 Photograph crime scenes/physical evidence	15.5	7.6
2–6 Photograph surveillance targets	15.2	7.2
2–14 Clean and maintain assigned weapons	14.2	7.9
2–10 Utilize a crime scene processing kit	13.9	7.7
2–2 Operate assigned vehicles	13.8	6.8
2–8 Utilize latent fingerprint kit	11.1	6.9
2–11 Photograph individuals for identification purposes	10.8	6.9
2–7 Maintain photographic equipment and accessories	10.6	6.0
2–9 Utilize rolled ink fingerprint impressions equipment	8.7	6.0
2–5 Perform minor maintenance of assigned vehicles	8.6	6.7
2–1 Operate a mobile radio	8.4	4.3

Florida Department of Law Enforcement Special Agent Task Inventory (*cont.*)

Function	Task Importance Value (TIV)	Standard Deviation (SD)
Reports and Forms		
3–13 Prepare affidavits and warrants (attest, search, wiretap)	29.8	9.1
3–19 Obtain written statements, written admissions, and written confessions	23.6	9.0
3–7 Prepare FDLE Case Reports	21.9	7.5
3–12 Prepare investigative summaries	21.0	9.0
3–10 Prepare intelligence reports	16.8	7.3
3–20 Obtain signed waiver of counsel forms from suspects prior to custodial interviews	16.3	8.1
3–11 Initiate and maintain surveillance logs	15.3	6.4
3–9 Prepare Expenditure Reports	15.1	8.6
3–8 Prepare Attest/Booking Reports	14.9	7.3
3–14 Prepare consent to search forms	13.2	7.5
3–18 Prepare evidence receipts	11.6	6.7
3–6 Prepare Assistance Rendered Reports	11.1	6.5
3–17 Initiate and maintain chain of custody forms	13.0	7.1
3–16 Prepare requests for Crime Lab Services	9.7	5.8
3–15 Prepare fingerprint cards	9.3	5.1
3–5 Prepare FDLE Lead Sheets	8.7	6.2
3–2 Prepare Weekly Activity Reports	8.6	6.4
3–1 Prepare Daily Activity Reports	8.4	7.5

From Frank Sistrunk and Philip L. Smith, *Multimethodological Job Analysis for Criminal Justice Organizations* (Tampa: Center for Evaluation Research, University of South Florida, 1982), pp. 88–97.

5 Worker (Job) Specification

A worker specification is one of the principal derivatives of job analysis. It spells out, in written form, the knowledges, skills, abilities, and other human characteristics (KSAOs) that are necessary for effective job performance. This chapter is concerned with the *what*, *why*, and *how* of worker specifications.

The following are the specific goals of this chapter:

1. To define a set of terms that are relevant to the study and construction of worker specifications.
2. To present an inventory of human characteristics that can serve as a basis for decisions relating to worker specifications.
3. To show the uses of worker specifications in human resource management.
4. To review the approaches, techniques, and methods in deriving worker specifications.
5. To review the legal mandates that need to be taken into account in formulating and using worker specifications.
6. To provide the human resource director with specific suggestions for compiling worker specifications that meet the requirements of the law and that are also effective from a business perspective.

5.1 Terminology of Worker Specification

All organizations need to have some understanding of the qualifications needed on the part of their employees for performing the jobs that comprise the organization. The following are the key terms that are encountered in the literature dealing with the study of human characteristics at work.

Human (worker) characteristic	For grammatical convenience, this term is used here in a collective sense to refer to aptitudes, abilities, skills, knowledges, personality, and other human attributes that are relevant in discussions of worker specifications.
Trait	Commonly viewed as a dimension of personality. When used in that way, it refers to stable and visible behavioral characteristics of individuals. It can also be used more generally to refer to physical and other attributes in describing people.

KSAO	An acronym of the following words: knowledges, skills, abilities, and other human characteristics. It is used for grammatical convenience to refer to work-related human characteristics.
Worker (job) specification	Descriptions of human characteristics that are considered relevant for effective performance of the job. (Note: Such specifications are also commonly referred to as job specifications. However, since the objects of such descriptions are workers, this practice leads to unnecessary confusion. They are therefore referred to here as worker specifications.)
Test	Any device, procedure, or mechanism that is used in differentiating individuals over specific human characteristics. The concept can encompass a paper-and-pencil test, an interview, an oral examination, or even an application blank.
Subject matter experts (SMEs)	Managers, employees, and other human sources with specialized or expert knowledge about the job and other relevant elements of the work situation.

The terms just defined relate to the most general concepts encountered in worker specification activity. The discussion that follows presents the derivative terms that expand on the basic notions.

Before proceeding further, the distinction between a worker specification and a test needs to be emphasized. Specifications spell out, in varying degrees, the types (and possibly even the amounts) or human characteristics considered essential for job performance. Tests, on the other hand, are specific devices for finding out whether or not and the extent to which particular individuals possess those characteristics. To illustrate, the specification might state that knowledge of advanced calculus is essential for effective job performance. Whether or not individuals possess this knowledge would be measured through tests. These tests could be in form of written examinations, work samples, study of work history, or even interview questions. The links between specific human characteristics and tests and testing procedures are explored in the next chapter. At this stage, our concern is with the derivation of worker specification, which is the first step in differentiating individuals for the purposes of hiring, promotion, and other human resource management concerns.

5.2 Worker Specification: Overview

Much is available to the job analyst in the form of techniques and methods for deriving worker specifications. Before examining these, however, it is worthwhile to gain an overview of the potential contents of worker specifications, their uses in human resource management, and the approaches that are followed in deriving them.

CONTENTS OF WORKER SPECIFICATIONS

A worker specification spells out the human characteristics that are considered relevant to successful job performance. The task of developing specifications would be greatly simplified if a complete list were available of all the actual and potential human capabilities. Unfortunately, such a list is not available. Humans have proven to be difficult to describe, and the range and interdependencies of their potentials have eluded classifiers.

To aid this discussion, Exhibit 5.1 shows some interrelations between two sets of known human characteristics and potential job outcomes. While not exhaustive, the characteristics shown in this illustration have figured prominently in discussions of human effectiveness at the workplace. Details about their interdependencies are covered in the discussion that follows.

Aptitudes and Abilities. These are the basic concepts in the description of human capabilities and serve as the point of departure for the understanding of the others. The term *aptitude* refers

EXHIBIT 5.1 Interrelations Between Two Sets of Human Characteristics and Job Outcomes

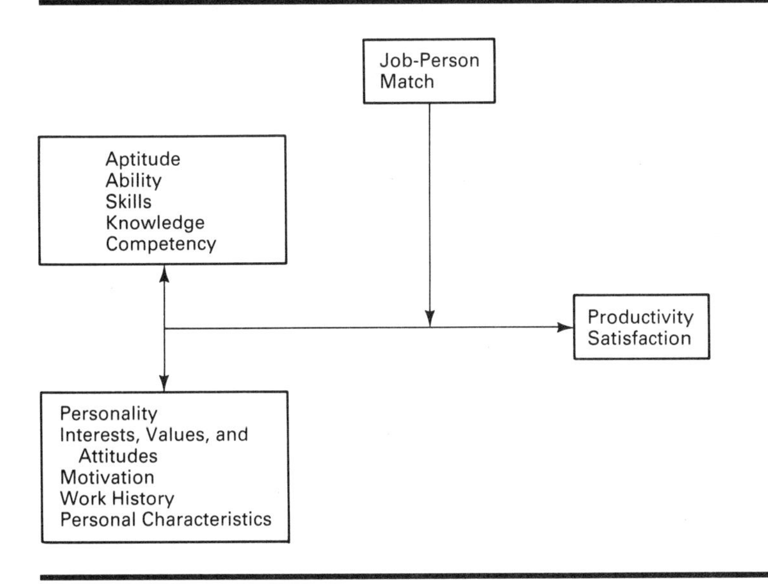

to a potential or capacity for doing or learning something. Aptitudes can be mental or physical. The search for aptitudes is a search for finding out what a species (or a member within the species) is capable of doing.

The fact that a person possesses a particular aptitude, however, does not mean that the person is going to be able to perform an activity related to that aptitude. This brings up the relevance of the notion of *ability*. When contrasted conceptually with aptitude, ability refers to a readiness to perform developed through training or experience. Thus, the basic human aptitudes of speaking, singing, and dancing can all be enhanced through training.

Although aptitude and ability are conceptually distinct terms, attempts to use them typically result in loss of their distinctiveness. Also, several other terms have arisen that enable depictions of varying combinations of human capabilities. The meanings of the terms contained in this total package, and their interrelationships, are as follows:

Aptitude	Capability; innate attribute; basic equipment.
Ability	Readiness to perform or learn; a present competence to perform a behavior or task.
Skills	Physical and motor aptitudes and abilities; proficiency at doing something.
Knowledge	A body of information possessed by an individual that can be applied directly to the performance of a job task.
Competency	A knowledge, skill, or ability, or a particular combination of the three; this characteristic can also be extended to include a circumstance that can influence a person's ability to work (e.g., possession of a driver license enabling a worker to drive a car, if required to do so by employer).

Personality and Related Characteristics. The foregoing characteristics reflect ways of looking at human readiness and potential for performing and learning. While useful from that perspective, they are not sufficient for understanding or predicting the behavior of particular individuals. This is where the other set of human characteristics shown in Exhibit 5.1 come into the picture. Collectively, this set provides clues relating to the reasons behind the level of abilities attained by individuals and the prospects of their being able and willing to use them in the future. To

EXHIBIT 5.2 Sixteen Primary Personality Traits

1. Reserved .... Outgoing
2. Less intelligent .... More intelligent
3. Affected by feelings .... Emotionally stable
4. Submissive .... Dominant
5. Serious .... Happy-go-lucky
6. Expedient .... Conscientious
7. Timid .... Venturesome
8. Tough-minded .... Sensitive
9. Trusting .... Suspicious
10. Practical .... Imaginative
11. Forthright .... Shrewd
12. Self-assured .... Apprehensive
13. Conservative .... Experimenting
14. Group-dependent .... Self-sufficient
15. Uncontrolled .... Controlled
16. Relaxed .... Tense

From S. P. Robbins, *Essentials of Organizational Behavior* (Englewood Cliffs, N.J.: Prentice-Hall, 1984), p. 15.

simplify, measures of aptitudes and abilities reveal what a person is capable of doing and the level of proficiency attained in particular areas; the measures of personality and related characteristics explain how the person attained the current level of proficiency and the chances that the person will successfully use the ability in the future in the service of the organization.

The meanings of this second set of characteristics and their interrelations with each other are given next. Examples are given in the accompanying illustrations.

EXHIBIT 5.3 Interests, Values, and Attitudes

Interests are preferences for particular activities. Examples of statements relating to interests are as follows:

1. I would rather repair a clock than write a letter.
2. I like to supervise the work of others.
3. I would enjoy keeping a stamp collection.
4. I prefer outdoor work to work in an office.

Values reflect preferences for "life goals" and "ways of life." Examples of statements that express values are as follows:

1. I consider it more important to have people respect me than to like me.
2. A person's duty to family comes before duty to society.
3. I do not think it is right for some people to have much more money than others.
4. Service to others is more important to me than personal ambition.

Attitudes are feelings about particular social objects such as physical objects, types of people, particular people, social institutions, and government policies. Statements exemplifying attitudes are as follows:

1. The United Nations is a constructive force in the world today.
2. Trade unions have too much effect on our economy.
3. All public schools should be fully integrated.
4. Fraternities and sororities do more harm than good.

From Jum C. Nunnally, *Psychometric Theory*, 2nd ed. (New York: McGraw-Hill Book Company, 1978), pp. 588–590.

Personality	In the popular literature, personality is used loosely to encompass a diverse set of qualities, ranging from social charm to character and ability. The professional literature, on the other hand, takes a limited view. There is insistence that this term be kept apart from aptitudes and abilities. As conceived by psychologists, personality refers to relatively consistent and stable dispositions to respond in distinctive ways to other persons, objects, and situations. Differences in personality are measured by placing individuals on scales of response traits. Exhibit 5.2 provides examples of personality traits that can be used for differentiating individuals on this characteristic (Krech, Crutchfield & Ballachey, 1962, p. 104; Nunally, 1978, pp. 544–587).
Interests	Preferences for particular activities. Typical areas of research have been hobbies, recreational patterns, and vocational pursuits. Exhibit 5.3 gives statements that exemplify interests in comparison with those that exemplify values and attitudes.
Values	Preferences for life goals and ways of living; notions of what is desirable and undesirable. See Exhibit 5.3 for examples.
Attitudes	Beliefs and feelings about persons, social groups, organizations, social institutions, and other objects in the environment. A distinguishing feature of attitudes is that they tend to be centered on particular targets. Examples are given in Exhibit 5.3.
Motivation	A willingness to expend energy and to use abilities in the service of desired activities and goals. Motivated workers contribute high levels of effort in attaining the missions of their jobs. The interrelations among motivation, ability, and performance concepts are shown in Exhibit 5.4.
Work history	Experiences obtained by the individual in work settings beginning with the first gainful employment. Work history can cover changes in earnings, job titles, promotions, and experiences with different methods and levels of work.

EXHIBIT 5.4 Interrelations Between Motivation and Performance: A Simplified View Based on Expectancy Theory

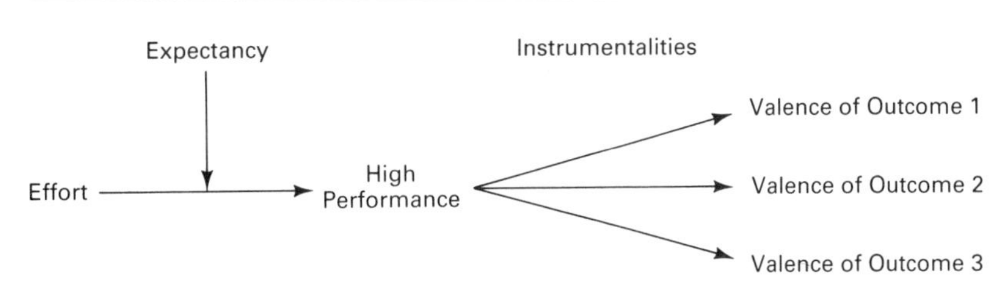

Definitions of the various components of the diagram are as follows:

Effort	= the motivation to perform.
Valence	= attractiveness of rewards or outcomes that performance could lead to.
Instrumentality	= feelings concerning the likelihood that performance will lead to certain results.
Expectancy	= estimation of the probability that changes in effort will lead to changes in actual performance.

From H. G. Heneman III and D. P. Schwab, "Work and Rewards Theory," in *ASPA Handbook of Personnel and Industrial Relations*, Vol. II, pp. 6-4—6-5 (Washington, D.C.: The Bureau of National Affairs, Inc., 1975).

Personal characteristics	A residual category that can accommodate job-relevant characteristics not covered by the above. The following types of items could be included in this category: physical characteristics such as height and weight, socioeconomic background, sex, and age.

This discussion illustrates the choices available in regard to human characteristics that could be included in worker specifications. Actual worker specifications range widely in scope and detail. The details can range from simply indentifying the required KSAO to describing levels and degrees of the KSAO required. The special agent KSAOs presented in Appendix 5.1 illustrate the simplest version of specifications, which merely identifies the knowledges, skills, and abilities required for effective performance of the special agent job. These statements can be expanded to cover levels of KSAOs required and the degrees within those levels. These differences are illustrated in the examples provided under the techniques and methods section that follows.

PURPOSES SERVED IN HUMAN RESOURCE MANAGEMENT

Worker specifications are a primary tool of human resource management. The general rationale behind written worker specifications is nicely captured in the following quote from R. J. Burke in an article published in 1916:

> In purchasing materials, a certain quantity and quality is secured for a certain price and the material is usually bought because (it is) best adapted for its particular, intended use. Specifications are drawn up giving exact kind, sizes, dimensions, etc., as required by intended use and for given money.
>
> In purchasing labor, does not the same relation between commodity, service, and price hold true? Labor should be purchased solely because the individual man has attributes, qualities and degree of fitness that make him an efficient selection for the particular job at an economical price. (R. J. Burke, 1916, p. 176)

EXHIBIT 5.5 Uses of Worker Specifications

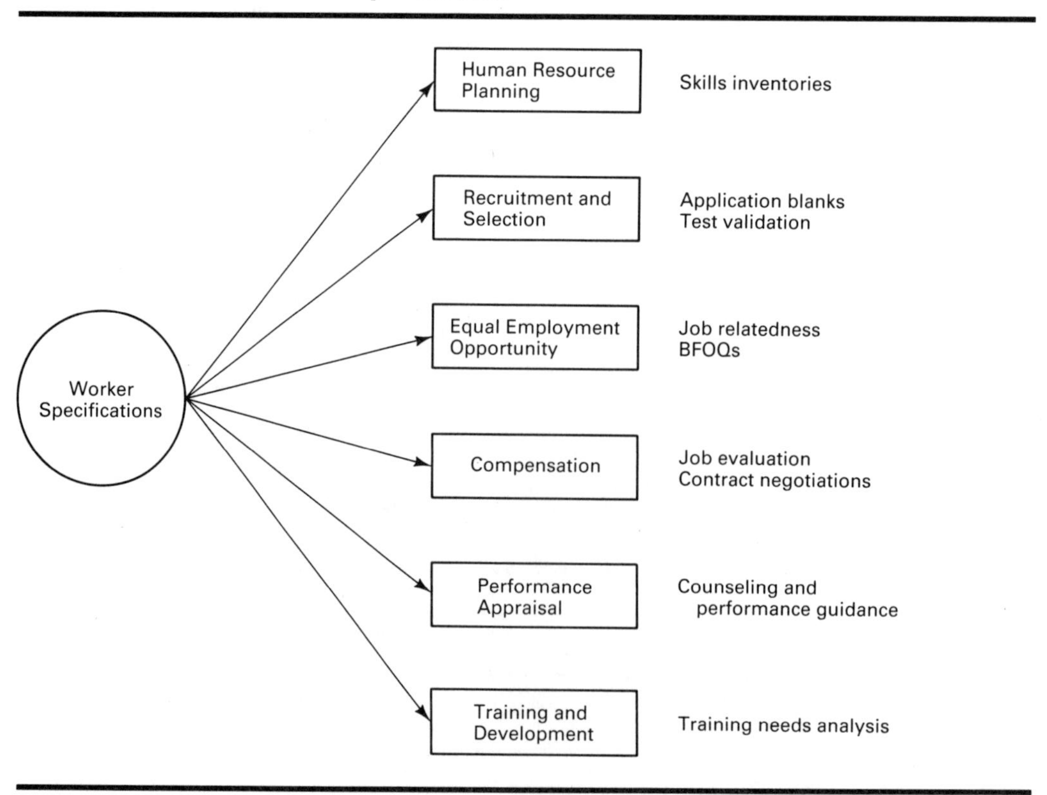

In human resource management, worker specifications have historically been associated with hiring. In recent years, however, additional and varied uses have been discovered for this document, and its importance has arisen in the human resource management process. The multiple uses of the worker specification in modern human resource management are shown in Exhibit 5.5

In human resource planning, worker specifications can provide the required KSAO compositions of the labor force for inclusion in human resource (skills) inventories. In recruitment and selection, KSAOs provide the information needed for the formulation of application blanks and for the validation of tests. Closely related to the test validation concern are the equal employment opportunity (EEO) requirements of job-relatedness and bona fide occupational qualities (BFOQs). Both are serviced by systematically derived KSAOs. The derivation of compensable factors requires understanding of both job and worker variables involved in job performance. Worker specifications can provide the worker-related variables essential for formulating compensable factors. These can be used in the performance of the compensation and labor relations functions. KSAOs can provide supervisors with a basis for counseling employees during performance appraisal. Training needs are established by comparing worker specifications in the abstract with the realities found within the labor force. Systematically articulated worker specifications are thus a prerequisite for training effectiveness.

The uses of the worker specification just documented result when this document is viewed by itself. Its versatility and effectiveness, however, increase considerably when it is used in conjunction with the job description, duties and responsibilities, and other products of job analysis. The multiplicity of uses of the products of job analysis, viewed as a set, are covered in the next chapter of this book.

APPROACHES TO WORKER SPECIFICATION

A considerable amount of effort has been expended by job analysts over the years in developing procedures for deriving worker specifications. However, there has not yet emerged a standard or generally accepted way of arriving at worker specification. There currently exist a variety of techniques and methods for fulfilling this activity. In general, the available resources can be grouped roughly under two approaches: job oriented and worker oriented. Under both approaches, it is assumed that the derivation of worker specification is an inferential process. Also, both approaches rely on subject matter experts (SMEs) for making the inferences. There are significant differences, however, between these two approaches with reference to where they begin the process, the actions required of the SMEs, and the tools and techniques used in drawing the inferences. These differences are illustrated schematically in Exhibit 5.6, which is used hereafter as a guide for this discussion.

Job-Oriented Approach. The distinguishing characteristic of the job-oriented approach to worker specification is that it relies on written, explicit descriptions of jobs for fulfilling this activity. Under this approach, the starting point is the construction of a description of the job for which the specification is to apply. The description then serves as the basis for understanding the nature of the demands made on the worker by the job situation. These demands are then compared against lists of KSAOs. The SMEs serve as the judges or the authority for the inferences that are drawn.

Variations within this approach revolve around structure and scope of instruments used, amount of quantification attained, and the methods and modes of data analysis. The job analysis systems that fall within this group are the three functional job analysis systems and the health service mobility study.

Worker-Oriented Approach. The starting point of this approach is some inventory, either ready-made or developed on the spot, of work-related behaviors, KSAOs, or critical incidents and elements. The items within the inventory are compared against other instruments, superior workers, or perhaps even a job description to arrive at worker specifications. The variations

EXHIBIT 5.6 Approaches to the Derivation of Worker Specifications

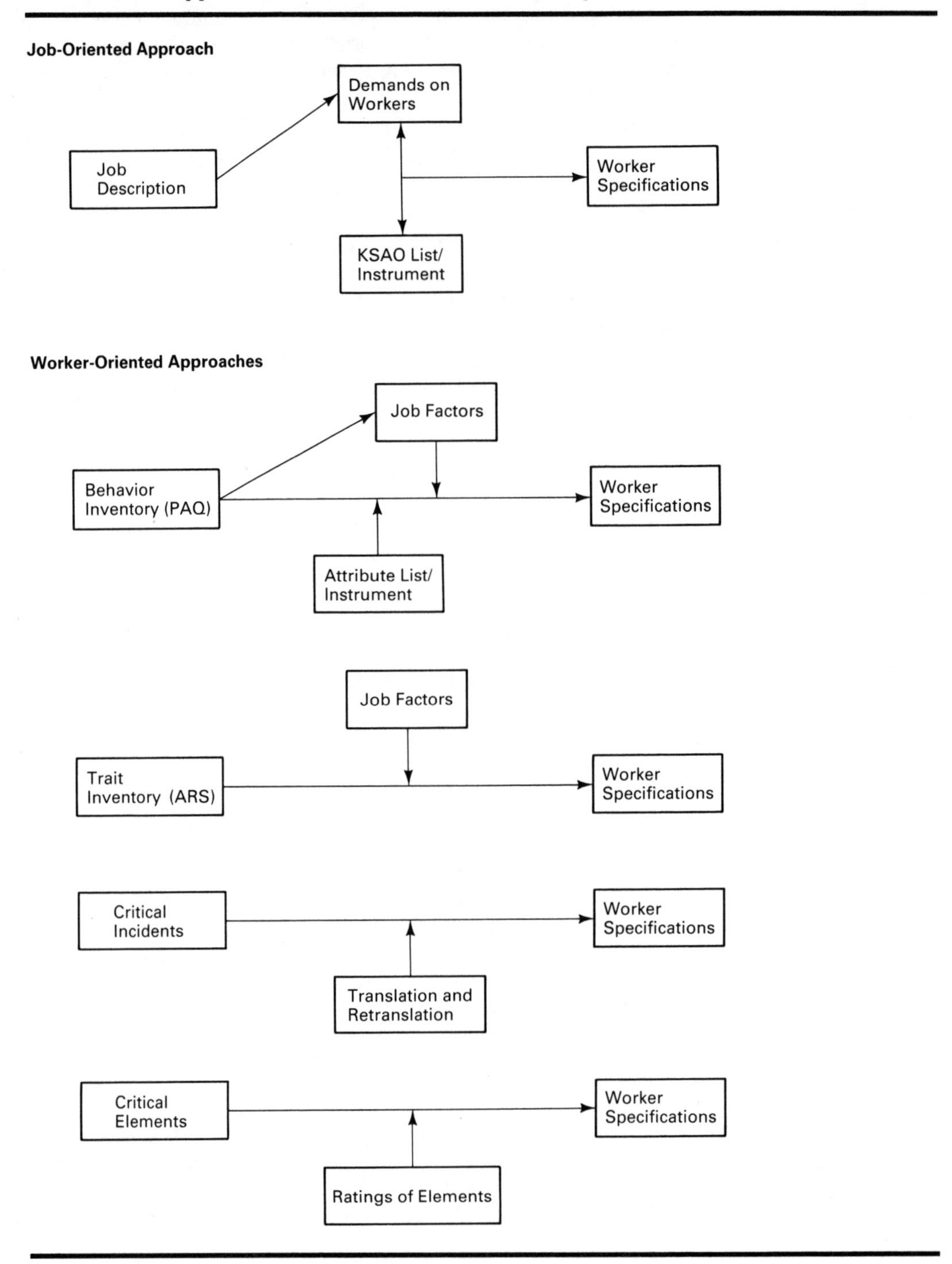

within this approach are many and revolve around whether they are behavior based or trait based. Job descriptions, if used at all, are brought in for verification or cross-checking. They are not the starting point of the analysis as in the job-oriented approach. The worker-oriented systems that are discussed in the paragraphs that follow are the Position Analysis Questionnaire, the Ability Requirements Scales, the critical incidents technique, and the job elements method.

5.3 Functional Job Analysis

Functional job analysis, (FJA) provides many valuable tools for deriving worker specifications. The primary FJA instruments that relate to worker specification issues are reproduced in Appendix J at the back of the book. The following discussion focuses on showing how those instruments are used in arriving at worker specifications.

DOL SYSTEM

This system contains specific provisions for systematically deriving worker specifications. To aid in the illustration of how the worker specification process works under this system, a completed specification is provided in Exhibit 5.7. The job in question is one that we have encountered before: dough mixer. (Descriptions of tasks involved in this job were shown in Exhibit 4.12 in Chapter 4; they are hence omitted in Exhibit 5.7.)

The DOL system is a job-oriented system. Worker specifications are derived directly from the job description. Three job factors are required for the derivation of specifications: job summary, tasks, and work performed ratings. In addition, the job analysis schedule has provisions for narrative descriptions of context factors (see U.S. Department of Labor, 1972, Ch. 7).

Six categories of human characteristics are recognized by the DOL system for the purposes of worker specification. These are training time, aptitudes, interests, temperaments, physical demands, and environmental conditions. Definitions of these characteristics, and explanations of the accompanying rating scales are as follows.

Training Time. This category refers to the amount of general educational development (GED) and specific vocational preparation (SVP) required for a worker to acquire the KSAOs necessary for average performance in a particular job.

GED Education of a general nature that does not have a recognized, specific occupational objective. GED contributes to the worker's reasoning development, ability to follow instructions, and acquisition of "tool" knowledges such as language and mathematical skills. The GED scale is reproduced in Appendix J-3. It consists of three factors: reasoning, mathematical, and language. Each of these is broken down

EXHIBIT 5.7 Specifications for the Job of Dough Mixer

Establishment Job Title: DOUGH MIXER
Industry Assignment: Bakery Products
SIC Code and Title: 2051 Bread and Other Bakery Products
DOT Code: 520–782

Job Summary

Operates mixing machine to mix ingredients for straight and sponge (yeast) doughs according to established formulas, directs other workers in fermentation of dough, and cuts dough into pieces with hand cutter.

Worker Trait Ratings (Specifications)

GED	1	(2)	3	4	5	6					
SVP	1	2	3	(4)	5	6	7	8	9		
Aptitudes	G3	V3	N3	S3	P3	Q4	K3	F3	M3	E4	C4
Temperaments	D	F	I	J	(M)	P	R	S	(T)	V	
Interests	(1a)	1b	2a	2b	3a	3b	4a	(4b)	5a	(5b)	
Physical demands		S	L	M	(H)	V	2	(3)	(4)	5	(6)

From U.S. Department of Labor, *Handbook for Analyzing Jobs* (Washington, D.C.: U.S. Government Printing Office, 1972), pp. 42–43.

into six levels. The GED score is assigned as a composite of the three factors. Note that the dough mixer job (Exhibit 5.7) received a GED score of 2.

SVP Competencies required for average performance in a specific job-worker situation. SVP excludes orientation training, but can encompass any of the following: vocational education, apprentice training, in-plant training, on-the-job training, and experience in other jobs. SVP is measured in training time that is broken down into nine levels. Level 1 is short demonstration (anything from a couple of hours up to 30 days); level 9 is over 10 years. The dough mixer job is given an SVP rating of 4, which is over 3 months up to and including 6 months (Exhibit 5.7).

Aptitudes. Refer to specific capacities and abilities required of a worker to perform or to learn to perform a task or duty adequately. The system recognizes 11 aptitudes; these are given in Appendix J-5. Note that aptitudes are scaled into five levels, where 1 equals the top 10 percent of the population and 5 is the lowest 10 percent.

The aptitude ratings of the dough mixer job are shown in Exhibit 5.7. The letters (G, V, N, etc.) identify the aptitudes described in Appendix J-5, and the numbers show the ratings according to the five levels. In general, the dough mixer job requires level 3 or medium degrees of aptitudes.

Temperaments. This characteristic refers to ability to adapt to different work situations and demands. In practice, however, descriptions of temperaments are portrayals of behavioral demands of the workplace. Ten such descriptions are given; they are reproduced in Appendix K-1.

The rating task in regard to temperaments consists of identifying the situation that is descriptive of the job in question. Thus, for the dough mixer, two temperament categories were found to be relevant: M = adaptability to making generalizations, evaluations, or decisions based on measurable or verifiable criteria; and T = adaptability to situations requiring the precise attainment of set limits, tolerances, or standards.

Interests. Refer to preferences for certain types of work activities or experiences, with accompanying rejection of contrary types of activities or experiences. The system provides for five pairs of interest factors so that a positive preference for one factor of a pair also implies rejection of the other factor of that pair (Appendix K-2). The interest factors that were found to be relevant to the dough mixer job in Exhibit 5.7 were 1a = a preference for activities dealing with things and objects; 4b = a preference for activities that are carried on in relation to processes, machines, and techniques; and 5b = a preference for activities resulting in tangible, productive satisfaction.

Physical Demands. This item serves as a means of expressing simultaneously both the physical demands of the job and the physical capacities a worker must have to perform the job. Six categories of physical demand factors are recognized in the system; these are shown in Appendix J-7, along with the accompanying rating scales. The ratings received by the dough mixer job on physical demands are given at the bottom in Exhibit 5.7.

The first factor (strength) deals with whether the work is sedentary, light, medium, heavy, or very heavy. The definitions of these categories and illustrations are given at the bottom of Appendix J-7. The bracket around H in the physical demands section of Exhibit 5.7 indicates that the dough mixer job falls into the ''heavy'' category, which is defined as follows: H (heavy)—lifting 100 lb maximum, with frequent lifting and/or carrying of objects weighing up to 50 lb.

The remaining five physical demand factors (2 to 6 in Appendix J-7) tap other aspects of physical and sensory activities. They are rated according to a frequency scale, also shown in Appendix J-7. For the dough mixer's job, items within factors 3, 4, and 6 were found to be present and important (bracketed ratings at bottom of Exhibit 5.7).

Environmental Conditions. In the DOL system, environmental conditions are linked with the study of physical demands. However, these two factors can be viewed separately, and we have treated them as such in this book. Commentary relating to the DOL environmental conditions scale was provided in the section on job context in Chapter 4. The DOL scale relating to this factor is reproduced in Appendix I-1.

Evaluation of DOL. We have attempted to explain in detail the contents and the mechanics of the DOL system as they relate to worker specification. Several reasons influenced this depth of coverage. To begin with, this is the most established system of job analysis. It has influenced job analysis practice at state and local levels of government. It is also comprehensive, simple to use, and expandable. The developers have anticipated most of the significant organizational needs for job information and have made provisions for addressing them. No other system, to our knowledge, can match the array of ideas, descriptions of job situations, and techniques that are outlined in this system. All the other systems in existence have used or adapted materials contained in this system. The details just provided are thus useful as a comparative framework for understanding the workings of the other systems reviewed next (Wilson, 1974).

No system is perfect, and the DOL system contains some limitations. An obvious limitation is the crudeness of some of its scales. Thus, the scales dealing with temperaments, interests, and physical demands can benefit by substitution of the letter symbols with numbers. Inclusion of physical demands and working conditions under worker traits gives rise to severe terminological confusion. In completing this portion of the schedule, it is difficult to separate descriptions of the physical and environmental demands from prescriptions relating to worker specifications.

Perhaps the most severe limitation of the DOL system's worker specification procedure lies in the realm of the rating activity. The system does require active participation of SMEs for the completion of this task. But it does not spell out specific rules relating to who should do the ratings, the desired number of SMEs, methods for tabulation of agreement among raters, and criteria for accepting the results. The absence of such rules locks the system into the observational method of data gathering, with all the attendant advantages and disadvantages of that method (see Chapter 2).

SIDNEY FINE'S FJA

Fine's system contains several aids for deriving worker specifications. Its major offerings in this realm are twofold: a set of GED scales and a classification of work relevant KSAOs.

GED Scales. The GED scales contained in Fine's system are very similar in content to the GED scales found in the DOL system. They are reproduced in Appendix J-4 after the DOL scales. Note that Fine's GED scales contain language that is closer to common experiences and everyday speech. They are somewhat more behavioral in description than the corresponding DOL scales.

An example of output that results from Fine's system was provided in Chapter 3, Exhibit 3.3. Additional details of relevance to worker specification activity are added to that illustration and given in Exhibit 5.8. Fine's GED scales are to be used task by task. The task in Exhibit 5.8 received a rating of 3 for reasoning development, 1 for mathematical development, and 4 for language development. Thus, in performing this task, the job incumbent can get by with low understanding of mathematics and a moderate level of reasoning ability, but he or she needs a fairly high level of language facility.

Skills. Fine's system also provides for identification of KSAOs other than GED factors. Human performance at work is conceived as involving three types of skills: adaptive, functional, and specific content.

Adaptive skills	These are the competencies that enable an individual to manage the demands for comformity and/or change in relation to the physi-

EXHIBIT 5.8 Job Analysis Results from Fine's FJA

Sample Task

Data	People	Things	Data	People	Things		Reas.	Math.	Lang.	
W.F.—Level			W.F.—Orientation			Instr.	G.E.D.			Task No.
3B	3A	1A	35%	60%	5%	3	3	1	4	W.E.6

GOAL:

OBJECTIVE:

TASK: Suggests/explains to client reasons for making favorable appearance, and specific areas in which he needs improvement to conform to local standards/expectations, in order that client makes job applications appropriately dressed and groomed.

Performance Standards	Training Content
Descriptive: • Information given client is complete, accurate, and clear. • Appropriate approach/manner/attitude.	Functional: • How to explain grooming standards to client applying for job. • How to persuade client to meet appropriate grooming and dress standards.
Numerical: • In less than *X*% of cases, prospective employers report inappropriate dress and grooming as a result of inaccurate, incomplete, or unclear information provided by worker. • Less than *X*% complaints of worker's manner.	Specific: • Knowledge of client's situation. • Knowledge of local grooming and dress standards.

From Sidney A. Fine, *Functional Job Analysis: A Desk Aid* (Kalamazoo, Mich.: W. E. Upjohn Institute, 1973), p. 20. Copyright © by Sidney A. Fine. Reprinted by permission.

cal, interpersonal, and organizational arrangements and conditions in which the job exists. Included are management of oneself in relation to authority; to impulse control; to moving toward, away from, or against others; to time (e.g., punctuality and self-pacing); to care of property; to dress (e.g., style and grooming). These skills, rooted in temperament, are in the family situation and among one's peers and reinforced in the school situation.

Functional skills — These are the competencies that enable an individual to relate to things, data, and people (orientation) in some combination according to personal preferences and to some degree of complexity appropriate to abilities (level). They include skills like tending or operating machines; comparing, compiling, or analyzing data; and exchanging information with or without consulting and supervising people. These skills are normally acquired in educational, training, and avocational pursuits and are reinforced in specific job situations.

Specific content skills — These are the competencies that enable an individual to perform a specific job according to the standards required to satisfy the market. These skills are normally acquired in an advanced technical training school or institute, by extensive on-the-job experience or

> on a specific job. They are as numerous as specific products, services, and employers who establish the standards and conditions under which those products and services are produced (Fine & Wiley, 1971, pp. 79–80).

Exhibit 5.8 shows the functional and specific content skills that go with the task that is described in it. Note that what Fine calls adaptive skills are very similar in conception to the personality, interest, and motivational factors grouped together in Exhibit 5.1. He postulates the following interrelations among the three sets of skills:

> In effect, the degree to which a worker can use his functional skills effectively on a job is dependent on the degree to which his adaptive skills enable him to accept and relate to the specific content skill requirements. (Fine & Wiley, 1971, p. 80)

Fine's system is a variation of functional job analysis. It thus carries with it the advantages and disadvantages of the parent approach (see, also, Olson et al., 1981).

5.4 Health Services Mobility Study

The Health Services Mobility Study (HSMS) procedures for worker specification are linked to its view of tasks that was reviewed in the previous chapter. The system offers 18 scales, 1 of which is designed to measure task frequency, 1 deals with levels of knowledge, and the remaining 16 deal with generic human skills. (Several of the HSMS scales are reproduced in various appendices at the back of the book.)

DEFINITIONS

The HSMS offers an interesting slant in the study of human attributes relevant to work. As a point of departure, the HSMS system draws a distinction between skills and knowledges:

> . . . a skill is a teachable, behavioral attribute that is displayed when an individual carries out a mental or physical activity in performing a task. We assume that the activity can be evaluated for the degree or amount of skill it requires. We also assume that skills can be learned incrementally. (Gilpatrick, 1977b, pp. 5–1—5–2; the page references in the following paragraphs are to this source)
>
> In the HSMS (knowledge) is used to mean detailed information, facts, concepts, and theories that are parts of specific disciplines or subject areas and information on how things function and/or how to use them. (p. 7–2)
>
> While skills and knowledge are both teachable, skills require practice if they are to be learned. Knowledge is learned primarily through didactic instructional means . . . Applying or using knowledge in a job task requires skills. (p. 5–2)

These definitions emphasize that a skill is an attribute that is displayed in task performance, while knowledge is information that is useful in task performance. The influence of these definitions is evident in the scaling format of the HSMS. Consider the HSMS decision-making scales shown in Appendix E. In the design of these scales, decision making is not considered as a basic human ability, but rather as a demand placed by the task on the performer. The starting point is the task, not a human trait or capability.

PROCEDURES AND OUTPUT

The HSMS contains an elaborate network of rules, guidelines, and steps for establishing levels of skills required in task performance. Skills are to be identified task by task using ready-made scales. The following are the general rules for scaling tasks for skills:

1. Each of the elements of the task, including all contingencies and instances of the task are considered as part of the task for scaling. (The reader should refer back to the HSMS task description in Chapter 4.)
2. The analyst must consider the necessary minimum condition that must be met before a task can be rated above zero on each scale, each of the scaling principles of each scale, and the increments along each scale.

EXHIBIT 5.9 A Completed HSMS Skill Scaling Sheet for a Task

Task Name Conducting radiographic barium study of upper GI tract, non-pediatric patient. Task Code No. 3

Institution ______ Analysts ______

(Values shown in parentheses are circled on the sheet.)

Scale	0	1	1.5	2	2.5	3	3.5	4	4.5	5	5.5	6	6.5	7	7.5	8	8.5	9
	Circle Appropriate Scale Value for Each Scale																	
1 Frequency	0	1		2		3		4				6		7		8		9
2 Locomotion	(0)		1.5							5				7				9
3 Object Manipulation	(0)		1.5				3.5			5					7.5			9
4 Guiding or Steering	(0)		1.5			3					5.5			7				9
5 Human Interaction	0	1				3				(5)				7				9
6 Leadership	0	(1)				3			4.5				6.5				8.5	
7 Language: Oral Use	0			2				4							(7.5)			9
Insert name(s) of language(s): English																		
8 Language: Reading Use	0			2						(5)				7				9
Insert name(s) of language(s): English																		
9 Language: Written use	0			2						(5)			6.5					9
Insert name(s) of language(s): English																		
10 Decision: Methods	0		1.5			(3)			4.5					7				9
11 Decision: Quality	0		1.5	2			3.5				5.5			(7)				9
12 GIS: Figural	0	1					3.5			5				(7)				9
13 GIS: Symbolic	(0)		1.5				3.5			5				7				9
14 GIS: Taxonomic	0			(2)							5.5			7				9
15 GIS: Implicative	0	1		2				4		(5)						8		9
16 Error: Financial	0	(1)						4				6			7.5			9
Insert error: — omitted from this example.																		
17 Error: Human	0	1		2		3					(5.5)			7		8		9
Insert error: — omitted from this example.																		

Check here if this is a master sheet . . . (X)

Circle the preentered scale value chosen for each scale.

From Eleanor Gilpatrick, *The Health Services Mobility Study Method of Task Analysis and Curriculum Design*, Research Report No. 11, Vol. 2 (New York: Hunter College, City University of New York, The Research Foundation, 1977), p. 6–16.

3. The task is scaled with the highest scale value required by any element or instance of the task for a given skill, assuming appropriate and acceptable standards for performance of the task (rather than common, current, or superior performance (Gilpatrick, 1977b, p. 6–5).

The scaling of the skill requirement of each task is to be attained according to sets of rules, procedures, and special problems pertinent to the task. These are far too numerous to be reviewed here. Exhibit 5.9 provides an example of a completed skill scaling sheet for a task. The scale values assigned to the task are circled in this illustration.

EVALUATION

The foundation for the HSMS specification activity is provided by systematically derived and extensive task descriptions. Skills (teachable, behavioral attributes) are to be derived directly from the demands of the tasks. The focus of the system is thus on identifying those attributes that are clearly demanded by the task. Even in the definition of skills, the concern is with identifying types and levels of behavioral accommodations required of the worker rather than on specifying abstract human traits. This feature enhances the chances of deriving specifications that meet the test of job-relatedness, which has emerged as an important equal employment opportunity concern.

A couple of limitations of the HSMS from a human resource management perspective can be noted. To begin, derivation of skill requirements under this system is tied to its procedures for describing tasks. Analysts who find the HSMS scales (given in appendices at back of the book) attractive thus need to make sure that they first define tasks according to the system's requirements. Also, about half of its skills are most relevant to health care work and hence may not have much appeal for analysts in industrial situations.

5.5 Position Analysis Questionnaire

The Position Analysis Questionnaire (PAQ) is a worker-oriented job analysis system. It contains a fund of information that is of direct relevance to worker specification. This consists of the PAQ itself, which is made up of 187 job elements or work-related human behaviors that are organized into six broad divisions; these were given, along with the accompanying rating scales, in Chapter 3 (Exhibits 3.8 and 3.9). The PAQ list of behaviors is intended to embrace the spectrum of human behaviors at work. In addition, the developers of the PAQ have assembled a list of 68 work-relevant human attributes that are matched against the PAQ elements. To appreciate what the PAQ package has to offer in worker specification activity, it is useful to review briefly the general approach and its mechanics. (In the discussion that follows, the term attribute is treated synonymously with knowledges, skills, abilities, and other human characteristics, or KSAOs.)

PAQ APPROACH TO SPECIFICATION

The PAQ is part of a comprehensive program of job analysis. The general procedure for establishing the human attribute requirements of jobs is described as follows by the authors of the PAQ:

1. The development of a reasonably objective job analysis method by which a given job can be characterized in terms of each of various job elements of a "worker-oriented" nature. (The PAQ represents the objective job analysis method or instrument.)
2. Identification of human "attributes" that are most relevant to personnel selection.
3. The rating, for each job element, of the degree to which each attribute is relevant to the element.
4. The computation of the mean or median of the ratings of each attribute (as relevant to each job element in the job analysis instrument) and the subsequent derivation of an attribute

profile for each job element (this consisting of the mean or median attribute ratings for all attributes).

5. The analysis of any given job with the job analysis instrument (in this case the PAQ).
6. The computation, for each job, of a composite job attribute profile based on some summation or ''building up'' of the attribute profiles of the job elements that are part of the job (Mecham & McCormick, 1969, p. 2; all the page references that are given in the following discussion are to this source).

In considering these steps, it is important to emphasize that the first four steps are part of the general approach for establishing attribute requirements of the elements in the PAQ. The PAQ elements, and the accompanying attributes, are then to be used for computing job attribute profiles for individual jobs or steps 5 and 6.

SELECTION OF ATTRIBUTES

In keeping with the general plan, the developers of the PAQ identified 68 attributes. These are not the attributes that go with any specific job. Rather, they are human attributes of a generic nature considered to be potentially relevant to performance in different kinds of work activities. The primary source of these attributes was the *Dictionary of Occupational Titles* (Vol. II, 1965). These 68 attributes were selected through a screening process that involved participation by 29 psychologists who judged a more tentative list for their discreetness, measurability, relevance to jobs, and acceptability of the definition used (p. 4).

Forty-one of the 68 attributes are of an aptitude nature; the remaining 27 consist of interest or temperament factors characterized by different types of job situations to which people must adjust at work. Examples of the PAQ attributes within these two groupings are the following:

Attributes of an Aptitude Nature	Attributes of an Interest or Temperament Nature
1. Verbal comprehension	42. Variety of duties
8. Intelligence	47. Dealing with people
11. Aesthetic judgment	51. Empathy
22. Olfactory acuity	58. Working alone
39. Explosive strength	60. Stage presence

RATING PROCEDURES

Establishment of the relevance of the selected attributes to the PAQ elements (steps 3 and 4 of the general procedure) was attained as follows. A number of raters were asked to rate the relevance of each of the 68 attributes to each of the 187 elements in the PAQ, one by one, according to the following scale:

0 = Attribute is of no relevance to job element
1 = Very limited or nominal relevance
2 = Limited relevance
3 = Moderate relevance
4 = Substantial or considerable relevance
5 = Extreme or extensive relevance

The raters who participated in the study were psychologists or graduate students in industrial psychology. Each attribute was rated by at least 8 and not more than 18 raters (p. 5).

OUTPUT

The attributes requirements of each of the 187 elements of the PAQ were tabulated in the form of means and medians. A portion of the results are given in Exhibit 5.10. For each of the PAQ elements (listed on the left side of the table) are presented the attribute scores relating to three attributes—verbal comprehension, auditory acuity, and manual dexterity. Given the structure of the relevance scale, higher scores signify greater relevance of the attribute to the element against which it is rated. Thus, high levels of verbal comprehension are required for jobs that involve written materials, decision making, and staff functions. This attribute received low scores for job elements that entail assembling, finger manipulation, and repetitive activities. Auditory acuity is of substantial relevance for negotiating, signaling, and staff functions. Manual dexterity received moderate relevance scores for handling devices, for dealing with powered land vehicles, and for doing precision work.

Establishment of the attribute requirements of the PAQ elements completed the first four of the six steps outlined. It shows the types of KSAOs that go with the elements within the PAQ. It is important to emphasize, however, that this is a generalized body of knowledge. To find out the attribute requirements of particular jobs (steps 5 and 6), the analyst needs to establish the relevance of the PAQ elements of the job. To illustrate, suppose that a job received high scores on decision making (PAQ element 36 in Exhibit 5.10) according to the rating procedures in the PAQ. The analyst then automatically has access to the corresponding scores relating to the 68 attributes, 3 of which are shown in Exhibit 5.10.

EVALUATION

As a tool in worker specification activity, the PAQ brings with it some positive features. The PAQ elements cover a wide range of work-relevant human behaviors. The rating scales contained in the instrument are extensive and systematically stated. The elements and the accompanying scales jointly provide a convenient way of isolating the behavioral demands of jobs. Experience with the use of the PAQ suggests that the instrument can be used in a wide range of jobs and work situations for estimating attribute requirements. (A review of research in support of this claim is provided by McCormick, 1979, pp. 259–263.)

Negative features of the PAQ are its length, complexity, and finite nature of its elements and attributes. The instrument is about 28 pages in length and requires fairly high levels of reading abilities on the part of the respondents. Its inventory of job elements and human attributes,

EXHIBIT 5.10 Ratings of Three Human Attributes for a Sample of PAQ Elements

	Attribute					
	(1) Verbal Comprehension		(21) Auditory Acuity		(28) Manual Dexterity	
PAQ Elements	Mean	Median	Mean	Median	Mean	Median
1. Written Materials	4.73	5.00	0.00	0.00	1.39	1.00
36. Decision Making	4.55	5.00	1.33	0.00	0.46	0.00
53. Handling Devices	0.27	0.00	0.56	0.00	3.85	4.00
72. Powered Land Vehicles	1.09	1.00	2.89	3.00	3.15	3.00
100. Negotiating	4.46	4.50	4.22	4.50	0.00	0.00
108. Signaling	2.55	3.00	4.11	4.50	2.77	3.00
133. Staff Functions	4.36	4.00	3.78	4.00	0.69	0.00
145. Physical Hazards	0.00	0.00	1.89	0.00	1.31	0.00
178. Precision	1.36	1.00	0.56	0.00	3.08	3.00
189. Job Structure	3.36	3.50	0.89	0.00	0.46	0.00

From R. C. Mecham and E. J. McCormick, *The Rated Attribute Requirements of Job Elements in the Position Analysis Questionnaire* (Lafayette, Ind.: Department of Psychological Sciences, Purdue University, 1969), p. 11.

although extensive in coverage, is fixed in content. It thus cannot be relied upon in all job situations (see Ash & Edgell, 1975; Arvey & Begalla, 1975; Taylor, 1978; Levine et al., 1983).

5.6 Ability Requirements Scales

Trait inventories represent another worker-oriented approach to worker specification (Exhibit 5.6). The starting point of this approach typically is a ready-made inventory of abilities, skills, or traits. The general procedure is for the SMEs to arrive at a job-relevant human characteristic by matching the items in the inventory against jobs factors.

Several trait inventories currently exist, varying greatly in terms of stage of development, scope, and applicability. The Ability Requirement Scales, discussed in the paragraphs that follow, is one of the most established and developed methods in this approach. Others that fall within this group are the Job Components Inventory, the Generic Skills Project of the Canadian Department of Manpower Administration, and Threshold Traits Analysis. (Source references for these inventories were given in Exhibit 3.4 in Chapter 3.)

The ARS resulted from a longstanding program of research involving the identification of perceptual-motor ability requirements in human task performance conducted by E. A. Fleishman and his associates. The general objective of this research was to identify the fewest independent ability categories that might be most useful and meaningful in describing performance in the widest variety of tasks (Fleishman & Quaintance, 1984, p. 162; the page references in the following paragraphs are to this source).

DEFINITIONS

The unit of analysis of the ARS are human abilities that are distinguished from skills as follows:

> An *ability* refers to a more general capacity of the individual related to performance in a variety of human tasks . . . [it] is a general trait of the individual that has been inferred from certain response consistencies. Both learning and genetic components underlie ability development.
>
> In contrast, a *skill* is defined as the level of proficiency on a specific task or group of tasks. The development of a given skill or proficiency on a given task is predicated in part on the possession of relevant basic abilities. (pp. 162–163)

As as tool in worker specification, the ARS approach provides a list of human abilities and a set of aids in estimating human ability requirements. The original system contained 37 abilities grouped roughly under four categories: mental abilities (e.g., verbal comprehension), physical abilities (e.g., stamina), psychomotor abilities (e.g., choice reaction time), and abilities having to do with the way incoming sensory material is perceived (e.g., spatial orientation). Appendix J-6 shows the current and expanded list of abilities and provides their definitions.

PROCEDURES AND OUTPUT

According to the ARS, worker specifications can be derived in one of two ways. The first, labeled the rating scale approach, makes use of rating scales that accompany each of the abilities. Exhibit 5.11 provides examples of two of the rating scales: static strength and verbal comprehension. The scales can have either 5 or 7 points, signifying degrees of the ability. The basic procedure consists of having SMEs rate ability requirement of the tasks involved in the job. Exhibit 5.12 shows the ability requirements results for two of the abilities: oral comprehension, which is very similar to verbal comprehension, and static strength. Thus, a high degree of oral comprehension is essential for tasks that require understanding a lecture on navigation in space. Conversely, low degrees of this ability are required in understanding a McDonald's hamburger commercial.

The second approach to using the ARS in worker specification consists of using flow diagrams

EXHIBIT 5.11 Ability Rating Scales for Two Abilities

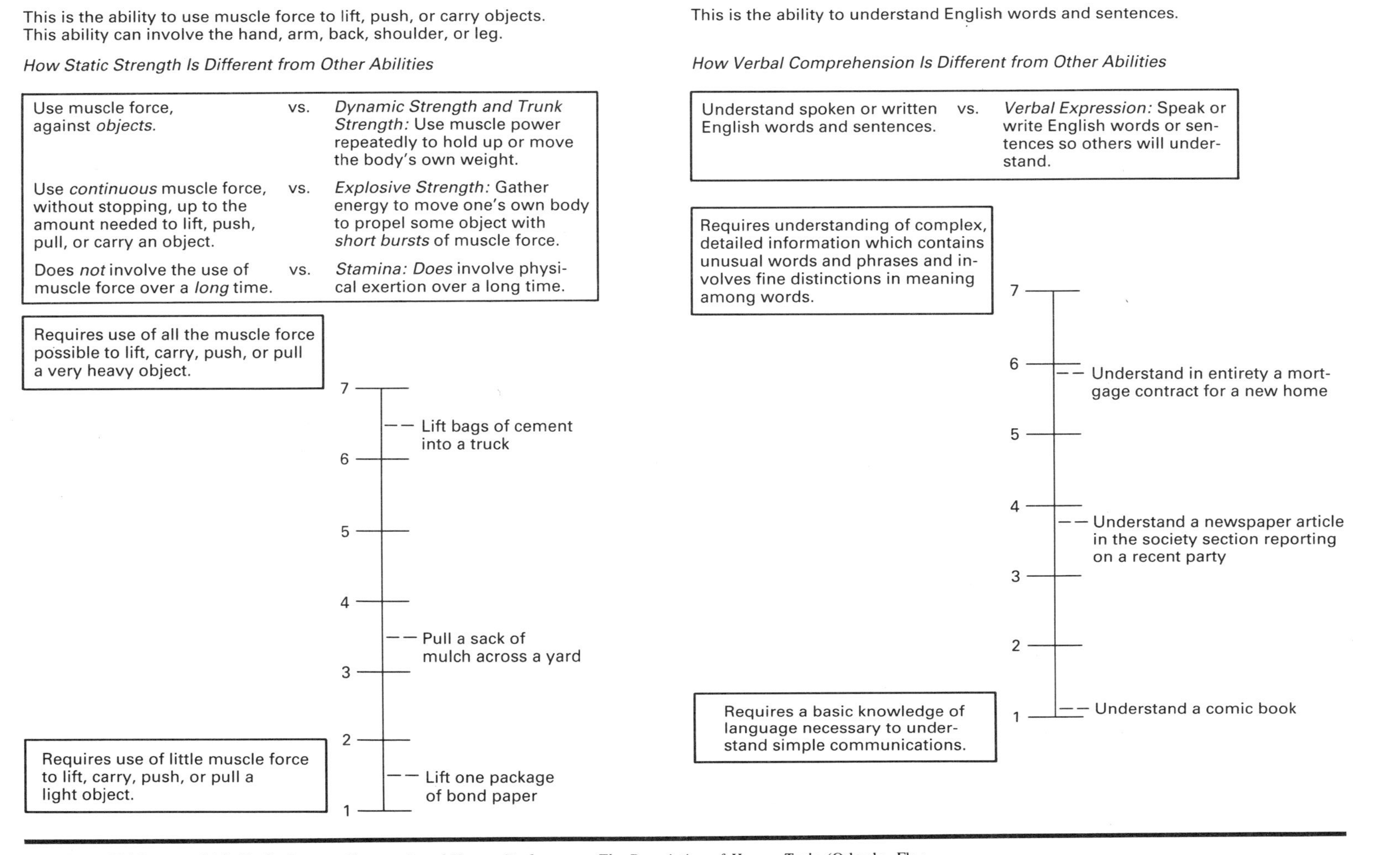

From E. A. Fleishman and M. K. Quaintance, *Taxonomies of Human Performance: The Description of Human Tasks* (Orlando, Fla.: Academic Press, 1984), pp. 319–320, as adapted from G. C. Theologus, T. Romashko, and E. A. Fleishman, *Development of a Taxonomy of Human Performance: A Feasibility Study of Ability Dimensions for Classifying Human Tasks*, American Institutes for Research Technical Report, *JASA Catalog of Selected Documents in Psychology*, 1973, 3, 25–26 (Ms. No. 321). Reprinted by permission.

EXHIBIT 5.12 Tasks Representing Different Ability Categories

Selected Ability-Task Items	Mean	Standard Deviation
1. *Oral Comprehension*		
Understand a lecture on navigating in space.	6.28	.75
Understand instructions for a sport.	3.48	1.09
Understand a McDonald's hamburger commercial.	1.17	.60
32. *Static Strength*		
Lift up the front end of a V.W.	6.15	1.26
Push open a stuck door.	3.30	1.10
Lift a dining room chair.	1.48	.70

From E. A. Fleishman and M. K. Quaintance, *Taxonomies of Human Performance: The Description of Human Tasks* (Orlando, Fla.: Academic Press, 1984), pp. 465, 470.

or decision trees. Exhibit 5.13 shows a portion of a flow diagram dealing with some perceptual abilities. This approach requires the SMEs to make a series of branching, binary decisions that result in assessing the presence or absence of an ability. The rating scales (Exhibit 5.11) are then used to assess the amount or degrees of the abilities required. The combined use of decision trees and scales enhances the validity of the results. Specifically, it has been found to reduce "false positives" or the tendency of SMEs, when allowed to rely soly on rating scales, to include abilities that should not be included (p. 331).

EVALUATION

The ARS system brings a couple of notable strengths to the worker specification process. The list of abilities developed by Fleishman and his associates is viewed by many as being the most comprehensive and up-to-date statement of human capabilities. It has much empirical support and is currently figuring prominently in research dealing with establishment of ability requirements of tasks. The scales and decision flow diagrams that accompany the list of abilities simplify the task of worker specification (see McCormick, 1979; Bemis et al., 1983).

The limits of ARS in worker specification are fairly visible. The list of abilities contained in the system (Appendix J-6), although extensive, is by no means complete. It specifically ignores a wide set of abilities that are relevant to managerial and other complex decision-making roles. The decision trees, exemplified in Exhibit 5.13, are difficult and time consuming to construct. They also might be inappropriate for describing dynamic job situations that involve simultaneous interactions with multiple job elements and interfaces. Imagine trying to construct one of these for managerial work!

The two worker-oriented systems (the PAQ and the ARS) rely on ready-made inventories as basis for deriving worker specifications. The PAQ is an inventory of generalized human behaviors at work, while the ARS contains a list of abilities. The systems that are described in the following two sections, which are also worker-oriented systems, approach the task in a markedly different manner. The starting point of these systems is the identification of critical job performance requirements expressed in behavioral or trait terms. These are then refined to yield KSAOs for the jobs in question.

5.7 Critical Incidents Technique

The critical incidents technique (CIT) provides an approach to developing worker specification from firsthand, behavioral data job by job. The starting point of this approach is the gathering of critical incidents, which are translated into behaviors and then into KSAOs.

EXHIBIT 5.13 Decision Flow Diagram Dealing with Some Perceptual Abilities

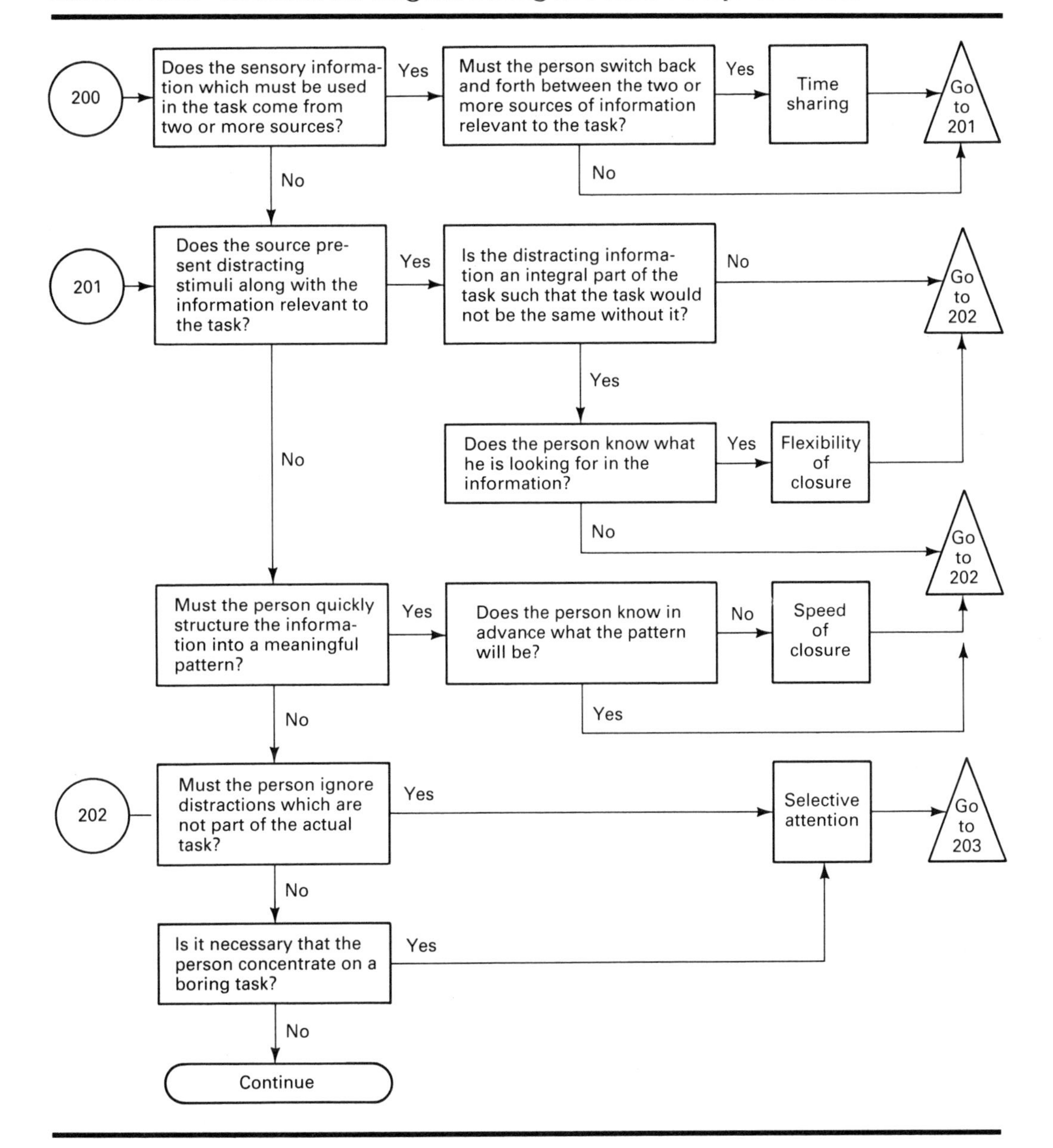

From E. A. Fleishman and M. K. Quaintance, *Taxonomies of Human Performance*: *The Description of Human Tasks* (Orlando, Fla.: Academic Press, 1984), p. 332, as adapted from S. M. Mallamad, J. M. Levine, and E. A. Fleishman, "Identifying Ability Requirements by Decision Flow Diagrams," *Human Factors*, 1980, 22 (1), 59–61. Copyright 1980, by the Human Factors Society, Inc., and reproduced by permission.

CRITICAL INCIDENTS DEFINED

John C. Flanagan, the original developer of the technique, defined a critical incident as follows:

> By an incident is meant any observable human activity that is sufficiently complete in itself to permit inferences and predictions to be made about the person performing the act. To be critical, an incident must occur in a situation where the purpose or intent of the act seems fairly clear to the observer and where its consequences are sufficiently definite to leave little doubt concerning its effects. (Flanagan, 1954, p. 27)

To be included in the analysis, both good and bad incidents are accumulated. Exhibit 5.14 gives examples of critical incidents that might occur in a couple of job situations.

PROCEDURES

The general procedures to be followed in developing and using critical incidents information as outlined by Flanagan are given in Exhibit 5.15. Their application in developing worker specifications consists of several stages. The first stage in the process is the development of the critical incidents. The sources of incidents could be supervisors, job incumbents, and other persons who are familiar with the job or have had opportunities to observe events surrounding the job. Incidents can be gathered through interviews or by observation. When data are gathered for job analysis purposes, it is common to assemble groups of SMEs. Each SME then recalls a story or anecdote and describes (1) what led up to the incident and the setting in which it occurred, (2) exactly what the employee did that was so effective or ineffective, (3) perceived consequences of the critical behavior, and (4) whether such consequences were actually within the control of the employee. It is quite common for such sessions to yield hundreds, and even thousands, of incidents (Dunnette, 1966, p. 79).

After the incidents are developed, they are then translated into behavioral categories or dimensions that are expressed in KSAO terms. The translation phase is an inherently qualitative undertaking, with the judgment of SMEs being an integral part of the translation. Recent refinements of the CIT call for inclusion of two groups of SMEs in the translation. The first group, which could include the job analyst, contributors of the incidents, or anybody else judged to be knowledgeable about the job, is asked to cluster the incidents into five to ten homogeneous categories or dimensions of behaviors that are implied in the incidents. When the CIT is used

EXHIBIT 5.14 Critical Incidents in Two Job Situations

Critical Incidents in Job of Accountant II

1. When a misunderstanding developed between data processing and accounting, the employee met with the data processing manager, explained the problem, and developed compromise solutions.
2. The employees located information requested by other departments and the federal government and responded to the requests in a prompt and friendly manner.
3. When a part of the job was to answer employee telephone calls regarding retirement withholding, the employee bluffed his way through the inquiries rather than seek assistance to learn the correct answers to the questions.*

Critical Incidents in Job of Salesman

1. A salesman received a complaint from a customer about the quality of a particular type of tape. He failed to look into the matter or write up a formal complaint. The defective tape was returned to the jobber and no credit was issued to the jobber or to the retailer involved. While the account was not lost, the customer was dissatisfied for a long time.
2. A large customer complained about our tape and decided to try out a competitor's tape. The complaint was justified and a substitution run was recommended. The salesman told the customer about this new run and said it would come in the next order. He did not tie this down with the jobber, however, and the jobber shipped more of the old run when the customer's order came through. As a result, the customer felt that the salesman could not be trusted and withdrew his account.
3. A salesman driving down the street saw a truck containing equipment for which company products might be used. He followed the truck to find the delivery point, made a call on this account, which was a new one, and obtained an order.†

* From F. Sistrunk and P. L. Smith, *Multimethodological Job Analysis for Criminal Justice Organizations* (Tampa: Center for Evaluation Research, University of South Florida, 1982), pp. 168–169.

† Reprinted, by permission of the publishers, from *Personnel*, September/October 1957, © 1957 American Management Association, New York. All rights reserved.

EXHIBIT 5.15 Critical Incidents Technique: Form and Procedure

Form for Use by an Interviewer in Collecting Effective Critical Incidents

"Think of the last time you saw one of your subordinates do something that was very helpful to your group in meeting their production schedule." (Pause till he indicates he has such an incident in mind.) "Did his action result in increase in production of as much as one percent for that day?—or some similar period?"

(If the answer is "no," say) "I wonder if you could think of the last time that someone did something that did have this much of an effect in increasing production." (When he indicates he has such a situation in mind, say) "What were the general circumstances leading up to this incident?" ______________________

"Tell me exactly what this person did that was so helpful at that time." ______________________

"Why was this so helpful in getting your group's job done?" ______________________

"When did this incident happen?" ______________________

"What was this person's job?" ______________________

"How long has he been on this job?" ______________________

"How old is he?" ______________________

The Five Procedural Steps of the Critical Incidents Technique

a. Determination of the general aim of the activity. This general aim should be a brief statement obtained from the authorities in the field which expresses in simple terms those objectives to which most people would agree.

b. Development of plans and specifications for collecting factual incidents regarding the activity. The instructions to the persons who are to report their observations need to be as specific as possible with respect to the standards to be used in evaluating and classifying the behavior observed.

c. Collection of the data. The incident may be reported in an interview or written up by the observer himself. In either case it is essential that the reporting be objective and include all relevant details.

d. Analysis of the data. The purpose of this analysis is to summarize and describe the data in an efficient manner so that it can be effectively used for various practical purposes. It is not usually possible to obtain as much objectivity in this step as in the preceding one.

e. Interpretation and reporting of the statement of the requirements of the activity. The possible biases and implications of decisions and procedures made in each of the four previous steps should be clearly reported. The research worker is responsible for pointing out not only the limitations but also the degree of credibility and the value of the final results obtained.

From J. C. Flanagan, "The Critical Incidents Technique," *Psychological Bulletin*, vol. 51 (1954), pp. 327–358.

to develop worker specifications, the dimensions could consist of significant interfaces (e.g., contact with the public), a knowledge, an ability, a skill, or a personal trait.

The second group of SMEs is then instructed to retranslate (or reallocate) the critical incidents. This group is provided with names and descriptions of the dimensions, but not the incidents that fall within each dimension. This step provides an index of the validity of the first translation. The criterion for keeping an item within a particular dimension is the extent of agreement between the results of the two groups. Typically, an incident is retained if some percentage (usually 50 percent to 80 percent) of the group assigns it to the same dimension as did the first group (based on Schwab et al., 1975; Landy et al., 1976; Mussio & Smith, 1973; Bouchard, 1972).

OUTPUT

The steps that follow the development of the dimensions depend on the purposes for which the CIT is being used. Most of the applications of the CIT have been in the development of performance appraisal scales, particularly Behaviorally Anchored Rating Scales (BARS). Exhibit 5.16 provides an example of an ability relevant to clerical work that was derived from a critical incidents exercise. The ability was inferred from the eight critical incidents listed in the illustration.

EVALUATION

The major strength of the CIT as a basis for developing worker specifications is that the incidents themselves reflect actual occurrences of on-the-job behavior. They thus present the realities underlying the determinants of effective and ineffective performance and provide a logical basis for inferring critical KSAOs.

EXHIBIT 5.16 An Ability Derived from a Critical Incidents Checklist

JOB: Clerk Typist I
DIMENSION: Ability to Work Accurately and Neatly

Critical Incidents:

1. Notices an item in a letter or report that didn't appear to be right, checks it, and corrects it.
2. Produces a manuscript with square margins on each side, making it look like a printed book.
3. Notices and corrects an incorrect address on a mailing roster to clients.
4. Uses a secretary's manual whenever in doubt about proper usage.
5. Misfiles charts, letters, etc., on a regular basis.
6. Types key information showing size, location, and other data in reversed order because of carelessness.
7. Continually fails to use the dictionary "when in doubt" of a word's spelling because is never in doubt.
8. Makes typing errors and crooked margins so flagrant as to necessitate the retyping of 600–800 pages.

From S. J. Mussio and M. K. Smith, *Content Validity: A Procedural Manual* (Minneapolis: Civil Service Commission, 1973), p. 82. Reprinted by permission.

The disadvantages of the CIT are fairly evident. To begin, there is a danger that essential employee behaviors may be excluded by the participants, particularly in instances where they are instructed to relate only extremes of job performance. Also, since the critical incidents are reports of past occurrences, they are subject to distortion. It takes a great deal of skill on the part of the analyst to sort out the factual from the impressionistic. Perhaps the most significant problem with the CIT is the subjectivity that is inherent in the translation exercises. For this reason, the retranslation step is a very essential part of the exercises. While it may not remove all subjectivity, it does provide a second opinion and a cross-check (Mussio & Smith, 1973).

5.8 Job Elements Method

The Job Elements Method (JEM) was developed by Ernest S. Primoff of the U.S. Office of Personnel Management. The general objective of this method was to develop tests that could be used in selection of employees for jobs in the federal government. Several steps in the method, however, relate to development of worker specifications; these are discussed in the paragraphs that follow.

JOB ELEMENTS DEFINED

A central concept in the JEM is the notion of job element, which is defined as follows:

A job element may be

A knowledge, such as knowledge of accounting principles
A skill, such as skill with woodworking tools
An ability, such as ability to manage a program
A willingness, such as willingness to do simple tasks repetitively
An interest, such as interest in learning new techniques
A personal characteristic, such as reliability or dependability (Primoff, 1975, p. 2)

A job element could thus consist of just about any human characteristic that is relevant to job performance. Primoff's original formulation of the method contained a standard set of job elements that were designed for use with trades and industrial jobs. The method was later modified to serve as a procedure for developing job elements for any job (Primoff, 1975).

DEVELOPMENT OF JOB ELEMENTS

After the job is selected, job elements are contributed by supervisors, job incumbents, personnel specialists, and other SMEs. The following considerations are used in selecting SMEs: knowledge of the requirements of the job, knowledge of the characteristics of both new and experienced employees, freedom from bias (such as a preconceived opinion that the job is done better by men than by women), willingness to consider many aspects of the job and many ways to measure potential productivity, and willingness to emphasize abilities and skills rather than the credentials evidencing those abilities and skills (Primoff et al., 1982, p. 9).

The persons selected as SMEs are organized into a panel that convenes for three or four sessions. The analyst briefs the panel members on the purposes of the meetings and the basic procedures of the JEM. The following points relating to element development are routinely covered:

- Panel members are expected to suggest elements that are important to job success, so that applicants may be selected on the basis of their ability rather than how long they worked or where they went to school.
- Each member of the panel rates each of the accumulated suggestions with respect to its usefulness in choosing successful employees.
- Applicants will be evaluated on how well they meet the elements.
- If tests are used in selection, they will be based on the elements.

The following directions are to be read by the analyst to the panel members before they offer their suggestions:

> We would like you to list the abilities, knowledges, skills, and personal characteristics that are necessary for the job of ______________.
>
> What ability must an employee have?
> What makes an employee superior?
> In what areas have you had trouble when employees are weak?
>
> I don't want to influence you, so I'll give you an example for a different job. Suppose we wanted to rate a grocery cashier. We might consider accuracy, knowledge of stock, ability to be pleasant, and reliability. Each of these is an element.
> Now, I would like you to suggest elements for the job of ______________.

The elements suggested by the panel are written on a flipchart or chalkboard and are numbered consecutively. During this phase, discussion of the elements is discouraged. Pauses are to be used by the analyst to elicit additional elements by asking probing questions. After the panel has listed all the elements that it apparently can, attention is directed toward the development of subelements. These are the particular items that can be inserted into tests or checklists for personnel decisions. The following are examples of subelements of the element accuracy in the grocery store job:

> Grocery cashier accuracy:
>
> Accuracy in figuring cost of one item, when the price is 3 for 59 cents.
> Accuracy in pressing key on the cash register.
> Accuracy in making change.

The list of subelements is expanded element by element through additional probing questions and by getting the panel to consider possible differences in grade levels. If the list of elements generated by the panel is felt by the analyst to be incomplete, lists of elements identified in prior studies are shown to them for stimulating additional ideas. After the elements and subelements are described, the panel moves to rate them according to a standardized procedure (Primoff, 1975, pp. 7–11; page references in the following paragraphs are to this source).

RATING OF ELEMENTS

The basic instrument for rating the elements and subelements is the Job Element Blank, a copy of which is reproduced in Exhibit 5.17. The elements are rated in terms of four categories that pertain to job success, with the raters indicating the degree of relationship between elements and job success in a single step. These four categories are

> Barely acceptable—What relative proportion of even barely acceptable workers is good in the element?
>
> Superior—How important is the element in picking out the superior worker?
>
> Trouble—How much trouble is likely if the element is ignored when choosing among applicants?
>
> Practical—Is the element practical? To what extent can we fill our openings if we demand it? (p. 3)

As shown in Exhibit 5.17, each of the categories is scored according to a three-point scale that can be translated for numerical scoring as follows: + = 2, $\surd$ = 1, and 0 = 0.

OUTPUT

Results of the ratings for the foregoing categories are analyzed to determine those elements, and the subelements that define them, that have the maximum likelihood of identifying among applicants those who will be superior for the particular job. The analysis is done according to a formula that emphasizes the difference between barely acceptable and superior ability and elements with a high total in the analysis have a wide spread in ability. The analysis can be done through a computer using a specially prepared FORTRAN program or by using a hand calculator. Exhibit 5.18 shows the results of a tabulation of values for KSAOs used in developing a Police Office Examination.

The following are some of the interpretations that can be made of the results. Note that all the values are calculated on the basis of formulas derived from empirical research and that interpretations are made on the basis of transmuted values that allow for standardized comparisons.

- A high Barely Acceptable value indicates that most barely acceptable workers are satisfactory in the element.
- A high Superior value indicates that the element is important in selecting superior employees.
- A high Trouble Likely value indicates that the element is a consideration, especially at the lower end of ability; applicants weak in the element may be very weak employees.
- The purpose of the Item Index is to find elements that will select superior workers. Item Index values indicate the extent to which a tentative subelement is a useful factor within an element. If an item is not an element, but has a satisfactory Item Index, it may be used as content for any examining instrument.
- The Total Value indicates whether the item is broad and is an element, or is relatively narrow and is a subelement. High Total Values are considered to be major elements. They are too broad to allow applicants to describe their abilities with precision, and therefore applicants are asked to give evidences of their ability in various subelements.
- If an element or subelement should rate high in Superior and Trouble Likely, but low in Practical and Barely Acceptable, then it might be a valuable subject for an on-the-job training program. Such elements can also be used later in performance evaluation to recognize achievements when the employee's abilities are developed through training or on-the-job experience.

EXHIBIT 5.17 Job Element Blank

Page No. __ __ (col. 1 2)

Job:
Grade:

Rater Name and Grade:
Title and Location:

Rater No. __ __ __ (col. 3 4 5

Job No. __ __ __ 6 7 8)

Date:

Element No. (Do not punch)	Barely acceptable workers (B) + all have √ some have 0 almost none have	To pick out superior workers (S) + very important √ valuable 0 does not differentiate	Trouble likely if not considered (T) + much trouble √ some trouble 0 safe to ignore	Practical. Demanding this element, we can fill (P) + all openings √ some openings 0 also no openings	Columns	S × P	T	Item Index (IT) SP + T	Total Value (TV) IT + S − B − P	P' (+ = 0 √ = 1 0 = 2)	SP'	Training Value (TR) S + T + SP' − B
						(These columns for use in hand calculation of values)						
					9–12							
					13–16							
					17–20							
					21–24							
					25–28							
					29–32							
					33–36							
					37–40							
					41–44							
					45–48							
					49–52							
					53–56							
					57–60							
					61–64							
					65–68							
					69–72							
					73–76							
					77–80							

Note: For all categories except P', + counts 2, √ counts 1, 0 counts 0. For category P', + counts 0, √ counts 1, 0 counts 2.

From Ernest S. Primoff, *How to Prepare and Conduct Job Element Examinations* (Washington, D.C.: U.S. Civil Service Commission, Personnel Research and Development Center, U.S. Government Printing Office, 1975), p. 12.

EXHIBIT 5.18 Ratings of Police Officer KSAOs According to the Job Element Method

Element	B	S	T	P	TV	IT	TR
Have good physical coordination (*S*)	60	63	79	92	53	65	46
Have no major physical incapacities (*RS*)	81	44	96	94	23	59	33
Ability to engage in weaponless physical contact (*S*)	68	68	80	87	55	66	49
No fear of firearms (*S*)	73	49	81	90	27	56	33
Ability to compare signatures	39	58	27	50	29	29	50
Ability to recover from glare of oncoming lights (*S*)	74	43	71	89	15	50	25
Have sufficient height to see over roofs of cars (*SC*)	92	30	71	95	14	43	6
Ability to work outdoors in bad weather for long periods (*S*)	72	53	67	92	26	54	29
No unusual vocal characteristics (lisp, high-pitched)	66	37	62	94	4	44	19
Ability to change car tire (*SC*)	94	23	57	95	32	33	4
Ability to function in tear gas	50	52	51	61	31	41	44
Ability to read and understand memoranda (*S*)	70	62	71	88	42	61	37
Ability to determine reasonable grounds for arrest (*TS*)	60	89	48	44	56	42	88
Ability to express oneself verbally (*S*)	63	81	82	93	79	77	56
Ability to understand statistical data	44	55	37	62	28	36	43
Ability to recall facts (*S*)	58	91	75	85	89	77	68
Ability to enforce laws (*S*)	71	81	81	79	71	70	61
Ability to administer first aid	66	58	49	68	28	44	37
Have empathy (*S*)	44	79	60	82	72	64	60
Have self-reliance (*S*)	51	89	76	91	93	80	65
Ability to function while in physical danger (*E*)	58	94	90	86	101	84	76
Ability to accept discipline (*S*)	46	84	86	92	93	80	68
Have honesty (*RS*)	76	85	98	95	86	86	58
Possess good judgment (*E*)	46	96	86	93	111	88	75
Have leadership ability (*TS*), (*S*)	25	92	53	71	90	62	86
Have good moral character (*S*)	65	75	89	95	74	78	54

Note: Part of a tabulation of values in a police officer examination, marked to show elements (*E*), subelements (*S*), rankable screenouts (*RS*), training subelements (*TS*) and screenouts (*SC*). Relevant values are underscored.

From Ernest S. Primoff, *How to Prepare and Conduct Job Element Examinations* (Washington, D.C.: U.S. Civil Service Commission, Personnel Research and Development Center, U.S. Government Printing Office, 1975), p. 24.

- Screenouts are subelements that specify a detailed requirement that applicants must possess to be eligible (see Exhibit 5.18 for examples of Screenouts). There are two types of Screenouts: true screenouts—applicants with valid driver's license are eligible, those without such licenses are ineligible; and rankable screenouts—subelements for which lack of a certain minimum rating will screen out applicants, but higher ratings will result in additional credit. Thus, typists must have a specified amount of Ability to Type, but superior applicants will be given credit for greater skill.
- Training Value of an element or subelement indicates the extent to which it relates to superior work but is not practical to expect. A high Training Value implies that the agency will have to give on-the-job training. Elements or subelements may be considered for inclusion in a training program in the order of their Training Values.

EVALUATION

A major strength of the JEM is clarity of procedures. The details provided merely skim the surface of what is available in terms of rules, formulas, and standardized values for transmuting results. The element ratings are linked systematically to a testing program that emphasizes past achievements rather than credentials and experience. More is said about the JEM's testing program in the next chapter.

The most significant flaw, and perhaps the Achilles heel, of the JEM is its sole reliance on SME opinions in generating elements. The system has no provisions whatsoever for job descriptions. In fact, an implicit rule of this system is that the SMEs are to focus on superior and minimally acceptable *employees* that they have known in the past rather than on tasks and other job factors. This rule assumes that the SMEs agree on the tasks that the future employee is to perform, and that they are willing and able to base their specifications on their knowledge of the tasks.

This feature has gotten the JEM in trouble on the equal employment opportunity front. Specifically, the system has been found to be deficient on the job-relatedness principle. Thus, in *United States* v. *State of New York* (1978), a case in which the JEM was used in the development of the New York State Police trooper examination, the Court declared that the "sole use of the job element method of job analysis and test development for other than blue-collar jobs does not comport with generally accepted standards of the psychological profession." The decision found that use of the JEM was susceptible to bias because it failed to establish sufficient linkage between observable work behaviors (job tasks) and other characteristics identified as important for job success. Primary reliance on the judgment of incumbent personnel contributed to the possibility of exclusionary selection procedures (Bemis et al., 1983, pp. 132–138).

In response to these developments, Primoff has drafted a supplement that combines the JEM with techniques from FJA and CIT. The supplement assures a complete description of the work behaviors of the job and provides operational definitions of the knowledges, skills, and abilities, which may be used either to develop a new examination or to document an existing one (Primoff et al., 1982, p. 1).

5.9 Worker Specifications and the Law

Worker specifications are on the forefront of the current debates on equal employment opportunity. This is because the central thrust of worker specification activity is on determining the types of people that the organization plans to recruit and to maintain in its labor force. And this is a subject in which the law has expressed a special interest in recent years. In fact, so pervasive is the interest in this subject that the bulk of the legal materials that have accumulated in the EEO arena deals in some way with industrial practices relating to matching jobs and people (Bernardin & Cascio, 1984).

Before proceeding further with this review, it is pertinent to remind the reader of the distinction made earlier between specifications and tests. Our focus here is on specifications; legal issues pertinent to the translation of specifications into tests are implied in some of the points raised in the paragraphs that follow. However, they are dealt with in greater detail in the next chapter.

The legal concerns involved in worker specification are many. The pivotal concern, however, is with the potential that organizations have for using specifications for exercising biases and prejudices in hiring, promotion, and other job-worker matching activities. Thus, the congressional hearings that preceded the passage of the Civil Rights Act of 1964 revealed widespread patterns of institutional discrimination against blacks, women, and other minorities. Since then, many horror stories have been uncovered and reported about persistence of discrimination in just about all walks of life (see Gregory and Katz, 1979, pp. 546–582; Feldacker, 1983, pp. 395–443).

Keeping in mind that the potential for unfair discrimination is the central legal concern, we can now outline the legal developments that affect worker specification activity.

· Although hiring decisions have been the focal points of the debates, the coverage of the law now extends to just about all activities dealing with matching jobs and people. The scrutiny of the law has extended to performance appraisal, compensation, training, and human resource planning (Ledvinka, 1982).

· The pivotal legal decision in this arena was rendered in the *Griggs* v. *Duke Power Company* case (1971). The phrases used by Chief Justice Burger in expressing the majority opinion have had a great impact on thinking on this subject. We reproduce here the issues faced by the Court in this case and the interpretations of some of the provisions of Title VII of the Civil Rights of 1964.

> We granted the writ in this case to resolve the question whether an employer is prohibited by the Civil Rights Act of 1964, Title VII, from requiring a high school education or passing of a standardized general intelligence test as a condition of employment in or transfer to jobs when (a) neither standard is shown to be significantly related to successful job performance, (b) both requirements operate to disqualify Negroes at a substantially higher rate than white applicants, and (c) the jobs in question formerly had been filled only by white employees as part of a longstanding practice of giving preference to whites.
>
> Congress provided, in Title VII of the Civil Rights Act of 1964, for class actions for enforcement of provisions of the Act. . . . The objective of Congress in the enactment of Title VII is plain from the language of the statute. It was to achieve equality of employment opportunities and remove barriers that have operated in the past to favor an identifiable group of white employees over other employees. Under the Act, practices, procedures, or tests neutral on their face, and even neutral in terms of intent, cannot be maintained if they operate to ''freeze'' the status quo of prior discriminatory employment practices.
>
> Congress did not intend by Title VII, however, to guarantee a job to every person regardless of qualifications. . . . What is required by Congress is the removal of artificial, arbitrary, and unnecessary barriers to employment when the barriers operate invidiously to discriminate on the basis of racial or other impermissible classification.
>
> The Act proscribes not only overt discrimination but also practices that are fair in form, but discriminatory in operation. The touchstone is business necessity. If an employment practice which operates to exclude Negroes cannot be shown to be related to job performance, the practice is prohibited. . . . good intent or absence of discriminatory intent does not redeem employment procedures or testing mechanisms that operate as ''built-in headwinds'' for minority groups and are unrelated to measuring job capability. . . . Congress directed the thrust of the Act to the *consequences* of employment practices, not simply the motivation. More than that, Congress has placed on the employer the burden of showing that any given requirement must have a manifest relationship to the employer in question.
>
> The facts of this case demonstrate the inadequacy of broad and general testing devices as well as the infirmity of using diplomas or degrees as fixed measures of capability. History is filled with examples of men and women who rendered highly effective performance without the conventional badges of accomplishment in terms of certificates, diplomas, or degrees. Diplomas and tests are useful servants, but Congress has mandated the commonsense proposition that they are not to become masters of reality.
>
> Congress has not commanded that the less qualified be preferred over the better qualified simply because of minority origins. Far from disparaging job qualifications as such, Congress has made such qualifications the controlling factor, so that race, religion, nationality, and sex become irrelevant. What Congress has commanded is that any tests used must measure the person for the job and not the person in the abstract. (Adapted from Twomey, 1986, pp. 7–11; Commerce Clearing House, 1983, p. 25, 171)

Most of the legal issues encountered in choosing KSAOs, and the posture of the Court relating to them, are implied in the foregoing excerpt. Many other cases and developments have taken place since the *Griggs* case was decided. Using the preceding opinion as basis, we highlight some of these developments.

- Discrimination is not outlawed in itself. In fact, there is a healthy recognition of the fact that organizations both need to, and are entitled to, have preferences in regard to the qualifications of their labor forces.
- While the employer's right to have preferences in regard to employee characteristics is recognized, this is no longer viewed as an absolute right. The employer may not specify any characteristic that it chooses. The following characteristics are protected under various laws: race, color, sex, national origin, age, and handicaps. This means these characteristics may not be used as basis for personnel decisions without some justification stemming from business necessity.

EXHIBIT 5.19 Analysis of Legal Decisions Relating to Use of Educational Achievement as a Selection Requirement

Independent Variable	Defendant Won[a]	Plaintiff Won[a]	Total[b]
Educational Level			
10th grade	0	100	1
H.S. Diploma	27	73	55
Apprenticeship	0	100	1
Some college	25	75	4
Bachelor's	47	53	15
Master's	100	0	4
Ph.D.	100	0	3
Legal Authority			
Title VII	33	67	68
ADEA	0	0	0
Civil Rights—1866	50	50	6
Amendment 5	100	0	2
Amendment 14	57	43	7
Adverse Impact			
4/5 rule	13	87	31[c]
Potential applicant flow	15	85	39
Labor market	19	81	21
Internal comparisons	8	92	26
Disparate treatment	67	33	6
None	100	0	18
Adjudication Strategies			
Prove A.I., burden shifts	17	83	58[d]
No A.I., burden shifts	100	0	9
Burden shifts	0	0	0
A.I. only investigated	79	21	14
Defense Strategies			
Assert validity	60	40	19
Business necessity	53	47	15
Quality of work force	20	80	5
Affirmative action	60	40	5
Content validity	50	50	4
Criterion-related validity	60	40	5
None	0	100	30
Total	36	64	83

[a] Numbers are percentages.
[b] Numbers indicate number of cases.
[c] More than 83 cases because most plaintiffs used multiple methods to prove adverse impact.
[d] Less than 83 because adjudication strategy was not specified in 2 cases.

From R. Merritt-Haston and K. N. Wexley, "Educational Requirements: Legality and Validity," *Personnel Psychology*, vol. 36 (1983), p. 748.

· Employer requirements relating to human characteristics need to be linked with demands stemming from objective, observable job factors. Practically, this means that the KSAOs demanded of employees must stem from the needs of the job and not from value preferences of the employer. Abstract traits such as dependability, cooperation, and industry thus have no place in worker specifications (Cascio & Bernardin, 1981).

· Educational requirements (e.g., high school diploma, college degree), a traditional favorite of the employers, come within the jurisdictional realm of Title VII as well as the *Uniform Guidelines*. The rationale behind the use of educational requirements as a criterion for personnel decision making is that level of education is indicative of aptitude and ability, and hence predictive of success in learning a new job. Use of educational achievement as a criterion in personnel decision is permissible. However, employer success in defending this criterion hinge on a number of factors. Exhibit 5.19 provides a summary of outcomes of 61 cases in which educational requirements were challenged. All these cases occurred between 1969 to 1982. The conclusions stated by the researchers about these findings were as follows:

The defendant (employer) is *least* likely to win if the following conditions exist:

The educational requirement in question involves some college or less.
The job is entry level.
The complaint is filed under Title VII.
Adverse impact is established.
The defendant can only claim it wanted to improve the quality of its work force.
The defendant has no defense at all.

In contrast, the defendants are *most* likely to win when

A Master's or Ph.D. requirement is being challenged.
A highly technical job, one that involves risk to safety of the public, or one that requires advanced knowledge, is involved.
The complaint is filed under Amendment Five or Fourteen.
Adverse impact cannot be established.
A disparate treatment complaint is filed.
A defense can be offered that involves assertion of validity, evidence of criterion-related validity, or an effective affirmative action program (Merritt-Haston & Wexley, 1983, pp. 751).

· Employers need to be prepared to demonstrate business necessity in the choice of KSAOs. Two principles guide deliberations related to demonstration of business necessity: bona fide occupational qualifications (BFOQ) and job-relatedness.

The BFOQ principle is contained in Section 703(e) of the Civil Rights Act and states that religion, sex, or national origin may be used as basis for personnel decision making only in those instances when they serve as qualifications that are reasonably necessary for the normal operations of the business or for the propagation of a particular religion. In deciding the BFOQ status of a characteristic, the employer needs to go considerably beyond expressions of preferences or the showing of a convenience. Potential employees are entitled to challenge employer preferences in regard to these characteristics. In determining whether an employer has acted illegally, the shifting burdens are as follows. The employee has the initial burden of proving a prima facie case under criteria developed in the *McDonnell Douglas* case. These are (1) that the person belonged to a protected group under Title VII, (2) that the person applied for and was qualified for a job for which the employer was seeking applicants, (3) that despite being qualified, the person was rejected, and (4) that after the person was rejected, the position remained open and the employer continued to seek applicants from others with the rejected applicants qualifications. If the employee is able to establish a prima facie case, the employer then has the burden of setting forth a nondiscriminatory reason for the rejection. In doing so, the employer does not have to prove that it acted for a nondiscriminatory reason; the requirement merely is that the employer articulate, through the introduction of evidence, the reasons for the plaintiff's rejection. If the employer sets forth a nondiscriminatory reason, the burden once again shifts to the employee to prove that the reason given is a pretext for unlawful discrimination (Feldacker, 1983, pp. 395–402; the summary of the *McDonnell Douglas* principles are from this source).

The job-relatedness principle resulted directly from the *Griggs* v. *Duke Power Company* case. It deals with disparate impact discrimination. In such cases, the employer is not engaged in discrimination that is overt, intentional, or the result of consciously prejudiced actions. Rather, it results from personnel practices that bring about unequal consequences for people of different races, color, religion, sex, or national origin. Examples of such discrimination are a screening procedure that excludes a greater proportion of women or minorities than white males, a job evaluation system that results in higher pay for men, and a promotion system that favors a particular group. The *Griggs* case established such consequences to be a form of illegal discrimination (see Ledvinka, 1982).

Job-relatedness is a defense against disparate impact discrimination. This principle is activated only in the presence of *adverse impact.* There is thus no general requirement for personnel practices continuously to meet tests of business necessity, validity, or fairness. The shifting burden of proof in impact discrimination proceedings is as follows. The plaintiff has the initial burden of proving that a practice or procedure has disparate impact. This can be done by showing that the protected group constitutes a significantly smaller percentage of the company's work force than the general population or through the use of the 4/5 rule developed by the *Uniform Guidelines.* If there is disparate impact, the burden shifts to the employer. The employer has two options: eliminate the unequal impact or present evidence that the procedure is valid. The first option is met through the adoption of affirmative action programs. Employers who choose to defend their practices are required by the EEOC *Uniform Guidelines* to show that they are valid according to the validation procedures spelled out in the *Uniform Guidelines.*

Even if the employer proves the challenged procedure to be job related, the plaintiff can still prevail by demonstrating the existence of alternative methods that can satisfy the employer's legitimate business needs without the undesirable adverse consequences on the protected group. The Supreme Court's opinion expressed in the *Griggs* case implies that proof of an alternative method can be taken to indicate that the employer's purported business reason was a pretext for unlawful discrimination (Feldacker, 1983, p. 404).

The law of employer-employee relations is a constantly changing and expanding body of law. The developments noted, however, appear to be of an enduring nature. Collectively, they call for objectivity in the derivation of worker specifications. The following section presents some ways in which this requirement can be met.

5.10 Suggestions Relating to Worker Specifications

The preceding sections reviewed the *what, why,* and *how* of worker specifications and presented the legal requirements and obligations that go with this activity. This final section identifies some issues of managerial concern and offers some suggestions for assuring that the specifications that are derived contribute toward sound human resource management.

WRITING WORKER SPECIFICATIONS

A worker specification spells out the human characteristics that are needed for effective job performance. Considerable choice is available in regard to scope of factors covered, level of details provided, and form of the specification. The following are some suggestions relating to composing worker specifications. (This discussion draws heavily on specification guidelines provided in Bemis et al., 1983, pp. 77–88.)

Basic versus Special Competencies. In composing the worker specification, it is useful to distinguish between basic competencies and special competencies. A basic competency refers to the KSAOs that are needed to perform the job adequately or minimally. A special competency, on the other hand, refers to the KSAOs that are needed to perform the job in a superior manner. Exhibit 5.20 gives examples that illustrate the difference between these two types of competencies.

Writing Style. The manner in which the competency is described will have a bearing on its understandability and usefulness. The following are some suggestions for writing competencies:

- Begin the sentence with the competency, that is,

  Skill in . . .
  Ability to . . .
  Knowledge of . . .

EXHIBIT 5.20 Basic and Special Competencies: Clerk Typist/Receptionist

Duties/Tasks	Competencies	Tasks That Require This Competency
I. Typing	BASIC COMPETENCIES	
1. Types letters, memos, and reports	1. Knowledge of typing format.	1, 2, 3
2. Types/transcribes letters, memos, and reports	2. Ability to type final copy from handwritten material.	1, 3
3. Types forms and form letters	3. Eye-hand dexterity to operate electric typewriter.	1, 2, 3
4. Proofreads and corrects	4. Ability to type forms.	3
II. Answering telephone/greeting visitors 5. Answers telephone	5. Eye-hand-foot coordination to simultaneously operate typewriter and transcribing equipment.	2
6. Greets visitors III. Filing	6. Ability to use standard references (dictionary, style manual).	1, 2, 3, 4, 5, 6
7. Files 8. Searches files/pulls documents	7. Ability to speak/understand spoken English language sufficient to answer telephone, greet visitors, and transcribe dictated copy.	2, 5, 6
	8. Knowledge of organizational filing procedures and system.	7, 8
	9. Knowledge of correct English language usage (grammar, spelling, punctuation) sufficient to identify and correct errors and type dictated copy.	2, 4
	10. Ability to proofread and correct own work.	4
	11. Ability to operate multi-line telephone (hold, transfer, and connect calls).	5
	12. Ability to read English language sufficient to understand style manual and instructions for typed copy, and to file documents by subject.	1, 2, 3, 4, 7
	13. Ability to alphabetize sufficient to file and retrieve material	7, 8
	14. Ability to recognize and differentiate between numbers and series of numbers sufficient to file and retrieve material.	7, 8
	15. Ability to use English language to read/write/type specific information on forms.	3, 5
	16. Ability to compare and perceive differences between two sets of copy.	4
	SPECIAL COMPETENCIES	
	1. Ability to work with interruptions (e.g., phone or visitors) when typing.	All
	2. Ability to format or lay out handwritten dictated material on typed page.	1, 2, 3
	3. Ability to work with minimal supervision/instruction	All
	4. Ability to identify and correct grammar, spelling, and punctuation errors in original copy.	1, 2, 3
	5. Ability to apply/adapt instructions or procedures from one assignment to another	All
	6. Social skills as demonstrated by pleasant handling of callers and visitors.	5, 6

From S. E. Bemis, A. H. Belenky, and D. A. Soder, *Job Analysis* (Washington, D.C.: The Bureau of National Affairs, 1983).

- Ensure that specifications contain particulars relating to types and levels of competencies needed. Here are some examples:

  Ability to read at the sixth grade level on a standardized reading test

  Ability to read highway traffic signs and labels

  Knowledge of criterion-related validation procedures provided in the *Uniform Guidelines*

- Show the links between the ability and the task to be performed. This is particularly relevant in cases where general abilities are to be used in particular ways in the job. The following are some of the abilities requirements for the tasks involved in the job of housing inspector:

  Ability to read and interpret housing plans, blueprints, and specifications

  Ability to translate the language of the housing code into terminology appropriate to the layman

  Ability to communicate verbally with people from varied socioeconomic and educational levels (Mussio & Smith, 1973)

- Emphasize the underlying characteristic desired rather than the perceived determinants of the characteristic. Thus, if knowledge of mathematics is relevant, highlight the types and levels of this knowledge required rather than training, education, and experience. This is because years of experience or education may not assure that the particular competency that is desired is present in the applicant; and conversely, individuals without these visible symbols may in fact possess the required characteristics. Besides, as pointed out earlier, sole reliance on educational requirements may not be legally defensible (Bemis et al., 1983, p. 83; Merritt-Haston & Wexley, 1983; Gordon & Johnson, 1982).
- When specifying licenses, citizenship, and other special requirements, cite the authority that mandates these requirements. In cases where they are mandated by governmental authorities, union contracts, and other external agencies, the specification should state the exact requirement and identifying details about the agency involved.

CRITERIA FOR INCLUSION OF KSAOS ON SPECIFICATIONS

All the job analysis methods can, and typically do, result in large numbers of potentially job-relevant human characteristics. The following are some criteria that can be used in retaining characteristics:

- Link tasks with other job factors. Preference should be given to characteristics that can be clearly linked with specific tasks, context, and other job factors. The absence of this link creates doubt about the relevancy of the characteristic.
- Importance to job performance. Potential characteristics are not all equally important to job performance. Some are critical, while others are good to have. Specifications should distinguish characteristics in regard to their importance to job performance. Recruiters, trainers, and other users can thus engage in making informed trade-offs in selecting individuals.
- Consider the marketplace. Preference should be given to those characteristics that are available in the marketplace. Even the highest-scoring characteristic is useless if it is not present among the applicants for the job.
- Sensitivity. To be included, a characteristic must be discriminating, that is, capable of distinguishing between superior, average, and unacceptable levels of performance.

In applying these criteria, it is useful to work out a format and rules for decision making. The illustrations given in the special agent KSAO study reproduced in Appendix 5.1 show how this can be done.

CHOOSING LEVELS OF KSAOS

Some work-related human characteristics are qualitative. Examples include sex, race, and nationality. When these are relevant to the personnel decision, they can be readily spelled out in yes or no terms. Others, however, are quantitative and come in degrees. Examples of these include aptitudes, abilities, and skills. For these characteristics, more is typically better. Thus, the higher the level of ability, the greater the chances of an individual being able to perform or learn a task.

The quantitative characteristics present a problem in human resource decision making. Since more is better, there is a temptation to favor applicants with higher levels of these characteristics. Thus, applicants with college degrees may be preferred over those with high school diplomas. More years of experience can be taken to be superior to fewer years of experience.

While this temptation is there, it is important to guard against falling into this mode of thinking. For one thing, more may not necessarily be better in some instances. Thus, ten years of experience at a routine and repetitive task may not necessarily create greater competency than six months of experience. In other instances, more may be irrelevant. Thus, years of formal education may be irrelevant beyond the basic levels. This is so for manual and clerical jobs where the types of KSAOs developed through college education are simply not relevant to the job requirements. In still other instances, more might actually result in harmful consequences. Thus, hiring college graduates and other highly trained persons to do work that does not utilize their competencies can result in job dissatisfaction (see Schein, 1978; Gordon & Johnson, 1982).

In coming to grips with this issue, the best guide for the analyst is to stay as close as possible to the central mandate of the worker specification enterprise: specify the characteristics that are relevant to the job situation to be encountered by the worker. The following considerations can be taken into account when fulfilling this mandate.

- *Career ladders and opportunities*. For dead-end jobs, the best strategy is to stay with the basic levels of competencies. Going beyond the basic levels is to invite dissatisfaction and unhappiness. On the other hand, if the hiring is for an entry-level job, with opportunities for advancement, investment in higher levels of competencies might be both justified and essential.
- *Promotion policy*. This is a corollary of the point just noted. Some organizations are committed to a policy of promotion from within; others choose to go outside for filling vacancies. In some instances, this choice is dictated by the job itself. Thus, senior technicians cannot be promoted to engineering jobs, since the latter typically require college degrees and licensure. In other instances, hiring from the outside is the result of conscious managerial preferences, and is adhered to even in instances where mobility is possible. Organizations that are committed to hiring from the outside should stay with minimum level requirements. Those who practice promotion from within, on the other hand, should seek persons with high levels of competencies.
- *Rate of change in organization*. Investments in higher levels of abilities are justified in instances where the rate of change in regard to products and methods is high. The greater the rate of change, the greater the need for adaptability on the part of the labor force.

SELECTION OF SUBJECT MATTER EXPERTS

The derivation of worker specifications ultimately relies on the exercise of human judgment. It is important, therefore, to choose SMEs whose competence and credibility is beyond question. The critical requirement here is that the persons chosen to serve as SMEs have some legitimate claim for serving in that capacity. The following are some of the ways in which potential SMEs can meet this test. (Some of the factors discussed next were recognized in the section on JEM.)

- *Experience at the job*. Job incumbents and supervisors meet this test. It is particularly helpful if the supervisors are persons who have been promoted from the ranks and can demonstrate that they have firsthand knowledge of the work.

- *Experts.* This category includes human resource managers, job analysts, researchers, and other professionals who can lay claim to specialized knowledge of the industry, labor markets, or job structures. Although lacking firsthand familiarity with the job, such persons can bring outside perspectives and knowledge of comparable job situations to the worker specification activity.
- *Freedom from bias.* Regardless of other qualifications, persons serving as SMEs must be willing to set aside preconceived notions. Bias can creep into the deliberations in the form of racial, sexual, age, and other stereotypes. A specific danger is that experiences with prior job incumbents can color perceptions about KSAO requirements. The freedom from bias requirement is difficult to meet in its entirety. Nevertheless, efforts must be made to get persons serving as SMEs to examine their attitudes and to approach their mandate with open minds.
- *Minorities.* The presence of women, blacks, and other minorities in worker specification activity adds to its credibility and fairness; it is also desirable from a legal perspective.
- *Comprehension levels.* Worker specification is a specialized activity. It requires the SMEs to respond to stimuli, typically in written form, that depict job-worker situations. It is important, therefore, that the persons selected to play this role be able to understand the written word.

In considering the qualifications of SMEs, it is important to emphasize that no one characteristic is sufficient in itself. Thus, an experienced but illiterate worker would not be of much use as an SME. The testimony of minorities can enrich the process if it brings particular viewpoints that might otherwise be missed. The credibility of these sources, however, can be eroded if their representatives are unable to be objective or if they use the activity as a forum for futhering the interests of their constituency.

VERIFICATION

The techniques of worker specification described in the preceding sections are inherently systematic. There is no guarantee, however, that they will always yield results that are reliable, valid, and fair. It is good practice, therefore, to subject both the process and the results to tests of verification.

The ultimate test of the validity of a KSAO is the extent to which it fulfills the purposes for which it is derived (Exhibit 5.5). That is the firing line test, but one that cannot be administered outside its uses. Here are a couple of internal checks that can be run before the KSAOs are actually incorporated into the human resource program.

- Ask the SMEs to repeat their ratings a second time and compare the results. The results can be judged to be reliable if there are no significant differences in the ratings.
- Classify the SMEs according to sex, race, nationality, and other potentially biasing traits and compare their results. An unbiased estimate can be said to exist if the differences are not statistically significant.
- Ask a different group of persons to comment on the relevance of the KSAOs for the job in question. High levels of agreement between the first group and this second group can be interpreted as favoring judgment of validity.

DOCUMENTATION

Efforts at systematizing the worker specification mechanism are totally useless unless documentation is provided. Ideally, documentation should cover all the procedures and techniques that were used, and the decision rules that were followed. The following are some of the areas for which documentation should be routinely provided:

- Listing of the job factors taken into account in generating worker specifications and a description of the procedures and rules followed in choosing the factors.

- Listing of the human characteristics considered in arriving at the specifications and a description of the procedures and rules followed in choosing specifications.
- Summary of the biographical information on the SMEs.
- Summary of key statistical results, including attempts at verification, that formed the basis for the decisions relating to the selected KSAOs (Sistrunk & Smith, 1982).

APPENDIX 5.1 FLORIDA DEPARTMENT OF LAW ENFORCEMENT SPECIAL AGENT KSAOS

The materials presented in this appendix illustrate the use of the inventory method in generating KSAOs. The job for which the KSAOs were generated was that of special agent in the Florida Department of Law Enforcement. Portions of the methodology used in this study, and the results relating to tasks involved in the special agent's job, were reproduced in Chapter 4. This appendix begins with the details relating to the procedures followed in generating, rating, and analyzing KSAOs. The special agent KSAOs and their ratings are presented at the end of the appendix.

This study has a couple of notable features. To begin with, it is a multimethodological investigation that makes use of concepts and procedures from established systems of job analysis. Note the structure of the KSAO rating form (Exhibit 5.A). Some of the rating factors are from the Job Elements Method; they were supplemented with a rating scale (right side of the illustration). The method specifies in advance not only how the data are to be gathered (text and Exhibit 5.A) but also how they are to be analyzed (Exhibit 5.B). The documentation section contains a sample form for collecting information about SMEs (Exhibit 5.C).

KSAO Generation, Rating, and Analysis

The following are the general procedures involved in the generation and use of KSAOs through the inventory method. (Compare with those used in the development of tasks presented in Appendix 4.1.)

A. PREPARATION FOR A MEETING

1. Six SMEs should be contacted (four incumbents and two supervisors) who have had at least two years of experience and exposure to a variety of assignments at several locations. If female and minority SMEs are available, their inclusion is very desirable for legal reasons.
2. Establish a meeting time and place. Set aside one full day.
3. Secure a large writing pad, easel, tape, and two magic markers.
4. Make six copies of the task and function importance listing, one for each SME.

B. THE MORNING SESSION SHOULD BE DEVOTED TO GENERATING KSAOS FOR EACH FUNCTION

If there are four hours available in the morning and ten functions, each function should be considered for no more than 20 to 25 minutes. KSAOs generated for one function would not be repeated for another. Each KSAO should be numbered. As a general target, no more than 100 KSAOs should be generated for the entire job.

EXHIBIT 5.A KSAO Rating Form

Subject Matter Expert Name: ______________________ Date: ____________

KSAO Number	Is this KSAO necessary for newly hired workers?	Is this KSAO practical to expect in the labor market?	Trouble Likely To what extent is trouble likely if this KSAO is ignored in selection relative to other KSAO's for this job?	Distinguish Superior from Average To what extent do different levels of the KSAO distinguish the superior from the average worker relative to other KSAO's for this job?
			1 = Very little or none 2 = To some extent 3 = To a great extent 4 = To a very great extent 5 = To an extremely great extent	
	Circle one	Circle one	Circle one	Circle one
	Yes No	Yes No	1 2 3 4 5	1 2 3 4 5
	Yes No	Yes No	1 2 3 4 5	1 2 3 4 5
	Yes No	Yes No	1 2 3 4 5	1 2 3 4 5
	Yes No	Yes No	1 2 3 4 5	1 2 3 4 5
	Yes No	Yes No	1 2 3 4 5	1 2 3 4 5
	Yes No	Yes No	1 2 3 4 5	1 2 3 4 5
	Yes No	Yes No	1 2 3 4 5	1 2 3 4 5
	Yes No	Yes No	1 2 3 4 5	1 2 3 4 5
	Yes No	Yes No	1 2 3 4 5	1 2 3 4 5
	Yes No	Yes No	1 2 3 4 5	1 2 3 4 5
	Yes No	Yes No	1 2 3 4 5	1 2 3 4 5
	Yes No	Yes No	1 2 3 4 5	1 2 3 4 5
	Yes No	Yes No	1 2 3 4 5	1 2 3 4 5
	Yes No	Yes No	1 2 3 4 5	1 2 3 4 5
	Yes No	Yes No	1 2 3 4 5	1 2 3 4 5
	Yes No	Yes No	1 2 3 4 5	1 2 3 4 5
	Yes No	Yes No	1 2 3 4 5	1 2 3 4 5
	Yes No	Yes No	1 2 3 4 5	1 2 3 4 5

From F. Sistrunk and P. L. Smith *Multimethodological Job Analysis for Criminal Justice Organizations* (Tampa: Center for Evaluation Research, University of South Florida, 1983), p. 71.

EXHIBIT 5.B Actions for KSAO Results

Combination	Yes/No Q. 1 Essential for New Workers	Yes/No Q. 2 Practical	Rating. 2 Distinguish Superior from Average Performance	Action Required
1.	4 or more Yes responses	4 or more Yes responses	Mean ≥ 1.50	Consider in compensatory selection procedure
2.	4 or more Yes responses	4 or more Yes responses	Mean ≤ 1.50	Consider as a pass-fail qualifier
3.	4 or more Yes responses	3 or more No responses	Mean ≥ 1.50	Consider special recruitment or job redesign
4.	4 or more Yes responses	3 or more No responses	Mean < 1.50	Consider job redesign or special recruitment
5.	3 or more No responses	4 or more Yes responses	Mean ≥ 1.50	Consider training for those who need it
6.	3 or more No responses	4 or more Yes responses	Mean ≤ 1.50	Drop KSAO from consideration
7.	3 or more No responses	3 or more No responses	Mean ≥ 1.50	Consider training for all new workers
8.	3 or more No responses	3 or more No responses	Mean ≤ 1.50	Drop KSAO from consideration

From F. Sistrunk and P. L. Smith, *Multimethodological Job Analysis for Criminal Justice Organizations* (Tampa: Center for Evaluation Research, University of South Florida, 1983), p. 74.

C. THE AFTERNOON SESSION SHOULD BE SPEND FIRST REVIEWING THE KSAOS FOR REDUNDANCY AND POSSIBLE REDUCTION

Then each SME will independently rate each KSAO, listing its number on the KSAO rating form (Exhibit 5.A) and completing the required ratings. For each KSAO in turn, each SME will answer two yes/no questions and provide two ratings.[1]

Yes/No Question 1. Is this KSAO necessary for newly hired workers?

Yes/No Question 2. Is this KSAO practical to expect in the labor market?

Rating 1. To what extent is trouble likely if this KSAO is ignored in selection relative to other KSAOs for this job?

Rating 2. To what extent do different levels of the KSAO distinguish the superior from the average worker relative to other KSAOs for this job?

D. ANALYSIS OF THE KSAO RATINGS

1. KSAOs important for consideration in selection are identified in the following manner (i.e., all three conditions must be met):
   a. Four or more of the six SMEs state that the KSAO is necessary for newly hired workers ("Yes" to Yes/No Question 1).
   b. Four or more of the six SMEs state that the KSAO is practical to expect in the labor market ("Yes" to Yes/No Question 2).
   c. The mean rating on rating 2 (Distinguish Superior from Average) is greater than or equal to 1.50.
2. All KSAOs important for consideration in selection (as identified in D.1) should be included

[1] Rating scale values for both ratings are 1 = very little or none, 2 = to some extent, 3 = to a great extent, 4 = to a very great extent, 5 = to an extremely great extent.

EXHIBIT 5.C Subject Matter Experts Background Information Form

Name ______________________ Phone (   ) ______________________
Age __________ Sex (circle one) Male Female
Ethnic Origin (circle one): American Indian Black White
Asian/Pacific Islander Hispanic
Other (Specify) ______________

Education: Describe your general education, including college degrees and associated majors, and any occupation—specific training, licenses, or certificates in the space below.

____

____

____

____

____

Work Experience
Present occupation ______________________
Place of employment ______________________ Phone (   ) ______________
Address ______________________
Time in present occupation: years, ________ months
Brief description of duties: ______________________

____

____

____

Previous work experience: In the space provided, please describe any previous work experience you have had that is *relative to the job under study*. Be sure to include job titles, brief descriptions of job duties, and the approximate number of years and months of experience in each. ______________

____

____

____

____

____

____

I certify that the information I have given or will give in connection with the job analysis is truthful and correct to the best of my knowledge.

Signature ______________________ Date ______________

From F. Sistrunk and P. L. Smith, *Multimethodological Job Analysis for Criminal Justice Organizations* (Tampa: Center for Evaluation Research, University of South Florida, 1982), pp. 76–77.

in an examination plan or test budget. Weights for exam components are determined as follows:

a. Multiply the mean Trouble Likely (rating 1) value by the Distinguish Superior from Average (rating 2) value, yielding a KSAO importance value. This value will range from 1 to 25.
b. Total all importance values and compute percentages based on the importance values for each KSAO. The percentages are the relative weights for the respective KSAO exam components.

3. Exhibit 5.B shows the possible actions required for KSAOs, depending on the KSAO rating results. As shown, this process has implications not only for selection but for job design, training, and recruitment.

KSAOs meeting the criteria of either combination 1 or 2 should be considered for assessment in the selection procedure, with those meeting combination 2 criteria incorporated only as pass-fail qualifiers. KSAOs meeting the criteria for either combination 3 or 4 should be considered in the development of special recruitment efforts for the job or as targets in job redesign efforts (i.e., design the need for such KSAOs out of the job in question). KSAOs meeting the criteria of combinations 5 and 7 should be considered for inclusion in either training programs for particular workers who do not possess adequate level of the KSAO in question (combination 5) or for all new workers (combination 7). KSAOs meeting the criteria for either combination 6 or 8 should be dropped from further consideration.

This concludes the KSAO analysis phase.

Documentation

A report should be written describing both the process and results of the job analysis. In addition to the report, Subject Matter Expert Background Information forms (Exhibit 5.C) from the participating SMEs should be kept. The raw data should be kept for five years after completion of the study.

A. INFORMATION FOR INCLUSION IN THE TASK INVENTORY SECTION OF THE REPORT

1. Brief description of the task inventory development, covering the sources of task statements and the task statement review process, including a summary of biographical information on the SMEs. (See Exhibit 5.C for a sample form to collect this information.)
2. Summary biographical information on the inventory respondents.
3. Means, standard deviations, and ranges on each task for each of the four rating scales and the task importance (composite) index.
4. The function importance values and the respective tasks arranged in rank order of importance.

B. INFORMATION FOR INCLUSION IN KSAO SECTION OF THE REPORT

1. Brief description of the KSAO generation and rating procedure.
2. Summary biographical information on the SMEs.
3. A listing of the KSAOs subjected to the rating process and the summary rating information for each KSAO, Frequencies for the Yes/No rating should be included, as well as means, standard deviations, and ranges for the two ratings.
4. The KSAOs identified as important for consideration in the selection process.
5. The KSAOs identified as important for consideration in training.
6. The KSAOs identified as important for job redesign and special recruitment considerations.

Eighty-five KSAOs were identified for the job of special agent (Exhibit 5.D). They are broken down into knowledge, skills, and abilities and are grouped under nine dimensions. The ratings of the KSAOs are given in Exhibit 5.E. The asterisks signify factors that are particularly important.

EXHIBIT 5.D Special Agent KSAOs

Legal Proceedings

1. K of DLE report writing procedures
2. K of applicable statutes and laws (state, federal, local)
3. A to orally communicate

EXHIBIT 5.D Special Agent KSAOs (*cont'd*)

4. K of court policy and procedures
5. K of defense and prosecution tactics
6. A to present facts
7. K of case preparation
8. A to organize and plan
9. A to write technical reports and correspondence
10. A to work with others
11. A to understand system procedures (geographical)
12. A to write routine reports and correspondence
13. A to define problems, establish facts, and draw valid conclusions

Practice and Procedures

14. K to undercover law enforcement
15. A to identify self-limitations/boundaries (related to self-confidence, self-reliance)
16. A to withstand long hours of work
17. Good physical fitness
18. Mental fitness
19. A to withstand stress
20. Emotional stability
21. A to adapt to various situations, circumstances, roles
22. A to analyze problems quickly and take appropriate action under stress
23. K of laws and procedures of arrest
24. K of laws and procedures of search and seizure
25. A to coordinate joint force effort
26. S in operation of weapons
27. A to establish rapport with others (i.e., other law enforcement agencies)
28. K of laws and procedures of interrogation
29. A to record and observe events accurately and completely
30. K of subject (person) being interviewed
31. A to speak clearly and audibly
32. A to take command of situations (aggressive)
33. K of news media relations
34. K of DLE policies and regulations
35. K of functions of DLE
36. A to complete routine forms and records
37. A to follow oral and written directions
38. A to add, subtract, multiply, and divide numbers
39. S in operation of xerox machine
40. S in operation of tape recorder
41. S in operation of radio equipment
42. A to apply principles to solve practical problems
43. A to draw charts, graphs, and diagrams
44. K of laws and procedures of evidence
45. K of laws and procedures of extradition
46. K of laws and procedures of suspect identification (line-ups)
47. S in operation of motor vehicle
48. K of narcotics and controlled substances
49. K of functions and services of other agencies
50. K of evidence collection (crime scene preservation)
51. S in operation of cameras
52. A to collect evidence (includes preservation and packaging)
53. K of criminal justice systems and procedures
54. S in operation of fingerprinting equipment
55. S in operation of surveillance equipment
56. K of surveillance techniques

EXHIBIT 5.D Special Agent KSAOs (*cont'd*)

Intelligence

57. A to cultivate informants
58. A to handle sensitive public contacts
59. A to solve complex problems involving many variables
60. A to maintain and control informants (all types)
61. K of psychology of people
62. A to gather and evaluate information

Evidence Collection and Preservation

63. K of DLE crime lab functions and services
64. K of crime scene analysis
65. A to identify evidence (vs. property)
66. K of forensic science
67. K of document identification

Self-development

68. A to read and comprehend policies, procedures, technical reports
69. A to identify self strengths and weaknesses

Public Contacts

70. K of first aid
71. A to handle routine public contacts
72. K of instructional methods
73. A to deliver lectures, talks, etc., to a variety of audiences
74. K of public relations (community relations)
75. K of emergency commitment procedures

Equipment Use and Maintenance

76. A to fire authorized department weapons at department qualifying standards
77. S in operation of special protective devices
78. A to identify malfunctions in equipment and have it repaired

Reports and Forms

79. K of purchasing procedures (vs. I&E funds)
80. A to write legibly

Miscellaneous

81. S in operation of calculator
82. S in operation of teletype
83. K of state geography
84. K of crimes against persons investigation
85. K of crimes against property investigation

Key: K = knowledge, S = skills, A = abilities.

From F. Sistrunk and P. L. Smith, *Multimethodological Job Analysis for Criminal Justice Organizations* (Tampa: Center for Evaluation Research, University of South Florida, 1983), pp. 100–102.

EXHIBIT 5.E Results of Special Agent KSAO Ratings

KSAO Number	Essential for New Hires? (Question 1 Response)	Practical to Expect in Labor Market? (Question 2 Response)	Trouble Likely If KSAO Ignored in Selection? (Rating 1 Response)	Does KSAO Distinguish Superiors from Average? (Rating 2 Response)	KSAO Importance Value	Percent-age	Action Required
1	Y	N	3.7	3.2	11.84	.0156	3
2	Y	Y	3.5	3.3	11.55	.0152	1
3*	Y	Y	4.0	3.3	13.20	.0174	1
4	Y	Y	2.8	3.0	8.40	.0111	1
5	Y	Y	3.0	3.3	9.90	.0131	1
6	Y	Y	3.8	4.4	16.72	.0220	1
7	Y	Y	3.0	3.2	9.6	.0127	1
8	Y	Y	3.0	3.2	9.6	.0127	1
9	Y	Y	3.0	2.7	8.10	.0107	1
10*	Y	Y	4.0	4.2	16.80	.0221	1
11	Y	Y	2.3	2.3	5.29	.0070	1
12	Y	Y	3.2	3.5	11.20	.0148	1
13*	Y	Y	4.5	3.7	16.65	.0219	1
14	N	N	2.0	3.2	6.40	.0085	7
15	Y	Y	3.0	3.2	9.60	.0127	1
16*	Y	Y	3.7	3.7	13.69	.0180	1
17	Y	Y	2.5	2.8	7.0	.0092	1
18*	Y	Y	3.7	3.7	13.69	.0180	1
19*	Y	Y	3.8	3.3	12.54	.0165	1
20*	Y	Y	4.2	3.5	14.70	.0194	1
21	Y	Y	3.2	3.5	11.20	.0148	1
22*	Y	Y	3.5	4.2	14.70	.0194	1
23*	Y	Y	4.0	3.7	14.80	.0195	1
24*	Y	Y	3.7	3.8	14.06	.0185	1
25	N	N	2.2	2.7	5.94	.0078	7
26	Y	Y	3.7	2.8	10.36	.0137	1
27	Y	Y	3.3	3.5	11.55	.0152	1
28	Y	Y	3.0	3.5	10.50	.0138	1
29	Y	Y	3.0	3.8	11.40	.0150	1
30	N	N	2.2	3.3	7.26	.0096	7
31	Y	Y	3.3	2.7	8.91	.0117	1
32*	Y	Y	3.2	4.0	12.80	.0169	1
33	Y	N	1.8	2.2	3.96	.0052	3
34	Y	N	3.0	3.8	11.40	.0150	3
35	Y	N	2.8	3.8	10.64	.0140	3
36	Y	Y	3.2	3.0	9.60	.0127	1
37*	Y	Y	4.0	4.2	16.80	.0221	1
38	Y	Y	3.3	2.0	6.60	.0087	1
39	N	N	1.2	1.2	1.44	.0019	8
40	N	N	1.8	1.7	3.06	.0041	7
41	Y	Y	3.0	2.8	8.40	.0111	1
42*	Y	Y	3.5	4.0	14.00	.0184	1
43	Y	Y	1.8	2.3	4.14	.0055	1
44*	Y	Y	3.8	4.0	15.20	.0200	1
45	N	N	2.0	2.5	5.0	.0066	7
46	Y	Y	2.7	3.7	9.99	.0132	1
47	Y	Y	4.0	1.3	5.20	.0069	2
48	Y	Y	2.7	3.2	8.64	.0114	1
49	N	N	2.2	2.8	6.16	.0081	7
50	Y	Y	3.2	3.3	10.56	.0139	1
51	N	N	2.2	2.0	4.40	.0058	7
52	Y	Y	2.7	2.5	6.75	.0089	1
53	Y	Y	2.7	3.3	8.91	.0117	1
54	N	N	2.0	2.3	4.60	.0061	7
55	Y	Y	2.8	2.8	7.84	.0103	1
56	Y	Y	2.5	3.3	8.25	.0109	1
57	Y	Y	2.8	4.0	11.20	.0148	1
58*	Y	Y	3.5	3.7	12.95	.0171	1

* Most important KSAOs (those with KIVs of 12 or higher) are highlighted.

EXHIBIT 5.E Results of Special Agent KSAO Ratings (*cont'd*)

KSAO Number	Essential for New Hires? (Question 1 Response)	Practical to Expect in Labor Market? (Question 2 Response)	Trouble Likely If KSAO Ignored in Selection? (Rating 1 Response)	Does KSAO Distinguish Superiors from Average? (Rating 2 Response)	KSAO Importance Value	Percent-age	Action Required
59*	Y	Y	3.7	3.5	12.95	.0171	1
60*	Y	Y	3.7	3.7	13.69	.0180	1
61	N	N	2.3	3.0	6.90	.0091	7
62	Y	Y	3.0	3.3	9.90	.0131	1
63	N	N	2.2	3.0	6.60	.0087	7
64	N	N	2.0	2.8	5.60	.0074	7
65	Y	Y	2.7	3.2	8.64	.0114	1
66	N	N	2.0	3.0	6.0	.0079	7
67	N	N	1.8	2.5	4.50	.0060	7
68	Y	Y	3.2	3.0	9.60	.0127	1
69	Y	Y	2.7	3.2	8.64	.0114	1
70	N	N	1.8	1.5	2.70	.0034	7
71	Y	Y	2.5	2.7	6.75	.0089	1
72	N	N	1.8	1.8	3.24	.0043	7
73	N	N	2.0	2.3	4.60	.0061	7
74	Y	Y	2.0	2.0	4.0	.0053	1
75	N	N	1.8	2.2	3.96	.0052	7
76*	Y	Y	4.2	3.2	13.44	.0177	1
77	Y	Y	3.0	2.8	8.40	.0111	1
78	Y	Y	2.8	2.0	5.60	.0074	1
79	Y	N	2.3	3.0	6.90	.0091	3
80	Y	Y	3.8	2.8	10.64	.0140	1
81	N	N	1.5	1.5	2.25	.0030	7
82	N	N	1.3	1.3	1.69	.0023	8
83	N	N	1.8	2.3	4.14	.0055	7
84	Y	N	2.5	3.0	7.50	.0099	3
85	Y	Y	2.3	2.8	6.44	.0085	1

* Most important KSAOs (those with KIVs of 12 or higher) are highlighted.

From F. Sistrunk and P. L. Smith, *Multimethodological Job Analysis for Criminal Justice Organizations* (Tampa: Center for Evaluation Research, University of South Florida, 1983), pp. 103–106.

6 Uses of Job Information

The uses to which information acquired through job analysis can be put in human resource management have been pointed out in general terms in the preceding chapters, particularly Chapters 4 and 5. The purpose of this chapter is to extend that discussion and to show the linkages between job analysis products and key human resource management functions. The following are the specific goals of this chapter:

1. To crystalize further the role of job analysis in the performance of key human resource management functions.
2. To highlight applications of job analysis in human resource management activities of particular significance in the current context.

6.1 Plan of Approach

Job analysis has potential for servicing the informational needs of a very wide range of managerial functions and concerns. An exhaustive coverage of all its potential applications is beyond the scope of any one book. Since this text addresses the human resource director, we focus our attention in this chapter on a set of functions that are at the heart of modern human resource management. These were listed in Exhibit 1.3 and have been discussed in general terms in various parts of the book.

ORGANIZATION OF THE CHAPTER

The plan of this chapter is as follows. A section is devoted to each of functions noted in Exhibit 1.3. A common sequence is adhered to in each exposition:

- *Introduction to the function.* Each discussion begins with an analysis of the "what" and "why" of the function, showing its place and contributions to the human resource management process.
- *Legal requirements and mandates.* Explanation of the legal influences impinging on the function, with particular reference to the requirements of civil rights/equal employment opportunity (EEO) laws (see Exhibit 1.6, in Chapter 1).
- *Role of job analysis.* Overview of the potential contributions of job analysis in the performance

of the function. (A standard format is followed for showing the job information needs of the function.)

- *Selected issues and applications*. Focus on application of job analysis to current and emerging issues of concern to human resource management.

A NOTE ON JOB ANALYSIS METHODS AND SYSTEMS

The methods and systems of job analysis that comprise the tool kit of modern job analysis have been reviewed at length in the previous chapters. Additionally, the appendices at the end of the book provide a collection of instruments that can be used in job analysis activities. To avoid repetition, discussion of methods and systems is kept to a minimum; it is limited to highlighting particular applications wherever appropriate.

6.2 Equal Employment Opportunity

Equal employment opportunity has emerged as a significant concern of modern human resource management. The impetus behind this development is a national recognition that every person has a right to equality of opportunity at the workplace without regard to race, religion, color, national origin, sex, or any other personal characteristic. A package of laws passed by the government, beginning with the Civil Rights Act of 1964, has now made EEO a governmental mandate. These laws, along with related constitutional mandates and agency orders, were reviewed in Chapter 1 and are hence not repeated here (see particularly Exhibit 1.6). Our focus is on analysis of the provisions of the *Uniform Guidelines* and the case law that has arisen in relation to the implementation of the civil rights/EEO package.

EEO: MANDATE AND PROCEDURAL REQUIREMENTS

As noted in Chapter 1, there are two sides to the EEO mandate: prevention of unfair discrimination and promotion of upward mobility of minorities through affirmative action and other proactive programs.

Unlawful Discrimination. The law does not ban discrimination in itself. What is prohibited is unfair discrimination. Two forms of unfair discrimination are recognized: disparate treatment and disparate impact. Disparate treatment takes place when an employer treats members of certain groups less favorably than members of other groups. The groups that are of particular concern to the policy makers are women, blacks, older people, and religious, nationality, and other minorities that have traditionally been excluded or discriminated against in employment. Under disparate treatment cases, proof of discriminatory motive is essential. Disparate impact, on the other hand, exists when an employer's apparently neutral employment practices have a significantly disparate (adverse) impact on a protected group and the employment practice is not shown to be job related by the employer. Here, discriminatory motive is not the issue. The concern, rather, is with the impact of the practices on the representation of the protected groups in the employer's labor force. (Note that disparate impact can also be referred to as adverse impact.)

Separate provisions and rules have been developed for establishing proof of discrimination under the two forms of unfair discrimination. The requirements for establishing proof under disparate treatment were spelled out in the *McDonnell Douglas Corp.* v. *Green* case decided in 1972. The initial burden is on the plaintiff to establish a prima facie case. To do this, the plaintiff must show (1) that he or she belongs to a group protected from discrimination by Title VII; (2) that he or she was qualified and applied for the job for which the employer was seeking applicants; (3) that despite being qualified, he or she was rejected by the employer; and (4) that after being rejected, the position remained open and the employer continued to seek applications from other persons whose qualifications were similar to those of the plaintiff. Once a prima facie case is established, the burden then shifts to the employer to articulate some legitimate, nondiscriminatory reason for its actions. If the employer provides such a reason, the plaintiff is then afforded the opportunity to demonstrate that the supposedly valid reason given by the employer was really a pretext or a cover-up for a discriminatory decision. (For a review of case law that refines these criteria, see Twomey, 1986, p. 41.)

The requirements relating to proof of discrimination under the disparate (adverse) impact form of discrimination were first enunciated in *Griggs* v. *Duke Power Company*. The process consists roughly of three stages. To begin with, the burden of establishing a prima facie case is on the plaintiff. This is done by showing, through statistical analysis, that an apparently neutral employment practice at issue produced a significantly discriminatory impact. If the plaintiff succeeds in showing adverse impact, the burden shifts to the employer to demonstrate that the requirement in question is justified on the basis of job-relatedness or business necessity. Even if the employer meets this test, the plaintiff can still prevail by showing that the employer was using the practice as a mere pretext for discrimination. This is done by showing that alternative methods of making personnel decisions exist that would satisfy the employer's legitimate needs without inflicting undesirable adverse consequences on a protected group. This third phase brings the proceedings into the arena of disparate treatment or intentional discrimination. The claims are then processed under the *McDonnell Douglas* rules (based on Feldacker, 1983, pp. 395–409; Twomey, 1986; Ledvinka, 1982).

Affirmative Action. Affirmative action addresses the second concern of the EEO laws. This deals with the promotion of upward mobility of the protected groups. It is thus not enough for the employer to assure that the decision-making tools are job related and free from bias. The employer must take the additional step of finding ways to facilitate movement of the minority groups into jobs and organizational levels that have traditionally been closed to them.

The *Guidelines* address the affirmative action obligation of the employers. They emphasize that equal employment opportunity is the law of the land. Public sector employers are expected to go beyond validation of selection procedures. They must take proactive steps to remedy the effects of prior discrimination and the achievement of affirmative action objectives. Affirmative action is not a requirement for private sector employers in the absence of adverse impact. However, private sector employers are encouraged to adopt and implement affirmative action programs on a voluntary basis (Section 13).

Section 15(2) of the *Guidelines* spells out the steps involved in the construction and operation of an affirmative action plan. As these have received wide circulation within the human resource management professions, detailed coverage of their contents is not essential. Basically, the process consists of three components. It begins with a formal and public commitment by the employer to a policy of nondiscrimination and the setting of goals. Integral aspects of this stage are dissemination of the plan, allocation of resources, and assignment of responsibility for accomplishing its goals. The next steps deal with work force availability and utilization analysis. Here, the employer studies its labor force to see if disparities exist in the utilization of minorities. If disparities are found to exist, the employer initiates affirmative steps to remedy the situation. These can include new recruitment programs, job redesign, revamping of selection instruments, training, and career planning. Audits and controls are to be conducted to assure compliance with overall goals of the plan (Hall & Albrecht, 1979).

Job analysis is not specifically mentioned in the provisions of the *Guidelines* that deal with affirmative action. The benefits that it can provide to the affirmative action planner, however, are fairly evident. Comprehensive job descriptions can provide the information needed for tracing mobility paths, for uncovering roadblocks to upward mobility, and for classification of jobs. This information can in turn be used for deriving KSAOs, for analyzing training needs, and for providing career guidance and counseling. The uses of job information for such purposes are discussed in general terms in the sections that follow.

JOB ANALYSIS AND EQUAL EMPLOYMENT OPPORTUNITY: OVERVIEW

Job analysis has a central role to play in EEO. To appreciate this role, it is important to note the very broad view expressed in the *Guidelines* about employment decisions and selection procedures. Briefly, an *employment decision* is any personnel action taken by the employer affecting the employment relationship—it encompasses hiring, promotion, demotion, referral, retention, training, transfer, certification, and membership in employee organizations. A *selection procedure* is any measure or combination of measures or procedures used as a basis for making employment decisions; this can include paper-and-pencil tests, application forms, interviews, performance tests, training programs, and physical, educational, and work experience requirements (Sections 2B and C and 16Q).

In EEO deliberations, job analysis is viewed as a tool for enhancement and verification of the appropriateness of selection procedures. Exhibit 6.1 shows the specific EEO requirements and the job information that are needed for meeting them.

Discrimination. Job analysis is accorded official recognition in the *Uniform Guidelines* in this regard. Technically, job analysis becomes relevant when the employer is charged with unfair discrimination. Under a disparate treatment charge, job analysis can provide the information needed to demonstrate the BFOQ status of the challenged selection procedure. It is also the chief vehicle for demonstrating the job-relatedness of selection procedures under a disparate impact charge. Specific procedures are contained in the *Guidelines* for demonstrating job-relatedness. (These are examined in greater detail later in this chapter.)

EXHIBIT 6.1 Job Analysis and Equal Employment Opportunity: Overview

For the performance of the human resource management function or activity noted, this information is
Essential = √√
Useful = √
Not relevant = ○

JOB FACTORS	
Job identification data	√√
Job summary: Mission	√
Job Outputs: Products	√√
Services	√√
MTEWA	√
Materials and substances	√
Techniques and methods	√
Guidelines and controls	√√
Tasks	√√
Behaviors	√√
Contacts	√√
Context	
Work flow and plant layout	√
Physical environment	√
Job interrelations	√√
Terms and conditions	√
Legal requirements	√
WORKER CHARACTERISTICS	
Knowledges	√√
Abilities and skills	√√
Values, beliefs, and attitudes	√
Interests	√
Personal characteristics	√√

Job analysis provides the information for isolating the criterion and predictor variables needed for
- Demonstration of job-relatedness of selection procedures.
- Validation of selection procedures (same as above).
- Demonstration of BFOQ status of predictors, particularly of sex, age, education, and other personal characteristics.
- Verification of differential validity.
- Fulfilling the documentation requirements of the *Guidelines*.

In affirmative action programs, job analysis can provide the data required for fulfilling the following affirmative steps:
- Redesign of jobs in ways that provide opportunities for upward mobility of minority members that lack journeymen level KSAOs to progress in the field.
- Revamping selection procedures to reduce or to eliminate exclusionary effects on protected groups.
- Efforts to provide career advancement training, both classroom and on-the-job, to employees locked into dead-end jobs.

Affirmative Action. Job analysis is not specifically mentioned in the *Guidelines* with reference to affirmative action. However, the *Guidelines* do recommend a set of affirmative steps that the employer can take when selection procedures are found to have an exclusionary effect. The steps that require systematically gathered job information for their completion are noted in Exhibit 6.1.

SELECTED ISSUES IN EEO

Job analysis has many applications in EEO activities. Here we discuss two of the applications that have emerged as significant concerns in recent years.

Validation Strategies. Under the EEO laws and rules, validation is called for in cases of disparate impact. Once the plaintiff has successfully made a prima facie case of disparate impact, the employer has a choice. It can either modify or eliminate the procedure that is claimed to produce the disparate impact, thus taking it out of the coverage of the *Uniform Guidelines.* If the employer chooses not to do that, then it must justify the continued use of the procedure on grounds of *business necessity*. Practically, this means that the employer must validate the selection procedure, that is, show that a clear relationship exists between performance on the selection procedure and performance on the job. For practical purposes, validity is the same as job-relatedness.

Three validation strategies are recognized in the *Guidelines*: criterion related, content, and construct. The definitions of these three strategies provided in the *Guidelines* are as follows:

Criterion-related validity	Demonstrated by empirical data showing that a selection procedure is predictive of or significantly correlated with important work behaviors.
Content validity	Demonstrated by data showing that the content of a selection procedure is representative of important aspects of performance on the job.
Construct validity	Demonstrated by data showing that the selection procedure measures the degree to which candidates have identifiable characteristics that have been determined to be important for successful job performance (Sections 16D, E, F).

The job analytic procedures that are recommended for each of these three validation strategies in the *Guidelines* are reproduced in their entirety in Appendix L. Basically, job analysis serves as the vehicle for uncovering and processing information relating to the job and its incumbents that is needed for demonstrating job-relatedness. (The reader should review the contents of Appendix L before proceeding further.)

Extensive job study is required in the case of content and construct validation. For both strategies, job analysis is relied upon for uncovering the important or critical tasks and work behaviors that are required for successful job performance, their relative importance, and the products that result from the work. This requirement is extended under construct validation to identifying the constructs believed to underlie the successful performance of the job behaviors. Each construct is to be named and defined, so as to distinguish it from other constructs. A full job analysis is not required for criterion validation. The concern here is with identifying predictors and performance criteria that can be measured in statistical terms. A "review of information" is considered sufficient for choosing these measures. (For more details on the mechanics of validation, see: Schwab, 1980; American Psychological Association, 1980; Arvey, 1979; Dreher & Sackett, 1983.)

Validity Generalization. Validity generalization refers to the degree to which the inferences from results of selection procedures used in one situation can be transported to other situations. An instrument can be said to attain generalizability when it can be shown that it yields valid results in similar job situations across different organizations. (Note that generalizability and transportability tend to be interchangeably used in the literature.)

Validity generalization has great appeal to employers. To begin, test validation is costly in terms of time, money, and other resources. Also, individual employers, particularly those employing a small number of workers, do not have access to large enough samples to meet the technical requirements spelled out in the *Guidelines*. Perhaps the central attraction of validity generalization is the possibility of avoiding unnecessary and wasteful duplication of effort and expenditure of resources. If a device has been found to be valid in a particular context, and if the situation in which it is to be used resembles the original site of the validation, then it makes sense to use it. To conduct validity studies in every instance might in fact be similar to reinventing the wheel over and over again.

The *Guidelines* permit transportation of personnel devices across organizations by employers. Users may rely on validity studies conducted elsewhere under the following conditions.

- Evidence from the available studies indicates that the procedure is valid according to the validation standards contained in the *Guidelines* (Sections 7B and 14B).
- Incumbents in the user's job and the incumbents in the job or group of jobs on which the validity study was conducted perform substantially the same major work behaviors. Job analysis is the key to verification of job similarity.
- The device has been checked for fairness according to the procedures spelled out in the *Guidelines* (Sections 14 and 15, particularly Section 14B-8).
- Variables that could affect the applicability of the procedure to the new setting are appropriately taken into account. The user must consider variables such as performance standards, work methods, and representativeness of the employee populations and samples. The burden is on the employer to demonstrate the similarity between the two job contexts. If significant variations exist between the employer's job situation and the conditions under which the validation studies were conducted, the employer may not use the device or must conduct an internal validity study.

Validity generalization has figured prominently in legal deliberations and the professional research on test validation. The legal response is summarized by Kleiman and Faley (1985). The issue was specifically addressed in four cases: *Dickerson* v. *U.S. Steel Corp.* (1978), *Ensley Branch* v. *Seibels* (1980), *Rivera* v. *City of Wichita Falls* (1982), and *Pegues* v. *Mississippi State Employment Service* (1980). In the first three cases, the judges were guided by the standards set forth in the *Uniform Guidelines*, which place the burden on the employer to demonstrate the similarity between the two job contents and contexts. In *Ensley Branch*, the employer was found to meet the tests in the *Guidelines*. However, the two other employers failed to do so. In *Dickerson*, the test in question was ruled not be "transportable" since the employer presented no evidence demonstrating the similarity between the two job settings. In *Pegues*, the judge's ruling was influenced by the current validity generalization research reviewed in an authoritative publication of the American Psychological Association (1980) that was extensively reviewed by the employer's expert witness. In upholding the job-relatedness of the examination in question, the judge stated

> Empirical research has demonstrated that validity is not perceptibly changed by differences in location, differences in specific job duties or applicant populations. Plaintiff's allegations that validity is specific to a particular location, a particular set of tasks, and to a specific applicant population . . . is not true. (cited in Kleiman & Faley, 1985, p. 827)

Validity generalization has received considerable support in the professional literature. Variables that had previously been assumed to create differential impacts have proven not to be significant. Moreover, numerous studies have shown that, at least under some circumstances, between-study variance in observed validity coefficients can be explained to a great extent by measurement and sampling error (see Schmidt et al., 1985).

6.3 Job Design

To design a job is to structure the relations among the things, substances, methods, people, and other elements of the job situation. A job can be said to be designed when what the worker does, how he or she does it, where, and the sequence of activities and the interrelations of the job with other jobs are specified. Job design is inherently a prescriptive activity (Buchanan, 1979; Davis & Taylor, 1979).

The need for designing jobs systematically and consciously stems from several factors. To begin, organizations are rational undertakings. This means that organizations in today's society come about for the attainment of specific purposes. Since jobs are the building blocks of organizations, they need to be structured to aid the attainment of those purposes. Without structure, there is a possibility that the design of jobs might not be in alignment with the needs of the organization. This is a pervasive concern and stems from the very nature of organizations.

A second reason behind job design is the nature of modern technology. The machines, tools, equipment, and work aids (MTEWA) that form technological underpinnings of modern enterprises are highly specialized and expensive. Consider MTEWAs such as typewriters, computers, and word processors. Not only are they expensive to purchase, but their operation demands the use of specialized skills and abilities. To get maximum benefits from these devices, it is essential to know, in fairly specific terms, how they are to be used and the precise goals to be attained.

Perhaps the most urgent stimulus behind recent concerns with job design is the knowledge that the structure of the work has potentials for affecting the physical and psychological well-being of the workers. The potential for physical harm from poor job design is readily apparent. In addition, the modern workplace, particularly the factory, harbors a wide array of substances and other things that have potential for adversely affecting the health and safety of workers. Thus, a highly publicized article in *U.S. News & World Report* (February 1979) claimed that thousands of workers are currently being exposed to health hazards such as arsenic, asbestos, radiation, and lead that have potential for causing cancer and lung and kidney diseases.

The potential psychological consequences of job design have received considerable attention in recent years. The underlying issue here is the place accorded to the worker within the basic structure of the relationships. The choice in this regard is considerable and can be viewed on a continuum. At one end of the continuum can be placed jobs that relegate the worker essentially to the role of an adjunct to machines. The worker is viewed as the proverbial cog in a wheel, with little opportunity for exercise of talents and skills. At the other end can be placed jobs that are designed to facilitate active involvement of the worker in their performance. Latitude is allowed in regard to what the worker is to attain, how, and scheduling of activities. This approach makes it possible for the worker to exercise a broader range of capabilities and interests (for job design options and practices, see Davis & Taylor, 1979).

JOB DESIGN AND THE LAW

Job design practice is currently being affected by two bodies of laws: Occupational Safety and Health Act (OSHA) of 1970 and antidiscrimination laws, particularly Title VII of the Civil Rights Act of 1964. Under OSHA, the employer has the general duty to furnish employees with a place of employment that is free from recognized hazards that cause or are likely to cause death or serious physical harm. In addition, the employer has the specific duty of complying with safety and health standards provided under the act and as revised by enforcing agency (see Schuler, 1984, pp. 458–486).

The EEO laws do not directly address the job design function. But job redesign is mentioned in the *Uniform Guidelines* as part of the affirmative steps that an employer can take to remedy imbalances in employment of minorities. Thus, Section 17(3)(c) encourages employers to make a systematic effort to organize work and redesign jobs in ways that provide opportunities for persons lacking "journeyman"-level knowledge or skills to enter and, with appropriate training, to progress in a career field.

JOB ANALYSIS AND JOB DESIGN: OVERVIEW

Job analysis is ideally suited for aiding organizations in coping with problems stemming from work design. Exhibit 6.2 shows the job and person factors that are relevant to job design issues. Basically, the two principal products of job analysis (job descriptions and worker specifications) provide the baseline data needed for diagnosis and problem finding. (The interrelations between job analysis and job design were covered in Chapter 1; see particularly Exhibit 1.12.)

SELECTED ISSUES IN JOB DESIGN

Job analysis has been found to be useful in tackling many job design issues. We discuss three principal areas of application of job analysis in job design: quality of work life (QWL), job redesign, and job-person matching.

Quality of Work Life. This is a catchall that encompasses concerns covering both physical and psychological quality of the work environment. The model shown in Exhibit 6.3 captures the sources, concerns, and outcomes of work design that form the substance of the QWL movement. An implicit assumption of this model is that the way in which jobs are arranged has potential for affecting a set of outcomes of interest to society, organizations, and workers.

Roughly two types of factors are instrumental in bringing about the conditions that lead to undesirable outcomes: physical and psychological. Exhibit 6.4 provides a summary of work arrangements, practices, and hazards that are known to be instrumental in causing accidents. All these are reachable through the breakdown of the context variables contained in our job description schedule.

EXHIBIT 6.2 Job Analysis and Job Design: Overview

For the performance of the human resource management function or activity noted, this information is
Essential = √√
Useful = √
Not relevant = O

JOB FACTORS		
Job identification data	√√	Job analysis provides information for performing the following job design activities: Quality of work life programs. Job redesign. Job-person matching.
Job summary: Mission	√	
Job Outputs: Products	√√	
Services	√√	
MTEWA	√	
Materials and substances	√	
Techniques and methods	√	
Guidelines and controls	√√	
Tasks	√√	
Behaviors	√√	
Contacts	√√	
Context		
Work flow and plant layout	√√	
Physical environment	√√	
Job interrelations	√√	
Terms and conditions	√√	
Legal requirements	√√	
WORKER CHARACTERISTICS*		
Knowledges	√	
Abilities and skills	√	
Values, beliefs, attitudes	√	
Interests	√	KSAO data are useful for understanding the fit between job demands and worker capabilities and preferences.
Personal characteristics	√	

EXHIBIT 6.3 A Model of Occupational Ill-Health in Organizations

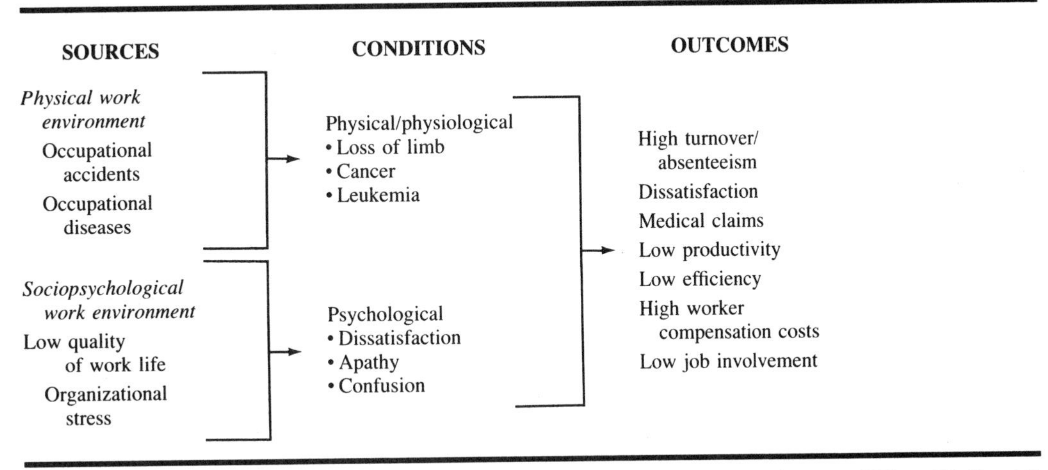

From R. S. Schuler, *Personnel and Human Resource Management* (St. Paul, Minn.: West Publishing Company, 1984), p. 464.

EXHIBIT 6.4 Work Arrangements, Practices, and Hazards That Cause Accidents

Code	Category	Definiition
850	TRAINING	Accident caused by lack of familiarity with safe operating procedures due to: absence of, incorrect, or ineffective training (at any level—management supervisory or employee). Examples of training deficiencies are
51		a. Lack of knowledge of the hazards involved.
52		b. Failure to demonstrate proper action.
53		c. Failure to warn against hazardous action.
54		d. Failure to provide retraining, including follow-up supervision, as necessary.
55		e. Failure to properly motivate supervision of employees.
860	WORK METHODS	Accident caused by work procedures (often a deviation from generally accepted safe practices) planned, directed, or condoned by management. Examples of deficient work methods are
61		a. Failure to formulate work procedures.
62		b. Improper selection of equipment, tools, materials, etc.
63		c. Failure to provide adequate help for material handling.
64		d. Improper assignment of personnel (disregard of employee physical limitations or skills).
65		e. Excessive production demands.
870	CONSTRUCTION MAINTENANCE	Accident caused by a defect in the physical condition of a structure, tool, machine, or component. Defect may result from
71		a. Deterioration.
72		b. Damage.
73		c. Lack of preventive maintenance.
74		d. Deficient design.
75		e. Deficient quality control.
76		f. Use of improper materials.
880	GUARDING	Accident caused by deficient guarding against contact with or exposure to mechanical, chemical, electrical, radiation, etc., hazards. Guarding includes stationary hazards protection (handrails, guard rails, toe boards, etc.) Examples of deficient guarding include
81		a. Substandard design or material.
82		b. Broken or damaged.
83		c. Never provided or missing.
84		d. Inadequate preventive maintenance.

EXHIBIT 6.4 Work Arrangements, Practices, and Hazards That Cause Accidents (*cont'd*)

Code	Category	Definition
890	ENVIRONMENTAL HAZARDS	Accident caused by general hazards of the workplace, which commonly affect anyone in the area regardless of his assignment. Examples of hazards are:
91		a. Excessive noise.
92		b. Improper illumination.
93		c. Inadequate ventilation.
94		d. Inadequate aisles or exits.
95		e. Inadequate clearance for moving persons or objects.
900	MENTAL/ PHYSICAL CONDITION	To be used only for an accident *clearly* caused by the mental and/or physical state of a person, whether that mental or physical state was brought about by natural or unnatural (drugs, alcohol, etc.) causes.
910	MALICIOUS ACT	To be used only for an accident *clearly* caused by an employee's deliberate and malicious act (contrary to reason or accepted practice.)
920	PERSONAL HUMAN ERROR	To be used only for an accident *clearly* caused by a human failure to follow known safe practices. Human errors may include a. Haste that is not employer motivated. b. Sudden or short lived inattention or distraction. c. Violation of rules and procedures where the rule was in effect before the accident and training was sufficient to properly motivate the employee. *Note*: Before using this category, determine that the accident cause should not be more properly classified elsewhere such as Work Methods or Training.
930	CAUSED BY OTHERS	To be used only for an accident *clearly* caused by person or agents not under the influence or control of the employer. Includes accidents caused by natural events such as earthquakes, tornadoes, floods, bites or stings from animals or insects, etc. *Note*: Equipment or employees of others on the premises should be under the control or influence of management. Therefore, an accident caused by such outside employees or equipment should be classified elsewhere.
940	UNCLASSIFIED	Not elsewhere classified or insufficient information to classify.

From The Bureau of National Affairs, Inc., *Safety Policies & the Impact of OSHA*, PPF Survey No. 117 (Washington, D.C.: The Bureau of National Affairs, Inc., 1977), p. 51. Copyright © 1977 by The Bureau of National Affairs. Reprinted by permission.

Job Redesign To redesign jobs is to alter the structure of the relations among things, substances, methods, people, and other elements of the job situation. Job redesign assumes the existence of jobs as concrete organizational units. The focus in redesign activity is to bring about a better alignment of the jobs with the needs of the organization and its people.

Job redesign may be instigated for one of two reasons: to remedy experienced inefficiencies and problems or as part of a program of change. The first of these would be triggered by developments such as low rates of productivity and high rates of absenteeism, turnover, accidents, grievances, and conflicts. The focus here would be on identifying the roots of such problems and in bringing about alterations in work design that aid in their control or elimination.

Job redesign can also be instigated as a part of a planned program of change. Such a program could result from alterations in the mission of the organization, pursuit of new products or services, introduction of different types of technology, or some other systemwide development. In such instances, the focus of the redesign effort would be on aligning the job with the emergent needs of the company. In some instances, existing jobs might be absorbed into different departments or perhaps even eliminated altogether.

Job analysis has potential for serving both these needs. When the redesign effort is directed at solving experienced problems, the job analyst could be a part of the team charged with diagnosing the source of the problem and in formulating solutions. The specialized contribution that the analyst provides these activities is the job description. Appendices B through I provide the instruments that can be used in diagnostic and descriptive activity. The checklist of questions given in Appendix H can be particularly valuable in diagnostic activity.

The responsibilities of the job analyst in a program of planned change that is not inspired by experienced problems, but that is directed at alterations in the fundamental mission and structure of the organization, are somewhat difficult to pinpoint. Here the analyst could serve as a resource person, sharing his or her knowledge of the job and skill composition of the labor force with the organizational planners, industrial engineers, and others involved in organizational redesign. In such instances, a "top-down" approach to job design is necessary. Sidney Gael has described how such an approach would work:

> When jobs do not yet exist, a panel of experts can use an organization's objectives as a starting point, a top-down approach, and identify the outputs that must be produced to attain objectives and the functions that must be performed to produce the outputs. Functions can then be broken down into tasks. With the top-down approach, it is not necessary to refer to jobs at all to analyze tasks and functions. The panel of experts, in this case, provides the details about function and task attributes, such as task importance, whereas in a bottom-up approach, task attribute information can be provided by job incumbents and supervisors. (quoted in Klatt et al., 1985, p. 130)

The efficacy of the top-down approach stems from the fact that few functions are entirely new. Even under circumstances where jobs are entirely new, it is frequently possible to describe the activities required quite accurately through the use of experts. Thus, activities involved in future jobs were forecast routinely by the U.S. Air Force and the National Aeronautics and Space Administration for space missions long before any space flights became a reality (Sidney Gael in Klatt et al., 1985, p. 130).

Job-Person Matching. This is a very popular and current concern of behavioral scientists. It rests on the commonplace but important notion that the demands made by jobs and the opportunities provided by them should match the abilities, needs, and aspirations of the persons assigned to perform them. The underlying postulate is that the greater the match, the greater the rates of productivity and satisfaction.

The matching of jobs and persons is a pervasive and important concern of human resource management in general. Aspects of it, however, can be isolated for analytic purposes. As a job design issue, the focus of job-person matching is on enhancing the fit between jobs in existence and current employees.

A large body of literature has recently accumulated on job-person matching. While alternative views exists, the Job Characteristics Model as proposed by Hackman, Lawler, Oldham, and their associates serves as the basis for much of the current research on the subject. This model was introduced in Chapter 3 (see particularly Exhibit 3.11). The dynamics behind job-person matching are summarized in five propositions: (1) to the extent that individuals believe that they can obtain outcomes that are valued by them by engaging in some particular behavior, the likelihood that they will actually engage in that behavior is enhanced; (2) outcomes are valued by individuals to the extent that they satisfy the physiological or psychological needs of the individual or to the extent that they lead to other outcomes that satisfy such needs or are expected by the individual to do so; (3) thus, to the extent that conditions at work can be arranged so that employees can satisfy their own needs best by working effectively toward organizational goals, employees will in fact tend to work hard toward the achievement of these goals; (4) most lower-level needs can be, and often are, reasonably well satisfied for individuals in contemporary society on a continuing basis and, therefore, will not serve as motivational incentives except under unusual circumstances; (5) individuals who are capable of higher-order need satisfaction will in fact experience such satisfaction when they learn that they have, as a result of their own efforts, accomplished something that they personally believe is worthwhile or meaningful (summarized from Hackman & Lawler, 1971, pp. 259–265).

Based on these propositions, the Job Characteristics Model identifies three properties of

EXHIBIT 6.5 Job Information Essential for Job Redesign to Enhance the Job-Person Match

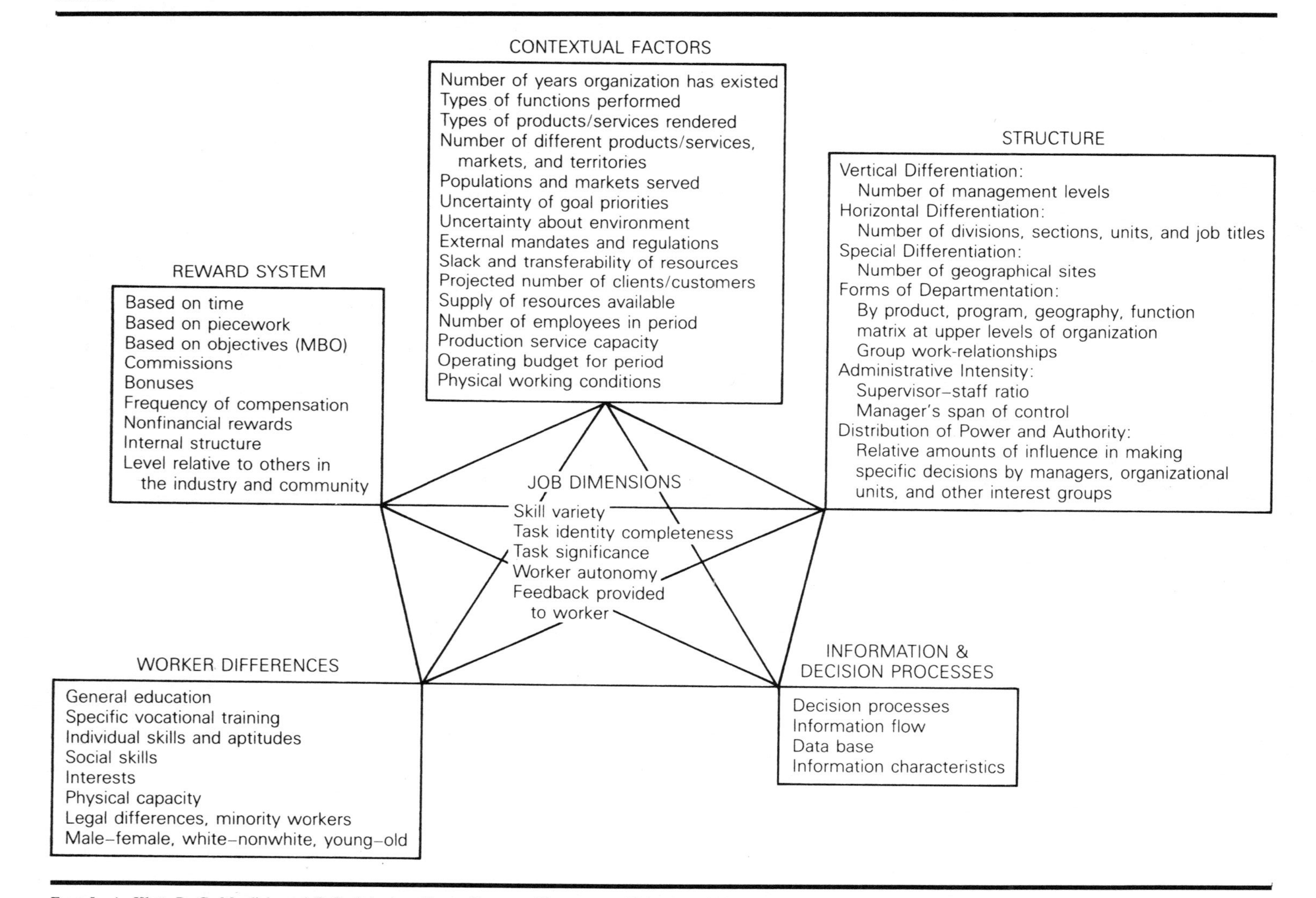

From L. A. Klatt, R. G. Murdick, and F. E. Schuster, *Human Resource Management* (Columbus, Ohio: Charles E. Merrill Publishing Company, 1985), p. 142. Copyright © 1985 by Bell & Howell Company, and based on J. R. Hackman and G. R. Oldham, "Motivation Through the Design of Work: Test of a Theory," *Organizational Behavior and Human Performance*, 16 (1976), 256, and A. H. Van de Ven and D. L. Ferry. Reprinted by permission.

jobs that have motivating potential: (1) the job must allow the worker to feel personally responsible for a meaningful portion of the work, (2) the job must provide outcomes that are intrinsically meaningful or otherwise experienced as worthwhile to the individual, and (3) the job must provide feedback about what is accomplished (Hackman & Oldham, 1980).

The tools provided by the Job Characteristics model for diagnosing the motivation potentials of jobs and the need patterns of the job incumbents are the Job Diagnostic Survey (JDI) and the Job Rating Form (JRF). The latter is reproduced in Appendix E-6. An elaborate set of principles and guidelines are provided for implementing job redesign by using data acquired from these instruments (see Hackman & Oldham, 1980).

The job analyst can participate in the job-person matching process by providing objective descriptions of jobs and ability and skill requirements. Exhibit 6.5 contains a summary of the types of job-related information that is relevant to discussions of job redesign, particularly with the goal of enhancing the job-person match. In this diagram, the required informational needs are linked with the five core job characteristics found in the Hackman and Oldham model (shown in Exhibit 3.11 in Chapter 3). The instruments given in Appendices B through I are relevant to this analysis. The Job Rating Form (Appendix E-6) would be particularly relevant to job-person matching efforts that rely on the Job Characteristics Model.

6.4 Human Resource Planning

Human resource planning consists of a set of activities directed at assuring the availability of human resources to achieve future organizational objectives. It is a forward-looking process through which management strives to have the right number and the right kinds of people, at the right places, at the right time, doing things that result in both the organization and the individual receiving maximum long-run benefit (Vetter, 1967, p. 15).

The steps and activities involved in human resource planning are shown in Exhibit 6.6. The stimulus behind human resource planning is provided by strategic management decisions at the total organizational level. These translate into a corporate plan that spells out the future demand for human resources. This demand is then compared with the human resource supply, both internal and external. The comparison yields the future net personnel requirements (NPRs).

EXHIBIT 6.6 The Human Resource Planning Process

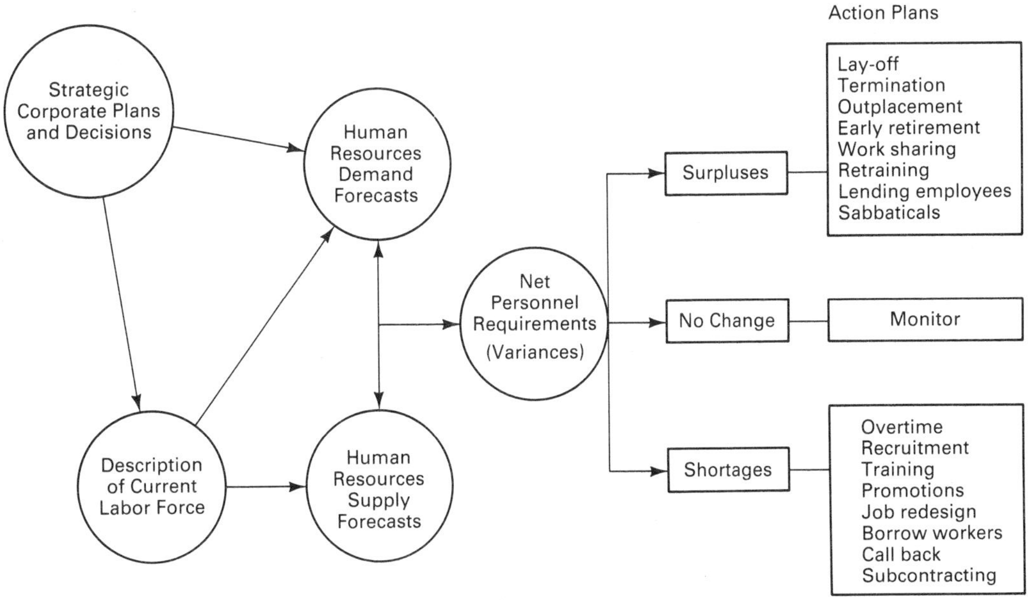

Action Plans

Strategic Corporate Plans and Decisions

Human Resources Demand Forecasts

Net Personnel Requirements (Variances)

Description of Current Labor Force

Human Resources Supply Forecasts

Surpluses

No Change

Shortages

Lay-off
Termination
Outplacement
Early retirement
Work sharing
Retraining
Lending employees
Sabbaticals

Monitor

Overtime
Recruitment
Training
Promotions
Job redesign
Borrow workers
Call back
Subcontracting

Three possibilities can be encountered in regard to the future NPRs: no change, surplus, and shortage. Each possibility is handled through different action plans. The "no change" condition is met by monitoring. The expectation of surpluses leads to actions such as outplacement, layoffs, early retirement, and transfers. When shortages are expected, the organization would have to hire from the outside, grant additional overtime to existing employees, or train for movements within the company.

Human resource planning thus has two major components. The first is an estimation of the future NPRs through forecasting of demand and supply. The second is the formulation of action plans for meeting the future requirements.

HUMAN RESOURCE PLANNING AND THE LAW

Human resource planning has potential for affecting the terms and conditions of employment of the labor force. It is thus within the purview of the civil rights/EEO laws and requirements. A more specific place for human resource planning in the EEO arena is in affirmative action. In the public sector, employers are obliged to undertake affirmative action regardless of disparate impact. Private employers are frequently required to undertake affirmative action in remedying proven cases of unfair discrimination. They are also encouraged to undertake such programs on a voluntary basis to remedy disparities in employment. Section 17(2) of the *Guidelines* specifies that the first step in affirmative action is work force analysis to determine the utilization status of the minorities. If substantial disparities are found, the employer is encouraged to undertake affirmative steps; chief among these are establishment of long-range goals and timetables, active recruitment of minorities, redesign of jobs to provide mobility opportunities, revamping of selection procedures to reduce or eliminate exclusionary effects, widening of the labor market pool, and career advancement and training.

JOB ANALYSIS AND HUMAN RESOURCE PLANNING: OVERVIEW

Job analysis has the potential for providing the basic data needed for human resource planning. Exhibit 6.7 shows the job and person factors that are relevant to human resource planning and the key uses to which they could be put in planning activities. To arrive at the NPRs, the planner needs data on both the jobs and the people occupying them. The information contained in job descriptions is critical for estimating future demand for human resources. Typically, job titles form the basis of demand forecasts. Knowledge of current outputs (types, quantities, and quality standards) can provide the foundation for anticipating changes in product lines and mixes of the future. Information relating to the "hows" of jobs (MTEWAs down to contacts in Exhibit 6.7) and context factors can provide the baseline data for the instigation of action plans that call for basic changes in the structure of the organization.

Information contained in worker specifications can be used in many areas of human resource planning. Adaptation to anticipated changes being the primary thrust of human resource planning, knowledge of the current capabilities, interests, and demographic composition of the labor force can provide the foundation of career planning, affirmative action, retraining, and other actions aimed at maintaining a fit between future job needs and human talents. (For a more complete breakdown of the data base essential for human resource planning, see *ASPA Handbook of PAIR*, Vol. IV, 2–66–2–68.)

SELECTED ISSUES IN HUMAN RESOURCE PLANNING

With the foregoing as an overview of the potential uses of job information in human resource planning, we now turn to some specific applications. Our concern in pursuing applications is not with showing the "hows" of human resource planning, but rather with highlighting the role of job analysis in selected areas that are of current interest.

Human Resource Forecasting and Matching. Job analysis has an obvious as well as a hidden role in forecasting and matching activities. To illustrate, consider the requirements forecast

EXHIBIT 6.7 Job Analysis and Human Resource Planning: Overview

For the performance of the human resource management function or activity noted, this information is
Essential = √√
Useful = √
Not relevant = ○

JOB FACTORS		
Job identification data	√√	Job and worker KSAOs information is essential for deriving net personnel requirements (variances) and for action planning. Examples are Job or work system redesign. Job elimination. Combining jobs and functions (job restructuring). Process modifications. Introduction of new technology. Job/role planning.
Job summary: Mission	√	
Job outputs: Products	√	
Services	√	
MTEWA	√	
Materials and substances	√	
Techniques and methods	√	
Guidelines and controls	√	
Tasks	√√	
Behaviors	√	
Contacts	√	
Context:		
Work flow and plant layout	√	
Physical environment	√	
Job interrelations	√√	
Terms and conditions	√	
Legal requirements	√√	
WORKER CHARACTERISTICS		
Knowledges	√√	Information on current worker KSAOs is essential for describing current labor force. Examples are Human resource inventories. Internal labor force description. Job/role planning. Career planning. Affirmative action planning.
Abilities and skills	√√	
Values, beliefs, attitudes	√	
Interests	√	
Personal characteristics	√√	

and resource matching plan shown in Exhibit 6.8. An obvious contribution of job analysis to such an undertaking would be job titles and other identification information. This is a basic requirement of all forecasting efforts and is one of the areas in which the planner relies on the analyst.

But note that for the company to meet even the modest goals of this matching plan, it needs some very accurate and current information on the contents of jobs and the competencies required for performing them. Thus, to arrive at the "responsibility levels" shown in Exhibit 6.8, this planner would first have to group jobs into families according to some relevant job descriptor. The feasibility of doing this hinges on the existence of job descriptions.

Note also that the feasibility of this matching plan shown at the bottom of Exhibit 6.8 hinges on the planner having access to information on the "promotability" of the internal candidates. Assessment of promotability, however, hinges on the existence of a systematic program of performance appraisal that in turn is not possible without job analysis. This is so because the criteria required for appraising performance can only be formulated through objective study of the outputs, methods, guidelines and controls, tasks, and other components of jobs. (More is said on this subject later in the section dealing with performance appraisal.)

Human Resource Information Systems. The computer now makes it possible to store and process large amounts of data. The growing availability of this device has raised hopes relating to the development of data banks or Human Resource Information Systems (HRIS) that can house critical job and employee data of relevance to personnel decision making. (Note that such systems are also referred to as skills inventories, job banks, and personnel inventories.

EXHIBIT 6.8 Human Resources Requirements and Matching Plan

Sample Manpower Requirements Forecast

Job/Skill Function: Marketing
Year: 197–

Responsibility Level	Number of Positions at Beginning* of Year	Increase (Decrease) in Staffing	Retirements†	Unscheduled Terminations	Primary‡ Open Positions to Be Filled	Vacancies Resulting from Promotions and Their Effects on Subsequent Levels						Total Positions to Be Filled
1	10	0	3	2	5	—	—	—	—	—	—	5
2	20	2	7	1	10	5	—	—	—	—	—	15
3	40	4	9	5	18	5	10	—	—	—	—	33
4	60	6	11	10	27	5	10	18	—	—	—	60
5	80	8	13	15	36	5	10	18	27	—	—	96
6	100	10	15	20	45	5	10	18	27	36	—	141
7	120	12	17	25	54	5	10	18	27	36	45	195
Totals	430	42	79	78	199	30	50	72	81	72	45	549

* Provides a check on each year's calculations.
† Requiring replacements.
‡ Primary open positions to be filled is the sum of increases (decreases) in staffing, retirements requiring replacements, and unscheduled terminations.

Sample Manpower Requirements/Resources Matching

Job/Skill Function: Marketing
Year: 197–

Responsibility Level	Total Employees at Beginning of Year	Total Promotable Candidates Available*	Retirements Among Promotables	Promotable Candidates Available for Promotion This Year†	Total Positions to Be Filled‡	Positions Filled with Promotable Candidates from Next Level	Positions Filled with Unpromotable Candidates from Next Level	Promotable Candidates Without Promotion Opportunity§	Requirements/ Resources Imbalance
1	10	5	1	4	5	1	0	0	0
2	20	10	1	9	15	15	0	8	+8
3	40	20	2	18	33	30	3	3	0
4	60	30	0	30	60	37	23	0	−3
5	80	40	3	37	96	48	48	0	−23
6	100	50	2	48	141	141	0	12	−48
7	120	160	7	153	195	195‖	0	5	+12
—	—	—	—	—	—	—	—	—	5
Totals	430	215	16	199	549	467	77	25	—

* For illustrative purposes, 50 percent of all position incumbents are assumed promotable in this year, or are promotable candidates carried over from the previous year when they did not have a promotion opportunity.

† For illustrative purposes, a simplifying assumption is made that the only turnover expected is scheduled retirements.

‡ From manpower requirements forecast (marketing/197.).

§ Promotable candidates without promotion opportunities during this year are carried forward to the next year and added to promotable candidates available for promotion this year.

‖ At the lowest organization level, positions filled with promotable candidates represents the function recruiting requirements; either external or from company positions below the lowest level included in the planning effort (e.g., nonexempt).

From E. H. Burack and J. W. Walker, eds., *Manpower Planning and Programming* (Boston: Allyn & Bacon, Inc., 1972), pp. 170–171.

Also, they can vary greatly in scope of coverage and place within the human resource management system.) (See Cascio, 1982, pp. 77–80; Burack & Mathis, 1980, pp. 245–290.)

Roughly four types of information are needed for operating such systems. First, it is essential to select and describe the jobs of strategic interest to management. Second, it is essential to describe the history and organizational context of the jobs. Third, the knowledges, skills, abilities, and other human characteristics (KSAOs) required for effective job performance need to be identified. Fourth, data corresponding to the KSAOs about the job incumbents have to be gathered and entered into the computer. Exhibit 6.9 contains ASPA's summary of the components of

EXHIBIT 6.9 Components of a Data Base for a Human Resource Information System

PERSONAL DATA

Name
Pay number or social security number
Sex
Date of birth
Physical description of employee (height, weight, color of eyes, etc.)
Names, sex, and birth dates of dependents
Marital status
Employee association participation
United Fund/Community Chest participation
Minority group classification

RECRUITING DATA

Date of recruiting contact
Responsible recruiter or interviewer
Source of candidate referral (newspaper ad, employment agency, etc.)
Product line experience
Managerial or supervisory experience
Foreign languages spoken, written, read
Publications authored
Special skills or hobbies of potential value to the business
Patents held
Elective governmental positions
Security clearances held

EDUCATIONAL DATA

College degree, high school diploma, level of educational attainment
Field of degree
Date of degree
Schools attended
Special employer sponsored courses completed
Professional licenses held

COMPENSATION/WORK ASSIGNMENT DATA

Exempt/nonexempt or hourly/salaried classification
Current salary or pay rate
Date of current salary level
Date and amount of next forecast salary/pay increase
Previous pay rates and dates effective
Previous dollar and percent increase and dates of increase
Organizational reporting level
Position title
Supervisor/individual contributor status
Job code
Hours worked
Premium time hours worked

PERFORMANCE EVALUATION/PROMOTABILITY DATA

Personal interests
Work preferences
Geographical preferences (for multiplant operations)
Level of aspiration
Rank value of contribution in current work group
Special nominations and awards
Appraisal reports
Date of last appraisal
Growth potential as rated by manager
Previous promotions considered for, and dates of consideration
Dates of demotion
Date of referral of candidate or application to interested management
Names of supervisors or managers referred to
Date of interview(s)
Date of offer of employment
Date added to payroll
Reasons for selection/rejection of candidate
Test scores and interviewer ratings
Number of jobs open for which candidate was potentially qualified
Number of other applicants for same open job or jobs

WORK EXPERIENCE DATA

Names and locations of previous employers
Prior employment chronology
Military service
Job skills possessed
Reason for demotion
Date of last internal transfer
Dates considered for apprenticeship or other special training
Reasons for elimination from consideration for apprenticeship or other special training
Dates of, type, and reason for disciplinary action

LENGTH OF SERVICE/LAYOUT DATA

Date hired by employer (actual or adjusted for lost service)
Seniority date (if different from date of hire)
Date of layoff
Last pay rate
Recall status

EMPLOYEE ATTITUDE/MORALE DATA

Productivity/quality measures
Absenteeism record
Tardiness record
Suggestions submitted (usually to a formal suggestion plan)
Grievances
Anonymous inquires/complaints
Perceived fairness of management practices regarding employees
Perceived fairness and soundness of management philosophy
Attitudes about credibility/honesty of management
Attitudes toward work, pay, supervisor, etc.

UNION MEMBERSHIP DATA

Union membership/representation status
Controlling union contract
Union officer status
Dues checkoff status

LOCATION/CONTACT DATA

Home address
City and state
Zip code
Home phone
Present component and work assignment
Geographic location of work assignment
Office phone
Emergency notification

BENEFIT PLAN DATA

Medical and/or life insurance plan participation
Pension plan participation
Savings plan participation (U.S. bonds, etc.)
Pay for time not worked (vacation, illness, lost-time accidents, personal time off, death in family, jury duty, military reserve duty, etc.)
Tuition refund plan participation
Etc.

SEPARATION FROM PAYROLL DATA

Date of removal from payroll
Reason for leaving
Forwarding address
Name and address of new employer
Amount of pay increase obtained with new employer
Eligibility for rehire

EXHIBIT 6.9 Components of a Data Base for a Human Resource Information System (*cont'd*)

SAFETY/ACCIDENT DATA

Noise level (in decibels) in work area
Exposure to noxious fumes or chemicals on job
Record of injury (date of accident, date reported, nature of injury, cause of injury, record of medical attention given, name of attending physician)
Classification of injury (disabling or nondisabling, days of work lost, lost time charged)
Physical limitations resulting from injury
Workmen's compensation claim data

OPEN JOBS OR POSITIONS DATA

Job request control number
Job title
Position or job code
Educational requirements
Experience requirements
Permissible salary range
Date by which position must be filled

WORK ENVIRONMENT DATA

Average educational level of co-workers
Average salary of co-workers
Number of job openings in component
Percent employees terminating employment (for some standard period)
Accident frequency and severity rates for position or component
Relative frequency of job changes in component
Manager's or supervisor's age
Manager's or supervisor's years supervisory experience
Selection or inheritance of employee by present manager
Relative frequency of manager's or supervisor's disciplinary actions
Manager's or supervisor's tendency toward strict or lenient rating of employees
Amount of overtime worked in component
Percent of employees dissatisfied with work, pay, supervisor, etc. in component

POSITION/JOB HISTORY DATA

Job or position ID number
Job or position code
Date job or position was established
Permanent/temporary classification of job
Identity of past incumbents in the job
Dates of change in job incumbents
Dates of vacancies in positions
Type of change involved for each person leaving the position (newly hired, lateral transfer, promotion from another position)
If a promotion, identity of position promoted from
Location of job in organization structure
Manager or supervisor to whom position reports

LABOR MARKET DATA

Analysis of local manpower availability
Unemployment levels by skill, occupation, age, sex, etc.
Predicted future manpower needs
Identification of scarce and surplus manpower pools
Wage and salary, shift differentials, etc.

From *ASPA Handbook of Personnel and Industrial Relations*, Vol. IV, *Planning and Auditing Pair* (Washington, D.C.: The Bureau of National Affairs, Inc., 1976), pp. 2-66—2-68.

data base required for HRIS. (The classification of factors shown in this exhibit does not follow the breakdown already suggested. However, the details contained in this illustration can be readily linked to the four informational categories just noted.)

The first three of these needs are clearly within the mandate of job analysis. In fact, they are covered in the two principal products of job analysis: job descriptions and worker specifications. However, since the computer can only accommodate numerical data, the scope of these descriptions would be somewhat limited. Alternatively, elaborate coding schemes would have to be developed. (See the *ASPA Handbook on PAIR*, Vo. IV, for ideas on how qualitative and quantitative data can be prepared for computer usage.)

Even though HRISs have been in existence for some time in the corporate sector, examples of their workings are not generally publicly available. Exhibit 6.10 shows the operations of a Skills Index, which was part of a larger HRIS at North American Rockwell. In this case, the use of the index is illustrated in filling a vacancy. Note that the process begins with a review of the job description and worker specification (identified as ''man requirements'' in the exhibit).

Job/Role Planning. This is a career planning strategy proposed by Edgar H. Schein (1978). It is based on the assumption that jobs and people are constantly in a state of change. Jobs evolve over time, reflecting the changing needs of the organization as it adjusts to changes in its environment. People likewise go through career stages, from being recruits to ultimately retiring. And during those stages, changes take place in their needs, aspirations, and vocational preferences.

Balance between organizational and individual needs is maintained during the association through sets of matching processes (Exhibit 6.11). Each state (or season) of a person's life requires different matching actions on the part of both the organization and the individual. But note that a continuing requirement in all these stages, and their corresponding interactions, is information about jobs and the KSAOs required for performing them.

EXHIBIT 6.10 Skills Index Used in Search Mode

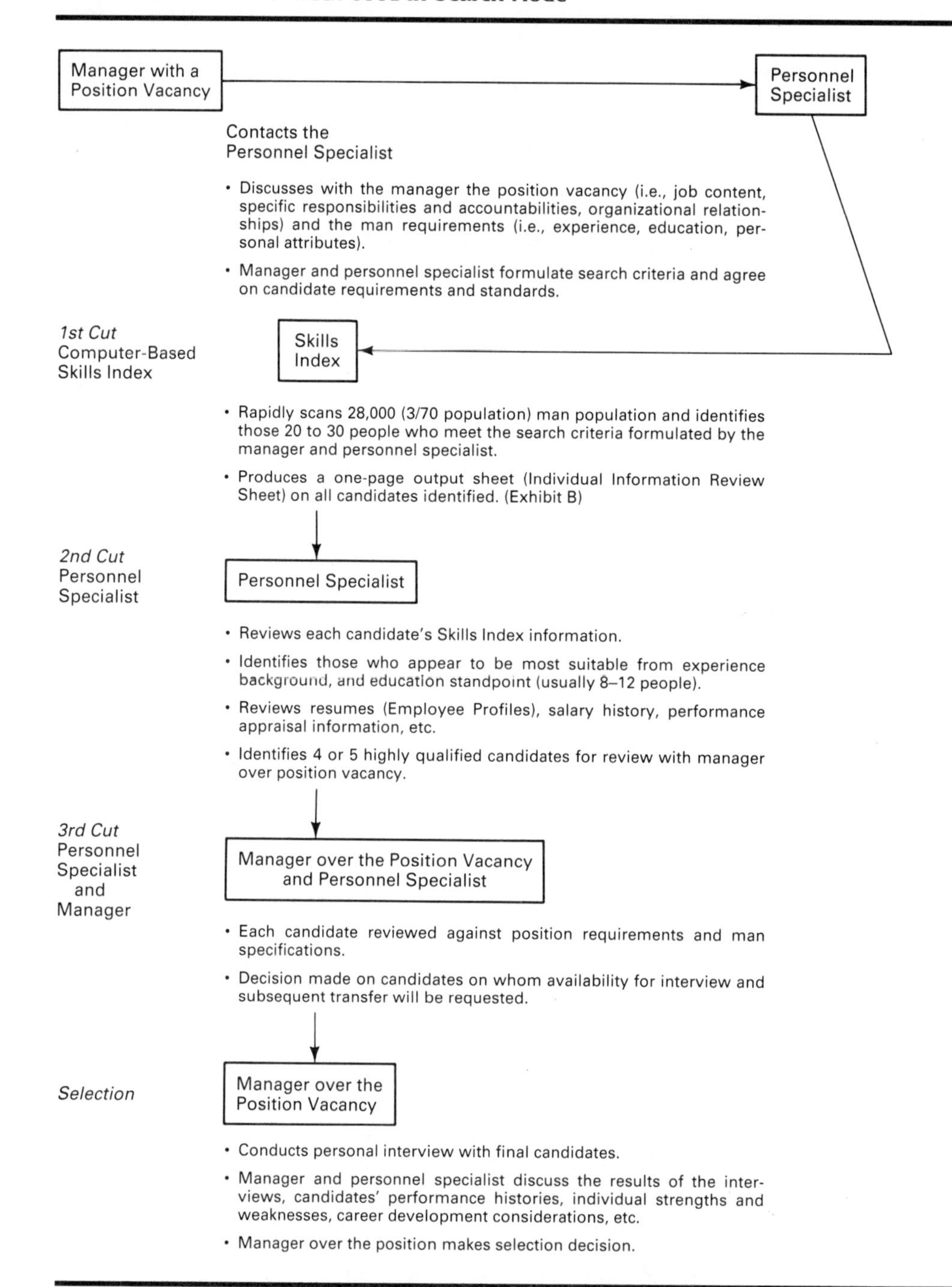

From E. H. Burack and J. W. Walker, eds., *Manpower Planning and Programming* (Boston: Allyn and Bacon, Inc., 1972), pp. 212–213. Copyright © E. H. Burack and J. W. Walker. Reprinted by permission.

So pervasive is the need for job information in the career planning process that Schein recommends that the human resource planner devote a portion of the effort to studying the evolution of jobs, independent of the people who may by occupying them. The purpose in doing so would be to ensure that the persons occupying such jobs in the future have the necessary skills, motives, and values required for performing them. He calls this activity job/role planning. In its current stage, job/role planning is tailored for managerial jobs. However, it can be readily adapted for other jobs. The process consists roughly of six steps.

EXHIBIT 6.11 Human Resource Planning and Development: A Temporal Development Model.

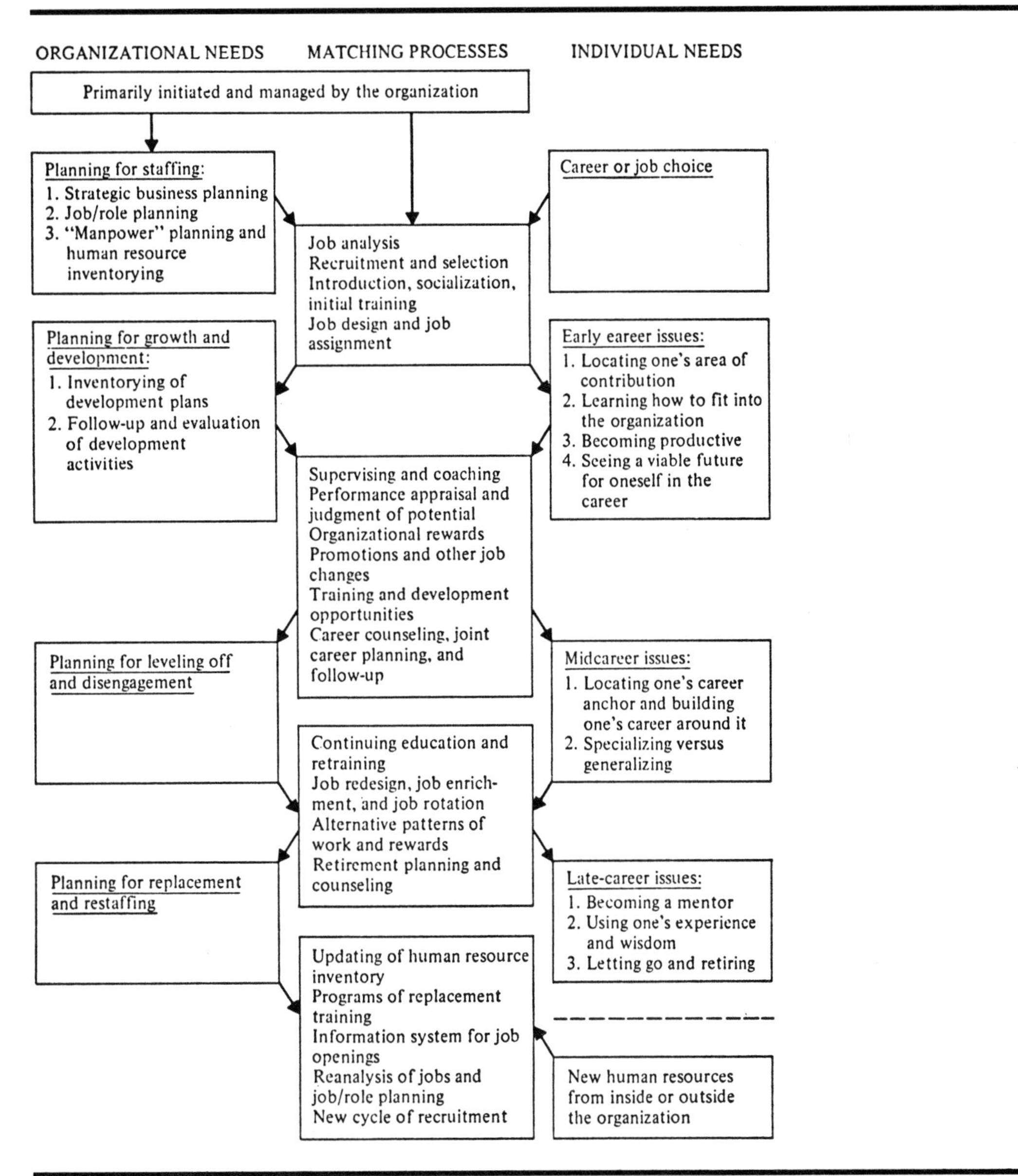

From Edgar Schein, *Career Dynamics*, © 1978, Addison-Wesley Publishing Company, Inc., Reading, Massachusetts. Page 201, Fig. 15.1. Reprinted with permission.

Step 1. Project into the future the major changes that will be occurring in the organization and its various environments.

Schein recommends that managers pay particular attention to technology, economic conditions, political-legal conditions, and sociocultural conditions and values. This analysis results in a forecast or a look into the future to project out the implications of the present.

Step 2. Develop a list of the key dimensions presently characterizing the job of the general manager.

Based on information obtained through observation and surveys of general managers, Schein proposes 11 dimensions as being relevant to job/role planning for managerial jobs. These dimensions are organized in questionnaire form as shown in Exhibit 6.12. This questionnaire is to be filled out by persons actually occupying managerial roles.

Step 3. Identify those dimensions that will be most affected by changes projected in Step 1, including the adding of new dimensions that may not have been thought of in Step 2.

Once the change-sensitive dimensions are identified, two actions are taken. First, knowledgeable persons are asked to comment on how the job will change in the future. The next step is identification of the dimensions showing the greatest amount of change from the present job description to future job protection.

Step 4. Identify the personal characteristics that will be relevant to effective performance on the key dimensions identified in Step 3.

This step consists of finding answers to the following question: Given the new characteristics of the managerial job just outlined, what skills, abilities, motives, and attitudes will be required to perform it successfully? Schein provides a questionnaire consisting of 45 items broken down into four basic categories: (1) motives and values—degree to which the person really wants to be a manager, is involved with the managerial career, and is comfortable in performing some of the duties and responsibilities of management; (2) analytical abilities and skills—problem solving and decision making, particularly by reliance on others; (3) interpersonal and group skills—communication, leadership, selecting subordinates, handling conflict, and interpersonal processes; (4) emotional skills—ability to work under pressure, tolerance for ambiguity, risk taking, persistence, and ability to take painful decisions. This questionnaire, called the Managerial Characteristic Profile, is reproduced in Appendix J-9 at the back of this book. In using this instrument, Schein recommends that room should be left under each major category for the planning team or individuals doing the rating to write in additional dimensions.

The Managerial Characteristics Profile is to be used to identify the motives, values, and skills relevant to effective performance of the dimensions identified in Step 3. For each key

EXHIBIT 6.12 Managerial Job/Role Profile

Each of the following dimensions expresses a key element of the managerial role.

1. Think about your present job/role. Rate your *present behavior* in your job by placing an *X* through the number that best describes your present behavior.
2. Now go back over the items and decide *ideally* what your present role requires of a manager. Rate each of the items on how the job role *should* be performed by putting a *circle* around the number that best expresses your opinion.

	Low				High
1. Degree to which I *integrate the efforts of others* who are technically more competent than I am.	1	2	3	4	5
2. Degree to which I have to rely on *secondhand information* that is gathered by my subordinates.	1	2	3	4	5
3. Degree to which I have to *monitor the thinking and decision making* of my subordinates rather than doing the thinking and decision making myself.	1	2	3	4	5
4. Degree to which I *facilitate the "processes" of management and decision making* rather than make day-to-day decisions.	1	2	3	4	5
5. Degree to which I identify problems and ensure that the right problems are worked on by others rather than solve the problems *brought to me* by others.	1	2	3	4	5
6. Degree to which I work with and in groups of various sorts (committes, meetings, task forces, etc.).	1	2	3	4	5
7. Degree to which I operate as a consultant/catalyst in my day-to-day managerial role.	1	2	3	4	5
8. Degree to which I am *dependent on my subordinates* for total performance rather than it being within my own control.	1	2	3	4	5
9. Degree to which my level of *responsibility* (accountability) *is greater than* my direct degree of control.	1	2	3	4	5
10. Degree to which I *actively manage the selection and development of my key subordinates.*	1	2	3	4	5
11. Degree to which I spend time considering the *long-range health of the organization* rather than the day-to-day performance of it.	1	2	3	4	5

From Edgar Schein, *Career Dynamics*, © 1978, Addison-Wesley Publishing Company, Inc., Reading, Massachusetts. Page 233, Table 16.1. Reprinted with permission.

dimension identified, a new list of relevant skills can then be constructed as the preliminary to the next step.

Step 5. Determine the degree ot which the present candidates for future opening possess the personal characteristics identified in Step 4.

Assessment of present candidates for future needs can be done in various ways. Schein discusses four methods: (1) self-ratings by present managers; (2) ratings by supervisors; (3) assessment centers, with or without psychological testing; and (4) global judgments by persons who know the candidates.

Whichever method is used, a decision must be reached as to whether the motives, values, and skills deemed necessary for future performance in the job being analyzed are (1) already present in some candidates; (2) developable in some candidates in a reasonable time frame; or (3) neither present nor developable, in which case a decision must be made to recruit from outside the organization or look for another source of candidates.

Step 6. Generate a plan for development of personal characteristics needed or for recruitment of new individuals with those skills, if development seems impractical.

This is the implementation step, and to complete it, the organization must (1) set about to select the candidates who are seen to have the requisite skills into the jobs when they open up, (2) launch the right development plans to have candidates ready when the jobs open up, or (3) plan to do whatever internal or external recruiting is necessary to generate qualified candidates (this summary is from Schein, 1978, pp. 221–242).

The concept of career planning has been around in one form or the other for some time. While it has always received wide support, the major stumbling block has been the absence of a plan of approach or method for instigating it. Job/role planning, as developed by Schein, offers a concrete approach to this subject. Although directed in its present form at managerial jobs, the basic plan can be modified and adapted to most job situations.

6.5 Recruitment and Selection

Recruitment and selection are two of the universally recognized functions of human resource management. The thrust of these functions is on meeting the current staffing needs of the organization. Recruitment refers to attracting and screening of candidates to determine eligibility, while selection involves choosing of candidates from those considered to be eligible.

The stimuli behind recruitment and selection activity is provided by human resource planning (Exhibit 6.7). When shortages are anticipated, the preoccupation is with hiring from the outside. The surplus condition calls for contracting of the existing labor force. The "recruits" under this condition are members of the internal labor force. The preoccupation is with terminating, retraining, and replacing those employees who do not suit the emerging job structure of the company. Under the no-change condition, there is no recruitment to be done from the outside. The preoccupation here is with finding candidates for promotion, transfer, and other routine internal movements.

Recruitment and selection have been traditionally thought of as functions that respond to expansions of the labor force. Our view, discussed already, emphasizes that they are ongoing activities. They happen all the time, with the thrust of the activity changing according to the immediate needs of the organization. This encompassing view of recruitment and selection is in keeping with the realities of the current economic conditions and employment patterns. It is also in harmony with the view expressed in the *Uniform Guidelines*.

RECRUITMENT, SELECTION, AND THE LAW

Most of the legal mandates and requirements that affect recruitment and selection activities have already been covered in previous discussions, particularly the section in this chapter dealing with equal employment opportunity. Our thrust in this section is with capturing the essence of the legal mandate as it relates to recruitment and selection in its broadest terms. We begin by noting that the primary concern of the employment relations laws is with assuring that all those who pursue opportunities in the employment arena are given a chance to do so without regard to race, religion, nationality, sex, and other purely personal characteristics. The following are the major substantive and procedural requirements specified in the *Uniform Guidelines* (1978).

- A very broad view is taken of a *selection decision*. It encompasses all decisions relating to hiring, discharge, compensation, training, promotion, demotions, referrals, retentions, licensing and certification, transfer, and training (Section 2B).
- A *selection procedure* encompasses virtually any decision-making tool, KSAO requirement, or even a construct that is used as a basis for a selection decision (Section 16Q).
- Selection procedures having *adverse impact* are considered to be discriminatory unless justified. Continued use of such procedures has to be defended through validation according to procedures provided for in the *Guidelines* (Sections 5, 6, 14, and 15; see Appendix L).
- Use of religion, sex, national origin, or age as selection criteria has to be justified on grounds of *business necessity*. The burden is on the employer to demonstrate that the criterion used in a bona fide occupational qualification (BFOQ). The courts have construed the BFOQ exception narrowly, tolerating its use only in the most justified cases. Race is not mentioned in the EEO laws as a potential exception; hence race may not be used as a BFOQ (Feldacker, 1983, p. 397).
- Employers are obligated to assure *fairness* of selection procedures. Selection 14B-8 of the *Uniform Guidelines* defines unfairness as follows:

> When members of one race, sex, or ethnic group characteristically obtain lower scores on a selection procedure than members of another group, and the differences in scores are not reflected in differences in a measure of job performance, use of the selection procedure may unfairly deny opportunities to members of the group that obtains the lower score.
>
> The *Guidelines* recognize that fairness with reference to selection procedures is a developing concept and that large samples are required for conducting fairness studies. Small businesses, therefore, are not required to conduct such studies. (For alternative views on fairness of selection procedures, see Arvey, 1979; Ledvinka, 1982; Reilley & Chao, 1982; Lawshe, 1983; Schmidt & Hunter, 1982; Norborg, 1984.)

- Employers in the public sector are required to undertake affirmative action to assure equal employment opportunity, while those in the private sector are encouraged to do so.

JOB ANALYSIS, RECRUITMENT, AND SELECTION: OVERVIEW

Job analysis has always had a prominent place as a tool in recruitment and selection activities. In recent years, it has also emerged as a requirement for meeting the legal mandates, particularly those contained in the *Uniform Guidelines*. Exhibit 6.13 provides an overview of the job and person factors that are relevant to recruitment and selection and the major uses that can be made of them in those activities.

- The primary operational use of job information in recruitment and selection is in the derivation of KSAOs required for effective job performance. This has been a time-honored use of job information. The techniques, methods, and processes involved in translating job information into KSAOs were discussed in Chapter 5.
- Job descriptions and specifications can serve as tools for training and guiding recruiters, supervisors, and others involved in the selection and placement decisions. The objective, written information derived through job analysis, can supplement the firsthand knowledge of the job situation held by these specialists.
- Job descriptions and specifications provide the information needed for constructing application blanks, inventories, checklists, and other instruments needed for human resource decision making.

EXHIBIT 6.13 Job Analysis and Recruitment and Selection: Overview

For the performance of the human resource management function or activity noted, this information is
Essential = √√
Useful = √
Not relevant = ○

JOB FACTORS		
Job identification data	√√	Job descriptions are used to derive worker specifications.
Job summary: Mission	√√	Job descriptions and worker specifications are used jointly in the following areas in recruitment and selection:
Job outputs: Products	√√	Selection plans for matching jobs and people.
Services	√√	Development of application blanks and other instruments.
MTEWA	√	Guides for recruiters and supervisors in hiring and placing workers.
Materials and substances	√	
Techniques and methods	√	Providing workers with realistic job previews (RJPs).
Guidelines and controls	√√	EEO concerns
Tasks	√√	Demonstration of job-relatedness of selection procedures.
Behaviors	√√	Investigations of fairness.
Contacts	√√	Promoting mobility of minorities.
Context		
Work flow and plant layout	√	
Physical environment	√	
Job interrelations	√√	
Terms & conditions	√√	
Legal requirements	√√	
WORKER CHARACTERISTICS		
Knowledges	√√	KSAOs can sometimes be used to make inferences about job tasks, behaviors, and characteristics
Abilities and skills	√√	
Values, beliefs, and attitudes	√√	
Interests	√√	
Personal characteristics	√√	

· Job information can serve as basis for providing workers with realistic previews of jobs. This is a relatively new development that shows promise of cutting down on turnover and reducing the dysfunctions associated with hasty and uninformed job acceptances. The basic procedure consists of exposing applicants to descriptions of the realities that they can expect to encounter at the job, if they should accept the offer. The expectation is that those who accept the job after being so informed would stay longer, adapt, and possibly experience greater levels of job satisfaction (Wanous, 1973, 1980; Breaugh, 1983).

· Job analysis is an integral part of the requirements for demonstration of job-relatedness (validation) of selection procedures, for establishing the BFOQ status of sex, age, and other personal characteristics and for fairness investigations (*Uniform Guidelines*, 1978).

· Information relating to horizontal and vertical linkages among jobs can be used for identifying mobility paths and other avenues of upward mobility for minorities. This addresses the second goal of the EEO laws (see Anderson et al., 1981; Boehm, 1981).

SELECTED ISSUES IN RECRUITMENT AND SELECTION

The many uses that can be made of systematically derived job information in recruitment and selection have been pointed out now and in previous discussions. Rather than expand on each of these, we limit our discussion to a couple of areas of application that are of particular significance and current interest to the professionals in the field.

Synthetic Validity. The need for having selection procedures that are valid, reliable, and fair is now widely recognized and strongly emphasized by the *Uniform Guidelines*. Unfortunately, businesses are not always able to meet the technical validation requirements for every device that is used, or needs to be used, due to constraints of time and other resources. But to operate with devices that are not validated could result in poor selection decisions, and possibly open the doors to legal retaliation from protected minorities in the presence of disparate impact.

Synthetic validation is one of the ways in which organizations can cope with at least a portion of their needs in personnel selection. It provides an approach to validation of tests, particularly the paper-and-pencil variety. It rests on the assumption that jobs that make common demands on employees in the form of work activities require similar KSAOs. Thus, teachers and salespersons share the basic requirement of verbal fluency. Both clerks and teachers need some level of numerical aptitude.

Capitalizing on the fact that different jobs make common demands on workers, synthetic validity provides a means for inferring validities of tests across job titles. According to M. H. Trattner of the U.S. Office of Personnel Management, there are currently three versions of synthetic validity: the original formulation by C. H. Lawshe, which goes by the commonly used label of synthetic validity; a version offered by McCormick and his associates known as Job Component Validity; and a variation linked with the J-Coefficient of Primoff's Job Element Method (Trattner, 1982).

All three versions of synthetic validity suffer from certain deficiencies that place them in conflict with the requirements in the *Guidelines*. Lawshe's version rested on the assumption of "natural selection," which postulated that employees who do not possess a high degree of an aptitude that is critical for occupational success will, by one mechanism or the other, be weeded out of that occupation. The traits exhibited by current employees of jobs can thus implicitly be assumed to exemplify those required for successful job performance. This is inconsistent with the *Guidelines*, which specify, in part, that validity of tests is to be demonstrated by correlating test results with actual work behaviors. McCormick's Job Component Validity also fails to meet the requirements of the *Guidelines*. This is so because the job components in this instance are standardized through the use of the PAQ; the links between job success and test scores is not direct. The problem with Primoff's version stems from the fact that it focuses directly on worker characteristics and not on required work behaviors (Trattner, 1982).

Taking these limitations into account, Trattner has proposed a fourth version of synthetic validity. Basically, it is a modification of Primoff's J-Coefficient, with the focus shifted from worker characteristics to job required behaviors as the starting point. Exhibit 6.14 reproduces the methodological and statistical details contained in an example used by Trattner to demonstrate how the J-Coefficient can be used for calculating synthetic validity of a test. The job in this instance is that of file clerk. We use these details to show the procedures involved in synthetic validation and to highlight the innovations suggested by Trattner.

EXHIBIT 6.14 Synthetic Validity: Calculation of the J-Coefficient of Test t for the Selection of File Clerks

(a) Generalized work behaviors performed in lower-level clerical occupations

a. Types simple copy
b. Operates switchboard
c. Performs simple calculations
d. Files material
e. Receives and directs visitors
f. Makes and assembles photoreproductions
g. Sorts mail and messages
h. Completes commercial and administrative documents
i. Operates card sorter
j. Keypunches data

EXHIBIT 6.14 Synthetic Validity: Calculation of the J-Coefficient of Test t for the Selection of File Clerks (*cont'd*)

(b) Rating scale to be used by SMEs for rating importance of work behaviors for file clerks

0—not performed	4—moderate importance
1—no importance	5—important
2—little importance	6—very important
3—some importance	7—critical

(c) Statistics required for calculation of J-Coefficient for file clerks

Intercorrelation of Work Behavior (r_{ij})											**Correlation of Test t with Work Behavior Score (Validity Coefficient of Test for Measuring Work Behavior) (r_{ti})**	**Mean Importance Ratings of Work Behavior for File Clerks (w_i)**
	a	*b*	*c*	*d*	*e*	*f*	*g*	*h*	*i*	*j*		
a		.20	.30	.40	.20	.30	.40	.20	.30	.40	.30	2
b			.20	.30	.40	.20	.30	.40	.20	.30	.40	0
c				.20	.30	.40	.20	.30	.40	.20	.50	0
d					.20	.30	.40	.20	.30	.40	.30	7
e						.20	.30	.40	.20	.30	.40	0
f							.20	.30	.40	.20	.50	4
g								.20	.30	.40	.30	0
h									.20	.30	.40	0
i										.20	.50	0
j											.30	0

(d) Formula for correlation of weighted sum of work behavior scores with a test score

$$r_{t(wsi)} = \frac{\sum_{i=1}^{q} w_i r_{ti}}{\left[\sum_{i=1}^{q} w_i^2 + \sum_{\substack{i=1 \\ i \neq j}}^{q} \sum_{j=1}^{q} r_{ij} w_i w_j\right]^{1/2}}$$

where:

$r_{t(wsi)}$ = correlation of a weighted sum of standardized work behavior scores with a test score.
w_i = importance weight for a work behavior.
r_{ti} = correlation of a test score with a work behavior score.
r_{ij} = intercorrelation of work behavior scores.
$1, i, j, q$ = work behaviors performed in a class of occupations.

(e) Calculation of validity of Test t for file clerks

$$r_{r(wsi)} = \frac{\begin{array}{r} \sum_{i=1}^{q} w_i r_{ti} \\ 2\,(.30) = .6 \\ 7\,(.30) = 2.1 \\ 4\,(.50) = \underline{2.0} \\ 4.7 \end{array}}{\left[\begin{array}{ll} \sum_{i=1}^{q} w_i^2 + & \sum_{i=1}^{q} \sum_{j=1}^{q} r_{ji}\, w_i w_j \\ & i \neq j \;\; .40\,(2)(7) = 5.6 \;\; (a.v.d) \\ \quad 4 & \quad\;\; .30\,(2)(4) = 2.4 \;\; (a.v.f) \\ \quad 49 & \quad\;\; .40\,(7)(2) = 5.6 \;\; (d.v.a) \\ \quad \underline{16} & \quad\;\; .30\,(7)(4) = 8.4 \;\; (d.v.t) \\ \quad 69 & \quad\;\; .30\,(4)(2) = 2.4 \;\; (f.v.a) \\ & \quad\;\; .30\,(4)(7) = \underline{8.4} \;\; (f.v.d) \\ & \qquad\qquad\qquad\quad 32.8 \end{array}\right]^{1/2}}$$

$$r_{t(wsi)} = \frac{4.7}{[69 + 32.8]^{1/2}} = .466$$

From M. H. Trattner, "Synthetic Validity and Its Application to the *Uniform Guidelines* Validation Requirements," *Personnel Psychology*, Vol. 35 (1982), pp. 383–398.

An important requirement in synthetic validation is the identification of the important elements of the job that influence the pattern of the required KSAOs. In Trattner's version, this is a two-step procedure. It begins with identification of generalized work behaviors common to a class of jobs or occupation. The work behaviors common to lower-level clerical occupations, of which the file clerk is a part, are given in section (a) of our illustration. The behaviors that are important for the job in question are then isolated by subject matter experts (SMEs) through use of a rating scale (b). The behaviors judged to be important for the job of file clerk are shown in the right-hand column in the table under section (c). The statistical values of work behaviors and test results needed for the calculation of the J-Coefficient are also shown in the table under section (c). These are obtained by measuring the performance of employees in several different jobs within the class on both the work behaviors judged to be important for the specific job and the selection test. The formula given under section (d) is used for calculating the J-Coefficient, which is taken thereafter as the validity coefficient of the test. In this case, the validity of Test t for the job of file clerk was estimated to be .466, as shown under section (e).

It is important at this stage to emphasize that synthetic validity is an evolving concept. Its major attraction is that it does not require situation specific predictor and criterion scores. Once the validity of a test is established according to procedures such as those illustrated in Exhibit 6.14, it can thereafter be used whenever the work behaviors for which it was validated are found to exist. But this is also its major disadvantage. It enables the user to demonstrate construct validity, with all the attractions and limitations of that validation strategy. It may be essential to follow this up with various manipulations of the data, or even resort to criterion-related validity to attain sufficient confidence in the results (for some ideas on how to proceed further, see Trattner, 1982).

Alternative Selection Strategies. Although a wide variety of concepts and tools have been available for making selection decisions, industry has traditionally relied heavily on two criteria: composite of education and experience (E&E) and psychological testing. Both raise numerous problems when examined in light of the current legal and other institutional demands. The E&E criterion fails to take into account individual differences in responses to common educational and work experiences leading to differences in quality of achievements. Also, heavy reliance on E&E has potential for accentuating disparities, since women, blacks, and other minorities have historically been denied employment opportunities on equal terms.

Psychological testing offers an alternative to blind reliance on credentials. Unfortunately, such testing has developed an unsavory reputation in industry due to persistent misuse. Also, the development of psychological tests that meet the legal requirements currently in force takes time, effort, money, and an immense amount of discipline. Industry is typically not willing to spend such energies on this tool (Wigdor & Garner, 1982).

For these reasons, a search has been in motion for some time for alternative selection procedures that can remedy the defects of those traditionally used and that also assure desirable levels of validity and fairness as required by the *Guidelines*. We comment next on two developments in which job analysis plays a critical part.

Work Sample Tests. As the name implies, work sample tests measure worker competency by taking a sample of behavior under realistic simulations of job conditions. Work sample tests can be sorted roughly into two categories: motor work samples, which require physical manipulation, and verbal work samples, which require communication or interpersonal skills. Examples of motor work sample concerns are carving dexterity test for dental students, shorthand and stenography for office workers, and map reading for traffic control officers. Examples of verbal work sample concerns are knowledge of law for law students, ability to follow oral directions, and speech interview for foreign students (Landy, 1985, p. 132).

Preliminary research on the validity of work sample tests has been quite encouraging. Large percentages of the studies using the work sample approach report validities in excess of .50. It appears, however, that motor work samples were better at predicting job proficiency, while verbal work samples were better at predicting training success (Landy, 1985, pp. 132–133).

Job analysis has a central role in the development of work sample tests. For both types of work sample tests, the first step is the objective study of the task and behavioral demands of the job. Job analysis provides the following information for developing work sample tests: a description of what the worker does, the methods and techniques followed, tools and equipment used, the outputs expected, and the required KSAOs. In short, the construction of two principal products of job analysis (descriptions and specifications) are a prerequisite for the development of work sample tests. (A short guide for construction of job sample tests is given in Plumlee, 1975).

Experience to date indicates that work sample tests that are based on systematic job study not only yield valid predictions of performance, but are also more liable to be perceived as being fair by applicants because of their clear face validity (see Campion, 1972; Schwartz, 1977; Schmidt et al., 1977; Cascio & Phillips, 1979).

Behavioral Consistency Method (BCM). Also known as "unassembled" and "nontest" selection, the Behavioral Consistency Method (BCM) draws on the familiar bit of conventional wisdom that states the best indicator of future performance is past performance. A distinction can thus be made between "signs" and "samples" of performance. Signs are conventional predictors such as education, experience, and aptitudes. Samples, on the other hand, are behaviors that are similar to the actual behaviors to be performed on the job. (The BCM is a variation of the Job Elements Method; see Appendix A for a discussion of the differences.)

The thrust of this approach in selection activity is on uncovering actual evidence of job-related achievements on the part of applicants. The principles that guide this approach are explained in a pioneering study that both developed and tested this approach (Schmidt et al., 1979).

- The best predictor of future behaviors of a given kind is a measure of past behaviors of a similar nature. A distinction is made between "exposures" and "behaviors." Exposures consist of education and experience that may, or may not, have called for the exact behaviors to be performed at the job. Behaviors, on the other hand, are actual achievements of the individual that are related to the requirements of the job in question.
- The rating procedure to be used in selection would place a strong emphasis on identifying and crediting past achievements that are actually job related. Achievements offered by the applicant for consideration are not required to be accomplished on the same or similar jobs. Even education and experience can be offered where they can be legitimately cited as indices of achievement that are behaviorally related to the job in question.

Detailed procedures are provided for acquiring and rating applicant achievements. Briefly, the KSAOs required for effective job performance are identified through the procedure used in the Job Elements Method, described in Chapter 5. Benchmark achievements are then developed and rated for each of the KSAOs. A portion of a benchmark achievements form for one of the KSAOs (Analytical and Quantitative Reasoning Abilities) of the job of budget analyst is given on the top of Exhibit 6.15. Applicants are asked to describe their achievements as they relate to each of the KSAOs according to a supplemental achievement form. The portion of the form that relates to Analytical and Quantitative Reasoning Abilities is shown at the bottom of Exhibit 6.15. Note the details asked of the applicants. The "examiners" then rate the applicants' achievements according to the benchmarks developed in making the selection decision.

The BCM approach, although relatively new, has received considerable support in the literature. It promises to remedy the major defects of conventional selection procedures. It fits squarely into the content validity requirements of the *Uniform Guidelines* and has potential for introducing job-relatedness, openness, and fairness in selection. Preliminary empirical evidence is also quite encouraging. Thus, the study by Schmidt et al. (1979), from which the foregoing was taken, compared the BCM approach with two other approaches and reported it to be superior in terms of content validity, lower estimated long-term costs, and higher interrater reliability. A study by Hough et al. (1983) tried out a very similar achievement-based selection strategy for positions held by attorneys in a large federal agency. In this instance, three "alternative" selection procedures developed through job analysis were compared with three "traditional" procedures. One of the alternative procedures, called the Accomplishments Record, was singled out by the authors as displaying high criterion-related validity, fairness, and other administrative merits.

EXHIBIT 6.15 Excerpts of Procedures Used in the Behavioral Consistency Method of Unassembled Examining for the Job of Budget Analysis

Portion of Benchmark Achievements for Item 1 in the Achievement Form
Item 1—Analytical and Quantitative Reasoning Abilities

Budget analysts must analyze complex technical data and other information, using logic and quantitative reasoning abilities. In doing this, they must be able to distinguish essential from nonessential information.

Benchmarks

2.25

(a) The operating budget for fiscal year 1974 was required for the general manager's review by September 1, 1973. I issued the call for estimates to the department supervisors, met with them individually and collectively to develop their anticipated costs based on a 5% cost level increase. Their estimates were submitted to me, and I analyzed, consolidated, and prepared them for presentation to the general manager and his submission to the president. (2.25)
(b) As a part of assigned duties, required to prepare quarterly status reports on various research projects based on submission of basic information from branch scientists, from other planning documents, and from previously reported data.
(2) In late 1963 while reviewing a research report on the aspects of microbiological studies, it appeared that a major objective had been achieved much earlier than anticipated. Subsequent discussions with team leaders confirmed that, although the researcher did state that to be, such had not occurred.
(3) Had these data been erroneously reported, the laboratory would have been subject to some embarrassment, to say the least. As it happened, reports were corrected and studies continued as planned.
(4) Finding the error was my achievement; correcting it was entirely the responsibility of the research team leader. (2.25)

Portion of the Supplemental Achievement Form (to be filled out by applicants)
Item 1—Analytical and Quantitative Reasoning Abilities

Budget analysts must analyze complex technical data and other information, using logic and quantitative reasoning abilities. In doing this, they must be able to distinguish essential from nonessential information. On a separate sheet of paper, give examples of your past achievements demonstrating these abilities.

DO NOT COMPLETE the following rating until you have described your achievements relevant to this factor. Remember to use a separate sheet of paper to describe these achievements. Do not forget to include, *for each achievement*,

1. What the problem or objective was.
2. What you actually did, and when (approximate date).
3. What the outcome or result was.
4. The estimated percentage of this achievement that you claim credit for.
5. The name, address, and telephone number of somebody who can verify the achievement.

The statements I have provided on this factor are accurate descriptions of my own achievements and the above rating reflects what I believe to be a fair evaluation of the achievements described.

Signature: ______________________ Date: ________________

From F. L. Schmidt, J. R. Caplan, S. E. Bemis, R. Decuir, L. Dunn, and L. Antone, *The Behavioral Consistency Method of Unassembled Examining* (Washington, D.C.: U.S. Office of Personnel Management, 1979), pp. 47, 53.

6.6 Performance Appraisal

Within organizational situations, individual performance can be viewed in two principal ways. First, with reference to the success attained by the individual in producing the outputs expected of the job. Successful performers from this perspective thus are those individuals who produce higher levels and/or better quality goods and services. The second way of viewing individual performance is in terms of tasks, functions, or behaviors that go with the job. Here, the focus is on what the individual did (or failed to do) in regard to behavioral expectations. Good employees are thus individuals who engage in behaviors that are valued by the organization.

Performance appraisal thus consists of sets of activities directed at assessing the accomplishments of workers with reference to job-relevant outputs and/or activities and behaviors that are valued by the organization. The steps and decisions involved in performance appraisal consist of the following.

- *Choice of the performance dimension for appraisal*: The options in this regard are outputs (products or services), tasks, or behaviors or a combination of these (see distinctions in Exhibits 2.1 and 2.2, in Chapter 2).
- *Specification of the criteria and standards to be used in appraisal*: Criteria refer to the operational translation of the performance dimension, and standards spell out the quantity and quality of performance expected of the individual.
- *Design of the appraisal instrument*: This is the performance appraisal form, and it specifies what is to be appraised and how. The choice here ranges from checklists to highly structured instruments with scales and other rating provisions.
- *Choice of appraisers*: Supervisors and other superiors are typically assigned the responsibility for performance appraisal. However, in recent years many organizations have experimented with peer, subordinate, and even self appraisals (Carroll & Schneier, 1982; Bernardin & Beatty, 1984; Landy & Farr, 1983).
- *Rules for conduction appraisals and making decisions*: These can encompass dates, times, and places of appraisal as well as guidelines for interpreting performance data.
- *Follow-up actions*: Steps for correcting poor performance, counseling employees, or enhancing performance during future periods.

The results of performance appraisals can be used for various purposes. The most logical and common use of appraisals is for personnel decisions relating to compensation, promotion, retention, and discipline. Appraisal data can also be used for predicting future performance, for establishing training needs and objectives, and as criteria in personnel research (Cascio, 1982, p. 310).

Performance Appraisal and the Law

Performance appraisal practices of industry have come under increasing legal scrutiny in recent years. Lawmakers, government agencies, the courts, arbitrators, and other third parties have intervened in regulation of the conduct of the performance appraisal function. The general concern of third-party involvement has been with encouraging objectivity and fairness of appraisal practices and decisions. Our review of these developments is limited to the provisions of the *Uniform Guidelines* and case decisions and interpretations. (For more complete analyses of the state of the law relating to performance appraisal, see Bernardin & Beatty, 1984, pp. 42–61; Edwards, 1979.)

Uniform Guidelines. Performance appraisal practices are covered in the *Guidelines* in a fairly direct way. The following are the major provisions of the *Guidelines* affecting this function.

- Performance appraisal decisions qualify as "employment decisions," and performance appraisal procedures qualify as "selection procedures" (Sections 2A and 16Q).
- Since performance appraisal decisions and procedures are considered to be covered by law, all the provisions of the *Guidelines* relating to discrimination, adverse impact determination, job-relatedness, BFOQ, fairness, and affirmative action have relevance for the conduct of this function. The employer is thus obligated to respect all the mandates of equal employment opportunity in conducting performance appraisals.
- A very broad view is taken of criteria in the *Guidelines*. This term encompasses production rate, error rate, tardiness, absenteeism, length of service, success in training, and paper-and-pencil tests (Section 14B-3).
- A measure can be both a predictor or a criterion, depending on the purposes to be served. Thus, employee success in a training program can be considered as a predictor if used for subsequent job assignments. It becomes a criterion when used to judge the accomplishments of the employee as a training participant. This is simply another way of emphasizing that performance decisions qualify as employment decisions, with all the attendant EEO requirements and expectations of employers. (This issue was deliberated at various levels in the *Washington* v. *Davis* case decided by the Supreme Court in 1976; see Bernardin & Beatty, 1984, p. 129.)

Case Law Relating to Performance Appraisals. Performance appraisal has figured prominently in employment litigation in recent years. In the paragraphs that follow, we present the common concerns and prescriptions that have arisen through legal decisions as revealed in authoritative reviews of cases.

An analysis of important cases led Holley and Field (1975) to suggest that inappropriate use of evaluations may occur for any one or more of the following reasons: (1) the performance rating method has not been shown to be job related or valid; (2) the content of the performance rating method has not been developed from thorough job analysis; (3) raters have not been able consistently to observe the ratees performing their work; (4) ratings have been based on raters' evaluations of subjective or vague factors; (5) racial, sexual, and other such biases of raters may have influenced the ratings given to ratees; and (6) ratings have not been collected and scored under standardized conditions (p. 428).

Cascio and Bernardin (1981) attempted to trace the implications of performance appraisal litigations for personnel decisions. Their review of case law led them to offer the following prescriptions: (1) appraisal of job performance must be based upon an analysis of job requirements as reflected in performance standards; (2) appraisal of job performance only becomes reasonable when performance standards have been communicated and understood by employees; (3) clearly defined individual components or dimensions of job performance should be rated, rather than undefined, global measures of job performance; (4) performance dimensions should be behaviorally based, so that all ratings can be supported by objective, observable evidence; (5) when using graphic ratings scales, avoid abstract trait names (e.g., loyalty, honesty) unless they can be defined in terms of observable behaviors; (6) keep graphic rating scale anchors brief and logically consistent; (7) as with anything else used as a basis for employment decisions, appraisal systems must be validated and psychometrically sound, and the ratings must be given by *individual* raters; and (8) provide a mechanism for appeal if an employee disagrees with a supervisor's appraisal (p. 211).

A review by Kleiman and Durham (1981) focused on the standards used by the courts in their assessment of performance appraisal systems when used as a basis for promotion decisions. They offered the following suggestions for developing legally and professionally acceptable appraisal systems for use in promotional decisions: (1) *adverse impact*—employers should keep accurate records of eligibility of employees for promotions and adopt a strong EEO posture; (2) *preparedness to defend system*—regardless of adverse impact, employers should be continually prepared to defend their systems; (3) *use of objective data*—these data add to defensibility of the system, if such data are relevant; (4) *use of subjective ratings*—if these are to be used, employers should rely on qualified raters and demonstrate job-relatedness through a careful job analysis of the promoted positions; (5) *construct validity*—regardless of the job analytic procedure used, the employer must also collect data on the ratings to demonstrate that the appraisal instrument had construct validity, that is, it measures the characteristics that it was intended to measure (pp. 118–119).

This brief review of the *Guidelines* and case law illustrates that performance appraisal procedures now have to meet some very stringent requirements to gain legal acceptance. It also highlights the indispensability of job analysis as a tool in developing valid and legally defensible appraisal systems. (Also, see Edwards, 1979; Schneier, 1978; Schuster & Miller, 1982; Bernardin & Beatty, 1984, pp. 42–61.)

JOB ANALYSIS AND PERFORMANCE APPRAISAL: OVERVIEW

Job analysis has an indispensible part to play in performance appraisal. Exhibit 6.16 provides an overview of the job information that is needed for performance appraisal and the specific uses to which it can be put. Roughly five categories of uses are made of job information in performance appraisal:

- *Formulation of criteria of performance.* This is universally acknowledged to be the primary application of job analysis in performance appraisal.
- *Development of rating methods and instruments for appraising performance.* All the systems of job analysis reviewed earlier have something of value to offer in this application. The critical incidents technique is particularly suitable for reaching the behaviors involved in successful job performance (see Bernardin & Beatty, 1984).

EXHIBIT 6.16 Job Analysis and Performance Appraisal: Overview

For the performance of the human resource management function or activity noted, this information is
Essential = √√
Useful = √
Not relevant = ○

JOB FACTORS		Job information is used in the following areas in performance appraisal:
Job identification data	√√	Development of criteria and standards for appraising performance.
Job summary: Mission	√	Development of performance appraisal instruments.
Job outputs: Products	√√	Meeting EEO requirements relating to job-relatedness (validity) and fairness investigations.
Services	√√	Administrative concerns:
MTEWA	√	Raters—who should rate?
Materials and substances	√	Purposes to be served by ratings.
Techniques and methods	√	Frequency of appraisals.
Guidelines and controls	√√	Timing of appraisals.
Tasks	√√	Modes of data processing.
Behaviors	√√	Research on performance, motivation, and productivity.
Contacts	√√	
Context		
Work flow and plant layout	√	
Physical environment	√	
Job interrelations	√√	
Terms & conditions	√	
Legal requirements	√√	
WORKER CHARACTERISTICS		
Knowledges	√√	
Abilities and skills	√√	
Values, beliefs, and attitudes	√	
Interests	√	
Personal characteristics	√√	

- *Verification of job-relatedness of criteria and instruments.* A primary concern here is with meeting the requirements of the *Uniform Guidelines* concerning job-relatedness and fairness of criterion measures and methods.
- *Decisions relating to administrative and practicality concerns such as who should appraise, purposes to be served by appraisals, frequency of appraisals, timing of appraisals, and modes of processing performance data.*
- *Research on performance, productivity, and motivation.* This is an emerging concern, but the role of the job analyst in fulfilling this function is not as yet sufficiently understood (this component was influenced by Bernardin & Beatty, 1984, pp. 15–39; Landy & Farr, 1983).

SELECTED ISSUE: PERFORMANCE CRITERIA

Of the various uses just discussed, the development of criteria and standards is the most central to the operation of effective performance appraisal systems. We dedicate the rest of this section to this concern.

Broadly viewed, a performance criterion is a measure of success on the job. It provides both a definition of employee success as well as a yardstick for appraising it in absolute or relative terms. An absolute assessment of success shows how close the employee came to meeting the performance expectations of the assessor. Relative success, on the other hand, refers to the position of the employee on the performance measure in comparison with other employees.

Classification of Criteria. Viewed as measures of success, criteria can be sorted into various categories. The following are the categories typically discussed in the literature.

- *Output criteria*—jobs are primary action units or vehicles for the production of the goods and services needed by the organization to attain its goals. The outputs that a particular job is organized to produce provide a logical basis for appraising the performance of the worker assigned to the job. When used as criteria of performance, outputs provide measures of the success attained by the employee in meeting the basic mission of the job. As emphasized earlier, job outputs can consist of products or services. Output criteria can thus be quantitative or qualitative, tangible or intangible. Exhibit 6.17 provides a collection of results-based performance criteria that are used under management-by-objectives (MBO) appraisal methods.
- *Input criteria*—inputs refer to the material, ideational, and human resources used in the manufacture of the job outputs. With reference to assessment of human performance, two kinds of inputs are relevant to job performance: worker competencies and behaviors undertaken by the worker in task performance. Of these two, current thinking favors the latter. This is so because competencies merely provide assessment of the potential for performance; they are not in themselves performance viewed in an action sense. To put it another way, what the worker does is more important in measuring performance than what the worker is capable of doing. Use of competencies as criteria of performance frequently places the focus on abstract traits that are difficult to measure and that lie outside the immediate control of the worker.
- *Behavioral criteria*—these consist of activities, contacts, interfaces, and other forms of behaviors engaged in by the worker in job performance. The focus here is squarely on the actions undertaken by the worker in meeting the obligations of the role. Whether a behavior is an ouput or input would depend on the context. Thus, number of telephone calls per day made by a salesperson can be viewed as an input into the selling function. Calls per day can also be viewed as indices of productivity or output. (The distinction between tasks and behaviors that was made earlier is critical in understanding the role of behavior in job performance; see Chapter 2, particularly Exhibit 2.2.)

Criteria for Criteria. An interesting body of literature has emerged recently addressing the issue of criteria for appraisal of criteria. Next we present the criteria that are commonly used in appraising the worth of performance measures as criteria of performance.

EXHIBIT 6.17 Results Used as Measures in Management by Objectives

Type A units sold
Transfers due to unsatisfactory performance
Training programs
Minority persons hired
Warranty claims
Items entered in a ledger
Days off the job
Mileage per replacement vehicle
Turnover
Sales
Tools replaced
Reduction in expenses from previous period
Extent of contribution and amount of innovation in the project (i.e., highly creative ideas)
Rejects
Pedestrian-vehicle accidents
Visits to the first-aid room
Cost of material used in training
Reports completed by X date
Community complaints received
Maintenance budget plus or minus
Grievances received
Profit by product line
Mileage per replacement tire
Potential contribution to total sales and profits
Returned goods
Research projects completed on time and within budget
Traffic accidents
The rate at which individuals advance
Transfers at employee's request
Employees ready for assignment
Units constructed
Days tardy
Earnings on commissions
Length of service
EEOC complaints received
Units produced
Claims received and processed
Containers filled to capacity
Discharges
Plus or minus budget
Dollar savings realized from projects
Burglaries
Errors in filing
Housing units occupied
Cost of each research project against budget
Damaged units shipped
Value of new cost-reducing procedure
Days sick
Percentage of profits to sales
Garbage cans emptied
Contributions and suggestions made via the suggestion program
Ratio of maintenance cost to product cost
Calls per day
Penetration of the market
Number of repairs on warranty
Time to reach expected results
Injury accidents
Letters typed
Minority persons trained
Cost of maintenance per machine
Number of promotable persons
Number of new versus old units sold
Successful completion of a course
Number of crimes against persons
Number of disgruntled customers
Results of a morale or attitude survey
Cost of spoiled work
Calls answered
Return of invested capital
Gallons used per vehicle
Amount of downtime
New customers per month
Customers maintained for one year
Customers paid by end of month
Delinquency charges
Percentage of deliveries on schedule
Number of customer complaints as a percentage of monthly purchase orders
Percentage of rejects in total monthly volume
Ratio of factory repair time to total production hours per month
Number of units service-free during warranty period
Cost per unit of output per month
Equipment utilization time as a percentage of monthly available hours

From H. John Bernardin and Richard W. Beatty, *Performance Appraisal: Assessing Human Behavior at Work* (Boston: Kent Publishing Company, 1984), pp. 193–194.

- *Relevant*—this is the ultimate concern in choosing criteria. The measures that are used should be logically and statistically related to job success. Ideally, they should provide direct assessments of job performance (i.e., the criteria and the performance factor should be the same). When such direct measurement is not possible, the measures that are used should reflect the behavioral demands or requirements for attaining the ultimate results that are desired.
- *Measurable*—criteria that do not lend themselves to measurement open the doors to bias and unfairness in appraisals. Such criteria do not have a place in performance appraisal in the modern context.
- *Objective*—as much as possible, performance criteria should minimize the influence of human judgment in assessing performance. Both the *Uniform Guidelines* and case law tend to favor reliance on objective measures of performance.
- *Sensitive*—criteria measures should be capable of discriminating between effective and ineffective performance. They should bring out the variability in achievement of different workers. (For more complete discussions of criteria for criteria, see Cascio, 1982; Bernardin & Beatty, 1984, pp. 131–142).

Responsibilities of the Job Analyst. Job analysis has a definitive role in the derivation of performance criteria. The following are the major contributions that the job analyst can make in formulating criteria that meet the foregoing tests.

- *Identification of the critical dimensions of the job that are relevant to performance appraisal.* In this regard, job analysis is the key to understanding the outputs, the inputs, and the context variables that are relevant to performance appraisal. This is the starting point for formulation of criteria. Although all job analysis systems have something of value to offer in this regard, functional job analysis and the critical incidents technique have proven to be particularly useful in isolating the job dimensions relevant to successful job performance (see, particularly, Olson et al., 1981).
- *Understanding the linkings among job components and performance effectiveness.* Job analysis is the basis for bringing out the behavioral, procedural, and process links involved in attaining the goals of the job.
- *Ranking of performance dimensions relevant to successful job performance.* This is both a managerial need as well as a legal requirement. To assure validity and fairness, the appraiser needs to know which tasks, behaviors, and other facets of human involvement are critical to job performance. (An example of how tasks can be rated for importance was given in Chapter 4, Appendix 4.1.)
- *Development of performance standards to measure levels of achievement.* Criteria of performance specify what is to be measured. Performance standards, on the other hand, spell out the expectations relating to quantity, quality, frequency, and timing. Job analysis is the key to understanding the standards of performance expected of the worker.

6.7 Compensation

Broadly viewed, to compensate employees is to reward them for their contributions to the organization. The focus of the compensation function, however, is on financial rewards such as pay and benefits. The compensation determination process consists of the following steps and decisions.

- *Defining objectives of compensation.* The primary objective of all compensation programs is to pay employees for producing the outputs that are expected of the job. Compensation programs can also be designed to retain competitiveness, to enhance productivity, to assure internal and external equity, to control costs, and to conform to the requirements of federal and local laws and guidelines.
- *Job evaluation* (rank ordering of jobs based upon their relative worth to the organization): Job evaluation is typically aimed at preserving internal equity of the wage structure.

- *Compensation surveys* (study of industry practices relating to wages, salaries, and benefits): Such surveys provide the employer with a basis for judging its comparative standing on compensation; they also address the issue of external equity.
- *Determining the wage structure*: This refers to the actual composition of the wage and salary package; it reflects the decisions that have been made relating to competitiveness, incentives, number and width of the pay grades, placing of jobs within pay grades, dollar amounts assigned to pay grades, and differentials among pay plans (French 1982, p. 427).
- *Administrative rules and procedures*: These address planning, budgeting, monitoring, and evaluating the compensation programs. Included in this section are rules for processing and delivering the wages, salaries, incentives, and benefits.

COMPENSATION AND THE LAW

Compensation practices of industry are subject to regulation through a wide variety of federal, state, and local laws and guidelines. We discuss in the paragraphs that follow its status under the EEO laws and requirements.

EEO Laws and Guidelines. The laws that have had the greatest impact on compensation decisions in recent years are the Equal Pay Act and the Civil Rights Act. The Equal Pay Act prohibits discrimination on the basis of sex when men and women perform equal work on jobs in the same establishment requiring equal skill, effort, and responsibility and that are performed under similar working conditions. Pay differences are allowed between equal jobs when they can be justified on the basis of differences in seniority, quantity and quality of performance, factors other than sex such as differences in training required for the job, and differences in working conditions such as hazards, heat, cold, and ventilation.

Title VII of the Civil Rights Act is much broader in coverage and intent than is the Equal Pay Act. It bans employment practices that discriminate against employees on the basis of race, color, religion, sex, or national origin. Compensation is included as a term or condition of employment. The Equal Pay Act was partially incorporated into Title VII via the Bennett Amendment, which allows wage differentials between men and women, if such differentials can be justified on the basis of the provisions of the Equal Pay Act. (For the full text of this provision, see Section 703(j) in Exhibit 1.7, Chapter 1.)

Since compensation is considered a term or condition of employment, all *employment decisions* that affect it come within the coverage of the act and the *Uniform Guidelines*. The procedures that are used in making these decisions thus also fall within the scrutiny of the law. The requirements of the *Guidelines* relating to job-relatedness of employment practices, fairness, affirmative action, and other EEO concerns are carried over into the compensation function.

Comparable Worth. The interpretation of the language of Title VII has been a problem. The crux of the issue is whether the jobs have to be equal or comparable in value to receive equal pay. The courts have gone back and forth on this issue of comparable worth. After reviewing leading cases on the subject, Milkovich and Newman offer the following summary:

> These court decisions imply that pay differentials between dissimilar jobs will not be prohibited under Title VII if the differences can be shown to be based upon the content of the work, its value to the organization's objectives, and the employer's ability to attract and retain employees in competitive external labor markets. They also suggest that the results from an employer's own job evaluation study . . . will be determinative unless the employer can demonstrate some business reason for deviating from their own study's results. (1984, p. 177)

The last sentence of the foregoing excerpt is of particular significance. It means that employers who conduct systematic job evaluation may not deviate from the results of their study without demonstrating business necessity. In other words, if the employer's own plan shows that two different jobs are of comparable worth, the employer is then obliged to pay comparable wages, unless differentials can be justified on the basis of market conditions or some other legitimate, business reason (see, also, Treiman & Hartmann, 1981).

JOB ANALYSIS AND COMPENSATION: OVERVIEW

Job analysis is clearly an integral part of the compensation function. Exhibit 6.18 provides a summary of the job information that is relevant for compensation decisions and the uses to which it can be put in compensation management. These are briefly discussed now.

- The primary use of job information in compensation is in deriving compensable factors and job families. A compensable factor is any job-related factor that is used as a criterion for determining the relative worth of the job within the job hierarchy. Compensable factors serve as the foundations of job evaluation. A job family is a grouping of jobs attained according to scores on common descriptors. Job families provide the basis of job classifications. Both these are derived from the two principal products of job analysis: job descriptions and worker specifications.
- Job analysis procedures have a vital role in assuring compliance with EEO requirements relating to fairness and equity in compensation. Helen Remick (1981) has provided a definition of comparable worth and a set of suggestions for minimizing bias in job evaluation systems. She offers the following operational definition of comparable worth:

> the application of a single bias-free point factor evaluation system within a given establishment, across job families, both to rank-order jobs and to set salaries. (p. 377)

According to Remick, bias in job evaluation systems can be minimized by checking in the following areas:

EXHIBIT 6.18 Job Analysis and Compensation: Overview

For the performance of the human resource management function or activity noted, this information is
Essential = √√
Useful = √
Not relevant = ○

JOB FACTORS		
Job identification data	√√	Job and KSAO information is essential for the following activities in compensation:
Job summary: Mission	√√	Derivation of compensable factors.
Job outputs: Products	√√	Derivation of job families.
Services	√√	Job evaluation.
MTEWA	√	EEO concerns relating to
Materials and substances	√	Pay equity and fairness.
Techniques and methods	√√	Justification of pay differentials.
Guidelines and controls	√√	Demonstrating job relatedness of compensable factors.
Tasks	√√	
Behaviors	√√	
Contacts	√	
Context		
Work flow and plant layout	√	
Physical environment	√√	
Job interrelations	√√	
Terms & conditions	√√	
Legal requirements	√√	
WORKER CHARACTERISTICS		
Knowledges	√√	
Abilities and skills	√√	
Values, beliefs, and attitudes	√	
Interests	√	
Personal characteristics	√√	

Factors chosen for analysis: Does the job evaluation system include factors usually associated with women's work (e.g., responsibility for people rather than things, literacy, the noise of office machines, or the poor working conditions created by many word processors)?

Factor weights: Are factors usually associated with women's work always given less weight? Can such differences be justified on basis other than sex?

Application: The best system in the world can be undone with a biased application. Are your job descriptions bias-free, or do men manage and women supervise, men interpret, and women use? Are the evaluators sensitive to the full scope of women's jobs.

Salary setting: Is a single salary scale used? If not, do the scales for women's jobs give consistently less return (lower salary) for worth (points)?

- Job analysis provides performance criteria and standards that can be used for justifying differentials among employees within the same job group. Job evaluation provides the wage and salary rates and ranges for jobs. Performance appraisal determines the earnings of particular individuals based on differences in accomplishments.

SELECTED ISSUES IN COMPENSATION

With the foregoing overview of the role of job analysis in compensation, we now examine a set of issues of particular consequence in today's context. The issues that are selected for detailed consideration are compensable factors, job families, and job evaluation.

Compensable Factors. This is a primary contribution of job analysis in the compensation process. A compensable factor is a job attribute that is actually used in appraising the worth of jobs. Exhibit 6.19 provides examples of compensable factors used in six job evaluation systems. All the items contained in this illustration have been encountered in our discussions of job descriptions and worker specifications. The point that needs to be emphasized here is that in compensation decisions, they serve as basis for differentiating jobs.

Compensable factors provide the basis for evaluating jobs. The place that a job occupies within the job hierarchy is determined directly by its relative standing on the factors that comprise the system. This being the case, compensable factors need to measure up to the following criteria:

1. *Job-relatedness*—The factors must reflect the actual demands made by the job.
2. *Criticality*—The factors must capture the critical behavioral or contextual demands of the job.
3. *Universality*—The factor must be found in all the jobs included in the job evaluation system.
4. *Discriminality*—The factors must be found in varying amounts in all the jobs; attributes that exist in equal amounts would be worthless in comparing jobs.
5. *Independence*—The factors must not overlap in meaning; practically this means that scores on one factor should not correlate significantly with scores on the other factors; overlapping leads to double weighting of factors within the evaluation set.
6. *Acceptability*—The factors must meet the approval of the parties who are going to be affected by the results of the job evaluation; if complete acceptability is not possible, the factors must at least reflect the union, management, minority, and other relevant perspectives within the organization.
7. *Clarity of Terminology*—All those who are to be affected by the evaluation must understand and agree on the meaning of the factors; significant disagreements on this fundamental issue might erode the credibility and acceptability of the factors by the parties (based on Belcher, 1974, p. 136).

EXHIBIT 6.19 Summary of Compensable Factors Used in Six Job Evaluation Systems

Bass	NMTA (AAIM)	Hay and Purves	Henderson	FES
SKILL 1. Intelligence or mental requirements 2. Knowledge required 3. Motor or manual requirements 4. Learning time	SKILL 1. Education (5)[*] 2. Experience (5) 3. Initiative and ingenuity (5)	KNOW-HOW 1. Practical procedures, specialized knowledge, and scientific disciplines (8) 2. Managerial (4) 3. Human relations (3)	KNOWLEDGE 1. Education (8) 2. Experience (8) 3. Skill (8)	KNOWLEDGE REQUIRED BY THE POSITION (9)[†] 1. Nature or kind of knowledge and skills needed 2. How these knowledges and skills are used in doing the work
WORKING CONDITIONS 1. Physical application 2. Nervous application 3. Occupational working conditions	EFFORT 1. Physical demands (5) 2. Mental or visual demands (5)	PROBLEM SOLVING 1. Thinking environment (8) 2. Thinking challenge (5)	PROBLEM SOLVING 1. Interpretation (8) 2. Compliance (8) 3. Communication (8)	SUPERVISORY CONTROLS (5) 1. How the work is assigned 2. The employee's responsibility for carrying out the work 3. How the work is reviewed
RESPONSIBILITY 1. Relate directly to type of work performed in a machine shop business	RESPONSIBILITY 1. Equipment or process (5) 2. Material or product (5) 3. Safety of others (5) 4. Work of others (5)	ACCOUNTABILITY 1. Freedom to act (7) 2. Job impact on end results (4) 3. Magnitude (4)	DECISION MAKING 1. Interpersonal (8) 2. Managerial (8) 3. Asset (8)	GUIDELINES (5) 1. The nature of guidelines for performing the work 2. The judgment needed to apply the guidelines or develop new guides
	JOB CONDITIONS 1. Working conditions (5) 2. Unavoidable hazards (5)			COMPLEXITY (6) 1. The nature of the assignment 2. The difficulty in identifying what needs to be done 3. The difficulty and originality involved in performing the work
				SCOPE AND EFFECT (6) 1. The purpose of the work 2. The impact of the work product or service
				PERSONAL CONTACTS (4)[‡]
				PURPOSE OF CONTACTS (4)[‡]
				PHYSICAL DEMANDS (3)[‡]
				WORK ENVIRONMENT[‡]

[*] All numbers in parentheses refer to the number of degrees or profile statements that further define the subfactors.

[†] The unique design features of FES incorporate the subfactor descriptions directly into the description of the respective universal factor and the degrees (or levels as termed in FES) apply directly to the factors.

[‡] There are no subfactors for this factor.

From Richard I. Henderson, *Compensation Management: Rewarding Performance*, 4/e, © 1985, p. 282. Reprinted by permission of Prentice-Hall, Inc., Englewood Cliffs, New Jersey.

The steps involved in deriving compensable factors are fairly straightforward in conception; they can be summarized as follows.

- *Select participants*: Job evaluation is an inherently judgmental process requiring the participation of two types of persons: job analysts and evaluators. The role of the analyst in this process is to gather and provide the required job information, while that of the evaluators is to select and rate the compensable factors.
- *Analyze jobs*: The job description is the source of content and context factors, while the specification provides the KSAOs required for effective job performance.
- *Choose compensable factors*: The criteria for compensable factors given serve as yardsticks for retaining factors. It is quite common to use standardized lists of compensable factors, such as those shown in Exhibit 6.19, as guides for choosing factors.
- *Establish degrees and assign weights*: Degrees refer to levels or amounts of the factor found in the job, while weights reflect the differences in importance attached to each factor. (See factor breakdowns in the FES scales reproduced in the appendices at the back of the book for examples of degrees and weights.)
- *Incorporate the factors into the job evaluation system according to the factor structure requirements and rules of the system*. Most structured systems require that the factors be broken into both degrees and weights.

Job Families. A job family is simply a group or cluster of jobs that are in some manner related. Examples of job families that are commonly found in the industry are groupings of jobs contained in the U.S. Government's Standard Industrial Classification, the occupational classes contained in the *Dictionary of Occupational Titles* (1976), and the Census Classification. The following distinctions are also examples of job family groupings: white-color/blue-collar, managerial/nonmanagerial, and skilled/unskilled. (Note that the terms job families and job classifications can be used interchangeably; for a finer distinction, classification can be viewed as the process of arriving at job families.)

Recent interest in development of job families is tied very closely to the issue of validity generalization discussed earlier. Briefly, the *Uniform Guidelines* (1978) allow for grouping of jobs that have similar or substantially similar work behaviors to attain adequate sample sizes when verifying criterion-related validity of selection procedures. Job families have also been found to be useful in the performance of a wide range of human resource management functions such as compensation, personnel classification, career guidance, and performance appraisal (Pearlman, 1980, p. 6).

To serve their multiple purposes, job families need to be meet two tests: (1) The what, why, and how of the job classification undertaking must be clear and acceptable to the persons that are going to be affected by the results. This is so because unlike performance appraisal, selection, and other ongoing human resource activities, the development of job families is a relatively specialized concern. The need for doing it, how it is to be done, and the specific purposes that the resulting classifications are going to serve thus should be spelled out and publicized in advance. (2) The job families that result should be distinct entities. This is the ultimate substantive test of a job family grouping. For the groupings to be practically useful, there should be no significant overlap between members of one group with those of others. The greater the overlap, the less useful the classification. (For statistical and other methodological issues involved in constructing distinct family groupings, see McCormick, 1979; Pearlman, 1980; Cornelius et al., 1979; Arvey et al, 1981; Lee & Mendoza, 1981; Sackett et al., 1981; Stutzman, 1983; Taylor, 1978.)

The steps involved in development of job families are very similar in conception to those followed in job function development (Chapter 4, Exhibit 4.4), KSAO generation (Chapter 5), and other classifying activities that have been discussed in preceding sections and chapters. Our discussion of the job family development process is therefore limited to pointing out the particular needs of this activity.

- *Define purposes of classification*: This is important because, as noted, grouping of jobs into families can serve multiple purposes. In compensation, classification is typically resorted to for justifying pay differentials.
- *Choose jobs to be grouped*: For compensation purposes, jobs considered for grouping are usually the same as those that are to be systematically evaluated.
- *Identify descriptors*: Virtually any job factor qualifies as a descriptor. Contemporary practice, however, limits use of this term in classification activity to those factors that are consciously used as yardsticks for grouping jobs. The choice in regard to descriptors covers the entire gamut of job content, job context, and person factors that have been discussed in prior chapters. Descriptors serve as "criteria" for family groupings; they should thus meet all the tests required of criteria (see criteria for criteria under performance appraisal).
- *Scale descriptors according to their measurement properties*: The distinctions between qualitative and quantitative and levels of measurement (nominal, ordinal, interval, and ratio) drawn in Chapter 2 are relevant to this step. In classifying activity, descriptors can be rated for their presence or absence, degrees found in jobs, relative importance, criticality, or significance. It should be apparent that quantification is an inherent part of classifying activity.
- *Rate jobs according to the scale format decided in the prior step and tabulate the results*: The success experienced in attaining distinctive groupings would hinge entirely on how well the preceding steps have been completed.

Job Component Method of Job Evaluation. The four traditional methods of job evaluation (ranking, classification, factor comparison, and point) have received wide coverage in human resource management and compensation textbooks. It is not essential, therefore, to analyze them in this presentation. Instead, we dedicate the rest of this section to a relatively new method offered by McCormick and his associates known as the Job Component Method (JCM) of job evaluation.

The JCM is actually a variation of the synthetic validation strategy discussed earlier. Its most common applications have been in validation of tests and other selection procedures. An adaptation of the basic strategy for job evaluation purposes was presented by McCormick to the Committee on Occupational Classification and Analysis of the National Research Council. (The reader should review the discussion relating to synthetic validity under the recruitment and selection section of this chapter before proceeding further; take particular note of the procedures summarized in Exhibit 6.14.)

The four traditional methods of job evaluation just noted all require the gathering of job-oriented information about jobs for making compensation decisions. Under the JCM, a job inventory takes the place of such information. The general procedures that are followed under the JCM of job evaluation consist of four steps:

1. The analysis of a sample of jobs in terms of an appropriate structured questionnaire with job elements consisting of tasks or basic human behaviors, and usually working conditions. The individual job elements, or statistically related groups thereof, can be considered as job components.
2. The derivation, for this sample of jobs, of money values for the individual components, in particular indexes of the extent to which the individual components contribute to the going rates of pay for the jobs. (This is a statistical procedure.)
3. The analysis with a structured job analysis questionnaire of specific jobs for which evaluations are to be made.
4. The derivation of an index of the total monetary value for each such job. This is done by "building up" the total value for each job from the indexes of the relevance of the individual components to the job, in combination with the money values of the components as previously derived from the original sample of jobs as described in steps 1 and 2 (quoted verbatim from Treiman & Hartmann, 1981, p. 122).

Under McCormick's version of the JCM, the PAQ would serve as the structured job analysis questionnaire. Whichever questionnaire is used, the JCM procedures result in statistically derived indexes of total job values (McCormick, 1979, pp. 317–321).

6.8 Training and Development

The training and development function addresses the ongoing needs of organizations for ensuring that the competencies of their employees are in line with the demands of their jobs. The difference between training and development hinges on specificity of objectives. Training is a relatively more specific activity; it is aimed at assuring a fit between worker competencies and specific task and other job demands that are of current relevance. Development, on the other hand, is directed at enhancing the adaptive capabilities of individuals; the concern is with enabling individuals to adapt to anticipated changes or to complex job situations.

The training and development process consists roughly of three phases and activities: training needs analysis, training, and evaluation of training effectiveness.

Training Needs Analysis. This is a four-stage process consisting of the following levels of analysis and activities:

- *Organizational analysis*: The unit of analysis is the entire enterprise, and the preoccupation is with isolating the ''wheres'' of training or the segments of the labor force in need of training. The sources for determining the ''where'' of training are organizational goals and objectives; human resource inventories; indices of organizational climate such as strikes, grievances, turnover, and customer complaints; and efficiency indices such as costs of labor and materials, waste, down time, and exit interviews (Moore & Dutton, 1978, p. 534).
- *KSAO requirements*: The unit of analysis here is the job or jobs that are identified as deserving attention through organizational analysis. The operational concern is with finding out what the employees need to be taught to perform the job at the desired levels. The first step here is job description. This is then used to arrive at the KSAOs needed for successful job performance. (The discussion in Chapter 5 of this book is particularly relevant to this step.)
- *Person analysis*: This step is concerned with finding out how the employees stand with respect to the desired KSAOs. This is done by matching the required KSAOs with the assessments of employees provided through performance appraisals, work sampling, interviews, specially designed questionnaires, and tests of job knowledge, proficiency, and achievement (Moore & Dutton, 1978, pp. 539–540).
- *Training objectives*: Comparison of the required with the actual yields information about the objectives to be attained through training. These can be stated in terms of KSAOs (e.g., improve specific competencies) or in terms of outputs (e.g., reduce production costs by 7 percent by a certain date after completion of training).

Training. The information acquired through the training needs analysis phase is used to devise the training program and to conduct the training. This phase includes the following activities and decisions:

- *Criteria of training effectiveness*: Derived from the training objectives.
- *Training program*: Selection of training methods and techniques, and design of training schedules and activities.
- *Conduct of training*: Implementation of training program.

Evaluation. The criteria of training effectivness resulting from the training objectives serve as basis for this phase. An integral aspect of this phase is evaluation of the feedback from the trainees and their supervisors, peers, and other co-workers (Goldstein, 1986).

TRAINING AND THE LAW

Under the *Uniform Guidelines*, training decisions qualify as employment decisions. All the provisions and requirements of the *Guidelines* relating to EEO and affirmative action thus apply to the training function. The legal status of the potential sources of differential impacts and discrimination against minorities in training are as follows.

Training as a Requirement. The issue here is whether certain types of training and educational preparations may be specified by employers as entry requirements at the time of hiring or as conditions for promotion and job assignments. This issue was first addressed in *Griggs* v. *Duke Power* in 1971. It has been subsequently debated and refined in several other cases. The current legal position on this subject is that such requirements need to be justified on the grounds of job relevancy in case of adverse impact. Job relevancy of training is demonstrated by showing that persons with the required training perform the job better than persons without such training. A criterion-related validity strategy is thus appropriate for demonstrating relevancy of training as a requirement (Bartlett, 1979; Russell, 1984; Merritt-Haston & Wexley, 1983).

Selection for Training. A potential for discrimination exists when selection for entry into a training program is based on tests, application blanks, and other selection procedures. If the use of any such procedure results in adverse impact, then continued use of the procedure must be justified through validation.

The Training Process. The content and procedures used in the training program have potential for causing adverse impact. Thus, the training equipment may be designed with physical characteristics of the average male as norms, thus taking them out of the reach of average women. Racism and sexism could creep into training materials leading to differential training performance.

If the training process results in adverse impact, its contents and procedures become suspect. The employer must then redesign the training materials or be prepared to demonstrate that the differences in training results actually lead to differentials in job performance (Bartlett, 1979).

Decisions Based on Training Outcomes. Results relating to trainee performance in training programs can be used by employers for making personnel decisions such as retention, placement, promotion, and compensation. If performance in training is used as a basis for making such decisions, then it becomes in fact a selection measure and is thus subject to the jurisdiction of the *Guidelines* (Bartlett, 1979; Russell, 1984).

JOB ANALYSIS AND TRAINING: OVERVIEW

Job analysis is an integral part of training and development activities. Exhibit 6.20 provides an overview of the job and person factors that are relevant to training activities and the uses to which they can be put in the training process. The most direct applications of job analysis in this area are in the phase of training needs analysis that deals with identification of the KSAOs required for effective job performance. The job analyst plays a supportive role in fulfilling the EEO requirements relating to validation of training programs under conditions of adverse impact.

SELECTED ISSUE: TRAINING NEEDS ANALYSIS

The functions that job analysis can serve in meeting the EEO requirements relating to the validation of training programs are similar in substance to those encountered in the validation of any selection procedure. As this issue has been covered in prior discussions, nothing further is said on that subject in this discussion. Instead, we dedicate the rest of this section to the direct applications of job analysis in training needs analysis.

As noted earlier, the training needs analysis phase of training consists roughly of three

EXHIBIT 6.20 Job Analysis and Training and Development

For the performance of the human resource management function or activity noted, this information is
Essential = √√
Useful = √
Not relevant = ○

JOB FACTORS		
Job identification data	√√	The primary use of job information in training and development activities is in identifying KSAOs required for effective job performance; these form the basis for identifying training needs of employees.
Job summary: Mission	√	Job analysis is useful in the following areas of EEO:
Job outputs: Products	√√	Justifying training as a criterion and predictor.
Services	√√	Identifying potential biases in training processes and decisions based on training outcomes.
MTEWA	√√	
Materials and substances	√√	
Techniques and methods	√√	
Guidelines and controls	√√	
Tasks	√√	
Behaviors	√√	
Contacts	√√	
Context		
Work flow and plant layout	√	
Physical environment	√	
Job interrelations	√√	
Terms & conditions	√	
Legal requirements	√√	
WORKER CHARACTERISTICS		
Knowledges	√√	
Abilities and skills	√√	
Values, beliefs, and attitudes	√	
Interests	√√	
Personal characteristics	√√	

levels of analysis: organizational, job, and person. The following are the applications of job information in each of these levels of analysis.

Organizational Analysis. This level of analysis is directed at finding out the "where" of training activity. Job information can be fruitfully used in the following areas in locating the needs for training.

- *Human Resource Information Systems (HRIS)*: The role of job analysis in the development of HRIS was covered in the section on human resource planning earlier in this chapter. The components of the data base required for such systems were shown in Exhibit 6.9. In training needs analysis, these systems could provide data on the composition of the labor and the locations of skill shortages and deficiencies.
- *Context information*: To locate labor force segments in need of training, the trainer needs to gather data on sources of cost overruns, accidents, down time, and process problems. The portion of the job description that deals with job context is particularly helpful in gathering such information.

KSAO Requirements. This is an integral step in training needs analysis. The focus of job analysis in this phase is with identifying the KSAOs required for job performance. These are to be derived from descriptions of the jobs. The following are the job factors that are considered to be particularly relevant in deriving KSAOs for training purposes.

- *Task characteristics*: According to Goldstein (1986), the task characteristics and attributes that are of particular relevance in establishing KSAOs are frequency of task performance, importance or criticality of tasks, difficulty of learning and performing the tasks, and place of task in the organization (p. 41).
- *Performance criteria and standards*: Yardsticks by which performance in the job is measured. In establishing training objectives, performance results could provide the baseline data needed for appraising training effectiveness.

Person Analysis. This phase is concerned with assessing the extent to which current employees possess the types and levels of KSAOs required for successful job performance. The major contribution of the job analyst to this phase is the KSAOs generated in the job analysis phase.

Appendices

Twelve appendices (A through L) accompany the book. Appendix A contains a description of the systems of job analysis that were referred to in earlier discussions. The details about the systems presented in that appendix should be viewed as supplementary to the applications shown in the text. The appendix contains information, largely of a background nature, that adds to the understanding of the systems, but that would have proven to be distracting if it had been presented in the body of the book itself.

Appendices B through K present ready-made instruments and other materials that can be used in job analysis activity. Two criteria were used in choosing the materials found in these appendixes. First was the relevance of the materials to the job analysis concerns of human resource management; this was a deciding factor and flows from the purposes of this handbook. Second was the feasibility of use for in-house purposes. The literature currently contains dozens (perhaps hundreds) of questionnaires, checklists, forms, and other ready-made materials that can be used in job analysis activity. Unfortunately, many of these require reliance on large samples and are time-consuming in application. The instruments that are included can be used directly by a job analyst or an in-house team of subject matter experts. Data sources and sample sizes can be increased at the option of the analyst for verification and validity checks.

Appendices B through I present instruments that deal with study of job factors. Their breakdown follows the flow of the discussions in Chapters 3 and 4 of the text. Appendices J and K present a set of instruments and other resources for studying worker characteristics. Their choice and organization was influenced by the discussion on worker specification in Chapter 5.

Appendix L is an excerpt from the *Uniform Guidelines on Employee Selection Procedures*. It presents portions of the *Guidelines* that pertain to job analysis.

Systems of Job Analysis

Job analysis systems vary widely in regard to their objectives, theoretical foundations, and methods of data gathering and analysis. The descriptions provided here are overviews of the systems. In the interest of space, details covered in the text are not repeated here. The exhibits provided in this appendix illustrate the basic concepts of the systems. Details covered in the text are referenced. Key publications relating to the system are presented at the end of each description. The following systems are described:

- ARS: Ability Requirements Scales
- BCM: Behavioral Consistency Method
- CIT: Critical Incidents Technique
- CODAP: Comprehensive Occupational Data Analysis Programs
- FJA: Functional Job Analysis
  - DOL—U.S. Department of Labor
  - Fine's Functional Job Analysis
  - JIMS—Job Information Matrix Systems
- HSMS: Health Services Mobility Study
- JEM: Job Elements Method
- PAQ: Position Analysis Questionnaire
- TTA: Threshold Traits Analysis Technique
- VERJAS: Versatile Job Analysis System
- WPSS: Work Performance Survey System

ARS—Ability Requirements Scales

Developed by E. A. Fleishman and his associates.

The ARS is a worker-oriented job analysis system. Its unit of analysis is human abilities and traits. The latest version of the system contains descriptions of 52 abilities and traits; these are described in Appendix J.6. Each ability is scaled on either 5- or 7-point scales. (Examples of ARS scales are given in Chapter 5.)

The ARS was developed as a means for classifying tasks according to abilities required in their performance. The system is expected to be applicable to all tasks and is to serve as a vehicle for distinguishing individual differences in performance and learning ability.

The primary use of the ARS has been in establishing ability requirements of tasks. The basic procedure consists of having subject matter experts (SMEs) rate tasks according to the ability scales. Flow diagrams and decision trees can also be used. (A decision tree appears in Chapter 5.)

Fleishman, E. A., & Quaintance, M. K. (1983). *Taxonomies of Human Performance: The Description of Human Tasks*. Orlando, Fla.: Academic Press.

BCM—Behavioral Consistency Method

Developed by Frank L. Schmidt, James Caplan, Stephen E. Bemis, and their associates at the U.S. Office of Personnel Management.

This system is a variation of the JEM. The similarities between the two systems are that they both attempt to measure only the most differentiating dimensions of worker characteristics that underlie superior and marginal performance, obtain this information (job elements) from SMEs, and obtain the information used in ranking from the applicants. The differences between the two are as follows:

Behavioral Consistency Method	Job Elements Method
1. Assessments of applicants are made solely on past achievements.	Variety of different kinds of information, including written tests are used.
2. Method does not purport to measure broad job element dimensions; samples behavior from achievement areas or domains.	Method purports to measure broad job elements.
3. It does not use self-ratings by applicants.	It uses self-ratings by applicants.
4. It requires greater verification of information.	It requires lesser verification of information.

The BCM is used primarily for identifying worker competencies in the selection of experienced professional and managerial applicants for midlevel government jobs. See applications in Chapter 6.

Schmidt, Frank L., Caplan, J. R., Bemis, S. E., Decuir, R., Dunn, L., Antone, L. L. (1979). *The Behavioral Consistency Method of Unassembled Examining*. Washington, D.C.: U.S. Office of Personnel Management.

U.S. Civil Service Commission (1977). *BRE Examination Preparation Manual*. Washington, D.C.: Bureau of Recruiting and Examining.

CIT—Critical Incidents Technique

Developed initially by John C. Flanagan during his association with the Aviation Psychology Program of the U.S. Army Air Forces in World War II. After the war, Flanagan expanded the technique in association with colleagues at the American Institute for Research and the University of Pittsburgh.

Critical incidents are effective or ineffective occurrences of a behavioral nature that have a bearing on performance. Exhibit 5.15 in Chapter 5 provides a sample of a form that can be used in collecting effective critical incidents and the five steps of the critical incidents procedure. Although the unit of analysis prescribed by Flanagan was behavior, the logic of the technique is now used in specifying knowledges, skills, abilities, and other human characteristics (KSAOs) required for effective job performance, job activities, and other job elements.

Flanagan, John C. (1954). The critical incident technique. *Psychological Bulletin*, 51, 327–358.
Kirchner, Wayne K., & Dunnette, M. D. (1957). Identifying the critical factors in successful salesmanship. *Personnel*, 34, 54–59.

CODAP—Comprehensive Occupational Data Analysis Program

Developed by Raymond E. Christal and his associates at the U.S. Air Force Human Resource Laboratory, Brooks Air Force Base, Texas.

CODAP is a task inventory. The system has two components: (1) the task inventories and (2) CODAP. The task inventories constitute the basic data gathering instruments. The contents of inventories include tasks for occupational groups or job families. CODAP consists of a series of interactive computer programs for analyzing, organizing, and reporting on data gathered from the task inventory.

A task is defined as a meaningful unit of work that is recognizable to the worker. In compiling tasks, a list of duties (or large segments of work) is first prepared. Tasks are then assigned to the duties. These could come from other task inventories or from new task statements prepared through the aid of subject matter experts. Each task is scaled on a 7-, 9-, or 11-point scale of "relative time spent." The "relative time spent" estimates are converted to "percent time spent" estimates that serve as the basis of judgments about jobs. Other scales can also be included, but the "relative time spent" is a requirement for the use of CODAP. An example of CODAP output is provided in Exhibit 3.7 in Chapter 3.

CODAP is used by the Air Force for collecting job data from very large populations of workers in scattered locations. The underlying approach is versatile and can be readily adapted for job classification, evaluation, design, and other job-related concerns.

Christal, R. E. (1974). *The United States Air Force Occupational Research Project* (AFHRL-TR-73-75). Lackland Air Force Base, Tex.: Air Force Human Resources Laboratory.
Christal, R. E., & Weissmuller, J. J. (1976). *New Comprehensive Occupational Data Analysis Programs (CODAP) for Analyzing Task Factor Information* (AFHRL Interim Professional Paper No. TR-76-3). Lackland Air Force Base, Tex.: Air Force Human Resource Laboratory.

FJA—Functional Job Analysis

Functional Job Analysis is a label given to an approach to job analysis developed by the U.S. Department of Labor in response to the Wagner-Peyser Act of 1935.

This act created the U.S. Employment Service, which was to serve as a nationwide public employment service. Three major responsibilities were imposed on the service: (1) the facilitation of the movement of unemployed persons into profitable employment; (2) the provision of occupational guidance to individuals seeking a vocational field and to employers having special recruitment problems; and (3) reduction of the waste of trial-and-error recruitment through taking into account, first, the worker qualifications that are necessary to successful job performance and, second, recruiting relationships between occupations. To fulfill its responsibilities, the Service found it necessary to develop a system of job analysis, which has since gone through many revisions. (Note that this system is also referred to in the literature as the U.S. Training and Employment Service (USTES) system after the agency that was originally involved in its development. However, the USTES is no longer in existence, and hence the system is now referred to by the name of the parent agency, the U.S. Department of Labor.)

Functional Job Analysis currently consists of three systems: U.S. Department of Labor, referred to hereafter as DOL; Sidney Fine's FJA; and JIMS.

DOL—DEPARTMENT OF LABOR

The DOL system is perhaps the most comprehensive job analysis system in existence. Its theoretical foundations are based on the data, people, and things schema of Functional Job Analysis. It contains elaborate techniques for describing jobs and people and for matching jobs and people. Just about all the systems that have come into being since the DOL's development have borrowed heavily from its terminology and techniques. It serves as the chief inventory of ideas, techniques, and terminology for job analysts in all sectors. (Detailed coverage of the applications of this system in job description, worker specification, and other job analysis concerns are given in Chapters 3 to 5 of this book.)

U.S. Department of Labor (1972). *Handbook for Analyzing Jobs.* Washington, D.C.: U.S. Government Printing Office.

Wilson, Michael (1974). *Job Analysis for Human Resource Management: A Review of Selected Research and Development.* Washington, D.C.: U.S. Government Printing Office.

SIDNEY FINE'S FUNCTIONAL JOB ANALYSIS

Developed by Sidney A. Fine during his association with the USTES during and after World War II.

Fine's FJA is a job-oriented system that is based on a systematically articulated theory of jobs and people. The primary elements in the FJA conceptual system are the following:

1. A fundamental distinction must be made between *what gets done* and *what workers do* to get things done.
2. What workers do, insofar as their job content is concerned, they do in relation to three primitives: things, data, and people.
3. In relation to each primitive, workers function in unique ways. Thus, in relation to things, workers draw on physical resources; in relation to data, on mental resources; and in relation to people, on interpersonal resources.
4. All jobs require the worker to relate to each of these primitives in some degree.
5. Although the behavior of workers or the tasks performed by them can apparently be described in an infinite number of ways, there are only a small number of definitive functions involved. Thus, in interacting with machines, workers function to feed, tend, operate, or set up; and in the case of vehicles or related machines, to drive-control them. Although each of these functions occurs over a range of difficulty and content, essentially each draws on a relatively narrow and specific range of similar kinds and degrees of worker characteristics and qualifications for effective performance.
6. The functions appropriate to each primitive are hierarchical and ordinal, proceeding from the simple to the complex. Thus, to indicate a particular function, say, compiling (data), as reflecting the requirements of a job is to say that it includes the requirements of lower functions such as comparing and excludes the requirements of higher functions such as analyzing.
7. The three hierarchies provide two measures for a job:
   Level: This is a measure of relative complexity in relation to things, to data, and to people.
   Orientation: This is a measure of relative (proportional) involvement with things, data, and people.
8. The hierarchies of functions reflect a progression *from much prescription* and little discretion

in worker instructions at the least complex level *to much discretion* and little prescription at the most complex level.

9. Human performance is conceived as involving three types of skills: adaptive, functional, and specific content.
   Adaptive skills are those competencies that enable an individual to manage the demands for conformity and/or change in relation to the physical, interpersonal, and organizational arrangements and conditions in which the job exists.
   Functional skills are those competencies that enable an individual to relate to things, data, and people (orientation) in some combination according to personal preferences and to some degree of complexity appropriate to abilities (level).
   Specific content skills are those competencies that enable an individual to perform a specific job according to the standards required to satisfy the market (Fine & Wiley, 1971, pp. 78–80).

Fine's FJA has proven to be a highly versatile system with applications in just about all the job analysis concerns. Its applications are illustrated in Chapters 3 to 5. The latest revision of Fine's worker functions scales is reproduced in Appendix B-2.

Fine, S. A., & Wiley, W. W. (1971). *An Introduction to Functional Job Analysis*. Kalamazoo, Mich.: W. E. Upjohn Institute for Employment Research.

JIMS—JOB INFORMATION MATRIX SYSTEMS

Developed by Dale Yoder and his associates at California State University, Long Beach, California.

JIMS is an extension of the DOL system. It contains standardized procedures for describing: what workers do, what they use, their responsibilities, the working conditions, and the knowledges required.

A notable application of JIMS has been in the construction of standardized lists of job tasks of common occupations and job families. These can be used as supplementary aids to in-depth job studies or as abbreviated methods for collecting job information in situations where complete job analyses are not required or not feasible. (These are described in the publication by C. E. Wesson referenced here.)

Stone, C. H., & Yoder, D. (1970). *Job Analysis, 1970*. Long Beach: Bureau of Business Services and Research, California State University.
Wesson, C. E. (1973). *Task Analysis Inventories: A Method for Collecting Job Information*. Washington, D.C.: U.S. Government Printing Office.

HSMS—Health Services Mobility Study

HSMS was initiated in 1967 under a one-year grant by the Office of Economic Opportunity. The grant carried the charge that the project investigate impediments to upward occupational mobility in New York City municipal hospitals and that it suggest means of overcoming obstacles to such mobility. The director of the study was Dr. Eleanor Gilpatrick, a professor at the Hunter College's School of Health Sciences.

Ten years later, the Health Services Mobility Study (HSMS) is ending its research and development activities. During that time, HSMS examined the occupational structure of New York City Muncipal Hospitals and investigated the problems of skill shortages and credentialing. It then undertook to design a method to promote occupational mobility by tying job requirements to curriculum design in a single system.

HSMS has developed, field tested, and applied a method to analyze work (task analysis) and design job ladders. It moved on to develop a method for curriculum design using task data and for the design of educational ladders to parallel job ladders. It eventually expanded the method to show how to make job structures and curricula responsive to quality standards and the needs of the consumers, and to show how occupational mobility can be economically attractive to employers. It then completed the system by showing how task data and curriculum objectives produced by the method can be used as inputs to the development of performance evaluation instruments and for the selection of content for, and validation of, occupational proficiency tests.

HSMS has made theoretical contributions to the fields of job analysis, curriculum development, and occupational testing. It has helped to promote the concepts of upward occupational and educational mobility, and has developed a design for a safe practice, quality assurance program in diagnostic radiology. (Gilpatrick, 1977a, iv)

The task analysis concepts and methods of the HSMS are described in Chapter 4. Key instruments from the system are reproduced in Appendices C, E, F, G, I, and J. The source referenced here provides extensive guides to the publications of the HSMS.

Gilpatrick, Eleanor (1977). *The Health Services Mobility Study Method of Task Analysis and Curriculum Design*, Research Report No. 11, Vol. 1. New York: City University of New York, Hunter College and the Research Foundation.

JEM—Job Element Method

Developed by E. S. Primoff of the U.S. Office of Personnel Management.

JEM draws on Wilhelm Wundt's rule that states that "we cannot understand the complex phenomena before we have become familiar with the simple ones." The simple aspects of jobs are job elements or those worker characteristics that influence success in a job. The JEM notion of job elements is extremely broad, encompassing knowledges, skills, abilities, willingnesses, interests, and personal characteristics and traits.

Job elements are collected through job incumbents, co-workers, supervisors, and other subject matter experts. The method does not contain any provisions for the gathering of task information.

This system is used primarily for constructing and administering examinations for selection of workers in federal, state, and local governments. It seeks to provide detailed descriptions of job elements that differentiate highly effective workers from marginal workers. Examples of applications are given in Chapter 5 of this book.

Eyde, Lorraine D., Primoff, E. S., & Hardt, R. H. (1981). *A Job Element Examination for State Troopers*. U.S. Office of Personnel Management, Personnel Research and Development Center. Washington, D.C.: U.S. Government Printing Office.

Primoff, Ernest S. (1975). *How to Prepare and Conduct Job Element Examinations*, U.S. Civil Service Commission, Personnel Research and Development Center. Washington, D.C.: U.S. Government Printing Office.

PAQ—Position Analysis Questionnaire

Developed by Ernest J. McCormick and his associates at the Department of Psychological Sciences, Purdue University.

The PAQ was consciously designed to be a worker-oriented system. It rests on the assumption that there is "some underlying behavioral [as opposed to technological] structure or order to the domain of human work":

If there is some such underlying behavioral structure, such structure presumably would have to be characterized in terms of the manner in which more specific "units" of job-related variables tend to be organized across jobs. Thus, the "building blocks" or common denominators of any dimensional structure must consist of relatively unitary, discrete job variables of some class that can be identified and quantified as they relate to individual jobs. (McCormick et al., 1972, p. 348)

The job ''units'' comprising the PAQ are ''generalized human behaviors''; they are referred to as job elements. Exhibit 3.8 in Chapter 3 contains a summary of the major divisions and subdivisions of the PAQ, the number of job elements contained in each, and examples of job elements. The theoretical framework that binds the job elements is as follows:

> A worker-oriented element can, in effect, be viewed collectively within the framework of the stimulus-organism-response paradigm or, in more operational terms, information input, mediation processes, and output. (p. 349)
>
> The primary frame of reference underlying the development and organization of the PAQ followed the information-input, mediation, and work-output model mentioned above, there being individual job elements relating to each of these. Additionally, there were job elements relating to the interpersonal activities associated with jobs, to the nature of the work situation or job context, and to certain miscellaneous aspects of the work. (pp. 348–349)

The inventory of job elements contained in the PAQ provide a basis for inferring the behavioral requirements of jobs. Its primary uses have been in job evaluation and worker specification activity. Examples of applications of the PAQ to human resource management functions are provided in Chapters 3 and 5.

McCormick, Ernest J., Jeanneret, P. R., & Mecham, R. C. (1969). *The Development and Background of the Position Analysis Questionnaire (PAQ)*. Lafayette, Ind.: Purdue University, Occupational Research Center.

McCormick, Ernest J., Jeanneret, P. R., & Mecham, R. C. (1972). A study of job characteristics and job dimensions as based on the Position Analysis Questionnaire (PAQ). *Journal of Applied Psychology Monograph*, 56, 347–368.

TTA—Threshold Traits Analysis Technique

Developed by Felix M. Lopez and his associates, Port Washington, New York.

TTA is within the family of worker-oriented job analysis systems. Its particular focus is on identification of human traits that predispose individuals to perform effectively on various types of jobs.

The theoretical preconceptions underlying TTA were developed after an extensive review of the literature that led to the following conclusions:

1. Every position possesses two broad aspects. The first relates to the tasks or activities that an incumbent must perform, and the second, to the demands or conditions under which those tasks are performed. A complete position description must include all the relevant tasks and demands of that position.
2. For personnel selection, placement, development, motivation and compensation purposes, a position description must identify the human attributes necessary to perform position functions in a clearly acceptable manner.
3. To facilitate such identification, it is necessary to group positions into classes (jobs) on the basis of the similarities of the traits required according to a practical trait taxonomy that can be applied across all types of jobs and occupational groupings.
4. Factor analytic studies of job analysis data, as well as human attribute data, had so far yielded essentially three broad trait categories or dimensions including motor and physical skills, cognitive abilities and personality or motivational factors. (Lopez et al., 1981, p. 482)

The TTA conceptual schema consists of 21 job functions organized into 5 major work domains and 33 traits that define the human characteristics necessary to perform a given job. The list of traits included in this system reflects primary competencies; it omits such secondary characteristics as education and years of experience.

Lopez, Felix M., Kesselman, G. A., & Lopez, F. E. (1981). An empirical test of a trait-oriented job analysis technique. *Personnel Psychology*, 34, 479–502.

VERJAS—Versatile Job Analysis System

Developed by Stephen E. Bemis, Ann Holt Belenky, and Dee Ann Soder.

Described by the authors as a job analysis melting pot in both origin and use, VERJAS draws on other systems to construct an empirically and legally defensible job analysis system with specific procedures and forms. The system has provisions for describing three aspects of jobs: job contents, job requirements, and job context. It utilizes concepts from the DOL and FJA systems for describing expected job behavior. Concepts from the Factor Evaluation System (FES) are used for describing job context. The suggested format for describing worker competencies is based on the Behavioral Consistency Method and Primoff's Job Element Method. (Applications are shown in Chapter 4 of this book.)

Bemis, Stephen E., Belenky, A. H., & Soder, D. A. (1983). *Job Analysis: An Effective Management Tool*. Washington, D.C.: The Bureau of National Affairs.

WPSS Work Performance Survey System

Developed by Sidney Gael at the American Telephone & Telegraph Company.

The WPSS is a computer-aided job inventory. The units of analysis are tasks and job functions. It relies primarily on interviews with job incumbents and content analysis of written materials for its data base. Observation plays a minor role in data gathering and serves mainly to familiarize job analysts with the job environment.

The task attributes studied by the WPSS are importance or significance, time spent, frequency of performance, and difficulty. Task scales have 7 points.

At AT&T, the WPSS has been used mainly to establish the way that a given job is actually performed throughout the Bell System telephone companies, both overall and at different locations. The following general applications are claimed for the system: job descriptions, design and redesign of jobs, placement, establishing staffing requirements, determining training needs, comparing actual to desired performance within jobs, and performance evaluation.

Gael, Sidney (1983). *Job Analysis: A Guide to Assessing Work Activities*. San Francisco, Jossey-Bass.
Gael, Sidney (1977). *Development of Job Task Inventories and Their Use in Job Analysis Research*. New York: AT&T Company. JSAS Catalog of Selected Documents in Psychology, 7(25) (Ms. No. 1445).

B Functional Job Analysis: Worker Functions

Functional job analysis (FJA) has been in the forefront of job analysis activity since the 1940s. Extensive coverage of its assumptions, approach, and applications were presented in Chapters 3 to 6. This appendix contains the worker functions scales of the three FJA systems: DOL, Sidney Fine's version, and JIMS. The worker function scales of the DOL (B.1) form the basis of the *Dictionary of Occupational Titles* (1977) and related Department of Labor publications on the occupational structure of the U.S. economy.

Sidney Fine's version of the worker functions hierarchy (B.2) follows the basic format of the DOL system. However, his descriptions of the functions are somewhat more behavioral in statement; they are suggestive of the human involvement in the work.

JIMS description of worker functions (B.3) provides a grammatical extension of the hierarchy. Descriptions of the functions are rendered more operational by breaking them down into activity verbs. This extension allows for a more discriminating identification of worker involvement in the functions.

APPENDIX B.1 WORKER FUNCTIONS: DEPARTMENT OF LABOR

EXPLANATION OF DATA, PEOPLE, AND THINGS

Much of the information in this publication is based on the premise that every job requires a worker to function in some degree to data, people, and things. These relationships are identified and explained below. They appear in the form of three listings arranged in each instance from the relatively simple to the complex in such a manner that each successive relationship includes those that are simpler and excludes the more complex.* The identifications attached to these relationships are referred to as worker functions, and provide standard terminology for use in summarizing exactly what a worker does on the job.

A job's relationship to data, people, and things can be expressed in terms of the lowest numbered function in each sequence. These functions taken together indicate the total level of complexity at which the worker performs. The fourth, fifth, and sixth digits of the occupational code numbers reflect relationships to data, people, and things, respectively.† These digits express a job's relationship to data, people, and things by identifying the highest appropriate function in each listing as reflected by the following table:

DATA (4th digit)	PEOPLE (5th digit)	THINGS (6th digit)
0 Synthesizing	0 Mentoring	0 Setting up
1 Coordinating	1 Negotiating	1 Precision working
2 Analyzing	2 Instructing	2 Operating-controlling
3 Compiling	3 Supervising	3 Driving-operating
4 Computing	4 Diverting	4 Manipulating
5 Copying	5 Persuading	5 Tending
6 Comparing	6 Speaking, signaling	6 Feeding, offbearing
	7 Serving	7 Handling
	8 Taking instructions, helping	

DEFINITIONS OF WORKER FUNCTIONS

DATA. Information, knowledge, and conceptions, related to data, people, or things, obtained by observation, investigation, interpretation, visualization, and mental creation. Data are intangible and include numbers, words, symbols, ideas, concepts, and oral verbalization.

0 Synthesizing: integrating analyses of data to discover facts and/or develop knowledge concepts or interpretations.

1 Coordinating: Determining time, place, and sequence of operations or action to be taken on the basis of analysis of data; executing determination and/or reporting on events.

2 Analyzing: Examining and evaluating data. Presenting alternative actions in relation to the evaluation is frequently involved.

3 Compiling: Gathering, collating, or classifying information about data, people, or things.

* As each of the relationships to people represents a wide range of complexity, resulting in considerable overlap among occupations, their arrangement is somewhat arbitrary and can be considered a hierarchy only in the most general sense.

† Only those relationships that are occupationally significant in terms of the requirements of the job are reflected in the code numbers. The incidental relationships that every worker has to data, people, and things, but that do not seriously affect successful performance of the essential duties of the job, are not reflected.

From U.S. Department of Labor, *Dictionary of Occupational Titles*, 4th ed. (Washington, D.C.: U.S. Government Printing Office, 1977).

Reporting and/or carrying out a prescribed action in relation to the information is frequently involved.

4 Computing: Performing arithmetic operations and reporting on and/or carrying out a prescribed action in relation to them. Does not include counting.

5 Copying: Transcribing, entering, or posting data.

6 Comparing: Judging the readily observable functional, structural, or compositional characteristics (whether similar to or divergent from obvious standards) of data, people, or things.

PEOPLE. Human beings; also animals dealt with on an individual basis as if they were human.

0 Mentoring: Dealing with individuals in terms of their total personality in order to advise, counsel, and/or guide them with regard to problems that may be resolved by legal, scientific, clinical, spiritual, and/or other professional principles.

1 Negotiating: Exchanging ideas, information, and opinions with others to formulate policies and programs and/or arrive jointly at decisions, conclusions, or solutions.

2 Instructing: Teaching subject matter to others or training others (including animals) through explanation, demonstration, and supervised practice; or making recommendations on the basis of technical disciplines.

3 Supervising: Determining or interpreting work procedures for a group of workers, assigning specific duties to them, maintaining harmonious relations among them, and promoting efficiency. A variety of responsibilities is involved in this function.

4 Diverting: Amusing others. (Usually accomplished through the medium of stage, screen, television, or radio.)

5 Persuading: Influencing others in favor of a product, service, or point of view.

6 Speaking, signaling: Talking with and/or signaling people to convey or exchange information. Includes giving assignments and/or directions to helpers or assistants.

7 Serving: Attending to the needs or requests of people or animals or the expressed or implicit wishes of people. Immediate response is involved.

8 Taking instructions, helping: Helping applies to "nonlearning" helpers. No variety of responsibility is involved in this function.

THINGS. Inanimate objects as distinguished from human beings, substances or materials; machines, tools, equipment, and products. A thing is tangible and has shape, form, and other physical characteristics.

0 Setting up: Adjusting machines or equipment by replacing or altering tools, jigs, fixtures, and attachments to prepare them to perform their functions, change their performance, or restore their proper functioning if they break down. Workers who set up one or a number of machines for other workers or who set up and personally operate a variety of machines are included here.

1 Precision working: Using body members and/or tools or work aids to work, move, guide, or place objects or materials in situations where ultimate responsibility for the attainment of standards occurs and selection of appropriate tools, objects, or materials and the adjustment of the tool to the task require exercise of considerable judgment.

2 Operating, controlling: Starting, stopping, controlling, and adjusting the progress of machines or equipment. Operating machines involves setting up and adjusting the machine or material(s) as the work progresses. Controlling involves observing gages, dials, etc., and turning valves and other devices to regulate factors such as temperature, pressure, flow of liquids, speed of pumps, and reactions of materials.

3 Driving, operating: Starting, stopping, and controlling the actions of machines or equip-

ment for which a course must be steered, or which must be guided, in order to fabricate, process, and/or move things or people. Involves such activities as observing gages and dials; estimating distances and determining speed and direction of other objects; turning cranks and wheels; pushing or pulling gear lifts or levers. Includes such machines as cranes, conveyor systems, tractors, furnace charging machines, paving machines and hoisting machines. Excludes manually powered machines, such as handtrucks and dollies, and power assisted machines, such as electric wheelbarrows and handtrucks.

4 Manipulating: Using body members, tools, or special devices to work, move, guide, or place objects or materials. Involves some latitude for judgment with regard to precision attained and selecting appropriate tool, object, or material, although this is readily manifest.

5 Tending: Starting, stopping, and observing the functioning of machines and equipment. Involves adjusting materials or controls of the machine, such as changing guides, adjusting timers and temperature gages, turning valves to allow flow of materials, and flipping switches in response to lights. Little judgment is involved in making these adjustments.

6 Feeding, offbearing: Inserting, throwing, dumping, or placing materials in or removing them from machines or equipment which are automatic or tended or operated by other workers.

7 Handling: Using body members, handtools, and/or special devices to work, move or carry objects or materials. Involves little or no latitude for judgment with regard to attainment of standards or in selecting appropriate tool, object, or material.

APPENDIX B.2 WORKER FUNCTIONS: REVISED VERSION OF SIDNEY FINE'S WORKER FUNCTION SCALES

THINGS FUNCTION SCALE*

Physical interaction with and response to tangibles—touched, felt, observed, and related to in space; images/visualized spatially.

Level 1A—Handling

Works (cuts, shapes, assembles, etc.), digs, moves, or carries objects or materials where objects, materials, tools, etc., are one or few in number and are the primary involvement of the worker. Precision requirements are relatively gross. Includes the use of dollies, handtrucks, and the like. (Use this rating for situations involving casual or optional use of tools and other tangibles.)

Level 1B—Feeding, Offbearing

Inserts, throws, dumps, or places materials into, or removes them from, machines or equipment that are automatic or are tended/operated by other workers. Precision requirements are built in, largely out of control of worker.

Level 2A—Machine Tending I—Material Products and Processing

Starts, stops, and monitors the functioning of machines and equipment set up by other workers where the precision of output depends on keeping one to several controls in adjustment, in response to automatic signals according to specifications. Includes all machine situations where there is no significant setup or change of setup, where cycles are very short, alternatives to nonstandard performance are few, and adjustments are highly prescribed.

* The arabic numbers assigned to definitions represent the successive levels of this ordinal scale. The A, B. C, and D definitions are variations on the same level.

Level 2B—Machine Tending II—Data Processing and Duplicating

Starts, stops, monitors the functioning of machines and equipment that are preprogrammed to perform the basic functions involved in data processing and document copying and printing. Machines/equipment are activated at keyboard terminals or pushbutton control panels and can accomplish special effects for particular activities through the input of special codes. Nonproduction use of calculators, typewriters, and similar is included here.

Level 3A—Manipulating

Works (cuts, shapes, assembles, etc.), digs, moves, guides, or places objects or materials where objects, tools, controls, etc., are several in number. Precision requirements range from gross to fine. Includes waiting on tables and the use of ordinary portable power tools with interchangeable parts and ordinary tools around the home, such as kitchen and garden tools.

Level 3B—Operating, Controlling I

Starts, stops, controls, and adjusts a machine or equipment designed to fabricate and/or process data, people, or things. The worker may be involved in activating the machine, as in typing or turning wood, or the involvement may occur primarily at startup and stop as with a semiautomatic machine. Operating a machine involves readying and adjusting the machine and/or material as work progresses. Controlling equipment involves monitoring gauges, dials, etc., and turning valves and other devices to control such items as temperature, pressure, flow of liquids, speed of pumps, and reactions of materials. (This rating is to be used only for operations of one machine or one unit of equipment.)

Level 3C—Driving, Controlling

Starts, stops, and controls (steers, guides) the actions of machines in two-dimensional spaces for which a course must be followed to move things or people. Actions regulating controls require continuous attention and readiness of response to traffic conditions.

Level 3D—Starting up

Readies powered mobile equipment for operation, typically following standard procedures. Manipulates controls to start up engines, allows for warmup and pressure buildup as necessary, checks mobility where movement is involved, and working parts (as in construction equipment), brakes, gauges indicating serviceability (fuel, pressure, temperature, battery output, etc.) and visually checks for leaks and other unusual conditions. Includes reverse shutdown procedures.

Level 4A—Precision Working

Works, moves, guides, or places objects or materials according to standard practical procedures where the number of objects, materials, tools, etc., embraces an entire craft and accuracy expected is within final finished tolerances established for the craft. (Use this rating where work primarily involves manual or power handtools.)

Level 4B—Setting Up

Installs machines or equipment; inserts tools; alters jigs, fixtures, and attachment; and/or repairs machines or equipment to ready and/or restore them to their proper functioning according to job order or blueprint specifications. Involves primary responsibility for accuracy. May involve one or a number of machines for other workers or for worker's own operation.

Level 4C—Operating-Controlling II

Starts, stops, controls, and continuously modifies setup of equipment designed to hoist and move materials in multidimensional space, reshape, and/or pave the earth's surface. Manipulation of controls requires continuous attention to changing conditions, and readiness of response to activate the equipment in lateral, vertical, and/or angular operations.

DATA FUNCTION SCALE*

Data are information, ideas, facts, statistics, specifications of output, knowledge of conditions, techniques, and mental operations.

Level 1—Comparing

Selects, sorts, or arranges data, people, or things, judging whether their readily observable functional, structural, or compositional characteristics are similar to or different from prescribed standards, e.g., checking oil level, tire pressure, worn cables; observes hand signal of worker indicating movement of load.

Level 2—Copying

Transcribes, enters, and/or posts data, following a schema or plan to assemble or make things and using a variety of work aids. Transfers information mentally from plans, diagrams, instructions to workpiece or work site, e.g., attends to stakes showing a grade line to be followed while operating equipment.

Level 3A—Computing

Performs arithmetic operations and makes reports and/or carries out a prescribed action in relation to them. Interprets mathematical data on plans, specifications, diagrams, or blueprints, e.g., reads and follow specifications or stakes.

Level 3B—Compiling

Gathers, collates, or classifies information about data, people, or things, following a schema or system but using discretion in application, e.g., considers wind, weather (rain or shine), shape, weight, and type of load heights and capacity of boom in making lift.

Level 4—Analyzing

Examines and evaluates data (about things, data, or people) with reference to the criteria, standards, and/or requirements of a particular discipline, art, technique, or craft to determine interaction effects (consequences) and to consider alternatives, e.g., considers/evaluates instructions, site and climatic conditions, nature of load, capacity of equipment, other crafts engaged with in order to situate (spot) crane to best advantage.

Level 5A—Innovating

Modifies, alters, and/or adapts existing designs, procedures, or methods to meet unique specifications, unusual conditions, or specific standards of effectiveness within the overall framework of operating theories, principles and/or organizational contexts, e.g., improvises using existing attachments, or modifies customary equipment to meet unusual conditions and fulfill specifications.

Level 5B—Coordinating

Decides times, place, and sequence of operations of a process, system or organization, and/or the need for revision of goals, policies (boundary conditions), or procedures on the basis of analysis of data and of performance review of pertinent objectives and requirements. Includes overseeing and/or executing decisions and/or reporting on events, e.g., selects/proposes equipment best suited to achieve an output considering resources (equipment, costs, manpower) available to get job done.

Level 6—Synthesizing

Takes off in new directions on the basis of personal intuitions, feelings, and ideas (with or without regard for tradition, experience, and existing parameters) to conceive new approaches

* The arabic numbers assigned to definitions represent the successive levels of this ordinal scale. The A and B and C definitions are variations on the same level.

to or statements of problems and the development of system, operational, or aesthetic *solutions* or *resolutions* of them, typically outside of existing theoretical, stylistic, or organizational context.

PEOPLE FUNCTION SCALE*

The people scale measures live interaction among people, communication, interpersonal actions.

Level 1—Taking Instructions, Helping

Attends to the work assignment, instructions, or orders of supervisor. No immediate response or verbal exchange is required unless clarification of instruction is needed.

Level 2—Exchanging Information

Talks to, converses with, and/or signals people to convey or obtain information, or to clarify and work out details of an assignment, within the framework of well-established procedures, e.g., requests clarification of a signal, verbal (in person or on radio) or hand signal.

Level 3A—Sourcing Information

Serves as a primary and central source to external public or internal work force of system information that is crucial in directing/routing people or workers to their destination or areas of concern and makes it possible for system/organization to function.

Level 3B—Persuading

Influences others in favor of a product, service, or point of view by talks or demonstrations, e.g., demonstrates safety procedures required on a piece of equipment for compliance with new regulations.

Level 3C—Coaching

Befriends and encourages individuals on a personal, caring basis by approximating a peer or family-type relationship either in a one-to-one or small-group situation; gives instruction, advice, and personal assistance concerning activities of daily living, the use of various institutional services, and participation in groups, e.g., gives support or encouragement to apprentice or journeyman on unfamiliar piece of equipment.

Level 3D—Diverting

Amuses to entertain or distract individuals and/or audiences or to lighten a situation.

Level 4A—Consulting

Serves as a source of technical knowledge and provides such knowledge as well as related ideas to define, clarify, enlarge upon, or sharpen procedures, capabilities, or product specifications, e.g., informs project managers of effective and appropriate use of equipment to achieve output within constraints (time, money, etc.).

Level 4B—Instructing

Teaches subject matter to others or train others, including animals, through explanation, demonstration, and test.

Level 4C—Treating

Acts on or interacts with individuals or small groups of people or animals who need help (as in sickness) to carry out specialized therapeutic or adjustment procedures. Systematically observes results of treatment within the framework of total personal behavior because unique individual reactions to prescriptions (chemical, physical, or behavioral) may not fall within the range of

* The arabic numbers assigned to definition represent the successive levels of this ordinal scale. The A, B, and C definitions are variations on the same level.

prediction. Motivates, supports, and instructs individuals to accept or cooperate with therapeutic adjustment procedures when necessary.

Level 5—Supervising

Determines and/or interprets work procedure for a group of workers; assigns specific duties to them (delineating prescribed and discretionary content); maintains harmonious relations among them; evaluates performance (both prescribed and discretionary) and promotes efficiency and other organizational values; makes decisions on procedural and technical levels.

Leve 6—Negotiating

Bargains and discusses on a formal basis as a representative of one side of a transaction for advantages in resources, rights, privileges and/or contractual obligations, *giving and taking* within the limits provided by authority or within the framework of the perceived requirements and integrity of a program.

Level 7—Mentoring

Works with individuals having problems affecting their life adjustment to advise, counsel, and/or guide them according to legal, scientific, clinical, spiritual, and/or other professional principles. Advises clients of implications of analyses or diagnoses made of problems, courses of action open to deal with them, and merits of one strategy over another.

APPENDIX B.3 WORKER FUNCTIONS: JOB INFORMATION MATRIX SYSTEMS

Data		People		Things	
10	Synthesizing	20	Mentoring	30	Setting up
11	Coordinating	21	Negotiating	31	Precision working
12	Analyzing	22	Educating	32	Operating, controlling
13	Discriminating	23	Superintending	33	Driving, operating
14	Figuring	24	Diverting	34	Manipulating
15	Compiling	25	Persuading	35	Tending
16	Copying	26	Speaking/signaling	36	Feeding, offbearing
		27	Serving	37	Handling

The two digits preceding each item correspond to the two digits preceding each job task in the printout. These digits serve two major purposes: (1) they facilitate storage and retrieval and (2) they serve as coded identifiers of job task skill level. The first digit indicates the major area of the *worker function*: 1 = data, 2 = people, and 3 = things. The second digit identifies the *level of complexity* (in descending order) within that major area of *worker function*. Thus 20 is more complex than 27; 31 is more complex than 32.

Pages that follow first list activity verbs for data and people by function; thereafter each of these verbs is defined. All the activity verbs are listed alphabetically on page 253.

CLASSIFICATION OF "DATA" ACTIVITY VERBS

10. *SYNTHESIZING*
    Devise
        compose
        invent
        discover
        hypothesize
        plan
        design
    Solve
        calculate
        forecast
        interpret
        translate

11. *COORDINATING*
    Direct
        manage

From C. H. Stone and D. Yoder. *Job Analysis* (Long Beach: Bureau of Business Services and Research, California State College, Long Beach, 1970).

implement
control
regulate
authorize
execute
Decide
deliberate
determine
Develop
formulate
Organize
marshal
schedule

12. *ANALYZING*
Investigate
research
experiment
study

Scrutinize
examine
audit
scan
Evaluate
verify
appraise
test
Report
identify
recommend
summarize
suggest

13. *DISCRIMINATING*
Compare
rank
inspect
distinguish
contrast
select
choose
Classify
grade
index
segregate
sort
match
arrange

14. *FIGURING*
Estimate
Compute
Plot

15. *COMPILING*
Measure
time
weight
calibrate
Collect
accumulate
inventory
count
observe
smell
listen

16. *COPYING*
Record
post
tabulate
list
transpose
Duplicate
transcribe
quote

CLASSIFICATION OF "PEOPLE" ACTIVITY VERBS

20. *MENTORING*
Treat
prognosticate
diagnose
prescribe
Advise
counsel
console
reconcile
Arbitrate
judge

21. *NEGOTIATING*
Mediate
settle
debate
bargain
reason
confer

22. *EDUCATING*
Teach
lecture
tutor
explain
instruct
Coach
demonstrate
train

23. *SUPERINTENDING*
Supervise
lead
order
appoint
assign
enforce
rate

24. *DIVERTING*
Entertain
humor
interest
amuse
imitate

25. *PERSUADING*
Influence
motivate
convince
Promote
Solicit
Sell

26. *SPEAKING, SIGNALING*
Discuss
interview
consult
question
Inform
dictate
answer
describe
indicate
relay
request
Meet
greet

27. *SERVING*
Assist
usher
Attend
wait upon
Supply
provide

"DATA" ACTIVITY VERB DEFINITIONS*

10. *SYNTHESIZING* — Integrating analyses of data to discover facts and/or develop knowledge concepts or interpretations. (*DOT*)

Devise — To form in the mind by *new* combinations or applications of ideas or principles. (W)

---

* Source of each definition is indicated by code in which (*W*) means Webster's Third New International and New Collegiate dictionaries; (*F&W*) means S. I. Hayakawa and the Funk & Wagnalls Dictionary staff, *Modern Guide to Synonyms and Related Words* (New York: Funk & Wagnalls, 1968); and (*S*) identifies definitions developed by members of the research staff after consulting these and other sources. Note that verbs beginning with capital letters are regarded as "general," serving to classify the more specific but related verbs that begin with lowercase letters.

compose	To create by artisitc labor. (W) (e.g., a musical score or painting).
Invent	To fabricate something useful; usually as a result of ingenious thinking or experimentation. (W)
discover	Implies an intentional search; always suggests the acquiring of something that already exists but is new to the discoverer. (F&W)
hypothesize	[to form] a tentative assumption . . . in order to draw out and test its logical or empirical consequences. (W)
plan	To work out roughly in the mind a detailed means of achieving an objective or goal. (S)
design	To devise the form or shape of a physical object. (S)
Solve	To answer a question or work out a problem; explain any set of events by finding a workable way of dealing with them or by seeing the deeper meaning of them. (F&W)
calculate	To ascertain or determine by mathematical processes. *Calculate* is usually preferred in reference to highly intricate process and problematical rather than exact or definite result. (W) Not to be confused with *compute* under "Figuring."
forecast	To calculate or predict (some future event or condition) usually as a result of rational study and analysis of available pertinent data. (W) Not to be confused with the less complex *estimate* under "figuring."
interpret	Using "knowledge or insight to cast light on some baffling problem or puzzle . . . stressing personal judgment or understanding." (F&W)
translate	To transfer or turn from one set of symbols into another. (W)
11. *COORDINATING*	Determining time, place, and sequence of operations or actions to be taken on the basis of analysis of data; executing determinations and/or reporting on events. (*DOT*)
Direct	To exercise leadership and control at the highest level; authority is often delegated to others (e.g., corporate director). (S) Syn: administer.
manage	Often refers to the actual running or handling of specific affairs, and may imply delegated authority. (F&W)
implement	To give practical effect to and ensure actual fulfillment by concrete measures. (W)
control	The function of maintaining awareness and appraisal with respect to the effectiveness of the organization and its parts in accomplishing assigned missions. (Yoder, *Personnel Management & Industrial Relations*, 1962, p. 614)
regulate	Means to order or control by rule, method, or established mode. (F&W)
authorize	[to give] approval of a proposed course of action by an authority empowered either to permit or to forbid it. (F&W)

execute	To follow, carry out, or put into effect [the direction of others]. (F&W)
Decide	To arrive at a decision that ends uncertainty. (S)
deliberate	To reach a decision only after intense analysis; the variables involved are *highly abstract*; the consequences of the decision are considerable. (S)
determine	To reach a decision only after intense analysis; the variables involved are *readily* apparent but the consequences of the decision are considerable. (S)
Develop	Positive change in which an existing or rudimentary [idea] is improved, evoked, or perfected. (F&W)
formulate	Refers to an act . . . in which, the rough *plan* is spelled out, formalized, or put into words. (F&W)
Organize	To set up an *administrative* structure in order to form a coherent or functioning whole. (S)
marshal	Items are brought together and ordered for greatest efficiency or for the most forceful effect possible. (F&W)
schedule	To appoint, assign, or designate for a fixed future time. (W)
12. *ANALYZING*	Examining and evaluating data. Presenting alternative actions in relation to the evaluation is frequently involved. (*DOT*)
Investigate	To investigate is to make a *methodical*, searching inquiry into a *complex* situation in an effort to uncover the facts. (F&W)
research	To investigate to discover or interpret facts or to revise accepted laws or theories. (S)
experiment	To test a theory or hypothesis under controlled conditions. (S)
study	To attempt to learn all aspects of the subject or problem under scrutiny before making plans or taking definite action. (F&W)
Scrutinize	To look something *complex* over closely but not necessarily in a systematic method as in "Investigate." (S)
examine	[to scrutinize] to determine the . . . condition or nature of a thing. (W)
audit	To examine accounts or records. (F&W)
scan	[to survey] from point to point often suggesting a cursory overall observation. (W)
Evaluate	To determine or fix the value of through analysis of *complex* data. (S)
verify	To confirm or establish the authenticity or existence of by examination, investigation, or competent evidence. (W)
appraise	To judge tentatively or approximately the value, worth, or significance of. (W definition for "estimate")
test	To judge the performance of something relative to *readily* observable standards. (S)
Report	Implies giving an account of something with . . . formal

	attention to details and to accuracy in the presentation of the relevant facts and information. (F&W)
identify	To point out the salient characteristics of something or associate it with some other thing. The characteristics and association are not readily apparent. (S)
recommend	Indicates a positive declaration, based on analysis of complex data, in favor of a particular alternative or set of possibilities. (F&W)
summarize	To tell in, or reduce to, a summary. (W)
suggest	To call or bring to mind (as an idea, mood, or object) by a process of logical thought or natural association of ideas. (W)
13. *DISCRIMINATING*	Comparing and classifying information about data, people, or things. Reporting and/or carrying out a prescribed action in relation to the discrimination is frequently involved. (S)
Compare	To examine the *readily apparent* character or qualities of, especially to discover resemblances or differences . . . implies an aim of showing relative values or excellence by bringing our characteristic qualities whether similar or divergent. (W)
rank	To determine or assign the relative rank or class of. (W) Requires more discretion than *grade*.
inspect	[to compare critically] to a standard of excellence, quality, or the like, with a view toward noting discrepancies or deficiencies. (F&W)
distinguish	It suggests the making of even finer distinctions than *compare* or *contrast* and making them among things even more closely resembling each other. (S)
contrast	To compare with an aim of pointing out differences but not determining relative values. (S)
select	To decide on one, or a few, from several possibilities; variables are readily apparent and the consequences are not as great as in *determine* and *deliberate* under "Coordinate." (S)
choose	To decide on one of *two* alternatives; the variables and consequences are the same as in *select*. (S)
Classify	To group or segregate in classes that have systematic relations usually founded on common properties or characters. (W)
grade	To divide into groups based on ascending or descending order; relative rank or class is prescribed. (S)
index	To classify information, usually on the basis of subject matter or name, to facilitate reference. (S)
segregate	To separate or set apart from others or from the general mass. (W)
sort	Suggests the selection of items according to type; this process is closely related to the categorizing process indicated by "*classify*." (F&W)
match	To pair up or put in a set as possessing equal or harmonizing attributes. (W)

arrange	Most often indicates the shifting about of items according to plan, but without necessarily altering the items themselves. (F&W)
14. *FIGURING*	Performing arithmetic operations on and/or carrying out a prescribed action in relation to them. Does not include counting. (*DOT*)
Estimate	To determine *roughly* the size, extent, or nature of (W). Not the same as *forecast* in ''Synthesizing.''
Compute	To arrive at an answer by simple (arithmetic) means. (W) *Compute* is not to be confused with *calculate* (under ''Synthesize''), which applies to highly abstruse and problematical questions.
Plot	To determine the physical position of by mathematical means. (S)
15. *COMPILING*	Measuring and collecting information about data, people, or things. (S)
Measure	To ascertain the quantity, mass, extent, or degree of in terms of a standard unit or fixed amount, usually by means of an instrument or container marked off in the units. (W)
time	To determine . . . the time, duration, or rate of (W).
weigh	To ascertain the heaviness of usually by use of a balancing device. (S)
calibrate	To determine the graduations of. (W)
Collect	To bring data together into a group . . . implies careful selection. (S)
accumulate	To bring together by degrees or regular additions. (W)
inventory	To make an itemized report or record of; take stock of. (W)
count	To indicate or name by units or groups to find the total number of units involved. (W)
observe	To obtain data through visual inspection. (S)
smell	To examine the odor or scent of with the nose. (S)
listen	To pay attention to sound; perceive with the ear . . . to be alert to catch an expected sound. (W)
16. *COPYING*	Transcribing, entering, or posting data. (*DOT*)
Record	To make a written note or account of. (W)
post	To transfer (an entry or item) from one record to another. (W)
tabulate	To put into tabular form. (W)
list	To enumerate one after another. (S)
transpose	To change the relative place or normal order of. (W)
Duplicate	To make a duplicate, copy, or transcript of (W).
transcribe	To make a copy of (dictated or recorded matter) in longhand or on a typewriter. (W)
quote	To write (a passage) from another usually with credit acknowledgment. (W)

"PEOPLE" ACTIVITY VERB DEFINITIONS

10. *MENTORING*	Dealing with individuals in terms of their total personality to advise, counsel, and/or guide them with regard to problems that may be resolved by legal, scientific, clinical, spiritual, and/or other professional principles. (*DOT*)
Treat	To treat medically is to accept someone as a patient, to diagnose his illness, and to relieve it. (F&W)
prognosticate	To make a knowledgeable look at the symptoms of a disease in order to determine its likely outcome. (F&W)
diagnose	To identify (as a disease or condition) by symptoms or distinguishing characteristics. (W)
prescribe	To recommend (medical treatment) with authority. (W) (F&W)
Advise	To give a person facts that involve his own interests. (F&W)
counsel	To advise seriously and formally after consultation so as to avoid rash actions. (W)
console	To mitigate the serious grief felt by another. (F&W)
reconcile	To restore to friendship, compatibility, or harmony. (W)
Arbitrate	To act with absolute power to decide a dispute. (W)
judge	To hear and determine or decide in the case of (as a person) in or as if in a court of justice. (W) To make decisions or pass upon the merits of something. (F&W)
21. *NEGOTIATING*	Exchanging ideas, information, and opinions with others to formulate policies and programs and/or arrive jointly at decisions, conclusions, or solutions. (*DOT*)
Mediate	To attempt to bring extremes together or to function as a form of communication between them. (F&W)
settle	To reach a definite or final choice after a period of indecision or dispute. (F&W)
debate	To argue formally, usually under the control of a referee and according to a set of regulations. (F&W)
bargain	To negotiate over the terms of a purchase, agreement, or contract. (W)
reason	To argue or discuss in a careful and painstaking manner to persuade or explore a subject in depth. (F&W)
confer	To hold conversation or conference. Now typically on important, difficult, or complex matters. (W)
22. *EDUCATING*	Developing the growth or expansion of knowledge, wisdom, desirable qualities of mind or character, physical health, or general competence especially by a course of formal study or instruction. (W)
Teach	To apply a guided process of assigned work, discipline, directed study, and the presentation of examples. (F&W)
lecture	To deliver a discourse given before an audience especially for instruction. (W)

tutor	To teach, guide, or instruct on an individual basis and in a special subject or for a particular occasion or purpose. (W)
explain	To clarify or make acceptable to understanding something that is mysterious, causeless, or inconsistent. (W)
instruct	To guide training or to impart information or commands (F&W)
Coach	To train intensively by instruction, demonstration, and repeated practice. (W)
demonstrate	To make evident or reveal as true by reasoning processes, concrete facts and evidence, experimentation, operation, or repeated examples. (W)
train	To develop the body or mind systematically for the purpose of acquiring proficiency in some physical or mental pursuit. (F&W)
23. *SUPERINTENDING*	Determining or interpreting work procedures for a group of workers, assigning specific duties to them, maintaining harmonious relations among them, and promoting efficiency. (*DOT*)
Supervise	To stress guidance and the exercise of leadership of a group of workers. (F&W)
lead	To take a principal or directing part in; have charge or direction of. (W)
order	To issue commands. (W)
appoint	To designate (a person) in whom shall be vested the responsibility of performing a given task. (S) (Syn: designate)
assign	To delegate a task to one or more members of a group. (F&W)
enforce	[to require] operation, observance, or protection of laws, orders, contracts, and agreements by authority. (W)
rate	To evaluate the work performance of a subordinate relative to specific standards. (W)
24. *DIVERTING*	To draw the mind away from serious thoughts or pursuits; distracting the attention from work, worry, pain, or commonplace concerns and focusing it on pleasure. (F&W)
Entertain	To provide some occupation that will afford pleasure or relieve monotony or boredom. (F&W)
humor	To comply with someone's moods, fancies, or capricious demands, though they may seem extreme. (S)
interest	To excite or hold one's curiosity or attention. (F&W) To engage or attract the attention of someone. (W)
amuse	To provide any form of distraction that contents the mind. (F&W)
imitate	To repeat convincingly or tellingly the recognizable features of the model; suggests following a model or pattern without precluding some variation. (W)

25. *PERSUADING*	Influencing others in favor of a product, service, or point of view. (*DOT*)
Influence	To bring about a change in another's actions or thoughts by persuasion. (F&W)
motivate	To attempt consciously to stimulate the active interest or desire for something. (S)
Convince	To bring by argument to assent or belief. (W) Compels one's belief in its soundness because it satisfies the sense of logic or fitness. (F&W)
Promote	To influence in an aggressive and deliberate manner, usually with a specific aim in mind. (S)
Solicit	To move to action, serve as an urge or incentive to. (W)
Sell	To give up to another for money or other valuable consideration. (W)
26. *SPEAKING, SIGNALING*	Talking with and/or signaling people to convey or exchange information, includes giving assignments and/ or directions to helpers or assistants. (*DOT*)
Discuss	To talk over, usually in an informal, friendly way; discuss points to the elucidation of an issue rather than to the narrow presentation of one's own view. (F&W)
interview	To question or converse with especially to obtain information or ascertain personal qualities. (W)
consult	To clarify a question with emphasis on motive without necessarily suggesting ultimate agreement. (F&W)
question	To seek clarification or test knowledge of (S).
Inform	To call someone's attention to something or to cause him to receive knowledge of it. (F&W)
dictate	To speak or read for a person to transcribe or for a machine to record. (W)
answer	To speak or write in reply to. (W)
describe	To cite details that will create a visual image in the mind of an audience. (F&W)
indicate	To stress a rough approximation of literal meaning of a sign or word. (F&W)
relay	To pass along a message, signal. (W)
request	To ask for a stated need with an expectation of response. (S)
Meet	To come into the presence of. (W)
greet	To meet or receive with a salutation. (W)
27. *SERVING*	Attending to the needs or requests of the people or animals or the expressed or implicit wishes of people. Immediate response is involved. (*DOT*)
Assist	To give support or aid to especially in some undertaking or effort; aid. (W)
usher	To conduct to a place. (W)
Attend	To look after or take charge of. (W)
wait upon	To attend as a servant; to supply the want of. (W)

Supply — To provide what is needed, sometimes to make up a deficiency, replacing losses or depletions, filling a gap. (W)

provide — To equip, stock, or give in the interest of preparing with foresight. (W)

ALPHABETIC INDEX OF THE ACTIVITY VERB LIST*

Verb	Code	Verb	Code	Verb	Code
accumulate	15	Direct	11	Measure	15
Advise	20	discover	10	Mediate	21
amuse	24	Discuss	26	Meet	26
answer	26	distinguish	13	motivate	25
appoint	23	Duplicate	16	observe	15
appraise	12	enforce	23	order	23
Arbitrate	20	Entertain	24	Organize	11
arrange	13	Estimate	14	plan	10
assign	23	Evaluate	12	Plot	14
Assist	27	examine	12	post	16
Attend	27	execute	11	prescribe	20
audit	12	experiment	12	prognosticate	20
authorize	11	explain	22	Promote	25
bargain	21	forecast	10	provide	27
calculate	10	formulate	11	question	26
calibrate	15	grade	13	quote	16
choose	13	greet	26	rank	13
Classify	13	humor	24	rate	23
Coach	22	hypothesize	10	reason	21
Collect	15	identify	12	recommend	12
Compare	13	imitate	24	reconcile	20
compose	10	implement	11	Record	16
compute	14	index	13	regulate	11
confer	21	indicate	26	relay	26
console	20	influence	25	Report	12
consult	26	Inform	26	request	26
contrast	13	inspect	13	research	12
control	11	instruct	22	scan	12
convince	25	interest	24	schedule	11
counsel	20	interpret	10	Scrutinize	12
count	15	interview	26	segregate	13
debate	21	invent	10	select	13
Decide	11	inventory	15	Sell	25
deliberate	11	Investigate	12	settle	21
demonstrate	22	judge	20	smell	15
describe	26	lead	23	Solicit	25
design	10	lecture	22	Solve	10
determine	11	list	16	sort	13
Develop	11	listen	15	study	12
Devise	10	manage	11	suggest	12
diagnose	20	marshall	11	summarize	12
dictate	26	match	13	Supervise	23

* The first digit designates the major functional area: 1—data; 2—people. The second digit indicates the specific level of worker function where the activity verb is categorized.

C Worker Contacts and Interactions

Study of worker contacts can be made a part of a larger network of interrelations, or it can be pursued independently. Thus, the worker functions hierarchy of the FJA systems approaches the study of worker contacts as part of its integrated methodology. The four scales presented in this appendix enable analysis of contacts as an independent concern.

The two scales from the FES are part of the job classification program of the U.S. Office of Personnel Management. Each of these scales is broken down into levels, with more points assigned to higher levels. The Personal Contacts Scale (C.1) deals with face-to-face contacts and telephone and radio dialogue with persons that are not in the supervisory chain. The Purpose of Contacts Scale (C.2) covers exchange of factual information to situations involving significant or controversial issues and differing viewpoints, goals, or objectives.

The remaining two scales within this appendix are from the HSMS. The unit of analysis here is the task. The Human Interaction Scale (C.3) deals with the degree of sensitivity to others required of the performer. The Leadership Scale (C.4) measures the degree to which the performer is required to exercise leadership in dealing with subordinates.

An implicit assumption underlying the worker contacts scales is that jobs and tasks can be rated according to the quality of contacts. In general, the more important or sensitive and risky the contact, the higher the rating. The worker's ability to do damage or to advance the goals of the job are taken into account.

APPENDIX C.1 PERSONAL CONTACTS (FES)

This factor includes face-to-face contacts and telephone and radio dialogue with persons not in the supervisory chain. (NOTE: Personal contacts with supervisors are covered under Factor 2, Supervisory Controls.) Levels described under this factor are based on what is required to make the initial contact, the difficulty of communicating with those contacted, and the setting in which the contact take place (e.g., the degree to which the employee and those contacted recognize their relative roles and authorities).

Above the lowest level, points should be credited under this factor only for contacts which are essential for successful performance of the work and which have a demonstrable impact on the difficulty and responsibility of the work performed.

The relationship of Factors 6 and 7 persumes that the same contacts will be evaluated for both factors. Therefore, use the personal contacts which serve as the basis for the level selected for Factor 7 as the basis for selecting a level for Factor 6.

Level 6–1 *10 points*

The personal contacts are with employees within the immediate organization, office, project, or work unit, and in related or support units;

AND/OR

The contacts are with members of the general public in very highly structured situations (e.g., the purpose of the contact and the question of with whom to deal are relatively clear). Typical of contacts at this level are purchases of admission tickets at a ticket window.

Level 6–2 *25 points*

The personal contacts are with employees in the same agency, but outside the immediate organization. People contacted generally are engaged in different functions, missions, and kinds of work, e.g., representatives from various levels within the agency such as headquarters, regional, district, or field offices or other operating offices in the immediate installations;

AND/OR

The contacts are with members of the general public, as individuals or groups, in a moderately structured setting (e.g., the contacts are generally established on a routine basis, usually at the employee's work place; the exact purpose of the contact may be unclear at first to one or more of the parties; and one or more of the parties may be uninformed concerning the role and authority of other participants). Typical of contacts at this level are those with persons seeking airline reservations or with job applicants at a job information center.

Level 6–3 *60 points*

The personal contacts are with individuals or groups from outside the employing agency in a moderately unstructured setting (e.g., the contacts are not established on routine basis; the purpose and extent of each contact is different and the role and authority of each party is identified and developed during the course of the contact). Typical of contacts at this level are those with persons in their capacities as attorneys; contractors; or representatives of professional organizations, the news media, or public action groups.

Level 6–4 *110 points*

The personal contacts are with high-ranking officials from outside the employing agency at national or international levels in highly unstructured settings (e.g., contacts are characterized

---

From U.S. Civil Service Commission, *Instructions for the Factor Evaluation System* (Washington, D.C.: U.S. Government Printing Office, 1977), pp. 27–28.

by problems such as the officials may be relatively inaccessible; arrangements may have to be made for accompanying staff members; appointments may have to be made well in advance; each party may be very unclear as to the role and authority of the other; and each contact may be conducted under different ground rules). Typical of contacts at this level are those with members of Congress, leading representatives of foreign governments, presidents of large national or international firms, nationally recognized representatives of the news media, presidents of national unions, state governors, or mayors of large cities.

APPENDIX C.2 PURPOSE OF CONTACTS (FES)

In General Schedule occupations, purpose of personal contacts ranges from factual exchanges of information to situations involving significant or controversial issues and differing viewpoints, goals, or objectives. The personal contacts which serve as the basis for the level selected for this factor must be the same as the contacts which are the basis for the level selected for Factor 6.

Level 7–1 *20 points*

The purpose is to obtain, clarify, or give facts or information regardless of the nature of those facts, i.e., the facts or information may range from easily understood to highly technical.

Level 7–2 *50 points*

The purpose is to plan, coordinate, or advise on work efforts or to resolve operating problems by influencing or motivating individuals or groups who are working toward mutual goals and who have basically cooperative attitudes.

Level 7–3 *120 points*

The purpose is to influence, motivate, interrogate, or control persons or groups. At this level the persons contacted may be fearful, skeptical, uncooperative, or dangerous. Therefore, the employee must be skillful in approaching the individual or group in order to obtain the desired effect, such as gaining compliance with established policies and regulations by persuasion or negotiation, or gaining information by establishing rapport with a suspicious informant.

Level 7–4 *220 points*

The purpose is to justify, defend, negotiate, or settle matters involving significant or controversial issues. Work at this level usually involved active participation in conferences, meetings, hearings, or presentations involving problems or issues of considerable consequence or importance. The persons contacted typically have diverse viewpoints, goals, or objectives requiring the employee to achieve a common understanding of the problem and a satisfactory solution by convincing them, arriving at a compromise, or developing suitable alternatives.

APPENDIX C.3 HUMAN INTERACTION (HSMS)

This skill refers to the degree of sensitivity to others required of the performer in the task being scaled. The skills involves the performer's perception of the relevant characteristics or state of being of the other person(s), the performer's attention to feedback as the interaction occurs, and the performer's appropriate modification of his behavior so as to accomplish the task. The skill is involved if the task requires any personal contact or interaction with others.

(FES) From U.S. Civil Service Commission, *Instructions for the Factor Evaluation System* (Washington, D.C.: U.S. Government Printing Office, 1977), p. 29.

(HSMS) From E. Gilpatrick, *The Health Services Mobility Study Method of Task Analysis and Curriculum Design*, Research Report No. 11, Vol. 1 (New York: Hunter College, The Research Foundation, City University of New York, 1977), p. 2-21. Reprinted by permission.

The level of the skill rises as the degree of perceptiveness and sensitivity required of the performer rises, and as the subtlety of the feedback to which he or she must respond increases. The scale level is not determined by the level of knowledge required.

Scale Value	Descriptive Statement
0.0	The task does not require the performer to be in contact with or to interact with other people.
1.0	The task requires the performer to be in only *general contact* with other people. *Very little sensitivity to or perception of* the other person(s)' relevant general characteristics or state of being is required, and *little awareness of very obvious feedback is required* for the performer to adjust his behavior to perform the task.
3.0	The task requires the performer to interact with others in the performance of the task. The performer is required to be *somewhat sensitive to or perceptive of* the other person(s)' relevant general characteristics or state of being, and to be aware of *very obvious feedback* so as to adjust his behavior accordingly.
5.0	The task requires the performer to interact with others in the performance of the task. The performer is required to be *quite sensitive to or perceptive of* the other person(s)' relevant characteristics or state of being, and to be aware of *fairly obvious feedback* so as to adjust his behavior accordingly.
7.0	The task requires the performer to interact with others in the performance of the task. The performer is required to be *keenly sensitive to or perceptive of* the other person(s)' relevant characteristics or state of being, and to be aware of *fairly subtle or complex feedback* so as to adjust his behavior accordingly.
9.0	The task requires the performer to interact with others in the performance of the task. The performer is required to be *keenly sensitive to or perceptive of* the other person(s)' relevant characteristics or state of being, and to be aware of *very subtle or very complex feedback* so as to adjust his behavior accordingly.

APPENDIX C.4 LEADERSHIP (HSMS)

This skill refers to the degree to which leadership in interacting with subordinates is required on the part of the performer in the task being scaled. The skill is involved when the performer's task requires him to interact with subordinates so as to affect their work performance in order for the performer to achieve goals related to the task. The subordinate relationship may be *de facto* as well as formal.

The level of this skill rises in relation to three aspects of the performer's relationship with subordinates which are relevant to the task situation. These are: (1) power over subordinates' conditions of employment, (2) clearness of mutual channels of communication, and (3) clearness of subordinates' own relevant task procedures.

Low levels of Leadership are required when the performer has a great deal of power over the subordinates' conditions of employment, when the performer has very formal and clearly defined channels of communication with the subordinates relevant to the task situation, and when the tasks of the subordinates related to the performer's objectives are very clear cut, obvious, and require little discretionary judgment.

High levels of Leadership are required when the performer's power is low, when channels of communication are vague and undefined, and when the relevant subordinates' tasks are vague and require a great deal of discretionary judgment.

The level of Leadership required for the task being scaled is determined by the combination of ratings of high, medium or low for each of the three aspects. The parentheses for each statement indicate the various combinations for each scale value.

From E. Gilpatrick, *The Health Services Mobility Study Method of Task Analysis and Curriculum Design*, Research Report No. 11, Vol. 1 (New York: Hunter College, The Research Founation, City University of New York, 1977), p. 2-23. Reprinted by permission.

Scale Value	Descriptive Statement
0.0	The task does not require the performer to relate to subordinates.
1.0	The task requires the performer to relate to subordinates in order to achieve work goals. The performer is understood to have a *great amount of power* over the related subordinates' conditions of employment. *Channels of communication* between the performer and the subordinates are *very formalized and very well defined*. The subordinates' *related tasks are very clear cut, obvious and require little discretionary judgment*. (*Low range of Leadership needs on each of the three aspects*. Also included: *two lows and one medium*.)
3.0	The task requires the performer to relate to subordinates in order to achieve work goals. The performer is understood to have a *moderate amount of power* over the related subordinates' conditions of employment. The *channels of communication* between the performer and the subordinates are somewhat *formalized and moderately well defined*. The subordinates' *related tasks are very clear cut, obvious, and require little discretionary judgment*. (*Mid-range of leadership needs on two out of the three aspects and low on a third*. Also included: *two lows and one high*.)
4.5	The task requires the performer to relate to subordinates in order to achieve work goals. The performer is understood to have a *moderate amount of power* over the related subordinates' conditions of employment. The *channels of communication* between the performer and the subordinates are *somewhat formalized and moderately well defined*. The subordinates' *related tasks are moderately clear cut, requiring some discretionary judgment*. (*Mid-range of leadership needs on each of the three aspects*. Also included: *one low, one medium and one high*; and *two mediums and a high*.)
6.5	The task requires the performer to relate to subordinates in order to achieve work goals. The performer is understood to have a *moderate amount of power* over the related subordinates' conditions of employment. The *channels of communication* between the performer and the subordinates are *very informal, vague or irregular*. The subordinates' *related tasks are vaguely defined and require a great deal of discretionary judgment*. (High rating for *Leadership on two out of three aspects*.)
8.5	The task requires the performer to relate to subordinates in order to achieve work goals. The performer is understood to have *very little power* over the related subordinates' conditions of employment. The *channels of communication* between the performer and the subordinates are *very informal, vague, or irregular*. The subordinates' *related tasks are vaguely defined and require a great deal of discretionary judgment*. (*High ratings for leadership on all three aspects*.)

D Work Fields and the Sentence Analysis Technique

Both the work fields and the sentence analysis technique concepts are from the DOL system. Work fields are organizations of specific methods that are characteristic either of the machines, tools, equipment, or work aids used in the work or of the techniques designed to fulfill the objectives of the work. The DOL *Handbook* contains 100 work fields that have been organized for the purpose of classifying all the jobs in the economy. Appendix D.1 contains an alphabetical list and some examples of work fields.

The Sentence Analysis Technique (SAT) was devised to assist the analyst in stating job-worker situations in standard terms. The standardization is provided by the terminology of Functional Job Analysis. Examples of applications of the SAT are given in Appendix D.2. The outputs of the SAT contain the following standard features. First is a summary of the work, emphasizing the mission and objectives attained. This is followed by an analysis of the tasks involved. The task descriptions begin with an active verb, which is synonymous with the worker function. The analysis section also shows the object of the worker function, the work field in which the activity falls, and the products or services that result from the task.

APPENDIX D.1 WORK FIELDS: ALPHABETICAL LISTING AND EXAMPLES

ALPHABETICAL LISTING OF WORK FIELDS

051 Abrading
291 Accommodating
232 Accounting-Recording
295 Administering
211 Appraising
141 Baking-Drying
005 Blasting
071 Bolting-Screwing
053 Boring
153 Brushing-Spraying
034 Butchering
094 Calking
132 Casting
052 Chipping
031 Cleaning
161 Combing-Napping
263 Composing
146 Cooking-Food Preparing
003 Cropping
142 Crushing
135 Die Sizing
202 Developing-Printing
144 Distilling
242 Drafting
111 Electrical Fabricating-Installing-Repairing
112 Electronic Fabricating-Installing-Repairing
122 Electro-Mechanical Fabricating-Installing-Repairing
154 Electroplating
244 Engineering
183 Engraving
297 Entertaining
181 Eroding
182 Etching
041 Filling
145 Filtering-Straining-Separating
061 Fitting-Placing
082 Flame Cutting-Arc Cutting
062 Folding-Fastening
006 Gardening
063 Gluing
294 Healing-Caring
133 Heat Conditioning
012 Hoisting-Conveying
001 Hunting-Fishing
151 Immersing-Coating
192 Imprinting
282 Information Giving
271 Investigating
032 Ironing
165 Knitting
092 Laying
241 Laying out
272 Litigating
011 Loading-Moving
002 Logging
033 Lubricating
057 Machining
091 Masoning
121 Mechanical Fabricating-Installing-Repairing
131 Melting
292 Merchandising
055 Milling-Turning-Planing
004 Mining-Quarrying-Earth Boring
143 Mixing
136 Molding
072 Nailing
042 Packing
262 Painting
201 Photographing
134 Pressing-Forging
191 Printing
147 Processing-Compounding
293 Protecting
014 Pumping
231 Recording
251 Researching
073 Riveting
152 Saturating
056 Sawing
171 Sewing-Tailoring
054 Shearing-Shaving
083 Soldering
162 Spinning
021 Stationary Engineering
221 Stock Checking
101 Structural Fabricating-Installing-Repairing
264 Styling
243 Surveying
281 System Communicating
296 Teaching
013 Transporting
093 Troweling
298 Undertaking
102 Upholstering
164 Weaving
212 Weighing
081 Welding
163 Winding
043 Wrapping
261 Writing

CROPPING 003

Breeding, cultivating, growing, and marketing plant or animal life by any combination of Accounting, Recording; Appraising; Cleaning; Healing-Caring; Loading-Moving; Merchandising; Mixing; Packing; Protecting; Recording; Shearing-Shaving; Stock Checking; and Transporting. Jobs involved with only one of these work fields are listed thereunder.

From U.S. Department of Labor (1972). *Handbook for Analyzing Jobs*. Washington, D.C.: U.S. Government Printing Office, pp. 84–148

Methods Verbs

Baling	Driving (sheep)	Incubating	Rounding up
Branding	Dusting	Milking	Sorting
Breeding	Feeding	Mulching	Sowing
Budding	Fertilizing	Picking	Spraying
Candling	Grafting	Planting	Sterilizing
Castrating	Grazing	Plowing	Storing
Chilling	Grooming	Potting	Threshing
Culling	Harrowing	Pruning	Transplanting
Digging	Hatching	Reaping	Watering
Dredging			

Machines	Tools	Equipment	Work Aids
Combine	Branding iron	Incubator	Bee hives
Conveyor	Brushes		Hutches
Corn picker	Hoe		Pens
Cotton picker	Mattock		
Cultivator	Pitchfork		
Harvester	Plow		
Hay baler	Scythe		
Mowing machine	Shovel		
Tractor	Sickle		

Grows various herbs used for medicinal or flavoring purposes, such as mint, golden seal, wormwood, ginseng, belladonna, and digitalis.

Captures and raises frogs for consumption or for sale alive. Kills adult frogs and removes legs for marketing. Sells live frogs as breeding pairs and scientific specimens, and sells tadpoles as fishing bait.

Breeds, raises, and sells saddle horses, matched teams of draft animals, or race horses. Selects stallion and mare for breeding; breaks, trains, and grooms horses; exhibits stock at horse shows for sale.

Cultivates bees to produce honey or to sell for pollination of crops.

Plants and raises shade trees and ornamental plant stock, for sale to homeowners and landscape gardeners.

PRESSING-FORGING 134

(Forging-Pressing)

Shaping, severing, piercing, or forge-welding materials by a force pushed against or through them as in squeezing or punching, or by applying sharp blows as in hammering. Distinguish from Casting, Die Sizing, Ironing, and Molding.

Methods Verbs

Beating	Dimpling	Kneading	Spinning
Braking	Dishing	Molding	Squeezing
Clipping	Drawing	Pounding	Stamping
Coiling	Flaring	Punching	Striking
Compressing	Hammering	Rolling	Swaging
Crimping	Hitting	Shearing	Twisting

Machines	Tools	Equipment	Work Aids
Blanking press	Hammers	Coal forge	Anvils
Bull press	Sledges	Electric furnace	Calipers
Drop hammer	Pincers	Gas furnace	Diagrams
Forging press	Tongs	Oil furnace	Fixtures
Head machine	Wrenches		Gages
Impact hammer			Level
Notching press			Micrometers
Press brake			Punches
Restrike hammer			Rule
Upsetter			Shims
			Square

Tends power hammer or power press to shape metal stock.

Forge-welds metal parts by heating and hammering parts together.

Sets up and operates power brake to bend, notch, punch, form, roll, arc, or straighten metal plates and structural shapes to blueprint or sketch specifications.

Shapes metal bars into horseshoes by heating, hammering, and punching bars.

Hammers metal stock into specified size and shape on blacksmith's anvil.

ETCHING 182

Inscribing the surface of materials by the corrosive action of chemicals on exposed parts of material.

Methods Verbs

Corroding	Dusting	Scratching	Scribing
Desensitizing	Scoring		

Machines	Tools	Equipment	Work Aids
Etching machine	Spray guns	Drying chamber	Acid solutions
	Rubber stamp	Timers	Charts
		Etching tank	Formulas
		Scale (wt)	Litmus paper
			Magnifying glass
			Micrometers
			Stencils
			Templates

Etches artistic designs onto glass surfaces of articles, such as bowls, vases, and stemware, using acid solutions.

Tends machine that etches conductive patterns onto copper-faced plastic sheets.

Supervises and coordinates activities of workers engaged in etching trade name on razor blades.

Etches trademarks on stainless steel knives and forks, using rubber stamp and acid solution.

Dissolves exposed portions of metal objects in etching solutions to produce aircraft parts or sheets, using templates, micrometers, spray guns, and handtools.

WRITING 261

Reporting, editing, promoting, and/or interpreting ideas in written form.

Methods Verbs

Adapting	Depicting	Editing	Reading
Criticizing	Describing	Proofreading	Reporting

Machines	**Tools**	**Equipment**	**Work Aids**
Typewriter	Writing implements	Camera	Charts
		Tape recorder	Interview forms
		Two-way radio	Reference books

Reviews and rewrites news copy and edits copy to ensure conformance to accepted rules of style and syntax and to shorten or lengthen items to fit allocated space on newspaper pages.

Analyzes news and writes syndicated articles for newspaper publication.

Writes newspaper stories conforming to prescribed editorial techniques and format after collecting and analyzing facts about newsworthy events.

Composes advertising copy for radio or television commercial scripts.

Edits newspaper or magazine copy for errors in spelling, punctuation, or grammar, according to accepted rules of style and syntax.

COMPOSING 263

Expressing and interpreting ideas in musical form, or creating dynamics of movement to interpret music.

Methods Verbs

Arranging	Harmonizing	Scoring	Transposing
Copying	Orchestrating	Translating	Writing

Machines	**Tools**	**Equipment**	**Work Aids**
	Pencils	Tape recorder	Choral slide rule
	Pens		Piano
			Reference books
			Staff paper
			Various musical instruments

Creates and writes musical compositions.

Transcribes musical compositions or melodic lines to adapt or create particular style for orchestra, band, choral group, or individual.

Writes musical score for orchestra, band, or choral group, adapting arrangement for interpretation best suited to performers.

Creates original dances for ballet performance, musical show, or revue.

Copies musical parts onto staff paper from score written by arranger or orchestrator, for each instrument or voice within musical group.

INVESTIGATING 271

Securing and evaluating data about persons, places, or incidents for the purpose of solving criminal cases; settling claims; estimating credit risks; determining the qualifications, integrity, or loyalty of persons; or preparing reports for various operational purposes. Distinguish from *Researching*, which involves inquiry or examination into areas of fundamental knowledge.

Methods Verbs

Advising	Inspecting	Questioning	Scanning
Enforcing	Interviewing	Reporting	Searching
Inquiring	Measuring		

Machines	Tools	Equipment	Work Aids
Optical scanners		Camera	Charts
		Electronic equipment	Diagrams
		Tape recorder	Federal and state statute books
			Reference books

Inspect machinery, equipment, and working conditions in establishment for hazards, to prevent accidents and fires.

Interviews applicants seeking admission to public housing project to determine eligibility, according to prescribed admission standards.

Investigates business establishments and individuals to settle claims or ensure compliance with state and federal laws and regulations, such as those governing child labor, wages and hours, and financial responsibility.

Examines printed matter, letters, and press dispatches in time of war to ascertain that material contains no information of value to the enemy.

Investigates claims for loss or damages filed in conjunction with insurance policy to determine authenticity of claims.

PROTECTING 293

Protecting life and property (including animals and plants) against loss from fire, pests, and other natural hazards, and from negligence, criminal acts, and unlawful practices. *Protecting* includes maintaining peace and order; directing traffic; patrolling establishments or areas; apprehending lawbreakers; extinguishing various types of fires by water and chemical means; and demolishing property, exterminating pests and parasites by fumigating, burning, smothering, dusting, spraying, and draining swamps.

Methods Verbs

Burning	Dusting	Fumigating	Patrolling
Cautioning	Firefighting	Guarding	Policing
Draining			Spraying

Machines	Tools	Equipment	Work Aids
Boat	Axe	Alarms	Azimuth sighter
Motorcycle	Chisel	Call box	Caution sign
Patrol car	Crowbar	Camera	Ladder
Patrol wagon	Firearms	Hydrant	Map
Smoke ejectors	Hand cuffs	Radio	Protective clothing
	Hose nozzle	Respirator	Ticket book
		Telephone equipment	

Escorts individuals to provide protection from bodily injury or invasion of privacy, using physical force or firearms when necessary.

Patrols ski trails and slope areas to provide assistance and protection to skiers and report condition of ski trails, lifts, and snow cover on slopes.

Controls and extinguishes fires, protects life and property, and maintains equipment as employee of city, township, or industrial plant.

Circulates among patrons in place of entertainment to prevent improper dancing, skating, or similar activities and to detect persons annoying other patrons or damaging furnishings of establishment.

Sprays marshland, drainage ditches, or catch-basins with insecticide to control breeding of mosquitoes, using portable compressed-air spray tank.

TEACHING 296

Instructing and training people or animals in the acquisition of mental, physical, or social skills. Distinguish from Information Giving.

Methods Verbs

Demonstrating	Examining	Lecturing	Supervising
Directing	Grading	Planning (lessons)	Testing

Machines	Tools	Equipment	Work Aids
Braille Writer	Pen	Projector	Blackboard
	Pencil	Public address system	Chalk
	Pointer	Tape recorder	Charts
	Slate		Diagrams
	Stylus		Examinations
			Manuals
			Maps
			Publications
			Reference books
			Textbooks

Teaches groups of women basic principles of good carriage, balance, behavior, and grooming to improve appearance and demeanor.

Trains wild animals such as lions, tigers, bears, and elephants to perform tricks for entertainment of audience.

Teaches academic subjects such as English, mathematics, and foreign languages to pupils requiring private instructions, adapting curriculum to meet individual needs.

Teaches military subjects, such as employment and deployment of weapons, systems, military aspects of geopolitics, and passive defense, in military school, college, or university.

Instructs individuals or groups in theory and practice of proper automobile driving skills.

UNDERTAKING 298

Preparing bodies for burial and carrying out funeral services. Distinguish from Accommodating.

Methods Verbs

Embalming Pallbearing

Machines	Tools	Equipment	Work Aids
Hearse	Scalpel	Pump	Casket
Limousine	Suture	Retort furnace	Clay
	Trocar		Cosmetics
			Cotton
			Plaster of paris

Slides casket containing body into retort furnace, controls valves to attain extreme heat for specific length of time to cremate body, and scrapes ashes of casket and body from furnace.

Acts as one of group to carry casket from mortuary to place of funeral service and from place of service to place of interment.

Reshapes or reconstructs disfigured or maimed bodies, using materials such as clay, cotton, plaster of paris, and wax to prepare body for funeral services.

Interviews family or other authorized person to arrange details of funeral, such as preparation of obituary notice, selection of casket, location and time of burial, selection of pallbearers, procurement of religious official, and transportation of mourners.

Drives hearse to transport bodies to mortuary for embalming and from mortuary to place of funeral service or interment.

APPENDIX D.2 EXAMPLES OF APPLICATIONS OF THE SENTENCE ANALYSIS TECHNIQUE

ILLSTRATION A

Job Worker Situation. Composes narrative, dramatic, or lyric poetry for magazines, books, or other publications, usually on freelance basis, choosing own subject matter and suitable form to express personal feeling and individual experience, or to narrate story or event.

Analysis

Verb (Worker Function)	Immediate Object (MTEWA, Data, People)	Infinitive Phrase	
		Infinitive (Work Field)	Object of Infinitive (MPSMS)
Integrates	subject matter, form, style	to write	poetry.
Converses with	colleagues	to discuss	poetry.
Handles	writing materials	to write	poetry.

Classification

Hierarchy	Worker Function	Work Field	Code	MPSMS	Code
(Data)	Synthesizing (0)	Writing	261	Literature & Philology	784
People	Speaking-Signaling 6				
Things	Handling 7				

ILLUSTRATION C

Job Worker Situation. Assists legal representatives in preparation of written contracts covering other than standardized agreements. Reviews agreement for conformity to company rates, rules, and regulations. Writes agreement in contract form and obtains necessary legal department approval.

From U.S. Department of Labor (1972). *Handbook for Analyzing Jobs*. Washington, D.C.: U.S. Government Printing Office, pp. 183–206.

Analysis

Verb (Worker Function)	Immediate Object (MTEWA, Data, People)	Infinitive Phrase: Infinitive (Work Field)	Infinitive Phrase: Object of Infinitive (MPSMS)
Analyzes	agreement	to prepare	legal contract.
Talks with	legal representatives	to prepare	written contract.
Handles	legal papers, writing materials	to write	contracts.

Classification

Hierarchy	Worker Function	Work Field	Code	MPSMS	Code
(Data)	Analyzing (2)	Litigating	272	Legal	942
People	Speaking, signaling 6				
Things	Handling 7				

ILLUSTRATION E

Job Worker Situation. Computes wage data and operates posting machine to post data to payroll records. Computes earnings from time sheets and work tickets. Operates posting machine to post to payroll records deductions such as income tax witholdings, social security payments, insurances, credit union payments, and bond purchases. Enters net wages on earning record card, check, check stub, and payroll sheets.

Analysis

Verb (Worker Function)	Immediate Object (MTEWA, Data, People)	Infinitive Phrase: Infinitive (Work Field)	Infinitive Phrase: Object of Infinitive (MPSMS)
Computes	earnings, tax witholdings, social security payments, insurance, bond purchases	to record	payroll.
Takes instructions from	supervisor	to record	payroll.
Operates	posting machine	to record	payroll.

Classification

Hierarchy	Worker Function	Work Field	Code	MPSMS	Code
(Data)	Computing (4)	Accounting-recording	232	Bookkeeping	893
People	Taking Instructions 8				
(Things)	Operating-Controlling (2)				

ILLUSTRATION H

Job Worker Situation. Performs lay duties to assist ordained religious leaders. Visits members of congregation, especially sick, and provides welfare services. Preaches at and conducts religious meeings. Prepares candidates for acceptance by religious body.

Analysis

(Verb (worker Function)	Immediate Object (MTEWA, Data, People)	Infinitive Phrase: Infinitive (Work Field)	Infinitive Phrase: Object of Infinitive (MPSMS)
Evaluates	parish members' problems	to determine	spiritual guidance.
Preaches	sermons	to provide for	spiritual needs.
Counsels	parish members	to provide for	spiritual guidance.
Handles	books, magazines, pamphlets, papers	to provide for	spiritual needs.

Classification

Hierarchy	Worker Function	Work Field	Code	MPSMS	Code
(Data)	Analyzing (2)	Information Giving	282	Spiritual Services	954
(People)	Mentoring (0)				
Things	Handling 7				

ILLUSTRATION I

Job Worker Situation. Plans, administers, and directs intercollegiate athletic activities in college or university. Interprets and participates in formulating extramural athletic policies. Employs and discharges athletic coaches and other athletic department employees on own initiative or at direction of board in charge of athletics. Assumes responsibility for athletic publicity. Oversees and directs athletic coaches and members of coaching staff. Prepares budget estimates. Assumes immediate responsibility for receipts and expenditures of department, and for production of income, such as scheduling sports events, and controlling and managing ticket sales.

Analysis

Verb (Worker Function)	Immediate Object (MTEWA, Data, People)	Infinitive Phrase: Infinitive (Work Field)	Infinitive Phrase: Object of Infinitive (MPSMS)
Plans	athletic program	to administer	intercollegiate athletic activities.
Prepares and controls	budget	to administer	intercollegiate athletic activities.
Negotiates with	people	to formulate	extramural athletic policies.
Observes and directs	athletic coaches	to administer	intercollegiate athletic activities.
Handles	paper materials	to administer	intercollegiate athletic activities.

Classification

Hierarchy	Worker Function	Work Field	Code	MPSMS	Code
(Data)	Coordinating (1)	Administering	295	Educational	941
(People)	Negotiating (1)				
Things	Handling 7				

ILLUSTRATION K

Job Worker Situation. Supervises and coordinates activities of workers engaged in mixing chemicals and spraying crops to destroy harmful aspects and to control fungus diseases. Directs workers in methods of applying chemical solutions. Keeps records of chemicals used.

Analysis

Verb (Worker Function)	Immediate Object (MTEWA, Data, People)	Infinitive Phrase	
		Infinitive (Work Field)	**Object of Infinitive (MPSMS)**
Coordinates	data, concerning extermination of pests, parasites, and fungus diseases	to protect	crops.
Directs	workers	to spray	crops.
Handles	equipment, chemical	to spray	crops.

Classification

Hierarchy	Worker Function	Work Field	Code	MPSMS	Code
(Data)	Coordinating (1)	Protecting	293	Field crops, fruits, tree nuts	300
(People)	Supervising (3)				
Things	Handling 7				

ILLUSTRATION M

Job Worker Situation. Protects property, merchandise, or money of store or similar establishment by detecting thieving, shoplifting, or other unlawful practices; gathering information for use as evidence; and using own knowledge of city, county, and state laws.

Analysis

Verb (Worker Function)	Immediate Object (MTEWA, Data, People)	Infinitive Phrase	
		Infinitive (Work Field)	**Object of Infinitive (MPSMS)**
Gathers	information	to protect	Property of store.
Talks with	people	to detect	thieving, shoplifting, or other unlawful practices.
Talks with	police or management	to protect	property of store.
Handles	merchandise	to protect	property of store.

Classification

Hierarchy	Worker Function	Work Field	Code	MPSMS	Code
(Data)	Compiling (3)	Protecting	293	Retail trade	881
(People)	Speaking-Signaling (6)				
Things	Handling 7				

ILLUSTRATION O

Job Worker Situation. Sets up variety of machine tools such as gear hobbers, lathes, milling machines, boring machines, and grinders for other workers and machines' first-run workpiece. Changes worn cutting tools, and adjusts cutting speeds, feed rates, and depth of cut.

Analysis

Verb (Worker Function)	Immediate Object (MTEWA, Data, People)	Infinitive Phrase	
		Infinitive (Work Field)	Object of Infinitive (MPSMS)
Compiles	information about condition and placement of machine tools	to adjust	machines.
Takes instructions from	supervisor	to set up	machines.
Sets up	machine tools	to machine	metal.

Classification

Hierarchy	Worker Function	Work Field	Code	MPSMS	Code
(Data)	Compiling (3)	Machining	057	Metal Ferrous and nonferrous	530
People	Taking Instructions-Helping 8				
(Things)	Setting Up (0)				

ILLUSTRATION Q

Job Worker Situation. Operates cord or cordless switchboard to relay incoming, outgoing, and interoffice calls. On cordless switchboard, pushes switch keys to make connections and relay calls. On cord-type equipment, plugs cord in jacks mounted on switchboard. Supplies information to callers and records messages.

Analysis

Verb (Worker Function)	Immediate Object (MTEWA, Data, People)	Infinitive Phrase	
		Infinitive (Work Field)	Object of Infinitive (MPSMS)
Compares	switchboard operation with standards	to relay	calls.
Converses with	callers	to convey, to receive	information.
Operates	cord or cordless switchboard	to relay	incoming, outgoing, and interoffice calls.

Classification

Hierarchy	Worker Function	Work Field	Code	MPSMS	Code
Data	Comparing 6	System Communicating	281	Telephone Services	864
(People)	Speaking-Signaling (6)				
(Things)	Operating-Controlling (2)				

ILLUSTRATION S

Job Worker Situation. Installs draperies in customers' homes. Measures area to be covered by drapes in customer's home. Screws and bolts brackets and hangers onto wall, using handtools. Hangs and arranges drapes to enhance appearance of room.

Analysis

Verb (Worker Function)	Immediate Object (MTEWA, Data, People)	Infinitive Phrase	
		Infinitive (Work Field)	Object of Infinitive (MPSMS)
Measures	area to be covered	to determine	draping dimension.
Takes instruction from	customers, supervisor	to install	draperies.
Hangs, arranges	draperies	to install	draperies.
Manipulates	handtools	to install	brackets, hangers.

Classification

Hierarchy	Worker Function	Work Field	Code	MPSMS	Code
Data	Computing 4	Structural Fabricating-Installing-Repairing	101	Textile Products, n.e.c.	439
People	Taking Instructions-Helping 8				
(Things)	Manipulating (4)				

E Guidelines and Controls

In the job analysis literature, the focus of the study of guidelines and controls is approached by ascertaining the amount of discretion that is allowed to the worker in task performance. The six scales reproduced in this appendix provide differing ways of reaching this goal. The Scale of Worker Instructions (Appendix E.1) is from Sidney Fine's version of FJA. Fine's basic premise is that all tasks have prescribed and discretionary components. The prescribed components of a task represent those areas where the worker has no choice over what he or she does. The discretionary components, on the other hand, are those areas of tasks where the worker is expected, or even required to, use judgment in the planning and execution of the task. His scale combines these two interdependent concepts. Lower scores on this scale imply lesser amounts of discretion or more prescription. The highest score is a situation where the worker is given a need experienced by the organization. It is up to the worker to muster the resources, organization, and strategy for meeting the need.

The next two scales (E.2 and E.3) are from the FES system of the U.S. Office of Personnel Management. The Supervisory Controls Scale analyzes the pattern of supervision, with lower scores signifying tighter controls. The Guidelines Scale deals with the contents of instructions provided.

The scales in Appendices E.4 and E.5 are from the HSMS. These instruments are more focused than all the others included in this appendix. The Decision Making on Methods Scale deals with the "how" of task performance, including what is done, when, in what order, what is used, and who is involved. Scores higher than zero become relevant when the worker has discretion over any of the issues. At low scale values, the performer is allowed the latitude of choosing from among prescribed alternatives within the guidelines provided. At higher scale values, the discretion increases both in regard to range of possibilities and the formulation of guidelines for making the decision.

The Decision Making on Quality (E.5) Scale deals with the latitude allowed to the worker in affecting the quality of the task outcomes. Scale values are assigned according to the extent to which the performer is able to affect the outcomes personally and the extent to which the output is subject to review before it is passed on or consumed (Gilpatrick, 1977a, 1977b).

The Job Rating Form (JRF), given in Appendix E.6, is a companion instrument of the Job Diagnostic Survey (JDS). Both these instruments were developed by Hackman, Oldham, and their associates as a part of their action scheme for job redesign. The theoretical basis of these instruments were reviewed in Chapter 3 (see particularly Exhibit 3.11). Both instruments were designed to yield data on the key elements of the job characteristics theory outlined in the diagram in that exhibit. The JDS addresses all the elements of that theory; it measures the job characteristics and provides scores relating to employees' experienced psychological states, satisfaction with their jobs, and work context. It is to be completed by job incumbents, not by individuals outside the job. The JRF, on the other hand, is designed for use by analysts and other subject matter experts. It focuses only on the five core job characteristics (Exhibit 3.11). The resulting score provides an index of how the job stands in regard to these five characteristics. The scoring procedures to be used in the administration of the JRF are given on the page following the instrument. (Analysts who desire to experiment with the JRF as a tool in job analysis should refer to the discussions and guidelines provided in Hackman and Oldham, 1980.)

APPENDIX E.1 REVISED SCALE OF WORKER INSTRUCTIONS (FINE)

The Worker Instructions Scale defines *responsibility* in terms of the mix of specifications (that which is prescribed) and judgment (that which is specifically left to discretion) assigned to the worker. This can range across several levels in a given assignment (job) depending on the activity(ies).

Level 1

Inputs, outputs, tools, equipment, and procedures are all specified. Almost everything the worker needs to know is contained in the assignment. The worker is supposed to turn out a specified amount of work or a standard number of units per hour or day.

Level 2

Inputs, outputs, tools, and equipment are all specified, but the worker has some leeway in the procedures and methods used to get the job done. Almost all the information needed is in the assignment instructions. Production is measured on a daily or weekly basis.

Level 3

Inputs and outputs are specified, but the worker has considerable freedom as to procedures and timing, including the use of tools and/or equipment. The worker may have to refer to several standard sources for information (handbooks, catalogs, wall charts). Time to complete a particular product or service is specified, but this varies up to several hours.

Level 4

Output (product or service) is specified in the assignment, which may be in the form of a memorandum or of a schematic (sketch or blueprint). The worker must work out own way of getting the job done, including selection and use of tools and/or equipment, sequence of operations (tasks), and obtaining important information (handbooks, etc.). Worker may either do the work or set up standards and procedures for others to do it.

Level 5

Same as Level 4, but in addition, the worker is expected to know and employ theory so that he or she understands the whys and wherefores of the various options that are available for dealing with a problem and can independently select from among them. Worker may have to do some reading in the professional and/or trade literature to gain this understanding.

Level 6

Various possible outputs are described that can meet stated technical or administrative needs. The worker must investigate the various possible outputs and evaluate them in regard to performance characteristics and input demands. This usually requires creative use of theory well beyond referring to standard sources. There is no specification of inputs, methods, sequences, sources, or the like.

Level 7

There is some question as to what the need or problem really is or what directions should be pursued in dealing with it. To define the problem, to control and explore the behavior of the variables, and to formulate possible outputs and their performance characteristics, the worker must consult largely unspecified sources of information and devise investigations, surveys, or data analysis studies.

Level 8.

Information and/or direction comes to the worker in terms of needs (tactical, organizational, strategic, financial). Worker must call for staff reports and recommendations concerning methods of dealing with them. He or she coordinates both organizational and technical data to make decisions and determinations regarding courses of action (outputs) for major sections (divisions, groups) of his or her organization.

APPENDIX E.2 SUPERVISORY CONTROLS (FES)

''Supervisory Controls'' covers the nature and extent of direct or indirect controls exercised by the supervisor, the employee's responsibility, and the review of completed work. Controls are exercised by the supervisor in the way assignments are made, instructions are given to the employee, priorities and deadlines are set, and objectives and boundaries are defined. Responsibility of the employee depends upon the extent to which the employee is expected to develop the sequence and timing of various aspects of the work, to modify or recommend modification of instructions, and to participate in establishing priorities and defining objectives. The degree of review of completed work depends upon the nature and extent of the review, e.g., close and detailed review of each phase of the assignment; detailed review of the finished assignment; spotcheck of finished work for accuracy; or review only for adherence to policy.

Level 2–1 *25 points*

For both one-of-a-kind and repetitive tasks the supervisor make specific assignments that are accompanied by clear, detailed, and specific instructions.

The employee works as instructed and consults with the supervisor as needed on all matters not specifically covered in the original instructions or guidelines.

For all positions the work is closely controlled. For some positions, the control is through the structured nature of the work itself; for others, it may be controlled by the circumstances in which it is performed. In some situations, the supervisor maintains control through review of the work which may include checking progress or reviewing completed work for accuracy, adequacy, and adherence to instructions and established procedures.

Level 2–2 *125 points*

The supervisor provides continuing or individual assignments by indicating generally what is to be done, limitations, quality and quantity expected, deadlines, and priority of assignments. The supervisor provides additional, specific instructions for new, difficult, or unusual assignments including suggested work methods or advice on source material available.

The employee uses initiative in carrying out recurring assignments independently without specific instruction, but refers deviations, problems, and unfamiliar situations not covered by instructions to the supervisor for decision or help.

The supervisor assures that finished work and methods used are technically accurate and in compliance with instructions or established procedures. Review of the work increases with more difficult assignments if the employee has not previously performed similar assignments.

Level 2–3 *275 points*

The supervisor makes assignments by defining objectives, priorities, and deadlines; and assists employee with unusual situations which do not have clear precedents.

The employee plans and carries out the successive steps and handles problems and deviations in the work assignment in accordance with instructions, policies, previous training, or accepted practices in the occupation.

From U.S. Civil Service Commission, *Instructions for the Factor Evaluation System* (Washington, D.C.: U.S. Government Printing Office, 1977), pp. 18–20.

Completed work is usually evaluated for technical soundness, appropriateness, and conformity to policy and requirements. The methods used in arriving at the end results are not usually reviewed in detail.

Level 2–4 *450 points*

The supervisor sets the overall objectives and resources available. The employee and supervisor, in consultation, develop the deadlines, projects, and work to be done.

At this level, the employee, having developed expertise in the line of work, is responsible for planning and carrying out the assignment; resolving most of the conflicts which arise; coordinating the work with others as necessary; and interpreting policy on own initiative in terms of established objectives. In some assignments, the employee also determines the approach to be taken and the methodology to be used. The employee keeps the supervisor informed of progress, potentially controversial matters, or far-reaching implications.

Completed work is reviewed only from an overall standpoint in terms of feasibility, compatibility with other work, or effectiveness in meeting requirements or expected results.

Level 2–5 *650 points*

The supervisor provides administrative direction with assignments in terms of broadly defined missions or functions.

The employee has responsibility for planning, designing, and carrying out programs, projects, studies, or other work independently.

Results of the work are considered as technically authoritative and are normally accepted without significant change. If the work should be reviewed, the review concerns such matters as fulfillment of program objectives, effect of advice and influence of the overall program, or the contribution to the advancement of technology. Recommendations for new projects and alteration of objectives are usually evaluated for such considerations as availability of funds and other resources, broad program goals, or national priorities.

APPENDIX E.3 GUIDELINES (FES)

This factor covers the nature of guidelines and the judgment needed to apply them. Guides used in General Schedule occupations include, for example, desk manuals, established procedures and policies, traditional practices, and reference materials such as dictionaries, style manuals, engineering handbooks, the pharmacopoeia, and the *Federal Personnel Manual.*

Individual jobs in different occupations vary in the specificity, applicability, and availability of the guidelines for performance of assignments. Consequently, the constraints and judgmental demands placed upon employees also vary. For example, the existence of specific instructions, procedures, and policies may limit the opportunity of the employee to make or recommend decisions or actions. However, in the absence of procedures or under broadly stated objectives, employees in some occupations may use considerable judgment in researching literature and developing new methods.

Guidelines should not be confused with the knowledges described under Factor 1, Knowledge Required by the Position. Guidelines either provide reference data or impose certain constraints on the use of knowledges. For example, in the field of medical technology, for a particular diagnosis there may be three or four standardized tests set forth in a technical manual. A medical technologist is expected to know these diagnostic tests. However, in a given laboratory the policy may be to use only one of the tests; or the policy may state specifically under what conditions one or the other of these tests may be used.

From U.S. Civil Service Commission, *Instructions for the Factor Evaluation System* (Washington, D.C.: U.S. Government Printing Office, 1977), pp. 21–22.

Level 3–1 *25 points*

Specific, detailed guidelines covering all important aspects of the assignment are provided to the employee.

The employee works in strict adherence to the guidelines; deviations must be authorized by the supervisor.

Level 3–2 *125 points*

Procedures for doing the work have been established and a number of specific guidelines are available.

The number and similarity of guidelines and work situations requires the employee to use judgment in locating and selecting the most appropriate guidelines, references, and procedures for application and in making minor deviations to adapt the guidelines in specific cases. At this level, the employee may also determine which of several established alternatives to use. Situations to which the existing guidelines cannot be applied or significant proposed deviations from the guidelines are referred to the supervisor.

Level 3–3 *275 points*

Guidelines are available, but are not completely applicable to the work or have gaps in specificity.

The employee uses judgment in interpreting and adapting guidelines such as agency policies, regulations, precedents, and work directions for application to specific cases or problems. The employee analyzes results and recommends changes.

Level 3–4 *450 points*

Administrative policies and precedents are applicable but are stated in general terms. Guidelines for performing the work are scarce or of limited use.

The employee uses initiative and resourcefulness in deviating from traditional methods or researching trends and patterns to develop new methods, criteria, or proposed new policies.

Level 3–5 *650 points*

Guidelines are broadly stated and nonspecific, e.g., broad policy statements and basic legislation which require extensive interpretation.

The employee must use judgment and ingenuity in interpreting the intent of the guides that do exist and in developing applications to specific areas of work. Frequently, the employee is recognized as a technical authority in the development and interpretation of guidelines.

APPENDIX E.4 DECISION MAKING ON METHODS (HSMS)

This skill refers to the degree of responsibility required of a performer with respect to decisions he must make about how he does the task being scaled. *How* the task is done (the method) includes what is done, when, in what order, what is used, and who is involved. When the performer has any amount of latitude in deciding how to do the task, the skill is involved.

The skill rises as the choice of methods in the task situation are less and less obvious or specified; the skill rises as the circumstances of the task from one instance to another are more and more varied. The level of this scale is not determined by the level of knowledge required.

From E. Gilpatrick, *The Health Services Mobility Study Method of Task Analysis and Curriculum Design*, Research Report No. 11, Vol. 1 (New York: Hunter College, The Research Foundation, City University of New York, 1977), p. 2-31. Reprinted by permission.

Scale Value	Descriptive Statement
0.0	The performer is not required to decide on how to do any part of the task.
1.5	The performer is required to decide how to do all or part of the task. *Instances of the task vary little with respect to the methods to choose from*, and once the situation is known, the performer's *choice is obvious and/or specified*.
3.0	The performer is required to decide how to do all or part of the task. *Instances of the task vary little with respect to the methods to choose from*, and the performer's choice is arrived at by referring to *general guidelines for choosing* an appropriate method.
4.5	The performer is required to decide how to do all or part of the task. *Instances of the task vary somewhat with respect to the methods to choose from*, and the performer's choice is arrived at by referring to *general guidelines for choosing* an appropriate method.
7.0	The performer is required to decide how to do all or part of the task. *Instances of the task cover a wide range of circumstances calling for very different methods*, and the performer's choice is arrived at by referring to *general guidelines for choosing* an appropriate method.
9.0	The performer is required to decide how to do all or part of the task. *Instances of the task cover a wide range of circumstances calling for very different methods*, and once the situation is assessed, the performer must make his choice by *applying his own guidelines for selecting* an appropriate method.

APPENDIX E.5 DECISION MAKING ON QUALITY (HSMS)

This skill refers to the degree of responsibility required of the performer with respect to decisions he must make about the quality of the output he produces in the task being scaled. The scale refers to the performer's latitude beyond the minimum acceptable levels of task performance. The skill is involved when the performer has any effect on the quality of the task's output beyond minimum requirements.

The skill rises with the extent to which the performer can affect the output's quality. It is also affected by whether or not the output is subject to review or inspection by others before it is used. The level of this scale is not determined by the level of knowledge required nor by the possiblity of making errors.

Scale Value	Descriptive Statement
0.0	The performer is unable to affect the quality of the task's output.
1.5	The performer's exercise of choice in his standards of task performance can have only a *minor effect on the quality* of the task's output beyond minimum requirements, and the output is *subject to complete and automatic review or inspection by someone else before it is used*.
2.0	The performer's exercise of choice in his standards of task performance can have only a *minor effect on the quality* of the task's output beyond minimum requirements, and the output is *subject to review or inspection by someone else before it is used*.
3.5	The performer's exercise of choice in his standards of task performance can have only a *minor effect on the quality* of the task's output beyond minimum requirements, and the output is *not subject to review or inspection by anyone else before it is used*.
5.5	The performer's exercise of choice in his standards of task performance can have *considerable effect on the quality* of the task's output beyond minimum requirements, but the output is *subject to review or inspection by someone else before it is used*.
7.0	The performer's exercise of choice in his standards of task performance can have *considerable effect on the quality* of the task's output beyond minimum requirements, and the output is *not subject to review or inspection by anyone else before it is used*.
9.0	The performer's exercise of choice in his standards of task performance can *completely determine the quality* of the task's output due to the absence of minimum requirements, and the output is *not subject to review or inspection by anyone else before it is used*.

From E. Gilpatrick, *The Health Services Mobility Study Method of Task Analysis and Curriculum Design*, Research Report No. 11, Vol. 1 (New York: Hunter College, The Research Foundation, City University of New York, 1977), p. 2-33. Reprinted by permission.

APPENDIX E.6 THE JOB RATING FORM (HACKMAN & OLDHAM)

This questionnaire was developed as part of a Yale University study of jobs and how people react to them. The questionnaire helps to determine how jobs can be better designed, by obtaining information about how people react to different kinds of jobs.
You are asked to rate the characteristics of the following job:

____

Please keep in mind that the questions refer to the job listed above, and *not* to your own job. On the following pages, you will find several different kinds of questions about the job listed above. Specific instructions are given at the start of each section. Please read them carefully. It should take no more than 10 minutes to complete the entire questionnaire. Please move through it quickly.

SECTION ONE

This part of the questionnaire asks you to describe the job listed above as *objectively* as you can. Try to make your description as accurate and as objective as you possibly can.

A sample question is given below.

A. To what extent does the job require a person to work with mechanical equipment?

1 -------- 2 -------- 3 -------- 4 -------- 5 -------- ⑥ -------- 7

Very little; the job requires almost no contact with mechanical equipment of any kind.	Moderately	Very much; the job requires almost constant work with mechanical equipment.

You are to *circle* the number which is the most accurate description of the job you are rating.

If, for example, the job requires a person to work with mechanical equipment a good deal of the time—but also requires some paperwork—you might circle the number 6, as was done in the example above.

1. To what extent does the job require a person to *work closely with other people* (either ''clients'' or people in related jobs in the organization)?

1 -------- 2 -------- 3 -------- 4 -------- 5 -------- 6 -------- 7

Very little; dealing with other people is not at all necessary in doing the job.	Moderately; some dealing with others is necessary.	Very much; dealing with other people is an absolutely essential and crucial part of doing the job.

2. How much *autonomy* is there in the job? That is, to what extent does the job permit a person to decide *on his or her own* how to go about doing the work?

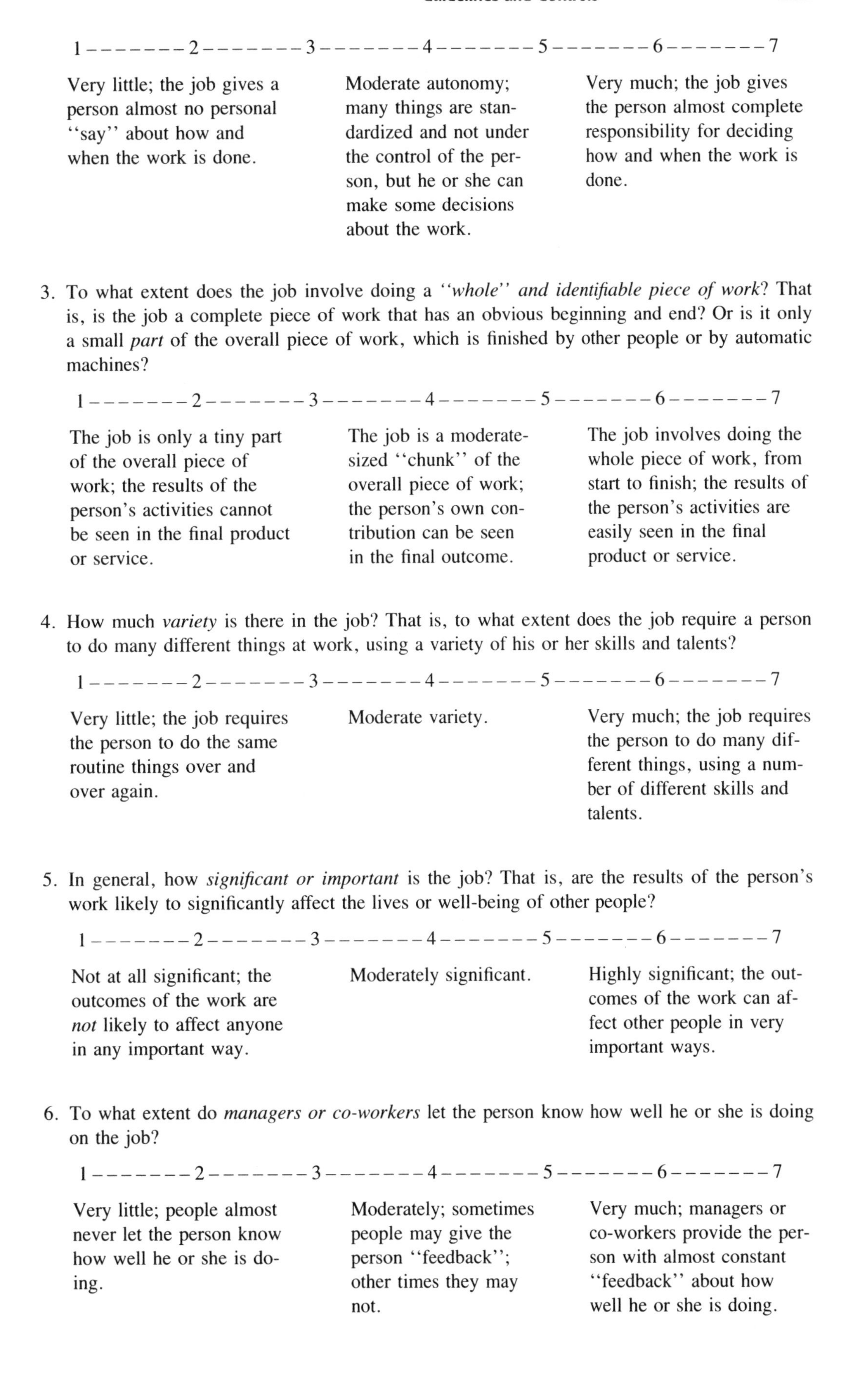

1 ------- 2 ------- 3 ------- 4 ------- 5 ------- 6 ------- 7

Very little; the job gives a person almost no personal "say" about how and when the work is done.	Moderate autonomy; many things are standardized and not under the control of the person, but he or she can make some decisions about the work.	Very much; the job gives the person almost complete responsibility for deciding how and when the work is done.

3. To what extent does the job involve doing a *"whole" and identifiable piece of work*? That is, is the job a complete piece of work that has an obvious beginning and end? Or is it only a small *part* of the overall piece of work, which is finished by other people or by automatic machines?

1 ------- 2 ------- 3 ------- 4 ------- 5 ------- 6 ------- 7

The job is only a tiny part of the overall piece of work; the results of the person's activities cannot be seen in the final product or service.	The job is a moderate-sized "chunk" of the overall piece of work; the person's own contribution can be seen in the final outcome.	The job involves doing the whole piece of work, from start to finish; the results of the person's activities are easily seen in the final product or service.

4. How much *variety* is there in the job? That is, to what extent does the job require a person to do many different things at work, using a variety of his or her skills and talents?

1 ------- 2 ------- 3 ------- 4 ------- 5 ------- 6 ------- 7

Very little; the job requires the person to do the same routine things over and over again.	Moderate variety.	Very much; the job requires the person to do many different things, using a number of different skills and talents.

5. In general, how *significant or important* is the job? That is, are the results of the person's work likely to significantly affect the lives or well-being of other people?

1 ------- 2 ------- 3 ------- 4 ------- 5 ------- 6 ------- 7

Not at all significant; the outcomes of the work are *not* likely to affect anyone in any important way.	Moderately significant.	Highly significant; the outcomes of the work can affect other people in very important ways.

6. To what extent do *managers or co-workers* let the person know how well he or she is doing on the job?

1 ------- 2 ------- 3 ------- 4 ------- 5 ------- 6 ------- 7

Very little; people almost never let the person know how well he or she is doing.	Moderately; sometimes people may give the person "feedback"; other times they may not.	Very much; managers or co-workers provide the person with almost constant "feedback" about how well he or she is doing.

7. To what extent does *doing the job itself* provide the person with information about his or her work performance? That is, does the actual *work itself* provide clues about how well the person is doing—aside from any "feedback" co-workers or supervisors may provide?

1 - - - - - - - 2 - - - - - - - 3 - - - - - - - 4 - - - - - - - 5 - - - - - - - 6 - - - - - - - 7

Very little; the job itself is set up so a person could work forever without finding out how well he or she is doing.	Moderately; sometimes doing the job provides "feedback" to the person; sometimes it does not.	Very much; the job is set up so that a person gets almost constant "feedback" as he or she works about how well he or she is doing.

SECTION TWO

Listed below are a number of statements which could be used to describe a job.
You are to indicate whether each statement is an *accurate* or an *inaccurate* description of the job you are rating.
Once again, please try to be as *objective* as you can in deciding how accurately each statement describes the job—regardless of your own *feelings* about the job.

Write a number in the blank beside each statement, based on the following scale:

How accurate is the statement in describing the job you are rating?

1	2	3	4	5	6	7
Very Inaccurate	Mostly Inaccurate	Slightly Inaccurate	Uncertain	Slightly Accurate	Mostly Accurate	Very Accurate

_______ 1. The job requires a person to use a number of complex or sophisticated skills.
_______ 2. The job requires a lot of cooperative work with other people.
_______ 3. The job is arranged so that a person does *not* have the chance to do an entire piece of work from beginning to end.
_______ 4. Just doing the work required by the job provides many chances for a person to figure out how well he or she is doing.
_______ 5. The job is quite simple and repetitive.
_______ 6. The job can be done adequately by a person working alone—without talking or checking with other people.
_______ 7. The supervisors and co-workers on this job almost *never* give a person any "feedback" about how well he or she is doing the work.
_______ 8. This job is one where a lot of other people can be affected by how well the work gets done.
_______ 9. The job denies a person any chance to use his or her personal initiative or discretion in carrying out the work.
_______ 10. Supervisors often let the person know how well they think he or she is performing the job.
_______ 11. The job provides a person with the chance to finish completely any work he or she starts.
_______ 12. The job itself provides very few clues about whether or not the person is performing well.
_______ 13. The job gives a person considerable opportunity for independence and freedom in how he or she does the work.
_______ 14. The job itself is *not* very significant or important in the broader scheme of things.

SCORING KEY FOR THE JOB DIAGNOSTIC SURVEY AND THE JOB RATING FORM

The scoring manual for the Job Diagnostic Survey (JDS) and the Job Rating Form (JRF) is presented below. For each variable measured by the JDS, the questionnaire items that are averaged to yield a summary score for the variable are listed.

Sections One and Two (the measures of the job characteristics) are identical for the Job Diagnostic Survey and the Job Rating Form, and therefore the same scoring key is used for both instruments.

A computerized scoring service for the JDS is provided by the Roy W. Walters and Associates consulting firm (Whitney Industrial Park, Whitney Road, Mahwah, N.J. 07430). The Walters organization also provides printed copies of the JDS.

I. JOB CHARACTERISTICS (for both the JDS and JRF).

A. *Skill variety*. Average the following items.

Section One: #4
Section Two: #1
#5 (reversed scoring—i.e., subtract the number entered by the respondent from 8)

B. *Task identity*. Average the following items:

Section One: #3
Section Two: #11
#3 (reversed scoring)

C. *Task significance*. Average the following items:

Section One: #5
Section Two: #8
#14 (reversed scoring)

D. *Autonomy*. Average the following items:

Section One: #2
Section Two: #13
#9 (reversed scoring)

E. *Feedback from the job itself*. Average the following items:

Section One: #7
Section Two: #4
#12 (reversed scoring)

F. *Feedback from agents*. Average the following items:

Section One: #6
Section Two: #10
#7 (reversed scoring)

G. *Dealing with others*. Average the following items:

Section One: #1
Section Two: #2
#6 (reversed scoring)

Worker Involvement in Job and Tasks

Study of the nature of worker involvement in the job or tasks is an implicit concern of all job analysis methodologies. The scales given in this appendix are targeted at specific concerns relating to worker involvement in tasks. In the interest of space, and to bring out the variations, different scales measuring the same dimension are combined within the appendices.

Part-of-Job Scales. These scales are usually used to study job tasks. However, they can be readily expanded to accommodate job functions, behaviors, things, and even context factors.

The part-of-job scales address a fundamental concern of job analysis (i.e., whether or not the factor is a part of the job). If the factor is not a part of the job, then nothing else is relevant—the analysis stops at that stage. The part-of-job scale was originally proposed by John K. Hemphill (1959). However, it has since become a generic tool and is now found in many variations. The simplest is a yes/no scale. This can be extended to ordinal or higher levels of measurements as shown in Appendix F.1. (These variations are based on Melching & Borcher, 1973; McCormick, 1979, pp. 119–123.)

Time Spent on Tasks. This is an ongoing and serious managerial concern. Early research on this dimension revealed that job incumbents were typically not able to report the absolute amounts of time spent on tasks with acceptable levels of precision. This finding led to the development of the Relative Time Spent Scales. These scales ask the workers to report the amount of time they spend on each task relative to the amount of time they spend on other tasks. The basic format of the Relative Time Spent Scale can be altered to accommodate more points as well as to pursue prescriptive concerns (Christal, 1974).

Common variations in the Relative Time Spent Scales are reproduced in Appendix F.2. The CODAP system of the U.S. Air Force uses the scale shown as F.2a. The scale shown under F.2b follows the same format, but uses slightly different anchors. The third scale (F.2c) pursues a prescriptive concern. It asks the respondents to indicate the amount of time that they should spend on the task.

Whichever format is used, responses can be converted into percentage of time spent values. (Examples of time spent results expressed as percentages were given in Exhibit 3.7 in Chapter 3.)

Frequency of Task Performance. This is another common managerial concern and is also relatively easy to assess in regard to tasks. The Task Frequency Scale giving in Appendix F.3 is from the HSMS. Another variation of this scale can be found in Gael (1983, p. 103).

APPENDIX F.1 PART-OF-JOB SCALES

Is (. . .) part of this job?

F-1a Yes ☐ No ☐

F-1b 0 = Definitely not (or not applicable)
1 = Minor part of the job
2 = . . .
3 = One of several other tasks (or . . .)
4 = . . .
5 = A substantial part of the job

F-1c 0 = Definitely not (or not applicable)
1 = Yes, but not a significant part
2 = . . .
3 = Yes, of average significance
4 = . . .
5 = Yes, a very significant part

F-1d 0 = Definitely not (or not applicable)
1 = Under unusual circumstances
2 = . . .
3 = Usually a part of the job
4 = . . .
5 = A regular part of the job

APPENDIX F.2 RELATIVE TIME SPENT ON TASKS

F-2a 0 = Not performed
1 = Extremely small amount of time
2 = Small amount of time
3 = Below-average amount of time
4 = Average amount of time
5 = Above-average amount of time
6 = Large amount of time
7 = Extremely large amount of time

F-2b 0 = Not performed
1 = Very much below average
2 = Below average
3 = Slightly below average
4 = About average
5 = Slightly above average
6 = Above average
7 = Very much above average

F-2c 0 = Should not be performed
1 = Should spend extremely small amount of time
2 = Should spend small amount of time
3 = Should spend below-average amount of time

(F.2) From F. Sistrunk and P. L. Smith, *Multimethodological Job Analysis for Criminal Justice Organizations* (Tampa: Center for Evaluation Research, University of South Florida, 1982).

4 = Should spend average amount of time
5 = Should spend above-average amount of time
6 = Should spend large amount of time
7 = Should spend extremely large amount of time

APPENDIX F.3 FREQUENCY OF TASK PERFORMANCE (HSMS)

This scale refers to the frequency with which the task being scaled is executed by the performer. Tasks which are regularly done should be scaled by using the wording outside of the parentheses in the statements presented below. Tasks which are done infrequently or in concentrated periods during the year should be scaled by using the wording within the parentheses; the figures represent conversions to a normal work year.

Scale Value	Descriptive Statement
0	Task is never done.
1	Task is done once per year or less.
2	Task is done more often than once per year, but less than once per month (no more than 11 times per year).
3	Task is done once per month or more, but less often than once per week (no more than 33 times per year).
4	Task is done once per week or more, but less often than once per day (no more than 180 times per year).
6	Task is done once per day or more, but less often than 5 times per day (no more than 912 times per year).
7	Task is done 5 times per day or more, but less often than 10 times per day (no more than 2,052 times per year).
8	Task is done 10 times per day or more, but less often than 50 times per day (no more than 11, 172 times per year).
9	Task is done 50 times per day or more (11,173 times per year or more).

Note: This scale is not used for clustering tasks. Ratings on this scale are relevant only at the level of the institution.

From E. Gilpatrick, *The Health Services Mobility Study Method of Task Analysis and Curriculum Design*, Research Report No. 11, Vol. 1 (New York: Hunter College, The Research Foundation, City University of New York, 1977), p. 2-13. Reprinted by permission.

G Job and Task Characteristics

Here we get into the evaluative aspect of job analysis. The concern behind the *characteristics* scales is to arrive as some evaluative judgment about a job that enables placing it within some conception of worth, goodness, or place within the organizational hierarchy. Such judgments are arrived at through the use of constructs or configurations of attributes that serve as the indices of evaluation.

A variety of constructs have been developed over the years to enable the passing of evaluative judgments about jobs. The following are the major constructs that have figured prominently in the job analysis literature. None of them, however, has yet acquired generally acceptable definitions. We, therefore, present samplings of the viewpoints that exist.

Difficulty	The amount of time it takes for individuals to learn to perform a task adequately (Christal, 1974, p. 14).
	The amount of physical or mental effort required to perform the task.
	How hard the task is to do or to learn to do effectively.
	The number of steps encompassed in the task sequence (Gael, 1983, pp. 98–100).
Importance	The contribution of the task to effective operations in your office (Gael, 1983, p. 100).
	Difficulty plus criticality plus actual time spent (Sistrunk & Smith, 1982, p. 68).
Criticality	The seriousness of consequences that arise from inadequate or incorrect performance of a task relative to other tasks (Sistrunk & Smith, 1982, p. 67)
Significance	Task importance plus task frequency plus task difficulty (Gael, 1983, p. 97).
	The degree to which the job has a substantial impact on the lives of other people, whether those people are in the immediate organization or in the world at large (Hackman & Oldham, 1980, p. 79).

The development of constructs to enable the passing of evaluative judgments on job factors has turned out to be an intellectually challenging aspect of job analysis. This type of analysis goes beyond merely documenting the what, why, and how of jobs to arriving at some sense of the worth of the factors under consideration. However, as can be seen from the definitions provided, construct building in job analysis is still in its formative stage.

The simplest way of acquiring evaluative ratings of job factors is by attaching a Likert-type rating scale to a construct such as significance, importance, or difficulty and letting the raters make the judgment on the basis of whatever meaning that they choose to give to the word. This basic format can be refined by providing more details on the meaning of the construct and by being discriminating in designing the anchors.

The scales given in this appendix exemplify the variations available in rating job/task characteristics. The Task Difficulty Scale (Appendix G.1) follows the simple format, relying on synonyms and antonyms of the word "difficult" ("easier," "harder") to elicit responses. It could be refined by building in the definition of difficuty provided above by Christal.

The Task Significance Scale (G.2) is from the WPSS system. It asks the rater qualitatively to consider task importance, frequency, and difficulty in arriving at a judgment about the significance of the task (Gael, 1983, pp. 97–108).

The next two scales (G.3 and G.4) are from the FES system. The Complexity Scale combines judgments about various concepts that are collectively suggestive of variety, intricacy, and multiplicity of steps or methods to arrive at a score for complexity. The Scope and Effect Scale covers the relation between the nature of the work and its effect on work products and services both inside the outside the organization.

Appendix G.5 contains a scale for measuring task criticality, which is equated with seriousness of consequences that may result from inadequate or incorrect performance of the task. Note, however, that the scale asks for absolute judgments at the extreme points (1, 2 and 6, 7) and relative judgments at the middle points (3, 4, and 5).

The last two scales are from the HSMS. The scale in Appendix G-6 deals with financial consequences of error, while that in G-7 measures consequences of errors to humans. Although couched in terms of consequences, the results could provide indices of criticality, significance, and importance.

APPENDIX G.1 TASK DIFFICULTY

Indicate the level of difficulty in doing this task correctly relative to all other tasks you perform in your current job assignment.

I think this task is

1 = one of the EASIEST tasks of all relative to all the tasks I am currently assigned to do.
2 = CONSIDERABLY EASIER than most tasks I perform in my current job assignment.
3 = EASIER than most tasks I perform in my current job assignment.
4 = ABOUT AVERAGE; one-half of the tasks are more difficult, one-half are less difficult.
5 = HARDER than most tasks I perform in my current job assignment.
6 = CONSIDERABLY HARDER than most tasks I currently perform.
7 = one of the MOST DIFFICULT tasks I perform relative to all other tasks I do.

APPENDIX G.2 TASK SIGNIFICANCE (WPSS)

Read each task statement carefully and decide whether or not the task is part of your present job. You are not expected to perform all the tasks listed, nor are all tasks performed in every Business Service Center. It is important that you think only of your present job, not previous jobs. Some tasks you perform are more significant for your job than others. Consider the following factors in judging the significance of a task to your job:

a. IMPORTANCE the contribution of the task to effective operations in your office.
b. FREQUENCY how often you perform the task.
c. DIFFICULTY how hard the task is to do or to learn to do effectively.

Combine these factors in your mind to determine the significance of a task and choose an appropriate rating according to the following.

0 = Definitely not a part of my job; I never do it.
1 = Under unusual or certain circumstances may be of a minor significance to my job.
2
3
4 = Of substantial significance to my job.
5
6
7 = Of most significance to my job.

Here is an example of how this is done:

	Task	Significance	Time Spent
001	Review a completed order.	0 1 2 3 4 ⑤ 6 7	________
002	Distribute incoming mail.	⓪ 1 1 3 4 5 6 7	________

For Task 001 in the example, a "5" was circled indicating that reviewing completed orders is somewhat more than of substantial significance to the job.

For Task 002, a "0" was circled, indicating that distributing incoming mail is not part of the job.

From F. Sistrunk and P. L. Smith, *Multimethodological Job Analysis for Criminal Justice Organizations* (Tampa: Center for Evaluation Research, University of South Florida, 1982).

(WPSS) From S. Gael, *Job Analysis: A Guide to Assessing Work Activities* (San Francisco, Calif.: Jossey-Bass, Inc.) Copyright © 1983 by Jossey-Bass, Inc. Reprinted by permission.

Even if you have the responsibility to see that a task is performed, but you do not perform the task, the "0" should be circled. The number you select should be your best estimate of the significance of the task to your job.

APPENDIX G.3 TASK COMPLEXITY (FES)

This factor covers the nature, number, variety, and intricacy of tasks, steps, processes, or methods in the work performed; the difficulty in identifying what needs to be done; and the difficulty and originality involved in performing the work.

Level 4–1 *25 points*

The work consists of tasks that are clear-cut and directly related.

There is little or no choice to be made in deciding what needs to be done.

Actions to be taken or responses to be made are readily discernible. The work is quickly mastered.

Level 4–2 *75 points*

The work consists of duties that involve related steps, processes, or methods.

The decision regarding what needs to be done involves various choices requiring the employee to recognize the existence of and differences among a few easily recognizable situations.

Actions to be taken or responses to be made differ in such things as the source of information, the kind of transactions or entries, or other differences of a factual nature.

Level 4–3 *150 points*

The work includes various duties involving different and unrelated processes and methods.

The decision regarding what needs to be done depends upon the analysis of the subject, phase, or issues involved in each assignment, and the chosen course of action may have to be selected from many alternatives.

The work involves conditions and elements that must be identified and analyzed to discern interrelationships.

Level 4–4 *225 points*

The work typically includes varied duties requiring many different and unrelated processes and methods such as those relating to well-established aspects of an administrative or professional field.

Decisions regarding what needs to be done include the assessment of unusual circumstances, variations in approach, and incomeplete or conflicting data.

The work requires making many decisions concerning such things as the interpreting of considerable data, planning of the work, or refining the methods and techniques to be used.

Level 4–5 *325 points*

The work includes varied duties requiring many different and unrelated processes and methods applied to a broad range of activities or substantial depth of analysis, typically for an administrative or professional field.

Decisions regarding what needs to be done include major areas of uncertainty in approach, methodology, or interpretation and evaluation processes resulting from such elements as continuing changes in program, technological developments, unknown phenomena, or conflicting requirements.

The work requires originating new techniques, establishing criteria, or developing new information.

From U.S. Civil Service Commission, *Instructions for the Factor Evaluation System* (Washington, D.C.: U.S. Government Printing Office, 1977), pp. 23–24.

Level 4–6 *450 points*

The work consists of broad functions and processes of an administrative or professional field. Assignments are characterized by breadth and intensity of effort and involve several phases being pursued concurrently or sequentially with the support of others within or outside of the organization.

Decisions regarding what needs to be done include largely undefined issues and elements, requiring extensive probing and analysis to determine the nature and scope of the problems.

The work requires continuing efforts to establish concepts, theories, or programs, or to resolve unyielding problems.

APPENDIX G.4 SCOPE AND EFFECT (FES)

Scope and Effect covers the relationship between the nature of the work, i.e., the purpose, breadth, and depth of the assignment, and the effect of work products or services both within and outside the organization.

In General Schedule occupations, effect measures such things as whether the work output facilitates the work of others, provides timely services of a personal nature, or impacts on the adequacy of research conclusions. The concept of effect alone does not provide sufficient information to properly understand and evaluate the impact of the position. The scope of the work completes the picture, allowing consistent evaluations. Only the effect of properly performed work is to be considered.

Level 5–1 *25 points*

The work involves the performance of specific, routine operations that include a few separate tasks or procedures.

The work product or service is required to facilitate the work of others; however, it has little impact beyond the immediate organizational unit or beyond the timely provision of limited services to others.

Level 5–2 *75 points*

The work involves the execution of specific rules, regulations, or procedures and typically comprises a complete segment of an assignment or project of broader scope.

The work product or service affects the accuracy, reliability, or acceptability of further processes or services.

Level 5–3 *150 points*

The work involves treating a variety of conventional problems, questions, or situations in conformance with established criteria.

The work product or service affects the design or operation of systems, programs, or equipment; the adequacy of such activities as field investigations, testing operations, or research conclusions; or the social, physical, and economic well being of persons.

Level 5–4 *225 points*

The work involves establishing criteria; formulating projects; assessing program effectiveness; or investigating or analyzing a variety of unusual conditions, problems, or questions.

The work product or service affects a wide range of agency activities, major activities of industrial concerns, or the operation of other agencies.

From U.S. Civil Service Commission, *Instructions for the Factor Evaluation System* (Washington, D.C.: U.S. Government Printing Office, 1977), pp. 25–26.

Level 5–5 *325 points*

The work involves isolating and defining unknown conditions, resolving critical problems, or developing new theories.

The work product or service affects the work of other experts, the development of major aspects of administrative or scientific programs or missions, or the well-being of substantial numbers of people.

Level 5–6 *450 points*

The work involves planning, developing, and carrying out vital administrative or scientific programs.

The programs are essential to the missions of the agency or affect large numbers of people on a long-term or continuing basis.

APPENDIX G.5 CRITICALITY OF ERROR

Indicate the seriousness of consequences that may result from inadequate or incorrect performance of task relative to all other tasks performed.

The consequences of error in performing this task are
1 = MINIMAL, NEGLIGIBLE, OR VERY SLIGHT
2 = MORE THAN SLIGHT, BUT NOT TOO SERIOUS
3 = SOMEWHAT SERIOUS relative to other tasks
4 = ABOUT AVERAGE IN SERIOUSNESS relative to other tasks
5 = SLIGHTLY ABOVE AVERAGE IN SERIOUSNESS
6 = EXTREMELY SERIOUS
7 = DISASTROUS (life threatening)

APPENDIX G.6 FINANCIAL CONSEQUENCES OF ERROR (HSMS)

This skill refers to the degree of responsibility carried by a performer with respect to the financial damage which could result from errors in his performance of the task being scaled. The error whose consequences would be rated would be the most serious likely error to be expected from a performer qualified to do the task. The skill is involved if errors in performance of the task have any financial consequences involving any output, equipment, materials, time, or other chargeable items. The level of this scale is not determined by the value of insurance claims or damage suits which would result from harm to humans.

Scale Value	Descriptive Statement
0.0	No likely error in the performer's task performance could result in financial damage to the institution.
1.0	The most serious likely error in the performer's task performance would result in *negligible financial damage* to the institution.
.	
.	
.	

From F. Sistrunk and P. L. Smith, *Multimethodological Job Analysis for Criminal Justice Organizations* (Tampa: Center for Evaluation Research, University of South Florida, 1982).

(HSMS) From E. Gilpatrick, *The Health Services Mobility Study Method of Task Analysis and Curriculum Design*, Research Report No. 11, Vol. 1 (New York: Hunter College, The Research Foundation, City University of New York, 1977), p. 2-43. Reprinted by permission.

4.0 The most serious likely error in the performer's task performance would result in financial damage to the institution of a *relatively moderate but manageable amount.*

.
.
.

6.0 The most serious likely error in the performer's task performance would result in financial damage to the institution of an amount considered to be *relatively difficult to absorb.*

.
.
.

7.5 The most serious likely error in the performer's task performance would result in financial damage to the institution of an amount considered to be *extremely serious and extremely difficult to absorb.*

.
.
.

9.0 The most serious likely error in the performer's task performance would result in financial damage to the institution of an amount so serious that *the institution would cease to exist.*

APPENDIX G.7 CONSEQUENCES OF ERROR TO HUMANS (HSMS)

This skill refers to the degree of responsibility carried by the performer with respect to the harm which could be done to humans as a result of errors in his performance of the task being scaled. The error whose consequences are rated would be the most serious likely error to be expected from a performer qualified to do the task. The skill is involved if errors in performance of the task result in any physical or mental harm to humans, including recipients, respondents, co-workers, or persons not directly related to the task. The performer is included. The level of this scale is not determined by any financial harm which could be done to persons.

Scale Value	Descriptive Statement
0.0	No likely error in the performer's task performance could result in harm to a human.
1.0	The most serious likely error in the performer's task performance would result in *physical or mental inconvenience.*
2.0	The most serious likely error in the performer's task performance would result in *very minor physical or mental harm, requiring little or no remediation.*
3.0	The most serious likely error in the performer's task performance would result in *minor physical or mental harm and would require remediation or treatment.*
.	
.	
.	
5.5	The most serious likely error in the performer's task performance would result in *considerable physical or mental harm and would require remediation or treatment.*
.	
.	
.	
7.0	The most serious likely error in the performer's task performance would result in *very serious physical or mental harm, or would put the affected person in danger of minor permanent damage.*
8.0	The most serious likely error in the performer's task performance would result in *serious permanent damage beyond the help of remediation or treatment.*
9.0	The most serious likely error in the performer's task performance would result in *immediate and inevitable death.*

From E. Gilpatrick, *The Health Services Mobility Study Method of Task Analysis and Curriculum Design*, Research Report No. 11, Vol. 1 (New York: Hunter College, The Research Foundation, City University of New York, 1977), p. 2-45. Reprinted by permission.

Checklist of Questions Relevant to Method Study

Method study consists of systematic recording and critical examination of existing and proposed ways of doing work, as a means of developing and applying easier and more effective methods and reducing costs. It is one aspect of a broad field known as work study (International Labour Organisation, 1979, p. 33). (Refer to discussions of work study in Chapters 1 and 4.)

The checklist given in Appendix H has developed over a course of time and experience gained by industrial engineers. It is a part of the ILO's handbook on work study and is commonly used around the world in designing and redesigning work systems. It covers just about all the issues encountered in the study of technological arrangements at work. Analysts who need to examine work systems in depth should find this checklist to be a valuable source of questions, ideas, and actions.

APPENDIX H.1 CHECKLIST OF QUESTIONS RELEVANT TO METHOD STUDY

Most of the questions listed below apply generally to method study investigations. The questions are listed under the following headings:

A. Operations
B. Design
C. Inspection Requirements
D. Material Handling
E. Process Analysis
F. Material
G. Work Organization
H. Workplace Layout
I. Tools and Equipment
J. Working Conditions
K. Job Enrichment

A. Operations

1. What is the purpose of the operation?
2. Is the result obtained by the operation necessary? If so, what makes it necessary?
3. Is the operation necessary because the previous operation was not performed correctly?
4. Is the operation instituted to correct a condition that has now been corrected otherwise?
5. If the operation is being carried out to improve appearance, does the additional cost give extra saleability?
6. Can the purpose of the operation be obtained in another way?
7. Can the material supplier perform the operation more economically?
8. Is the operation being performed to satisfy the requirements of all users of the product, or is it made necessary by the requirements of one or two customers only?
9. Does a subsequent operation eliminate the necessity for this operation?
10. Is the operation being performed as a result of habit?
11. Was the operation established to reduce the cost of a previous operation, or a subsequent operation?
12. Was the operation added by the sales department as a special feature?
13. Can the part be purchased at a lower cost?
14. Would adding a further operation make other operations easier to perform?
15. Is there another way to perform the operation and still maintain the same results?
16. If the operation has been established to correct a subsequent difficulty, is it possible that the corrective operation is more costly than the difficulty itself?
17. Have conditions changed since the operation was added to the process?
18. Could the operation be combined with a previous or a subsequent operation?

B. Design

1. Can the design be changed to simplify or eliminate the operation?
2. Is the design of the part suitable for good manufacturing practice?
3. Can equivalent results be obtained by changing the design and thus reducing cost?
4. Can a standard part be substituted?
5. Would a change in design mean increased saleability, an increased market?
6. Can a standard part be converted to do the job?
7. Is it possible to improve the appearance of the article without interfering with its utility?
8. Would an additional cost caused by improved appearance and greater utility be offset by increased business?
9. Has the article the best possible appearance and utility on the market at the price?
10. Has value analysis been used?

From International Labour Organisation, *Introduction to Work Study*, 3rd ed. (Geneva; ILO, 1979), pp. 417–423.

C. Inspection Requirements

1. What are the inspection requirements for this operation?
2. Does everybody involved know exactly what the requirements are?
3. What are the inspection details of the previous and following operations?
4. Will changing the requirements of this operation make it easier to perform?
5. Will changing the requirements of the previous operation make this operation easier?
6. Are tolerance, allowance, finish and other standards really necessary?
7. Can standards be raised to improve quality without unnecessary cost?
8. Will lowering standards reduce cost considerably?
9. Can the finished quality of the product be improved in any way above the present standard?
10. How do standards for this operation/product compare with standards for similar items?
11. Can the quality be improved by using new processes?
12. Are the same standards necessary for all customers?
13. Will a change in standards and inspection requirements increase or decrease the defective work and expense in the operation, shop or field?
14. Are the tolerances used in actual practice the same as those shown on the drawing?
15. Has an agreement been reached by all concerned as to what constitutes acceptable quality?
16. What are the main causes of rejections for this part?
17. Is the quality standard definitely fixed, or is it a matter of individual judgment?

D. Material Handling

1. Is the time spent in bringing material to the work station and in removing it large in proportion to the time used to handle it at the work station?
2. If not, could material handling be done by the operatives to provide a rest through change of occupation?
3. Should hand, electric or fork-lift trucks be used?
4. Should special racks, containers or pallets be designed to permit the handling of material with ease and without damage?
5. Where should incoming and outgoing materials be located in the work area?
6. Is a conveyor justified, and if so, what type would best be suited for the job?
7. Can the work stations for progressive steps of the operation be moved closer together and the material-handling problem overcome by gravity chutes?
8. Can material be pushed from operative to operative along the bench?
9. Can material be dispatched from a central point by means of a conveyor?
10. Is the size of the container suitable for the amount of material transported?
11. Can material be brought to a central inspection point by means of a conveyor?
12. Could the operative inspect his own work?
13. Can a container be designed to make material more accessible?
14. Could a container be placed at the work station without removing the material?
15. Can an electric or air hoist or any other lifting device be used with advantage?
16. If an overhead travelling crane is used, is the service prompt and accurate?
17. Can a tractor-trailer train be used? Could this or an individual railway replace a conveyor?
18. Can gravity be utilized by starting the first operation at a higher level?
19. Can chutes be used to catch material and convey it to containers?
20. Would flow process charts assist in solving the flow and handling problem?
21. Is the store efficiently located?
22. Are truck loading and unloading stations located centrally?
23. Can conveyors be used for floor-to-floor transportation?
24. Can waist-high portable material containers be used at the work stations?
25. Can a finished part be easily disposed of?
26. Would a turntable eliminate walking?
27. Can incoming raw material be delivered at the first work station to save double handling?
28. Could operations be combined at one work station to save double handling?

29. Would a container of standard size eliminate weighing?
30. Would a hydraulic lift eliminate a crane service?
31. Could the operative deliver parts to the next work station when he disposes of them?
32. Are containers uniform to permit stacking and eliminate excessive use of floor space?
33. Could material be bought in a more convenient size for handling?
34. Would signals, i.e., lights, bells, etc., notifying men that more material is required, save delay?
35. Would better scheduling eliminate bottlenecks?
36. Would better planning eliminate crane bottlenecks.
37. Can the location of stores and stockpiles be altered to reduce handling and transportation?

E. Process Analysis

1. Can the operation being analyzed be combined with another operation? Can it be eliminated?
2. Can it be broken up and the various parts of the operation added to other operations?
3. Can a part of the operation being performed be completed more effectively as a separate operation?
4. Is the sequence of operations the best possible, or would changing the sequence improve the operation?
5. Could the operation be done in another department to save the cost of handling?
6. Should a concise study of the operation be made by means of a flow process chart?
7. If the operation is changed, what effect will it have on the other operations? On the finished product?
8. If a different method of producing the part can be used, will it justify all the work and activity involved?
9. Can the operation and inspection be combined?
10. Is the job inspected at its most critical point, or when it is completed?
11. Will a patrol form of inspection eliminate waste, scrap and expense?
12. Are there other similar parts which could be made using the same method, tooling and setup?

F. Material

1. Is the material being used really suitable for the job?
2. Could a less expensive material be substituted and still do the job?
3. Could a lighter-gauge material be used?
4. Is the material purchased in a condition suitable for use?
5. Could the supplier perform additional work on the material that would improve usage and decrease waste?
6. Is the material sufficiently clean?
7. Is the material bought in amounts and sizes that give the greatest utilization and limit scrap, offcuts and short ends?
8. Is the material used to the best possible advantage during cutting, processing?
9. Are materials used in connection with the process—oils, water, acids, paint, gas, compressed air, electricity—suitable, and is their use controlled and economized?
10. How does the cost of material compare with the cost of labor?
11. Can the design be changed to eliminate excessive loss and scrap material?
12. Can the number of materials used be reduced by standardization?
13. Could the part be made from scrap material or offcuts?
14. Can newly developed materials—plastics, hardboard, etc.—be used?
15. Is the supplier of the material performing operations on it which are not necessary for the process?
16. Can extruded materials be used?
17. If the material was of a more consistent grade, could better control of the process be established?

18. Can a fabricated part be substituted instead of a casting to save pattern costs?
19. Is the activity low enough to warrant this?
20. Is the material free from sharp edges and burrs?
21. What effect does storage have on material?
22. Could a more careful inspection of incoming materials decrease difficulties now being encountered in the shop?
23. Could sampling inspection combined with supplier rating reduce inspection costs and delays?
24. Could the part be made more economically from offcuts in some other gauge of material?

G. Work Organization

1. How is the job assigned to the operative?
2. Are things so well controlled that the operative is never without a job to do?
3. How is the operative given instructions?
4. How is material obtained?
5. How are drawings and tools issued?
6. Is there a control on time? If so, how are the starting and finishing times of the job checked?
7. Are there many possibilities for delays at the drawing-room, tool-room and store-room and at the clerk's office?
8. Does the layout of the work area prove to be effective, and can it be improved?
9. Is the material properly positioned?
10. If the operation is being performed continually, how much time is wasted at the start and end of the shift by preliminary operations and cleaning up?
11. How is the amount of finished mateiral counted?
12. Is there a definite check between pieces recorded and pieces paid for?
13. Can automatic counters be used?
14. What clerical work is required from operatives for filling in time cards, material requisitions and the like?
15. How is defective work handled?
16. How is the issue and servicing of tools organized?
17. Are adequate records kept on the performance of operatives?
18. Are new employees properly introduced to their surroundings and do they receive sufficient instruction?
19. When workers do not reach a standard of performance, are the details investigated?
20. Are suggestions from workers encouraged?
21. Do the workers really understand the incentive plan under which they work?

H. Workplace Layout

1. Does the plant layout aid efficient material handling?
2. Does the plant layout allow efficient maintenance?
3. Does the plant layout provide adequate safety?
4. Is the plant layout convenient for setting-up?
5. Does the plant layout help social interaction between the operatives?
6. Are materials conveniently placed at the workplace?
7. Are tools pre-positioned to save mental delay?
8. Are adequate working surfaces provided for subsidiary operations, e.g., inspection and deburring?
9. Are facilities provided for the removal and storage of swarf and scrap?
10. Is adequate provision made for the comfort of the operative, e.g., fan, duckboard or chairs?
11. Is the lighting adequate for the job?
12. Has provision been made for the storage of tools and gauges?
13. Has provision been made for the storage of the operatives' personal belongings?

I. Tolls and Equipment

1. Can a jig be designed that can be used for more than one job?
2. Is the volume sufficient to justify highly developed specialized tools and fixtures?
3. Can a magazine feed be used?
4. Could the jig be made of lighter material, or so designed with economy of material to allow easier handling?
5. Are there other fixtures available that can be adapted to this job?
6. Is the design of the jig correct?
7. Would lower-cost tooling decrease quality?
8. Is the jig designed to allow maximum motion economy?
9. Can the part be quickly inserted and removed from the jig?
10. Would a quick-acting, cam-actuated mechanism be desirable for tightening the jig, clamp or vice?
11. Can ejectors be installed on the fixture for automatically removing the part when the fixture is opened?
12. Are all operatives provided with the same tools?
13. If accurate work is necessary, are proper gauges and other measuring instruments provided?
14. Is the wooden equipment in use in good condition and are work benches free from splinters?
15. Would a special bench or desk designed to eliminate stooping, bending and reaching reduce fatigue?
16. Is pre-setting possible?
17. Can universal tooling be used?
18. Can setting time be reduced?
19. How is material supply replenished?
20. Can a hand or foot air-jet be supplied to the operative and applied with advantage?
21. Could jigs be used?
22. Could guides or bullet-nosed pins be used to position the part?
23. What must be done to complete the operation and put away all the equipment?

J. Working Conditions

1. Is the light even and sufficient at all times?
2. Has glare been eliminated from the workplace?
3. Is the proper temperature for comfort provided at all times; if not, can fans or heaters be used?
4. Would installation of air-conditioning equipment be justified?
5. Can noise levels be reduced?
6. Can fumes, smoke and dirt be removed by exhaust systems?
7. If concrete floors are used, are duckboards or matting provided to make standing more comfortable?
8. Can a chair be provided?
9. Are drinking fountains with cool water provided and are they located nearby?
10. Has due consideration been given to safety factors?
11. Is the floor safe, smooth but not slippery?
12. Has the operative been taught to work safely?
13. Is the clothing suitable from a safety standpoint?
14. Does the plant present a neat and orderly appearance at all times?
15. How thoroughly is the workplace cleaned?
16. Is the plant unduly cold in winter, or stuffy in summer, especially on the first morning of the week?
17. Are dangerous processes adequately guarded?

K. Job Enrichment

1. Is the job boring or monotonous?
2. Can the operation be made more interesting?
3. Can the operation be combined with previous or subsequent operations to enlarge it?
4. What is the cycle time?
5. Can the operative do his own setting?
6. Can he do his own inspection?
7. Can he deburr his own work?
8. Can he service his own tools?
9. Can he be given a batch of tasks and do his own scheduling?
10. Can he make the complete part?
11. Is job rotation possible and desirable?
12. Can group layout be used?
13. Are flexible working hours possible and desirable?
14. Is the operation machine paced?
15. Can buffer stock be provided to allow variations in work pace?
16. Does the operative receive regular information about his performance?

I Context of Jobs

The study of the context of jobs is an integral part of job analysis. Documentation of the context in which the work is to be performed provides clues relating to the mental, physical, and emotional demands on the worker. This information can be used for refining the specifications relating to worker characteristics, techniques and methods, and expected rates of quantity and quality of output.

The need for studying job context has been widely recognized in the literature. However, there is a dirth of instruments that are directed specifically at documentation of environmental factors. Part of the problem is that a very wide range of factors qualify for inclusion as environmental influences. Also, the connections between environmental factors and job performance factors are not as yet sufficiently understood. (Refer back to discussions of context in Chapters 2 and 4, particulary Exhibits 2.3 and 4.15.)

The instruments contained in this appendix provide glimpses into different aspects of the work environment. The instrument from the DOL system (I.1) captures the physical factors. The FES work environment scale (I.2) focuses on the risks and discomforts encountered in the physical environment.

The Job Context Work Sheet from VERJAS (I.3) is the most comprehensive documentation of context factors. It encompasses degree of accountability, responsibility, and supervision as well as the physical, personal, and emotional demands on the worker. It thus combines various factors that have been conceptually separated in our discussions.

The excerpt from Primoff's Job Element Method (I.4) documents the working conditions encountered in performing manual work. This is a checklist whose components can be used for identifying factors of relevance to particular job situations.

APPENDIX I.1 ENVIRONMENTAL CONDITIONS (DOL)

Environmental Conditions		Comments
1. Environment Inside ______ % Outside ______ %		
2. Extreme cold with or without temperature changes	______	
3. Extreme heat with or without temperature changes	______	
4. Wet and/or humid	______	
5. Noise Estimated maximum number of decibels	______	
Vibration	______	
6. Hazards Mechanical	______	
Electrical	______	
Burns	______	
Explosives	______	
Radiant Energy	______	
Other	______	
	______	
7. Atmospheric Conditions Fumes	______	
Odors	______	
Dusts	______	
Mists	______	
Gases	______	
Poor Ventilation	______	
Other	______	

RATINGS: E. C.: I O B 2 3 4 5 6 7

PROTECTIVE CLOTHING OR PERSONAL DEVICES

From U.S. Department of Labor, *Handbook for Analyzing Jobs* (Washington, D.C.: U.S. Government Printing Office, 1972), p. 339.

APPENDIX I.2 WORK ENVIRONMENT (FES)

The "work environment" factor considers the risks and discomforts in the employee's physical surroundings or the nature of the work assigned and the safety regulations required. Although the use of safety precautions can practically eliminate a certain danger or discomfort, such situations typically place additional demands upon the employee in carrying out safety regulations and techniques.

Note: Regulations governing pay for irregular or intermittent duty involving unusual physical hardship or hazard are in Chapter 550, *Federal Personnel Manual.*

Level 9–1 *5 points*

The work environment involves everyday risks or discomforts which require normal safety precautions typical of such places as offices, meeting and training rooms, libraries, and residences or commercial vehicles, e.g., use of safe work practices with office equipment, avoidance of trips and falls, observance of fire regulations and traffic signals, etc. The work area is adequately lighted, heated, and ventilated.

Level 9–2 *20 points*

The work involves moderate risks or discomforts which require special safety precautions, e.g., working around moving parts, carts, or machines; with contagious diseases or irritant chemicals; etc. Employees may be required to use protective clothing or gear such as masks, gowns, coats, boots, goggles, gloves, or shields.

Level 9–3 *50 points*

The work environment involves high risks with exposure to potentially dangerous situations or unusual environmental stress which require a range of safety and other precautions, e.g., working at great heights under extreme outdoor weather conditions, subject to possible physical attack or mob conditions, or similar situations where conditions cannot be controlled.

From U.S. Civil Service Commission, *Instructions for the Factor Evaluation System* (Washington, D.C.: U.S. Government Printing Office, 1977), p. 31.

APPENDIX I.3 JOB CONTEXT WORKSHEET (VERJAS)

PART A—SCOPE AND EFFECT — Page ___ of ___ — Position No.: ______

	Factor	Notes	Tasks Which Require This Factor
I.	SUPERVISION RECEIVED Proximity: ☐ Visual ☐ Physical Sep. ☐ Geog. Sep. Frequency: ☐ Constant ☐ Hourly ☐ Daily ☐ Weekly ☐ Less Than Weekly	NOTES	
II.	GUIDELINES ☐ Not Applicable ☐ Applicable	NOTES	
III.	RESEARCH ANALYSIS REPORTS ☐ Not applicable ☐ Applicable	NOTES	
IV.	ACCOUNTABILITY CONSEQUENCES OF ERROR ☐ Not Applicable ☐ Applicable ☐ Life ☐ Property ☐ Injury ☐ Inconvenience ☐ Monetary	NOTES	
V.	PERSONAL CONTACTS ☐ Not Applicable ☐ Applicable	NOTES (INTERNAL) NOTES (EXTERNAL)	
VI.	SUPERVISION EXERCISED ☐ Not Applicable ☐ Applicable Number Supervised: ______ Skilled/Semiskilled; ______ Clerical; ______ Prof./Technical; ______ Other Nature: ☐ Hire/Fire ☐ Train ☐ Assignments ☐ Review Work ☐ Eval. Perf.	NOTES	

PART B—ENVIRONMENT

	Factor	Notes	Tasks Which Require This Factor
VII.	PHYSICAL DEMANDS ☐ Not Applicable ☐ Applicable Lifting: ☐ 10 lb max. ☐ 20 lb max. ☐ 50 lb max. ☐ 100 lb max. ☐ Over 100 lb Mobility: ☐ Standing ☐ Walking ☐ Sitting ☐ Stooping ☐ Reaching ☐ Kneeling ☐ Crouching ☐ Crawling ☐ Climbing	NOTES	
VIII.	WORK HAZARDS ☐ Not Applicable ☐ Applicable ☐ Mechanical ☐ Electrical ☐ Fire ☐ Chemical ☐ Explosives ☐ Radiation ☐ Atmospheric ☐ Weight	NOTES	
IX.	PERSONAL DEMANDS/STRESS ☐ Not Applicable ☐ Applicable ☐ Overtime ☐ Shift Work ☐ Split Shift ☐ Climate ☐ Stress ☐ Repetitious Operations	NOTES	

From S. E. Bemis, A. H. Belenky, and D. A. Soder, *Job Analysis* (Washington, D.C.: The Bureau of National Affairs, Inc., 1983), p. 72.

APPENDIX I.4 WORKING CONDITIONS RELEVANT TO EVALUATING MANUAL JOBS (JEM)

1. Do the Same Thing All Day, Like Stuffing Envelopes
2. Work Where You Can't Talk to Anyone Else
3. Work at a Desk All Day
4. Work Inside All the Time
5. Work Around Sick People
6. Work Where You Have to Cooperate with Others
7. Use Your Eyes in Close Work Examining Small Details
8. Work for a Long Period of Time Standing in One Place
9. Work Rotating Shifts (One Week Days, One Week Afternoons, One Week Nights)
10. Work Overtime
11. Work Seven Days in a Row
12. Work Weekends and Holidays
13. Work Outdoors in Cold Weather
14. Work Outdoors in the Rain
15. Work Outdoors in the Hot Sun
16. Having to Wear Protective Items Such as Goggles, Hood, Work Gloves
17. Work with Tools Where Hands Are Cramped
18. Work in a Narrow Space, in a Cramped Position
19. Work on Your Hands and Knees on the Floor
20. Work in a Room Where the Smell of Paint or Varnish Is Strong
21. Work in a Room Where There Are Strong Odors Caused by Chemicals Such as Plastics
22. Use Hand Tools That Require a Lot of Strength
23. Carry Heavy Items Such as Cables or Steel Bars
24. Work in a Close, Stuffy Room
25. Work Where Noise Is So Loud You Can't Hear Someone Speak
26. Work Where Safety Rules Are Strictly Enforced
27. Handle Tar-Like or Plastic Material That Is Hard to Wash Off Your Hands
28. Handle Sharp-Edged Pieces of Metal That Might Cut Your Hands
29. Handle Wood When You Might Get Splinters in Your Fingers
30. Hold Hot Metal with Tongs
31. Work with Hot, Molten Metals or Plastics
32. Work with Material That Causes a Lot of Dust in the Air
33. Shovel Snow
34. Ride in the Back of an Open Truck in the Snow and Rain
35. Work Around Gas Fumes From Trucks
36. Work in Smoke That Smarts Your Eyes
37. Work in the Mud
38. Work Where It's Damp
39. Take Stoppage Out of a Blocked Toilet
40. Clean Toilets
41. Handle Soiled Clothing
42. Work Around Odor of Decayed Garbage
43. Work in Raw Sewage in Sewers
44. Work Underground in Tunnels
45. Work in a Deep, Dark Pit
46. Work Where Clothes Become Dirty and Smelly
47. Use a Machine of Which a Part Might Break and Fly Off

From E. S. Primoff, *How to Prepare and Conduct Job Element Examinations* (Washington, D.C.: U.S. Government Printing Office, 1975), pp. 53–54.

48. Work Around Moving Machinery
49. Work 40 Feet or More Above Ground Such as on a Ladder, Scaffolding, Tall Mast, or King Post
50. Work Where Metal Chips Are Flying
51. Work with Chemicals Like Acids and Alkalis Which Can Burn the Skin
52. Work with Explosives or Chemicals That Can Blow Up If You Aren't Careful
53. Work Around High Electric Voltages

J Knowledges, Skills, and Abilities

Specification of the characteristics required of workers for effective job performance is one of the central concerns of job analysis. The instruments presented in this appendix are intended as aids in worker specification activity. None of them is individually complete. But as a set, they cover most of the KSAOs of interest in human resource management activity.

The scale from the FES system (J.1) is perhaps the most simplistic in conception. Even though labeled as a knowledge scale, it has parallel provisions for measuring both knowledge and skills.

The scale from the HSMS (J.2) is based on an implicit distinction between breadth of knowledge and depth of understanding. Breadth refers to the varieties of information that are organized within the category, such as facts, terms, definitions, special procedures, and the use of specialized equipment. Depth of understanding, on the other hand, refers to knowledge of the conceptual structure of the named category. It is synonymous with quality of knowledge, and it rises from "general awareness," to "considerable degree of understanding," and then to "a very deep understanding."

The two General Education Development (GED) Scales (J.3 and J.4) are from the DOL and Fine's FJA system, respectively. Both break down GED into three categories: reasoning, mathematical, and language.

The GED scale of the DOL (J.3) is intended to embrace those aspects of education (formal and informal) that contribute to the worker's (1) reasoning development and the ability to follow instructions and (2) acquisition of "tool" knowledges such as language and mathematical skills. GED is considered education of a general nature that does not have a recognized, fairly specific occupational objective. Ordinarily, such education is obtained in elementary school, high school, or college. It could also derive from experience and self-study (U.S. Department of Labor, 1972, p. 209).

Fine's GED scale (J.4) is similar in format to the DOL scale. However, the language used in differentiating the levels is closer to everyday speech.

It is important to emphasize that although the GED scales are labeled as education development scales, they are not tied to years of education. Rather, they reflect levels of reasoning, language, and mathematical skills, viewed in the abstract. They are functionally defined and have a constant meaning. It is implicitly assumed that persons can reach high levels of proficiencies in these areas without the benefit of formal education. The GED scales can be used to express job requirements, the level attained by a particular worker, or a worker's capacity to learn (Fine & Wiley, 1971, pp. 27–28).

Appendix J.5 contains a summary of the human characteristics that are a part of the DOL system's tool kit for the derivation of specifications. Although labeled as "aptitudes," this is really a list of universal human abilities that are relevant to job situations. The scale that is to be used in rating requirements of levels of these abilities is given at the bottom of the list. The DOL's handbook for analyzing jobs contains an extensive breakdown of the differences among the levels. Analysts who find these abilities relevant to their concerns should consult the DOL's manual (U.S. Department of Labor, 1972, pp. 231–294).

The DOL's list of abilities (J.5) is linked with the system's testing program. This is known as the General Aptitude Test Battery (GATB). The program provides norms for approximately 500 jobs. The GATB enables measurement of ability standings of individuals as a basis for selection decisions (U.S. Department of Labor, 1972, p. 233).

The list of abilities contained in Appendix J.6 are from Fleishman's Ability Requirements Scales (ARS). This list is the result of an ongoing program of research on job-related human abilities headed by Fleishman and his associates. The mechanisms for establishing the job relevance of these abilities consist of rating scales and flow charts, as discussed in Chapter 5. Analysts who find these abilities pertinent to their concerns should consult the ARS manual (see Fleishman & Quaintance, 1984).

The scales in Appendices J.7 and J.8 deal with physical abilities. Appendix J.7 gives the physical demand factors contained in the DOL system, along with the accompanying rating scales. The application of this instrument was illustrated in Chapter 5 (Exhibit 5.7). The physical demands factor found in the FES is given in J.8.

The last scale in this appendix (J.9) is from E. H. Schein's publication on career planning. It deals with KSAOs that are relevant to success at managerial work. It consists of 45 items broken down into four categories: motives and values, general abilities and analytical skills, interpersonal and group skills, and emotional skills. This scale should be of interest to job analysts who need to study managerial work, particularly as a part of career planning.

APPENDIX J.1 KNOWLEDGE REQUIRED BY THE POSITION (FES)

Factor 1 measures the nature and extent of information or facts which the workers must understand to do acceptable work (e.g., steps, procedures, practices, rules, policies, theories, principles, and concepts) and the nature and extent of the skills needed to apply those knowledges. To be used as a basis for selecting a level under this factor, a knowledge must be required and applied.

Level 1–1 *50 points*

Knowledge of simple, routine, or repetitive tasks or operations which typically includes following step-by-step instructions and requires little or no previous training or experience;

OR

Skill to operate simple equipment or equipment which operates repetitively, requiring little or no previous training or experience;

OR

Equivalent knowledge and skill.

Level 1–2 *200 points*

Knowledge of basic or commonly-used rules, procedures, or operations which typically requires some previous training or experience;

From U.S. Civil Service Commission, *Instructions for the Factor Evaluation System* (Washington, D.C.: U.S. Government Printing Office, 1977), pp. 16–17.

OR

Basic skill to operate equipment requiring some previous training or experience, such as keyboard equipment;

OR

Equivalent knowledge and skill.

Level 1–3 *350 points*

Knowledge of a body of standardized rules, procedures or operations requiring considerable training and experience to perform the full range of standard clerical assignments and resolve recurring problems;

OR

Skill, acquired through considerable training and experience, to operate and adjust varied equipment for purposes such as performing numerous standardized tests or operations;

OR

Equivalent knowledge and skill.

Level 1–4 *550 points*

Knowledge of an extensive body of rules, procedures or operations requiring extended training and experience to perform a wide variety of interrelated or nonstandard procedural assignments and resolve a wide range of problems;

OR

Practical knowledge of standard procedures in a technical field, requiring extended training or experience, to perform such work as: adapting equipment when this requires considering the functioning characteristics of equipment; interpreting results of tests based on previous experience and observations (rather than directly reading instruments or other measures); or extracting information from various sources when this requires considering the applicability of information and the characteristics and quality of the sources;

OR

Equivalent knowledge and skill.

Level 1–5 *750 points*

Knowledge (such as would be acquired through a pertinent baccalaureate educational program or its equivalent in experience, training, or independent study) of basic principles, concepts, and methodology of a professional or administrative occupation, and skill in applying this knowledge in carrying out elementary assignments, operations, or procedures;

OR

In addition to the practical knowledge of standard procedures in Level 1–4, practical knowledge of technical methods to perform assignments such as carrying out limited projects which involves use of specialized, complicated techniques;

OR

Equivalent knowledge and skill.

—Make decisions or recommendations significantly changing, interpreting, or developing important public policies or programs;

OR

Equivalent knowledge and skill.

Level 1–9 *1850 points*

Mastery of a professional field to generate and develop new hypotheses and theories;

OR

Equivalent knowledge and skill.

APPENDIX J.2 LEVELS OF KNOWLEDGE (HSMS)

This scale refers to the level of knowledge in a given subject category required of the performer in the task being scaled. The knowledge category is rated with this scale. To be rated above zero on the scale, the tasks must require knowledge beyond the simple memorization of the overt steps of the task.

The scale rises with the amount of detailed knowledge which must be consciously applied and with the depth of understanding required in the subject area, in terms of the subject area's content, the structure of its ideas, and its uses. ''Detailed knowledge'' covers such things as technical or special terms or facts. ''Consciously applied'' means that the performer is able to (but need not) articulate his use of the knowledge in the task situation.

The level of knowledge for a category is not determined by the level of any intellectual skills required, nor by the level for any other knowledge category required for the task, nor by the level of the category required for any other tasks of the job involved.

Scale Value	Descriptive Statement
0.0	The task does *not* require the performer consciously to apply knowledge in this subject category which has been gained in a *learning experience requiring more than the memorization of the overt steps of the specific task being scaled.*
1.5	The task requires that the performer consciously apply *a limited amount of detailed knowledge* in this subject category, including such things as technical or special terms, facts, or equipment.
2.5	The task requires that the performer have *a general awareness* of this subject category in terms of its content, the structure of its ideas, and its uses. The performer must consciously apply *a limited amount of detailed knowledge* in this subject area, including such things as technical or special terms, facts, or equipment.
3.5	The task requires that the performer have *a general awareness* of this subject category in terms of its content, the structure of its ideas, and its uses. The performer must consciously apply *a moderate amount of detailed knowledge* in this subject area, including such things as technical or special terms, facts, or equipment.
3.5	The task requires that the performer have *a general awareness* of this subject category in terms of its content, the structure of its ideas, and its uses. The performer must consciously apply *a moderate amount of detailed knowledge* in this subject area, including such things as technical or special terms, facts, or equipment.
5.5	The task requires that the performer have *a considerable degree of understanding* of this subject category in terms of its content, the structure of its ideas, and its uses. The performer must consciously apply *a moderate amount of detailed knowledge* in this area, including such things as technical or special terms, facts, or equipment.
7.0	The task requires that the performer have *a considerable degree of understanding* of this subject category in terms of its content, the structure of its ideas, and its uses. The performer must consciously apply *a very great*

From E. Gilpatrick, *The Health Services Mobility Study Method of Task Analysis and Curriculum Design*, Research Report No. 11, Vol. 1 (New York: Hunter College, The Research Foundation, City University of New York, 1977), pp. 2-47–2-48. Reprinted by permission.

amount of detailed knowledge in this subject area, including such things as technical or special terms, facts, or equipment.

8.0 The task requires that the performer have *a very deep understanding* of this subject category in terms of its content, the structure of its ideas, and its uses. The performer must consciously apply *a moderate amount of detailed knowledge* in this subject area, including such things as technical or special terms, facts, or equipment.

9.0 The task requires that the performer have *a very deep understanding* of this subject category in terms of its content, the structure of its ideas, and its uses. The performer must consciously apply *a very great amount of detailed knowledge* in this subject area, including such things as technical or special terms, facts, or equipment.

APPENDIX J.3 GENERAL EDUCATION DEVELOPMENT (DOL)

Level	Reasoning Development	Mathematical Development	Language Development
6	Apply principles of logical or scientific thinking to a wide range of intellectual and practical problems. Deal with nonverbal symbolism (formulas, scientific equations, graphs, musical notes, etc.) in its most difficult phases. Deal with a variety of abstract and concrete variables. Apprehend the most abstruse classes of concepts.	Advanced calculus: Work with limits, continuity, real number systems, mean value theorems, and implicit function theorems. Modern algebra: Apply fundamental concepts of theories of groups, rings, and fields. Work with differential equations, linear algebra, infinite series, advanced operations methods, and functions of real and complex variables. Statistics: Work with mathematical statistics, mathematical probability and applications, experimental design, statistical inference, and econometrics.	Reading: Read literature, book and play reviews, scientific and technical journals, abstracts, financial reports, and legal documents. Writing: Write novels, plays, editorials, journals, speeches, manuals, critiques, poetry, and songs. Speaking: Conversant in the theory, principles, and methods of effective and persuasive speaking, voice and diction, phonetics, and discussion and debate.
5	Apply principles of logical or scientific thinking to define problems, collect data, establish facts, and draw valid conclusions. Interpret an extensive variety of technical instructions in mathematical or diagrammic form. Deal with several abstract and concrete variables.	Algebra: Work with exponents and logarithms, linear equations, quadratic equations, mathematical induction and binomial theorem, and permutations. Calculus: Apply concepts of analytic geometry, differentiations and integration of algebraic functions with applications. Statistics: Apply mathematical operations to frequency distributions, reliability and validity of tests, normal curve, analysis of variance, correlation techniques, chi-square application and sampling theory, and factor analysis.	Same as Level 6.
4	Apply principles of rational systems* to solve practical problems and deal with a variety of concrete variables in situations where only limited standardization exists. Interpret a variety of instructions furnished in written, oral, diagrammatic, or schedule form.	Algebra: Deal with system of real numbers; linear, quadratic, rational, exponential, logarithmic, angle and circular functions, and inverse functions; related algebraic solution of equations and inequalities; limits and continuity, and probability and statistical inference. Geometry: Deductive axiomatic geometry, plane and solid; and rectangular coordinates. Shop Math: Practical application of fractions, percentages, ratio and proportion, mensuration, logarithms, slide rule, practical algebra, geometric	Reading: Read novels, poems, newspapers, periodicals, journals, manuals, dictionaries, thesauruses, and encyclopedias. Writing: Prepare business letters, expositions, summaries, and reports, using prescribed format and conforming to all rules of punctuation, grammar, diction, and style. Speaking: Participate in panel discussions, dramatizations, and debates. Speak extemporaneously on a variety of subjects.

* Examples of rational systems are bookkeeping, internal combustion engines, electric wiring systems, house building, nursing, farm management, and navigation.

From U.S. Department of Labor, *Handbook for Analyzing Jobs* (Washington, D.C.: U.S. Government Printing Office, 1972), p. 209.

Level	Reasoning Development	Mathematical Development	Language Development
		construction, and essentials of trigonometry.	
3	Apply commonsense understanding to carry out instructions furnished in written, oral, or diagrammatic form. Deal with problems involving several concrete variables in or from standardized situations.	Compute discount, interest, profit, and loss; commission, markup, and selling price; ratio and proportion, and percentage. Calculate surfaces, volumes, weights, and measures. Algebra: Calculate variables and formulas; monomials and polynomials; ratio and proportion variables; and square roots and radicals. Geometry: Calculate plane and solid figures; circumference, area, and volume. Understand kinds of angles, and properties of pairs of angles.	Reading: Read a variety of novels, magazines, atlases, and encyclopedias. Read safety rules, instructions in the use and maintenance of shop tools and equipment, and methods and procedures in mechanical drawing and layout work. Writing: Write reports and essays with proper format, punctuation, spelling, and grammar, using all parts of speech. Speaking: Speak before an audience with poise, voice control, and confidence, using correct English and well-modulated voice.
2	Apply commonsense understanding to carry out detailed but uninvolved written or oral instructions. Deal with problems involving a few concrete variables in or from standardized situations.	Add, subtract, multiply, and divide all units of measure. Perform the four operations with like common and decimal fractions. Compute ratio, rate, and percent. Draw and interpret bar graphs. Perform arithmetic operations involving all American monetary units.	Reading: Passive vocabulary of 5,000–6,000 words. Read at rate of 190–215 words per minute. Read adventure stories and comic books, looking up unfamiliar words in dictionary for meaning, spelling, and pronunciation. Read instructions for assembling model cars and airplanes. Writing: Write compound and complex sentences, using cursive style, proper end punctuation, and employing adjectives and adverbs. Speaking: Speak clearly and distinctly with appropriate pauses and emphasis, correct pronunciation, variations in word order, using present, perfect, and future tenses.
1	Apply commonsense understanding to carry out simple one- or two-step instructions. Deal with standardized situations with occasional or no variables in or from these situations encountered on the job.	Add and subtract two digit numbers. Multiply and divide 10's and 100's by 2, 3, 4, 5. Perform the four basic arithmetic operations with coins as part of a dollar. Perform operations with units such as cup, pint, and quart; inch, foot, and yard; and ounce and pound.	Reading: Recognize meaning of 2,500 (two- or three-syllable) words. Read at rate of 95–120 words per minute. Compare similarities and differences between words and between series of numbers. Writing: Print simple sentences containing subject, verb, and object, and series of numbers, names, and addresses. Speaking: Speak simple sentences, using normal word order, and present and past tenses.

APPENDIX J.4 REVISED VERSION OF SIDNEY FINE'S GENERAL EDUCATION DEVELOPMENT SCALE

REASONING DEVELOPMENT SCALE

The Reasoning Development Scale is concerned with knowledge and ability to deal with theory versus practice, abstract versus concrete, and many versus few variables.

Sidney Fine & W. W. Wiley, *An Introduction to Functional Job Analysis* (Kalamazoo, Mich.: W. E. Upjohn Institute, 1971), pp. 27–28.

Level 1

Have the commonsense understanding to carry out simple one- or two-step instructions in the context of highly standardized situations.

Recognize unacceptable variations from the standard and take emergency action to reject inputs or stop operations.

Level 2

Have the commonsense understanding to carry out detailed but uninvolved instructions where the work involves a *few* concrete/specific variables in or from standard/typical situations.

Level 3

Have the commonsense understanding to carry out instructions where the work involves several concrete/specific variables in or from standard/typical situations.

Level 4

Have knowledge of a system of interrelated procedures, such as bookkeeping, internal combustion engines, electric wiring systems, nursing, farm management, ship sailing, or machining.

Apply principles to solve practical everyday problems and deal with a variety of concrete variables in situations where only limited standardization exists.

Interpret a variety of instruction furnished in written, oral, diagrammatic, or schedule form.

Level 5

Have knowledge of a field of study (engineering, literature, history, business administration) having immediate applicability to the affairs of the world.

Define problems, collect data, establish facts, and draw valid conclusions in controlled situations.

Interpret an extensive variety of technical material in books, manuals, texts, etc.

Deal with some abstract but mostly concrete variables.

Level 6

Have knowledge of a field of study of the highest abstractive order (e.g., mathematics, physics, chemistry, logic, philosophy, art criticism).

Deal with nonverbal symbols in formulas, equations, or graphs.

Understand the most difficult classes of concepts.

Deal with a large number of variables and determine a specific course of action (e.g., research, production) on the basis of need.

MATHEMATICAL DEVELOPMENT SCALE

The Mathematical Development Scale is concerned with knowledge and ability to deal with mathematical problems and operations from counting and simple addition to higher mathematics.

Level 1

Counting to simple addition and subtraction; reading, copying, and/or recording of figures.

Level 2

Use arithmetic to add, subtract, multiply, and divide whole numbers. Reading scales and gauges as in powered equipment where readings and signals are indicative of conditions and actions to be taken.

Level 3

Make arithmetic calculations involving fractions, decimals, and percentages. Mentally acts upon dimensional specifications marked on material or stakes.

Level 4

Performs arithmetic, algebraic, and geometric procedures in standard practical applications.

Level 5

Have knowledge of advanced mathematical and statistical techniques such as differential and integral calculus, factor analysis, and probability determination.

Work with a wide variety of theoretical mathematical concepts.

Make original applications of mathematical procedures, as in empirical and differential equations.

LANGUAGE DEVELOPMENT SCALE

The Language Development Scale is concerned with knowledge and ability to speak, read, or write language materials from simple instructions to complex sources of information and ideas.

Level 1

Cannot read or write but can follow simple oral, *pointing out* instructions.

Sign name and understand ordinary, routine agreements when explained, such as those relevant to leasing a house; employment (hours, wages, etc.); procuring a driver's license.

Read lists, addresses, safety warnings.

Level 2

Read short sentences, simple concrete vocabulary; words that avoid complex Latin derivatives (exploded diagrams, comic books, action-type, i.e., Western, mystery magazines).

Converse with service personnel (waiters, ushers, cashiers).

Copy written records precisely without error.

Keep taxi driver's trip record or service maintenance record.

Level 3

Comprehend orally expressed trade terminology (jargon) of a specific technical nature.

Read material on level of the *Reader's Digest* and straight news reporting in popular *mass* newspapers.

Comprehend ordinary newscasting (uninvolved sentences and vocabulary with focus on events rather than on their analysis).

Copy written material from one record to another, catching gross errors in grammar.

Fill in report forms, such as Medicare forms, employment applications, and card form for income tax.

Level 4

Write routine business correspondence reflecting standard procedures.

Interview job applicants to determine work best suited for their abilities and experience; contact employers to interest them in services of agency.

Read and comprehend technical manuals and written instructions as well as drawings.

Conduct opinion research surveys involving stratified samples of the population.

Level 5

Write instructions for assembly of prefabricated parts into units.

Write instructions and specifications concerning proper use of machinery.

Write copy for advertising. Report news for the newspapers, radio, or TV.

Prepare and deliver lectures for audiences that seek information about the arts, sciences, and humanities in an informal way.

Level 6

Report, write, or edit articles for technical and scientific journals or journals of advanced literary criticism (e.g., *Journal of Educational Sociology*, *Science*, *Physical Review*, *Daedalus*).

APPENDIX J.5 APTITUDES (DOL)

Specific capacities and abilities required in order to learn or perform adequately a task or job duty.

G INTELLIGENCE: General learning ability. The ability to "catch on" or understand instructions and underlying principles. Ability to reason and make judgments. Closely related to doing well in school.

V VERBAL: Ability to understand meanings of words and ideas associated with them, and to use them effectively. To comprehend language, to understand relationships between words, and to understand meanings of whole sentences and paragraphs. To present information or ideas clearly.

N NUMERICAL: Ability to perform arithmetic operations quickly and accurately.

S SPATIAL: Ability to comprehend forms in space and understand relationships of plane and solid objects. May be used in such tasks as blueprint reading and in solving geometry problems. Frequently described as the ability to "visualize" objects of two or three dimensions, or to think visually of geometric forms.

P FORM PERCEPTION: Ability to perceive pertinent detail in objects or in pictorial or graphic material. To make visual comparisons and discriminations and see slight differences in shapes and shadings of figures and widths and lengths of lines.

Q CLERICAL PERCEPTION: Ability to perceive pertinent detail in verbal or tabular material. To observe differences in copy, to proofread words and numbers, and to avoid perceptual errors in arithmetic computation.

K MOTOR COORDINATION: Ability to coordinate eyes and hands or fingers rapidly and accurately in making precise movements with speed. Ability to make a movement response accurately and quickly.

F FINGER DEXTERITY: Ability to move the fingers and manipulate small objects with the fingers rapidly or accurately.

M MANUAL DEXTERITY: Ability to move the hands easily and skillfully. To work with the hands in placing and turning motions.

E EYE-HAND-FOOT COORDINATION: Ability to move the hand and foot coordinately with each other in accordance with visual stimuli.

C COLOR DISCRIMINATION: Ability to perceive or recognize similarities or differences in colors, or in shades or other values of the same color; to identify a particular color, or to recognize harmonious or contrasting color combinations, or to match colors accurately.

Aptitude amounts are expressed in terms of levels, which in turn reflect equivalent amounts of the aptitudes possessed by segments of the working population, as follows:

1 = the top 10% of the population; this segment possesses an extremely high degree of the aptitude

2 = the highest third, exclusive of the top 10% of the population; this segment possesses an above-average or high degree of the aptitude

3 = the middle third of the population; this segment possesses a medium degree of the aptitude, ranging from slightly below to slightly above average

4 = the lowest third, exclusive of the bottom 10% of the population; this segment possesses a below-average or low degree of the aptitude

5 = the lowest 10% of the population; this segment possesses a negligible degree of the aptitude

---

From U.S. Department of Labor, *Dictionary of Occupational Titles*, 3d ed. (Washington, D.C.: U.S. Government Printing Office, 1965), p. 653.

APPENDIX J.6 DEFINITIONS OF ABILITIES IN THE ARS (FLEISHMAN)

1. *Oral Comprehension* is the ability to understand spoken English words and sentences.
2. *Written Comprehension* is the ability to understand written sentences and paragraphs.
3. *Oral Expression* is the ability to use English words or sentences in speaking so others will understand.
4. *Written Expression* is the ability to use English words or sentences in writing so others will understand.
5. *Fluency of Ideas* is the ability to produce a number of ideas about a given topic.
6. *Originality* is the ability to produce unusual or clever ideas about a given topic or situation. It is the ability to invent creative solutions to problems or to develop new procedures to situations in which standard operating procedures do not apply.
7. *Memorization* is the ability to remember information, such as words, numbers, pictures, and procedures. Pieces of information can be remembered by themselves or with other pieces of information.
8. *Problem Sensitivity* is the ability to tell when something is wrong or is likely to go wrong. It includes being able to identify the whole problem as well as the elements of the problem.
9. *Mathematical Reasoning* is the ability to understand and organize a problem and then to select a mathematical method or formula to solve the problem. It encompasses reasoning through mathematical problems to determine appropriate operations that can be performed to solve problems. It also includes the understanding or structuring of mathematical problems. The actual manipulation of numbers is not included in this ability.
10. *Number Facility* involves the degree to which adding, subtracting, multiplying, and dividing can be done quickly and correctly. These can be steps in other operations like finding percentages and taking square roots.
11. *Deductive Reasoning* is the ability to apply general rules to specific problems to come up with logical answers. It involves deciding if an answer makes sense.
12. *Inductive Reasoning* is the ability to combine separate pieces of information, or specific answers to problems, to form general rules or conclusions. It involves the ability to think of possible reasons for why things go together.
13. *Information Ordering* is the ability to follow correctly a rule or set of rules to arrange things or actions in a certain order. The rule or set of rules used must be given. The things or actions to be put in order can include numbers, letters, words, pictures, procedures, sentences, and mathematical or logical operations.
14. *Category Flexibility* is the ability to produce many rules so that each rule tells how to group a set of things in a different way. Each different group must contain a least two things from the original set of things.
15. *Speed of Closure* involves the degree to which different pieces of information can be combined and organized into one meaningful pattern quickly. It is not known beforehand what the pattern will be. The material may be visual or auditory.
16. *Flexibility of Closure* is the ability to identify or detect a known pattern (like a figure, word, or object) that is hidden in other material. The task is to pick out the disguised pattern from the background material.

From E. A. Fleishman and M. K. Quaintance, *Taxonomies of Human Performance: The Description of Human Tasks* (Orlando, Fla.: Academic Press, Inc., 1984). as adapted from (1) Fleishman, E. A. *Development of ability requirement scales for the analysis of Bell System jobs*. Bethesda, Md.: Management Research Institute, 1975; (2) Fleishman, E. A. & Hogan, J. C. A taxonomic method for assessing the physical requirements of jobs: The physical abilities analysis approach (ARRO Final Report 3012/R78–7). Washington, D.C.: Advanced Research Resources Organization, June 1978; (3) Hogan, J. C., Ogden, G. D., & Fleishman, E. A. *Assessing physical requirements for establishing medical standards in selected benchmark jobs* (ARRO Final Report 3012/R78–8). Washington, D.C.: Advanced Research Resources Organization, June 1978; and (4) Schemmer, F. M. *Development of rating scales for selected visual, auditory and speech abilities* (ARRO Final Report 3064). Washington, D.C.: Advanced Research Resources Organization, June 1982. Reprinted by permission.

17. *Spatial Orientation* is the ability to tell where you are in relation to the location of some object or to tell where the object is in relation to you.
18. *Visualization* is the ability to imagine how something will look when it is moved around or when its parts are moved or rearranged. It requires the forming of mental images of how patterns or objects would look after certain changes, such as unfolding or rotation. One has to predict how an object, set of objects, or pattern will appear after the changes are carried out.
19. *Perceptual Speed* involves the degree to which one can compare letters, numbers, objects, pictures, or patterns, quickly and accurately. The things to be compared may be presented at the same time or one after the other. This ability also includes comparing a presented object with a remembered object.
20. *Control Precision* is the ability to move controls of a machine or vehicle. This involves the degree to which these controls can be moved quickly and repeatedly to exact positions.
21. *Multilimb Coordination* is the ability to coordinate movements of two or more limbs (for example, two arms, two legs, or one leg and one arm), such as in moving equipment controls. Two or more limbs are in motion while the individual is sitting, standing, or lying down.
22. *Response Orientation* is the ability to choose between two or more movements quickly and accurately when two or more different signals (lights, sounds, pictures) are given. The ability is concerned with the speed with which the right response can be started with the hand, foot, or other parts of the body.
23. *Rate Control* is the ability to adjust an equipment control in response to changes in the speed and/or directions of a continuously moving object or scene. The ability involves timing these adjustments in anticipating these changes. This ability does not extend to situations in which both the speed and direction of the object are perfectly predictable.
24. *Reaction Time* is the ability to give one fast response to one signal (sound, light, picture) when it appears. This ability is concerned with the speed with which the movement can be started with the hand, foot, or other parts of the body.
25. *Arm–Hand Steadiness* is the ability to keep the hand and arm steady. It includes steadiness while making an arm movement as well as while holding the arm and hand in one position. This ability does not involve strength or speed.
26. *Manual Dexterity* is the ability to make skillful coordinated movements of one hand, a hand together with its arm, or two hands to grasp, place, move, or assemble objects like hand tools or blocks. This ability involves the degree to which these arm–hand movements can be carried out quickly. It does not involve moving machine or equipment controls like levers.
27. *Finger Dexterity* is the ability to make skillful, coordinated movements of the fingers of one or both hands and to grasp, place, or move small objects. This ability involves the degree to which these finger movements can be carried out quickly.
28. *Wrist–Finger Speed* is the ability to make fast, simple repeated movements of the fingers, hands, and wrists. It involves little, if any, accuracy or eye–hand coordination.
29. *Speed of Limb Movement* involves the speed with which a single movement of the arms or legs can be made. This ability does not include accuracy, careful control, or coordination of movement.
30. *Selective Attention* is the ability to concentrate on a task one is doing. This ability involves concentrating while performing a boring task and not being distracted.
31. *Time Sharing* is the ability to shift back and forth between two or more sources of information.
32. *Static Strength* is the ability to use muscle force in order to lift, push, pull, or carry objects. It is the maximum force that one can exert for a brief period of time.
33. *Explosive Strength* is the ability to use short bursts of muscle force to propel oneself or an object. It requires gathering energy for bursts of muscle effort over a very short time period.
34. *Dynamic Strength* is the ability of the muscles to exert force repeatedly or continuously over a long time period. This is the ability to support, hold up, or move the body's own weight and/or objects repeatedly over time. It represents muscular endurance and emphasizes the resistance of the muscles to fatigue.
35. *Trunk Strength* involves the degree to which one's stomach and lower back muscles can support part of the body repeatedly or continuously over time. The ability involves the degree

to which these trunk muscles do not fatigue when they are put under such repeated or continuous strain.

36. *Extent Flexibility* is the ability to bend, stretch, twist, or reach out with the body, arms, or legs.

37. *Dynamic Flexibility* is the ability to bend, stretch, twist, or reach out with the body, arms and/or legs, both quickly and repeatedly.

38. *Gross Body Coordination* is the ability to coordinate the movement of the arms, legs, and torso together in activities in which the whole body is in motion.

39. *Gross Body Equilibrium* is the ability to keep or regain one's body balance or to stay upright when in an unstable position. This ability includes maintaining one's balance when changing direction while moving or standing motionless.

40. *Stamina* is the ability of the lungs and circulatory systems of the body to perform efficiently over long time periods. This is the ability to exert oneself physically without getting out of breath.

41. *Near Vision* is the capacity to see close environmental surroundings.

42. *Far Vision* is the capacity to see distant environmental surroundings.

43. *Visual Color Discrimination* is the capacity to match or discriminate between colors. This capacity also includes detecting differences in color purity (saturation) and brightness (brilliance).

44. *Night Vision* is the ability to see under low light conditions.

45. *Peripheral Vision* is the ability to perceive objects or movement towards the edges of the visual field.

46. *Depth Perception* is the ability to distinguish which of several objects is more distant from or nearer to the observer, or to judge the distance of an object from the observer.

47. *Glare Sensitivity* is the ability to see objects in the presence of glare or bright ambient lighting.

48. *General Hearing* is the ability to detect and to discriminate among sounds that vary over broad ranges of pitch and/or loudness.

49. *Auditory Attention* is the ability to focus on a single source of auditory information in the presence of other distracting and irrelevant auditory stimuli.

50. *Sound Localization* is the ability to identify the direction from which an auditory stimulus originated relative to the observer.

51. *Speech Hearing* is the ability to learn and understand the speech of another person.

52. *Speech Clarity* is the ability to communicate orally in a clear fashion understandable to a listener.

APPENDIX J.7 PHYSICAL DEMANDS (DOL)

Physical Demands			Comments
1. Strength			
a. Standing ______ %			
Walking ______ %			
Sitting ______ %			
b.		Weight	
Lifting ______		______	
Carrying ______		______	
Pushing ______		______	
Pulling ______		______	
2. Climbing		______	
Balancing		______	
3. Stooping		______	
Kneeling		______	
Crouching		______	
Crawling		______	
4. Reaching		______	
Handling		______	
Fingering		______	
Feeling		______	
5. Talking Ordinary		______	
Other		______	
Hearing Ordinary Conversation		______	
Other Sounds		______	
6. Seeing Acuity, Near		______	
Acuity, Far		______	
Depth Perception		______	
Accommodation		______	
Color Vision		______	
Field of Vision			

RATINGS: P. D.: S L M H VH 2 3 4 5 6

From U.S. Department of Labor, *Handbook for Analyzing Jobs* (Washington, D.C.: U.S. Government Printing Office, 1972), pp. 337–338.

RATING SCALES AND PROCEDURES

Frequency Scale (to be used for physical demand factors 1b and 2 to 6)
This activity or condition exists:
NP = Not present—does not exist
O = Occasionally—up to one-third of time
F = Frequently—from one-third to two-thirds of time
C = Constantly—two-thirds or more of time
Type of Work Scale
S = Sedentary—mostly sitting, but occasionally requires walking, standing, carrying or lifting light objects weighing 10 lb or less
L = Light—frequent walking, standing, pushing, pulling, and lifting or carrying objects weighing 10 to 20 lb maximum
H = Heavy—same as L with lifting or carrying of objects from 50 to 100 lb maximum
VH = Heavy—same as L with lifting or carrying of objects weighing from 50 lb to excess of 100 lb

APPENDIX J.8 PHYSICAL DEMANDS (FES)

The "Physical Demands" factor covers the requirements and physical demands placed on the employee by the work assignment. This includes physical characteristics and abilities (e.g., specific agility and dexterity requirements) and the physical exertion involved in the work (e.g., climbing, lifting, pushing, balancing, stooping, kneeling, crouching, crawling, or reaching). To some extent the frequency or intensity of physical exertion must also be considered, e.g., a job requiring prolonged standing involves more physical exertion than a job requiring intermittent standing.

Note: Regulations governing pay for irregular or intermittent duty involving unusual physical hardship or hazard are in Chapter 550, *Federal Personnel Manual.*

Level 8–1 *5 points*

The work is sedentary. Typically, the employee may sit comfortably to do the work. However, there may be some walking; standing; bending; carrying of light items such as papers, books, small parts; driving an automobile, etc. No special demands are required to perform the work.

Level 8–2 *20 points*

The work requires some physical exertion such as long periods of standing; walking over rough, uneven, or rocky surfaces; recurring bending, crouching, stooping, stretching, reaching, or similar activities; recurring lifting of moderately heavy items such as typewriters and record boxes. The work may require specific, but common, physical characteristics and abilities such as above-average agility and dexterity.

Level 8–3 *50 points*

The work requires considerable and strenuous physical exertion such as frequent climbing of tall ladders, lifting heavy objects over 50 pounds, crouching or crawling in restricted areas, and defending oneself or others against physical attack.

APPENDIX J.9 MANAGERIAL CHARACTERISTICS PROFILE (SCHEIN)

1. Rate yourself as you are now on each characteristic by putting an *X* through the appropriate number.
2. Rate where you *would like to be* by *circling* the appropriate number on the scales to the right of the items.

From U.S. Civil Service Commission, *Instructions for the Factor Evaluation System* (Washington, D.C.: U.S. Government Printing Office, 1977), p. 30.

(Schein) From Edgar Schein, *Career Dynamics*, © 1978, Addison-Wesley Publishing Company, Inc., Reading, Massachusetts. Pages 237, 238, and 239, Table 16.2. Reprinted with permission.

A. Motives and Values	**Low**				**High**
1. My desire to get a job done, my need for accomplishment.	1	2	3	4	5
2. My commitment to my organization and its mission.	1	2	3	4	5
3. My desire to work with and through people.	1	2	3	4	5
4. My career aspirations, ambitions.	1	2	3	4	5
5. My degree of involvement with my career.	1	2	3	4	5
6. My desire to function as a general manager free of functional and technical concerns.	1	2	3	4	5
7. The degree to which I feel comfortable about exercising power and authority.	1	2	3	4	5
8. My desire for a high level of responsibility.	1	2	3	4	5
9. My desire to take risks in making tough decisions.	1	2	3	4	5
10. My desire to monitor and supervise the activities of subordinates.	1	2	3	4	5

B. Analytical Abilities—Skills					
11. My ability to identify problems in complex, ambiguous situations.	1	2	3	4	5
12. My degree of insight into myself—my motives.	1	2	3	4	5
13. My degree of insight into myself—my strengths.	1	2	3	4	5
14. My degree of insight into myself—my weaknesses.	1	2	3	4	5
15. My ability to sense quickly what information is needed and how to get it in relation to any given problem.	1	2	3	4	5
16. My ability to assess the validity of information I have not gathered myself.	1	2	3	4	5
17. My ability to learn quickly from experience.	1	2	3	4	5
18. My flexibility, my ability to think of and implement different solutions for different kinds of problems.	1	2	3	4	5
19. My breadth of perspective—insight into a wide variety of situations.	1	2	3	4	5
20. My creativity, my ingenuity.	1	2	3	4	5

C. Interpersonal and Group Skills					
21. My ability to select effective key subordinates.	1	2	3	4	5
22. My ability to develop open and trusting relationships with subordinates;	1	2	3	4	5
23. with peers;	1	2	3	4	5
24. with superiors.	1	2	3	4	5
25. My ability to listen to others in an understanding way.	1	2	3	4	5
26. My ability to develop a climate of collaboration and team work among my subordinates;	1	2	3	4	5
27. among my peers;	1	2	3	4	5
28. among my superiors.	1	2	3	4	5
29. My ability to develop managerial processes which ensure high-quality decisions without my having to make the decisions myself.	1	2	3	4	5
30. My ability to create a climate of growth and development for my subordinates.	1	2	3	4	5
31. My ability to communicate my own thoughts and ideas clearly and persuasively.	1	2	3	4	5
32. My ability to communicate my feelings clearly.	1	2	3	4	5
33. My ability to diagnose complex interpersonal or group situations.	1	2	3	4	5
34. My ability to influence people over whom I have no direct control.	1	2	3	4	5
35. My ability to design management processes for intergroup and interfunction coordination.	1	2	3	4	5

D. Emotional Skills

36. The degree to which I am able to make up my own mind versus relying on the opinions of others.	1	2	3	4	5
37. My degree of tolerance for ambiguity.	1	2	3	4	5
38. My ability to assess the wisdom of proposed courses of action without having first-hand knowledge of the situation.	1	2	3	4	5
39. My ability to pursue a course of action even if it makes me uncomfortable.	1	2	3	4	5
40. My ability to take risks, to make a decision even if it may produce strong negative consequences.	1	2	3	4	5
41. My ability to confront and work through conflict situations (versus avoiding or suppressing them).	1	2	3	4	5
42. My ability to keep going after an experience of failure (losing a negotiation, a product failure, the loss of a good subordinate, etc.).	1	2	3	4	5
43. My ability to confront painful issues of social responsibility (EEO, product safety, environmental impact, etc.)	1	2	3	4	5
44. My ability to fire someone.	1	2	3	4	5
45. My ability to continue to function, to make decisions with incomplete information and in the face of continued environmental turbulence.	1	2	3	4	5

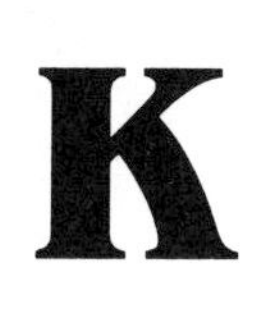

Interests and Other Motivational Characteristics

Effective job performance is the result jointly of capability and willingness. Information relating to knowledges, skills, and abilities takes care of the capability side of the requirement. By itself, however, capability does not assure effectiveness at work. The individual must also be willing to use his or her knowledges, skills, and abilities in the service of the organization. (Refer to discussion relating to interrelations among the determinants of human performance at work in Chapter 5.)

A rich variety of materials have been devised over the years for the measurement of interests, attitudes, values, personality, motivation, and other human characteristics that relate to willingness to contribute. Unfortunately, the bulk of these are in the form of instruments (tests, inventories, and questionnaires) that enable differentiation of individuals from each other over these characteristics. While they are an integral (and vital) part of the tool kit of human resource management, these materials do not relate to the immediate, first-level concern of the job analyst. This concern is with identifying the human characteristics, other than knowledges, skills, and abilities that go with successful job performance. (For inventories of instruments dealing with interests, values, personality, and related characteristics, see Guion, 1965; Crites, 1969; Nunnally, 1978; Anastasi, 1976.)

Viewed from this perspective, a relatively small number of instruments address the primary concern of the job analyst. The three that are included in this appendix were designed for use by analysts in specification activity. The first two are from the DOL system. The instrument in K.1, labeled as Temperaments, spells out the types of interpersonal and behavioral adaptations required of the worker performing the job. The Interest Scales in K.2 are designed to find out the activity preferences of individuals expressed in bipolar terms.

The list of attributes of an interest or temperament nature given in K.3 is from the PAQ package. They are linked with the elements in the PAQ. Their relevance to the PAQ elements is judged according to the scale of attribute relevance given in Chapter 5 in the section dealing with that instrument. A study was conducted by McCormick and his colleagues to find out specifically the requirement levels of these attributes that go with the elements of the PAQ. The results can be found in Marquardt and McCormick, 1972.

APPENDIX K.1 TEMPERAMENTS (DOL)*

D—DCP	Adaptability to accepting responsibility for the direction, control, or planning of an activity.
F—FIF	Adaptability to situations involving the interpretation of feelings, ideas, or facts in terms of personal viewpoint.
I—INFLU	Adaptability to influencing people in their opinions, attitudes, or judgments about ideas or things.
J—SJC	Adaptability to making generalization, evaluations, or decisions based on sensory or judgmental criteria.
M—MVC	Adaptability to making generalizations, evaluations, or decisions based on measurable or verifiable criteria.
P—DEPL	Adaptability to dealing with people beyond giving and receiving instructions.
R—REPCON	Adaptability to performing repetitive work, or to performing continuously the same work, according to set procedures, sequence, or pace.
S—PUS	Adaptability to performing under stress when confronted with emergency, critical, unusual, or dangerous situations; or situations in which working speed and sustained attention are make-or-break aspects of the job.
T—STS	Adaptability to situations requiring the precise attainment of set limits, tolerances, or standards.
V—VARCH	Adaptability to performing a variety of duties, often changing from one task to another of a different nature without loss of efficiency or composure.

APPENDIX K.2 INTERESTS (DOL)†

1a. A preference for activities dealing with things and objects	*vs*	1b. A preference for activities concerned with the communication of data
2a. A preference for activities involving business contact with people	*vs*	2b. A preference for activities of a scientific and technical nature
3a. A preference for activities of a routine, concrete, organized nature	*vs*	3b. A preference for activities of an abstract and creative nature
4a. A preference for working for the presumed good of people	*vs*	4b. A preference for activities that are carried on in relation to processes, machines, and techniques.
5a. A preference for activities resulting in prestige or the esteem of others	*vs*	5b. A preference for activities resulting in tangible, productive satisfaction

* Temperaments = adaptability requirements made on the worker by specific types of job-worker situations.

† Interest = tendency to become absorbed in an experience and to continue it, while an aversion is a tendency to turn away from it to something else.

From U.S. Department of Labor, *Handbook for Analyzing Jobs* (Washington, D.C.: U.S. Government Printing Office, 1972), pp. 8–9.

APPENDIX K.3 ATTRIBUTES OF AN INTEREST OR TEMPERAMENT NATURE (PAQ)*

42. *Variety of duties*: duties often characterized by frequent change.
43. *Repetitive/short-cycle operations*: operations carried out according to set procedures or sequences.
44. *Dealing with things/objects*: preference for situations involving activities which deal with things and objects rather than activities concerned with people or the communication of ideas.
45. *Processes/machines/techniques*: situations which are nonsocial in nature, being primarily concerned with methods and procedures often of a mechanical or chemical nature.
46. *Scientific/technical activities*: using technical methods or investigating natural phenomenon using scientific procedures.
47. *Dealing with people*: i.e., personal contacts beyond giving and receiving instructions.
48. *Social welfare*: working with people for their presumed good.
49. *Influencing people*: influencing opinions, attitudes, or judgments about ideas or things.
50. *Directing/controlling/planning*: operations involving the activities of others, or processes with which others are involved.
51. *Empathy*: seeing things from another person's point of view.
52. *Personal risk*: risk of physical or mental illness or injury.
53. *Conflicting/ambiguous information*: ability to tolerate and critically evaluate information of an uncertain or opposing nature.
54. *Pressure of time*: working in situations where time is a critical factor for successful job performance.
55. *Sensory alertness*: alertness over extended periods of time.
56. *Attainment of set standards*: attainment of set limits, tolerances, or standards.
57. *Working under specific instructions*: i.e., those that allow little or no room for independent action or judgment in working out job problems.
58. *Working alone*: working in physical isolation from others, although the activity may be integrated with that of others.
59. *Separation from family/home*: separation for extended periods of time.
60. *Stage presence*: speaking to or performing for an audience.
61. *Prestige/esteem from others*: working in situations resulting in high regard from others.
62. *Tangible/physical end-products*: working with material elements or parts which ultimately result in a physical product.
63. *Sensory/judgmental criteria*: arriving at generalizations, judgments, or decisions which require sensory discrimination or cognitive appraisal.
64. *Measurable/verifiable criteria*: arriving at generalizations, judgments, or decisions based on known or obtainable standards, characteristics, or dimensions.
65. *Interpretation from personal viewpoint*: interpretation of feelings, ideas, or facts in terms of personal viewpoint or values.
66. *Susceptibility to fatigue*: diminished ability to do work, either physical or mental, as a consequence of previous and recent work done.
67. *Dealing with concepts/information*: preference for situations that involve conceptual or informative ideas and the possible communication of these ideas to others.
68. *Creative activities*: preference for situations involving the finding of new solutions to a problem or new modes of artistic expression.

* As characterized by different types of job situations to which people must adjust.

From R. C. Mecham and E. J. McCormick, *The Rated Attribute Requirements of Job Elements in the Position Analysis Questionnaire* (Lafayette, Ind.: Purdue University, Department of Psychological Sciences, 1969).

Quotations from the *Uniform Guidelines* Pertaining to Job Analysis

The *Uniform Guidelines* published in 1978 cover a wide range of topics dealing with the broad subject of employee selection within the context of the Civil Rights Act and other EEO laws. This appendix presents the sections that relate directly to job analysis. The validation requirements contained in this appendix should be studied in conjunction with the mathematical mechanics presented in Appendix 2.1 at the end of Chapter 2.

APPENDIX L.1 QUOTATIONS FROM THE 1978 *UNIFORM GUIDELINES ON EMPLOYEE SELECTION PROCEDURES* PERTAINING TO JOB ANALYSIS

The complete reference, to which the abbreviations after each quote apply, is U.S. Equal Employment Opportunity Commission, U.S. Civil Service Commission, U.S. Department of Labor, & U.S. Department of Justice, *Uniform Guidelines on Employee Selection Procedures* (1978), Federal Register, vol. 43, no. 166 (1978), pp. 38295–38309.

JOB ANALYSIS IN GENERAL

The enforcement agencies will take into account the fact that a thorough job analysis was conducted (Sec. 9B, p. 38299)

Any validity study should be based upon a review of information about the job for which the selection procedure is to be used. The review should include a job analysis. . . . Any method of job analysis may be used if it provides the information required for the specific validation strategy used. (Sec. 14A, p. 38300)

JOB ANALYSIS FOR CRITERION-BASED VALIDITY

Evidence of the validity of a test or other selection procedure by a criterion-related validity study should consist of empirical data demonstrating that the selction procedure is predictive of or significantly correlated with important elements of job performance. (Sec. 5B, p. 38298)

Where appropriate, jobs with substantially the same major work behaviors may be grouped together for validity studies, in order to obtain an adequate sample. (Sec. 14B(1), p. 38300)

There should be a review of job information to determine measures of work behavior(s) or performance that are relevant to the job or group of jobs in question. These measures or criteria are relevant to the extent that they represent critical or important job duties, work behaviors or work outcomes as developed from the review of job information. (Sec. 14B(2), p. 38300)

Whatever criteria are used should represent important or critical work behavior(s) or work outcomes. Certain criteria may be used without a full job analysis if the user can show the importance of the criteria to the particular employment context. (Sec. 14B(3), pp. 38300–38301)

Where performance in training is used as a criterion, success in training should be properly measured and the relevance of the training should be shown either through a comparison of the content of the training program with the critical or important work behavior(s) of the job(s), or through a demonstration of the relationship between measure of performance in training and measures of job performance. (Sec. 14B(3), p. 38301)

Sole reliance upon a single selection instrument which is related to only one of many job duties or aspects of job performance will also be subject to close review. (Sec. 14B(6), p. 38301)

Where a job analysis is required a complete description of the work behavior(s) or work outcome(s), and measures of their criticality or importance should be provided (Essential). The report should describe the basis on which the behavior(s) or outcome(s) were determined to be critical or important, such as the proportion of time spent on the respective behaviors, their level of difficulty, their frequency of performance, the consequences of error, or other appropriate factors (Essential). Where two or more jobs are grouped for a validity study, the information called for in this subsection should be provided for each of the jobs, and the justification for the grouping (see Section 14B(1)) should be provided (Essential). (Sec. 15B(3), p. 38304)

The materials in this appendix are direct quotes from the *Uniform Guidelines on Employee Selection Procedures* (1978). All quotes have been selected because they pertain to job analysis directly or specify the kind of information that a job analysis should bring to a test development project.

JOB ANALYSIS FOR CONTENT VALIDITY

Evidence of the validity of a test or other selection procedure by a content validity study should consist of data showing that the content of the selection procedure is representative of important aspects of performance of the job for which the candidates are to be evaluated. (Sec. 5B, p. 38298)

A selection procedure can be supported by a content validity strategy to the extent that it is a representative sample of the content of the job. Selection procedures which purport to measure knowledges, skills, or abilities may in certain circumstances be justified by content validity, although they may not be representative samples, if the knowledge, skill, or ability measured by the selection procedure can be operationally defined as provided in Section 14C(4) below, and if that knowledge, skill, or ability is a necessary prerequisite to successful job performance. (Sec. 14C(1), p. 38302)

Thus, a content strategy is not appropriate for demonstrating the validity of selection procedures which purport to measure traits or constructs, such as intelligence, aptitude, personality, commonsense, judgement, leadership, and spatial ability. Content validity is also not an appropriate strategy when the selection procedure involves knowledges, skills, or abilities which an employee will be expected to learn on the job. (Sec. 14C(1), p. 38302)

There should be a job analysis which includes an analysis of the important work behavior(s) required for successful performance and their relative importance and, if the behavior results in work product(s), an analysis of the work product(s). Any job analysis should focus on the work behavior(s) and the tasks associated with them. If work behavior(s) are not deservable, the job analysis should identify and analyze those aspects of the behaviors that can be observed and the observed work products. The work behavior(s) selected for measurement should be critical work behavior(s) and/or important work behavior(s) constituting most of the job. (Sec. 14C(2), p. 38302)

To demonstrate the content validity of a selection procedure, a user should show that the behavior(s) demonstrated in the selection procedure are a representative sample of the behavior(s) of the job in question or that the selection procedure provides a representative sample of the work product of the job. In the case of a selection procedure measuring a knowledge, skill, or ability, the knowledge, skill, or ability being measured should be operationally defined. In the case of a selection procedure measuring a knowledge, the knowledge being measured should be operationally defined as that body of learned information which is used in and is a necessary prerequisite for observable aspects of work behavior of the job. In the case of skills or abilities, the skill or ability being measured should be operationally defined in terms of observable aspects of work behavior of the job. For any selection procedure measuring a knowledge, skill, or ability, the user should show that (a) the selection procedure measures and is a representative sample of that knowledge, skill, or ability; and (b) knowledge, skill, or ability is used in and is a necessary prerequisite to performance of critical or important work behavior(s). In addition, to be content valid, a selection procedure measuring a skill or ability should either closely approximate an observable work behavior, or its product should closely approximate an observable work product. If a test purports to sample a work behavior or to provide a sample of a work product, the manner and setting of the selection procedure and its level and complexity should closely approximate the work situation. The closer the content and the context of the selection procedure are to work samples or work behaviors, the stronger is the basis for showing content validity. As the content of the selection procedure less resembles a work behavior, or the setting and manner of the administration of the selection procedure less resemble the work situation, or the result less resembles a work product, the less likely the selection procedure is to be content valid, and the greater the need for other evidence of validity. (Sec. 14C(4), p. 38302)

A selection procedure which is supported on the basis of content validity may be used for a job if it represents a critical work behavior (i.e., a behavior which is necessary for performance of the job) or work behaviors which constitute most of the important parts of the job. (Sec. 14C(8), pp. 38302–38303)

Where a selection procedure supported solely or primarily by content validity is used to rank job candidates, the selection procedure should measure those aspects of performance which differentiate among levels of job performance. (Sec. 14C(9), p. 38303)

A description of the method used to analyze the job should be provided (Essential). The work behavior(s), the associated tasks, and, if the behavior results in a work product, the work products should be completely described (Essential). Measures of criticality and/or importance of the work behavior(s) and the method of determining these measures should be provided (Essential). Where the job analysis also identified the knowledges, skills, and abilities used in work behavior(s), an operational definition for each knowledge in terms of a body of learned information and for each skill and ability in terms of observable behaviors and outcomes, and the relationship between each knowledge, skill, or ability and each work behavior, as well as the method used to determine this relationship, should be provided (Essential). The work situation should be described, including the setting in which work behavior(s) are performed, and where appropriate, the manner in which knowledges, skills, or abilities are used, and the complexity and difficulty of the knowledge, skill, or ability as used in the work behavior(s). (Sec. 15C(3), p. 38305)

The evidence demonstrating that the selection procedure is a representative work sample, a representative sample of the work behavior(s), or a representative sample of a knowledge, skill, or ability as used as a part of a work behavior and necessary for that behavior should be provided (Essential). The user should identify the work behavior(s) which each item or part of the selection procedure is intended to sample or measure (Essential). Where the selection procedure purports to sample a work behavior or to provide a sample of a work product, a comparison should be provided of the manner, setting, and the level of complexity of the selection procedure with those of the work situation (Essential). (Sec. 15C(5), pp. 38305–38306)

JOB ANALYSIS FOR CONSTRUCT VALIDITY

Evidence of the validity of a test or other selection procedure through a construct validity study should consist of data showing that the procedure measures the degree to which candidates have identifiable characteristics which have been determined to be important in successful performance in the job for which the candidiates are to be evaluated. (Sec. 5B, p. 38298)

There should be a job analysis. This job analysis should show the work behavior(s) required for successful performance of the job, or the groups of jobs being studied, the critical or important work behavior(s) in the job or group of jobs being studied, and an identification of the construct(s) believed to underlie successful performance of these critical or important work behaviors in the job or jobs in question. Each construct should be named and defined, so as to distinguish it from other constructs. If a group of jobs is being studied, the jobs should have in common one or more critical or important work behaviors at a comparable level of complexity. (Sec. 14D(2), p. 38303)

The user should show by empirical evidence that the selection procedure is validly related to the construct and that the construct is validly related to the performance of critical or important work behavior(s). (Sec. 14D(3), p. 38303)

If a study pertains to a number of jobs having common critical or important work behaviors at a comparable level of complexity, and the evidence satisfies subparagraphs 14B(2) and (3) above for those jobs with criterion-related validity evidence for those jobs, the selection procedure may be used for all the jobs to which the study pertains. (Sec. 14D(4), p. 38303)

In determining whether two or more jobs have one or more work behavior(s) in common, the user should compare the observed work behavior(s) in each of the jobs and should compare the observed work product(s) in each of the jobs. . . . If the work behaviors are not observable, then evidence of similarity of work products and any other relevant research evidence will be considered in determining whether the work behavior(s) in the two jobs are the same. (Sec. 14D(4b), p. 38303)

A clear definition of the construct(s) which are believed to underlie successful performance of the critical or important work behavior(s) should be provided (Essential). This definition should include the levels of construct performance relevant to the job(s) for which the selection procedure is to be used (Essential). There should be a summary of the position of the construct in the psychological literature, or in the absence of such a position, a description of the way in which the definition and measurement of the construct was developed, and the psychological theory underlying it (Essential). Any quantitative data which identify or define the job constructs, such as factor analyses, should be provided (Essential). (Sec. 15D(3), p. 38306)

A description of the method used to analyze the job should be provided (Essential). A complete description of the work behavior(s) and, to the extent appropriate, work outcomes and measures of their criticality and/or importance should be provided (Essential). The report should also describe the basis on which the behavior(s) or outcomes were determined to be important, such as their level of difficulty, their frequency of performance, the consequences of error or other appropriate factors (Essential). Where jobs are grouped or compared for the purposes of generalizing validity evidence, the work behavior(s) and work product(s) for each of the jobs should be described, and conclusions concerning the similarity of the jobs in terms of observable work behaviors or work products should be made (Essential). (Sec. 15D(4), p. 38306)

Where a study pertains to a group of jobs, and on the basis of the study, validity is asserted for a job in the group, the observed work behaviors and the observed work products for each of the jobs should be described (Essential). Any other evidence used in determining whether the work behavior(s) in each of the jobs is the same should be fully described (Essential). (Sec. 15D(7), p. 38306)

A description of the important job behavior(s) of the user's job and the basis on which the behaviors were determined to be important should be provided (Essential). (Sec. 15E(1), p. 38307)

If a selection procedure is used to evaluate candidates for jobs at a higher level than those for which they will initially be employed, the validity evidence should satisfy the documentation provisions of this section 15 for the higher level job or jobs, and in addition, the user should provide: (1) a description of the job progression structure, formal or informal; (2) the data showing how many employees progress to the higher level job and the length of time needed to make this progression; and (3) an identification of any anticipated changes in the higher level job. In addition, if the test measures a knowledge, skill, or ability, the user should provide evidence that the knowledge skill or ability is required for the higher level job and the basis for the conclusion that the knowledge, skill, or ability is not expected to develop from the training or experience on the job. (Sec. 15G, p. 38307)

JOB ANALYSIS FOR VALIDITY GENERALIZATION

Criterion-related validity studies conducted by one test user will be considered acceptable for use by another user when . . . the incumbents in the user's job and the incumbents in the job or group of jobs on which the validity study was conducted perform substantially the same major work behaviors, as shown by appropriate job analyses both on the job or group of jobs on which the validity study was performed and on the job for which the selection procedure is to be used. (Sec. 7B(2), p. 38299)

Where jobs are grouped or compared for the purposes of generalizing validity evidence, the work behavior(s) and work product(s) for each of the jobs should be described, and conclusions concerning the similarity of the jobs in terms of observable work behaviors or work products should be made (Essential). (Sec. 15D(4), p. 38306)

JOB ANALYSIS DEFINITIONS

Job analysis. A detailed statement of work behaviors and other information relevant to the job.

Job description. A general statement of job duties and responsibilities.

Work behavior. An activity performed to achieve the objectives of the job. Work behaviors involve observable (physical) components and unobservable (mental) components. A work behavior consists of the performance of one or more tasks. Knowledges, skills, and abilities are not behaviors, although they may be applied in work behaviors.

Observable. Able to be seen, heard, or otherwise perceived by a person other than the person performing the action.

Knowledge. A body of information applied directly to the performance of a function.

Skill. A present, observable competence to perform a learned psychomoter act.

Ability. A present competence to perform an observable behavior or a behavior which results in an observable product.

Content validity. Demonstrated by data showing that the content of a selection procedure is representative of important aspects of performance on the job.

Construct validity. Demonstrated by data showing that the selection procedure measures the degree to which candidates have identifiable characteristics which have been determined to be important for successful job performance.

Criterion-related validity. Demonstrated by empirical data showing that the selection procedure is predictive of or significantly correlated with important elements of work behaviors. (Sec. 16, pp. 38307–38308)

Bibliography

Albemarle Paper Co. v. *Moody*, 10 FEP 1181 (1975).

Allen, R. E., & Keaveny, T. J. (1983). *Contemporary labor relations*. Reading, Mass.: Addison-Wesley.

American Psychological Association. (1980). *Principles for the validation and use of personnel selection procedures*. Berkeley, Calif.: APA.

American Psychological Association. (1974). *Standards for educational and psychological tests*. Washington, D.C.: APA.

American Psychological Association. (1954). Technical recommendations for psychological tests and diagnostic techniques. *Psychological Bulletin*, 51, 201–238.

Anastasi, Anne (1976). *Psychological testing*. New York: Macmillan.

Anderson, J. C., Milkovich, G. T., & Tsui, A. (1981). A model of intraorganizational mobility. *Academy of Management Review*, 6(4), 529–538.

Arvey, R. D. (1979). *Fairness in Selecting Employees*. Reading, Mass.: Addison-Wesley.

Arvey, R. D., & Begalla, M. E. (1975). Analyzing the homemaker job using the PAQ. *Journal of Applied Psychology*, 60(4), 513–517.

Arvey, R. D., Maxwell, S. E., Gutemberg, R. L., & Camp, C. (1981). Detecting job differences: A Monte Carlo study. *Personnel Psychology*, 34, 709–730.

Arvey, R. D., & Mossholder, K. M. (1979). A proposed methodology for determining similarities and differences among jobs. *Personnel Psychology*, 30, 363–374.

Ash, R. A. (1982). Job elements for task clusters. *Public Personnel Management*, 11(1), 80–90.

Ash, R. A., & Edgell, S. A. (1975). A note on the readability of the Position Analysis Questionnaire. *Journal of Applied Psychology*, 60, 765–766.

Ash, R. A., & Levine, E. L. (1980). A framework for evaluating job analysis methods. *Personnel*, 57, 53–59.

ASPA Handbook of Personnel and Industrial Relations, Vols. I–VIII. Washington, D.C.: The Bureau of National Affairs.

Astin, A. W. (1964). Criterion-centered research. *Educational and Psychological Measurement*, 24, 807–822.

Baehr, M. E. (1980). Job analysis: Objectives, approaches and applications. In E. L. Miller, E. H. Burack, and M. H. Albrecht (eds.), *Management of human resources*, pp. 269–291. Englewood Cliffs, N.J.: Prentice-Hall.

Baehr, M. E. (1967). *A factorial framework for job description*. Chicago: University of Chicago, Industrial Relations Center.

Banks, M. H., Jackson, P. R., Stafford, E. M., & Warr, P. B. (1983). Job Components Inventory and the analysis of jobs requiring limited skill. *Personnel Psychology*, 36(1), 57–66.

Barnes, E. M. (1980). *Motion and time study*, 7th ed. New York: John Wiley.

Bartlett, C. J. (1979). Equal employment issues in training. *Public Personnel Management*, November–December, 398–405.

Belcher, D. W. (1974). *Compensation administration*. Englewood Cliffs, N.J.: Prentice-Hall.

Bemis, S. E., Belenky, A. H., & Soder, D. A. (1983). *Job analysis: An effective management tool*. Washington, D.C.: The Bureau of National Affairs.

Bernardin, H. J., Alvarez, K. M., & Cranny, C. J. (1976). A re-comparison of behavioral expectation scales to summated scales. *Journal of Applied Psychology*, 61, 564–570.

Bernardin, H. J., & Beatty, R. W. (1984). *Performance appraisal*. Boston: Kent.

Bernardin, H. J., & Cascio, W. F. (1984). *An annotated bibliography of court cases relevant to employment decisions* (1980–1984). Authors.

Berwitz, C. J. (1975). *The job analysis approach to affirmative action*. New York: John Wiley.

Blum, M. L., & Naylor, J. C. (1968). *Industrial psychology*. New York: Harper & Row.

Boehm, V. R. (1981). Scientific parallelism in personnel mobility research: Preview of two approaches. *Academy of Management Review*, 6(4), 527–528.

Bouchard, T. J. (1976). Field research methods. In M. D. Dunnette (ed.), *Handbook of industrial and organizational psychology*, pp. 363–415. Chicago: Rand McNally.

Bouchard, T. J. (1972). *A manual for job analysis*. Minneapolis: Minnesota Civil Service Department.

Boulding, K. (1956). General systems theory—The skeleton of science. *Management Science*, 2, 197–208.

Breaugh, J. A. (1983). Realistic job previews: A critical appraisal and future research directions. *Academy of Management Review*, 8(4), 612–619.

Bridgeport Guardians v. *Police Department*, 16 FEP 486 (1977).

Brief, Arthur P., & Aldag, R. J. (1978). The Job Characteristics Inventory: An examination. *Academy of Management Journal*, 21(4), 659–670.

Brumback, G. B. (1971). Consolidating job descriptions, performance appraisals, and manpower reports. *Personnel Journal*, 50, 604–610.

Buchanan, D. A. (1979). *The development of job design theories and techniques*. New York: Praeger.

Buckley, Walter (ed.). (1968). *Modern systems research for the behavioral sciences*. Chicago: Aldine.

Burack, E. H., & Mathis, N. J. (1980). *Human resource planning: A pragmatic approach to manpower staffing and development*. Lake Forest, Ill.: Brace-Park Press.

Burack, E. H., & Walker, J. W. (eds.). (1972). *Manpower planning and programming*. Boston: Allyn & Bacon.

Bureau of National Affairs (1966). *Job analysis*, BNA Survey No. 79. Washington, D.C.: The Bureau of National Affairs.

Burke, R. J. (1916). Written specifications for hiring. *The Annals of the American Academy of Political and Social Science*, 65, 176–181.

Butler, J. L. (1975). Job analysis: (What + How + Why = Skills Involved). Unpublished manuscript, Stamford, Conn.

Byars, L. L., & Rue, L. W. (1984). *Human resource and personnel management*. Homewood, Ill.: Richard D. Irwin.

Campion, J. E. (1972). Work sampling for personnel selection. *Journal of Applied Psychology*, 56, 40–44.

Carlson, Suny (1951). *Executive behavior*. Stockholm: Strombergs.

Carroll, S. J., & Schneier, C. E. (1982). *Performance appraisal and review systems*. Glenview, Ill.: Scott, Foresman.

Carroll, S. J., & Taylor, W. H. (1969). Validity of estimates by clerical personnel of job time proportions. *Journal of Applied Psychology*, 53, 164–166.

Carroll, S. J., & Taylor, W. H. (1968). A study of the validity of a self-observational central signaling method of work sampling. *Personnel Psychology*, 21 (Autumn), 359–364.

Cascio, W. F. (1982). *Applied psychology in personnel management*. Reston, Va.: Reston.

Cascio, W. F., & Azad, E. M. (1981). *Human resources management: An information systems approach*. Reston, Va.: Reston.

Cascio, W. F., & Bernardin, H. J. (1981). Implications of performance appraisal litigation for personnel decisions. *Personnel Psychology*, 34, 211–226.

Cascio, W. F., & Phillips, N. F. (1979). Performance testing: A rose among thorns. *Personnel Psychology*, 32, 751–765.

Chance v. *Board of Examiners*, 4 FEP 596 (1972).

Christal, T. E. (1974). The U.S. Air Force occupational research project. *JSAS Catalog of Selected Documents in Psychology*, 4, 61.

Christal, T. E., & Weissmuller, J. J. (1977). New Comprehensive Occupational Data Analysis Programs (CODAP) for analyzing task factor information. *JSAS Catalog of Selected Documents in Psychology*, 7, 24–25 (Ms No. 1444).

Chruden, H. J. & Sherman, A. W. (1984). *Managing human resources*, 7th ed. Cincinnati: South-Western.

Cohen, J. (1977). *Statistical power analysis for the behavioral sciences*. New York: Academic Press.

Commerce Clearing House, *Labor law course*, 25th ed. Chicago: Commerce Clearing House, 1983.

Cook, T. D., & Reichardt, C. S. (1979). *Qualitative and quantitative methods in evaluation research*. Beverly Hills, Calif.: Sage.

Cooper, E. A., & Barrett, G. V. (1984). Equal pay and gender: Implications of court cases for personnel practice. *Academy of Management Review*, 9(1), 84–94.

Cornelius, E. T., III, & Lyness, K. S. (1980). A comparison of holistic and decomposed judgment strategies in job analysis by job incumbents. *Journal of Applied Psychology*, 65, 155–163.
Cornelius, E. T., III, Carron, T. J., & Collins, M. N. (1979). Job analysis models and job classification. *Personnel Psychology*, 32, 693–708.
Crites, John O. (1969). *Vocational psychology*. New York: McGraw-Hill.
Cronbach, L. J., Yalow, E., & Schaeffer, G. (1980). A mathematical structure for analyzing fairness in selection. *Personnel Psychology*, 33, 693–704.
Cronbach, L. J., & Gleser, G. (1965). *Psychological tests and personnel decisions*. Urbana: University of Illinois Press.
Cunningham, J. W., Tittle, T. C., Floyd, J. R., & Bates, J. A. (1971). *The development of the Occupational Analysis Inventory*, Research Monograph No. 6. Raleigh: North Carolina State University.
Dalton, Melville (1959a). Conflicts between staff and line managerial officers. *American Sociological Review*, 15(3), 342–351.
Dalton, Melville (1959b). *Men who manage*. New York: John Wiley.
Davis, L. E., & Taylor, J. C. (1979). *Design of jobs*, 2nd ed. Santa Monica, Calif.: Goodyear.
Davis v. *Washington*, 5 FEP 293 (1972).
Dickerson v. *U.S. Steel Corp.*, 472 F. Suppl. 1304 (E.D. Penn. 1978).
Division of Industrial-Organizational Psychology, American Psychological Association (1975). *Principles for the validation and use of personnel selection procedures*. Dayton, Ohio: The Industrial-Organizational Psychologist.
Donaldson v. *Pillsbury Company*, 554 F.2d 825 (8th Cir. 1977).
Dreher, G. F., & Sackett, P. R. (1981). Some problems in applying content validity evidence to assessment center procedures. *Academy of Management Review*, 6(4), 551–560.
Drucker, P. F. (1954). *The practice of management*. New York: Harper & Row.
Dunnette, M. D. (ed.). (1976). *Handbook of industrial and organizational psychology*. Chicago: Rand McNally,
Dunnette, M. D. (1966). *Personnel selection and placement*. Belmont, Calif.: Wadsworth.
Edwards, K. J. (1979). *Performance appraisal: Legal aspects*. Greensboro, N.C.: Center for Creative Leadership.
Ensley Branch v. *Seibels*, 22 FEP Cases 1207 (Fifth Circuit, 1980).
Faley, R. H. (1982). Sexual harassment: Critical review of legal cases with general principles and preventive measures. *Personnel Psychology*, 35(3), 583–600.
Feldacker, B. S. (1983). *Labor guide to labor law*, 2nd ed. Reston, Va.: Reston.
Feldman, D. C. (1984). The development and enforcement of group norms. *Academy of Management Journal*, 9(1), 47–53.
Fine, Sidney A. (1974). Functional job analysis: An approach to a technology for manpower planning. *Personnel Journal*, November, 813–818.
Fine, Sidney A. (1973). *Functional job analysis scales: A desk aid*. Kalamazoo, Mich.: W. E. Upjohn Institute.
Fine, Sidney A. (1967). *Guidelines for the design of new careers*. Kalamazoo, Mich.: W. E. Upjohn Institute.
Fine, Sidney, & Wiley, W. W. (1971). *An introduction to Functional Job Analysis*. Kalamazoo, Mich.: W. E. Upjohn Institute.
Firefighters Institute for Racial Equality v. *City of St. Louis*, 14 FEP 1486 (1977).
Flanagan, J. C. (1954). The critical incidents technique. *Psychological Bulletin*, 51, 327–358.
Fleishman, E. A. (1975). Toward a taxonomy of human performance. *American Psychologist*, 30, 1127–1149.
Fleishman, E. A., & Quaintance, M. K. (1984). *Taxonomies of human performance: The description of human tasks*. Orlando, Fla.: Academic Press.
Fombrum, C., Tichy, N. M., & Devanna, M. A. (1984). *Strategic human resource management*. New York: John Wiley.
French, W. L. (1982). *The personnel management process*, 5th ed. Boston: Houghton Mifflin.
Gael, Sidney (1983). *Job analyis: A guide to assessing work activities*. San Francisco: Jossey-Bass.
Gehm, J. W. (1970). Job descriptions: A new handle on an old tool. *Personnel Journal*, Vol. 49 (December), 983–985.
Ghiselli, E. E., Campbell, J. P., & Zedeck, S. (1981). *Measurement theory for the behavioral sciences*. San Francisco: W. H. Freeman.
Ghorpade, J., & Atchison, T. J. (1980). The concept of job analysis: A review and some suggestions. *Public Personnel Management*, 9(3), 134–144.
Gilpatrick, E. (1977a). *The Health Services Mobility Study method of task analysis and curriculum design*, Research Report No. 11, Vol. 1. New York: Hunter College, City University of New York.
Gilpatrick, E. (1977b). *The Health Services Mobility Study method of task analysis and curriculum design*, Research Report No. 11, Vol. 2. New York: Hunter College, City University of New York.
Glueck, W. F. (1979). *Personnel: A book of readings*. Dallas, Tex.: Business Publications.

Goldstein, I. L. (1986). Tıaining: Program development and evaluation. Monterey, Calif.: Brooks/Cole.
Goldstein, I. L. (1980). Training in work organizations. *Annual Review of Psychology*, 31, 229–272.
Gordon, M. E., & Johnson, W. A. (1982). Seniority: A review of its legal and scientific standing. *Personnel Psychology*, 35, 255–266.
Gordon, S. R. (1978). The impact of fair employment laws on training. *Training and Development Journal*, 32, 29–44.
Grego, N. R., & Rudnik, M. C. (1970). *Job description and certification for library technical assistants*. Chicago: Council on Library Technology.
Gregory, C. O., & Katz, H. A. (1979). *Labor and the law*, 3rd ed. New York: W. W. Norton.
Griffin, R. W., Welsh, A., & Moorhead, G. (1981). Perceived task characteristics and employee performance: A literature review. *Academy of Management Review*, 6(4), 655–664.
Griggs v. *Duke Power Company*, 401 U.S. 424 (1971).
Guardians Association v. *Civil Service Commission*, 23 FEP 909 (1980).
Guest, R. H. (1956). Of time and foreman. *Personnel*, 32, 478–486.
Guilford, J. P. (1965). *Fundamental statistics in psychology and education*. New York: McGraw-Hill.
Guilford, J. P., & Fruchter, B. (1973). *Fundamental statistics in psychology and education*. New York: McGraw-Hill.
Guion, Robert M. (1965). *Personnel testing*. New York: McGraw-Hill.
Haas, J. A., Porat, A. M., & Vaughan, J. A. (1969). Actual vs. ideal time allocations reported by managers: A study of managerial behavior. *Personnel Psychology*, 22, 66.
Hackman, J. R., & Lawler, E. E. (1971). Employee reactions to job characteristics. *Journal of Applied Psychology*, 55, 259–286.
Hackman, J. R., & Oldham, G. R. (1980). *Work redesign*. Reading, Mass.: Addison-Wesley.
Hackman, J. R., & Suttle, J. L. (1977). *Improving life at work*. Santa Monica, Calif.: Goodyear.
Hall, F. S., & Albrecht, M. J. (1979). *The management of affirmative action*. Santa Monica, Calif.: Goodyear.
Hart, M. B. (1985). Changing secretarial jobs and implications for teachers and administrators. *Business Education Forum*, 39(5), 5–8.
Hayes, W. L. (1973). *Statistics for the social sciences*. New York: Holt, Rinehart and Winston.
Heckmann, I. L., & Huneryager, S. G. (1962). *Management of the personnel function*. Columbus, Ohio: Charles E. Merrill.
Hemphill, J. K. (1959). Job descriptions for executives. *Harvard Business Review*, 37, 55–67.
Henderson, R. I. (1979). *Compensation management: Rewarding performance*. Reston, Va.: Reston.
Heneman, H. G., Schwab, D. P., Fossum, J. A., & Dyer, L. D. (1986). *Personnel/human resource management*, 3rd ed. Homewood, Ill.: Richard D. Irwin.
Henerson, M. E., Morris, L. L., & Fitz-Gibbon, C. T. (1978). *How to measure attitudes*. Beverly Hills, Calif.: Sage.
Holley, W. H., & Field, H. S. (1975). Performance appraisal and the law. *Labor Law Journal*, 26, 423–430.
Hough, L. M., Dunnette, M. D., & Keyes, M. A. (1983). An evaluation of three "alternative" selection procedures. *Personnel Psychology*, 36(2), 261–276.
International Labour Organisation (1979). *Introduction to work study*. Geneva: ILO.
Janger, A. R. (1977). *The personnel function: Changing objectives and organization*, Report No. 712. New York: The Conference Board.
Jenkins, G. D., Nadler, D. A., Lawler, E. E., & Camaan, C. (1975). Standardized observations: An approach to measuring the nature of jobs. *Journal of Applied Psychology*, 60, 171–181.
Jones, A. P., Main, D. S., Butler, M. C., & Johnson, L. A. (1982). Narrative descriptions as potential sources of job analysis ratings. *Personnel Psychology*, 35(4), 813–828.
Jones, J. J., & Decoths, T. A. (1969). Job analysis: National survey findings. *Personnel Journal*, 49(10), 805–809.
Katz, D., & Kahn, R. L. (1978). *The social psychology of organizations*, 2nd ed. New York: John Wiley.
Kelly, J. (1969). The study of executive behavior by activity sampling. *Human Relations*, 17, 277–287.
Kirkland v. *Department of Correctional Services*, 7 FEP 694 (1974).
Klatt, L. A., Murdick, R. C., & Schuster, F. E. (1985). *Human resource management*. Columbus, Ohio: Charles E. Merrill.
Kleiman, L. S., & Durham, R. L. (1981). Performance appraisal and the courts: A critical review. *Personnel Psychology*, 34(1), 103–122.
Kleiman, L. S., & Faley, R. H. (1985). The implications of professional and legal guidelines for court decisions involving criterion-related validity: A review and analysis. *Personnel Psychology*, 38, 803–834.
Kleiman, L. S., & Faley, R. H. (1978). Assessing content validity: Standards set by the courts. *Personnel Psychology*, 31, 701–713.
Klinger, D. E. (1979). When a traditional job description is not enough. *Personnel Journal*, 27, 243–248.

Krech, D., Crutchfield, R. S., & Ballachey, E. L. (1962). *Individual in society*. New York: McGraw-Hill.

Kezystofiak, F., Newman, J. M., & Anderson, G. A. (1979). A quantified approach to the measurement of job content: Procedures and payoffs. *Personnel Psychology*, 32, 341–357.

Kuriloff, A. H., Yoder, D., & Stone, C. H. (1975). *Communication in Task Analysis*, Technical Report No. 8. Los Angeles: California State University.

Landy, F. J. (1985). *Psychology of work behavior*, 3rd ed. Homewood, Ill.: Dorsey.

Landy, F. J., & Farr, J. L. (1983). *The measurement of work performance*. San Diego, Calif.: Academic Press.

Landy, F. J., Farr, J. L., Saal, F. G., & Freytag, W. R. (1976). Behaviorally anchored scales for rating the performance of police officers. *Journal of Applied Psychology*, 61, 752–758.

Lawshe, C. H. (1983). A simplified approach to the evaluation of fairness in employee selection procedures. *Personnel Psychology*, 36, 601–608.

Ledvinka, J. (1982). Federal regulation of personnel and human resources management. Boston: Kent.

Lee, J. A., & Mendoza, J. L. (1981). A comparison of techniques which test for job differences. *Personnel Psychology*, 34, 731–748.

Levine, E. L., Ash, R. A., & Bennett, N. (1980). Exploratory comparative study of four job analysis methods. *Journal of Applied Psychology*, 65, 524–535.

Levine, E. L., Ash, R. A., Hall, H., & Sistrunk, F. (1983). Evaluation of job analysis methods by experienced job analysts. *Academy of Management Journal*, 26(2), 339–347.

Levine, E. L., Bennett, N., & Ash, R. A. (1979). Evaluation and use of four job analysis methods for personnel selection. *Public Personnel Management*, 8, 146–151.

Lilienthal, R. A., & Rosen, T. H. (1980). *A design for validating selection procedures for groups of jobs*. Washington, D.C.: U.S. Office of Personnel Management.

Lopez, F. M., Kesselman, G. A., & Lopez, F. E. (1981). An empirical test of a trait-oriented job analysis technique. *Personnel Psychology*, 34, 479–502.

McCormick, E. J. (1979). *Job analysis: Methods and applications*. New York: AMACOM.

McCormick, E. J. (1970). Job analysis: An overview. *Indian Journal of Industrial Relations*, 1970 (July), 5–14.

McCormick, E. J., Jeanneret, P. R., & Mecham, R. C. (1972). A study of job characteristics and job dimensions as based on the Position Analysis Questionnaire (PAQ). *Journal of Applied Psychology*, 56, 347–368.

McCormick, E. J., Jeanneret, P. R., & Mecham, R. C. (1969). *Position Analysis Questionnaire*. West Lafayette, Ind.: Occupational Research Center, Purdue University.

March, J. G., & Simon, H. A. (1959). *Organizations*. New York: John Wiley.

Marquardt, L. D., & McCormick, E. J. (1972). *Attribute ratings and profiles of the job elements of the Position Analysis Questionnaire (PAQ)*, Department of Psychological Sciences, Report No. 1. West Lafayette, Ind.: Purdue University.

Mathis, R. L., & Jackson, J. H. (1985). *Personnel*, 4th ed. St. Paul, Minn.: West.

Mecham, R. C., & McCormick, E. J. (1969). *The rated attribute requirements of the job elements of the Positon Analysis Questionnaire (PAQ)*, Department of Psychological Sciences, Report No. 1. West Lafayette, Ind.: Purdue University.

Melching, W. H., & Borcher, S. D. (1973). *Procedures for constructing and using task inventories*, Center for Vocational and Technical Education, Research and Development Series No. 91. Columbus: The Ohio State University.

Mendleson, J. L. (1969). Improving executive job descriptions. *Management of Personnel Quarterly*, 8 (Spring), 26–35.

Merritt-Haston, R., & Wexley, K. N. (1983). Educational requirements: legality and validity. *Personnel Psychology*, 36(4), 743–753.

Milkovich, G. T., & Newman, J. M. (1984). *Compensation*. Plano, Tex.: Business Publications.

Miller, F., & Coghill, M. A. (1961). *The historical sources of personnel work: An annotated bibliography of developments to 1923*. Ithaca, N.Y.: NYSSILR, Cornell University.

Mintzberg, H. (1973). *The nature of managerial work*. New York: Harper & Row.

Moore, M. L., & Dutton, P. (1978). Training needs analysis: Review and critique. *Academy of Management Review*, 3(3), 532–545.

Morrissey, G. L. (1977). *Management by objectives and results for business and industry*, 2nd ed. Reading, Mass.: Addison-Wesley.

Mussio, S. J., & Smith, M. K. (1973). *Content validity: A procedural manual*. Chicago: International Personnel Management Association.

Nelson, E. C., Jacobs, E. R., & Breer, P. E. (1975). Study of the validity of the task inventory method of job analysis. *Medical Care*, 13, 104–113.

Niebel, B. W. (1982). *Motion and time study*. Homewood, Ill.: Richard D. Irwin.

Norberg, J. M. (1984). A warning regarding the simplified approach to the evaluation of test fairness in employee selection procedures. *Personnel Psychology*, 37, 483–486.

Nunnally, Jum C. (1978). *Psychometric theory*, 2nd ed. New York: McGraw-Hill.

Oldham, F., & Seglin, J. L. (1984). *Job descriptions in banking*. Boston: Bankers.

Olson, H. C., Fine, S. A., Myers, D. C., & Jennings, M. C. (1981). The use of functional job analysis in establishing performance standards for heavy equipment operators. *Personnel Psychology*, 34, 351–364.

Owen, P. R. (1983). The role of the deputy head in secondary schools. *Educational Management and Administration*, 11(2), 51–56.

Patterson v. *American Tobacco Company*, 586 F.2b300 (4th Cir. 1978).

Patton, M. Q. (1980). *Qualitative evaluation methods*. Beverly Hills, Calif.: Sage.

Pearlman, K. (1980). Job families: A review and discussion of their implications for personnel selection. *Psychological Bulletin*, 87, 1–28.

Pegues v. *Mississippi State Employment Service*, 488 F. Suppl. 239 (N.D. Miss. 1980).

Plumlee, L. B. (1975). *A short guide to the development of work sample and performance tests*, 2nd ed. Washington, D.C.: Personnel Research and Development Center, U.S. Office of Personnel Management, 80–83.

Prien, E. P. (1977). The function of job analysis in content validation. *Personnel Psychology*, 30, 167–174.

Prien, E. P. (1965). The development of a clerical position description questionnaire. *Personnel Psychology*, 18, 91–98.

Primoff, E. S. (1975). *How to prepare and conduct job-element examinations*. Washington, D.C.: U.S. Government Printing Office.

Primoff, E. S., Clark, C. L., & Caplan, J. R. (1982). *How to prepare and conduct job element examinations: Supplement*. Washington, D.C.: U.S. Government Printing Office.

Randhawa, B. S. (1978). Clustering of skills and occupations: A generic skills approach to occupational training. *Journal of Vocational Behavior*, 12, 80–92.

Redfern, G. B. (1984). Using job descriptions as an administrative tool. *Spectrum*, 2(1), 21–26.

Reilly, R. S., & Chao, G. T. (1982). Validity and fairness of some alternative selection procedures. *Personnel Psychology*, 35, 1–62.

Remick, H. (1981). The comparable worth controversy. *Public Personnel Management*, 10 (Winter), 377–383.

Rivera v. *City of Wichita Falls*, 665 F.2d (Fifth Circuit 1982).

Robbins, S. P. (1984). *Essentials of organizational behavior*. Englewood Cliffs, N.J.: Prentice-Hall.

Rowland, K. M., & Ferris, G. R. (1982). *Personnel management*. Boston: Allyn & Bacon.

Runyon, R. P., & Haber, A. (1976). *Fundamentals of behavioral statistics*. Reading, Mass.: Addison-Wesley.

Rusmore, J. T. (1973). Position description factors and executive positions. *Personnel Psychology*, 26 (Spring), 135–138.

Russell, James S. (1984). A review of fair employment cases in the field of training. *Personnel Psychology*, 37, 261–276.

Sackett, P. R., Cornelius, E. T., & Carron, T. J. (1981). A comparison of global judgment vs. task oriented approaches to job classification. *Personnel Psychology*, 34, 791–805.

Sawyer, J. (1966). Measurement and prediction, clinical and statistical. *Psychological Bulletin*, 66, 178–200.

Sayles, L. R. (1964). *Managerial Behavior*. New York: McGraw-Hill.

Scharf, S. (1976). The influence of lawyers, legal language, and legal thinking. *Personnel Psychology*, 29, 541–554.

Schein, E. H. (1978). *Career dynamics*. Reading, Mass.: Addison-Wesley.

Schmidt, F. L., Caplan, J. R., Bemis, S. E., Decuir, R., Dunn, L., & Antone, L. (1979). *The behavioral consistency method of unassembled examining*. Washington, D.C.: U.S. Office of Personnel Management.

Schmidt, F. L., Greenthal, A. L., Hunter, J. E., Berner, J. G., & Seaton, F. W. (1977). Job sample versus paper-and-pencil trades and technical tests: Adverse impact and examinee attitudes. *Personnel Psychology*, 30, 187–197.

Schmidt, F. L., & Hunter, J. E. (1982). Two pitfalls in assessing fairness of selection tests using the regression model. *Personnel Psychology*, 35, 601–607.

Schmidt, F. L., Pearlman, K., Hunter, J. E., & Hirsh, H. R. (1985). Forty questions about validity generalization and meta-analysis. *Personnel Psychology*, 38(4), 697–802.

Schneider, B., & Schmitt, N. (1986). *Staffing organizations*, 2nd ed. Glenview, Ill.: Scott, Foresman.

Schneider, B. S. (1976). *Staffing organizations*. Pacific Palisades, Calif.: Goodyear.

Schneier, D. B. (1978). The impact of EEO legislation on performance appraisals. *Personnel*, 55(4), 24–34.

Schoderbek, P. P. (1971). *Management systems*, 2nd ed. New York: John Wiley.

Schoderbek, P. P., & Plambeck, D. (1978). The missing link in management by objectives—continuing responsibilities. *Public Personnel Management*, 7(6), 19–25.

Schuler, R. S. (1984). *Personnel and human resource management*, 2nd ed. St. Paul, Minn.: West.

Schuster, M. H., & Miller, C. S. (1982). Performance evaluations as evidence in ADEA cases. *Employee Relations Law Journal*, 6, 561–583.

Schwab, D. P. (1980). Construct validity in organizational behavior. In B. M. Staw and L. L. Cummings (eds.), *Research in organizational behavior*, Vol. 2, pp. 3–44. Greenwich, Conn.: JAI.

Schwab, D. P., Heneman, H. G., & DeCotiis, T. (1975). Behaviorally anchored rating scales: A review of the literature. *Personnel Psychology*, 28, 549–562.

Schwartz, D. J. (1977). A job sampling approach to merit system examining. *Personnel Psychology*, 30, 175–185.

Scott, W. D., Clothier, R. C., & Spriegel, W. R. (1961). *Personnel management: Principles, practices, and point of view*. New York: McGraw-Hill.

Scott, W. R. (1981). *Organizations*. Englewood Cliffs, N.J.: Prentice-Hall.

Selltiz, C., Jahoda, M., Deutsch, M., & Cook, S. W. (1959). *Research methods in social relations*, rev. one-volume ed. New York: Holt, Rinehart and Winston.

Selznick, P. (1968). *Law, society, and industrial justice*. New York: Russell Sage.

Sharf, J. C. (1977). Fair employment implications for HRD: The case of *Washington* v. *Davis*. *Training and Development Journal*, 31, 16–21.

Shartle, C. L. (1959). *Occupational information*, 3rd ed. Englewood Cliffs, N.J.: Prentice-Hall.

Shaw, M. (1981). *Group dynamics*. New York: Harper & Row.

Shield Club v. *City of Cleveland*, 13 FEP 533 (1974).

Sistrunk, F., & Smith, P. L. (1982). *Multimethodological job analysis for criminal justice organizations*. Tampa: University of South Florida, Center for Evaluation Research.

Sovereign, K. L. (1984). *Personnel law*. Reston, Va.: Reston.

Sparks, C. P. (1982). Job analysis. In K. M. Rowland & G. R. Ferris (eds.), *Personnel management*, pp. 78–100. Boston: Allyn & Bacon.

Stanton, M. (1985). From franchise to programming: Jobs in cable television. *Occupational Outlook Quarterly*, 29(2), 26–32.

Stern, S. T. (1977). *Introduction to civil litigation*. St. Paul, Minn.: West.

Stogdill, R. M. (1969). Validity of leader behavior descriptions. *Personnel Psychology*, 22 (Summer), 153–158.

Stone, C. H., & Yoder, D. (1970). *Job Analysis, 1970*. Long Beach: California State University.

Stoner, J. A. F. (1982). *Management*, 2nd ed. Englewood Cliffs, N.J.: Prentice-Hall.

Stutzman, T. M. (1983). Within classification job differences. *Personnel Psychology*, 36, 503–516.

Sudman, S., & Bradburn, N. M. (1982). *Asking questions*. San Francisco: Jossey-Bass.

Sutermeister, R. A. (1976). *People and productivity*, 3rd ed. New York: McGraw-Hill.

Taylor, H. C., & Russell, J. T. (1939). The relationship of validity coefficients to the practical effectiveness of tests in selection: discussion of tables. *Journal of Applied Psychology*, 23, 565–578.

Taylor, L. R. (1978). Empirically derived job families as a foundation for the study of validity generalization, Study 1. *Personnel Psychology*, 31, 325–340.

Tead, O., & Metcalfe, H. C. (1933). *Personnel administration: Its principles and practice*. New York: McGraw-Hill.

Thompson, D. E., & Thompson, T. A. (1982). Court standards for job analysis in test validation. *Personnel Psychology*, 35(4), 865–874.

Tornow, W. W., & Pinto, P. R. (1976). The development of a managerial job taxonomy. *Journal of Applied Psychology*, 61, 410–418.

Trattner, M. H. (1982). Synthetic validity and its application to the *Uniform Guidelines* validation requirements. *Personnel Psychology*, 35(2), 383–398.

Treiman, D. J., & Hartmann, H. I. (eds.). (1981). *Women, work and wages: Equal pay for jobs of equal value*. Washington, D.C.: National Academy.

Turner, A. N., & Lawrence, P. R. (1965). *Industrial jobs and the worker*. Boston: Graduate School of Business Administration, Harvard University.

Twomey, D. P. (1986). *A concise guide to employment law*. West Chicago, Ill.: South-Western.

Uhrbrock, R. S. (1922). The history of job analysis. *Administration*, 3, 164–168.

Ulery, J. D. (1981). *Job descriptions in manufacturing industries*. New York: AMACOM.

Unglaube, J. M. (1983). Searching for senior administrators. *New Directions for Higher Education*, 11(2), 49–58.

Uniform Guidelines on Employee Selection Procedures. (1978). *Federal Register*, 43, 38290–38315.

Usery v. *Tamiami Trail Tours, Inc.*, 12 FEP 1233 (1976).

U.S. Department of Labor. (1977). *Dictionary of occupational titles*, 4th ed. Washington, D.C.: U.S. Government Printing Office.

U.S. Department of Labor (1973). *Task analysis inventories: A method for collecting job information*. Washington, D.C.: U.S. Government Printing Office.

U.S. Department of Labor. (1972). *Handbook for analyzing jobs*. Washington, D.C.: U.S. Government Printing Office.

U.S. Office of Personnel Management. (1979). *How to write position descriptions*. Washington, D.C.: U.S. Government Printing Office.

U.S. v. *City of St. Louis*, 14 FEP 1473 (1976).

U.S. v. *State of New York*, 21 FEP 1286 (1979).

Van Maanen, J. (ed.). (1983). *Qualitative methodology*. Beverly Hills, Calif.: Sage.

Vetter, E. W. (1967). *Manpower planning for high talent personnel*. Ann Arbor: University of Michigan Press.

Vulcan Society v. *Civil Service Commission*, 6 FEP 1045 (1973).

Wallace, M. J. (1983). Methodology, research practice, and progress in personnel and industrial relations. *Academy of Management Review*, 8(1), 6–13.

Wallace, M. J., Crandall, N. F., & Fay, C. H. (1982). *Administering human resources*. New York: Random House.

Wanous, J. (1980). *Organizational entry*. Reading, Mass.: Addison-Wesley.

Wanous, J. P. (1973). Effects of a realistic job preview on job acceptance, job attitudes, and job survival. *Journal of Applied Psychology*, 58, 327–332.

Wanous, J. P., & Dean, R. A. (1984). The effects of realistic job previews on hiring bank tellers. *Journal of Applied Psychology*, 69, 95–105.

Washington v. *Davis*, 12 FEP 1415 (1975).

Watkins v. *Scott Paper*, 12 FEP 1191 (1976).

Weahkee v. *Perry*, 587 F.2d 1256 (D.C. Div. 1978).

Wigdor, A. K., & Garner, W. R. (1982). *Ability testing: Uses, consequences, and controversies*. Part I: *Report of the Committee*. Washington, D.C.: National Academy.

Wiggins, J. S. (1973). *Personality and prediction: Principles of personality assessment*. Reading, Mass.: Addison-Wesley.

Wilson, M. (1974). *Job analysis for human resource management*, Monograph No. 4, U.S. Department of Labor. Washington, D.C.: U.S. Government Printing Office.

Yoder, Dale (1962). *Personnel management and industrial relations*, 5th ed. Englewood Cliffs, New Jersey: Prentice-Hall.

Youngman, M. B. (1983). Intrinsic roles of secondary school teachers. *British Journal of Educational Psychology*, 53 (Part 2), 234–246.

Zerga, J. E. (1943). Job analysis: A resume and bibliography. *Journal of Applied Psychology*, 27, 249–267.

Name Index

Subject Index